P9-CCQ-175

REPORTING CIVIL RIGHTS
PART ONE

REPORTING
CIVIL RIGHTS

PART ONE
AMERICAN JOURNALISM 1941–1963

THE LIBRARY OF AMERICA

Some of the material in this volume is reprinted
with permission of the holders of copyright and publication
rights. Acknowledgments are on pages 951–57.

The paper used in this publication meets the
minimum requirements of the American National Standard for
Information Sciences—Permanence of Paper for Printed
Library Materials, ANSI z39.48—1984.

Distributed to the trade in the United States
by Penguin Putnam Inc.
and in Canada by Penguin Books Canada Ltd.

Library of Congress Catalog Number: 2002027459
For cataloging information, see end of Index.
ISBN 1–931082–28–6

First Printing
The Library of America—137

Manufactured in the United States of America

Advisory board for *Reporting Civil Rights*

Contents

ix

Call to Negro America

"To March on Washington for Jobs and Equal Participation in National Defense"

July 1, 1941

GREETINGS:

We call upon you to fight for jobs in National Defense.

We call upon you to struggle for the integration of Negroes in the armed forces, such as the Air Corps, Navy, Army and Marine Corps of the Nation.

We call upon you to demonstrate for the abolition of Jim-Crowism in all Government departments and defense employment.

This is an hour of crisis. It is a crisis of democracy. It is a crisis of minority groups. It is a crisis of Negro Americans.

What is this crisis?

To American Negroes, it is the denial of jobs in Government defense projects. It is racial discrimination in Government departments. It is widespread Jim-Crowism in the armed forces of the Nation.

While billions of the taxpayers' money are being spent for war weapons, Negro workers are being turned away from the gates of factories, mines and mills—being flatly told, "NOTHING DOING". Some employers refuse to give Negroes jobs when they are without "union cards", and some unions refuse Negro workers union cards when they are "without jobs".

What shall we do?

What a dilemma!

What a runaround!

What a disgrace!

What a blow below the belt!

Though dark, doubtful and discouraging, all is not lost, all is not hopeless. Though battered and bruised, we are not beaten, broken or bewildered.

Verily, the Negroes' deepest disappointments and direst defeats, their tragic trials and outrageous oppressions in these

I

dreadful days of destruction and disaster to democracy and freedom, and the rights of minority peoples, and the dignity and independence of the human spirit, is the Negroes' greatest opportunity to rise to the highest heights of struggle for freedom and justice in Government, in industry, in labor unions, education, social service, religion and culture.

With faith and confidence of the Negro people in their own power for self-liberation, Negroes can break down the barriers of discrimination against employment in National Defense. Negroes can kill the deadly serpent of race hatred in the Army, Navy, Air and Marine Corps, and smash through and blast the Government, business and labor-union red tape to win the right to equal opportunity in vocational training and re-training in defense employment.

Most important and vital to all, Negroes, by the mobilization and co-ordination of their mass power, can cause PRESIDENT ROOSEVELT TO ISSUE AN EXECUTIVE ORDER ABOLISHING DISCRIMINATIONS IN ALL GOVERNMENT DEPARTMENTS, ARMY, NAVY, AIR CORPS AND NATIONAL DEFENSE JOBS.

Of course, the task is not easy. In very truth, it is big, tremendous and difficult.

It will cost money.

It will require sacrifice.

It will tax the Negroes' courage, determination and will to struggle. But we can, must and will triumph.

The Negroes' stake in national defense is big. It consists of jobs, thousands of jobs. It may represent millions, yes hundreds of millions of dollars in wages. It consists of new industrial opportunities and hope. This is worth fighting for.

But to win our stakes, it will require an "all-out", bold and total effort and demonstration of colossal proportions.

Negroes can build a mammoth machine of mass action with a terrific and tremendous driving and striking power that can shatter and crush the evil fortress of race prejudice and hate, if they will only resolve to do so and never stop, until victory comes.

Dear fellow Negro Americans, be not dismayed in these terrible times. You possess power, great power. Our problem is to harness and hitch it up for action on the broadest, daring and most gigantic scale.

In this period of power politics, nothing counts but pressure, more pressure, and still more pressure, through the tactic and strategy of broad, organized, aggressive mass action behind the vital and important issues of the Negro. To this end, we propose that ten thousand Negroes MARCH ON WASHINGTON FOR JOBS IN NATIONAL DEFENSE AND EQUAL INTEGRATION IN THE FIGHTING FORCES OF THE UNITED STATES.

An "all-out" thundering march on Washington, ending in a monster and huge demonstration at Lincoln's Monument, will shake up white America.

It will shake up official Washington.

It will give encouragement to our white friends to fight all the harder by our side, with us, for our righteous cause.

It will gain respect for the Negro people.

It will create a new sense of self-respect among Negroes.

But what of national unity?

We believe in national unity which recognizes equal opportunity of black and white citizens to jobs in national defense and the armed forces, and in all other institutions and endeavors in America. We condemn all dictatorships, Fascist, Nazi and Communist. We are loyal, patriotic Americans, all.

But, if American democracy will not defend its defenders; if American democracy will not protect its protectors; if American democracy will not give jobs to its toilers because of race or color; if American democracy will not insure equality of opportunity, freedom and justice to its citizens, black and white, it is a hollow mockery and belies the principles for which it is supposed to stand.

To the hard, difficult and trying problem of securing equal participation in national defense, we summon all Negro Americans to march on Washington. We summon Negro Americans to form committees in various cities to recruit and register marchers and raise funds through the sale of buttons and other legitimate means for the expenses of marchers to Washington by buses, train, private automobiles, trucks, and on foot.

We summon Negro Americans to stage marches on their

City Halls and Councils in their respective cities and urge them to memorialize the President to issue an executive order to abolish discrimination in the Government and national defense.

However, we sternly counsel against violence and ill-considered and intemperate action and the abuse of power. Mass power, like physical power, when misdirected is more harmful than helpful.

We summon you to mass action that is orderly and lawful, but aggressive and militant, for justice, equality and freedom.

Crispus Attucks marched and died as a martyr for American independence. Nat Turner, Denmark Vesey, Gabriel Prosser, Harriet Tubman and Frederick Douglass fought, bled and died for the emancipation of Negro slaves and the preservation of American democracy.

Abraham Lincoln, in times of the grave emergency of the Civil War, issued the Proclamation of Emancipation for the freedom of Negro slaves and the preservation of American democracy.

Today, we call upon President Roosevelt, a great humanitarian and idealist, to follow in the footsteps of his noble and illustrious predecessor and take the second decisive step in this world and national emergency and free American Negro citizens of the stigma, humiliation and insult of discrimination and Jim-Crowism in Government departments and national defense.

The Federal Government cannot with clear conscience call upon private industry and labor unions to abolish discrimination based upon race and color as long as it practices discrimination itself against Negro Americans.

NEGROES' COMMITTEE TO MARCH ON
WASHINGTON FOR EQUAL PARTICIPATION IN
NATIONAL DEFENSE.

2289 7th Avenue, New York City   EDgecombe 4-4340

Walter White	Richard Parrish
Rev. William Lloyd Imes	Dr. Rayford Logan
Lester B. Granger	Henry K. Craft
Frank R. Crosswaith	A. Philip Randolph
Layle Lane	

Negro Morale

by Roi Ottley

THROUGHOUT the urban areas of the country, the Negro communities are seething with resentment, expressed in the utterances of ordinarily conservative Negro leaders, and in the Negro press and periodicals. "Where there was once tolerance and acceptance of a position believed to be gradually changing for the better, now the Negro is showing a 'democratic upsurge of rebellion,' bordering on open hostility," says Harlem's Amsterdam-Star News.

This unrest has recently been brought to a head by twin factors which have come to the surface in the national emergency but whose roots lie deep in American life: the treatment of Negro members of the army and the frustration Negroes feel at being barred from jobs in the defense industries.

Negro newspapers describe the army situation as bad indeed. They cite as examples, race riots at Fort Oswego; fighting at Camp Davis; discrimination at Fort Devens; jim-crow conditions at Camps Blanding and Lee; stabbings at Fort Huachuca; killings at Fort Bragg; and the edict "not to shake a nigger's hand" at Camp Upton.

Nearly every day there are reports of Negroes going AWOL, particularly those stationed in Southern camps. For instance, The New York Times carried a story on August 18, 1941, that, following friction with the white population, forty-three Negroes of the Ninety-fourth Engineers (labor) Battalion from Chicago and Detroit departed from the maneuver area near Gurdon, Arkansas. In explaining the "racial difficulties" involved, Major Gen. Robert C. Richardson Jr., white, said that ". . . some of these Northern Negroes, not understanding the attitude of the Southerner, and apparently to avoid further trouble, left their command."

This is too pat an answer. It ignores the undercurrent of

feeling among all Negroes that comes to the surface at the least provocation; and it slides over the fact that the Northern Negro knows the Southern viewpoint all too well. A Negro who has lived in the freer atmosphere of the North and become aware of his political rights will not relinquish them or put up with abuse because he happens to be in the South. That he wears the uniform of the United States Army increases his self-respect.

To some Southerners such a man is a dangerous "nigger" who must be made to "know his place"—with violence and terror, if necessary. The prejudiced Southerner refuses to accord even the ordinary decencies to the Negro—uniform or no uniform—and is not impressed by the statements of administration leaders about extending democracy to the oppressed. In his view, democracy is not a way of life for all, but a luxury for better-class white people only.

The sharply differing views of the Northern Negro and the prejudiced white Southerner are now meeting head-on. This was revealed in the flare-up at Fort Bragg, North Carolina, the result of an affray in which a Negro soldier and a white military policeman were killed. In this instance, however, the killing of the white MP was the act of a Southern Negro whose resentment against injustice mounted to a desperate thrust for human dignity.

According to the best available accounts, this soldier, Ned Turman, voiced objections to an attack on a fellow Negro soldier and was cracked over the head with a club by a white MP. In wrestling to protect himself, the Negro managed to snatch his assailant's gun. Brandishing it, he stepped back and cried: "I'm going to break up you MP's beating us colored soldiers!" And with that he fired the fatal shot. He was immediately shot to death by another white MP, who also had participated in the fracas. After the shooting, whole companies not involved in the affair—their Negro officers included —were forced to stand all night with their hands above their heads while armed military policemen patroled the camp.

The daily newspapers, with the exception of New York's PM, maintained a silence that made the situation no less real. Few were the voices of white people protesting against such treatment of members of the country's army. Similar acts committed by Nazis outrage American opinion and result in columns and columns of newspaper comment.

Negroes, however, were outspoken about the affair to the point of being inflammatory. George S. Schuyler, a well known commentator who has few illusions about his race and its problems, spoke of the "racial hatred, official cowardice and hypocrisy" rampant in the "new so-called people's army," and held that "every American, whose soul was not corroded by Negrophobia should be enraged." After condemning "Hitlerism at Home," The Pittsburgh Courier, largest-selling Negro newspaper in the country, went on to say editorially that "Nothing short of the most drastic punishment of officers and enlisted men among the white military police will satisfy a justifiably aroused Negro people." The equally influential Baltimore Afro-American, in calling for mass action, observed that "One individual marching up and down Pennsylvania Avenue in front of the White House denouncing race prejudice is arrested as a crank. Ten thousand persons get respectful attention. When great batches of drafted men *desert* rather than serve in the army down in Dixie, the War Department will then do something."

In a typical letter to the editor of PM, a Negro man-in-the-street wrote: "When I read these things I am forced to wonder just how far removed is this brand of democracy that we practise from fascism, Nazism and barbarism. . . . Lest someone chide me for not being loyal, may I say that I am as loyal as America permits me to be."—"Negroes have been patient, loyal and patriotic," The Amsterdam-Star News remarked editorially, "but they will not be destroyed!"

The other most important cause for unrest in the Negro population is the lack of employment in the defense industries. In a statement to the President, the National Association for the Advancement of Colored People argued that "equitable employment of minority racial groups in defense industries was more than an issue of racial policy." When the administration appointed a Negro, Dr. Robert C. Weaver, to the Advisory Commission to the Council of National Defense, and appointed Judge William H. Hastie, a Negro, Civilian Aide to the Secretary of War, for the purpose of integrating Negroes into the defense program, The Crisis, official

organ of the NAACP, held that these acts "indicated a growing realization that colored Americans must be given the serious consideration they demand."

It soon became apparent, however, that the White House
statement—"It is the policy of the War Department that the
services of Negroes will be utilized on a fair and equitable
basis"—was not taken literally by those responsible for carrying it out. No real effort was made to utilize the vast reservoir
of Negro labor.

To procure jobs in the defense industries, A. Philip Randolph, president of the Brotherhood of Sleeping Car Porters,
called upon Negroes, in May, 1941, to "march onto Washington." "The administration leaders in Washington," he told
the writer at that time, "will never give the Negro justice until they see masses—ten, twenty, fifty thousand Negroes on
the White House lawn!" The Negro public agreed, and responded immediately. Both the NAACP and the National
Negro Congress supported the march actively. Walter White
brought his influence and prestige to the movement. Thousands of dollars were spent. Press and pulpit played decisive
roles in building up sentiment. The Pullman Porters became
couriers, carrying the word to Negro communities throughout the country.

The march was scheduled to take place on July 1, 1941. A
demonstration involving upwards of fifty thousand Negroes
in the nation's capital was filled with danger, and the administration recognized its gravity. Four days before the appointed day, Randolph was summoned to Washington. The
administration leaders made new pledges and persuaded him
to call off the march. A few days later President Roosevelt, in
a public statement, broadly condemned racial intolerance and
urged the country to drop its bars against the employment of
racial minorities.

The masses of Negroes were bewildered by the sudden turn
of events; indeed, many of Randolph's own colleagues were
disgruntled by the easy conclusion of the affair. Nothing tangible had been gained, they felt. The recent incidents at the
army camps and the chronic, acute unemployment bear them
out. Randolph lost much prestige as a leader. And Negroes
now appear to be taking the situation into their own hands

and stampeding their leaders, with the result that newer and younger men now are taking the helm. The Negro public is particularly critical in the Eastern urban areas.

Naïve attempts to mollify the natural resentment of Negroes have served only to aggravate the problems. Recently the War Department, noticing the gathering of ominous clouds, gave a forty-five-minute radio broadcast over a nationwide hook-up of NBC, featuring the Negro soldier. Officials in the War Department hoped this would soothe the wounded feelings of the race. Unhappily, the program missed fire. In reporting the event, The Chicago Defender, leading Midwestern Negro weekly, headlined its story, "Soft Soap." The Pittsburgh Courier called the affair a "flop." Roy Wilkins, editor of The Crisis, writing in The Amsterdam-Star News, said he tore up his studio admission tickets. "Who wants to fight," he wrote, "for the kind of 'democracy' embodied in the curses, the hair-trigger pistols and the clubs of Negro-hating hoodlums in the uniforms of military police?"

What Negroes wanted to hear, one paper commented icily, was not how racial separatism was being perpetuated in the army as outlined by Undersecretary of War Patterson, principal speaker on the radio program; nor did they need him to remind them that they were being compelled to defend a democracy almost nonexistent for most of them in many parts of the country. What they did want to hear was what the War Department was doing to put into practice the democracy preached by the administration. "Instead," said The Courier, "Negroes heard the old familiar platitudes, a eulogy of black soldiers who had won honors fighting for democracy, a little tap dancing and what amounted to praise of a jim-crow system that mocks the word democracy."

Negroes may differ among themselves on minor issues concerned with day-to-day living, but on the question of their rights—political, economic and moral—and the right to integration in American life, they present an almost solid bloc. For, as individuals, they face common problems, regardless of status. They have learned on many bitter occasions that no individual can rise far above the condition of the race; not even the most distinguished. Paul Robeson, the concert artist, and Big Jim, the stevedore, both feel the lash of prejudice.

This curious characteristic of American life has caused the manifestation of a Negro group consciousness and provided the economic basis for a feeling of solidarity among its members. Thus, the more fortunate members of the race have been forced into what might be called a united front with the masses. And they have been compelled by the very nature of this position into articulating the aspirations and demands of the underprivileged. Today, in the present national emergency, these demands are for a fair share of the jobs in the defense industries and for the protection of the Negro soldier against the violent prejudice of both the white civil and military populations throughout the country.

To dismiss this situation—a formidable bar to national unity—as only the inevitable discontent of a rapidly progressing, educated group of the race, is to be blind to the true picture. Casually to term the protests fulminations of "agitators" is to impute false motives to these people. The question of liberty, equality and the pursuit of happiness in a democracy is the point at issue, and the Negro is reacting in a positive way to the high-minded slogans currently heard.

Negroes—driven into the category of second-class citizens —feel, with logic on their side, that the American people should expend some of their crusading zeal within the borders of the United States.

The New Republic, November 10, 1941

"Will Two Good White Men Vouch for You?"

by Tolly R. Broady

On October 7, 1941, I appeared before the Board of Registrars in an Alabama county and this is a true account of what happened. After I had stated my desire to register, I was asked if I had "three hundred dollars worth of taxable property." I replied in the negative and added that it was my understanding that the property qualification was an alternative to the literacy qualification.

"No! you will have to have three hundred dollars worth of property or forty acres of land." After a lapse of a few minutes I asked if I would be permitted to file an application? "Yes, I will take your application but the board will have to pass on you and you don't have three hundred dollars worth of taxable property and that is one of the qualifications. Do you know two white persons who will vouch for you?"

"Yes," I replied giving her the names of two local shopkeepers.

"One of these persons will have to come in and sign for you," she explained.

I left the office of the board of registrars and went across the street to a radio shop where I had recently purchased a radio. After I had made known the nature of my visit the shopkeeper promised that he would go over later that afternoon and sign for me. On October 9 I called the radio shop and asked the proprietor whether he had found the time to go over and vouch for me the day before. He stated that he did not find such an opportunity but that he would try to find time that day. On October 10 and 13 I called with the same result. The polls closed on October 13, reopening November 4. On the morning of November 4, I called the shopkeeper and he told me to come to his place of business at 2:00 P.M. I went to the radio store at 2:00 and I was told that the owner was out of town.

I resolved that I had better try to get some one else to vouch for me, so I went over to one of the local clothing stores and asked to see the proprietor. After asking me several questions the clothing store proprietor said that he knew me but "not well enough to take an oath," but that if I could get the cashier at the bank, where I had an account, to telephone him he would be glad to go over. I went to the bank and explained the trouble I was having and he consented to call the clothing store owner. But every time the cashier called the owner of the shop would be out. A few days later I went to the postmaster and asked him to call the clothing store owner. He did while I waited. After he had finished talking over the telephone, I was told that I should go to the clothing store that day at 1:55 P.M.

At approximately 2:30 P.M., on November 12, I appeared once more before the board of registrars in the company of the clothing store proprietor. Before I had an opportunity to explain that I had at long last been successful in getting someone to vouch for me, a member of the board explained: "We have investigated your application and I find that you don't have three hundred dollars worth of property or 40 acres of land and that's one of the qualifications." I asked again if this property qualification was not an alternative to the literacy qualification under Article VIII, Section 181 of the State Constitution, and I then proceeded to quote the sections.

After I had finished quoting from the state constitution, the man I had brought over to vouch for me turned and said, "Boy, it doesn't make any difference whether you graduated from Harvard; if you don't have the property you can't register." Without further comment I turned and walked slowly from the office. The clothing store owner followed. "Well," he said, "I guess you got to get $300 worth of property or 40 acres of land somewhere." I replied that I had no such intentions and that I intended to register, since there were provisions in the constitution for determining one's qualifications. He looked a little stunned as I turned to leave him.

On November 13 I presented myself before the board of registrars in the company of two other electors and asked what were the qualifications for an elector. When I was told that you had to have the property qualification, one of the electors asked when the amendment had been passed making both qualifications necessary.

One of the board members replied that she knew nothing about amendments, but that she had "marked the place in the book" which gave the qualifications. She then proceeded to read the passages. When she had finished reading the first qualification, she was asked her interpretation of the "or" between the paragraphs. To this she replied that the board of registrars got their interpretation from the attorney general. We asked to see the ruling, or at least where we might get an official interpretation of the "or". We were referred to the probate judge after one member of the board stated that "this board will have to pass on you, and we register who we want to register."

We went to the probate judge's office and told him that we had been referred to him for an interpretation of whether the "or" in the state constitution meant "and" and the judge replied that it did, adding "that you must have both the property as well as the literacy qualification." He was then asked whether all of the voters on the qualified list had the property qualification. He evaded this question and told us that he knew everything about beef cattle and tags for automobiles. I asked whether or not they ever purged the list of voters, and he replied "only once a year." I asked if the question of whether the person was a holder of $300 worth of property when the list was purged was ever considered. Again he refused to answer but stated that we were only trying to get him into an argument with the board of registrars.

With still no information on whether *or* meant *and*, I started preparation for filing an appeal to have my qualifications as an elector determined. That same afternoon the telephone rang and I was told that if I would go down town that afternoon I would be able to get my registration certificate. The caller asked me not to divulge his name, if I contemplated court action. (This step had evidently been taken to forestall court action.) I did not go down town that afternoon and the next morning I received another telephone call, this time, from the board of registrars telling me to "come down about 10:00 o'clock, we got some more questions we would like to ask you." I replied, "Thank you very much."

The above experience is not unusual. It is on the contrary the usual thing for a Negro to be denied the right to register. It takes various forms but the end result is always the same.

The Crisis, January 1947

Non-Violence vs. Jim Crow

by Bayard Rustin

Recently I was planning to go from Louisville to Nashville by bus. I bought my ticket, boarded the bus and, instead of going to the back, sat down in the second seat back. The driver saw me, got up, and came back to me.

"Hey you, you're supposed to sit in the back seat."

"Why?"

"Because that's the law. Niggers ride in back."

I said, "My friend, I believe that is an unjust law. If I were to sit in back I would be condoning injustice."

Angry, but not knowing what to do, he got out and went into the station, but soon came out again, got into his seat, and started off.

This routine was gone through at each stop, but each time nothing came of it. Finally the driver, in desperation, must have phoned ahead, for about thirteen miles north of Nashville I heard sirens approaching. The bus came to an abrupt stop, and a police car and two motorcycles drew up beside us with a flourish. Four policemen got into the bus, consulted shortly with the driver, and came to my seat.

"Get up, you —— nigger!"

"Why?" I asked.

"Get up, you black ——!"

"I believe that I have a right to sit here," I said quietly. "If I sit in the back of the bus I am depriving that child—" I pointed to a little white child of five or six— "of the knowledge that there is injustice here, which I believe it is his right to know. It is my sincere conviction that the power of love in the world is the greatest power existing. If you have a greater power, my friend, you may move me."

How much they understood of what I was trying to tell them I do not know. By this time they were impatient and angry. As I would not move they began to beat me about the

15

head and shoulders, and I shortly found myself knocked to the floor. Then they dragged me out of the bus and continued to kick and beat me.

Knowing that if I tried to get up or protect myself in the first heat of their anger they would construe it as an attempt to resist and beat me down again, I forced myself to be still and wait for their kicks, one after another. Then I stood up, spreading out my arms parallel to the ground, and said, "There is no need to beat me. I am not resisting you."

At this three white men, obviously Southerners by their speech, got out of the bus and remonstrated with the police. Indeed, as one of the policemen raised his club to strike me, one of them, a little fellow, caught hold of it and said, "Don't you do that!" A second policeman raised his club to strike the little man, and I stepped between them, facing the man, and said, "Thank you, but there is no need to do that. I do not wish to fight. I am protected well."

An elderly gentleman, well-dressed and also a Southerner, asked the police where they were taking me.

They said "Nashville."

"Don't worry, son," he said to me. "I'll be there to see that you get justice."

I was put into the back seat of the police car, between two policemen. Two others sat in front. During the thirteen-mile ride to town they called me every conceivable bad name and said anything they could think of to incite me to violence. I found that I was shaking with nervous strain, and to give myself something to do, I took out a piece of paper and a pencil, and began to write from memory a chapter from one of Paul's letters.

When I had written a few sentences the man on my right said, "What're you writing?" and snatched the paper from my hand. He read it, then crumpled it into a ball and pushed it in my face. The man on the other side gave me a kick.

A moment later I happened to catch the eye of the young policeman in the front seat. He looked away quickly, and I took a renewed courage from the realization that he could not meet my eyes because he was aware of the injustice being done. I began to write again, and after a moment I leaned forward and touched him on the shoulder. "My friend," I said, "how do you spell 'difference'?"

He spelled it for me—incorrectly—and I wrote it correctly and went on.

When we reached Nashville a number of policemen were lined up on both sides of the hallway down which I had to pass on my way to the captain's office. They tossed me from one to another like a volley-ball. By the time I reached the office the lining of my best coat was torn, and I was considerably rumpled. I straightened myself as best I could and went in. They had my bag, and went through it and my papers, finding much of interest, especially in the *Christian Century* and *Fellowship*.

Finally the captain said, "Come here, nigger."

I walked directly to him. "What can I do for you?" I asked.

"Nigger," he said menacingly, "you're supposed to be scared when you come in here!"

"I am fortified by truth, justice and Christ," I said. "There is no need for me to fear."

He was flabbergasted and, for a time, completely at a loss for words. Finally he said to another officer, "I believe the nigger's crazy!"

They sent me into another room and went into consultation. The wait was long, but after an hour and a half they came for me and I was taken for another ride, across town. At the courthouse, I was taken down the hall to the office of the Assistant District Attorney, Mr. Ben West. As I got to the door I heard a voice, "Say, you colored fellow, hey!" I looked around and saw the elderly gentleman who had been on the bus.

"I'm here to see that you get justice," he said.

The Assistant District Attorney questioned me about my life, the *Christian Century*, the F.O.R., pacifism, and the war, for half an hour. Then he asked the police to tell their side of what had happened. They did, stretching the truth a good deal in spots and including several lies for seasoning. Mr. West then asked me to tell my side.

"Gladly," I said, "and I want *you*," turning to the young policeman who had sat in the front seat, "to follow what I say, and stop me if I deviate from the truth in the least."

Holding his eyes with mine, I told the story exactly as it

had happened, stopping often to say "Is that right?" or "Isn't that what happened?" to the young policeman. During the whole time he never once interrupted me, and when I was through I said, "Did I tell the truth just as it happened?" and he said, "Well——"

Then Mr. West dismissed me, and I was sent to wait alone in a dark room. After an hour, Mr. West came in and said, very kindly, "you may go, *Mister* Rustin."

I left the courthouse, believing all the more strongly in the non-violent approach, for I am certain that I was addressed as "Mister," as no Negro is ever addressed in the South; that I was assisted by those three men; and that the elderly gentleman interested himself in my predicament because I had, without fear, faced the four policemen, and said, "There is no need to beat me. I offer you no resistance."

Fellowship, July 1942

Thrown from Train, Attacked

by L. O. Swingler

MEMPHIS, Tenn. — (SNS) — Bodily thrown from a Frisco passenger train, the Sunnyland, by two Tupelo, Miss., police officers last Saturday evening following complaints of the conductor that he had been "sassed," Prof. Hugh M. Gloster, Professor of English at Morehouse College, Atlanta, and for many years a faculty member of LeMoyne College, was viciously beaten, his life threatened, and fined $10.00 while en route to Memphis to visit his mother, and friends.

He didn't reach Memphis until Sunday night. Taken immediately to Jane Terrell Memorial hospital by friends, it was disclosed that Mr. Gloster, who is one of the outstanding educators of the country, had suffered head and body bruises as the result of the unmerciful beating by the officers. His eyes were discolored from the attacks, his head badly bruised, and the examination showed injuries of the nose, face, right arm, legs, and right side.

The Tupelo officers, although Mr. Gloster was in the custody of the police for more than twelve hours, never offered any medical treatment for his injuries.

Mr. Gloster's experiences, reports of which have been shocking to a wide circle of friends in Memphis and Atlanta, grew out of a simple request he made of the train conductor for more accommodation to take care of the excessive number of colored passengers riding the Frisco between Amory, Miss., and Tupelo.

Mr. Gloster, coming from Atlanta, changed his train to the Frisco at Birmingham, around 10:15 Saturday night. By the time the train reached Amory, Miss., at 3:00 Sunday morning, the one coach for Negroes was over-crowded, and passengers stood congested in the aisle.

There were only two white passengers in the next coach, and Mr. Gloster asked the conductor if these passengers

19

couldn't be moved to the white section. During the course of the dispute between the conductor and Mr. Gloster, neither man used profanity but the trainman showed evidence of disturbance over the insistent request Mr. Gloster made for better riding conditions for colored passengers.

"I thought everything was settled until the train was a few miles out of Tupelo," Mr. Gloster stated. "When we were nearing Tupelo, the conductor came into the colored coach and took my ticket check from the window shade. I asked him why he was moving it in view of the fact that I was over a hundred miles from Memphis and the train had several other stops to make. He said (the conductor) that he merely wanted to make some corrections in his report," Mr. Gloster asserted.

When the train reached Tupelo, the conductor got off and called the police. Mr. Gloster said that he had no idea of this until some of the passengers told him that policemen were coming into the colored section.

"When the policemen, three of them, reached the colored coach, they asked, 'Where is the nigger?'" Prof. Gloster stated. "The conductor, pointing me out, said, 'There he is.'"

The prominent educator was then seized by the three officers, and the conductor, and pitched off the train. Afterwards, right in front of the door of the colored coach, Mr. Gloster was severely assailed for about five minutes. They took him to the squad car, and all the way to the police station, they beat their victim, cursed him, and asked if he had forgotten that he was a 'nigger.' One wanted to know whether he knew he was in Mississippi. Another suggested that he be taken out to the lake and beaten some more.

Mr. Gloster had to spend the rest of the night in a filthy jail cell where there were two other prisoners. The place was foul-smelling with blood, mercurochrome and body waste.

"Roaches crawled over me all night," Mr. Gloster stated, "and there was nothing but a dirty, smelly mattress on the bunk."

He was also searched at the jail. When one of the policemen opened his bag, he remarked that he should beat the "h . . out of me for having such a good bag," Mr. Gloster said.

They didn't take his money, about $42.00 in cash, but rambled all through his personal effects.

"As soon as I was brought to the office from the train, I asked for permission to get in touch with my people," Mr. Gloster said. "This request was refused by the officers, one of whom said they were going to put me in the chain gang.

"After sunrise the two day-officers came on duty and individually visited the cells. I asked the first if I might get in touch with my people, and he replied that I would have to wait until the chief came. When the second officer came by my cell, I asked him if I might call my relatives, and he said, 'So you're the nigger that sassed the conductor this morning. Don't you know you're in Mississippi? Have you ever been here before? If I'd been one of the arresting officer, I'd have beat your G . . . . D . . . . brains out.'"

Mr. Gloster later in the day (Sunday) was approached by a Frisco railroad agent, and asked to sign papers confessing that he was wrong and that he regretted recommending better riding accommodations to the conductor. The agent tried to impress upon Mr. Gloster that he had committed a grave wrong for which he could be kept in jail or put in the chain gang for disturbing the peace and trying to break the Jim Crow law.

"So under duress, and because I didn't know of any way to reach my people and didn't want to be further exposed to beating, I set down in my own handwriting a letter which he dictated and signed," Mr. Gloster continued.

"I never would have done this if I had not been under pressure or if I could have been sure that my people knew of my condition."

Mr. Gloster said that all along the agent was more interested in absolving his railroad line of any blame than he was anything else. He said that the agent even tore off the letterhead of the Frisco stationery before he gave him the paper to write the statement.

When given a choice of remaining in jail at Tupelo until the Amory Chief of Police sent for him or going back to Amory with the agent in order to stand trial, Mr. Gloster said that he told the Tupelo, Miss., Chief of Police that he preferred going to Amory, which was given jurisdiction over the case because it originated there.

In the meantime Mr. Gloster's brother-in-law, W. C. McFarlin, and Mrs. McFarlin, of Atlanta, had arrived on the scene. They accompanied Mr. Gloster and the agent back to Amory, and instead of taking the educator to jail, as intimated in Tupelo, the agent directed him to the Frisco office near the station.

Realizing that he had some cash money on him, the Frisco agent took Mr. Gloster in the Chief of Police's car to the home of the mayor. The mayor fined the Atlantan $10 and then told me the "case was a closed book," Mr. Gloster stated.

Mr. Gloster, during his teaching career in Memphis at LeMoyne, was active in community work. He served as General Chairman of the Boy Scout fund campaign in 1938, worked in the Red Cross drives, headed as president the local graduate chapter of Alpha Phi Alpha fraternity, served as assistant editor of the Sphinx Magazine, is founder of the Association of Teachers of Language of Negro Colleges, serving as its first president.

Atlanta Daily World, August 27, 1942

Out of Their Mouths

by Sterling A. Brown

I. The People Yes . . . Yes Indeed

Deep South—*a Soliloquy:*

"Why do you reckon white folks act like they do? I sit home studying them. A cracker is like this. He will cut his own throat just to see a Negro die along with him. Further and more, they're fussing and squabbling among theirselves so much that a man can creep up behind them unbeknownst to 'em and hit 'em on the head.

"Take Talmadge, that narrow-minded rascal. All this trouble, war, soldiers being killed by the thousands, hostages being killed, bombs falling on women and little children— and all he can do is woof about 'coeducation of the races' or 'segregation.' Somebody ought to dump him on his head in some sea or other.

"This war now. It looks like they don't want you in the navy, army, or marines. Just like before the war they didn't want you anywhere you could make a dime out of it. When those Japs first started out in the Pacific, I thought Negroes ought to thank their lucky stars that they weren't on those ships going down with the white folks. Then I got to studying and knew I was wrong. Onliest way we can get anything out of this war is to put all we can in it. That's my best judgment.

"The diffunce between the northern and the southern Negro is that the northern is a freeborn-minded Negro, but the southern is trained to say Yes-sir and No-sir all the time. That don't mean the southern Negro won't fight, but he's just more kinderhearted. The gurvenment is exchanging them, sending one to the north and one to the south.

"These crackers will chase a Negro like he was a jackrabbit. There ain't no right in their heart or soul.

"Do you think they will elect President Roosevelt for a

fourth term? They'd better, if they know what's good for the country. I don't wish him no hard luck, but I hope he will wear out in his job. But I hope that won't be for many a long year. Yessir, I hope he dies in the White House. But I hope he lives forever. He's the best friend the Negro ever had. Bar none, Lincoln, Washington, Teddy Roosevelt. And Mrs. Roosevelt, she's the greatest woman living today.

"The party—I don't give two cents for party. My question is who's gonna do most for me, my people, all the poor people. I'm a New Dealite.

"It's remarkable how the Negro continues to keep coming on. Right out of slavery, the Negro jumped into teaching college. Course he ain't perfect. Cutting, fighting, laziness. A lot of Negroes have gone to hell and destruction fooling around with numbers and that mess. But you can't fault the Negro for that. Not much diffunce between a man robbing you in the nighttime with a gun, and robbing you in the daytime with knowledge.

"The Negro's obstacles made a man out of him. Depression, lynching, all like that, the Negro kept coming, smiling and singing. They come on like the Japs before Singapore. You bend back the middle, the niggers (I mean Negroes) flow around the edges.

"I'm patriotic. I've got a boy in camp. Yessir, some of my blood is in the army. I love my country but I don't like the way they doing us down here in the South.

"I know all the professors. I guess I know more of the fine upstanding Negroes than any man in my field. I have seen 'em go from raggedy students to deans.

"I declare it's so hot today the hairs stick to your neck like flies to glue."

———

Old Mose had made the best crop of cotton he ever made, but still he came out even. The landlord told him he had done fine, and that he could start the next year out of debt. Old Mose didn't say nothing, just sat there looking. Old Cracker kept on making admiration over the crop and how fine it was to be out of debt. Mose didn't say nothing. Cracker kept throwing out chances for Mose to talk. Finally his curiosity got the best of him. "What you thinking about

Mose?" Mose just looked at him. Old Cracker banged his office desk and hollered, "What the hell you thinking about, Mose! If you don't tell me what you thinking, I'm gonna run you off my place." Mose said, "Oh, I was jes thinking, Mr. Landlord, jes thinking that the next time I ever say 'giddap' to a mule, he gonna be setting in my lap."

———

Store with newsstand, white operator, Negro neighborhood: "I lost eight sales on that *Ladies' Home Journal.* I wonder why did so many want that number?"

Magazine circulator: "Didn't you hear the governor's speech?"

Storekeeper: "No. Did they have an article on him? I read the *Saturday Evening Post* article."

Circulator: "No. He made a speech against the *Journal.*"

S.: "What for?"

C.: "Well, they had some pictures in it of colored people. Four or five pages. High-toned colored people getting ahead. When the governor spoke against it, that made all the white people want to see it. And it was already going like hot cakes among the colored."

S.: "Why doesn't somebody tell me these things? I wish . . ."

C.: "We don't know what's in these magazines until we get them. How do we know which way Governor Talmadge is going to jump? . . . I can't let you have but two *Supermans.* We can't keep anymore in stock."

———

A: "Little Orphan Annie has joined up, too. Did you see where she discovered the Negro?"

B: "Indeed I did. Harold Gray got around to it at last. At long last, too. The Asp, Punjab, that Chinaman and now the colored brother."

A: "You're never grateful for anything. He made the little Negro boy a sergeant, didn't he? And he showed that he was the one who found the car."

B: "Sure. But you never see him any more, do you?"

A: "Well, that was as far as he could go. Trouble with all you Negroes is you want little Annie to fall in love with that boy."

B: "Don't you put out that lie. Confidentially I think she's going to marry Daddy Warbucks when she grows up. Only reason I read the thing is for that."

———

"Uh-uh. Here it is. I see they have arrested Gandhi. He'll be a tough nut to crack.

"Used to make salt. Englishmen wanted them just to use English salt. Gandhi went down to the ocean and made salt out of the seawater. The English ordered him to stop making it. But he went right on making it.

"He's a man all right."

———

Negro Union Business Agent: "In the early 20's, when wages went up to a dollar an hour, the clamor went up as today for industrial training. The whites took over the Booker Washington idea. Most of our schools slept through the whole thing. The whites learned so fast and took over the jobs that had been called 'Negro jobs' so fast that the colored workers couldn't believe it. Now the white Technical High School and Boys High are giving from 25 to 30 courses in various trades, but over at Booker T. Washington they are hardly giving any. I blame our educators in part for that."

———

Negro bricklayer: "I know one local where whites and colored work together on the same scaffold, meet together in the same hall. They all kid and joke together. As a general rule there is brotherliness. Of course when the whistle blows, that just about ends. But the Negroes do have the whites' respect as good bricklayers."

———

Negro trade unionist: "Lots of white people are willing to work on the job with you side by side. Others object, and sometimes they talk so loud they scare the fairminded ones.

"Something about this working 'side by side' you ought to know. For instance, say I'm painting ceilings in here. The white man in the next apartment will be painting walls. But if I'm painting walls, he's painting ceilings. Just reverse and vice versa; I've seen it working both ways. Crazy ain't it?

"One trouble with the Negro worker, he doesn't know how to break into the union, he doesn't know what the labor movement is all about.

"Negroes and white workers just had to get together. Had to unite for strength. The smart white working men agree with that 100 percent. They want you on the job because you're entitled to it. They want you to get the same amount of pay. They're willing to go bargain with you. It's to their advantage. They wouldn't go out with you if it wasn't good business. But they don't play social equality. And most of them don't want you working side by side with them."

———

A: "Did you see this week's *Statesman*? A *great* educator, one of *your* people, is reported to have said, 'We want a separate little university of our own.'"

B: "He's gonna get it."

A: "Then he says, I quote: 'We came with the shackles of slavery about our wrists, today we are clothed with the American ballot, which makes us citizens of the greatest republic on earth.' Unquote."

B: "He said that?"

A: "Here it is."

B: "I don't want to read it. All I can say is that if the Negro is clothed with the ballot, he most certain sure is going around with his butt raggedy."

———

"The Negro starts out with two strikes on him."

"Well, it don't take but one to hit it."

———

Old woman: "Son, you worries too quick. You gotta learn how to take the sad stuff easy."

II. Southern Traditions

Southern White Editor: "These fellows come down here and instead of doing the job with common sense, they go at it in a crusading way. They just blow open prejudices. So the dyed-in-the-wool traditionalist backs up, god-damning this and that to hell. The way these crusaders go about they hurt some real friends of the Negro."

———

Negro journalist: "Some of these southern liberals used to want to accelerate Negro progress. Now it seems that all they want to do is put on the brakes.

"A lot of white women are up in arms because they have to bring up their own children."

———

Negro newspaper editor (backstage Louis Armstrong concert, City Auditorium): "Did you see that? White boy said to the Negro 'You go ahead,' and then drank out of the same water fountain. There's the paradoxical South for you. He was by himself. When they come in threes or fours, they won't do that. Scared of being called 'Nigger lover.'"

———

Little redheaded girl (Negro): "Ethel and I got on the elevator in the department store. You know Ethel is lighter than I am, and her hair is straighter. A white man got on, looked at me, and especially my hair. I was looking at him out of the corner of my eyes. He wasn't sure, and finally he took off his hat. We burst out laughing. Right away he put his hat back on his head."

———

On the train *Robert E. Lee*, headed South. In the Pullman washroom the whites had been neither hostile nor polite, but reserved. On leaving I overheard one say: "The price we have to pay for democracy!"

———

"If it had to happen—"

"Don't finish. That's what I wouldn't want to happen to a dog."

"No more would I, but what I'm saying is this. If it had to happen, it's best it happened to a great man like Roland Hayes. Shows Europe and the whole world how even our greatest, our potentates, ain't safer than our least ones."

"Them peckerwoods up in Rome (Ga.) ain't never heard of Roland Hayes or Europe either."

"Well, Europe is gonna hear of them peckerwoods."

———

Young Negro professor, working toward doctorate in American culture, closes his narrative of how he was thrown off the train and badly beaten at Tupelo, Miss. "He told me that I looked like a smart boy, that I ought to know better than to sass a white man in Mississippi. That he would fine me $5 for breaking the peace and $5.40 for costs of court, or else he would bind me over for the next court session. He advised me to pay the fine. After I paid it he said to me that he hoped I would profit by my experience."

Dr. P. talking: . . . "The road-cop pulled up and told me I'd been exceeding the speed limit, that he'd been pacing me on the whole trip. I told him the car wouldn't go much over 40. It was a red Chrysler with wire wheels, sorta fancy. I knew he didn't like the looks of it with me behind the wheel. Both of us argued back and forth. Finally he said, 'I don't know whether to shoot you or take you to jail.'

"I said, 'Well, it won't make any difference to me. One's about as bad as the other.'

"He said, 'You don't act like you're scared at all.'

"I spoke right up. 'Why you're the last man in the world I'd be scared of. You're the *law.* You're supposed to be my protection.'

"Man, that threw him off balance. He finally said, 'Well, Doc, you'd better watch yourself. There's a couple fellows in a pepped-up Ford (that's a Ford with a Frontenac head) on the road that are kinda mean. They'd like to pick you up in a car like this. So you take it easy now.'

"Then he growled at me, 'But you know damn well you were doing more than 40 miles an hour.'"

White liberal: "This Negro soldier was sitting on a seat opposite to a white man. The bus was not crowded, and he wasn't sitting in front of any white. But the driver came back and told him to move. He refused. The driver shouted, 'I'm gonna move you.' The Negro took his coat off and said, 'Well I'm fixing to go off and fight for democracy. I might as well start right now.' And I want to tell you that bus driver backed down. It did me good to see it."

Lawyer to Negro defendant who violated residential segregation: "You keep talking about the Bill of Rights. Do you know what the Bill of Rights is?"

Negro defendant: "I may not know exactly. All I know is that whatever it is, it's something the Negro ain't got."

———

FEPC HEARINGS.

Investigator: "You were first employed by the company seventeen years ago?"

Negro shipyard worker: "Yessuh."

Q: "You were upgraded for the first time within the past three months?"

NSW: "Yessuh. They made me a leaderman. . . ."

Q: "Why would you say that there has been so little upgrading?"

NSW: "Most of the men do not feel themselves capable."

Negroes in Amen Corner (whispers, low growls): "Why he's just a pimp for the company! Hurry up and get rid of that Negro. Put him off the stand."

———

BARBER SHOP. *The day that Life magazine appeared with pictures of Paul Robeson as Othello with a white actress as Desdemona:*

A: "Some Negro's going to get his head whipped before nightfall on account of that picture."

B: "I'll bet Talmadge is writing his Friday speech for the radio."

A: "Yeah. Gonna make Shakespeare out to be a communist, or a Rosenwald."

———

Young woman teacher (Negro): "Well the experiences I had were on the pleasant side. They used to set up a table for you in your space. But the porter came up and said they were going to serve me in the dining car. Had a sign on the table 'Reserved.' The steward pulled out my seat for me. The diner was full of white people; my table was right square in the midst of the car. As I sat down they put up the little curtain. But I could see the white folks eat, if I had been curious; and they could see me eat, if they were curious. And some of them were curious. The Pullman conductor tipped his hat when he came in the car this morning. Great day!"

Professor: "He must have thought you were Booker Washington's daughter."

III. This Is War

Negro taxi-driver (northern city, early months after Pearl Harbor): "Man, those Japs really do jump, don't they? And it looks like everytime they jump, they land."

Passenger: "More they land, the worse it's going to be for you and me. How's your rubber?"

T-D: "I know it's gonna be a long war. But one thing you've got to give those Japs, they showed the white man that a brown hand could handle a plane and a machine gun too."

P: "Yes, Hitler believes that they're fit to be allies of the great Nazis."

T-D: "Well, I reckon one's bad as the other, but they still can fight, and they've already knocked out a lot of the white man's conceit. And that's something."

———

Harlemite (shortly after Pearl Harbor): "All these radio announcers talking about yellow this, yellow that. Don't hear them calling the Nazis white this, pink that. What in hell color do they think the Chinese are anyway! And those Filipinos on Bataan? And the British Imperial Army, I suppose they think they're all blondes?"

———

Negro foreman (big as John Henry), Tuskegee Flying Field, talking about the Negro contractor for the building of the base:

"Have I anything to say about Mr. X.? I don't know what to say about him. I just don't have any words to tell you. He's a great man, that's all. Only way he can get shed of me is to fire me.

"I'll tell you something. I'm pastor of a little church. When I heard about this job, got a letter from Mr. X., I asked my church for a leave of absence. If they hadn't give it to me I was going to resign. You know when a preacher is willing to give up his church, he really must have heard a call."

———

Negro in charge of big government project: "The Negro has kept on saying: 'I can do it, I can do it.' But this is the kind of world where Negroes have got to say: 'Look, see what we've done!'"

First Negro: "They can't win the war that way. And they keep on messing around, they sure gonna lose it."

Second Negro: "That's all I've been hearing, 'they,' 'they,' 'they.' We've got to learn how to say 'We.'"

1 N: "I said it on purpose. When they let us work and fight for the country as much as we are willing and able, I'll stop calling it *their* war."

2 N: "You've got a point. They are shortsighted, no getting away from that. But it's still *our* war right on. They've taken some slow steps: employment, navy, new branches of the service."

1 N: "Slow steps won't win this war for them."

2 N: "Nor for *us*, either."

Civilian defense worker in a southern metropolis: "This was the first black blackout, the rest had been white blackouts. (Only houses of whites got orders.) Man, guns were going off every place. Airplanes dropping sacks of flour. One Negro said to me, 'They just dropped that flour on white folks' town. Showered it on the crackers, dodged the Negro sections. We'll be lucky if that's the way bombs fall.'"

IN A SMALL SOUTHERN TOWN:

Buying bus tickets in drugstore. White boys and colored en route to camp. Warm friendly atmosphere. All were talking about whipping the Japs. One Negro draftee holds spotlight with his badinage. Asks soda clerk for a coke. White boys drinking theirs look up. Noise and stir.

Soda Clerk: "Ain't got none."

Out front a truck is unloading cases on cases of coca-cola.

Negro: "You ain't got none? All that coca-cola I see and you say that? Now, that's bad stuff."

Clerk: "You want to make something out of it?"

The boy walks out into the streets. The screen door slams.

IN A BARBER SHOP:

A: "I see here by the paper that Bob Considine says 'The Little People fight on against Hitler tyranny.' All about the Belgian underground."

B: "What's that underground?"

A: "That's the way people get out of slavery. The name came from the Negroes here. A lot of slaves got away from the South by underground."

B: "Under the ground?"

A: "No. But under cover. At night time. Friends helped them. Some white folks, even."

B: "Never heard of it."

C: "That ain't all you never heard of."

B: "What do he mean by little people?"

A: "Frenchmen, Greeks, Jews—all of the little countries Hitler overcame and conquered."

B: "You got to be white to be little people?"

C: "You got to be white to be big people, too. You got to be white to be people. Period."

———

A: "Well, Bob Considine's all right."

B: "Whatcha mean, all right. He's white, ain't he?"

A: "Man, sometimes you sound like a black Talmadge."

B: "Don't you call me Talmadge. And don't call me black."

A: "If you was white, you'd be as hard on the colored as a hound dog is on fleas. Everybody white ain't bad."

B: "I would expect an old handkerchief head like you to say that."

C: "Considine used to be a sports writer, didn't he?"

A: "Yes. He was fair, too. He really wrote good stories about Joe Louis."

B: "It's easy for white folks to write good stories about Joe. What else could they write?"

C: "Yes, even that Pegler can find something good to say about Joe."

A: "Maybe they'll get around to writing something good about *Negroes* fighting against tyranny."

B: "Maybe they will. Then I'll be *for* them, same as you."

———

College Purchasing Agent: "I put a cracker salesman out of my office the other day. I was going to buy some stuff from him, $300 worth of it. He knew I was going to buy it, too. When I was just about ready to order he started getting confidential. He said, 'You know one thing. All this stuff was started by

these goddamn Jews. We get rid of these Jews everything will
be all right.'

"I said, 'That's just what Hitler is saying. I believe I'm not
going to buy anything today.'

"'What do you mean?'

"I mean I don't want anything from you.

"He got to stuttering. 'But—but you'

"I'm busy today.

"'Well, tomorrow,' he said.

"Today, tomorrow, from then on, far as you're concerned,
I'm busy. Now let me get to my work."

A Negro bragging at a gas station: "I done regist. Expect to
be called soon. That Hitler. Think he can whup anybody. I'm
gonna capture Hitler. I'm gonna deliver him to President
Roosevelt. At the front door of the White House."

The white bystanders applauded.

"Then I'm gonna fight for some rights over here."

The whites froze up.

A: "Yonder goes a Negro knows more about electricity
than the man that invented electricity."

B: "Yeah? What ditch is he digging in?"

FOLK TALES

"They're telling the story that a cracker running a lunchroom
at a railroad junction got a wire ordering lunches for 500 soldiers. He got together all the bread and eggs and chickens
and coffee and stuff he could. When the troop train pulled in
he saw they were Negroes. He ran to the officer in charge:
'You said 500 *soldiers.* Those are just Nigra boys.' The officer
told him they were soldiers in the uniform of their country.
Man kept on: 'You said *soldiers.* I can't serve those boys in my
place.' The captain wouldn't budge. Finally the man said to
the white officers, 'Well, y'all can come in and eat but I'll have
to put their food in boxes. I reckon I can stir up that many
boxes.'

"'No; these men must eat hot food.'

"But that cracker wouldn't give in. So the boys went unfed.

The story goes that all the townspeople went together and put in so much money apiece to save white supremacy and the lunchroom man's money."

—

On a border city trolley, a strapping white sailor, in a spic-and-span white suit, jumped up from the seat when an old Negro woman sat down beside him. He stood scowling, looking around for support.

"Thank you, son," she said. "But I didn't need the whole seat. I spread, but not that much. You know, you sure look cute in that pretty white suit Joe Louis bought you."

—

Taxi-driver, northern city: "One of the Negro soldiers came back on leave with his eyes blacked and hands all bruised and tore up. He said it was hell down there. You either took it or you fought back. Said a cracker yelled at him, 'You goddam nigger, get off the sidewalk down in the street where you belong.' Said everything, really lower-rated his mother. The soldier told me, 'I just couldn't take that. So I had to fight.' He could barely see out of his eyes but the skin was off his knuckles."

—

A: "I heard that the crackers made threats that if a Negro aviator ever lighted in their fields they'd burn the plane and lynch the pilot. Is there anything to that yarn?"

B: "That's stuff. It's really been just the opposite. They tell the story of a cadet who got lost in Florida. Some of these details may be wrong, but when you meet him he'll vouch for the rest. He lost his way and landed in a Florida field. He says that as soon as he came to a stop, a little white boy stuck his head over his wing and asked 'Are you a Jap?' But he proved to everybody's satisfaction that he was an American Negro.

"Since his orders were to stick by his plane whenever grounded, there he stayed. All of the people of the nearby town, white as well as Negro, looked out for him. The story goes that the next day when the lieutenant and the pilot found him, there was a picnic spread out on the wings of his plane: thermos bottle with lemonade, sandwiches, cake, everything. And some young white ladies were waiting on him.

The boys at primary swear that the cadet brought back a lot of canned goods in his plane. They say they're still eating them."

—

Attributed to Joe Louis by a public speaker: "There may be a whole lot wrong with America, but there's nothing that Hitler can fix."

The Race Riots

by Thomas Sancton

ALL these words of anguish which swirl and flow through the press and out upon the air waves in the wake of the Detroit race riot are useless. The thing is done. What we say about the riot can never raise thirty-one men and women from the grave. What we say about it can never heal smashed mouths and ruptured eyeballs. It can never quiet the terrors of a hundred thousand Negro children who will remember all their lives what happened to them here in America. It can never replace lost tanks and planes. It can never redeem the legion of lost Americans, the fascists of Detroit. It can never silence the Tokyo radio. We have lost a battle in Detroit. It was a clean defeat. Nothing was salvaged.

There will be many official and unofficial explanations of the riot. We shall hear over and over again about the first fistfight between a white man and a Negro on Belle Isle bridge; about the rumor which swept immediately through the Negro residential areas that a Negro baby had been thrown from the bridge; about a rumor which swept through the white sections that a Negro had killed a white girl on the island. Mayor Jeffries of Detroit has already given what looks like the official white-folks line-up on the day's events: The Negroes began the rioting, wrecked white property, attacked white men in the Negro section. Then, "The white people were slow getting started, but when they did get started they sure made up for lost time."

In the absence of a thorough, reliable report, it is impossible yet to tell exactly what took place during the riot and what the causes were. Most of the accounts in the daily press have been sent out by white reporters. They constitute a white-man's version of the riot. But what can we honestly say in the face of the abundant internal evidence of their news photographs, and the unintended implications of their stories?

Every one of the sixteen victims shot down by Detroit's predominantly Southern police force the first day of the rioting were Negroes. The news photographs of the flaming, exploding automobiles show the destruction of Negro property, not white. There are pictures of Negroes lying dead and wounded on the streets; begging for mercy; running like animals before white mobs armed with pipes and beer bottles. Almost without exception, the pictures of those arrested show only Negroes, men and women, lined up like cattle, hands above their heads. There is one revealing picture of a bewildered Negro man held by two policemen, and being struck by a white rioter; something speaks out from that picture beyond any force of argument; the white man knew the police were with him. There is a picture of a Negro cowering against a wall as two policemen came in fast with clubs. Twenty-five of the thirty-one dead are Negroes.

The local newspaper accounts contained paragraphs like this one from The Detroit News:

"Sturks and Hamilton [Detroit policemen] then entered the store and were confronted by two unidentified Negroes who began cursing the officers. The patrolmen fired simultaneously and both Negroes crumpled to the floor, dead."

Negroes must certainly have rioted, destroyed white property, fought back, when they had the chance, in defense of their lives. But it is the Negroes who do the suffering and the dying in American riots; the dark and agonizing knowledge of it hangs over them all the days of their lives. They don't start riots. They are the victims.

One feels the futility of trying to say anything of any usefulness or meaning about what happened in Detroit. A blind man could see it coming. For three years the country has witnessed an unending succession of warnings of race riots—from individuals ranging from reactionary white Southerners to radical Northern whites and Negroes. Most of the warners, it is true, had views of America and of democracy that were themselves irreconcilably in conflict; but all who gave any thought to the race problem knew that it had reached a dangerous crisis. And nowhere was the fact more apparent than in Detroit.

In the last three years Detroit has swollen and festered with all our accumulated national poisons. Detroit brought them to an ugly, pustulate head. There was race hate there older than the Nazi Party, older than the American Constitution; and there were new treasons and new traitors, rank with the fascist evil. Detroit is our fourth largest city, with two and a half million population in the greater industrial area. Hundreds of thousands of these were Negro families, who came up from Mississippi, Alabama, Tennessee, Louisiana during the last war and through the twenties. Special trains were run from Southern cotton fields to carry the Negro migration. Later, during the thirties and especially after present armament expansion began, white Southerners and other outlanders, by the hundreds of thousands, came to work in the plants. The old subdued, muted, murderous Southern race war was transplanted into a high-speed industrial background. I do not mean that the presence of Southern whites and Negroes was alone responsible for the Detroit tension, but it was one of the important factors. There were other raw, fascist-minded newcomers. There were other distinct, clannish groups like the Poles.

The Ku Klux Klan took on new life in Detroit. It signed up thousands of members, streamlined its organization, used the Communist boring tactics and heavily infiltrated the United Automobile Workers. The Southern Society, loyal to a similar ideology, built up a membership of some 16,000. The Black Legion flourished. Father Coughlin built up his first great following there—and a fat war chest for American fascism. Frank Norris, the hell-shouting, Negro-hating Texas preacher, opened a tabernacle in this fertile city and it prospered; he built up one of the biggest "congregations" in Detroit and began to commute back to Texas by airplane. Gerald L. K. Smith, once a Louisiana preacher, who fled with other political stooges when Huey Long was killed, at length found a spiritual home again in Detroit.

There was a coming together of sharks: race-hate preachers and various other kinds of shouters from the South; seditionists and anti-Semites from New York and Brooklyn and Boston; German traitors. The Nazi Bund grew up there. Fritz Kuhn and many of its other leaders found steady employment in the Henry Ford plant. Any capable agitator who wanted to get out a fascist propaganda sheet, or start an organization, could usually get financed by one industrialist or another. The Sunday broadcasts over Detroit's radio stations were a babble of racism, fundamentalism, ignorance and guile. They stank of an anti-democratic ferment going on below the city's surface. No city, North or South, could match this hellish Sunday symphony of the Detroit radio stations.

The National Workers' League was another organization which helped give Detroit its Nazi tone. The League's benevolent interest in workers manifested itself in projects like the incitement of the Sojourner Truth housing riot two years ago. In this instance, it will be remembered, occupants of a new Negro housing unit were stoned and driven temporarily from the area. The inciters of the riot tried to create the impression that white "neighbors" of the project had risen in a wave of spontaneous anger to block the project by force. A check of the license plates of some of these "neighbors" revealed that they came from as far as twenty-five miles away. And finally Parker Sage and Garland Alderman, officials of the National Workers' League, were indicted for inciting the riot: indicted, long months ago, but never brought to trial. A stiff jail sentence for the guilty in the Sojourner Truth incident would have been strong and simple American propaganda. Perhaps for that reason, none of the officials of Detroit had courage enough to carry through this case.

The Eleanor Club myth—stories of conspirational Negro groups organized by Mrs. Roosevelt—was deeply rooted in the city. This piece of propaganda is so perfectly tailored to the American race problems that it seems unbelievable it was not created in the German Propaganda Ministry. Beyond a mild and supremely negative announcement by Attorney General Biddle that the FBI had not been able to find the existence of any Eleanor Clubs, no effort remotely approaching adequacy has been made by the government to combat this effective enemy lie.

The Ethiopian Pacific League worked the Negro side of the street. This is a fifth-column organization started years before Pearl Harbor by the Japanese. It is tailored to Negro hate and ignorance with the same consummate expertness that the Eleanor Club lie was patterned for the whites. Led by

Negro traitors, a number of whom have been imprisoned, the League advanced the Japanese as the champions of all colored races and sought the aid of American Negroes against the whites. The basic loyalty of Negroes in this country is un-shaken; they are cynical of much hypocritical white oratory, and in their own minds millions of them are as earnest to win withheld rights and dignities in America as they are to win the war abroad; but basically they know it is a United Nations and not an Axis victory which contains the promise of a bet-ter life for them. Yet in quagmires of hate like Detroit, the Ethiopian movement has achieved some following, and there must certainly have been a few Negro provocateurs in the group of riot conspirators—traitors to America and traitors to the Negro people.

The city became gravely overcrowded as war work ex-panded. There was, and is, a housing scandal. Real-estate in-vestors—aided by industrialists who did not want their migratory workers to become entrenched and independent—blocked any chance for a strong and adequate federal housing program to take care of the most primary needs of the work-ers in the arsenal of democracy. Trailer camps grew up, and with them a sizable population of delinquent, rootless "trailer boys"—the cruel, pitiable, negative young savages who are good for riots and for fascist *Putsches*. Negroes and whites lived in overcrowded quarters. They competed for what little housing was available, competed for food in the markets, competed for seats in the movie houses. Negroes learned skills. (Yes, Negroes *can* learn them, and this is one of the el-emental causes of our race war.) Negroes were put in jobs where only white men had worked.

Sunday was a hot day in the city. The Belle Isle recreation island in the Detroit River was packed with sweltering, irrita-ble whites and blacks. A fight broke out on the bridge. Whites and Negroes joined. The provocateurs went to work through-out the city. The Detroit riot, which everyone knew was com-ing, had begun.

Here is a partial list of the race clashes which have occurred within the past few weeks:

Detroit—riot.

Beaumont—riot; two killed, seventy-five injured; Negro section of the city "stomped into the ground," according to a city official; war production cut down.

Mobile—riot; more than a score of Negro ship workers beaten; large shipyard thrown out of production for several days.

Camp Stewart, Georgia—riot between Negro soldiers and white military police; one white MP killed and four others wounded; caused by long-standing discriminations and friction and the alleged beating of the wife of a Negro soldier by a white MP.

Marianna, Florida—lynching; white men seize and beat to death a Negro prisoner whose conviction for the hammer-slaying of a white man was twice overturned by the state supreme court.

Los Angeles—riots against Mexicans and Negroes.

Newark, New Jersey—gang warfare between white and Negro youths; one Negro killed.

El Paso, Texas—clash between white soldiers and a group of Negro soldiers who were rushing to El Paso from Fort Bliss because they had heard false rumors of rioting; one Negro soldier killed and one white soldier critically wounded.

Fort Custer, Michigan—five Negroes of a quartermaster battalion were arrested for trying to seize arms and trucks to go to the aid of Detroit's Negroes.

Collins, Mississippi—ten Negro soldiers arrested, one clubbed, one shot, when a Negro baseball team returning to Camp Shelby was stopped by a white policeman for speeding.

Centreville, Mississippi—"investigation" of local conditions begun by army inspector general's office following trouble between townsmen and Negro soldiers at Camp Van Dorn; one soldier dead.

Philadelphia—four Negroes beaten by a mob of white boys.

Washington—race-riot rumors sweep the capital.

What has caused this mounting race crisis? Has it been the radical leadership of white and Negro individuals? Or has it been a general shift of the economic and spiritual position of the Negro group relative to the white group; a taking up of new bases, long desired by Negroes, but only made possible by the war? It seems to me the second answer is obvious. This shift cannot be divorced of course from the leadership and agitation of individuals; but the swift tides of war and race conflict sweeping through all countries of the world have caused both the change in Negro outlook and the ascendancy of aggressive Negro leadership.

One leading Southern writer views the situation thus: "A small group of Negro agitators and another small group of white rabble-rousers are pushing this country closer and closer to an interracial explosion," etc. And it seems to me that this is meaningless. Where does India fit into this picture? China? Japan? Where do the awakening colored millions of the earth, a two-thirds majority, of which the American Negroes are a part, fit into the picture? Does such reasoning deny they are awakening; does it believe that the white man's monopoly of technology, his knowledge of guns and ships and planes and trades, will remain hermetically sealed within his race forever? That if he continues to insist on his master-racism, his arrogance, his de-facto privilege and overlordship of the earth, that he will not be called on in a few brief decades to prove his racial superiority?

A Mississippi editor, in a less sophisticated editorial, reduces this reasoning to its essence: "It is blood on your hands, Mrs. Eleanor Roosevelt. More than any other person, you are morally responsible for those race riots in Detroit where two dozen were killed. . . . You have been personally proclaiming and practising social equality at the White House and wherever you go, Mrs. Roosevelt. In Detroit, a city noted for the growing impudence and insolence of its Negro population, an attempt was made to put your preachments into practice, Mrs. Roosevelt. . . ." And this too is meaningless. What are these words—"impudence," "insolence"? In whose framework do they repose? As we battle and struggle down the years through the islands of the Pacific, needing our colored allies, clinging to them, who is going to have the privilege of defining these words, Mississippi editors or the millions of dark Chinese and Indians who are with us against the millions of dark Japanese who are against us?

The causes of the Detroit race riot do not exist only as of today or yesterday, and only in relation to the war. They exist in time and history. In one paragraph, Charles S. Johnson, the sociologist, gives the story*:

Subject races may take over the standards, taboos and other cultural elements of the dominant group, including even the concept of their own inferior status. This, indeed, frequently happens in a slave, or caste, organization of society; and no urgent race problems arise as long as the subject races accept or rationalize their position. The symbols of authority, preserved in the etiquette of race relations and in the conventions, crystallize into customs, which are enforced by informal means. Such a status quo, however, cannot be maintained indefinitely. The process of acculturation will inevitably cause a disturbance of fixed racial roles; for the influences of penetrating economic, political and religious forces cannot be isolated; nor can these elements of a dominant culture divorce themselves from others which are bound up in the web of personal relationships. There is no avenue of escape from the social and biological consequences of contact. Mixed-blood populations and culturally marginal peoples emerge. Adoption of the dominant cultural standards and values produces new wants, new aspirations and new ambitions among the subject peoples.

Mr. Roosevelt is faced with a race problem as grave as the one which faced Lincoln. The tragedy is that he almost certainly does not know this. The President has shown greatness as a military leader, and history may accord him a fuller measure than we dream. Yet, if he continues to lose his grip on domestic issues, his failure as a President may in the end be even greater. If it happens, history must render a merciless verdict against the little group of yes-men and intriguers who are his immediate advisers.

What have they been telling Mr. Roosevelt for months and years about the race crisis?

Okay, Boss. Okay, okay, okay. It's all okay, Boss. Everything will blow over. Don't get excited. Don't get worried. Don't think unpleasant thoughts, Boss. It will all blow over. We'll dust off this Negro delegation for you.

Long ago, a year ago at least, when riot rumors and hyste-

*"Patterns of Negro Segregation," Harpers, $3.50.

ria had already swept the South; when cities like Memphis and Norfolk and others had all but been plunged into the first, inevitable race riots; when Ku Klux Klan oratory was lighting the fuses of Mobile and Beaumont and Detroit (and others yet to come); the President should have come to this nation and talked to us as he did on the coal strike, on black markets, on war bonds, on a score of other subjects which already have been buried by the rubble of history.

Why, in these months when the peril of open race war hung upon the air, hasn't Mr. Roosevelt come to us with one of his greatest speeches, speaking to us as Americans, speaking to us as the great mongrel nation; immigrants (and the descendants of immigrants) all of us; none of us the master race, none of us independent of the other; why hasn't he come to us and talked to us in the simple and genuine language that Lincoln might have used, why hasn't he come waking memories of the old American dream, of live and let live, of a land where all men are endowed with inalienable rights, of a country where all are created equal? We are a people often cruel and cynical; but a great moment does not fail to move us.

Why does not the President come to us NOW with such a speech? He must! The race situation is not okay, Mr. Roosevelt, whatever the subtle men whisper. There will be other riots in America. Only a strong federal policy may prevent them.

There are many things that could be done to create a strong federal policy. (Even this casual citing of possible methods seems futile when we cannot get a *speech* out of Mr. Roosevelt.) There has been recent competent study in the field by people like Carey McWilliams, whose book, "Brothers Under the Skin," develops impelling arguments for establishing race relations on the basis of an affirmative national policy. He suggests a National Fair Racial Practices Act paralleling the Wagner Act, with an enforcement arm like the National Labor Relations Board. McWilliams proposes the creation of a congressional committee to conduct a broad study of the race problem. It seems to me that a report making comprehensive recommendations by a board with prestige and ability, such as the TNEC reports, might also serve this purpose. Certainly a division could be created in the Interior Department, equipped with real authority and charged with permanent attention to the race problem.

There are many things that could be done without causing another civil war. But all of them, even the mildest, will meet with political resistance from the South. Whether Mr. Roosevelt will be able to measure the necessity against the political cost we shall see; he has failed miserably to do so in the past.

Negroes must continue to leave the South. Negroes have been a fearful element in white Southern thinking too long. When their numbers grow less in the South, when the white Southerner is no longer confronted with disturbing images like the rural towns on Saturday nights overrun by a sea of black faces, and when Negro labor is no longer so abundant and so cheap, the white South may begin to fear the Negro less and value him more; and then programs may be considered even in the South, with a fair chance of succeeding. One of the most callous and tragic elements that has grown up in the Southern character is the tendency to consider the Negro an actual beast of burden, with no rights at all, not even the right of leaving. Southerners hate the Negro, but rather than see their cheap labor vanish, they will "put up" with him forever—indeed, insist upon it. But a program similar to the Farm Security Administration is needed to lend Negro families money to get out of the South in large numbers and to help them settle in sections in the North and West. Here they will find no paradise, but at least will have a chance at a few of the decent things of life, and some education. Even though the greatest racist of them all, Senator Bilbo, proposes sending Negroes back to Africa, many Southerners would greet with howls of rage and anguish any proposal to aid the migration of dollar-a-day cotton pickers. (There are many instances of this in Southern newspapers, and in Southern books like the late Will Percy's "Lanterns on the Levee.")

But such a program must eventually be attempted. The race problem, centered as it has been in Southern states, has been a cyst in our national anatomy. We must break it up, absorb it. Like a wounded man who, in his pain, lashes out against those who would help, the Southern people turn on the proponents of any kind of change, and resent any discussion of the problem. This is the deepest tragedy in American history, a people of virtue and courage, who have been blinded.

Here is a revealing paragraph from an editorial in The Ruston, Louisiana, Leader, titled "California Bound." The editor blames the New Deal because his "black boy has left after ten years of good and faithful service . . . without warning, without providing any relief and in doing so he has put us in a terribly awkward situation."

. . . He has become the victim of our government's thoughtless program and has removed one more good laborer from the South where they are the muscle and backbone of our livelihood. Numbers of good Negro workmen have left the businesses and farms of this parish, possibly never to return, and the hardship which they are putting upon us who need them is going to ruin this section of the nation unless we find some way to remedy the situation. The bad part about this is that the very best of our Negroes are leaving. Those we have educated and trained to be useful not only to us but to be leaders among their own people are among the first ones to go chasing rainbows.

It is hard to convey in words how deep-seated and ineradicable such intellectual brutality can be in the South. But the migration of the Negro northward and westward must continue; and it must continue under the guidance of sound federal policy so that congestion in a few Northern cities will not lead to friction and riots as it has in the past. But even with the riots of the past, even with ghettos like Harlem, the Negro people have been helped by the migration northward.

The United States never needed more gravely than it does today a strong and intelligent federal policy on the race issue. What shield can it be, what group of men, what one individual, what set of circumstances, which stand between the President and this fact? Whatever it is, may its place be accursed in history.

As a nation we sat with vacant eyes and waited for Pearl Harbor. For two years we sat and watched the Detroit riot in the making. How many other riots will we wait upon before acting? The situation recalls the fatalism of Alexander Stephens of Georgia before the election of 1860: "Men will be cutting one another's throats in a little while. In twelve months we shall be in a war, the bloodiest in history. There are not virtue and patriotism and sense enough left in the country to avoid it."

The New Republic, July 5, 1943

Eyewitness Story of Riot:
False Rumors Spurred Mob

by Ralph Ellison

AT 3 a.m. this morning, I left the Eighth Av. Subway at 127th St. and St. Nicholas Av. When I came out, there was the sound of gunfire and the shouting as of a great celebration.

Groups of people stood on the corners looking in the direction of Eighth Av. with the timidity of people afraid of flying bullets. The fellow on my right said "Gee, is this still going on?" I asked him "What?" He said, "The rioting. I left Harlem and went to Brooklyn about 10 p.m. and already it was going on at 125th St. and Seventh Av."

"What happened?" I said.

He said: "A cop shot a Negro soldier out at Braddock's bar."

(Editor's Note: This evidently referred to the shooting of a Negro Army military policeman in the Braddock Hotel, which precipitated the outbreak. The M.P., Pvt. Robert Bandy, was shot in the back; his condition is serious.)

I asked if the soldier had been killed. He said, "Yes, he was killed. The mob has been breaking windows and the cops have been shooting them down ever since."

By that time we were walking toward 141st St. Many people stood nervously on the corners desiring to reach their homes which lay across Eighth Av., but were afraid. Through it all there was an unending sound of burglar alarms. Then the fire trucks came, the hook and ladders, with red headlights flashing, the bells ringing, going swiftly through the dark streets.

When we reached 141st St. and started through, there was again the sound of shots fired. Boys and men approached us running, carrying rolls of linoleum, mattresses, clothing. When we reached Eighth Av. the street was full of people. Windows were being broken, glass was falling, men and boys darted in and out of windows, taking what they wanted.

In the crowd they talked about the soldier, who was rumored to have been killed. Indignation was expressed on the indignity suffered by a Negro soldier and against the police of Harlem.

At this time, there were few policemen in the area between 138th St. and 145th St. on Eighth Av. The angry mob wreaked its revenge on pawnshops, grocery stores, second-hand furniture stores, shoe stores, fish stores, liquor stores, jewelry stores, hardware stores, and corner bars.

These were the things they took: roll after roll of gaudy linoleum, second-hand chairs, cheap coffee tables with blue mirror tops, articles of clothing and food.

In half an hour, it seemed that all of Harlem was awake. Women stood on stoops in their nightgowns and wrappers and when the fire trucks went through with their flashing lights, you could see them framed in their tenement windows.

Instructions were shouted among the mob as to what stores to attack. As in the riot of 1935, no Negro store was knowingly molested. Most Negro merchants who were awakened in time supervised signs of identification on their premises.

Two types of stores were selected for special consideration: Pawnshops and groceries. Pawnshops located at 145th St. and Eighth Av. were entered despite the iron grilles which protected the front of the stores.

About 4 o'clock squads of police officers came to the center of the street, breaking up attacks on individual stores. They were greatly outnumbered, and when they gave their attention to one end of the block, the looters quickly gave their attention to the other.

It was noticeable that though these officers fired their revolvers into the air, the crowd was in no mood to give them serious consideration. It would have been a mistake had any officer lost his head so much as to have shot into the mob.

Going through the crowd, it was very noticeable that this whole incident was a naive, peasant-like act of revenge. I heard one man, as he was about to throw an ash-can through a window, exclaim: "I don't have to do this. I make a fair salary as a longshoreman. I'm doing this for revenge."

In the distance there suddenly came the sound of a voice speaking over a loudspeaker.

Soon we saw a WNYC truck approaching. The speaker, speaking in the name of the Negro Neighbor Victory Committee, asked the people to return to their homes. He assured them that the soldier had not been killed, and that Mayor LaGuardia had promised that fair judgment would be done. The crowd applauded and cheered, then returned to its looting activities.

As the night went on, women began to participate, bringing mattresses away and clothing for their children. And at 6 a.m. the kids came out to search within the rubble. I saw one little boy shoot past with a handful of candy bars and a penny whistle.

The sidewalks along Eighth Av. were filled with broken glass, broken clocks, and articles of furniture and clothing.

The burglar alarms were still ringing, and the store owners started coming and standing around their stores in consternation. It is very noticeable that in this section, no physical violence was done to any individual because of his color or creed.

In talking with the people along the sidewalks, I get the impression that they were giving way to resentment over the price of food and other necessities, police brutality and the general indignities borne by Negro soldiers.

By daylight, the crowds had thinned. As I see it, the situation has not ended. Much will depend upon how well Mayor LaGuardia, working with Negro elements who would rather not see this type of thing, is able to reach the people of Harlem.

New York Post, August 2, 1943

Jim Crow in the Army*

by Lucille B. Milner

I am a Negro soldier 22 years old. I won't fight or die in vain. If I fight, suffer or die it will be for the freedom of every black, any black man to live equally with other races. . . . If the life of the Negro in the United States is right as it is lived today, then I would rather be dead.

Any Negro would rather give his life at home fighting for a cause he can understand than against any enemy whose principles are the same as our so-called democracy.

A new Negro will return from the war—a bitter Negro if he is disappointed again. He will have been taught to kill, to suffer, to die for something he believes in, and he will live by these rules to gain his personal rights.

STATEMENTS like these are found over and over in the hundreds of soldiers' letters received by organizations defending the rights of the colored people. It is impossible to read a dozen of these letters picked at random without feeling their tragic significance. The war attitude of the Negro reflects today's dilemma of his race, in an intensified and critical form. The Negro soldier is deeply patriotic, vividly conscious of our aims in this war, eager to get into the fighting areas. That seems an ideal attitude for a soldier to have, but the truth is that the morale of the colored men in our armed forces is far from ideal. For they are not allowed to express their patrio-

---

*The letters quoted in this article are in the files of organizations such as the National Association for the Advancement of Colored People. For obvious reasons the names and addresses of the senders are withheld. It is the policy of these organizations to forward copies of letters making serious charges to the proper authorities for investigation. Thus many of the conditions described in the actual letters quoted, or scores of similar ones, have been authenticated by high military and civil officers, and in some cases have been corrected.—L.B.M.

tism, their democracy and their militancy freely. They have fought bravely in every war, from the Revolution on, but still they are not treated like Americans.

The sense of being excluded from the mainstream of military service is expressed in their letters in phrases like these: "We really have nothing to soldier for." . . . "It is not like being in a soldier camp. It is more like being in prison." A soldier at an air base wrote: "Segregation in the Army is making enemies of the Negro soldier, demoralizing him. You may wonder why they don't rebel. They do, but individually, and as a result, they are either transferred to Southern parts, placed in the guardhouse or given a dishonorable discharge from the army. . . . We keep constantly in mind that army law is WHITE man's law."

The very set-up in our various services proves that a race that has been three centuries on our soil is still considered Negro, rather than American. The fault is not in our pronouncements but in our practice. The Selective Training and Service Act of 1940 said distinctly that there shall be no discrimination against any person because of race or color.

How is this principle reflected in military practice?

The Navy has refused to commission Negroes in any branch of service—in the Navy proper, the Marine Corps and the Coast Guard.* While it has admitted Negroes to its fighting ranks, Jim Crowism is practised in training and in service.

The Air Corps has discriminated against Negroes in the most complicated and costly way, building a segregated air base for Negroes when there was room in established training centers over the country. The annual output of Negro pilots was 200 when it could easily have been five times that number.

The Army trains and commissions colored and white candidates without discrimination, but Jim Crow rules over every Southern camp.

Colored women are excluded from every auxiliary service but the Wacs, and here there is segregation.

With the Army calling for thousands of nurses, they have held down the quota of colored nurses to about 200.

*On February 15, 1944, since this article was written, the Secretary of the Navy announced that 22 Negroes will be commissioned.

Briefly this is the set-up. It reflects no policy on the part of our command, for the simple reason that no policy exists. It reflects merely today's confusion and the inherited tradition of our services from the prewar days when Southern officers in the Army and Navy had a good deal to do with molding attitudes. The Negro serviceman feels that the general pattern he must follow is this: to be barred from the sea and the air except on "their" terms; to serve on the land mainly in labor or "service of supply" battalions; to endure Jim Crow in every guise, from subtle slights to brutality and death at the hands of both peace officers and military police; to be kept on American soil and excluded from combat service as long as "they" can contrive retraining, or transfer, or some other run-around; in combat service to be kept if possible behind the lines and always out of the headlines, the newsreels and the glory; to come back as a war casualty and find Jim Crow waiting in most of the hospitals in the South.

The racial attitude of the military is a curious anachronism. Despite the gains made on the civilian front in race relations during the last two decades, actual conditions in our camps, most of which are unfortunately in the South, show a reversion to dark and ignorant prejudice. A corporal writes from the Deep South: ". . . It is no secret that the Negro soldier in the South is as much persecuted as is his civilian brother; the conditions existing in this Godforsaken hole which is Camp . . . are intolerable, and may be considered on a par with the worst conditions throughout the South since 1865."

Certain inequalities may not seem important until you think what they mean to the soldiers: post movie theatres and post exchanges barring Negroes in some camps and segregating them in others; guest accommodations for whites only in Southern camps; the fact that in many parts of the South Negro MP's may not carry arms as the whites do; exclusion from the white USO even when none exists for the colored men; overwhelming and widespread troubles about transportation in buses and trains. Candidates for commissions in a few of the training schools may eat, sleep and study together without regard to color—but what then? The white officer is soon sent overseas, the colored officer is apt to be transferred to another camp for "further training." The practice seems to be to keep the Negroes, as far as possible, from overseas duty, to use them at their lowest rather than their highest skills and to retard promotion.

Segregation is the deepest issue between whites and blacks in the services. It is made more bitter by the fact that North and South as well as white and colored are thrown together in the camps and bases. Northern-born Negroes are appalled at meeting Jim Crow on his home ground for the first time, and as a rule the Northern whites are also shocked. But Southern Negroes crossing the Mason-Dixon Line for the first time are confused by the comparative freedom of conditions in the North and West; it is claimed that they become demoralized. Southern white officers and trainees coming North often turn into rabid missionaries for "keeping the niggers in their place."

The soldiers ponder and write a good deal about this crisscross. A private at an air base in the Pacific Northwest writes: "The next sore spot that may respond to lancing is the attitude of the Southern-born or (climate of opinion) Commanding Officers. They try to impose a Dixie viewpoint on a democratic community."

A white boy from New York who had never thought much about racial problems wrote from a Southern camp:

I feel bitter towards the South and the Southern boys. I used to think that when one talked about the Civil War being fought all over again it was a gag. Not any more. We just had another discussion about the Negro situation. It seems to be the big thing around here. Some Southern boys do believe that the Negro should be treated as a man. They say: "Give them education, give them all the rights we have, but always remember that a white man is always better than a colored man. Let the white man live in one place and the Negro in another." . . . A boy runs into a brick wall when he talks to a Southern boy about the Negro.

From a colored officer in the Deep South:

The only desire the Negro officers could possibly have is to get completely out of the South. Many of us have never been below the Mason-Dixon Line, and are now being subjected to chain-gang practices and disgraceful and embarrassing verbal abuse. . . . No nursing or recreational facilities have been organized for us. . . . To go to a nearby city is to invite trouble, not only from civilian police but more often from the military police, who are upheld in any discourtesy, breach of discipline, arrogance and bodily assault they render the Negro officers.

Another young white officer, born in the North, made it a point to discuss race relations with hundreds of men, white and black, gathered from every part of the country at a Southern camp. He reports some reactions:

A white private from Virginia: "Gosh, I just had to salute a damn nigger lieutenant. Boy, that burns me up."

A professedly progressive school-teacher from North Carolina: "Give the Negroes equality of opportunity by all means —by themselves."

A technical sergeant from Texas: "You people up North want to change things overnight. You are heading for a revolution."

The segregation question will be a burning postwar issue. Meanwhile our High Command has the Supreme Court behind it. It has voided laws creating Negro districts in cities, but upheld those compelling separate railroad accommodations, declaring that segregation is not discrimination when the facilities offered both races are substantially the same. Taking the same ground, the Interstate Commerce Commission recently dismissed a complaint filed by eighteen Negro seamen against the Atlantic Coast Line. The men asked for "a bold declaration that segregation in and of itself today must be regarded as constituting an unlawful discrimination." That puts the Negro attitude on segregation in a nutshell. The Commission responded, "What complainants asked us to decide is in its essence a social question and not a question of inequality of treatment."

This makes it lawful, if somewhat grotesque, for incidents like the following to happen. On a crowded troop train going through Texas the colored soldiers were fed behind a Jim Crow curtain at one end of the dining car. In the main section, along with the white folks, a group of German war prisoners dined—and no doubt fed their illusions of race superiority on that Jim Crow curtain.

The assignment of Negro units in the Army to menial jobs is a widespread practice. Colored inductees go to camp for military training and find themselves assigned to service units —cooking, shoveling coal, waiting on the white officers. Entering service, they may find themselves building the Burma Road, or African bases, or encountering winter temperatures of 50 degrees below zero hacking the Alaska Highway or the Canol pipeline out of the Canadian wastes. Meanwhile white units trained at the same time are in the fighting war, where the Negro longs to be. "The sight of masses of Negro soldiers constantly blocked off into separate groups and assigned to menial jobs," a white officer writes, "generates in the mind of the average soldier a powerful feeling of superiority and of being 'different'."

A highly trained Negro technologist turned up in the psychotic ward of a hospital. His Army service was picking up papers around the officers' quarters in a Southern camp. When he was transferred to radio work his mental troubles vanished. Another inductee, a brilliant bio-chemist, had a fantastic Army career. At the reception center on the Pacific Coast the officers proposed to use his years of medical training to the Army's advantage. He was sent to Camp A for training and assigned to a post in the biological laboratory. Before he could start work he was shipped further east to Camp B, and enrolled for technical training as an armorer. He passed this course with high honors, and was promptly shipped to Camp C—farther west—classed as corporal and assigned to the Army Air Forces. A week later he found himself at Camp D in the Southwest, assigned to labor detail. That meant losing his corporal's stripes gained in another division. He wrote his wife:

I find that this post is the "Port of Lost Hope." . . . Merciful God, I have not been so close to loss of faith as I am at this moment. . . . All this build-up for something to respect, only to be treated like a brainless gorilla fit for nothing more than a post-hole digger and a stringer of wire, a yard bird. . . . I swear if this was Guadalcanal or Australia or North Africa I would expect nothing and would give everything, even my life. . . . It is mockery, let no one tell you differently, this sudden opening up of the so-called exclusive branches of the services to Negroes. We are trained, become skilled —and then the oblivion of common labor.

It is no secret that the Air Corps wished no Negro inductees. But it was forced to let the color bar down late in

1940 and created ten "Aviation Squadrons (Separate)" which served no specific military need and were assigned to whatever odd jobs of common labor the various air fields could offer. There was no equivalent white organization and these Negro units would probably never have come into existence but for the necessity of making some provision for the Negroes enlisted in the Air Forces.

The Air Corps began by training Negroes for combat aviation in only one branch—pursuit flying. A segregated base was set up near Tuskegee Institute and advanced training was at Selfridge Field. Pursuit flying is the most difficult type of combat aviation. Perhaps the Air Corps was paying tribute to the Negro; possibly it was trying to discourage him. In any event, the pursuit flyers not only made good in training, but the Ninety-ninth Squadron, the first and only one sent abroad, has won special praise from Secretary of War Stimson and others for its fine spirit and the specialized dive bombing the men were called upon unexpectedly to perform when the squadron was on loan to the British Eighth Army in Italy.

In 1943, schools for bombardiers and navigators were opened to Negroes and the first squadron, known as Squadron 10, was graduated on February 26, 1944, at Hondo, Texas, and will now receive training as bombardiers.

In some respects the Navy, with its ancient and Southern-gentleman traditions, tallies with the policy of the modern Air Command. Between 1922 and 1942 Negroes were "the chambermaids of the Navy," acting as stewards, chefs and messboys. Several months after Pearl Harbor the Navy broke down and admitted colored men as apprentice seamen with the chance of becoming petty officers. It has let down the bars to women—but no dark-skinned women. There are no colored Waves, Spars or Marine Corps Auxiliaries. And since no Negro could be commissioned up to a few weeks ago, there are no Negro chaplains in the Navy.

The Navy trains its seamen in a Jim Crow station near the Great Lakes Naval Training Station. In creating this new all-Negro camp it was thought fitting to name it for a seagoing Negro, and history provided the name of Robert Smalls, a hero of the Civil War. Smalls was a slave who served as pilot of the Confederate gunboat Planter. Early in the war he and his Negro engineer smuggled their families aboard while the white captain was ashore at Charleston. Smalls took the gunboat through the Confederate blockade and delivered it to the Union officers at Port Royal. He was commissioned in the Navy and served for the duration.

At Camp Robert Smalls the colored men took their boot training with no hope of being commissioned like Smalls. Their chief comfort is their white commander, Lt.-Comdr. Daniel C. Armstrong, whose father founded Hampton Institute and brought him up to understand race problems.

It is reliably reported that a large proportion of the Seabees, a remarkable new arm of the service, is colored. Much of the work is stevedoring and the building of naval bases and many of the Negroes who enlisted after Pearl Harbor are highly skilled artisans, college and technical-school graduates. Racial discrimination is thinly camouflaged by ratings—the Negroes, whatever their qualifications, are kept in lower grades and the men are segregated by grades, not by color. Recently fifteen Negro Seabees who had worked more than a year constructing a naval base in the Caribbean were dishonorably discharged as "unfit." Their real offense was telling their battalion commander, in what he assured them was an off-the-record consultation, that they objected to the Jim Crow conditions at the construction base.

The fact that no Negroes have been commissioned in the Marine Corps and the Coast Guard has not discouraged many youngsters who see a chance for adventurous and tough service in these branches. If they want higher pay and complete surcease from Jim Crow, they join the Merchant Marine. Since the Navy is out of the picture, any Negro who has served fourteen months on a floating unit may enter an Officers' Candidate School in the Merchant Marine. At present three merchant ships with mixed crews are commanded by Negroes—the Booker T. Washington, the Frederick Douglass and the George Washington Carver.

It is hard to decide which is more cruel—this new pattern of murdering the ambition, the skills, the high potential contributions of the gifted Negro, or the old pattern of physical brutality which the Negro-baiters and Klan agents use against the colored man in uniform. Soldiers of both races have been killed in camp riots which have grown out of unequal conditions and mounting tensions. But the Negro soldier is much safer in camp than in some Southern towns or on common carriers. He "finds himself not only outside the protection of the law but even the object of lawless aggression by the officers of the law," in the opinion of Judge William H. Hastie, former Civilian Aide to the Secretary of War, who felt it necessary to resign his high post in protest against the Air Corps policy toward Negroes.

For instance, last Memorial Day at Centerville, Mississippi, the local sheriff intervened in a minor fracas between a white MP and a Negro soldier whose offense was having lost a sleeve button. The two were fighting things out, with the other MP's and the Negro's companions holding back. When the MP began to get the worst of things, he yelled at the sheriff, "Shoot the nigger." The sheriff fired point-blank at the Negro's chest, then asked the MP, "Any more niggers you want killed?"

Another ugly story based on the sworn testimony of eyewitnesses concerns the murder of a colored private in Hampton, Arkansas, last spring. He was trying to protect his sister from assault by a white man who was drunk. A deputy sheriff intervened, and though it was the white man who attacked him, it was the black man who was shot. The deputy sheriff was never apprehended.

Buses and trains mean even more to the Negro soldier than to the white in parts of the country where there is no local Negro population, and he must travel far, or else hope for a visit from his family, in order to mingle with his own kind. The soldiers' letters describe endless troubles with buses and trains. Even when they are being transferred as troops, they are often refused service in the railway restaurants and go hungry for twenty-four hours. The wife and two babies of a Negro chaplain traveled three days to join him without being able to buy anything but cold milk and sandwiches. One gentle little Negro woman, whose soldier-husband was refused coffee at a bus terminal, delivered a sermon to the snappish counter-girl. "Our boys can fight for you," she said. "They are spilling their blood for you on the battlefield, yet you can't serve them a cup of coffee." But the management still refused the coffee. "May the Lord forgive them, for they know not what they do," she said in a quiet tone as they turned and left.

From 1770, when the colored boy Crispus Attucks fell in the Boston Massacre, down through the Battle of San Juan Hill and the Meuse-Argonne offensive, the colored Americans have been collecting their traditions of war and their flags and decorations and trophies. As far as we will let them, they are fighting as Americans today, and yet they are fighting with a difference. This, from a soldier's letter, expresses what is in their hearts: "Those of us who are in the armed services are offering our lives and fortunes, not for the America we know today, but for the America we hope will be created after the war."

The New Republic, March 13, 1944

A Blueprint for First Class Citizenship

by Pauli Murray

HOWARD UNIVERSITY traditionally has been called the "Capstone of Negro Education." When 2,000 young Americans, fresh from 45 states and students from 24 foreign countries arrived there two years ago, their futures uncertain, their draft numbers coming up every day, and their campus surrounded by the dankest kind of degradation they were tempted to call their alma mater the "keptstone" of education. More than half of these students had come from northern or border states or western and middle-western communities. Many of them had never tasted the bitter fruits of jim crow. They were of a generation who tended to think for themselves as Americans without a hyphen.

Thrown rudely into the nation's capital where jim crow rides the American Eagle, if indeed he does not put the poor symbol to flight, these students were psychologically and emotionally unprepared for the insults and indignities visited upon them when they left the campus and went downtown to see the first-run shows, or stopped in a cafe to get a hotdog and a "coke". The will to be free is strong in the young, and their sensitive souls recoiled with a violence that reverberated throughout the war time campus.

The revolt against jim crow started with a mutter and a rumble. It was loudest in the Law School where men students, unprotected by any kind of deferment, were being yanked out of their classes and into a G.I. uniform. "I don't want to fight in a jim crow army." "I'd rather die first!" "I'll go to jail first." were some of the remarks daily. During the first tense days of war time conscription, classes were almost entirely disrupted by the feeling of futility and frustration that settled over these young men.

And then the spirit of revolt took shape. It started in the

fall of 1942 with the refusal of Lewis Jones, Morehouse graduate, to be inducted into a jim crow army and the editorial comment of John P. Lewis of *PM* on Lewis' stand. Stung into action, a letter signed by 40 Howard University students, supporting the spirit which led Lewis to take such action, was sent to editor Lewis. He did not print the letter although he wrote the students a courteous reply.

In January, 1943 three women students were arrested in downtown Washington for the simple act of refusing to pay an overcharge for three hot chocolates in a United Cigar store on Pennsylvania avenue. The young women sat down at the counter and ordered hot chocolates. The waitress refused to serve them at first and they asked for the manager. They were told the manager was out, and they replied they would wait, keeping their seats at the counter. After hurried legal consultation the "management" ordered the waitress to serve them, but upon looking at their checks they were charged twenty-five cents each instead of the standard dime charged for a packaged hot drink. The young women laid thirty-five cents on the counter and started for the door where they were met by a half dozen policemen, hauled off to a street corner, held until the arrival of a Black Maria, and landed in prison in a cell with prostitutes and other criminal suspects. It was not until they were searched and scared almost out of their wits that the dean of women at Howard University was notified and they were dismissed in her care without any charge lodged against them.

The flood of resentment against the whole system of segregation broke loose. Conservative administration members frowned upon this "incident" and advised the three young women they should not stage individual demonstrations against jim crow. It was suggested they should work through an organization concerned with such matters.

These young women of Howard were determined. Others joined them. They took the matter to the student chapter of the NAACP. In the meantime from the Law School issued a new trend of thought. The men had spent hours in their "bull sessions" discussing attack and counter-attack upon jim crow. One second-year student, a North Carolinian and former leader in NAACP, William Raines, had agitated for months for what he called "the stool-sitting technique." "If the white

people want to deny us service, let them pay for it," Raines
said. "Let's go downtown some lunch hour when they're
crowded. They're open to the public. We'll take a seat on a
lunch stool, and if they don't serve us, we'll just sit there and
read our books. They lose trade while that seat is out of circulation. If enough people occupy seats, they'll lose so much
trade, they'll start thinking."

While Raines was arguing another student, Ruth Powell,
from Boston, Mass., later chairman of the dynamic Civil
Rights Committee, was doing just this. She would sit for
hours and stare at the waitress who had refused her service.
She reported it disconcerted the management and sometimes
she might even be served.

When this point of view percolated the campus, the students
went into action. Raines went into the army but his idea went
on. A temporary Student Committee on Campus Opinion was
formed. A questionnaire was distributed throughout the campus on February 3, 1943, testing student and faculty reactions
to an active campaign against segregation in Washington, D.C.

292 students answered the questionnaire. 284 or 97.3% of
those said they did not believe Negroes should suspend the
struggle for equal rights until the end of the war. 256, or 97%
of those answering this question said they believed Negro students should actively participate in the struggle for equality
during war time. 218 said they would actively join a campaign
to break down segregation in Washington; 38 indicated they
would not join but would support others who did. Only 6
disapproved of the idea.

A Civil Rights Committee was formed in March under the
sponsorship of the Howard Chapter, NAACP. The students
unearthed an "Equal Rights Bill for the District of Columbia,
No. 1995," introduced by Congressman Rowan of Illinois and
a companion bill introduced in the Senate by the late Senator
Barbour from New Jersey.

The Civil Rights Committee undertook a campaign to
bring equal accommodations to the District of Columbia.
They set up five sub-committees, publicity and speakers' bureau, program and legislative, committee on correspondence,
finance, and direct action. They lobbied in groups with the
representatives and senators from their states. They made in-

genious little collection cans out of hot chocolate cups and collected pennies from their classmates to pay for paper and postage. They held pep rallies around campus and broadcast their campaign from the tower of Founders Library. They sponsored a Town Hall Meeting at Douglass Hall and brought in community speakers to lead a discussion on "Civil Rights" and the techniques by which they were to be attained.

Their most interesting project, and the one to draw the most fire, was the Direct Action sub-committee. There the "stool sitting" idea combined with the "sit-it-out-in-your-most-dignified-bib-and-tucker" idea to make a fundamental thrust at the heart of jim crow.

A committee of students surveyed the accommodations of the immediate Negro community on northwest U Street. They reported four stores which still excluded Negroes and catered to "White Trade Only." One of these cafes, the Little Palace Cafeteria, run by a Greek-American, was located at 14th and U Streets, NW, in the heart of the Negro section, and the stories told by Negroes of their embarrassment and mortification in this cafeteria were legion.

The direct action sub-committee spent a week studying the disorderly conduct and picketing laws of D.C. They spent hours threshing out the pros and cons of public conduct, anticipating and preparing for the reactions of the white public, the Negro public, white customers and the management. They pledged themselves to exemplary behavior, no matter what the provocation. And one rainy Saturday afternoon in April, they started out. In groups of four, with one student acting as an "observer" on the outside, they approached the cafe. Three went inside and requested service. Upon refusal they took their seats and pulled out magazines, books of poetry, or pencils and pads. They sat quietly. Neither the manager's panicky efforts to dismiss them nor the presence of a half dozen policemen outside could dislodge them. Five minutes later another group of three would enter. This pilgrimage continued until the Little Cafeteria was more than half-filled with staring students on the inside, and a staring public grouped in the street. In forty-five minutes the management had closed the cafeteria. The students took up their vigil outside the restaurant with attractive and provocative picket signs, "There's No Segregation Law in D.C."—"What's Your Story Little Palace?" "We die together—Why Can't We Eat Together?" and so on. The picketing continued on Monday morning when the restaurant reopened its doors. The students had arranged a picketing schedule and gave their free hours to the picket line. In two days the management capitulated and changed its policy.

In the spring of 1944, the Civil Rights Committee decided to carry the fight downtown into the heart of Washington. They selected a Thompson's cafeteria at 14th and Pennsylvania in the shadow of the White House. They took off a Saturday afternoon, dressed in their best, and strolled into Thompsons in two's and three's at intervals of ten minutes. They threw up a small picket line outside. Three white sympathizers polled the customers inside and found that only 3 out of 10 expressed objection to their being served. They scrupulously observed the picketing laws, and neither the jeers of undisciplined white members of the Armed Forces, nor cheers of WACs, WAVEs and other sympathetic members of the public brought any outward response. When 55 of them, including 6 Negro members of the Armed Forces, had taken seats at the tables, and the Thompson's trade had dropped 50 percent in four hours, the management, after frantic calls to its main office in Chicago, was ordered to serve them.

Before the Civil Rights Committee was able to negotiate with the local management of Thompsons with reference to a changed policy, the Howard University Administration, through the office of Dr. Mordecai W. Johnson, requested them to suspend their activities until there was a clarification of Administration policy. A hurried meeting of the Deans and Administrators was called and a directive issued requesting the students to cease all activities "designed to accomplish social reform affecting institutions other than Howard University itself."

The students were quick to take up this challenge. They then directed their efforts at "social reform" toward the Administration itself. They had already requested a discussion with representatives of the faculty and administration. They indicated their unwillingness to give up their direct action program, and appealed the ruling of the Administration to the Board of Directors which meets in October, 1944.

Out of the struggle, however, issued a new level of student responsibility and interest in campus affairs. The students did not win their total battle against Thompson's, but they achieved a moral victory for student-administration-faculty relationships. They learned interesting things about their University—for example, that 60 percent of its income is a grant from the Federal Government, that 22 percent comes from student fees and that 13 percent comes from campus enterprises, and that only 9 percent comes from gifts other than governmental aid. They learned that the enemies of Howard University in Congress seek to destroy it every time the voting of appropriations arrives. They also learned that Howard University is a beacon light to the Negro community and a significant contribution to the total community, and that everything done there is watched with intense interest. A Student-Faculty Administration has been set up to make recommendations on student affairs.

The question remains to be settled during the coming months whether Howard students shall participate in social action directed against the second-class citizenship to which they have been victimized. There are those who believe the energy and the dynamics of social change must originate in democratic institutions which form test-tubes of democracy and that there must be a realistic relation of one's activities in the community to one's studies in the classroom. There are others who believe that education is a static affair and must not be related to the community at large. Between these two points of view Howard University must make a choice.

But whatever the final outcome, Howard may be proud of those students who have led the way toward new, and perhaps successful techniques to achieve first class citizenship in one area of life in these United States.

The Crisis, November 1944

Adventures in Dining

by Langston Hughes

EATING in dining cars south of the Mason-Dixon line these days is, for Negroes, often quite an adventure. Until recently, for some strange reason, southern white people evidently did not think that colored travellers ever got hungry while travelling, or if they did get hungry they were not expected to eat. Until the war came along, and the Mitchell Case was won, most Southern trains made no arrangements at all for Negroes to eat in the diners.

But now some Southern trains do arrange for Negroes to eat at times by having one or two tables curtained off in the dining car, and serving colored travellers behind the curtain. But not all trains do this. Some expect Negro passengers to eat early, others expect them to eat late, and others still expect them not to eat at all, but just go hungry until they get where they are going.

I have just come out of the South, having been during this lecture season from the Carolinas to Texas. On some trains heading southward from Washington through Virginia, I have been served without difficulty at any table in the diner, with white passengers eating with me. Further South, I have encountered the curtain, behind which I had to sit in order to eat, often being served with the colored Pullman porters and brakemen. On other trains there has been no curtain and no intention for Negroes to eat.

Coming out of Chattanooga on such a train, I went into the diner on the first call for dinner because sometimes these days if you wait for the second call everything will be gone. As I entered the diner, I said to the white steward, "One, please." He looked at me in amazement and walked off toward the other end of the car. The diner was filling rapidly, but there were still a couple of empty tables in the center of the car, so I went ahead and sat down.

Three whites soon joined me, then all the seats in the dining car were taken. The steward came and gave the three whites menus, but ignored me. Every time he passed, though, he would look at me and frown. Finally he leaned over and whispered in my ear.

"Say, fellow, are you Puerto Rican?"

"No," I said, "I'm American."

"Not American Negro, are you?" he demanded.

"I'm just hungry," I said loudly.

He gave me a menu! The colored waiters grinned. They served me with great courtesy, a quality which I have always found our dining car waiters to possess.

A few days later, in the great state of Alabama, I was riding in a Pullman that was half sleeping-car and half diner. There were only six tables in the dining portion of the car so, when the Filipino steward announced luncheon, I got up and went forward. I took a seat at one of the middle tables. Two white Navy men and a WAVE occupied the table with me. The Filipino steward looked very perturbed.

He walked up and down the aisle and gave a menu to everybody but me. Then he gave order checks to everybody but me. Then he disappeared in the kitchen. Finally he came out and addressed me nervously in broken English.

"Chef want to see you in kitchen," he mumbled.

I said, "What?"

He repeated, "Chef want see you in kitchen."

"I have nothing to do with the kitchen!" I said. "Tell the chef to come here."

He disappeared again. Finally he came back and gave me a menu. Since he was both waiter and steward, he served me himself. Nothing more was said.

On some dining cars in Texas, I found that they have colored stewards, although they do not term them stewards, but "waiters-in-charge." It happened that I knew one "waiter-in-charge," an intelligent and progressive young Negro, who invited me to be his personal guest at dinner. He told me that he seated colored passengers right along with the others. Certainly there is great variation in railroad dining for the race these days in the South. Just exactly what to expect still remains a mystery for Negroes—but it has the aura of adventure.

I would advise Negro travellers in the South to use the diners more. In fact, I wish we would use the diners in droves— so that whites may get used to seeing us in diners. It has been legally established that Negro passengers have a lawful right to eat while travelling. If we are refused service or ejected on grounds of color, we can sue. Several cases have been won and damages assessed recently. So, folks, when you go South by train, be sure to eat in the diner. Even if you are not hungry, eat anyhow—to help establish that right. Besides, it will be fun to see how you will be received.

Chicago Defender, June 2, 1945

Our GI's in S. Pacific Fiercely Resent "Uncle Tom" Roles

by Charles H. Loeb

GUAM—It's a thing that leaves one with a feeling of deep shame at one's inability to describe it within the stiff limits of the printed word . . . this magnificently poignant gesture through which Negro servicemen overseas have been silently voicing their contempt for Negro artists who continue to play Uncle Tom roles in radio, films and theatre.

I've seen it happen in New Guinea, in the Philippines, on blood-swept Okinawa, and again here on Guam. Whether at some hastily-constructed theatre framed by tropic jungle, or in one of the elaborate affairs the Sea Bees have constructed here on Guam where the seats have backs and the sound is perfect, the reaction—and that gesture—are always the same.

The silent audience of GI's will be intent upon the screen, following the action, ribbing the actors in impossible situations, hurling juicy jibes at Hollywood's attempts to glamorize our war heroes . . . then it hits you between the eyes—that old familiar pattern.

Sometimes it's a dark-skinned "mammy" whose "yes'm" and "Noam's" will touch it off. Again it's a comely lady's maid in black uniform and white tea apron whose "Sho' is the truf" does the trick. Or maybe tonight it's a shuffling, elongated, masculine Uncle Tom, who thrusts the dirk into the heart of every brown-skinned Yank in the audience.

Silently, as unobtrusively as possible, as if moved by some invisible puppet master, dark shapes rise silently from among the audience and slink silently away to their quarters.

Of course you sit there and see the picture through, pretending that you wish to watch the reaction of the whites about you to what has transpired. Most of them are unaware of what has transpired, but here and there a few exchange knowing glances and low snickers.

Your sense of deep disgust wrestles with the deeper sympathy you feel for these Negro men over here so far away from home, and you pray for some impossible miracle that would permit the "deportation" of a select company of Negro movie stars to this station to witness this spectacle and share this shame.

Chairlady of the delegation (you pray) would be Hattie McDaniel. Along with this illustrious lady should be sent the internationally famous Clarence Muse, Stepin Fetchit, and Willie Best. Bringing up the rear of the party would be Pigmeat Markam, Ben Carter, Manton Moreland, and Jimmy "Remus" Basquette.

How you'd love to watch them squirm—or would they?—as they watched their images sabotage the Negro soldier's best efforts to wear their uniforms with distinction and dignity.

Resentment among GI's in the Philippines was particularly eloquent. Whenever I visited an outfit our Uncle Tomming Negro artists were on the pan.

Said one soldier in an engineering outfit on Luzon:

"We try for weeks to offset the vicious propaganda being used against us among these friendly Filipino people who have been told that we are all ignorant, servile, boisterous and illiterate. We tell them of our lawyers and doctors, our scientists and teachers, our business men and politicians. Then we invite them to our movies to see Negroes in roles that represent the worst that has been said about us. It's not only humiliating but disgusting. We can damn well do without any of them."

The criticism of movie roles carries over to such of our radio figures as are heard overseas. Rochester is a number one "so and so" to the men who wear the uniforms of Army, Navy and Marines. Sole difference in reaction may be measured in intensity and the clamor with which protests are made.

During my service in the Pacific I have heard a multitude of gripes from Negro servicemen. I have heard the segregation policy of the armed forces roundly lambasted. I have heard complaints about ratings and assignments, about restrictions and rotation, and the numberless other things that are the bane of military life, but the protest against those who permit themselves to be used as tools of the anti-Negro propagandists on the screen and radio is by far the most eloquent.

So extreme is the GI's reaction to our artistic Uncle Toms that even the comparatively innocuous "This Is the Army," came in for a round of criticism from GI's on this island, who are currently voicing resentment against the clowning of Sgt. James Cross, a Negro principal who does a singing bit, using a dustpan and mop as props.

Negro servicemen have not failed to note that the big soldier chorus in the production is composed entirely of whites, and that Negro participation in the "Stage Door Canteen" scene is limited to a single Negro soldier stationed near the wings.

And this despite the fact that it is generally known that off-stage the relations between Negro and white members of the cast are delightfully democratic.

And the movies over here could be such a fine morale builder!

New York Amsterdam News, September 1, 1945

It Was a Great Day in Jersey

by Wendell Smith

JERSEY CITY, N.J.—The sun smiled down brilliantly in picturesque Roosevelt Stadium here Thursday afternoon and an air of excitement prevailed throughout the spacious park, which was jammed to capacity with 25,000 jabbering, chattering opening day fans . . . A seething mass of humanity, representing all segments of the crazy-quilt we call America, poured into the magnificent ball park they named after a man from Hyde Park—Franklin D. Roosevelt—to see Montreal play Jersey City and the first two Negroes in modern baseball history perform, Jackie Robinson and Johnny Wright . . . There was the usual fanfare and color, with Mayor Frank Hague chucking out the first ball, the band music, kids from Jersey City schools putting on an exhibition of running, jumping and acrobatics . . . There was also the hot dogs, peanuts and soda pop . . . And some guys in the distant bleachers whistled merrily: "Take Me Out to the Ball Game" . . . Wendell Willkie's "One World" was right here on the banks of the Passaic River.

The outfield was dressed in a gaudy green, and the infield was as smooth and clean as a new-born babe . . . And everyone sensed the significance of the occasion as Robinson and Wright marched with the Montreal team to deep centerfield for the raising of the Stars and Stripes and the "Star-Spangled Banner" . . . Mayor Hague strutted proudly with his henchmen flanking him on the right and left . . . While the two teams, spread across the field, marched side by side with military precision and the band played on . . . We all stood up—25,000 of us—when the band struck up the National Anthem . . . And we sang lustily and freely, for this was a great day . . . Robinson and Wright stood out there with the rest of the players and dignitaries, clutching their blue-crowned baseball caps, standing erect and as still as West Point cadets on dress parade.

No one will ever know what they were thinking right then, but I have traveled more than 2,000 miles with their courageous pioneers during the past nine weeks—from Sanford, Fla., to Daytona Beach to Jersey City—and I feel that I know them probably better than any newspaperman in the business . . . I know that their hearts throbbed heavily and thumped a steady tempo with the big drum that was pounding out the rhythm as the flag slowly crawled up the centerfield mast.

And then there was a tremendous roar as the flag reached its crest and unfurled gloriously in the brilliant April sunlight . . . The 25,000 fans settled back in their seats, ready for the ball game as the Jersey City Giants jogged out to their positions . . . Robinson was the second batter and as he strolled to the plate the crowd gave him an enthusiastic reception . . . They were for him . . . They all knew how he had overcome many obstacles in the deep South, how he had been barred from playing in Sanford, Fla., Jacksonville, Savannah and Richmond . . . And yet, through it all, he was standing at the plate as the second baseman of the Montreal team . . . The applause they gave so willingly was a salute of appreciation and admiration . . . Robinson then socked a sizzler to the shortstop and was thrown out by an eyelash at first base.

The second time he appeared at the plate marked the beginning of what can develop into a great career. He got his first hit as a member of the Montreal Royals . . . It was a mighty home run over the left field fence . . . With two mates on the base paths, he walloped the first pitch that came his way and there was an explosive "crack" as bat and ball met . . . The ball glistened brilliantly in the afternoon sun as it went hurtling high and far over the leftfield fence . . . And, the white flag on the foul-line pole in left fluttered lazily as the ball whistled by.

Robinson jogged around the bases—his heart singing, a broad smile on his beaming bronze face as his two teammates trotted homeward ahead of him . . . When he rounded third, Manager Clay Hopper, who was coaching there, gave him a heavy pat on the back and shouted: "That's the way to hit that ball!" . . . Between third and home-plate he received another ovation from the stands, and then the entire Montreal team stood up and welcomed him to the bench . . . White hands slapping him on his broad back . . . Deep Southern voices from the bench shouted, "Yo sho' hit 'at one, Robbie, nice goin' kid!" . . . Another said: "Them folks 'at wouldn't let you play down in Jacksonville should be hee'ah now. Whoopee!" . . . And still another: "They cain't stop ya now, Jackie, you're really goin' places, and we're going to be right there with ya!" . . . Jackie Robinson laughed softly and smiled . . . Johnny Wright, wearing a big, blue pitcher's jacket, laughed and smiled . . . And, high up in the press box, Joe Bostic of the Amsterdam News and I looked at each other knowingly, and we, too, laughed and smiled . . . Our hearts beat just a bit faster, and the thrill ran through us like champagne bubbles . . . It was a great day in Jersey . . . It was a great day in baseball!

But he didn't stop there, this whirlwind from California's gold coast . . . He ran the bases like a wild colt from the Western plains. He laid down two perfect bunts and slashed a hit into rightfield . . . He befuddled the pitchers, made them balk when he was roaring up and down the base paths, and demoralized the entire Jersey City team . . . He was a hitting demon and a base-running maniac . . . The crowd gasped in amazement . . . The opposing pitchers shook their heads in helpless agony . . . His understanding teammates cheered him on with unrivaled enthusiasm . . . And Branch Rickey, the man who had the fortitude and courage to sign him, heard the phenomenal news via telephone in the offices of the Brooklyn Dodgers at Ebbetts Field and said admiringly— "He's a wonderful boy, that Jackie Robinson—a wonderful boy!"

When the game ended and Montreal had chalked up a 14 to 1 triumph, Robinson dashed for the club house and the showers . . . But before he could get there he was surrounded by a howling mob of kids, who came streaming out of the bleachers and stands . . . They swept down upon him like a great ocean wave and he was drowned in a sea of adolescent enthusiasm . . . There he was—this Pied Piper of the diamond—perspiration rolling off his bronze brow, idolizing kids swirling all around him, autograph hounds tugging at him . . . And big cops riding prancing steeds trying unsuccessfully to disperse the mob that had cornered the hero of the day . . . One of his own teammates fought his way through the howling mob and finally "saved" Robinson . . . It was Red Durrett, who was a hero in his own right because he had pounded out two prodigious home runs himself, who came to the "rescue." He grabbed Robinson by the arm and pulled him through the crowd. "Come on," Durrett demanded, "you'll be here all night if you don't fight them off. They'll mob you. You can't possibly sign autographs for all those kids."

So, Jackie Robinson, escorted by the red-head outfielder, finally made his way to the dressing room. Bedlam broke loose in there, too . . . Photographers, reporters, kibitzers and hangers-on fenced him in . . . It was a virtual madhouse . . . His teammates, George Shuba, Stan Breard, Herman Franks, Tom Tatum, Marvin Rackley and all the others, were showering congratulations on him . . . They followed him into the showers, back to his locker and all over the dressing room . . . Flash bulbs flashed and reporters fired questions with machine-gun like rapidity . . . And Jackie Robinson smiled through it all.

As he left the park and walked out onto the street, the once-brilliant sun was fading slowly in the distant western skies . . . His petite and dainty little wife greeted him warmly and kindly, "You've had quite a day, little man," she said sweetly.

"Yes," he said softly and pleasantly, "God has been good to us today!"

The Pittsburgh Courier, April 27, 1946

Lynch Law Back in Georgia—4 Murdered

by Tom O'Connor

MONROE, Ga., July 27.—I have just seen the first proof of Eugene Talmadge's election as Governor of Georgia. I saw it in the basement of Dan Young's funeral parlor (for colored) here in Monroe.

An embalmer was sewing up bullet holes in one of the girls, Dorothy Malcolm. He had already done his best to patch up the rifle and pistol bullet holes in the other girl and the two fellows lynched here Thursday night.

But nothing in the undertaker's art could put back the faces of Roger Malcolm or May Dorsey.

Shotgun shells fired point blank don't leave much face.

Their deaths or the death of some other Georgia Negro by lynch mob violence was inevitable.

When the votes were counted in the July 17 primary, and the minority candidate Talmadge was declared the Democratic nominee, the season on "niggers" was automatically opened, and every pinheaded Georgia cracker and bigoted Ku Kluxer figured he had a hunting license.

I don't know whether the murderers of Roger Malcolm and George Dorsey and their wives will ever be brought to trial.

I doubt it.

But in two hours in this town I've picked up enough clues as to the identity of the leader of the lynch mob and at least one of his henchmen that it would seem child's play for anyone with authority to have the guilty ones within 24 hours.

This morning in Washington, Atty. Gen. Tom Clark said he was ordering a full investigation of the lynching. At 7 p.m. the F.B.I. hadn't shown up. Two assistant United States attorneys dropped in from Macon and chatted with the Sheriff for an hour or so Friday afternoon, and then said they didn't think there had been a violation of any Federal law. They didn't think the Civil rights statute would apply.

I wonder if it would comfort what is left of those four young Negroes, lying naked on slabs in the basement of Dan Young's funeral parlor, to know that their civil rights had not been violated when they were jerked from an automobile by a mob of 25 or 30 men, taken down to a river bottom, lined up and riddled with rifle and pistol bullets and shotgun shells?

This was no spontaneous uprising of race hatred. It was a carefully organized mass murder, timed to the second, carried out with storm trooper efficiency. Here is the sequence of events:

On Sunday, July 14, Roger Malcolm, an uneducated Negro farmhand in his twenties, who worked on the farm of one Barney Hester in this cotton and corn section 40 miles east of Atlanta, got into a fight with his wife. He had been drinking.

The official story is that Dorothy Malcolm, Roger's wife, ran to the Hester house and appealed for help. The official story is, further, that Hester merely told Malcolm to calm down and quit causing trouble, whereupon Malcolm pulled out a knife and stabbed him.

The true story, as nearly as I can make it out, is that Hester started beating Malcolm first. But at any rate Hester was stabbed.

Malcolm was quickly caught and a mob gathered. They bound Malcolm with rope and there was talk of lynching him. But a white woman who had known him from childhood called the Sheriff. Sheriff E. S. Gordon and two deputies arrived in time, and Malcolm was taken to Monroe jail.

Three days later Talmadge was nominated—purely, simply and solely on the issue of keeping the Negro "in his place." This county voted for Talmadge. The farm section around "Hestertown" voted overwhelmingly for Talmadge—and Hestertown's Negroes didn't vote.

With Talmadge's victory, the threats to "get" Malcolm crescendoed. There was so much talk of lynching him that his relatives and neighbors thought a week ago that he already had been killed.

Yesterday Loy Harrison, a well-to-do farmer for whom Malcolm's sister-in-law and her husband worked, drove into town to bail Malcolm out of jail.

Dorsey, recently out of the Army, his wife, Mrs. Malcolm's sister, and Mrs. Malcolm came along.

They arrived at the courthouse at about 2 o'clock and by 2:10 the bond of $600 had been posted and the papers all signed to get Malcolm out. It was an extremely low bond—the charge was assault with attempt to commit murder—and Hester was still in the hospital, not yet out of danger.

For some reason not yet explained, Malcolm was not released immediately. Harrison went to get his car fixed and the women went shopping. They came back at 5 o'clock, got Malcolm and started in Harrison's car for his farm some ten miles away.

The rest of the story is as Harrison related it to the Coroner's inquest last night a few hours after the murders and again to officers.

They started out of town by one road, but "someone" told them to go another way. Harrison said he doesn't know who the "someone" was. They took the indicated road. Driving along the Moores Bridge Road they came to a bridge across the Apalachee River, dividing line between Walton and Coonee counties.

At the bridge there was a car drawn up across the road. Harrison stopped. Another car immediately swung in behind his. From those two cars, a Ford and a Chevrolet, and from two others about 25 or 30 men piled out.

Their leader, described by Harrison as a well-dressed, heavy set man in a brown double-breasted suit and smooth-toed shoes, came up and said:

"Get out, Charlie. We wants you, Charlie."

Harrison said he replied:

"That isn't Charlie, that's George." Whereupon the mob leader clapped his gun to Harrison's head and said:

"You shut up. This is our party. We ought to kill you too."

Harrison said they took the two men about 20 yards away off the road down toward the river bank, when one of the women cried out from the car, "Don't kill him, Mr. so and so."

Harrison maintained he did not catch the name the woman shouted. At any rate he reported the mob leader said:

"She recognized us. Get those women too. You, and you,

and you, and you, go back and bring them bitches along. You know what you're supposed to do."

The four men the leader had designated, responding like well drilled soldiers, pulled the two women from the car. The women must have fought hard; when I saw their bodies each had a broken arm.

Harrison said he was asked by the lynch leader if he recognized anyone, and he swore he didn't. He still swears he didn't.

"Mr. Harrison must have made mighty few acquaintances in these parts," a reporter remarked to Sheriff Gordon this afternoon. The Sheriff and his deputies all smiled broadly. The lynching occurred upon land which is part of the farm upon which Harrison was born and raised and still lives.

When the mob told Harrison to beat it after the murders, he drove to the nearest store and called the Sheriff.

The Sheriff sent some deputies and the coroner out but didn't go himself.

A drumhead inquest was held on the spot.

Harrison was the only one to testify. He said he hadn't recognized any one. The jury promptly brought in its verdict— "death by gunshot wounds from person or persons unknown."

"I'm ashamed to be a Georgian," is an expression I've heard more than once.

At Cheyenne, Wyo., Eugene Talmadge said: "Things like that are to be regretted."

PM, July 28, 1946

Race Justice in Aiken

by George McMillan

Aiken, S.C., November 13

ISAAC WOODARD'S demand that a Southern bus driver treat him like a man started a chain of events that were made to seem inevitable in Federal Court at Columbia, South Carolina, last week—even to the final event, the acquittal of the Batesburg police chief who blinded the Negro war veteran.

By speaking as he did on a bus that was making its way through the South Carolina piedmont Woodard threatened a way of life that is still taken for granted in that state.

While the case was being tried, the alleged acts of the police chief were overshadowed by the question of Woodard's behavior: in the ten hours after he was discharged from the army was it that of a "sober South Carolina Negro," or was it outside the pattern of conduct cut by South Carolina whites "for the inferior race to which Woodard belongs"?

In the turgid climate of the courtroom Woodard had to be acquitted of conduct unbecoming a Negro before Police Chief Lynwood Shull could be convicted of depriving Woodard of his constitutional right to "be secure in his person." Few in the courtroom knew, or seemed to care, that this was the first civil-rights case ever heard in South Carolina.

Every one of the witnesses who had been on or near the bus that night of February 12, 1946, was asked by the defense whether Woodard had talked profanely and obscenely "in front of, or in the hearing of, white ladies." All the defense witnesses said he had. The prosecution spent much of its time vainly trying to prove that Woodard was no more boisterous than the others in the group of understandably elated and hilarious men who had been discharged from the army that afternoon at Camp Gordon, Georgia.

The event that undoubtedly provoked Woodard into his angry argument with the bus driver was mentioned only indirectly at the trial. The bus driver had asked a white soldier who was sitting beside Woodard at the beginning of the journey to get up and move to the front. This man, known only by his nickname "Montana," did not appear as a witness for either prosecution or defense. With some other men aboard the bus, he had not only been discharged with Woodard but had also returned from the Pacific on the same troop transport.

It is easy to see how "Montana" and the other men felt for that moment in time a comradeship which overcame what must have seemed, if indeed they were conscious of it at all, the superficial ritual of segregation called for in the South Carolina setting.

One of the white veterans, Jennings Stroud, now a student at the University of South Carolina, did testify in Woodard's behalf. "Woodard was making noise," Stroud said, "but so were all of us."

The resentment aroused in Woodard when the bus driver asked Montana to move up front was perfectly natural. Later, when Woodard asked the driver to make a rest stop, the driver refused; he said, "Hell, no," according to the Negro. It was then that Woodard replied, "Dammit, you've got to talk to me like a man."

This reply of Woodard's, his claim that, though a Negro, he should be treated as a man, caused the driver—the conclusion is inescapable from the evidence at the trial—to single Woodard out for arrest at Batesburg. By the time Shull came on the scene to arrest Woodard the racial battle lines had been drawn, and Woodard stood convicted.

The defense was perfectly willing to let the jury decide between the word of Shull and that of Woodard. Only the two participants were able to make any assertion about what happened during their altercation. The blows were struck around the corner from the bus stop, in the dark, on a deserted block of tiny Batesburg's business district. The jury could take Shull's word that Woodard was still profane and resisted arrest by grabbing Shull's pellet-loaded blackjack; or it could take Woodard's word that he was merely protesting that Shull had no reason to arrest him, and that he grabbed Shull's blackjack only after Shull had already hit him.

The all-white jury had to choose between the word of a

white man and the word of a Negro. Shull was acquitted in twenty-eight minutes.

Two facts which helped to bring the case to national attention went undisputed. Woodard is permanently blind, and Shull struck the blow which blinded him.

The Nation, November 23, 1946

Literacy Tests: Southern Style

by Jack H. Pollack

Since the Civil War most Southern states, at one time or another, have used economic pressures, white primaries, poll taxes, "grandfather clauses," intimidation and even outright violence to keep the ballot from Negroes. It is now more than a generation since Mississippi Senator James K. Vardaman shamelessly shouted: "I am just as much opposed to Booker T. Washington as a voter with all his Anglo-Saxon re-enforcements as I am to the cocoanut-headed, chocolate-colored typical little coon who blacks my shoes every morning. Neither is fit to perform the supreme function of citizenship." And long before Senator Bilbo's widely ballyhooed campaign last year—"the best way to keep the nigger from voting is to see him the night before election"—the visible or implied warning sign at Southern polling places was: "Negroes, Vote at Your Own Risk."

Should any of these threats and dodges fail to discourage persistent Negro ballot-seekers, Dixie voting officials have one trump card with which to disfranchise them. It is a tricky "literacy test," which has been used increasingly of late against Negroes—and even some whites who are union members. Though not all Southern states use this artifice, most of them are legally authorized to do so by discriminatory amendments in their state constitutions. Some of the states which set forth literacy requirements for voters exempt Confederate veterans and their "lawful descendants."

Before a Southern Negro is allowed to vote, he must often be "approved" by a (white) Board of Registrars, a Board which proves difficult to locate in many county areas. Some rural registrars even keep their registration books at their homes; and in Arlington County, Virginia—which is adjacent to our nation's capital—at least one precinct's registration place is situated in a white woman's front parlor: the applicant will find a bellicose husband and a ferocious-looking police dog standing by during "registration." It takes an exceedingly brave Negro to brave these barriers.

Other registration places are in county courthouses, which Negroes also have trouble entering. A frequent ruse is not to furnish seats for Negro applicants in the Board of Registrars' office. In Mississippi, as the Bilbo hearings revealed, Negroes are often turned away for being "loaded with liquor" or for carrying an imaginary "concealed weapon."

After filling out the necessary forms—and paying their poll tax where it is required—white applicants are usually automatically approved. But Negroes, even after meeting all other requirements, must pass the "literacy test." The Southern quizmasters conducting them are given sweeping interrogatory powers by their respective state statutes.

For example, Mississippi law requires "a reasonable interpretation" of the Constitution by the would-be voter, and registrars have made the most of this loophole. Clifford R. Fields, a 62-year-old Natchez registrar and a white primary diehard, confessed: "I asked Negroes to read sections of the Constitution of the state of Mississippi where it explains the re-election of the Governor. I did not require it of whites."

"Do you think it fair to make it harder for a colored person to vote than a white person?" Republican Senator Bridges asked.

"Yes, I think so," replied Fields.

Another Mississippi registrar, circuit clerk D. P. Gayden of Rankin County, testified: "No, sir, I don't keep any qualified Negroes from voting. I know my duty under the law." Asked why in that event only a handful of Negroes were registered in his county, he smilingly explained: "They just don't try to qualify."

II

Despite the opposition of liberal Governor Folsom, Alabama took a long step backward in November 1946 when it passed the Boswell Amendment, requiring voting applicants to "understand and explain" any section of the U. S. Constitution *to the satisfaction* of the Board of Registrars. Outgoing Gov-

ernor Sparks confided that this tightening of voting requirements would "prevent a flood of Negro registration."

Named after its author, State Representative E. C. Boswell
of Geneva, the Boswell Amendment was an attempt to circumvent a 1944 Supreme Court decision which had ruled the
Texas white primary unconstitutional. Ex-Governor Frank H.
Dixon stumped the state for it crying, "We face the elimination of our segregation laws, zoning laws . . . we will see our
children in mixed schools, our legislature with Negro minorities, our juries of mixed races—should we fail to pass the
Boswell Amendment." State Democratic Committee Chairman Gessner McCorvey was quoted by the Associated Press
as asking that "only properly qualified persons register."

Designed to keep the crucial Democratic primary predominantly white and to get around the Supreme Court ruling, the
Boswell Amendment requires the prospective voter to be a
Constitutional authority. He must be able not only to read,
write and interpret but also "understand and explain the Constitution" as well as be "of good character," and understand
"the duties and obligations of good citizenship." Under the
Boswell Amendment, as Stetson Kennedy (the author of
Southern Exposure) pointed out, "the machine-appointed registrars might conceivably go so far as to deny registration to
Alabama's Supreme Court Justice Hugo Black on the grounds
that he did not 'understand and explain' the Constitution to
their satisfaction, or was not of 'good character' or did not
'understand the duties and obligations of good citizenship.'"

Illustrative of the mentality which sponsored the Boswell
law is the statement of Roy Harris, political mentor of Gene
and Herman Talmadge: "If our system is held unconstitutional, we will change the law at the next session of the legislature—by only a period or comma. If the Supreme Court
invalidates that law, too, then we will rewrite it again for the
next primary. That will go on *ad infinitum*."

Voting in Alabama has never been easy for Negroes. During the 1946 primary election—several months before the
Boswell Amendment was enacted—more than a hundred
Birmingham Negro World War II veterans marched in double
file to the Jefferson County Courthouse, to present their discharge papers as evidence of "literacy." The vast majority was

rejected. Among those turned down were Negro officers, many with high school and college training, property owners and operators of successful businesses. They were asked such questions as: "What kind of government have we?"; "How is a Congressman elected?"; "What must a political party do to win?"

Though the building's façade bore an inscription quoted from Jefferson, proclaiming "equal and exact justice to all men," veteran after veteran was disqualified for inability to "interpret" the Constitution to the Board's satisfaction. After trying to interpret it, they were told, "If you're registered, you'll hear from us. We're taking your application under advisement." In most cases, that was the last they heard.

The most common "question" used in Southern "literacy tests" is: "Read, repeat, or interpret the Federal or State Constitution." This question has been used so often that many Negro teachers are training their students to recite both constitutions parrot-like, until they know them letter-perfect. But as one Georgia official reflected, "Negroes can still be required to write the Constitution and then be disqualified if they leave out any commas."

Barred for years on these grounds, a South Carolina Negro decided to memorize the entire Federal and State Constitutions—with all the punctuation. Though he finally came to know both documents far better than his examiners, he was turned down because the registrar was permitted, under his broad powers, to insist that the Constitution be recited in Chinese.

However, one Alabama Negro college graduate reputedly upset the applecart. As Louis E. Burnham, secretary of the Southern Negro Youth Congress, tells the story, he was asked to recite the preamble to the Constitution. Clearing his throat and gathering his thoughts, he began, "Four score and seven years ago, our forefathers . . ."; and ended grandiloquently with ". . . government of the people, by the people and for the people shall not perish from the earth."

Stunned by the applicant's fluency, the three registrars exchanged incredulous glances. Finally, the chairman slapped his thigh, hit the bull's-eye in the spittoon and exclaimed, "Dog-gone, if he don' know that there Constitution! Let's pass him, boys!"

III

Next to the Constitutional bogey, the most frequent trap "question" in Southern literacy tests is to translate—and spell correctly—obscure Latin phrases. A Negro veteran who recently tried to register in Jackson, Mississippi, was asked, "What is the meaning of *Itar, E. Quar Tum Entertia Ventricular*?" Shortly afterwards, another Negro was asked, "What does a writ of *Certiorari, Writ Error Coraim Nobis, Subpoena Duces Tecum* mean?"

The richest Negro in Mississippi, according to Walter Winchell, is Dr. S. D. Redmond of Jackson, who reveals that registrars reject Negro applicants for not properly answering such "intelligent questions" as "Boy, what's the meaning of *delicut status quo rendum hutt*?"

If the bewildered applicant ponders the phrase, the registrar continues: "Maybe that's too hard for you. Here's an easy one. If the angle plus the hypotenuse equals the subdivided of the fraction, then how many children did your mother miss having?" Should the applicant by some miracle answer this successfully, the registrar will snap: "Boy, since you're so smart, tell me what's going to happen to you if you don't get the hell out of here!"

During the Bilbo hearings in Mississippi, a stream of Negro war veterans testified that they were barred from voting by such questions as "What is a writ of habeas corpus?" and "What is an *ex post facto* law?" A Jackson Negro attempting to register was greeted with: "Now let's see whether you're up on your civics. What does *ipso facto* mean?"

"That means I don't vote," replied the Negro, departing.

Another Jackson Negro, Herman L. Caston, testified that while he was pondering a "question" about slavery, he was told, "It doesn't matter how you answer, it still won't be satisfactory to me." A Louisville, Mississippi, Negro, John L. Hatchorn, though deemed eligible, was advised: "Take it easy, boy. You're not gonna vote in this here election." Of the

350,000 Mississippi Negroes eligible, only about 3000 were allowed to register—and even that small number made some whites uneasy.

Reverend C. M. Eiland, a 52-year-old Mississippi Negro Baptist minister testified with almost classic understatement: "My father was a slave, and when he was freed, bought property and paid taxes. I have paid taxes for 25 years. I've never been arrested or in any kind of trouble. I sort of feel that as a citizen, I ought to have the right to vote."

In Alabama, during the 1944 registration, George S. Mitchell of the Southern Regional Council was given circumstantial accounts of the questions Birmingham registrars asked of a Negro woman school teacher. One trick question was, "How many rooms does the White House have?" She was allowed to leave, looked it up and returned with the correct answer, but was still refused registration. Aubrey Williams, editor-publisher of the Montgomery, Alabama, *Southern Farmer* reports that some applicants have been asked, "How many *windows* does the White House have?"

But the prize Alabama story concerns Jessie L. Dennis, a decorated Negro war hero who was asked during last year's Alabama primary: "What is the Government?" "The Government is the people," he answered with classic simplicity.

His answer was counted wrong and he was told to apply at the next registration.

Even in North Carolina, perhaps the most progressive Southern state, where registrars are given five cents for every person registered, attempts are made to keep down the number of voters through "literacy" devices, especially in the rural areas. The state constitution requires that the applicant "satisfy" the registrar as to his eligibility. A group of Negro citizens in a small coastal town in Pamlico County wrote to secretary Mary Price of the Committee for North Carolina in Greensboro:

When eight of us went to register this is what happened. The man said we would have to read and write any parts of the Constitution and answer any question that he might ask. We said that we were prepared to do so. He then changed and said that he would have to appoint a day, call a judge and we would have to answer him to satisfaction. We asked him to set the date. He then changed and told us to come back to the building in one and one-half hours. We returned at the hour named and he told us that each one would have to write five pages of the Constitution of the U.S. When we began to write, he left the room, after telling us beforehand that we would have to write before him. We had to write from Article I, Legislative Department (every word) to Treason, Sec. 3 under Art. III, Judicial Department. The white men who came with us stayed on the outside and made sport. Please help us. We want to try again to register.

Although ballot-seekers denied registration on "literacy" grounds can usually appeal to the courts, they rarely if ever do. Among other difficulties, the election is generally over before a decision can be rendered. Negro illiteracy in the South has been cut from 95 per cent in 1865 to 10 per cent in 1940, but you'd never know it from the enormous number of Negroes who have never been able to pass "literacy tests."

The American Mercury, May 1947

Not So Deep Are the Roots

by James Peck

THE ROOTS of racial segregation in the upper South are not too deep to be uprooted without dynamite. This was shown recently when sixteen Negroes and whites took a 2-week bus trip through Virginia, North Carolina, Tennessee and Kentucky, in which Negroes sat in front and whites in the rear.

We had the legal backing of a U.S. Supreme Court decision of last June outlawing jim-crow in interstate travel. We found, however, that the bus companies are treating that decision as if it did not exist.

There were twelve arrests during the trip and a number of threatened arrests. In such instances buses were delayed up to two hours while police were summoned, company attorneys notified and warrants were drawn up. During these tense delays, with attention focused on the issue, we were in a strategic position to determine just how deep the roots are—both among passengers and the townspeople who gathered outside.

The deeper you go in the South, the deeper are the roots. As a Negro told us on the first lap of our trip: "Some bus drivers are crazy: and the farther South you go, the crazier they get." And as a white from South Carolina commented about a Negro in our group who was sitting in front: "In my state he would either move or be killed."

But this was the upper South and in the twenty-six buses we rode, not a single act of hostility occurred. In only one instance—at Chapel Hill, N.C.—was there an act of hostility outside the bus. During the trip we came in direct contact with a large number of people.

There was the pretty blonde from Winston-Salem who spoke up for us aboard the bus on which arrests occurred at Chapel Hill. There was the girl who, finding no seat, asked the driver of a Statesville-Asheville bus how come a Negro was sitting in front. Being the only driver we encountered who recognized the existence of the Supreme Court decision, he said: "Don't blame me; blame those bastards up in Washington." The woman did not protest.

On that same bus was a portly white man traveling with his family who said in a loud voice: "I wish I was the driver." But at Chapel Hill a white passenger got off the bus, went into the station, and protested to the driver against his ordering arrests.

Then there were the majority of white passengers who made no comment at all upon seeing Negroes in front. Aboard buses where drivers ignored our Negroes sitting in front, passengers did likewise.

Inevitably, we encountered a few Uncle Toms—Negroes of the "yahsir massah" type. At Oxford, N.C., where an arrest was threatened, an aged Negro teacher, sweating under his stiff white collar, pleaded with Bayard Rustin, one of our Negroes sitting in front: "Please move. Don't do this. You'll get to Durham just the same whether you sit in front or in back." When the bus moved on without our being arrested he became abjectly apologetic. But in the rear of that same bus Negro passengers were audibly supporting Rustin. One Negro woman threatened to sue the bus company for being unnecessarily delayed.

In Petersburg, Va., a decrepit Negro porter tried to ingratiate himself by boarding the bus while an arrest was being made and saying: "We know how to deal with him. We ought to drag him off." But in Culpeper, Va., a Negro woman courageously boarded the bus and asked the Negro being arrested if he needed any help. She later came right into the office of the justice of the peace where we were putting up bail and again offered aid.

Then there were the many Negro passengers who made no comment at all. There were also the hundreds of Negroes who supported us by attending the meetings in various towns called by the NAACP to hear our group report on the trip. At the end of these meetings men and women came up to congratulate us with tears in their eyes. At the student meetings both Negroes and whites pledged to carry on by traveling in an unsegregated manner when they go home to another state.

Neither bus drivers nor police showed any hostilities in making the arrests. As a National Trailways driver told Conrad Lynn, when he refused to move to the back of a bus at Petersburg: "Personally, I don't care where you sit, but I have my orders from the company." A cop there told Rev. Ernest Bromley, white North Carolina minister in our group who was defending Lynn's position: "I am just not Christian enough."

Both northerners and southerners are surprised that the sole act of hostility against us was at Chapel Hill, which they associate with liberalism and Dr. Frank P. Graham, head of the University of North Carolina. We were surprised too, until we later learned that our action on the bus was but one of a series of recent acts against the jimcrow pattern at Chapel Hill. It just happened to be our action which exploded the growing hatred of the poor whites, who tenaciously hold on to their only privilege in our society—that of being recognized as superior to the Negroes.

The explosion might have occurred when Eleanor Roosevelt, rather than eat at a segregated function at the university, got Coca Cola and sandwiches and ate on the steps. It might have occurred when Dorothy Maynor, noted Negro singer, gave a concert on the campus at which seating was unsegregated. It might have occurred when Rev. Charles Jones, courageous white minister who housed our group, permitted an interracial CIO union meeting in his church.

But it just happened to occur on a grey Sunday afternoon when four of our group were arrested aboard a bus for Greensboro.

It was a particularly quiet Sunday afternoon in the little town and the white cab drivers were hanging around the bus station with nothing to do. Then they saw the bus held up and got wind of what was going on. Here was something over which they could work out their frustration. Two ringleaders started haranguing the other drivers. They started milling around closer to where the bus was parked.

When I got off the bus to put up bail and call our attorney, five of the drivers surrounded me. "Coming down here to stir up the niggers," snarled a big guy with steel-cold grey eyes. With that he slugged me a resounding blow on the side of the head. A couple of the bus passengers who were standing around protested and the five withdrew. I later learned that the sentiment among passengers aboard the bus was predominantly in our favor.

From the windows of the courthouse, as I looked at the mob of cab drivers, I recalled how of the 31 indicted two months ago in Greenville, S.C., for lynching a Negro, 28 of them were cab drivers. Every few minutes a driver would come into the courthouse, allegedly to get a drink. On one occasion he said: "They'll never get a bus out of here."

When we finally left the courthouse in Rev. Jones's car, twelve of the drivers piled into three cabs and sped after us. We succeeded in getting to Rev. Jones's home first. When we got inside and looked out of the window, we saw two of the drivers getting out with big sticks. Others started to pick up rocks by the roadside when one of the mob, apparently scared, motioned to them to lay off.

They drove away. But a few minutes later Rev. Jones, who was already marked as a "nigger lover" because of the CIO meeting in his church, received an anonymous phone call. "Get the niggers out of town by nightfall or we'll burn down your house," threatened a quivering voice. The following day he got a phone call threatening him with murder.

He managed to secure cars to get us out of town and then removed his wife and two children to safety. A number of the university students offered to stay at his house and protect him from any acts of violence. But none of the threats materialized and the only further act was the throwing of a rock at Rev. Jones's assistant as he approached his home.

A contrast to Chapel Hill was Culpeper, Va., where another arrest was made. As would happen in any small town, a crowd gathered around the bus station and started talking about it. But the discussion was quite calm and at no point was there even a threat of what occurred in Chapel Hill. A couple of white townspeople even sided with our Negro in standing up for his rights. One of them told him: "If I had been you I would have fought them before letting them take me off the bus." After bail was put up, we walked around the small town completely unmolested.

Most of the other arrests occurred in larger towns such as

Asheville, N.C. There, I and Dennis Banks, a Negro musician from Chicago, were sentenced to 30 days on the chain gang on a charge of violating the state's jim-crow law.

"Thirty days?" said Police Judge Sam Cathey, reputed to be a corrupt politician who remains in office because he is blind and nobody has ever dared run against him. Then he turned to the district attorney and asked: "Is that the maximum sentence under the law?" When the DA nodded, Judge Cathey said: "Then it is 30 days, under supervision of the State Highway Commission."

He then made a little speech which started: "We pride ourselves on our race relations here." Our lawyer, Curtiss Todd, is a Negro from Winston-Salem. It was the first time a Negro lawyer had appeared in that court, there being no Negro lawyers in Asheville. It was also unheard of to see a Negro lawyer defending a white man and to see a white and a Negro defendant sitting together in court. Never have I seen a look of hatred like the one a court attaché gave me as we were being locked up after the trial.

Trial of the Chapel Hill case came up on the very same day on which defense attorneys in Greensville, S.C., were presenting their final arguments for the 29 men acquitted two days later of lynching Willie Earl.

The identical appeals to prejudice and denunciations of northern interference featured in the final summation of T. J. Phipps, prosecutor in Chapel Hill.

He opened with: "I have good friends among the 'nigras' —that is among the better element." He went on to state that the Negroes had been brought over from Africa as savages and had been civilized by the whites. Then came a lengthy argument to show that the Negroes really want jimcrow.

At one point he said: "I will now quote from a decision in a case in which a 'nigra' raped a white girl," and then paused conspicuously. The decision had no bearing on the question of segregation in interstate travel. At only one point in his half-hour summation did he touch on the legal aspects of the case.

The trial ended with Judge Henry Whitfield sentencing Igal Roodenko, white, to 30 days on the chain gang and Bayard Rustin, Negro, to costs. He later told our attorney off the record that he has much more contempt for a white man than for a Negro in such situations.

A month later, in sentencing the other two men arrested in Chapel Hill, the judge demonstrated still more contempt for a southern white man who opposes the prevailing prejudices. He sentenced Joe Felmet a white from Asheville to six months on the chain gang, which is six times the legal maximum. However, he was forced to reduce this to 30 days when the prosecutor pointed out that 30 days is the maximum under the state jim-crow law. At the same time he reduced the sentence of Andrew Johnson, the Negro convicted along with Felmet, from $50 and costs to $25 and costs.

Our lawyers in the Chapel Hill cases were C. Jerry Gates, Herman Taylor, and Edward Avant. The case in Asheville was defended by Curtiss Todd of Winston-Salem. Our Virginia cases are being handled by Martin, Hill & Robinson, the Richmond firm which successfully carried the Irene Morgan case to the Supreme Court. All are NAACP attorneys.

Appeals on the Chapel Hill and Asheville cases come up within the next few months. The three Virginia cases—Petersburg, Amherst and Culpeper—have been continued indefinitely pending decision of the Virginia Supreme Court in the Lottie Taylor case. A false arrest suit is planned in Durham where three of us were arrested and then released without charges.

In view of last June's Supreme Court decision, we hope to win these cases, to subsequently sue the bus companies for damages, and to thus discourage them from persisting in their jim-crow seating regulations. But more than that we hope that our trip will encourage others to help break down the jim-crow pattern by traveling interstate in an unsegregated manner.

This method was enthusiastically supported at our first meeting in Richmond, Va., by Charles Webber, president of the Virginia CIO Council. It was also indorsed by Moss Plunkett, outstanding Virginia liberal, at our Roanoke meeting. Our trip was sponsored by the Congress of Racial Equality and the Fellowship of Reconciliation.

The Crisis, September 1947

When I Was a Child

by Lillian Smith

EVEN its children know that the South is in trouble. No one has to tell them; no words said aloud. To them, it is a vague thing weaving in and out of their play, like a ghost haunting an old graveyard or whispers after the household sleeps— fleeting mystery, vague menace, to which each responds in his own way. Some learn to screen out all except the soft and the soothing; others deny even as they see plainly, and hear. But all know that under quiet words and warmth and laughter, under the slow ease and tender concern about small matters, there is a heavy burden on all of us and as heavy a refusal to confess it. The children know this "trouble" is bigger than they, bigger than their family, bigger than their church, so big that people turn away from its size. They have seen it flash out like lightning and shatter a town's peace, have felt it tear up all they believe in. They have measured its giant strength and they feel weak when they remember.

This haunted childhood belongs to every southerner. Many of us run away from it but we come back like a hurt animal to its wound, or a murderer to the scene of his sin. The human heart dares not stay away too long from that which hurt it most. There is a return journey to anguish that few of us are released from making.

We who were born in the South call this mesh of feeling and memory "loyalty." We think of it sometimes as "love." We identify with the South's trouble as if we, individually, were responsible for all of it. We defend the sins and sorrows of three hundred years as if each sin had been committed by us alone and each sorrow had cut across our heart. We are as hurt at criticism of our region as if our own name were called aloud by the critic. We have known guilt without understanding it, and there is no tie that binds men closer to the past and each other than that.

98

It is a strange thing, this umbilical cord uncut. In times of ease, we do not feel its pull, but when we are threatened with change, suddenly it draws the whole white South together in a collective fear and fury that wipe our minds clear of reason and we are blocked off from sensible contact with the world we live in.

To keep this resistance strong, wall after wall has been thrown up in the southern mind against criticism from without and within. Imaginations close tight against the hurt of others; a regional armoring takes place to keep out the "enemies" who would make our trouble different—or maybe rid us of it completely. For it is a trouble that we do not want to give up. We are as involved with it as a child who cannot be happy at home and cannot bear to tear himself away, or as a grown-up who has fallen in love with his own disease. We southerners have identified with the long sorrowful past on such deep levels of love and hate and guilt that we do not know how to break old bonds without pulling our lives down. *Change* is the evil word, a shrill clanking that makes us know too well our servitude. *Change* means leaving one's memories, one's sins, one's ancient prison, the room where one was born. How can we do this when we are tied fast!

The white man's burden is his own childhood. Every southerner knows this. Though he may deny it even to himself, yet he drags through life with him the heavy weight of a past that never eases and is rarely understood, of desire never appeased, of dreams that died in his heart.

In this South I was born and now live. Here it was that I began to grow, seeking my way, as do all children, through the honeycomb cells of our life to the bright reality outside. Sometimes it was as if all doors opened inward. . . . Sometimes we children lost even the desire to get outside and tried only to make a comfortable home of the trap of swinging doors that history and religion and a war, man's greed and his guilt had placed us in at birth.

It is not easy to pick out of such a life those strands that have to do only with color, only with Negro-white relationships, only with religion or sex, for they are knit of the same fibers that have gone into the making of the whole fabric, woven into its basic patterns and designs. Religion . . . sex . . . race . . . money . . . avoidance rites . . . malnutrition . . . dreams—no part of these can be looked at and clearly seen without looking at the whole of them. For, as a painter mixes colors and makes of them new colors, so religion is turned into something different by race, and segregation is colored as much by sex as by skin pigment, and money is no longer a coin but a lost wish wandering through a man's whole life.

A child's lessons are blended of these strands however dissonant a design they make. The mother who taught me what I know of tenderness and love and compassion taught me also the bleak rituals of keeping Negroes in their place. The father who rebuked me for an air of superiority toward schoolmates from the mill and rounded out his rebuke by gravely reminding me that "all men are brothers," trained me in the steel-rigid decorums I must demand of every colored male. They who so gravely taught me to split my body from my feelings and both from my "soul," taught me also to split my conscience from my acts and Christianity from southern tradition.

Neither the Negro nor sex was often discussed at length in our home. We were given no formal instruction in these difficult matters but we learned our lessons well. We learned the intricate system of taboos, of renunciations and compensations, of manners, voice modulations, words, feelings, along with our prayers, our toilet habits, and our games. I do not remember how or when, but by the time I had learned that God is love, that Jesus is His Son and came to give us more abundant life, that all men are brothers with a common Father, I also knew that I was better than a Negro, that all black folks have their place and must be kept in it, that sex has its place and must be kept in it, that a terrifying disaster would befall the South if ever I treated a Negro as my social equal and as terrifying a disaster would befall my family if ever I were to have a baby outside of marriage. I had learned that God so loved the world that He gave His only begotten Son so that we might have segregated churches in which it was my duty to worship each Sunday and on Wednesday at evening prayers. I had learned that white southerners are a hospitable, courteous, tactful people who treat those of their own group with

consideration and who as carefully segregate from all the rich-
ness of life "for their own good and welfare" thirteen million
people whose skin is colored a little differently from my own.

I knew by the time I was twelve that a member of my family would always shake hands with old Negro friends, would
speak gently and graciously to members of the Negro race unless they forgot their place, in which event icy peremptory
tones would draw lines beyond which only the desperate
would dare take one step. I knew that to use the word "nigger" was unpardonable and no well-bred southerner was
quite so crude as to do so; nor would a well-bred southerner
call a Negro "mister" or invite him into the living room or eat
with him or sit by him in public places.

I knew that my old nurse who had patiently cared for me
through long months of illness, who had given me refuge
when a little sister took my place as the baby of the family,
who comforted me, soothed, fed me, delighted me with her
stories and games, let me fall asleep on her deep warm breast,
was not worthy of the passionate love I felt for her but must
be given instead a half-smiled-at affection similar to that
which one feels for one's dog. I knew but I never believed it,
that the deep respect I felt for her, the tenderness, the love,
was a childish thing which every normal child outgrows, that
such love begins with one's toys and is discarded with them,
and that somehow—though it seemed impossible to my agonized heart—I too, must outgrow these feelings. I learned to
give presents to this woman I loved, instead of esteem and
honor. I learned to use a soft voice to oil my words of superiority. I learned to cheapen with tears and sentimental talk of
"my old mammy" one of the profound relationships of my
life. I learned the bitterest thing a child can learn: that the human relations I valued most were held cheap by the world I
lived in.

From the day I was born, I began to learn my lessons. I was
put in a rigid frame too intricate, too complex, too twisting
to describe here so briefly, but I learned to conform to its
slide-rule measurements. I learned that it is possible to be a
Christian and a white southerner simultaneously; to be a
gentlewoman and an arrogant callous creature in the same
moment; to pray at night and ride a Jim Crow car the next

morning and to feel comfortable in doing both. I learned to believe in freedom, to glow when the word *democracy* is used, and to practice slavery from morning to night. I learned it the way all of my southern people learn it: by closing door after door until one's mind and heart and conscience are blocked off from each other and from reality.

I closed the doors. Or perhaps they were closed for me. Then one day they began to open again. Why I had the desire or the strength to open them or what strange accident or circumstance opened them for me would require in the answering an account too long, too particular, too stark to make here. And perhaps I should not have the insight or wisdom that such an analysis would demand of me, nor the will to make it. I know only that the doors opened, a little; that somewhere along that iron corridor we travel from babyhood to maturity, doors swinging inward began to swing outward, showing glimpses of the world beyond, of that clear bright thing we call "reality."

I believe there is one experience in my childhood which pushed these doors open, a little. And I am going to tell it here, although I know well that to excerpt from a life and family background one incident and name it as a "cause" of a change in one's life direction is a distortion and often an irrelevance. The profound hungers of a child and how they are filled have too much to do with the way in which experiences are assimilated to tear an incident out of a life and look at it in isolation. Yet, with these reservations, I shall tell it, not because it was in itself so severe a trauma, but because it became for me a symbol of buried experiences that I did not have access to. It is an incident that has rarely happened to other southern children. In a sense, it is unique. But it was an acting-out, a special private production of a little script that is written on the lives of most southern children before they know words. Though they may not have seen it staged this way, each southerner has had his own dramatization of the theme.

I should like to preface the account by giving a brief glimpse of my family and background, hoping that the reader, entering my home with me, will be able to blend the ragged edges of this isolated experience into a more full life picture and in doing so will see that it is, in a sense, everybody's story.

I was born and reared in a small Deep South town whose population was about equally Negro and white. There were nine of us who grew up freely in a rambling house of many rooms, surrounded by big lawn, back yard, gardens, fields, and barn. It was the kind of home that gathers memories like dust, a place filled with laughter and play and pain and hurt and ghosts and games. We were given such advantages of schooling, music, and art as were available in the South, and our world was not limited to the South, for travel to far places seemed a simple, natural thing to us, and usually there was one of the family in a remote part of the earth.

We knew we were a respected and important family of this small town but beyond this knowledge we gave little thought to status. Our father made money in lumber and naval stores for the excitement of making and losing it—not for what money can buy nor the security which it sometimes gives. I do not remember at any time wanting "to be rich" nor do I remember that thrift and saving were ideals which our parents considered important enough to urge upon us. Always in the family there was an acceptance of risk, a mild delight even in burning bridges, an expectant "what will happen now!" We were not irresponsible; living according to the pleasure principle was by no means our way of life. On the contrary we were trained to think that each of us should do something that would be of genuine usefulness to the world, and the family thought it right to make sacrifices if necessary, to give each child adequate preparation for this life's work. We were also trained to think learning important, and books, but "bad" books our mother burned. We valued music and art and craftsmanship but it was people and their welfare and religion that were the foci around which our lives seemed naturally to move. Above all else, the important thing was what we "planned to do with our lives." That each of us must do something was as inevitable as breathing for we owed a "debt to society which must be paid." This was a family commandment.

While many of our neighbors spent their energies in counting limbs on the family tree and grafting some on now and then to give symmetry to it, or in reliving the old bitter days of Reconstruction licking scars to cure their vague malaise, or in fighting each battle and turn of battle of that Civil War which has haunted the southern conscience so long, my father was pushing his nine children straight into the future. "You have your heritage," he used to say, "some of it good, some not so good; and as far as I know you had the usual number of grandmothers and grandfathers. Yes, there were slaves, far too many of them in the family, but that was your grandfather's mistake, not yours. The past has been lived. It is gone. The future is yours. What are you going to do with it?" Always he asked this question of his children and sometimes one knew it was but an echo of the old question he had spent his life trying to answer for himself. For always the future held my father's dreams; always there, not in the past, did he expect to find what he had spent his life searching for.

We lived the same segregated life as did other southerners but our parents talked in excessively Christian and democratic terms. We were told ten thousand times that status and money are unimportant (though we were well supplied with both); we were told that "all men are brothers," that we are a part of a democracy and must act like democrats. We were told that the teachings of Jesus are real and important and could be practiced if we tried. We were told also that to be "radical" is bad, silly too; and that one must always conform to the "best behavior" of one's community and make it better if one can. We were taught that we were superior not to people but to hate and resentment, and that no member of the Smith family could stoop so low as to have an enemy. No matter what injury was done us, we must not injure ourselves further by retaliating. That was a family commandment too.

We had family prayers once each day. All of us as children read the Bible in its entirety each year. We memorized hundreds of Bible verses and repeated them at breakfast, and said "sentence prayers" around the family table. God was not someone we met on Sunday but a permanent member of our household. It never occurred to me until I was fourteen or fifteen years old that He did not see every act and thought and chalk up the daily score on eternity's tablets.

Despite the strain of living so intimately with God, the nine of us were strong, healthy, energetic youngsters who filled our days with play and sports and music and books and managed to live much of our lives on the careless level at which young lives should be lived. We had our times of profound anxiety of course, for there were hard lessons to be learned about the body and "bad things" to be learned about sex. Sometimes I have wondered how we ever learned them with a mother so shy with words.

She was a wistful creature who loved beautiful things like lace and sunsets and flowers in a vague inarticulate way, and took good care of her children. We always knew this was not her world but one she accepted under duress. Her private world we rarely entered, though the shadow of it lay at times heavily on our hearts.

Our father owned large business interests, employed hundreds of colored and white laborers, paid them the prevailing low wages, worked them the prevailing long hours, built for them mill towns (Negro and white), built for each group a church, saw to it that religion was supplied free, saw to it that a commissary supplied commodities at a high price, and in general managed his affairs much as ten thousand other southern businessmen manage theirs.

Even now, I can hear him chuckling as he told my mother how he won his fight for Prohibition. The high point of the campaign was election afternoon, when he lined up the entire mill force of several hundred (white and black), passed out a shining silver dollar to each one of them, marched them in and voted liquor out of our county. It was a great day in his life. He had won the Big Game, a game he was always playing with himself against all kinds of evil. It did not occur to him to scrutinize the methods he used. Evil was a word written in capitals; the devil was smart; if you wanted to win you outsmarted him. It was as simple as that.

He was a practical, hardheaded, warmhearted, high-spirited man born during the Civil War, earning his living at twelve, struggling through bitter decades of Reconstruction and post-Reconstruction, through populist movement, through the panic of 1893, the panic of 1907, on into the twentieth century accepting his region as he found it, accepting its

morals and its mores as he accepted its climate, with only
scorn for those who held grudges against the North or pitied
themselves or the South; scheming, dreaming, expanding his
business, making and losing money, making friends whom he
did not lose, with never a doubt that God was always by his
side whispering hunches as to how to pull off successful deals.
When he lost, it was his own fault. When he won, God had
helped him.

Once while we were kneeling at family prayers the fire siren
at the mill sounded the alarm that the mill was on fire. My father did not falter from his prayer. The alarm sounded again
and again—which signified that the fire was big. With quiet
dignity he continued his talk with God while his children
sweated and wriggled and hearts beat out of their chests in
excitement. He was talking to God—how could he hurry out
of the presence of the Most High to save his mills! When he
finished his prayer, he quietly stood up, laid the Bible carefully
on the table. Then, and only then, did he show an interest in
what was happening in Mill Town. . . . When the telegram
was placed in his hands telling of the death of his beloved favorite son, he gathered his children together, knelt down, and
in a steady voice which contained no hint of his shattered
heart, loyally repeated, "God is our refuge and strength, a
very present help in trouble. Therefore will we not fear,
though the earth be removed, and though the mountains be
carried into the midst of the sea." On his deathbed, he whispered to his old Business Partner in Heaven: "I have fought
the fight; I have kept the faith."

Against this backdrop the drama of the South was played
out one day in my life:

A little white girl was found in the colored section of our
town, living with a Negro family in a broken-down shack.
This family had moved in only a few weeks before and little
was known of them. One of the ladies in my mother's club,
while driving over to her washerwoman's, saw the child
swinging on a gate. The shack, as she said, was hardly more
than a pigsty and this white child was living with ignorant and
dirty and sick-looking colored folks. "They must have kidnapped her," she told her friends. Genuinely shocked, the

clubwomen busied themselves in an attempt to do something, for the child was very white indeed. The strange Negroes were subjected to a grueling questioning and finally grew frightened and evasive and refused to talk at all. This only increased the suspicion of the white group, and the next day the clubwomen, escorted by the town marshal, took the child from her adopted family despite their tears.

She was brought to our home. I do not know why my mother consented to this plan. Perhaps because she loved children and always showed tenderness and concern for them. It was easy for one more to fit into our ample household and Janie was soon at home there. She roomed with me, sat next to me at the table; I found Bible verses for her to say at breakfast; she wore my clothes, played with my dolls and followed me around from morning to night. She was dazed by her new comforts and by the interesting activities of this big lively family; and I was as happily dazed, for her adoration was a new thing to me; and as time passed a quick, childish, and deeply felt bond grew up between us.

But a day came when a telephone message was received from a colored orphanage. There was a meeting at our home, whispers, shocked exclamations. All afternoon the ladies went in and out of our house talking to Mother in tones too low for children to hear. And as they passed us at play, most of them looked quickly at Janie and quickly looked away again, though a few stopped and stared at her as if they could not tear their eyes from her face. When my father came home in the evening Mother closed her door against our young ears and talked a long time with him. I heard him laugh, heard Mother say, "But Papa, this is no laughing matter!" And then they were back in the living room with us and my mother was pale and my father was saying, "Well, work it out, honey, as best you can. After all, now that you know, it is pretty simple."

In a little while my mother called my sister and me into her bedroom and told us that in the morning Janie would return to Colored Town. She said Janie was to have the dresses the ladies had given her and a few of my own, and the toys we had shared with her. She asked me if I would like to give Janie one of my dolls. She seemed hurried, though Janie was not to leave until next day. She said, "Why not select it now?" And in dreamlike stiffness I brought in my dolls and chose one for Janie. And then I found it possible to say, "Why? Why is she leaving? She likes us, she hardly knows them. She told me she had been with them only a month."

"Because," Mother said gently, "Janie is a little colored girl."

"But she can't be. She's white!"

"We were mistaken. She is colored."

"But she looks——"

"She is colored. Please don't argue!"

"What does it mean?" I whispered.

"It means," Mother said slowly, "that she has to live in Colored Town with colored people."

"But why? She lived here three weeks and she doesn't belong to them, she told me she didn't."

"She is a little colored girl."

"But you said yourself that she has nice manners. You said that," I persisted.

"Yes, she is a nice child. But a colored child cannot live in our home."

"Why?"

"You know, dear! You have always known that white and colored people do not live together."

"Can she come over to play?"

"No."

"I don't understand."

"I don't either," my young sister quavered.

"You're too young to understand. And don't ask me again, ever again, about this!" Mother's voice was sharp but her face was sad and there was no certainty left there. She hurried out and busied herself in the kitchen and I wandered through that room where I had been born, touching the old familiar things in it, looking at them, trying to find the answer to a question that moaned in my mind like a hurt thing. . . .

And then I went out to Janie, who was waiting, knowing things were happening that concerned her but waiting until they were spoken aloud.

I do not know quite how the words were said but I told

her that she was to return in the morning to the little place where she had lived because she was colored and colored children could not live with white children.

"Are you white?" she said.

"I'm white," I replied, "and my sister is white. And you're colored. And white and colored can't live together because my mother says so."

"Why?" Janie whispered.

"Because they can't," I said. But I knew, though I said it firmly, that something was wrong. I knew my father and mother whom I passionately admired had done that which did not fit in with their teachings. I knew they had betrayed something which they held dear. And I was shamed by their failure and frightened, for I felt that they were no longer as powerful as I had thought. There was something Out There that was stronger than they and I could not bear to believe it. I could not confess that my father, who had always solved the family dilemmas easily and with laughter, could not solve this. I knew that my mother who was so good to children did not believe in her heart that she was being good to this child. There was not a word in my mind that said it but my body knew and my glands, and I was filled with anxiety.

But I felt compelled to believe they were right. It was the only way my world could be held together. And, like a slow poison, it began to seep through me: *I was white. She was colored. We must not be together. It was bad to be together. Though you ate with your nurse when you were little, it was bad to eat with any colored person after that. It was bad just as other things were bad that your mother had told you. It was bad that she was to sleep in the room with me that night. It was bad. . . .*

I was suddenly full of guilt. For three weeks I had done things that white children are not supposed to do. And now I knew these things had been wrong.

I went to the piano and began to play, as I had always done when I was in trouble. I tried to play Paderewski's *Minuet* and as I stumbled through it, the little girl came over and sat on the bench with me. Feeling lonely, lost in these deep currents that were sweeping through our house that night, she crept closer and put her arms around me and I shrank away as if my body had been uncovered. I had not said a word, I did not say one, but she knew, and tears slowly rolled down her little white face. . . .

And then I forgot it. For more than thirty years the experience was wiped out of my memory. But that night, and the weeks it was tied to, worked its way like a splinter, bit by bit down to the hurt places in my memory and festered there. And as I grew older, as more experiences collected around that faithless time, as memories of earlier, more profound hurts crept closer and closer drawn to that night as if to a magnet, I began to know that people who talked of love and Christianity and democracy did not mean it. That is a hard thing for a child to learn. I still admired my parents, there was so much that was strong and vital and sane and good about them and I never forgot this; I stubbornly believed in their sincerity, as I do to this day, and I loved them. Yet in my heart they were under suspicion. Something was wrong.

Something was wrong with a world that tells you that love is good and people are important and then forces you to deny love and to humiliate people. I knew, though I would not for years confess it aloud, that in trying to shut the Negro race away from us, we have shut ourselves away from so many good, creative, honest, deeply human things in life. I began to understand so slowly at first but more and more clearly as the years passed, that the warped, distorted frame we have put around every Negro child from birth is around every white child also. Each is on a different side of the frame but each is pinioned there. And I knew that what cruelly shapes and cripples the personality of one is as cruelly shaping and crippling the personality of the other. I began to see that though we may, as we acquire new knowledge, live through new experiences, examine old memories, gain the strength to tear the frame from us, yet we are stunted and warped and in our lifetime cannot grow straight again any more than can a tree, put in a steel-like twisting frame when young, grow tall and straight when the frame is torn away at maturity.

As I sit here writing, I can almost touch that little town, so close is the memory of it. There it lies, its main street lined with great oaks, heavy with matted moss that swings softly even now as I remember. A little white town rimmed with

Negroes, making a deep shadow on the whiteness. There it lies, broken in two by one strange idea. Minds broken in two. Hearts broken. Conscience torn from acts. A culture split in a thousand pieces. That is segregation. I am remembering: a woman in a mental hospital walking four steps out, four steps in, unable to go further because she has drawn an invisible line around her small world and is terrified to take one step beyond it. . . . A man in a Disturbed Ward assigning "places" to the other patients and violently insisting that each stay in his place. . . . A Negro woman saying to me so quietly, "We cannot ride together on the bus, you know. It is not legal to be human in Georgia."

Memory, walking the streets of one's childhood . . . of the town where one was born.

from Killers of the Dream (1949)

Jim Crow in the North

by George S. Schuyler

PEOPLE in the North tend to look down on Southerners in the matter of discrimination against the Negro, and to pride themselves upon the civilized treatment accorded to him in communities north of Mason and Dixon's Line. The facts, unfortunately, give little cause for condescension or pride. The Negro is still pretty much a second-class citizen all over the country, and the whole concept of civil rights continues to be largely a dream to men and women who are colored. Much progress has been made in the past twenty-five years—and this progress has by no means been confined to the North. Nevertheless, conditions in the North are still, as we shall see, very far from ideal. I am reporting on those conditions, not out of any desire to aggravate racial feelings, but only to set the record straight. What I have to say is directed primarily at the millions of complacent white folk in the big Northern cities who are totally unaware of any color problem in their midst. The Southerners, at least, know they have a problem.

A survey of Jim Crow in the North might logically begin with New York. No state of the union draws Southern migrants more magnetically than New York. The Southern Negro has heard of the state's civil-rights laws, of its cosmopolitanism, of its reputation for being liberal. He knows that when he gets to New York he will be putting the hated Jim Crow laws and "For Colored" signs behind him. What he finds, however, are other forms of discrimination—more subtle, not sanctified by state law, but nevertheless almost inescapable.

In New York City, the supposed center of American enlightenment, he will find his choice of living quarters restricted to those in the "black ghetto." He will find that open racial discrimination is practiced in two of the major housing developments—both of which, incidentally, enjoy considerable tax exemption. Liberals asked that they be granted the exemption only on the condition that they practice "the policy of non-discrimination," but so far the courts have not held this to be necessary.

In November 1948 he would have noted bitterly that a veterans housing project a short distance from New York City was charged with forcing "upon unwilling tenants and purchasers a racial restrictive clause" requiring them to "subscribe to a denial of fundamental democratic principles." The clause in question reads: "No dwelling shall be used or occupied except by members of the Caucasian race, but the employment and maintenance of other than Caucasian domestic servants shall be permitted." Thus, the only Negro veterans who will be allowed in the development will be maids and janitors.

This particular development happens to be insured by the Federal Housing Authority. However, protests to FHA Commissioner Franklin D. Richards have been futile. In February 1949, Walter White, secretary of the National Association for the Advancement of Colored People, addressed a strong protest to President Truman, and in an accompanying 4000-word brief charged that the FHA "has continued to lend full support to the perpetuation of ghettos," and that, moreover, it has stated that "it would continue to give its support to such [racially restrictive] projects." Mr. Truman did not reply. In March 1949, Thomas G. Grace, the New York State FHA Director, told a protesting group of liberals that the agency did not have the power to bring builders to terms with Negro buyers. He said that Federal approval of a mortgage could not be withdrawn if the owner wrote into a lease or deed a clause barring occupancy to any racial, religious or national group.

Jim Crow in the North exists in the unlikeliest places. In New York City a special fact-finding committee of the National Conference of Christians and Jews reported to the mayor, not long ago, that the Brooklyn-Queens YMCA had some units which refused membership to Negroes, even though Negroes predominated in the neighborhoods of those units, and even though the need of Negroes for such facilities was desperate. The same committee reported that, despite New York's civil-rights laws, "some hotels, cabarets and eating places still find methods of preventing full use of their facilities by Negroes." The committee concluded that the discrimination "can in almost every instance, be traced back to segregation or apathy."

It is difficult to assess the practical effectiveness of New York's civil-rights laws. In December 1948 two groups investigating the city's race relations reported that one out of five New Yorkers interviewed had personally experienced job discrimination. Most experts believe that the state FEPC law is easy to circumvent, and these particular investigators reported: "Discrimination is believed to exist in all branches of industry and occupations in New York City, especially in heavy industry, public utilities and finance."

So much for New York City. In the rest of the state the situation is generally worse. It is practically impossible to find a colored clerk in a department store in Albany, and Negroes in that city are pretty well restricted in job opportunities. Negroes have also learned not to expect too much from Syracuse —not long ago a colored woman filed suit against a hotel there for turning her away. In the main, the pattern of segregation and employment discrimination is solidly fixed all throughout upper New York State, in both the urban and rural areas. It is abetted even by many labor unions, and it extends even to the use of recreational facilities.

This latter question is becoming a real sore point with Negroes, many of whom live in slums and so have special need of places where they can relax. At least 95 per cent of the privately owned resorts, bathing beaches, bowling alleys and other places of public recreation in New York State do their best to keep out Negroes. The White Plains YWCA is "solving" its Negro problem by letting Negro women use its swimming pool one evening a week.

II

Historically, New England has always been regarded as the most liberal section of the country in its treatment of Negro citizens. It was the stern Puritan conscience of this area that produced the Abolitionist movement in the early nineteenth century. Today there is little open discrimination in New England, especially in Maine, New Hampshire and Vermont, where Negroes are few in numbers. However, Negroes are not wanted at most resorts in these states, and where there is any question of competition, employment opportunities for Negroes are sharply limited.

In Massachusetts, Rhode Island and Connecticut, where there are more Negroes, the color bar is camouflaged but quite potent. It is only since 1940 that Negroes in these states have been able to breach the employment barrier to the extent of getting white-collar and skilled jobs. The enactment of fair-employment-practice laws in Massachusetts and Connecticut has helped appreciably.

It is easier for Negroes in New England to live where they choose than in any other section of the country, but even here there are some formidable barriers. The ghetto situation in New Haven is notorious. In Providence there are "understandings" which discourage purchases and rentals by Negroes in white areas. Some Providence realtors maintain special lists of sub-standard houses to be kept open for Negro occupancy; this procedure ensures that the colored areas will always have the worst slums.

A similar situation exists in Hartford, where it is virtually impossible for a Negro to rent a home outside the colored area. It is somewhat easier for a Negro to buy a home outright, but if word gets around that such a purchase is contemplated, pressure is often placed on bankers to withhold loans. Some Negroes find that they can buy property only if they have a white friend who is willing to act as a "front man" for them.

The pattern of Jim Crow in the North begins to emerge more clearly when we leave the comparatively enlightened regions of the Northeast and begin to consider facts and figures for the country as a whole. There is hardly a state in the whole North that can take pride in its treatment of our most abused minority.

The problem of obtaining decent housing is becoming a desperate one for Negroes all through the North and West. The decision of the U.S. Supreme Court last year to outlaw restrictive covenants was an immense help. But the battle is far from won. In Kansas, where John Brown once risked his life to help colored men, the state legislature recently passed an act specifically authorizing certain types of restrictive agreements. In Southern California, the regional office of the Anti-Defamation League has been fighting the attempts of real estate organizations in the Los Angeles area to circumvent the Supreme Court decision. The League reported recently that "a campaign of terrorism, vandalism and discrimination has begun to prevent Southern California families from enjoying [their] rights." Among the Negro victims of this campaign have been Nat ("King") Cole, the musician, who bought an $85,000 residence; Paul R. Williams, an eminent architect; Dr. Carl A. Dent, a Santa Monica physician who is reportedly afraid to occupy his new home; Dr. Pauline O. Roberts, who had a cross burned in front of her elegant new residence by some local patriots; and Mr. and Mrs. Ben Eustus, who were driven from their house when it was fired by vandals.

These cases are admittedly extreme, but of 55 cities outside the South reporting on residential restrictions for Negroes, there were only a few where purchases might be made with any freedom. Among these were Massillon and Columbus, in Ohio, Sacramento and San Francisco, in California, Morristown, New Jersey, and Albany and White Plains in New York. Even in these cities the privilege was almost always qualified, and purchases were usually much easier to arrange than rentals. In most other cities the black ghettos are expanding rather than disintegrating.

The school situation is also appalling in the North, where, contrary to the popular conception, there are plenty of racially segregated public schools. New Jersey and Indiana have recently abolished Jim Crow schools, but they still exist in Delaware, Pennsylvania, Kansas, Arizona, New Mexico, Maryland, Missouri and the District of Columbia. Actually, because of the expansion of solid Negro urban districts, there are more segregated schools in the North than ever before.

Naturally, there is a tendency to assign Negro schoolteachers to Negro schools, which often have sub-standard equipment and inferior curricula. In several Northern, Eastern and Western cities, no Negro teachers at all are hired. In Lansing, Michigan, the mayor answered a criticism on this score by saying that the city's schools had Negro janitors and that that was enough.

On the college level, most schools have fairly rigid Negro quotas, and Negroes who are admitted are subjected to various forms of segregation. An Amherst chapter of a student fraternity was expelled from the national organization last year for admitting a Negro to membership. When the National Interfraternity Conference met in New York City last December it postponed taking any stand on this issue for another year.

III

Things have improved somewhat since the day when Booker T. Washington commented that "in the North the Negro can spend a dollar but cannot earn it, while in the South he can earn a dollar but cannot spend it." But the employment situation is still bad in the North. A survey of 55 cities showed that in only 19 of them were Negroes employed as clerks or store salesmen. (The prejudice in this connection was least in New York City, but even here the number of such Negro employees was usually held carefully to a token half dozen or so.) The rise of closed labor unions has aggravated the problem considerably. The same survey showed that only 10 of the 55 cities were without discriminatory unions. The worst offenders are the unions of skilled workers, but inconsistencies, evasions and run-arounds are practiced by all types.

Finding a hotel to stop at is another of the Northern Negro's considerable problems. In about half the cities of the North, Negroes are never accepted. In the others they are accepted but made to feel that they are unwelcome. As a general rule, the only way a Negro can get a hotel room is to make an advance reservation. Sometimes even this is not enough. In Springfield, Lincoln's home, it is reported that five colored state legislators cannot get accommodations at any decent hotel. In Olympia, the capital of Washington, the famous "Wings over Jordan" choir members were barred from both of the city's hotels.

All hotels in Washington, D.C., now have a rigid color bar. There is a rather unusual history to this story. In 1872 the popularly-elected District Assembly passed a stiff civil-rights law, and until past the turn of the century, Negroes were welcome in all the capital's public places. But around 1904, this law "mysteriously disappeared from the compiled statutes of the District, and cannot be found in the present codes." There is no record that it was ever repealed, but it is certainly not enforced today.

Buying a meal in the North is almost as difficult as getting a hotel room. There are probably fewer than twenty cities in the country where Negroes are not completely barred from white-owned restaurants. Refusal is usually bold and callous; even where civil-rights laws exist, restaurant owners know that custom is with them. Negro legislators were not admitted to the Capitol Building lunchroom in Springfield until 1947, and, unless there has been a very recent change, the sixty-odd colored employees of the state of Illinois are still kept out. At the five-and-ten-cent stores in Topeka, white customers sit down to eat at the lunch counters, but Negroes must stand. At some soda fountains in that city, Negroes cannot get service whether they sit or stand.

To the widely-publicized Four Freedoms, American Negroes would like to add a fifth—Freedom of Recreation. In the event of another war, black boys may have to fight on the beaches, but neither in war nor peace are they allowed to bathe on them. Along the Atlantic and Gulf coasts, from New Jersey to Mexico, there are less than half a dozen spots where Negroes may enjoy bathing privileges. Almost everywhere, mountain resorts are closed to colored people. The same applies to bowling alleys and even, in some cases, to motion-picture theatres. At this late date there are upwards of a dozen Northern cities in which Negroes are either barred from theatres or segregated in them. (The national capital, of course, is included in this list.)

An especially ugly situation developed in the Palisades Amusement Park, which is right across the Hudson River from New York's Harlem. For the last three summers a non-violent direct-action group called New York's Committee on Racial Equality has been campaigning to break down the banning of Negroes from the swimming pool at Palisades. The Committee's pickets were rebuffed, insulted, and finally beaten up by police and jailed. In February 1948 a Federal judge ruled that the anti-discrimination provisions of the Federal Civil Rights Law did not apply to privately owned amusement parks. But finally, at the end of 1948, the New Jersey Supreme Court ruled that the discrimination was illegal. It remains to be seen whether New Jersey's new laws, outlawing Jim Crow completely throughout the state, will be enforced and obeyed.

New Jersey's new civil-rights law forbids segregation in the state's National Guard units. New York and Connecticut have also taken this step recently, but there are still segregated units in Massachusetts, the District of Columbia, Ohio, Illinois and California. The U.S. Army controls the various State Guards, but the present administration, like its predecessors, stands solidly behind the tradition of Jim Crow in uniform.

Since the bulk of Christian churches are Jim Crow institutions, it is not surprising that the YMCA and YWCA should also be guilty of discrimination. The YWCA's record is much better than that of the YMCA, only half of whose branches accept Negro members. And even these memberships rarely include the use of swimming pools, cafeterias or dormitories. Whenever possible, colored applicants are sweetly referred to the special Negro branches.

IV

Rabelais and Swift would have been convulsed by the prodigious effort expended in their country to prevent citizens of opposite sexes and colors from legally consummating their affection. Inasmuch as 80 per cent of American Negroes have some white blood, the reasons given for the restrictions are rather hypocritical. To prove the alleged aversion of the two races to intimate association, 29 states of the union (16 of them outside the South) have illegalized mixed marriages. The most savage penalties, as a matter of fact, are in the North. Georgia hands out a maximum sentence of one year for the offense, and Tennessee and Texas five years, but in Indiana, North Dakota and South Dakota, the rap is ten years.

All 29 states refuse to recognize even those interracial marriages which have been consummated elsewhere.

Another bitter pill for the Northern Negro is the hospital situation. In general, hospitalized Negroes are segregated. In San Francisco, Los Angeles and Wilmington, Negroes are not permitted to enter hospitals unless they are prepared to pay for private rooms. In other cities the pattern of discrimination works differently. Trenton, Columbus, and Harrisburg *insist* that Negroes go into the wards; they are not allowed private rooms. Kansas City, Missouri, bars Negroes from all hospitals except two: one a municipally-owned Jim Crow institution, the other a private hospital owned by Negroes. St. Louis bars them from some hospitals and segregates them in others. Fort Wayne segregates them in all hospitals but one. Even in large cities like New York and Chicago, there are various forms of subtle and exasperating bias.

Three winters ago, a Washington, D.C., colored woman in the throes of childbirth and unable to reach a city hospital was rushed to a church-supported institution. She was refused admission with firm Christian resolution, and her baby was delivered on the sidewalk. The somewhat contrite staff then made partial amends by supplying the mother and child with a covering sheet until the city ambulance took them away.

In this respect, as in others, the Negro from Washington, D.C., is heavily penalized. He must either accept space in a segregated ward or travel to Philadelphia or New York. Aside from Freeman's Hospital, a Negro institution, the nation's capital has only two private or semi-private rooms available to colored people. It is ironical to recall that sixty years ago the eleven hospitals in Washington served all races equally. Today three of the twelve private institutions totally exclude Negroes, and the remainder segregate them.

The Negro who wants to be a doctor finds difficulties in his way all along the line. He will have difficulty finding a school that will accept him and more difficulty finding a hospital in which he can gain interne experience. (However, Negro nurses are freely accepted in most hospitals.)

The crowning indignity to the Northern Negro is the treatment he receives from the proprietors of snooty cemeteries and mortuaries; even in death he cannot escape from Jim

Crow. However, it remained for Washington, D.C., to reach the depths of indecency. There, according to report, "a dog cemetery has erected a color bar against the burial of dogs belonging to colored people. In announcing this policy, the owner stated that he assumed the dogs would not object, but he was afraid his white customers would."

Apparently even a white dog is barred if its owner is black!

The American Mercury, June 1949

Men Who Shame Our State and Flag

by Ralph McGill

Two persons from Bainbridge came to see me.

They were solemn and sad, worried and a little bit afraid.

They had a right to be.

This was their story. A short time ago a 15-year-old Negro boy had been arrested on his return from a stay of two weeks in Ashburn. Frightened, cowed and very much alone, he was taken roughly, he says, to jail.

In a sworn statement from a hospital bed, he said that after arrest he was told he had insulted a white woman. He had not, and he denied it as strongly as he could. The officer then called up a number and had the boy talk into the telephone. "Does that sound like him?" he asked.

The boy said the county officer then hit him with his fist and locked him up. There was no warrant and no charge made.

He says he asked the county officer what he was charged with doing and the officer said to him that if it were up to him the boy would never see his daddy again. That's pretty hard on a boy of 15.

Apparently there was no charge or evidence against him because the next night the boy was released—late, about 10:30 p.m.

In his statement he said that when he came down the steps from the jail two men were waiting. They both hit him and one put a sack over his head. They took him to a car. During the drive they struck him and cursed him. After a while they reached some woods and got out, dragging him with them.

Now, whatever his race, this was but a 15-year-old boy. He was, one may assume, very much afraid and in a state of terror. Any boy would have been. He was all alone and knew he might be killed.

The boy was beaten, very heavily, with a strap and a club.

He was asked if he believed in civil rights. He said he didn't know what they were and had never heard of them. The odds are the men who were mistreating him so brutally didn't know what they were either. They asked him if he knew of any niggers insulting white women. He says they told him they were going to beat him until they killed him if he didn't tell. He said, truthfully, he didn't know any. They asked him who he ran around with and he told them. He is afraid they will be beaten, although the boy swears that neither he nor they have ever insulted or sought to insult anyone. He says they then asked him how old he was and he said 15 and they each whipped him hard for every year of his age. They then told him to run.

It was after midnight and dark. The 15-year-old boy tried to run, but kept falling down because he was almost unconscious and badly beaten. He says he hid in some bushes all night and the next morning, feverish and sick, asked for some water at a white farmer's house. The man gave him the water and asked him what the matter was. He said nothing was the matter. He went on to a Negro's house and these people bathed him and dressed his badly wounded back and put him to bed. They also called the deputy.

The boy and the deputy found the place where he had been whipped. They also found his shoes which had come off during the beating.

The deputy called the sheriff at Bainbridge and the boy's father, and the boy was put in the hospital at Bainbridge, with raw wounds from the beating.

The case is being "investigated."

As I have said here before, the Klan, or a manifestation of the Klan, is a cancer which will sicken and harm any town which does not rise to put it down.

Bainbridge is a fine city. Its colored and white populations always have got on well together. Its people do not approve of vicious ruffians taking the law into their own hands. The good people must not be afraid of the Klan element, which has pack courage, but only pack courage.

The pattern of this was typical. The law had nothing against the boy. But the outlaws, those of the Klan mentality, wanted to beat and slug someone in order to terrorize the

Negro population, rather than allow the law to run down any law violation by any Negro or persons in the town, suspected of saying obscene things over the telephone, which was the offense being investigated.

It could easily have been determined if the boy had been away. If he had been guilty it could have been proved. The boy in question was released because he was not involved.

But, the point to note is that two men knew when the boy would be released and were waiting. That is in the pattern.

What has happened there—as has happened in a few more places—is that a group of men have put themselves above the law.

Somebody at the jail let the men know when the boy would be released.

The people of Bainbridge and the county can join together and say they vote for sheriffs and for courts and they want them to handle their cases. They can demand of the sheriff that he run this down and arrest the guilty men and present the evidence to the grand jury. They can ask the sheriff why prisoners released from his jail can be picked up at the door, a sack put over their head, and then taken away by force and violence at the very door of the building which houses the law enforcement offices of the county. Many persons in the county are outraged and aroused. That's what we need.

Georgia can't go on advertising to the Nation that mobs can mock our law and our courts. We aren't the sort of people these evil persons try to make us seem.

Let the law find the guilty and try them legally, by law, and jail them by law.

We can't go on allowing violent and lawless men to dominate us. The flag of the United States and the flag of Georgia are supposed to fly over our courthouses and public buildings. Let's remember that. They are supposed to stand for law and justice.

The Atlanta Constitution, August 18, 1949

Florida's Legal Lynching

by Ted Poston

On September 8, in the palm-surrounded Lake County courthouse in Tavares, Samuel Shepherd and Walter Irvin, twenty-two-year-old Negro war veterans, heard themselves sentenced to death for the capital crime of rape. Charles Greenlee, sixteen years old, who had never seen Shepherd and Irvin until they found themselves in a mob-threatened cell together, received life imprisonment for the same crime.

Sentence was pronounced by Circuit Court Judge T. G. Futch, who, incidentally, owed his election to the support of the Negro voters of Lake County. The state was represented during the three-day trial by County Prosecutor Jess Hunter. An all-white jury accepted without question the unsupported word of Mrs. Norma Lee Padgett, a seventeen-year-old white farm housewife, that she had been raped by four Negroes in the back seat of a 1946 Mercury sedan in the early morning hours of July 16. There was no medical testimony, no presentation of objective evidence like her clothes or the car in which the crime allegedly occurred. The word of one white girl was believed against that of three Negro youths who insisted that they had never seen her before.

Mrs. Padgett's charges set off a three-day reign of terror, beginning July 16, in which local hoodlums, aided by unmasked klansmen from adjacent Orange County and distant Georgia, burned and pillaged Negro homes in Groveland, Stuckey's Still, and neighboring communities and struck terror into the hearts of thousands of Negro citrus workers who had hesitated about harvesting the crop at the low prevailing wage rate. After the rioting was finally quelled by the National Guard, word was sent to at least a dozen fairly successful Negro farmers to "leave everything and get out now and stay out." Their prospering independence was a bad example in a community which thrives on keeping its workers in a state of semi-peonage.

The National Association for the Advancement of Colored People, which first exposed the frame-up of Shepherd, Irvin, and Greenlee—and the wanton murder of Ernest Thomas, twenty-seven, the fourth suspect, by a deputized mob ten days after the alleged rape—will fight the convictions all the way up to the United States Supreme Court if an aroused public will contribute the $20,000 estimated as the cost of the appeals.

Through the N.A.A.C.P.'s entrance into the case several precedents were established. Two Negro lawyers, Franklin H. Williams of the association's national office, and Horace E. Hill of Daytona Beach, recently admitted to the Florida bar, appeared among the defense counsel in the third-floor courtroom in Tavares. Prospective jurors were forced to concede that Negro lawyers should have the same rights in Lake County courts as white lawyers, "even to the cross-examination of all witnesses, including white ladies." (None of them relished the prospect, but in their anxiety to serve on what they jokingly called the "lynch jury" they consented.) And for the first time in the history of Florida, and probably of the whole South, an all-white jury, which had been expected to bring in its verdict in five minutes, deliberated for two hours before it decided to convict three Negroes on the unsupported word of a white woman. Rather than face the fury of their neighbors, the jurors finally "compromised," but in recommending "mercy" for Charles Greenlee they admitted that the prosecution had not proved its case.

The chief defense counsel was Alex Akerman, Jr., a successful civil lawyer in nearby Orlando, the state's Republican leader, and a native Southern liberal. By raising the question of the systematic exclusion of Negroes from grand and petit juries in Lake County, Akerman prepared the way for the United States Supreme Court to order a new trial. Jess Hunter, the wily state's attorney, anticipated this question when the N.A.A.C.P. entered the case, and for that reason he placed a Negro truck driver on the grand jury which indicted the youths. This Negro, the first ever summoned for such duty, indicated a reluctance to attend, but the sheriff sent out

word that "he'll come or I'll go get him." Hunter also put
the names of three Negroes—something that had never been
done before—on the first two panels of 300 veniremen summoned for prospective jury duty at the trial, but he called
only one, a gray-haired old handyman. The court clerk
begged defense counsel to excuse this "boy," whom he called
"one of the best niggers in Lake County," so that he could attend his father-in-law's funeral.

Akerman fought brilliantly but in vain for a change of venue
to a less prejudiced county and for a postponement to give the
defense time to investigate new evidence uncovered a few days
before the trial opened. This evidence indicated strongly that
Norma Lee Padgett had never been raped by anyone, and that
her story was an attempt to cover up a fight she had had with
her husband, Willie Padgett, from whom she was estranged.

Akerman dared the county prosecutor to introduce as evidence the oral "confessions" obtained from the two older
boys after they had been beaten and tortured by "deputies" in
a nearby woods and had been strung up by their arms and
savagely thrashed in the basement of the combined jail and
courthouse in which the trial was held. Hunter, a highly intelligent prosecutor who deliberately cultivates a backwoods
manner, rejected the challenge because he knew that such
confessions had been ruled inadmissible by the United States
Supreme Court, and that their use would have made the
court's reversal of a guilty verdict inevitable. He thus placed
Florida on a slightly higher legal level than New Jersey, where
six Trenton Negroes were convicted of murder on the basis of
similarly elicited "confessions."

The difficulties encountered in securing a white attorney
were indicative of the feeling of terror that had been built up
by the inflammatory editorials and cartoons in the Florida papers. In the first two weeks after the N.A.A.C.P. entered the
case Franklin H. Williams, its assistant special counsel, traveled up and down the state trying to get a white lawyer who
could not be lambasted by local newspapers as an "outsider
interfering in local affairs."

A prominent Miami criminal attorney, approached indirectly through a liberal white Southerner, replied that he
would not consider "studying" the case unless the N.A.A.C.P.

paid him a retainer of $25,000, an impossible sum for an organization which was able to raise only $1,500 in defense funds; it actually spent more than $5,000 in the trial just concluded. A lawyer in Inverness demanded a $10,000 fee but called up before his offer could be accepted or rejected to say that his wife would not let him act in a rape case involving a white woman and Negro men.

The liberal son of a prominent Florida politician reluctantly decided that he could not take the case. "Although I disagree with many of my father's political beliefs and actions," he said, "I just can't take a step which would undoubtedly bring about his defeat in the next election." This man did act as an undercover investigator for the defense.

After a labor lawyer who has done some work for the C.I.O. refused to conduct the defense unless his partner also received a fee, Williams came back to Alex Akerman, Jr., who had been approached earlier without success. "A lawyer's first responsibility is to his existing clients," Akerman now told Williams, "and I have six clients whose interests might be prejudiced if I took this case." When Williams learned that the six clients were young Negro students in whose behalf Akerman was suing the University of Florida, he would not leave the Orlando attorney's office until he consented to undertake Florida's "little Scottsboro case." During the trial Jess Hunter intimated that Akerman had been paid by the N.A.A.C.P. to challenge the racial ban against Negroes at the University of Florida, but Akerman proved that he had instituted the suits as a private attorney, acting out of his belief in the justice of equal educational opportunities. He showed such fervor in the Tavares defense that another young white Florida lawyer, Joseph E. Price, Jr., volunteered his services without a fee.

The conviction of Shepherd and Irvin with a mandatory death sentence was almost a foregone conclusion. On their return to civil life both had refused to work in the local citrus groves for substandard wages. If either boy had had a chance, it disappeared when he walked to the witness stand, disdainful and unbroken despite the beatings he had received, and scorned the charge that he had assaulted Norma Lee Padgett. Conviction, even with a "mercy" recommendation, must have come as a sharp surprise to the sixteen-year-old Green-lee, for from the moment he began his testimony it was evident that the unlettered but articulate youngster believed that "if you just tell the good white folks the truth and make them understand, then everything will be all right." Akerman proved conclusively that the youth was twenty miles away from the scene of the alleged rape at the time it was said to have occurred, but it was Greenlee's frank, simple story which kept the jury deliberating for two hours.

Dispassionately, and using the time-table established by state witnesses, Akerman also proved that Shepherd and Irvin could not have been near the alleged rape scene on that July morning; but neither one had Greenlee's persuasiveness on the stand.

Ironically, the life-imprisonment sentence for Greenlee almost brought further tragedy to Lake County. Incensed that even one of the defendants had escaped the chair, five carloads of white men chased the two Negro defense lawyers and two Negro reporters forty miles over the road to Orlando on the night of the verdict.

The Nation, September 24, 1949

Cicero Nightmare

by Homer A. Jack

Chicago, July 18

FOR the first time in more than three decades the National Guard has been used to quell a race riot in the Chicago area. The Cicero outbreak was not like other race riots; 10,000 suburbanites went beserk, but not a single Negro was within miles of the scene.

Once the base of Al Capone's operations, Cicero with a population of 70,000 is today a city of many small homes, owned largely by second-generation Americans of Czechoslovak, Polish, Italian, and Dutch ancestry. Thousands of Negroes work in the great factories of the area, making Western Electric telephones, Hot Point stoves, Thor washing machines, and so on, but none of them live in Cicero. For years "the race issue" has been a convenient gimmick for Cicero politicians. The present political machine defeated an attempt to overturn it in 1948 by distributing a fake notice the night before the election which read: "The town board of Cicero has denied us the American right to live in Cicero for more than eighty years. Vote for the City Government [the reform group] next Tuesday, so that we colored people may enjoy the privilege of living in the town of Cicero."

Early in June, Harvey E. Clark, Jr., a twenty-nine-year-old Chicago bus driver recently graduated from Fisk University, rented an apartment in a twenty-unit building in northwest Cicero. Clark did not expect any more violence than Negroes usually encounter in "new" areas, but when he arrived at the apartment he was greeted by policemen, who prevented him from moving in. An hour or so later Cicero's Chief of Police appeared. Shoving Clark and the rental agent into a car, he is said to have threatened them, "Get out of Cicero and don't come back."

For this clear violation of the federal civil-rights statutes, the Chicago National Association for the Advancement of Colored People promptly filed suit in behalf of Clark against the city of Cicero, demanding $200,000 damages. On June 26 Federal Judge John P. Barnes issued a preliminary injunction restraining the city's officials from interfering with Clark's plans to occupy the apartment he had rented. Judge Barnes warned the Chief of Police: "If you don't obey the order, you're going to be in serious trouble. You are going to exercise the same diligence in seeing that these people move in as you did in trying to keep them out."

On Tuesday, July 10, the Clarks, protected by a small police detail, moved their furniture into the apartment. While they were away from the apartment in the afternoon, a crowd of some 500 persons gathered in front of the building unmolested by the police. Vandals then broke every window in Clark's third-floor apartment while the crowd cheered. The police did nothing.

On the following day nine white families, tenants in the building, moved out. That evening at least 2,000 people gathered around the premises, benignly watched by details of Cicero and Cook County police. Hoodlums again went into action. Breaking into Clark's apartment, they tossed the furniture and the family's possessions, including Clark's honorable discharge from the air force, out of the third-story window. One of the vandals swaggered out of the building with the Clarks' marriage certificate. The police looked on as the crowd burned the furniture but again made no arrests.

On Thursday afternoon the remaining ten white families moved out of the apartment building, and Governor Adlai Stevenson, at the request of Sheriff John Babb, ordered five companies of the Illinois National Guard into Cicero. Several hundred soldiers had arrived by 7 p.m., but owing to a misunderstanding did not reach the scene of the rioting until 10 p.m. They then waited an hour or so longer before making an attempt to disperse the angry crowd of more than 5,000 people. During that time a gang of fifty or so young toughs, in full view of Cicero and Cook County police and only a few yards from soldiers standing shoulder to shoulder with drawn bayonets, threw bricks and stones over the heads of the crowd, the soldiers, and the police at the apartment building. One member of the gang used the spotlight of a police squad car to light up their targets. Every time crashing glass marked a successful hit a roar of approval went up from the crowd. During the lulls one could hear kids breaking bricks on the sidewalk so they could have three "heaves" instead of one.

Mingling in the crowd was Joseph Beauharnais, head of the White Circle League. Telling everybody who would listen that the community must be kept "white," he passed out cards which described the White Circle League as "dedicated to safeguarding and maintaining the Dignity, Social Edicts, Customs, Heritage, and Rights of the White Race in America." One of its aims, the cards said, was "to preserve white neighborhoods for white people and to bring about complete separation of the black and white races."

At 11:30 p.m. the soldiers slowly pushed the crowd back, out of stone's-throw distance. Then another section of the crowd surged forward to within fifty feet of the building and threw "Molotov cocktails" and other incendiary flares into the upper-story windows. Several times the building caught fire, but firemen extinguished the flames. By 12:30 an uneasy "cease-fire" had been obtained, the crowd having been pushed back two blocks or more. Four police cars had been overturned, and nineteen persons had been injured. Seventy persons were arrested, ten charged with assault to kill. Of those arrested, more than half were under twenty-five years of age and about half came from Cicero and neighboring suburbs.

On Friday evening, July 13, the 500 soldiers and 120 Cicero and Cook County police for the first time demonstrated professional policing techniques. Barbed wire was erected for a block each way around the apartment; an area thirty blocks square was declared under martial law, and people who did not keep moving were arrested for unlawful assembly. Although no great crowds gathered that evening, forty-seven persons were arrested. Today Cicero is quiet, but there is talk that "the building will be razed forty-eight hours after the troops are withdrawn."

Various citizen groups are demanding federal and Cook County grand-jury investigations. The Chicago N.A.A.C.P. has sent a representative to Washington to demand federal prosecutions, and large damage suits will be pressed against the city of Cicero. In Chicago the Church Federation issued a statement praising the restraint of 500,000 Negroes in the area. "As leaders of the churches of Cook County," it said, "we hang our heads in shame." The leaders of the estimated 10,000 Protestant and 30,000 Roman Catholic church members in Cicero remained silent for the most part. One churchman privately admitted that the god worshiped in Cicero is the unencumbered deed and that the town's real churches are its savings-and-loan associations.

The Chicago N.A.A.C.P. is raising $6,000 to compensate the Clarks for the loss of their furniture and personal effects, accumulated through many years. Clark intends to return to Cicero; public opinion in Chicago holds that anything less would be a complete victory for lawless racism. But it is anybody's guess how soon Clark or any other Negro will find it safe to live in Cicero. The war there might last longer than the war in Korea.

The Nation, July 28, 1951

Mrs. Means Married Woman

by Hodding Carter

ONE fall day in 1951 our receptionist-switchboard operator said a Negro woman wanted to see me. I told her to send the caller in. She was a well-dressed woman in her thirties and not too much at ease.

I am sure she expected a rebuff after I asked what I could do for her, for she told her story with not a little difficulty. She identified herself as the wife of a Negro physician who had settled in Greenville some months earlier and had established a good practice and a position of leadership among Greenville's Negroes. She had been named chairman, she said, of the Negro section of the Red Cross drive, and what she had come to see me about was our newspaper's failure to identify Negro married women with a *Mrs.*, giving instead either their unadorned names, as Lucy Jones and Mary Smith, or departing from factual reporting, listing only the initials of their husbands if their own first names could not be learned.

She ended with a request that if her name should come up in any further stories about the Red Cross or anything else, we either give her recognition as a married woman and a self-respecting citizen or not print her name at all.

I might have brushed her aside with the usual comment that this was the established policy of the paper and of most Southern newspapers from time immemorial. Or I might have evaded the issue by saying that I would like time to think about it since, if I complied, I would be violating one of the longest-lasting of deep Southern taboos.

But I took neither of these courses because I felt that something very consequential was happening in my office, something important for more than just the unusual fact that a Negro woman was asking me, with dignity and reasonableness, to recognize in our news columns that she was married.

"Mrs.," she said, "just means married woman." For behind
her request was the persistent, long-unanswered demand that
we—not just we of Mississippi, or of the South, but the Western white people who are an amalgam of so many anciently
blended bloods—recognize that what the darker peoples of
the world require and must get from us is a recognition of
their right to human dignity and self-respect. That demand, I
thought, is part and parcel of the tangled reasons why Americans and Englishmen and Turks and Filipinos and Puerto
Ricans are dying in Korea; dying in battle against an Oriental
people to whom face was paramount and in whom the social
condescension and racial vindication of imperialism had
aroused murderous hatred of the Westerner, a hatred fanned
by the Communist incitement into a will to destroy all the
good which had at least partly offset the mistakes and the evils
of Western exploitation of the Orient. Through this doctor's
wife, I thought, speak the people of India, of Egypt and Iran,
Morocco and Malaya, and Africa and Mexico and of every
land where the white conqueror and the white trader and governor have drawn a demeaning line across another's country.

Face, dignity, self-respect—the words became a chant in my
ears: *Face, dignity, self-respect. Mrs. means married women,
China, Africa, India, Malaya.* I asked myself, am I more
afraid of what some of my newspaper readers might say—I
knew what some readers most certainly would say—than I am
of this bursting resentment, this cascading protest of the
people of color against our denial of dignity? I asked myself
also: What have I got to be afraid of? Afraid that somebody
will write or telephone to us to cancel their subscriptions to a
damned, nigger-loving paper? Afraid of economic reprisal or
social retaliation? Afraid that our usefulness in larger matters
will be impaired by our violation of the taboo against permitting a Negro self-respect?

I had faced these fears in other trials, and I knew I wasn't
afraid. I knew that this was my own self, wrestling with the
credo that I had been taught with my first words, and now I
was trying to break away from that union of pride and condescension and habit and caution that lies behind the refusal
to give all married women a common dignity of recognition
and offers instead a conscience-saving substitute. . . . *I love*

Negroes as long as they keep their place. Why my old nurse was just like my mother. I was raised with the funniest little nigger boy and we used to fish together, but Mrs. doesn't mean married woman, it means a white married woman, and the other kind are just named Nellie, and their husbands are named Jim, and when he grows old we call him Uncle unless he is a doctor or a professor or a judge or a congressman or an officer in the armed forces, anything but a Mr. married to a Mrs., because that's different, and if you give them an inch, they'll take a mile.

All right, I thought, let's see what will happen. I said to the Negro doctor's wife, "You're right. There's no sense in it, and we'll change." I'll not soon forget the look in her face; not gratitude, which would have been out of place; not relief or triumph, but a look, instead, of surprise and accomplishment and great dignity. She said, "Thank you, Mr. Carter," and left.

I mulled over the way to tell the staff. I knew that other Southern newspapers, large and small, had taken this step, some time before, a step which had been denounced by certain Southerners as a blatant acknowledgment of "social equality" and a letting down of needful bars. The Atlanta papers used Mrs. and so did most of the newspapers in North Carolina; but our nearest big-city-newspaper neighbors didn't, despite their unchallenged control of the metropolitan field; and maybe they hesitated because their non-city subscribers lived principally in rural Mississippi and Louisiana and western Tennessee, and the management, being smarter than I was, had decided that the deep South wasn't ready.

Wasn't ready. . . . That was another shibboleth. Maybe Greenville hadn't been ready, fifteen years before, when we published a news picture of Jesse Owens, who was coming to the Delta to demonstrate, at a little all-Negro town's seventy-fifth-anniversary fete, the co-ordination that had just won him four Olympic firsts. The next day I was told, violently and often, that Mississippi newspapers didn't print pictures of Negroes. But we kept on printing such pictures when we saw fit, and now nobody even bothers to mention it. Some had cautioned us that our people weren't ready when we urged the extension of the ballot to qualified Negro citizens and the removal of the poll tax; when we bespoke the equalization of education in Mississippi and the rightfulness of the Supreme Court's order to admit Negro students to Southern graduate schools, and the wisdom of employing Negro policemen in our town, as we now do, and of spending tax money, dollar for dollar, to build Mississippi's first Negro public swimming pool, and Negro hospital facilities and schools and playgrounds. I looked back over each debatable issue and I remembered some people had said we Mississippians weren't ready; and Bilbo braying every night during that campaign summer of 1946 that I was a mongrelizer, a homoculous (it means "mud-dwelling") liar, and telling my fellow Deltans that I ought to be skinned and put in a basket and toted out of town. But nobody had skinned me, nobody had toted me out of town, nobody had ostracized me or promised economic retaliation; only a few had threatened me, and they anonymously.

So what was I afraid of? Was it so unconventional in Greenville, Mississippi, in 1952, to admit in print that a married Negro woman was a Mrs.?

On the joined principles that there is strength in unity and that misery loves company, I telephoned the Atlanta headquarters of the Southern Regional Council, a sensibly motivated inter-racial organization which, without fanfare or much capital, has been a notable instrument in bringing the races closer together and in insisting on first-class citizenship for the Negro in America.

I asked the Council for a list of Southern newspapers which used the courtesy titles with Negro names. When I read the list which arrived airmail, special delivery, the next afternoon, I was both surprised and strengthened in my abrupt resolve of the day before. About a hundred Southern newspapers were using the titles, altogether or to a limited degree. These newspapers ranged from the South's largest to many which were smaller than ours and were published in regions considerably less tolerant than the Delta. The accompanying letter said that the list was not complete. So at least a hundred newspapers in the South and Southwest, out of some three hundred dailies and two thousand weeklies, were also violating the taboo. If they could, I told myself, we could.

When I talked to the staff after making the decision, Charlie Kerg—who is loyal to the *Democrat-Times*, the United States and the Greenville Bucks of the Cotton States League, in that order—said that he'd go along. David Brown, who is from small-town Louisiana, George Stroud, who writes agricultural and general county news and is from Arkansas, and Bob Tims, the newest staff member, who went from the Mississippi Gulf Coast to the Air Force and afterwards to Harvard and Oxford, each asked me why we hadn't done it before, and commented that it was high time. Lou Crump suggested a campaign to teach everybody good manners to everybody else, chortled that it was just grand, and dared an imaginary host of enemies to start anything. Gene Roper, older than the rest, and a veteran of copy and editorial desks of a dozen larger newspapers in the South, was cautious in his comment, saying the innovation might stir up unnecessary trouble. But nobody objected, either in the news department or the advertising department —where I had half expected a protective protest—or in the composing room upstairs although there was a good deal of comment.

Of course there was considerable talk when the first *Democrat-Times* appeared under the unannounced new policy. I must say our readers got the full treatment, although unintentionally. The second lead story had to do with the Red Cross campaign. A late story had come in from the Negro division of the Red Cross. Gene used it in bold-faced type, Mrs. and all, as a bulletin preceding the original story.

That night I had several telephone calls, not from critics but from friends who wondered whether we might really have gone too far this time. I told them that we'd wait and see. It had all become for me a fantastic exaggeration of nothing, this worrying about such a change in the day of the atom and the hydrogen bomb, in the mid-century of freedom's peril, in the hour of world doubting by black man, brown man, yellow man, white man, as to where they should ally themselves, whether with the power of world communism which promises bread and revenge, or with Western democracy which struggles toward the ideal of man's dignity.

The next day another friend dropped by to tell me that while he personally approved of the new policy, he had heard a great deal of criticism, and that some of our advertisers didn't like it. I thanked him, and after he left, I telephoned several of our larger advertisers. When they sent out bills or mail advertising to Negro customers and prospective customers, did they or did they not use the courtesy titles? They did, answered all but two. Did they let Negroes try on dresses or suits or gloves in their stores? Two did. Did they or didn't they try to get and hold Negro business? They did try. Did they want to reach as many Negroes as possible through the advertising columns of the *Democratic-Times*? They did. Did they know that in the past fifteen years, while our over-all circulation had grown from thirty-one hundred to nearly thirteen thousand, our Negro subscription list had increased from less than three hundred to more than five thousand? No, they didn't. And did they really object to our using "Mrs." before the names of Negroes in those relatively infrequent stories of Negro participation in community life, Negro educational achievements or War Department stories that Private Willie Johnson, son of Mrs. George Johnson, had been seriously wounded near Panmunjon? No, they really didn't.

Of course, a good many of my fellow citizens did object. But they were wraiths as concerns any bad effect upon our circulation, our advertising lineage, our friendships and the even tenor of our lives. It took me a long time to find this out, or to decide to want to find it out, and it may seem to the non-Southerner, or even to some of my fellow Southerners, that I am devoting too much time to too-small an incident and too-minor a decision. But I do not think that the incident was really small or that the decision that came from it was inconsequential.

A few months later I met a gaunt young priest, just returned from a year's brutal captivity under the Chinese Reds. He was a missionary priest serving the Negroes of eastern Arkansas, across the river from us. He was an intense, consecrated man, and because I wanted to talk with him, I asked if I could drive him home after he had spoken to a service club of his experiences in captivity before the Reds had sentenced him, almost miraculously, to perpetual banishment instead of death.

As we drove along he asked me what I did, and when I told

him that I published the Greenville paper, he smiled and said that he had just heard something about me from one of his Negro Catholic parishioners who had come to see me a few months before. She was the doctor's wife, who proudly had told the new priest of her visit and its results.

"We talk about face as if it were important only to the Chinese," Father Sullivan said. "It's as important to all of us as to any Chinese alive, whether we know it or not. What you've done is more important to our Negro brothers than if you'd built them six new high schools. I think it's more important to God."

I think so too.

from *Where Main Street Meets the River* (1953)

Thurgood Marshall and the 14th Amendment

by James Poling

THURGOOD MARSHALL, as special counsel for the National Association for the Advancement of Colored People, spends much of his time expertly pleading civil rights cases before the judges of our higher courts. His secretaries have spent a lot of *their* time pleading with him, in an effort to bring a little order into his life outside the courtroom. It is inevitable that the bench and his secretariat should see him through different eyes.

Lucille Ward, who became Marshall's first secretary when he opened his law practice in 1933, says, "I haven't seen him in a long time, but I bet he still needs a haircut, his pants pressed, and hasn't yet learned how to spell 'separate.' And I bet he still speaks in court like the man who wrote the grammar book and yet commits felonious assault on the king's English in private." She was right on all counts.

And Alice Stovall, his present secretary, says, "There's never a dull or lazy moment, except when I have to travel with him. Then I'm always left alone on the train while he spends his time in the dining car, gossiping with the crew—he was once a dining-car waiter, you know. If we have a layover, changing trains, I sit by myself in the station, by preference, while he goes off to see one of those they-went-that-a-way pictures; any one will do, even singing cowboys."

From the more austere elevation of the bench, Federal Judge William H. Hastie says, "Marshall is unquestionably our greatest civil liberties lawyer. He's been more instrumental than any other man in professionalizing the area of law dealing with civil rights, and certainly no other lawyer and practically no member of the bench has his grasp of the doctrine of civil rights law."

It is said by those who are qualified to speak that Thurgood Marshall's jitterbugging is real gone. Others, equally qualified, say that when he takes his stand before a lectern in the

U.S. Supreme Court, the justices of our highest tribunal lean forward in their seats and the courtroom is jammed with class-cutting law students. His elderly uncle, Fearless Williams, sees no contradiction here. "It's just that Thurgood's fun-lovin' and likes to socialize," he says. "But he can't kick up much. He once told me, 'Isn't it nice no one cares which twenty-three hours of the day I work?'"

Marshall's associates have good reason for letting him choose his own working hours. The National Association for the Advancement of Colored People has achieved goals in recent years which, according to Benjamin Fine, education editor of the New York Times, "would have been considered impossible ten years ago." And much of its progress can be attributed to Marshall's successful prosecution of civil rights cases before the highest courts of the land.

The NAACP is conducting a thoughtfully planned, carefully executed campaign against those state laws which support racial discrimination. Contrary to general belief, the association has neither the time, money nor inclination to go to the aid of every Negro in trouble. It is primarily interested in cases involving a violation of a man's constitutional rights which, in terms of the Fourteenth (or Equal Rights) Amendment, look as if they can be carried to a successful conclusion in the U.S. Supreme Court. The NAACP has won 30 of the 33 cases it has carried to that tribunal since 1915, and the ultimate aim of the campaign is a series of Supreme Court rulings that will render null and void all of the discriminatory laws now to be found in the statutes of many states.

Today, Negroes vote with relative ease in every state in the Union except Louisiana, Alabama and Florida—where registration is still made difficult for them, either by physical intimidation or by subjecting them to an intelligence-test question like, "How many windows in the White House?" Over a million Southern Negroes now have the franchise, as against the 250,000 who voted in the 1944 elections. Negro teachers, who have earned as low as $407.81 a year, now have salaries equal to white teachers in North Carolina, Maryland, West Virginia and Louisiana, with test cases pending in Virginia, Texas and Florida. Segregation in interstate travel has been declared unlawful. Negroes can now purchase and *occupy* any piece of property, if they can find a willing seller. Largely as the result of various court decisions, by February of 1952, Negroes were able to attend graduate schools at the universities of Texas, Louisiana, Oklahoma, Missouri, Maryland, North Carolina, Delaware, Virginia, Tennessee and Kentucky. West Virginia and Arkansas had voluntarily admitted Negroes into their graduate schools, and the trustees of the University of Delaware had gone beyond the court order and opened up their undergraduate school to Negroes. Test cases on the university level are now pending in Georgia and South Carolina, and a case is being processed in Florida. Nothing has as yet been done in Alabama or Mississippi, because no Negro has yet offered himself as a plaintiff.

And much of this has been accomplished by a man whose personal philosophy is, "I intend to wear life like a very loose garment, and never worry about nothin'."

But Marshall, at forty-three, is no dual personality to intrigue the psychiatric-minded. He is a tall, burly, gregarious man, light-skinned and lighthearted, and if he is paradoxical it might almost be said to be deliberate. He has consciously chosen to follow a hedonistic, nonworrying philosophy. And he has, just as consciously, dedicated himself to the extremely worrisome task of fighting racial discrimination.

Apparently, Marshall's determined gaiety in the face of the gravity of the project he has embarked on has never lessened his effectiveness. He is, as a matter of fact, well aware that it throws many people off guard. But Elmer Carter, of the New York State Commission Against Discrimination, says, "It's very important that we Negroes have a man who is at home in the Supreme Court and equally at home with the man on the street. Thurgood can talk on terms of equality with a social scientist like Sweden's Gunnar Myrdal, but he talks the argot of Harlem with the man on the street corner. He creates confidence on all levels of Negro life."

When Marshall took over as special counsel for the NAACP, in 1938, he came into a New York office which he describes as "very tush-tush." Obviously, this was no atmosphere for a man wearing a loose garment. "I changed things," he says, "and I think I've done a pretty good job of busting up that formality. Now I can operate in my natural-born way."

His associates are almost idolatrous in their praise of this method of operation. His work frequently takes him into tense, emotionally torn localities where mob rule is an ever-present threat. Those who work with him are convinced that it is only because he is always his unpretentious, natural-born self that he has been able to escape serious trouble while, at the same time, winning respect and understanding from opponents on all levels of life.

During his first year on the job, he flew to Austin, Texas, to protest the exclusion of a Negro from jury duty. Instead of becoming involved in litigation, he went directly to Governor James Allred. That executive was so impressed with Marshall's forthright presentation of his argument that he not only ordered out the Texas Rangers to defend the rights of Negroes to jury duty, but he voluntarily asked the FBI to study the situation.

In 1941, Marshall appeared in Hugo, Oklahoma, to defend W. D. Lyons, a Negro handy man accused of wiping out three of a family of five and setting fire to their house to conceal the crime. The NAACP undertook Lyons' defense because it had reason to believe he was a framed victim of racial prejudice.

Feeling was running so high in the community that the local Negroes, as sometimes happens when Marshall appears on the scene, organized to protect him; a different sleeping place was arranged for each night and an unofficial guard was established over him. These precautions turned out, however, not to be necessary.

At the beginning of the second day of the trial, the father of the murdered white woman, E. O. Colclasure, came forward and offered himself to Marshall as a defense witness! He testified that he had heard a state trooper say he had beaten a confession out of Lyons with a blackjack. And on the third day the superintendent of schools even declared a half holiday so that his students could go to court "and hear that cullud lawyer."

The case was fought to the Supreme Court, where Lyons' life sentence was allowed to stand—he had made another confession at a time when he was not under duress. It was one of the two cases Marshall has lost in the Supreme Court, of the 12 he has personally argued before that tribunal—a record that lawyers regard as extraordinary. (In Taylor vs. Alabama, after getting Taylor's death sentence for rape commuted to a life sentence by Governor Folsom, Marshall failed in his attempt to win Taylor his freedom in the Supreme Court, when its justices voted 4 to 4 in a split decision, after one member of the tribunal had disqualified himself.)

In the 10 cases in which Marshall has been victorious, in four instances he successfully defended individuals against criminal charges. In the other six cases he won far-reaching, highly significant verdicts against segregation in education, housing, transportation and at the polls. He has also taken part, not as the "lawyer of record," but as a consultant, in 11 other Supreme Court cases, 10 of which were victories.

Many authorities—including men as careful in their choice of words as Morris Ernst, general counsel for the Civil Liberties Union, lawyer Arthur Spingarn, and attorney Earl G. Harrison, former vice-president of the University of Pennsylvania —regard Marshall as one of our finest civil rights constitutional lawyers. He has become recognized as such a formidable courtroom opponent that the state of South Carolina has just paid him an indirect compliment of the highest order. Rather than rely on its own legal staff, the state has retained John W. Davis, onetime Presidential candidate on the Democratic ticket and long recognized as the dean of the American bar, to defend it from the attack Marshall has launched on segregation in the state's high and elementary schools.

There are many reasons why Marshall is regarded as such a formidable opponent. Important among them is his objectivity; the clarity of his reasoning is never befogged by his emotions. When he discusses race relations he says, "I think we make our greatest mistakes through oversimplifications. We find it too easy to regard the South as all bad and the North as all good. We've made tremendous inroads in the South in recent years—particularly among the younger white people and the enlightened older ones—but we can't direct all of our efforts at the South. There is still a lot to be accomplished in the North.

"A lawsuit is an educational process in itself. It educates not only the defendant and his lawyers, it also enlightens the general public in the area. When we were fighting to get Heman

Sweatt into the University of Texas, more than 200 white students set up an NAACP branch on the campus. They even built and manned a booth on the campus, to collect funds to help defray our legal expenses. They were a little worried the first day, when they saw a policeman, on the opposite side of the street, eying the booth for a long time . . . until he walked over to the booth, said, 'If you kids want that cullud man in your school so bad, you sure got a right to have him,' and handed them five dollars. It's such suits that bring home to many people the fact that Negroes have rights as Americans which must be respected.

"If we can keep up the educational process, as well as the legal suits, I've no doubt of our eventual victory. Even in the most prejudiced communities, I think the majority of people have some respect for truth and some sense of justice, no matter how deeply hidden it is at times."

Marshall knows, of course, that he is engaged in a hard, sometimes bitter, struggle, but he is equipped for this, too. He comes from a fighting family. His great-great-grandfather, according to family legend, was a captive from the toughest part of the Congo, who made his personal objections to slavery so widely known in Maryland that his master finally told him, "Look, I brought you here, so I guess I can't very well shoot you, as you deserve. And since I can't, with a clear conscience, sell anyone as ornery as you to another slaveholder, I'm going to set you free. Now, get out of this county."

Thurgood's paternal grandmother may have originated the sit-down strike. When a Baltimore court ruled that a utility company had the right to erect an electric pole in front of the Marshall grocery store, she took a kitchen chair, placed it over the spot marked for the pole, and calmly seated herself. After a few days of this the company put the pole elsewhere. And the Baltimore Sun, in its issue of August 6, 1875 (an era when Negroes were more frequently seen than heard in the South), reported that Isaac O. B. Williams—Marshall's maternal grandfather—had risen at a civic mass meeting to protest an unwarranted incident of police brutality that had resulted in a Negro's death.

And Marshall has the intelligence with which to back up his fighting heritage. He graduated with honors from Douglas

High School in Baltimore, where he was born July 2, 1908. His mother, Mrs. Norma Marshall, is now in her twenty-fifth year as a teacher in Baltimore's primary schools; his father, William Marshall, who died in 1950, was a steward at the exclusive Gibson Island Country Club, on Chesapeake Bay.

After high school Marshall attended Lincoln University, in Oxford, Pennsylvania, where he is remembered for the manner in which he prepared for examinations—by devoting the nights prior to them to pinochle. Despite this, he graduated *cum laude.*

During his senior year at Lincoln, he also had the boldness, considering that he was working his way through school— either as a baker, dining-car or country-club waiter—to get married. The bride was Vivien "Buster" Burey, who left the University of Pennsylvania to become his wife.

Marshall then abandoned pinochle to study law at Howard University, Washington, D.C., where he graduated *magna cum laude.* "I'd got the horsin' around out of my system," he explains, "and I'd heard lawbooks were to dig in. So I dug, way deep."

He had civil rights law in mind when he began to practice before the Maryland bar in 1933, although he knew such cases seldom earned a lawyer anything but respect. Some people claim he built up the largest law practice in Baltimore and still couldn't pay his rent. Lucille Ward and Sue Tilghman, the two secretaries who worked for him at that time, say, "He had a genius for ignoring cases that might earn him any money. Sometimes we'd get our $7.50 a week, sometimes we'd just get carfare, other times we were out-of-pocket at the end of the week. But we loved that man."

Marshall hadn't liked the fact that the laws of his home state had forced him to go out of the state to get a legal education and, during his Howard years, he laid preliminary plans for opening up the University of Maryland Law School to Negroes. In 1934, he met Donald Murray, a young Negro who thought it was just the law school for him. Now that he had a plaintiff, Marshall went to work in earnest. "He turned into a working machine," Miss Tilghman says. In 1935, he brought suit against the University of Maryland and won the case so convincingly the state didn't even bother to appeal it to the Supreme Court. At twenty-seven, Marshall had made the first breach in the wall of segregation which surrounds much of our public school system.

In 1936, the NAACP implemented its campaign against discrimination by retaining its first special counsel, the late Charles Houston. He had been dean of Howard University Law School when Marshall was there, and he brought the young lawyer with him as his assistant, at a yearly salary of $2,400 (Marshall now earns $12,000, or about one sixth of what it has been estimated he could earn in private practice).

When Houston retired to private practice in 1938, Marshall not only took over the strategy of the campaign, but also became its leading tactician. Today, over 500 cases a year pass across his desk, and at this writing he is either attorney of record or "of counsel" in 40 cases now in court. To assist him, he has a staff of three assistant counsels, two field-workers, a law-research clerk, and a socioeconomic analyst. A National Legal Committee of 45 volunteer attorneys—men like Morris Ernst, Bartley Crum, Arthur Garfield Hays and Samuel I. Rosenman—is also available to him.

His somewhat oversimplified explanation of his success is, "This is way deep in church—I wouldn't want anyone to find out—but the only reason I ever look good is just 'cause I get expert advice, then follow it."

Since taking office, the cases Marshall has pleaded or supervised have been argued on specific discriminatory points, such as the destruction of Jim Crowism in travel, obtaining the franchise, or opening up the educational system at the university level. While these cases have had individually stated goals, their over-all effect has been far-reaching.

In winning favorable rulings, for example, from the Supreme Court in the cases of Sweatt vs. University of Texas and Sipuel vs. University of Oklahoma, Marshall did far more than win entrance into the schools of their choice for Ada Sipuel and Heman Sweatt. Those rulings can now be used to pry open the door of any university that attempts to bar Negroes. Thus, the accumulated decisions won in all areas of discrimination by Marshall and his associates have gradually weakened the state laws supporting segregation.

However, in his attack on South Carolina's school system,

now pending before the Supreme Court, Marshall has finally succeeded in reaching a position hitherto denied him because of complicated legal technicalities, where he can ask the courts for a sweeping ruling to the effect that segregation is, in itself, a form of inequality and, therefore, unconstitutional.

When the case was first heard, May 28, 1951, before a three-judge federal court in Charleston, it was lost by a 2-to-1 verdict. Judge J. Waties Waring (Collier's, April 29, 1950), a courageous jurist whose stand on the racial question has won him social ostracism in Charleston, found, in his dissenting opinion, that "segregation is, *per se*, inequality." If the Supreme Court should reverse this 2-to-1 verdict, its ruling could abolish segregation at all educational levels.

A federal judge, who for obvious reasons cannot be named, has said, "It's going to be hard for the Supreme Court to side-step the issue. And it's going to be equally hard for them to face it, with the present-day political situation what it is. The case sort of puts them on the spot, and Thurgood has maneuvered that very cleverly."

The speed and bluntness with which Marshall is attacking discrimination has alarmed some Negroes who fear, if victory in the courts is won too rapidly, that it may lead to physical violence and rioting in areas where prejudice is still deep-rooted. Others feel it is strategically unwise to move too fast at this time. Marjorie McKenzie, columnist of the powerful Negro paper, The Pittsburgh Courier, writes of the South Carolina case:

"This was no ordinary test case. . . . It was a bare-bones challenge to the legality of segregation under the state's police power. . . . (There are those who) look upon the NAACP's moves with honest irritation and alarm . . . they involve risk where none was necessary. . . . The judicial system is part of a political structure and is, accordingly, not unresponsive to political forces. . . . (We are putting) premature pressure on the courts."

However, the great majority of the Negro press is stanchly behind the NAACP-Marshall program.

Even if he loses the decision in the South Carolina case, Marshall will not be left impotent. The U.S. Supreme Court has recently shown that it regards segregation in a public

school system as illegal *unless* Negroes are provided with facilities equal to those provided white students. And Marshall,
in a series of cases, has demonstrated it isn't hard to prove
that equal facilities are rarely available. Thus, while it would
take time, and cases would have to be filed state by state and
possibly county by county, the NAACP is now in a position to
make it very expensive for taxpayers in those states wishing to
maintain segregated schools.

The Office of Education of the Federal Security Agency
roughly estimates that it would cost the states with segregated
school systems $1,500,000,000 to bring their Negro school
plants up to the present level of their white school plants.
Furthermore, an additional annual $61,000,000 would be re-
quired to achieve over-all teacher equality.

In a speech before the Institute on Race Relations, meeting
at Fisk University, July, 1950, Marshall said, "We now have the
tools with which to destroy all governmentally imposed racial
segregation. . . . To hear some people talk, one would get
the impression that the majority of Americans are lawless people who will not follow the law as interpreted by the Supreme
Court. This is simply not true."

South Carolina has already heeded his words. The state has
appropriated $75,000,000 to be spent in bringing its Negro
schools up to the level of its white schools.

Adroit maneuvering is part of his stock in trade. One of his
wiliest moves saved a man's life. A few years ago the grapevine
reached him late one night, at a poker game in a Washington,
D.C., hotel room, with detailed information of a lynching
party that was forming in a Southern city, even as his long-
distance adviser spoke.

As is his custom, when incidents of racial violence occur,
Marshall immediately alerted the FBI, the Department of
Justice, and the secretary on duty at the White House—and
discovered, to his dismay, that neither the FBI nor the
Department of Justice had the authority to move with
enough rapidity to save the man. He then performed an instantaneous cerebral tour de force; he put through a long-
distance call to an influential Southern lawyer representing
strong anti-Negro factions.

When he had the man on the phone, he said, "Look, just

two sets of people can't afford a lynching at this time—us Ne-groes and you people. You're right in the midst of a Dixiecrat political campaign and a lynching's going to make your peo-ple look awful bad." The man's answer was, "Check! Give me the details and get off the phone so I can get moving. Call you back in half an hour." In 20 minutes Marshall's telephone rang and he was told, "The state troopers made it in time. Call this number in a few minutes; your man will be there, unharmed." And he was, although he was still too shaken to talk.

Wiliness and adroitness are not unusual attributes for a lawyer, and Marshall seems to have gained the respect and ad-miration of the legal fraternity as much for his honesty and high sense of ethics as for his cleverness, eloquence and ex-treme skill in logic and argumentation.

As Judge Charles D. Breitel, of the New York Supreme Court, puts it, "I've got so much respect for his integrity I'd accept his word on anything."

Morris Ernst once had a disagreement with Marshall. Ernst had devised a clever twist on what were known as "Lower Thirteen" cases. There was a time in some Southern states when a Negro, in quest of railroad sleeping accommodations, was sold a drawing room for the price of a lower berth, so that he could be kept segregated. Ernst wanted to build a case by having an eminent white man—he had a famous writer in mind—stand behind a Negro at a ticket window. After the Negro had been sold a drawing room at a reduced price, the writer would ask for a drawing room to the same destination and, naturally, be charged the full price. He would then protest—and a case could be filed in which the issue was dis-crimination against a white man.

"The idea amused me to beat hell," Ernst says, "and I thought Thurgood—well, with that belly laugh of his, which is about the first thing most leaders at the bar lose—I natu-rally thought he'd go for the idea, too. But he flatly rejected it—because it was rigged and because it was a trick. I realize now he was right. He knows we're in a battle to change the nation's folkways and he wants to do it soundly and, if pos-sible, with dignity."

Arthur Spingarn, the white attorney who is president of the

NAACP, says Marshall once refused to employ a means of destroying a witness' credibility that he'd suggested, because, "I wouldn't want anyone to say that about me and I don't want to say it about anyone else." When Spingarn protested that the attack was based on verified fact, Marshall's answer was simply, "I don't care. I just don't like to use that kind of orneriness."

Thurgood is so sentimental that he sends Christmas cards to dogs with whom he is acquainted, and he can be soft even in court—which is surprising, considering the deep emotional involvement he has in all of his cases. In one appellate case, the lawyer making the argument for the opposition had his memory fail him at a critical point. The court fell silent as the judge grimly waited for the man to cite the legal precedent necessary to support his contention. The man grew more and more embarrassed and confused as he pawed futilely at his notes—until Marshall could stand it no longer. Picking up a lawbook, he leafed through it to the case he knew his opponent had in mind, then silently handed the book to him.

Charles Thompson, dean of the graduate school of Howard University, says he has only seen Marshall discomfited in court once—when, in Sweatt vs. University of Texas, he had to cross-examine the white librarian of the university's law school. She was nervous when she took the stand, on the verge of tears when she took the oath, and she grew more and more confused as the questioning proceeded—even though Marshall's cross-examination was fumbling and inept, compared to his usual relentless attack on an opposition witness. But he has an alibi. He says, "That poor woman like to tore her handkerchief to shreds on the stand. She was a good woman and you could tell she didn't want to lie. Give me the mean ones that want to lie—then I romp."

Not that he is always sweetness and light. Opposing counsel occasionally shows signs of being outraged at the very fact of having to argue against a Negro lawyer. Then Marshall, with a straight face, abandons such conventional phrases as, "My esteemed opponent . . . the learned counsel for the state," and falls back on the now obsolete court formality, "My brother in law . . . my brother before the bar . . .", with sardonic emphasis on the noun.

He has had considerable experience with various forms of unpleasantness. The following telegram addressed to then Attorney General Tom Clark in 1946 tells its own story of the tactics he sometimes encounters:

LAST NIGHT AFTER LEAVING COLUMBIA, TENNESSEE, WHERE WE SECURED ACQUITTAL OF ONE OF TWO NE-GROES CHARGED WITH CRIMES GROWING OUT OF FEBRUARY DISTURBANCES THREE LAWYERS, INCLUDING MYSELF, WERE STOPPED OUTSIDE OF COLUMBIA IN THE NIGHT BY THREE CARLOADS OF OFFICERS INCLUDING DEPUTY SHERIFF, CONSTABLES AND HIGHWAY PATROL-MEN. ALLEGED PURPOSE WAS TO SEARCH CAR FOR WHISKY. WHEN NO WHISKY FOUND WE WERE STOPPED BY SAME OFFICIALS TWO MORE TIMES AND ON LAST OC-CASION I WAS PLACED UNDER ARREST FOR DRIVING WHILE DRUNK AND RETURNED TO COLUMBIA. MAGIS-TRATE REFUSED TO PLACE ME IN JAIL AFTER EXAMINING ME AND FINDING I WAS EXTREMELY SOBER. THIS TYPE OF INTIMIDATION OF DEFENSE LAWYERS CHARGED WITH DUTY OF DEFENDING PERSONS CHARGED WITH CRIME CANNOT GO UNNOTICED. THEREFORE, DEMAND IMMEDIATE INVESTIGATION ALL CRIMINAL CHARGES AGAINST OFFICERS PARTICIPATING IN LAST NIGHT'S OUTRAGE.

Although the federal investigation was hamstrung, locally, from the outset, and nothing could be done about the situation, Marshall returned to Columbia the following week and procured the acquittal of the second Negro.

A few years earlier there had been an outbreak of police brutality in Hempstead, New York. Ted Poston, who covered the story for the New York Post, said four cars of men were searching for Marshall. "I was riding with Marshall," said Poston, "and it didn't faze him in the slightest. Three times that caravan of cars passed right by houses we were in. I wanted to get away from there, fast. But all that guy did was make more and more outlandish jokes about what that mob would do to us if it caught us. Not that he was foolhardy. Once he got statements from the witnesses, and had them safely hidden in a spare tire, he drove out of there without honoring the speed laws." And with the aid of those statements, the state's attorney general quickly restored order in Hempstead.

Of these and similar incidents Marshall says, "I can testify there's times when you're scared to death. But you can't admit it: you just have to lie like hell to yourself. Otherwise, you'll start looking under the bed at night."

In 1949, Marshall's own behavior—variously described by his friends as "his integrity," "his idealism" and "his damned stubbornness"—stirred up some unpleasantness that resulted in his being deprived of his greatest ambition. He would like to be a federal judge and, in August, 1949, it looked as if his ambition was about to be realized.

On August 4, 1949, Ted Poston said in the New York Post that he had learned from authoritative sources that Thurgood Marshall was about to become the first Negro appointed to a federal judgeship in the continental United States. This was news to the Tammany leader in the 13th Manhattan Assembly District, although some other Democratic leaders knew that Marshall's name had been suggested to the White House.

The Tammany leader let it be known that he wanted to see Marshall. Thurgood bluntly refused to see the man. As one politician says, "The guy's unrealistic on this politics business. Hell, he's got to at least shake hands with someone. You got to have clearance. We begged him to at least spend three bucks, or whatever it is, and join the Carver Democratic Club. But he wouldn't."

As a result of his determination not to play ball with them, Harlem's Tammany leader opposed Marshall's appointment so vigorously that nothing more was ever heard of it.

He says, "Look, I had the three bucks to join the Carver Club. But in my book a federal judge is a different animal—he shouldn't have to play patty-cake with the clubhouse boys."

If Marshall did have a spare three bucks with which to join the Carver Club, it was surprising. To his friends' charge that he is as foolish as a man can be with money, he enters the strong denial, "If I had more money I could be more foolish." But he has learned to turn his checks over to his wife, and this works pretty much to his satisfaction. "I'm supposed to have my allowance," he explains, "but I always manage to borrow a little extra and I never, never pay it back. Only thing is, Buster won't give me any money to buy electric trains and we don't have any children to buy them for. Course, she has a point; she asks me when I'd have the time to fool with 'em."

When he registered this complaint he didn't know that his relatives were presenting him with an elaborate Diesel-drawn electric train set for Christmas. His family had never been able to afford electric trains in his youth and he has always dreamed of someday acquiring one for himself. But now that he has one, he hasn't, as Mrs. Marshall predicted, much leisure to devote to it.

Marshall makes a great show of despising work or physical exertion, and contends, "There's no call for a man to ever lift anything much heavier than a poker chip." But he's been working steadily since he took his first job as an errand boy at Hale's Grocery Store, in Baltimore, at the age of seven.

Today, he travels over 50,000 miles a year and, according to Arthur Spingarn, "He's making a damn' fool of himself, the way he works. He argues five times as many cases as the ordinary lawyer. He got off a plane from Kansas City at 3:00 A.M. yesterday; at 6:30 A.M. he was on a train headed for New Hampshire. When you urge him to slow down, you always get the same answer, 'Man, there's a job to get done.'" He has had two temporary fillings in his teeth for the past seven years because he hasn't had time to get back to the dentist to have the job finished.

On June 28, 1947, Marshall was so ill he barely managed to get through his speech of acceptance of the Spingarn Medal (annually awarded for the highest achievement by an American Negro during the preceding year). It was given to Marshall primarily for his work in winning the franchise for the Negroes of the South. After the award presentation he was flown from Cincinnati to New York where it was discovered at Harlem Hospital that he'd had a breakdown from overwork, with a resultant virus pneumonia of the worst type.

In the midst of his convalescence he received two gifts that deeply moved him: a piggy-bank geranium from Mrs. Eleanor Roosevelt, and a huge ham, sent by the Negro citizens of Columbia, Tennessee.

A man who works his schedule inevitably has a limited home life and but little time for play. His infrequent evenings spent in his New York apartment are usually dedicated to small dinner parties, or endless hours of arm-waving argument and discussion with his close friends, or solitary musical binges, during which he loads his record player with a catholic assortment of recordings ranging from Rachmaninoff to Louis Armstrong.

Where play is concerned Marshall is, like Barkis, always willing. His outside divertissements are simple—poker, a trip to the race track, or a baseball, hockey or football game. He hates night clubs and is intolerant of pretentious formal social functions. His greatest pleasure is derived from the Pokino Gang, a group of six couples, friends of long standing, who get together on Saturday nights. They generally start out playing penny-ante Pokino, a game which seems to be a combination of bingo and stud, and end up "just woofing and having general fun."

Marshall's favorite aunt, Mrs. Media Dodson, says, "Thurgood's wonderful to behold when he comes back from a hard case and gets together with the Pokinos. There he is, singing —though he can't turn a tune any more than an alligator— dancing, telling funny jokes and things.

"Everyone just says, 'This is Thurgood's night; look at him go.'"

It is probably just as well he can go on an occasional night. Mrs. Marshall says, "He's aged so in the past five years; his disposition's changed, he's nervous where he used to be calm —this work is taking its toll of him. You know, it's a discouraging job he's set himself."

However, Thurgood's discouragement doesn't show through the very loose garment he wears in public. "Mama taught me a lot," he says, "and I remember how she used to say, 'Boy, you may be tall but if you get mean I can always reach you with a chair.' Well, there's a lot of tall, mean people still around but the Fourteenth Amendment to the Constitution of the United States is a mighty big chair and I figure I can still reach a lot of 'em."

Collier's, February 23, 1952

from

Jim Crow's Last Stand

by Carl T. Rowan

Southland Braces for Final Battle on Segregation

SUMMERTON, S.C.—The short, ebony-skinned Methodist minister, the Rev. J. W. Seals, leaned against the counter of a small grocery store in this rural Clarendon county community and told me:

"We ain't asking for anything that belongs to these white folks. I just mean to get for that little black boy of mine everything that any other South Carolina boy gets. I don't care if he's as white as the drippings of snow."

An hour earlier, two blocks up Summerton's main street, David McClary, white livestock, feed and fertilizer dealer, had told photographer Bonham Cross and me:

"This fight on segregation is wrong, and it's gonna work to the detriment of these Nigras. We got a good bunch of Nigras here, and we got along fine till these outside influences came in here and started propagandizing. Segregation is our way of life. Both races want it. And if that court rules we got to mix 'em, we're gonna make every effort to avoid it."

Behind those remarks lies the deep, even bitter, turmoil that engulfs the southland today as it braces for the decisive battle that both whites and non-whites have termed "Jim Crow's last stand."

Amid visible tension, the south awaits the United States supreme court's answer to one question:

Is it a violation of the United States Constitution for states to require racial separation of children in public schools?

"Mister, we live in hope," said Mrs. Rebecca Brown, quick-tongued, grandmotherish proprietor of the little store. "That court has got to cut this segregation out, cause I'm telling you, we Negroes have caught hell long enough."

A few days earlier, Gov. Herman E. Talmadge of Georgia had said in a public speech that a court ruling against segregation would be "nothing less than a major step toward national suicide."

Such a ruling would be "the most foolhardy sociological calamity in our national history," Talmadge asserted.

By the time we reached this little town, after thousands of miles of travel, photographer Cross and I had heard other white southerners express views akin to Talmadge's. And we had talked to many Negroes who shared the views and determination of the minister and Mrs. Brown.

In our travels from Kansas to Delaware, and here into the "black belt" of the deep south where Negro school children outnumber white school children eight to one, we had seen two things clearly:

The court's answer involves the hopes and dreams of millions of Negroes who have come to believe that all the social and economic ills that beset them stem directly from segregation. More and more they have come to believe that there can be no justice, no equality of opportunity, under state-imposed segregation.

The answer also involves the deepest emotions of millions of whites who fear the results, real or imagined, of the ending of legalized segregation. These fears embrace employment, politics, social life, sex—the entire gamut of southern life.

And we had learned by the time we reached Clarendon county—certainly the cornerstone of the court dispute—that the issue becomes woefully complex and complicated because all Negroes do not want to see segregation ended; nor do all whites want to see it maintained.

But there is general awareness among members of both races that the cases now before the court are the most momentous on the race question since the Dred Scott case of pre-Civil war days. They may rank as the most important in our history.

On Dec. 7 attorneys will begin three days of re-argument of the case, which has been under deliberation by the supreme court for more than a year.

The decision may come immediately, or not until next

spring. Whenever it comes it will be welcomed by thousands, cursed by like numbers and, as a Virginia editor put it, "God only knows the results."

This is the legal picture:

Negro parents, on behalf of their children, brought suit in five places—Clarendon county of South Carolina; Prince Edward county, Virginia; New Castle county, Delaware; Topeka, Kan.; and the District of Columbia—challenging the legality of segregation in the public schools.

In the first four localities the parents, represented by lawyers of the National Association for the Advancement of Colored People (NAACP), charge that enforced segregation violates section one of the fourteenth amendment to the Constitution which states:

> *"All persons born or naturalized in the United States and subject to the jurisdiction thereof, are citizens of the United States and of the state in which they reside. No state shall make or enforce any law which shall abridge the privileges or immunities of citizens of the United States; nor shall any state deprive any person of life, liberty, or property, without due process of law; nor deny to any person within its jurisdiction the equal protection of the laws."*

Negro parents are asking the court to rule that state-imposed segregation denies to Negro children "equal protection of the laws."

The District of Columbia case is brought under the fifth amendment, which forbids that any citizen under federal jurisdiction (the district is governed by congress) be deprived of life, liberty or property without due process of law.

Lawyers for Negro parents contend that the Washington board of education has no right to operate separate schools because the laws of congress "took segregation for granted" but never required it. They add that had congress required segregation such a law would be invalid because it is in conflict with the fifth amendment.

Technically, what the court decides will affect only the five localities involved in the lawsuits. But the ruling actually will determine the course of race relations in almost every state in the union.

A ruling against segregation would have the effect of ending legalized Jim Crow in public schools in 21 states and the District of Columbia.

(The term "legalized Jim Crow" is important because there are informal patterns of school segregation still prevalent in the north, even in states which prohibit Jim Crow. This will be discussed in detail in a later article.)

The significance of these school cases goes beyond segregation in education. And it extends far beyond the south. The NAACP has, in the past 15 years, won several battles before the supreme court which all but knocked away the legal foundation of segregation. This is what Thurgood Marshall, chief NAACP lawyer, now asks the court to say:

> *The fourteenth amendment was designed to remove the race line from government. It decreed that the laws of all states must be the same for Negroes as for whites. It removed for all time the right of individual states to make laws based solely on the classification of race, because laws singling out a certain race of citizens are, of themselves, discriminatory.*

The south's major spokesman, John W. Davis, a noted constitutional lawyer, contends that there is no basis whatsoever for reaching the NAACP conclusions. This is what he asks the court to say:

> *The fourteenth amendment never was intended to do away with segregation in schools. It is a proper use of the police powers of a state to separate the races if the state believes segregation to be in the interest of common welfare. Segregation in schools is not in conflict with the Constitution as long as equal facilities are provided for the two races. A state has as much right to classify pupils by race as it does to classify them by sex or age.*

Should the court agree with Davis, the pattern of segregation would not be drastically affected. Progress in education in the south probably would continue at what Negroes regard as a pitifully slow pace. In other areas it would continue to be what Gov. Hugh White of Mississippi calls "pathetic and in some cases inexcusable."

Should the supreme court agree with the NAACP, the end would be in sight for legalized segregation in education throughout the nation.

Eventually, it would mean the end of government-imposed racial separation in every other area of life in both the north and south.

Only the formality of new lawsuits would be required to establish a rule that Texas cities cannot tell Negro taxpayers that they may use municipal golf courses only on certain days of the week.

Or that North Carolina cities cannot deny Negroes the right to use any or all publicly-supported recreation centers.

It would mean that California, Indiana and Michigan municipalities could not segregate Negroes in, or deny them admission to public housing projects, as is now being done.

It would mean the end of Jim Crow in intrastate travel (segregation in interstate travel already has been outlawed by the court).

A decree that statutes based solely on the classification of race are contrary to the fourteenth amendment also would mean that laws in North and South Dakota (and 27 other states) prohibiting "mixed marriages" are unconstitutional.

The issues of recreation, golf, housing or marriage are not involved directly in the cases now before the court. But millions of southerners realize that the court is being asked to rule, for the first time in 57 years, on the legality of segregation itself.

So the court is on trouble-strewn ground, for racial segregation has been, and is, the southland's most entrenched institution. Its roots go deep in southern custom and tradition. In scores of seldom-mentioned ways, segregation has become a part of laws governing the most routine matters of life. For example:

• Florida and North Carolina require that textbooks used by Negroes and whites be stored separately, and that they never be interchanged.

• Oklahoma requires that separate telephone booths for Negroes be provided wherever whites demand such separation.

• Louisiana and South Carolina require segregation at the circus.

• Mississippi forbids anyone to print or to circulate printed or written matter advocating social equality or intermarriage between Negroes and whites. Penalty: a $500 fine and/or six months in jail.
• Alabama, Mississippi and South Carolina require Negro nurses for Negro patients and white nurses for white patients.
• Alabama, Arkansas, Florida, Georgia, North Carolina and South Carolina forbid the chaining together of Negro and white chain gang prisoners.
• West Virginia and Alabama require separation of Negro and white paupers.
• North Carolina and Virginia prohibit interracial fraternal organizations.
• Fifteen states require segregation in hospitals.

This is the structure that is in danger of crumbling before the court's edict. Southerners, white and Negro, say it is certain to crumble if Negroes and whites attend the same schools where they play the same games, read the same books and are taught the same lessons by the same teachers.

Can all this be ended by a supreme court ruling? If so, how? Will there be chaos? Fighting in the streets? Cross and I heard predictions of both chaos and strife. We also heard equally strong denials, from southerners of both races.

Thus, the high court faces this dilemma:

To order that segregation is unconstitutional and that Negroes must be integrated into the public schools of the south might provoke disturbances and strife which would halt, or even set back, the progress made in race relations in the past 15 years.

Already, South Carolina and Georgia have taken steps to abolish the public schools and set up a "private school" system if integration is ordered. Similar threats have been made elsewhere.

To rule that segregation is constitutional would, in the opinion of the recent Truman administration, subject the country to continued embarrassment in world councils and greatly handicap the state department in its conduct of international affairs.

"It is in the context of the present world struggle between

freedom and tyranny that the problem of racial discrimination must be viewed," said the Truman administration in a brief submitted to the court.

"The existence of discrimination against minority groups in the United States has an adverse effect upon our relations with other countries. Racial discrimination furnishes grist for the Communist propaganda mills, and it raises doubts even among friendly nations as to the intensity of our devotion to the democratic faith."

The Eisenhower administration Friday also submitted a brief to the court asking it to outlaw segregation.

Much of the drama connected with next week's court sessions stems from the fact that the court has indicated it is aware of this dilemma and that it considers the disposition of these five cases of the utmost importance to the nation.

After months of deliberation, the court called the lawyers back for argument on these five questions:

1. Did the people who wrote and approved the Fourteenth amendment understand that it would mean an end to school segregation?

2. Did they intend to give congress or the courts the power to abolish separate schools?

3. Does the supreme court have the power to interpret the Fourteenth amendment as requiring an end to school segregation?

4. If so, does the court have the right to permit a gradual changeover from segregated to integrated schools?

5. If so, how should the change be worked out?

What these questions reveal about the court's position no one is sure. Sen. Walter F. George (D., Ga.) says they mean the court already has decided to rule against segregation.

Gov. James F. Byrnes of South Carolina is telling associates he has no fear whatsoever that the court will rule segregation unconstitutional.

The Norfolk Virginian-Pilot commented in an editorial:

The court's announcement gives strong reasons "for the southern states to adjust their own thinking, their own emotions, and their own habits to the seemingly increasing possibility that the end of segregation in public schools is nearer now than ever before."

What photographer Cross and I wanted to see was whether southerners generally share the Virginian-Pilot's viewpoint.

Will the people accept integration?

What is happening in Topeka, Kan., where the school board last September announced that it would end segregation voluntarily?

What is happening in Delaware where integration is under way as the result of a lower court ruling?

Has the nation's capital changed enough in the last few years for integration of pupils to take place easily?

And what about South Carolina, which is typical of the deep South—does the large Negro population create an extra problem that must be considered by the court?

Have the schools been equal under segregation? Do they approach it now? Can the south afford segregation?

These were questions for which we sought answers in our visits to schools and homes; in our chats in honky-tonks and churches; in random conversation with passengers at airports or with taxi drivers.

We learned of violence, dismissals from jobs, mortgage foreclosures in the bitterness immediately following filing of the lawsuits.

We heard glowing reports that integration does work.

We saw deep cleavages in Negro communities as colored citizens whose jobs exist primarily because of segregation asked, "Has anybody thought about what will happen to me and my family."

We reached South Carolina convinced that the people of the southland sense that they live on the eve of a strange, new chapter in race relations, the area's—and the nation's—gravest social problem.

Segregation Due to Fade Out in Topeka Schools

Topeka, Kan.

What will happen in the southland if the United States supreme court rules that segregation in public schools must be abolished?

• Will blood run in the streets of Dixie, as some southerners have predicted?

• Will "the American Confederate army" march in armed rebellion, as Grand Dragon Bill Hendrix of the Southern Knights of the Ku Klux Klan predicts?

• Will the ruling inject new life into the hate organizations of men who ride through the night, spreading terror under the cloak of bedsheets and darkness, as some southern journalists have hinted in what members of the National Association for the Advancement of Colored People (NAACP) call "a not-too-subtle attempt to intimidate the court?"

• Will it destroy the public school systems in several southern states, as has been indicated in South Carolina and Georgia?

• Or is the NAACP right when it tells the court there will be no explosion? That the people of the southland are far more ready for integration than the Talmadges and Byrneses would have the court believe? That southerners, like other Americans, generally are law-abiding people and could be expected to conform to a supreme court ruling?

These were the questions on my mind as I reached Topeka. And I knew they were important questions because a study of previous arguments, and questioning by the justices, indicated that the supreme court is weighing gravely the question of what results each ruling might produce.

And as I reached Topeka I knew that there is no single answer to the question, because an order to end segregation would meet with far less hostility in Kansas than in South Carolina.

This was a safe assumption, I felt, even though the Topeka I had lived in as a navy trainee exactly a decade earlier was a pretty segregated city.

Ten years ago Topeka was a paradox. There was no Jim Crow in some areas where you expected it; segregation had deep roots where it was not expected.

There was no segregation on city buses, or in any public transportation. But I was unable to go to a movie or into a restaurant with white navy buddies. Hotels, bowling alleys and other public recreation facilities were closed to Negroes.

"But there has been tremendous progress in race relations in the decade since I was here," I told myself. "Perhaps Topeka has changed, too, and that certainly has considerable bearing on this case."

But then I remembered the testimony of Paul Wilson, assistant attorney general of Kansas, when he appeared before the United States supreme court last December to defend the Kansas statute which permits segregated elementary schools.

Under questioning by the justices, he pointed out that segregated primary schools existed in nine of Kansas' cities of the first class (more than 15,000 population) and in the high schools of Kansas City.

Wilson also told the court that Kansas has about 73,000 Negroes in a population of about two million, and that two-thirds of these Negroes live in cities of the first class.

Justice Frankfurter asked Wilson what would be the consequences of a ruling reversing the Kansas decision. Wilson replied:

"In perfect candor, I must say to the court that the consequences would probably not be serious. As I pointed out, our Negro population is small. We do have in our Negro schools Negro teachers, Negro administrators, who would necessarily be assimilated in the school system at large. That might produce some administrative difficulties. I can imagine no serious difficulty beyond that."

Wilson then pointed out to the court that what was involved was not a question of whether segregation could be ended, but whether Kansas and other states have a right to segregate if they deem it wise.

The issue, he argued, is whether the doctrine of "separate but equal" laid down in the case of Plessy vs. Ferguson in 1896 is still the law of the land, or whether 21 states and the District of Columbia "have been wrong for 75 years" when they believed that separate facilities, though equal, were legal within the meaning of the fourteenth amendment.

Justice Burton: "Don't you recognize it as possible that within 75 years the social and economic conditions and the personal relations of the nation may have changed so that what may have been a valid interpretation of them 75 years ago would not be a valid interpretation of them constitutionally today?"

Wilson: "We recognize that as a possibility. We do not believe that (the) record discloses any such change."

Burton: "But that might be a difference between saying that these courts of appeal and state supreme courts have been wrong for 75 years?"

Wilson: "Yes, sir. We concede that this court can overrule the . . . Plessy doctrine, but nevertheless until (it is) overruled (it is) the best guide we have."

Frankfurter: "As I understood my brother Burton's question or as I got the implication of his question, it was not that the court would have to overrule those (separate but equal) cases; the court would simply have to recognize that laws are kinetic, and some new things have happened, not deeming those decisions wrong, but bringing into play new situations toward a new decision."

Wilson: "We agree with that proposition. But, I repeat, we do not think that there is anything in the record here that would justify such a conclusion."

Almost a year after Wilson's remarks, I knew before reaching Topeka that there had been a major development which would indicate the accuracy of Wilson's remark that an order to end segregation in Kansas would produce no calamity.

After a bitter election contest a new school board took office in Topeka. In a move that surprised thousands across the nation (including NAACP attorneys and probably Wilson), the new board announced this fall that it was ending segregation voluntarily in Topeka schools.

That knowledge left me with three questions:

How much has Topeka changed in other areas—enough to make the transition in schools simple, or do the non-segregated schools represent an opening wedge in a drive to end other areas of segregation?

How is non-segregation in the schools working?

What about those Negro teachers and administrators—are they being, or will they be, assimilated into the system at large?

I got my answer to the first question in my first few hours here.

"I'll be staying at the Jayhawk hotel. Call me there," I said to Charles S. Scott, Negro attorney whom I telephoned for an interview on the cases.

"No you won't," he said. "They won't permit Negroes to stay there. I'll probably be calling you at the Dunbar (the all-Negro hotel)."

"But I have a telegram from the Jayhawk confirming my reservation."

"Well, good luck. We'll be waiting to learn how you come out," said Scott.

A few minutes later I walked to the desk of the Jayhawk, where the woman clerk asked, "Did you want something?"

"Yes, I believe you have a reservation for Rowan," I said, already filling out a registration card.

The clerk appeared flustered. For several seconds she stared at the reservation book. Then she asked, "How do you spell that?"

I spelled my name. She turned and handed the bellboy a key.

As we rode alone on the elevator, the bellboy said, "Well, I'll be durned. I know of a couple of cases where football teams insisted that their Negro players be allowed to stay here. But this is the first time I know of them admitting a single Negro."

Scott was equally surprised. He said a court case charging another Topeka hotel with discrimination is pending.

He added that Negroes still can attend only one "white" movie theater and that they must sit in a special portion of the balcony.

A few hours later I learned first-hand about the policy in Topeka restaurants. It was early evening as we sat studying documents and discussing aspects of the Topeka court case. I asked Scott if it was necessary to return to the hotel, or could I get food elsewhere.

"Where can you eat? That's a tough question in Topeka," he replied.

He drove me to a little restaurant on Fourth street, in the heart of what Topekans call "the Negro drag." It was closed.

"Ugh," said Scott in disappointment. "That doesn't look like much of a place, but it's clean. It's the only place in this area I'd take you to. Say, you can get some food at my house."

"Thanks, but no. I see no reason why we should impose on your wife in a town full of restaurants."

"To tell the truth, I can think of only one place where we could eat. That's the Pennant cafeteria, and it's closed too . . . Perhaps the Jolly cafe."

Scott and I walked into the Jolly cafe, removed our coats and were taking seats in a booth when the Chinese man behind the cash register walked over.

Wringing his hands in front of him, he said timidly: "Very sorry. I cannot do this. Lose my customers."

"Beg your pardon?" said Scott.

"My customers, they do not want me to do this."

"We see no indication that your customers are concerned one way or the other."

"But that is what I am told. The customers do not like it. That is policy."

"Is that your policy?"

"No, the owner. He tells me that."

"Where is the owner? Could we have a word with him?"

"The owner, he died. Nobody own it now. I am very sorry. Best I can do is serve if you go to kitchen."

The lawyer and I walked out.

"This is so embarrassing," said Scott. "But it is the best answer I can give to people who ask why we are fighting school segregation. As it is, I have to pray each day that no guest comes to town. There isn't a single decent place to take them to eat. No places of recreation.

"And it stems from Jim Crow schools, because when segregation is part of the pattern of learning it permeates every area of life."

Scott recalled being told that one first class eating place, the Ranch House, had agreed to serve Negroes after conferences with an interracial delegation.

When we walked into the Ranch House a hostess asked, "Have you reservations?"

When we answered no she walked to the rear of the restaurant, obviously to see the manager. She returned and asked us to follow her. She led us to a private room.

"Be seated," she said, and walked away hastily.

"Do you want to eat here?" asked Scott.

"I'm not that hungry," I said. We walked back to the hostess and I asked, "Is it necessary that we eat in the private room?"

Tears came into her eyes.

"I'm sorry, but it's the manager," she said. "I told him that two colored men were here and that if I had to turn you away I was quitting. He said to take you into a private room."

"Could we have a word with the manager?"

She led us to a young man who was slicing a piece of beef.

"I just wanted to ask if the only place we can eat is in the private room," I said.

The young owner was not hostile. He said he wanted to do the right thing, but he feared customer reaction.

"You fellows have come out here to make a guinea pig of me. But you never think of my business," he said.

I assured him that we were not trying to make a guinea pig of him, that I had never heard of his place before in my life.

"We're just searching for one place in Topeka where two Americans can eat without dropping their heads in shame," said Scott.

"Do you really resent eating in the private room? I never knew that. Quite often some of the Negro teachers call in advance so we can get a private room ready. They know the food and service is the same," said the proprietor.

"It is—but the implication is not the same," I said. "When you put me in that private room when there are dozens of places in the main dining room, I sense that you have a special reason. And thinking about that special reason doesn't make me feel good, or dignified, or quite a full-fledged American."

"I agree with you—so help me God," said the proprietor. "I even tried serving Negroes without the private room. Always there were a few whites who would complain. But nobody ever came up with a pat on the back. But I want you to know I want to do right. If you want to eat in the main dining room, go ahead.

"Put these gentlemen in front of the fireplace," he said to the hostess.

I thought as I ate that this could be the beginning of Jim Crow's last stand in the restaurants of Topeka. But I still did not know how integration was faring in the elementary schools.

Superintendent Wendell Godwin had a quick answer to that question.

"Non-segregation is working fine where we have tried it. We've had no complaints, not even a ripple."

I asked if the move to integrate was the result of the lawsuit.

"I doubt if the suit had any relationship to the move to end segregation," he said. "We acquired a new school board over the past few years, and some of the new members say they always felt that to segregate school children wasn't right.

"On Sept. 3, Mr. Jacob Dickinson, the new board president, moved to abolish segregation. He was backed, 5 to 1, with the only dissent coming from a member who said he only thought we should wait until after the court case is ruled out.

"We decided to begin integration in the Southwest and Randolph school districts this year. Those are what you would call the elite neighborhoods, if Topeka has any elite neighborhoods."

"How many Negro children now are enrolled in elementary school, and how many are in mixed schools?" I asked.

The superintendent said that of 828 Negroes in the elementary schools of Topeka, 15 now go to mixed schools.

I asked Godwin if Negroes thought this was enough, or only "token" integration. I asked if there was any truth to reports that in "non-elite" districts where the Negro population is heavier Negroes soon would be permitted to go to the school nearest them, and that some whites would be shifted to what now are all-Negro schools.

Godwin answered:

"There has been no discussion on this by the board. The end of segregation will depend on the forbearance of both Negroes and whites. What we want is evolution, not revolution. After all, there might arise some incidents which would be unfortunate."

The superintendent then said the board has "no timetable for ending segregation (although I had been told by some white and Negro citizens that such a timetable had been drafted) but what we do have a lot of is sincerity. We think that is what counts. Our board doesn't think segregation makes sense. If there is any place where the races can get along together, it is in the elementary schools."

What about Negro teachers, will they be integrated, too? Godwin was asked.

"I wouldn't care to speculate on that," he said.

Later I saw Dickinson, the board president. He left little doubt that the board is sincerely opposed to segregation.

I told him that people across the nation were curious as to whether Topeka still will defend the legality of segregation before the supreme court next Monday.

"I suppose the attorney general will be there, but he won't be talking for Topeka," Dickinson said. "If Topeka files anything it will be a brief saying that we have ended segregation, but that we are interested in the question of gradual elimination. What we want is evolution, not revolution."

How do the Negro teachers fit into this picture? I asked.

"That teacher issue is the toughest of all," Dickinson admitted.

Here I had touched on the issue that had created a deep cleavage in Topeka's Negro community.

It was the source of personal feuds; of charges by militant Negroes that the teachers were timid "Uncle Toms"; that some of them were working under cover to preserve segregation and their jobs; of charges by some Negro teachers that a few "class-conscious" members of the NAACP were leveling such charges because they resented the education and social status of the teachers.

I talked to three of Topeka's 20-odd Negro teachers, all of whom worked in the all-Negro schools. They agreed that Negro teachers were concerned, even afraid, about what might happen to their jobs.

I knew why, for in my pocket was a copy of a letter to six Negro teachers. It was dated March 13, 1953, when it was expected that the supreme court might rule on the legality of segregation in public schools, and it was signed by Superintendent Godwin.

The letter was a big clue to why some Negroes support Jim Crow. It had considerable bearing on the Topeka situation, and it would have far more meaning in Delaware, Washington, D.C., Virginia and South Carolina.

I knew that the letter to six teachers was part of a bigger story of which I would not know all the details until many days later.

The letter also was just a symbol of the uncertainty, the confusion, existing today in what must be called the social upheaval of even the border state of Kansas.

Lurking beneath the upheaval, the many indications that for Jim Crow in Kansas everything is over but the funeral, there was vocal dissatisfaction.

"We're going to argue before that court just as hard as if 15 students never were integrated voluntarily," said Scott. "What we want the court to tell us is what our rights are under that Constitution.

"Once we know, we won't have to worry about the next city election and whether the next school board will decide that this integration is a passing fancy.

"We want it so no new school board can resurrect Jim Crow."

Delaware Wants Its Schools To Be "Separate, Equal"
Hockessin, Del.

From the first moments of her life, Shirley Bulah was in the public eye. Her mother left her on a doorstep in nearby Wilmington, Del.

Today the 9-year-old fourth grader is still in the public eye. She is at the center of the fuss and furor as Delaware grapples with the problem of color in the classroom.

The United States supreme court is being asked what are the rights of Shirley Bulah under the Constitution. It is not really a question of what rights Negroes have, because the court has said repeatedly that constitutional rights belong to the individual, not to groups.

So the great social issue before the court is about this little girl and others like her across the southland.

Mr. and Mrs. Fred Bulah, who rescued Shirley from the doorstep, argue that Shirley is entitled to attend the best and nearest school provided by the state. They went to court, and the results are sure to change the lives of almost every citizen in this state.

What began as merely an effort to get bus transportation for Negro children has ended in what the vast majority of citizens believe is the death of Jim Crow in schools of this state.

This is the story as Mrs. Bulah, a brown-skinned, bespectacled woman of 56, with button-on shoes and slightly graying hair, tells it:

A few years ago our granddaughter came to stay with us while going to high school. Every day she had to walk two miles to catch a bus for Wilmington. I couldn't figure that out, 'cause every school day I saw a bus picking up white kids a block away.

I talked to some colored neighbors and they said their children walked two miles, too.

"Why don't you all get together and see if you can't get a bus," I says to one lady.

"Aw, Mrs. Bulah, you know they ain't gonna give us no bus," she says to me.

"Well, I'm telling you, if it was my daughter in school they'd have to tell me something," I says to her.

First thing I know Shirley is a big girl and in school. Come rain or shine she's got to walk two miles to the colored elementary school. Most of the kids didn't actually walk two miles. They took the short cut through the thicket and across the cornfield.

I would always drive Shirley, but one day I got out there a-slipping around in the snow.

I said, "Shucks, why should I do this?" So I wrote school officials about a bus to pick up Shirley.

I never got an answer, so I wrote the governor. I got back some forms to fill out and have Shirley's teacher sign them. Do you know what that colored teacher told me?

She said, "Mrs. Bulah, you're just wasting your time."

Sure enough, the people at the state office of education wrote me that no bus went to my daughter's school.

"Then why can't she go to school where there is a bus?" I wrote them.

They said the state constitution forbids white and colored children going to the same school. They told me I was the only Negro ever to complain. I said first one or not, something had to be done about that constitution.

You see, I only got to the 10th grade in a one-room school in South Carolina. I meant for my daughter to get a better education than I got.

I contacted attorney Louis Redding of the National Association for the Advancement of Colored People (NAACP) and was told that the NAACP would not fight to get a Jim Crow bus to go to a Jim Crow school, but that if I wanted to challenge segregation it would back me.

"What happened when you filed the suit?" Mrs. Bulah was asked.

"Oh, things got hot in the Negro community. And once when I was delivering eggs (we raise chickens and get about 60 dozen eggs a week), this white lady, Mrs. Sarah Nurse, says to me, 'Why you fighting to get into the white school? Yours is as good as ours.'

"I told her no it wasn't equal, in no way, shape, form or fashion."

The court of chancery later ruled that the Negro school was substantially inferior to the white school in teacher training, pupil-teacher ratio, extra-curricular activities, physical plant and esthetic considerations and the extra burden of time and distance suffered by Negroes in attending school.

The court thus ordered that Negroes must be admitted to the white elementary school in Hockessin and the white high school in Claymont, a community to be discussed later. This ruling was upheld by the state supreme court.

In September 1952 Shirley Bulah was a pupil at school 29, representing a crack in the seam of a generations-old pattern that was law, custom and social tradition.

"How is non-segregation working out?" I asked Mrs. Bulah.

"Just wonderful," she said. "Shirley now goes to the white children's parties, and they come here to Shirley's parties. Why, Shirley is in the Brownies now. She's the only Negro in this area in the group."

"How is Shirley doing in her school work?" Mrs. Bulah was asked.

"She's improved in every way. She reads so much better. She gets Bs and Cs in her classes. She's getting along fine."

"Do you go to parent-teacher meetings," she was asked.

"Oh, yes. I and Mrs. Woolfolk, a colored lady with a child

in the first grade, was there just the other night. They sure treated us fine.

"You know, they put a number under each glass. And somebody else had the same number under their glass. That was your partner. Mrs. Woolfolk had a white lady for a partner and I had a white lady named Mrs. Walker. I and Mrs. Walker and Mrs. Woolfolk and her partner sure had a fine time.

"I tell you, if they don't want us there they sure haven't showed it."

"What about the white people to whom you sold eggs. Did any of them stop buying from you?" I asked.

"Not a one," said Mrs. Bulah. "A lot of the white folks congratulated me.

"Now take this Mrs. Nurse. She said, 'Well, Mrs. Bulah, I see you won.'

"And I said, 'I told you I was going to fight to the end.' And she said, 'Well, Mrs. Bulah, I'm glad.'

"I didn't even know her husband was home. But he heard us and walked out and said to me, 'Mrs. Bulah, we never had anything against you. We know that you are decent-living people. You keep your child clean. But there are a lot of dirty hoodlums that I didn't want near my child.'

"And I says to him, 'Look, Mr. Nurse, you know you've got as many dirty people in your race as I have.'

"And he says to me, 'Yes, I know. Some of them even put lice in my daughter's hair. But we have to let them ride the same bus. They're of our race. They have nowhere else to go.'"

All through this narration by Mrs. Bulah I had to remember one thing. None of this change was final. The Delaware courts had not ruled that segregation itself is unconstitutional.

They had said simply that Shirley Bulah was not getting what was due her under the "separate but equal" principle that still remained the law of the land until the nation's supreme court ruled otherwise.

The court even suggested that if state officials can show later that facilities for Negroes are equal to those for whites the court might find reason to restore the old pattern of separate schools.

Nobody expects this to happen, but it remains a legal fact that segregation, per se, is still legal in Delaware.

But in reaching this decision the court of chancery made a finding of fact which, along with a similar finding by the Kansas court, highlights a very dramatic point in the dispute now before the nation's highest court.

In both Delaware and Kansas, the courts reached conclusions that, in fact, there can be no equality under enforced segregation.

Said the three-judge United States district court for Kansas:

> *"Segregation of white and colored children in public schools has a detrimental effect upon the colored children. The impact is greater when it has the sanction of law; for the policy of separating the races is usually interpreted as denoting the inferiority of the Negro group.*
>
> *"A sense of inferiority affects the motivation of a child to learn. Segregation with the sanction of law, therefore, has a tendency to retard the educational and mental development of Negro children and to deprive them of some of the benefits they would receive in a racially-integrated school system."*

After hearing testimony of psychiatrists, psychologists and educators, some of them from Delaware, the same finding was made by the court of chancery in that state.

But in both states the courts held that, in view of the 1896 ruling in the case of Plessy vs. Ferguson, they must ignore this finding and interpret the word "equal" as referring only to physical facilities.

In Kansas, where Negroes and whites admitted physical facilities were equal, the court allowed segregation to continue.

In Delaware, where physical facilities were not equal, the court ordered "temporary" integration.

But in each case they tossed into the laps of nine men this pressing new question:

If segregation, of itself, creates inequality, if it does put roadblocks in the minds of the segregated children, how can there ever be equality under segregation? Does not the "separate but equal" doctrine then become only a joke?

Before the supreme court is a brief signed by 32 of the

nation's top social scientists (including Dr. Arnold Rose, professor of sociology at University of Minnesota) explaining why there can be no equality under segregation.

Attorneys for the southern states have attempted to belittle this testimony by describing a social scientist as "someone who always finds what he was looking for in the first place and then wraps it in scientific terminology."

But the NAACP is relying heavily upon the testimony of social scientists, and on the findings of the Kansas and Delaware courts, because it provides a second death-dealing shot at Jim Crow.

The high court could rule that any classification based on color is in conflict with the Constitution and thus overrule the "separate but equal" doctrine.

Failing this, it could rule that there is nothing in the Constitution that would rule out the "separate but equal" doctrine. But since it has been shown that separation and equality cannot exist together, then separation must go.

Either ruling would mean the abolition of Jim Crow public schools.

There is, of course, no guarantee that the court will reach either of those decisions. It could decide that the Constitution does permit segregation with equality, and that there are no substantial reasons why equality is not possible under segregation.

What do Delaware citizens look for? Said the Wilmington Morning News in an editorial last Oct. 23:

"The days of racial segregation in Delaware schools are numbered; there is hardly a doubt of that. The University of Delaware, private and parochial schools and certain public schools influenced by court decisions have opened their doors to Negro students.

"The state supreme court has ruled that segregation provisions of the Delaware constitution cannot be enforced to make Negro children endure seriously unequal educational opportunities; the United States supreme court is unlikely to upset this verdict. The trend of the times is against segregation."

How aware of this are the Negroes of Delaware? I wondered.

How may Negro parents grew up with their minds full of

"roadblocks" that make them feel unable to cope with an integrated society?

How many Negroes feel, even subconsciously, that the trend of the times that endangers Jim Crow also endangers their livelihood?

I remembered Kansas, and that letter to six teachers. And I thought of the part of the Shirley Bulah story that I had not yet told, and realized anew that one day soon the voice of the nation's high tribunal would severely shake thousands of lives on both sides of the color line.

Some Negro Teachers Favor School Segregation

Hockessin, Del.

Mrs. Fred Bulah, Negro housewife whose stubborn fight against inequality led to the ending of segregation in the elementary school here, is something less than a hero to other Negro parents in the area.

She is the symbol of petty hatreds, color-consciousness and the personal antagonisms that beset Negro communities like this everywhere. One must understand this conflict within a race to get a full meaning of the cases before the supreme court and of what a ruling outlawing segregation is likely to do in southern communities.

Photographer Bonham Cross and I visited Hockessin school 29, and although more than a year had passed since the courts ordered integration, only six Negro pupils were in the school.

The vast majority of Negroes still were in the all-Negro school.

"Why haven't more parents sent their children to the integrated school?" I asked Mrs. Bulah.

"Just tetched in the head, I guess," she said.

I found by checking around that there's more to it than that. Sarah Bulah is Fred Bulah's second wife, and as such has never been fully accepted in this little rural community.

And there was evidence that these Negroes, living in a color-conscious society, also were color-conscious.

"Some of the colored people were whispering that, just because Shirley is fair complexioned, we thought she was white, and that we were suing because we didn't want her to associate with colored children," Mrs. Bulah told me.

The talkative woman, who had had a 10th-grade education and who showed remarkable keenness of mind, then said that if I really wanted to know why Negroes were choosing Jim Crow I should see the Rev. Martin Luther Kilson, pastor of Chippey African Union Methodist church.

"He tried to talk me out of sending my daughter to the white school," she said, "and he's been talking to other parents."

We found the Negro minister behind his parsonage, wearing bow tie, boots and a blue toboggan cap. He was chopping wood.

I explained to him that we were interested in the school situation and wondered how he, a community leader, felt about it.

"Ain't much leadership you can do in this Negro community," the preacher said. "Some of 'em you can lead, some you can't."

Have you been trying to lead for or against segregation? he was asked.

"I'll tell you, I was for segregation. Mainly because nobody started out to get integration. All we wanted was a bus for the colored. Redding (attorney Louis Redding) and some members of the National Association for the Advancement of Colored People (NAACP) encouched (his word) this issue of segregation."

Why have some Negroes fallen out with Mrs. Bulah because she contested segregation? he was asked.

"The old residents didn't feel good about this newcomer (Mrs. Bulah has lived here only 11 years) coming in here and making bad feelings among their white friends.

"Now, I hated to see them tamper with that little old colored school there (next to his church). It was so handy. These folks around here would rather have a colored teacher. They didn't want to be mixed up with no white folks.

"Now that board of education has tampered with things till they've almost tore up that little old colored school."

So you advise your members not to go to the white school? I asked the minister, who said he entered the ministry 32 years ago after taking a correspondence Bible course.

"Well, I'll tell you. When they started this segregation case I didn't appreciate the idea. But a wise man changes. So many things have changed my mind lately. I think this integration is working better.

"They say this integration is working like a clock. And the school board says the children are doing better in mixed schools, so I suppose it has been an improvement. If I was to do any recommending today, I would tell my members to go on over to that white school."

This was the stand of a Negro minister, who, with his church, often is cited by backers of segregation as proof that Negroes like to keep to themselves.

On this journey I already had heard it said twice that in a segregated society the Negro teacher and the Negro preacher are the forces most active in preserving segregation.

I knew that I would have to reserve judgment there, because I expected to hear a different story about ministers in South Carolina. But what about the teachers?

Mrs. Bulah says that the two teachers in the Negro school became "unhappy" when she sued to end segregation.

"Suddenly I found that Shirley was not passed from the third to the fourth grade by her Negro teacher, although she had been promoted from first to second, and second to third grades with good marks," says Mrs. Bulah.

There is no way for one to conclude that the child was failed because the Negro teacher considered her a threat to her job, but there is evidence of insecurity among Negro teachers wherever segregation exists.

I recalled Topeka, Kan., and the letter to the six teachers and I realized that the fears of Negro teachers are not completely unjustified.

Last March 13, when it was thought that a supreme court ruling on the segregation cases would come at any time, superintendent Wendell Godwin of Topeka wrote six teachers:

"Due to the present uncertainty about enrollment next year in schools for Negro children, it is not possible at this time to offer you employment for next year. If the supreme court should rule that segregation in the elementary grades is unconstitutional, our board will proceed on the assumption that the majority of people in Topeka will not want to employ Negro teachers next year for white children.

"If it turns out that segregation is not terminated, there will be nothing to prevent us from negotiating a contract with you at some later date this spring. You will understand that I am sending letters of this kind to only those teachers of the Negro schools who have been employed during the last year or two.

"It is presumed that, even though segregation should be declared unconstitutional, we would have need for some schools for Negro children, and we would retain our Negro teachers to teach them.

"I think I understand that all of you must be under considerable strain, and I sympathize with the uncertainties and inconveniences which you must experience during this period of adjustment. I believe that whatever happens will ultimately turn out to be best for everybody concerned."

Negro attorney Charles S. Scott had told me that "many Negro teachers in Topeka are scared. We don't get much help out of them."

This was why.

While Gov. Herman Talmadge of Georgia and Gov. James Byrnes of South Carolina and other southerners only had warned that an attack on segregation would cost Negro teachers their jobs, Topeka officials admitted they would proceed under a policy that a Negro teacher is to teach only Negroes.

If this was a serious matter in Topeka, where 28 Negroes held teaching posts, how grave a factor it must be in the city of Washington where 1,822 Negroes teach, I thought. And what conflict it must create in Virginia, Delaware and South Carolina where thousands of Negroes earn their livelihood by teaching!

To understand the confusion in the mind of the teacher, the American observer would have to understand that for decades the southern Negro who could afford college usually trained to teach. That was the only profession where he could be sure of a job; segregation was his guarantee.

And because teaching was open to Negroes while other professions were closed, the Negro teacher became a leader, a spokesman; his social status in his community was much higher than that of the white teacher in the white community.

What could one expect the Negro teacher to do when segregation, the institution that made all this possible, was threatened?

McKinley L. Burnett, NAACP president in Topeka, had one answer. He says Harrison Caldwell, generally regarded as "top man" among Topeka's Negro teachers, denounced plans for integration. He accuses Caldwell of trying to start a Jim Crow junior high school.

The school board says this charge is untrue.

But when asked what role Negro teachers play in the Topeka situation, Caldwell said: "Frankly, I'm a little confused. I don't think Negro teachers know what to do. I don't see how any member of any minority group could favor segregation. But employment is an important factor, too. If you press me, I'll have to admit that the cause is more important than my job. But I think you can understand why Negro teachers don't know what to do."

I called two of the six teachers and asked them for an interview. Both stated frankly that they were afraid to talk for publication about the issue. When I promised not to use their names, one—a man—explained the situation this way:

"When I look at this campaign against segregated schools I keep wondering if anybody is thinking about the Negro teacher. Here I've spent more than five years going to college to prepare to teach, and I know I'm qualified, yet I have no idea when my job will end.

"I think there is no doubt that the Negro teacher will get the short end in this integration deal. Count the Negro teachers in Minneapolis, in any northern city or state. They don't have a lot of Negroes teaching whites. They won't here.

"I can get another job. My wife and I had jobs in California for this fall when we thought we would be dropped, but then the court didn't end segregation, so we were rehired. Sure, we can find another job. But a teacher wants to settle down in a town and start raising a family and arranging a home like other human beings."

I asked Burnett, the NAACP president, if anyone had thought of the Negro teachers.

"From the very start we have told the school board here that we won't be satisfied with any halfway integration. It's got to be both teachers and pupils," he said.

What will you do if the court rules against segregation and the board drops these six teachers?

"I don't believe they're going to try anything. They know we ain't going to stand for no foolishness," said Burnett, who works eight hours daily as a veteran's hospital employe and eight hours a day as a state highway department worker.

I recalled that the letter to the six teachers was written when the school board was composed of three veteran members and three new members. Perhaps the present "anti-segregation board" would not find it necessary to drop the Negro teachers.

"This teacher issue is the toughest of all," said Jacob Dickinson, board president who had made the motion to end segregation voluntarily in the elementary schools.

"I voted to send out that letter at the time because it seemed the only way we could get integration. The board was split three to three, and my feeling was that we ought to sacrifice six teachers to start integration if it had to be done.

"If six teachers had to be sacrificed for their race, we hoped they would understand. I believed that, in the long run, everybody would profit.

"But now I'm not sure we'll have to drop anybody. If everything goes right, I think we can handle this integration without ever hurting any person."

This would seem to reassure all but the insecure teacher, the Negro who realizes that his preparation has not been comparable to that of the white teacher.

It does not remove the fear and conflict from the minds of Negro teachers who realize, even subconsciously, that they are products of inferior schools and that they have been teaching in school systems where the demands on their abilities have not always been great.

These teachers fear the competition of an integrated society, and we had learned early in our journey that they attempt to justify the segregated school.

It was not a teacher, but a Negro social worker who handles

youth on a segregated basis, who outlined this reason for supporting segregation:

"The elementary school age is one in which youngsters are
deeply impressed. They are having their characters molded.
They get their outlook on life. It is here that they build up
ambition and self-confidence.

"Now I think they need to be encouraged at this age. They
need a pat on the back when they do something well. So I
think it better that they have Negro teachers who are likely to
be sympathetic to them. It would crush the souls of the little
darlings to have them taught by someone who despised them
because of their color."

This woman had touched on one of the little tragedies of
this many-sided issue. We found out what she meant here in
Hockessin.

When Cross and I tried to visit school 29, the principal told
us she could not talk to us or allow us to take pictures unless
we got the approval of her superiors.

I called George R. Miller, Jr., state superintendent of public instruction, at Dover to get permission to visit the integrated school.

"Let me call you back," he said. "I want to see if I can
think of any reasons for keeping you out that I can't think of
on the spur of the moment."

A few moments later he called to say he had checked the
state board members and it was their feeling that we could go
talk to the principal but could take no pictures. He said the
board members didn't want to do anything to jeopardize the
case before the court.

We walked into school 29 and asked a teacher where we
would find the principal. She asked a young girl to direct us
to the office of "Miss Moore."

As we reached the classroom of Miss Moore, a teaching
principal in the four-teacher school, a frail little woman with
angular facial features came running behind us. As I put my
hand on the knob the woman grabbed my arm and shoved
me toward Cross.

"Let me talk to her, let me talk to her!" she shouted almost
hysterically.

Cross and I sat for several minutes while, we later learned, long distance calls buzzed across the state. We could not understand this inasmuch as Miller had promised to call Miss Moore to say it was permissible for her to grant an interview.

We sat for 20 minutes. At intervals the frail woman walked past us, tossing angry glances more at Cross than at me.

Finally the principal and the other three teachers walked into the auditorium. Miss Moore said all the excitement resulted from the fact they had been bothered by impostors.

We sought to explain that we had not intended to cause any disturbance, and we took out credentials. But we never got a conference with the principal because the woman with the angular face took over.

"Are you the first grade teacher?" I asked.

She looked startled, then acquired a "how did you know this?" expression. She answered yes.

I never told her that I knew because members of the Negro community had told me that three of the teachers are eminently fair, "but the first grade teacher is definitely anti-Negro."

Most of the six Negro youngsters in the school are in the first grade.

Mrs. Mary Woolfolk is a Negro mother who has a child in the first grade, and she admits concern as to how her child will be affected by an obviously hostile teacher.

But Mrs. Woolfolk expresses the belief that the damage done in a year by such a teacher is not nearly so great or permanent as the damage done by a lifetime of segregation.

Other parents expressed the belief that hostile teachers almost always will be in the minority because most teachers will try to be fair out of professional pride. The few whose prejudices go too deeply for this will be far less willing to let their colleagues know it than is the teacher at the Hockessin school, they say.

Whether this is true at all, and certainly whether it would be true in South Carolina or other areas of the deep south, was a debatable matter. But a few miles away, in Claymont, Del., there was much evidence to support arguments that integration works, and that the white teacher is not waiting eagerly to crush the spirit of little black boys and girls.

"We think a lot of these (Negro) children because they are our children, too," said Harvey E. Stahl, superintendent of schools in Claymont, where the state courts ordered Negroes admitted to the high school.

"We've had no incidents, I'm happy to say. Our teachers have been most helpful. And a very, very capable Negro teacher, Mrs. Pauline Dyson, has helped us to make the necessary adjustments."

I was aware that Stahl was going to say what he felt, that he would ignore the word passed around by the state superintendent's office that school officials should say nothing to jeopardize the state's chances of getting the United States supreme court to rule that segregation can be restored.

"Last year 11 Negroes were in school," Stahl went on. "There are 20 this year. They've worked in very well, indeed.

"We've had no more incidents among the races than we have just among children. As a rule, children don't have racial prejudices. They have to be taught."

The superintendent told how he first learned the school was to be integrated when he heard of the state supreme court's ruling in a news broadcast the night of Aug. 28, 1952 —a few days before school was to open.

"I began trying to reach the attorney general to find out what we had to do. He was on vacation. Finally we got word from the state office that we would have to admit the Negro pupils.

"I asked the Negro parents to meet with me, and I told them that the eyes of the state and nation were going to be upon us. I told them that Negroes would have to do their part and my race would have to do its part.

"We're going to do our part here at the school, I told them, and almost in unison those Negro parents said they would do their part. And they have.

"Then I was told not to admit Negroes until the United States supreme court ruled, but I was committed to these parents. I refused to back down.

"My friends said, 'Stahl, you'll have some serious difficulties.'

"That's awful. Talk like that by citizens creates a disturbing influence. I knew that deep down in their hearts some of my fellow educators were hoping that we would fail. But we haven't.

"We've got to do a tremendous job of educating some of our educators.

"You tell all your readers that integration is working well. I knew all along that Claymont was the best school they could have picked in which to try integration.

"You tell them we're happy to be the guinea pigs. And you might add that if every community had a Negro teacher like Mrs. Dyson they wouldn't have any problems."

Even on the social level Claymont had met no great problems.

Stahl reported that the junior prom had been an interracial event and that the class president invited one Negro couple to his table so as to make sure the Negroes wouldn't be bunched off to themselves.

We left the high school to look for Mrs. Dyson, whose good works had earned her the community's designation of "outstanding woman of the year."

We found her in a little one-teacher elementary school which recently had had a room added. There had been no appropriation for window shades for the new room, so Mrs. Dyson was busy teaching the pupils arithmetic, which for that day consisted of measuring the windows and figuring out how much material they would need to make curtains.

When informed that the superintendent had given her much of the credit for the success of integration, she said modestly: "I only did what I thought was right."

Don't you ever worry about what the end of segregation might do to teaching jobs? she was asked.

"I'm not the least bit worried," she said, "for I'm sure of one thing. What affects one of us affects us all. If integration is good for boys and girls, it also is good for teachers.

"I just tell my boys and girls that education helps us to live with people. If we cannot do that we are not educated, no matter how much we know."

Segregation Retreats Without Pain in Washington, D.C.
Washington.

It should mean very little for me to report to American readers that in 1953 a Negro walked into the Mayflower hotel here and got a room.

But that fact does have considerable meaning today as the

nation's highest court weighs the burdensome question of whether this nation is to continue half segregated and half integrated.

The hotel story has meaning because it gives the supreme court a clue as to the trends of the times. It is an indication that the Washington described in 1947 as "a graphic illustration of a failure of democracy" is fading out of existence. Jim Crow is fading with it.

The Washington about which I write today is not the same city, racially speaking, about which I wrote less than three years ago.

How different it is from the city in which I was refused service at a hot dog stand.

How far removed it is from the city where three years ago a Negro could see a movie at a first-run theater only if he faked an accent and pretended to be a foreigner.

It is not a perfect city. Negro slums still are a festering eyesore in the shadows of the Capitol—squalid evidence that equality of housing opportunity does not exist.

Any Negro who has tried to get a job in public transportation knows that equality of job opportunity still does not exist.

But Americans—and foreigners—ought to know that this is not the Washington Ralph Bunche found too steeped in Jim Crowism for him to move his family here a few years ago so he could accept a government post.

Perhaps the hotels best describe where Washington stands today.

Most first class hotels accept Negro guests, although they are in the transition period where they employ the "basement policy" Negroes have recognized in many cities farther north.

Under this policy, it is customary for Negroes to be given a room on the second floor, or the lowest floor available, unless the Negro is aware of what is being done and specifically requests a higher room.

(The lower floors are less desirable because they are closer to the noise of the street, and often linen closets, meeting rooms and other service operations are housed on these floors. More important to the uneasy hotel management, Negro guests are less conspicuous in hotel traffic if they ride only a floor or two on the elevator.)

Clarence Mitchell, director of the Washington bureau of the National Association for the Advancement of Colored People (NAACP), reports that his office recently was asked to check on hotel facilities for a group of Negro children who planned to visit Washington. The vast majority of Washington hotels said they would take school groups "in the event only a small percentage of the children are Negroes."

Still, this is a change from a few years ago when groups having any Negro members were turned away.

Washington hotels have come a long way from policies of a few years ago when a Puerto Rican government official slept on a cot in a government office because hotels refused him.

What has all this to do with the question before the supreme court as to whether the Constitution permits the District of Columbia and four states to require Negroes to attend separate schools?

This is how the federal government explained it in a brief submitted to the court last December:

> *"The problem of racial discrimination is particularly acute in the District of Columbia, the nation's capital. The city is the window through which the world looks into our house. The embassies, legations and representatives of all nations are here, at the seat of the federal government. Foreign officials and visitors naturally judge this country and our people by their experiences and observations in the nation's capital; and the treatment of colored persons here is taken as the measure of our attitude toward minorities generally."*

What the justice department of a Democratic administration was saying is simply that the solidarity of the free world, and the heart of this free world's search for peace, is involved, in some measure, in the cases before the court.

On Nov. 27, in a supplementary brief submitted to the supreme court at the court's suggestion, the present Republican administration endorsed the same belief.

Attorney General Brownell pointed out that he had been asked to speak only on the five questions slated for re-argument beginning Monday, but he made it clear that there is bipartisan agreement on these principles outlined by his predecessor:

1. The issue now before the court "raises questions of the first importance in our society. For racial discriminations imposed by law, or having the sanction or support of government, inevitably tend to undermine the foundations of a society dedicated to freedom, justice and equality."

2. "In these days, when the free world must conserve and fortify the moral as well as the material sources of its strength, it is especially important to affirm that the Constitution of the United States places no limitation, express or implied, on the principle of the equality of all men before the law."

3. From 1946 to the time the brief was filed last December, damage to our country's foreign relations has increased because of suspicions and resentment in other countries to treatment of minorities in the United States.

To impress upon the court the seriousness of the latter point, the justice department included in its brief a letter from the secretary of state dated Dec. 2, 1952, which said in part:

"The United States is under constant attack in the foreign press, over the foreign radio, and in such international bodies as the United Nations because of various practices of discrimination against minority groups in this country. As might be expected, Soviet spokesmen regularly exploit this situation in propaganda against the United States, both within the United Nations and through radio broadcasts and the press, which reaches all corners of the world.

"Some of these attacks against us are based on falsehood and distortion; but the undeniable existence of racial discrimination gives unfriendly governments the most effective kind of ammunition for their propaganda warfare. The hostile reaction among normally friendly peoples, many of whom are particularly sensitive in regard to the status of non-European races, is growing in alarming proportions. In such countries the view is expressed more and more vocally that the United States is hypocritical in claiming to be the champion of democracy while permitting practices of racial discrimination here in this country.

"The segregation of school children on a racial basis is one of the practices in the United States that has been singled out for hostile foreign comment in the United Nations and elsewhere. Other peoples cannot understand how such a practice can exist in a country which professes to be a staunch supporter of freedom, justice and democracy. The sincerity of the United States in this respect will be judged by its deeds as well as by its words."

In the year since Dean Acheson wrote that letter there have been several deeds in Washington to minimize criticisms of the kind of democracy practiced here.

At 8 a.m. last June 10 Washington restaurants ended a decades-old policy of Jim Crow.

The supreme court had ruled, after appeals to do so from the present administration, that the policy of barring Negroes from District restaurants was illegal.

In one edict the court did what hundreds of citizens had failed to do in years of hard work; it did what many citizens said "just can't be done overnight."

Newspaper reporters made the better restaurants their beat the days after the ruling, looking for the "deluge" of "dirty Negroes" upon the better eating places. They waited for the trouble some residents said surely would come in a city that is one-third Negro.

The trouble never came.

"Nobody thinks about it any more, except maybe to comment that the old policy seems as queer as a $7 bill," a waitress in the Mayflower hotel coffee shop told me.

There have been other deeds which seem major to people who have lived here, who know how deeply segregation has been ingrained under a Congress where at least one member admitted he sought re-election because he wanted to keep Washington a segregated city.

Last spring, without publicity, the three main downtown theaters began admitting Negroes. Two legitimate theaters now are open on a non-segregated basis. Recently, two neighborhood chains ended their ban on Negroes.

A few movie people admit that these steps were not taken completely out of devotion to democracy. Television moved into homes on a non-segregation basis and the movie houses realized that Negroes represented a major source through which they might bolster sagging revenues.

Two weeks ago the district board of commissioners announced that race no longer is to be a factor in hiring and firing in jobs under its jurisdiction, except in schools, recreation and the fire department.

Thus these three areas represent the only phases of official Washington where segregation is entrenched. Most residents believe that if the court ends segregation in schools, non-segregation in these areas will follow almost automatically.

All this, too, has a bearing on the issues to be reargued before the high court next Monday, for most people involved admit that supreme court justices are influenced by such practical considerations as what they think the effect of a particular ruling will be.

Happenings in Washington in the past few years have indicated clearly that, even where the Negro population is large, old and deep-rooted policies of segregation can be swept away without ugly conflict.

The same had been evident in Kansas and Delaware, despite long-used arguments that segregation is the best policy because to keep the races apart prevents friction. In an editorial entitled "It Works," the Wilmington (Del.) Morning News had this to say about that argument:

"It (non-segregation) works. People are people, and some in all races are pretty poor specimen. But the decent ones generally get along fine—if they are not pitted against each other by artificial restrictions imposed by law or custom . . .

"Most of our so-called race problems are the result of laws which deprive people of the freedom to associate as freely as they wish. Remove the restrictions, the compulsions, and the problems solve themselves because most people of all races are decent. Experience with such change proves that the consequences so direly predicted rarely materialize. Race relations don't get worse, they get better."

Most Washington residents would agree that this had been the case. We had heard the same in Topeka. And in Delaware, the Morning News could find first-hand evidence in the nearby towns.

In fact, immediately following the court order that Hockessin and Claymont had to admit Negroes to schools there, citizens of Arden, Del., voted overwhelmingly to end segregation.

The state attorney general promptly notified them that they had no authority to end segregation in violation of the state constitution inasmuch as no court had ordered them to integrate.

Arden ignored the attorney general and apparently he decided he would avoid trouble by ignoring Arden.

Dr. Leon V. Anderson, a Negro physician who practices in

Wilmington, has two youngsters in the Arden elementary school, as well as four in the Claymont high school.

"This has changed the future of my children," he says of the new integration policies. "That stigma is off of them. This business of being shunted here and there because of your color is gone.

"That does something to your dignity. It gets under your skin.

"Now they are no different—just children. And they are doing better work.

"The work is harder at Claymont than at Howard (the Negro high school in Wilmington that his children formerly attended). Merle, my 16-year-old, graduates in June. She will have spent two years at Claymont. It has been tough on her because she had to work so hard to offset poor schooling in earlier years.

"Think what a difference it makes to be in a class of 15 to 20 pupils at Claymont when you've been used to classes with as many as 70 pupils at Howard."

I got the impression, from a visit to the office of Superintendent Hobart M. Corning here, that Washington school administrators feel the day is not far off when Negro parents in the district will get an opportunity to find out if integration is all Anderson says it is.

Officially, the school board says its policy is "wait and see." But it is significant that, while waiting, it has asked organizations and citizens to present their ideas on how to go about integrating the schools should the court order it.

This involves not only deciding where 58,000 Negro and 44,878 white pupils will go, but also whether 1,822 Negroes and 4,723 whites will continue to teach—and where.

In his brief to the high court, Brownell suggested that the District of Columbia, Kansas and Delaware should find the changeover to non-segregation "a relatively simple matter, requiring perhaps only a few months to accomplish."

Here, he said, "there can plainly be no valid justification for delay in ending exclusion of colored children from schools which they would otherwise be entitled to attend."

In other areas, Brownell said, a longer period of time may be needed.

Photographer Bonham Cross and I would leave Washington for some of the other areas—Virginia and South Carolina —with the knowledge that the United States government—as "friend of the court"—had leveled a mighty, bipartisan voice against racial custom and tradition in a great social debate that involves—the government believes—the foundations of the free world.

Negroes Who Support End of Segregation Fear Reprisals
Summerton, S.C.

Along the highway and the clay roads moved a procession the likes of which few northern readers ever have seen.

Traveling by white mule, horse-drawn surrey, wagon and team, Negroes moved by the hundreds into this little town of about 1,500 population. This Saturday, like every Saturday, they would do a week's shopping, visit a few relatives and exchange a bit of gossip. A few would have a week-end bit to drink.

This scene of country life, reminiscent of a way of life which went out with Henry Ford's tin horse, was a picture of outward calm. But it belied the smoldering hostility, the racial tension, that grips this country.

Just how deep the bitterness goes I learned upon visiting the Rev. E. E. Richberg, pastor of Liberty Hill African Methodist Episcopal (AME) church, a modern brick structure with 1,156 members that looked as much out of place in this area as would the Empire State building in the South St. Paul stockyards.

Mr. Richberg himself seemed out of place. He was a calm, obviously well-educated man in a county where others of his race knew of little but poverty, ignorance and disease.

"I'm sure you'll be told the Negro here doesn't want integration," Mr. Richberg said as I sat in his study. "Many of the Negro farm tenants and sharecroppers are afraid of reprisals, so they don't go around proclaiming that they want integration."

Have they any reason to fear reprisals? I asked.

The minister explained the background to the dispute before answering.

He told how facilities for Negro pupils were grossly inferior, a fact that South Carolina officials admitted in court. At

Scott's Branch school in Summerton, he continued, there was one teacher more than there were classrooms.

"This meant that any period of the day there was one teacher and a group of students walking outdoors, or through the building, waiting their turn to get into a classroom," said Mr. Richberg.

There was no chapel or place to study.

"Negro parents became disgusted and called a mass meeting at St. Marks AME church. From there, a meeting was held in the home of Harry Briggs and 67 parents signed a petition asking for equal facilities.

"As a result, eight Negro teachers lost their jobs.

"Farmer Lee Richardson, a petition signer, owed some money to David McClary, white livestock, seed and fertilizer dealer. McClary, nephew of the school superintendent, immediately ordered Richardson to pay up.

"Richardson could not pay at this time of the year, when no such demand ever had been made, and McClary was about to take Richardson's two mules. Negroes in the community took up a collection and paid McClary.

"James Brown, a truck driver–salesman for Esso-Standard Oil Co. here, was fired. H. B. Sprott, the proprietor, came to my church to fill the oil tanks and I asked why Brown was fired. He told me he hated to do it because Brown had been a faithful employe for 10 years, never coming in a penny short, but that the white people made him fire Brown.

"He said the whites told him they were 'not going to feed him to fight white folks.'

"Brown picked up his family and moved to Detroit.

"In the meantime, Negro cooks and maids—members of my church—would bring me word Sundays that the white folks said I'd 'better watch what you say. You're up there preaching NAACP instead of the gospel.'

"My son applied for a teaching job in the county. He never got a reply."

Mr. Richberg then explained that the Rev. J. A. DeLaine, Negro pastor of Antioch AME church, was the real leader of the anti-segregation movement.

"He was fired as principal-teacher of Silver school. Later his two sisters, Mrs. Carrie D. Martin and Mrs. Rowena Oliver, were fired from teaching jobs at Liberty Hill school right here by my church."

Records also show that Mr. DeLaine was sued for slander by S. I. Benson, former principal of the Negro school who was accused of "financial irregularities" by members of the 1949 graduating class and their parents.

Benson left the school under peculiar circumstances when the board of education apparently ruled that the parents' grievances were justified. However, when Mr. DeLaine led Negro parents into court he was sued for slander by Benson and the witnesses against him were the white school officials who also were the defendants in the school equalization case.

After two years of litigation, the Rev. DeLaine was ordered to pay Benson $2,700.

Then his wife and niece were fired from teaching jobs.

The bishop moved Mr. DeLaine to Lake City, S.C., "to get him out of the line of fire," so the minister rented his Summerton home to Fleming funeral home.

In October 1951 Mr. DeLaine's home, an adjoining building, a garage and his furniture were burned mysteriously about 3 a.m. Insurance money was taken by the courts to settle the slander judgment against the preacher.

I wanted the story of some Summerton whites. If all this had taken place because 67 Negro parents signed petitions demanding equal facilities, what would happen if the court ruled out segregation?

Photographer Bonham Cross and I walked into the office of McClary and saw a half dozen Negroes waiting to transact business. Leaning against the building outside was his Negro helper.

How do you feel about this suit to outlaw racial segregation in the public schools? I asked the young merchant.

"I think the Nigras were involved out of ignorance. I see a lot of 'em and they tell me they didn't know what they was signing."

Well, let's suppose the court outlaws segregation? Then what?

The young man twisted uneasily in his seat. The look of

distrust with which he had greeted us had not disappeared completely. Then he said:

"This fight on segregation is wrong, and it's gonna work to the detriment of these Nigras. We got a good bunch of Nigras here, and we got along fine till these outside influences came in here and started propagandizing. Segregation is our way of life. Both races want it. And if that court rules we got to mix 'em, we're gonna make every effort to avoid it."

You say Negroes want it. I understand that since 1914 Negroes in this state, with perhaps the lowest per capita income in the nation, have given more than $45,000 to finance this fight on segregation. Why have these people given their nickels and dimes?

"Propaganda. Propaganda from the pulpit. Propaganda from a few local Negroes who think this thing can be done pretty fast. But we don't think it can. I tell you it's gonna work to the detriment of these Nigras."

I hear that it already has worked to the detriment of some, I said. Is it true that you foreclosed a mortgage on two mules owned by a man named Richardson?

McClary straightened up in his seat and stared at me. Then he leaned back and began to tap the desk with a pencil.

"When you're in business you give a lot of credit. You have to collect sometime. That foreclosure had nothing to do with that petition he signed."

McClary quickly shifted the conversation, asserting that "the Negro schools around here are better than the white schools. Why down in Winnsboro, the whites done sued for equal facilities." He chuckled.

"Why, these Nigras have got what's due 'em. We white folks pay about 95 per cent of the taxes."

I believe that Negroes now agree that schools in this county are equal so that the issue before the court will be clearly one of whether segregation itself is constitutional, I said. I also understand that the schools built here for Negroes were financed by a statewide 3 per cent sales tax. Negroes probably pay their share of that, don't they?

"Well, I suppose now it is financed by a sales tax. But in other things we pay about 95 per cent of the taxes."

Is that because you make most of the money? I asked.

"No," he said almost indignantly, "there are about the same number of Nigras here as in New York city up there in Harlem. Nigras are better off here than there."

Will bureau of census per capita income figures back that up? I asked.

"Well, if not, it's only because South Carolina is a poor state," he said.

If Negroes are making money here why aren't they paying taxes? I asked.

"Bureau of internal revenue people told me they can't check up on these Nigras."

The bureau got any Negro agents working in this area (where the great majority of inhabitants are Negroes)? I asked.

"No," he said. "You got to remember this," he said, again shifting the subject, "Nigras outnumber us whites about eight to one around here. That's why we're for segregation."

If Negroes are in such majority, I asked, why are no Negroes ever elected to political office?

"Oh, we got 'em outnumbered about two to one here in Summerton. Most of the Nigras are tenant farmers."

What about elections on the county level?

"Most of the Nigras don't think about voting, I guess."

(In South Carolina, the Negro was without a vote until the 1948 ruling by now-retired Federal Judge J. Waties Waring of Charleston that the "white primary" was illegal. Even today, various registration devices and even intimidation are used to keep the Negro from voting in rural areas where Negroes outnumber whites.)

McClary refused to let Cross take his picture. As we left he restated his remark that "a good bunch of Nigras" live here and that "we never had any trouble till the NAACP came along."

Outside the door I stopped to talk to McClary's Negro helper, to ask his views on segregation. He said he didn't even know there was a case coming up on the subject.

Next door we saw H. C. Carrigan, who is serving his 12th term as mayor. This was his story:

"We people down here in the deep south don't have as big a problem as the papers say we have. The colored people have made wonderful progress. Their schools are superior to ours.

"The colored people want their own churches, schools and teachers. That's what they really want. This NAACP has been very active down here. And the colored churches have been kicking up a fuss, too.

"But Negroes want segregation. I've got several farms and they all have Negroes on them. I share-crop with them and they are all as happy as can be. You couldn't run them off."

I've heard that some Negroes lost their jobs for signing that petition leading to the court suit, I said. Is that true?

"I wouldn't be surprised," said the mayor.

"But we have no ax to grind," said Mayor Carrigan. "Now I had a colored boy in here for drunk driving. That boy's got a good old daddy. Been knowing him all my life. Daddy's a good old boy. I could have fined that boy $100 and loss of license for six months. I gave him the minimum fine of $55. We treat our Negroes fine. After all, 75 per cent of my business is with colored people."

It was midafternoon when Cross and I walked out. Now the streets were almost filled with Negroes—come to spend their dollars with the McClarys, Carrigans and Sprotts.

Leaning against Carrigan's building was John Myers, a Negro who said he farmed.

"How do you stand on this school segregation issue?" I asked.

"I believe I'd rather have the schools the way they is. I hates to say it, but Negroes is doing all right now, far as I can see."

Farther down the street we stopped farmer G. H. Henry, whose color and high cheek bone indicated some Indian ancestry, a characteristic of many Negroes we had seen here. Henry said he was "in the thick of the fight" to end segregation.

I told him I had just talked to a farmer at Carrigan's office who said he preferred segregation.

Henry pushed his face close to mine and barked:

"We got too damn many Negroes around here who ain't nothing but a white man's tool. They ought to've been dead before they were born then they wouldn't be around to raise so many children to grow up ignorant because their parents are cowards enough to say they don't want their children to have their just dues."

We walked into a small grocery store where the owner, Mrs. Rebecca Brown said Negroes live for the day that the court will rule out segregation.

The mayor just told me that you Negroes tell him you didn't mean to sign that petition, that you got tricked into this suit by the NAACP, I said to her.

"He's a liar and the truth ain't in him," exclaimed the grandmotherish Negro storekeeper. She started to take off her apron as she added, "And let's go back up there. I'll tell him to his face."

No. No need for that, I said to her.

"I was just in his no good office the other day," she argued on. "He doubled my taxes. Doubled 'em from $4 to $8. I can't figure out what for. Negroes have got no streets. I can't get city water. You can't get a darned thing here but a hard time. And you ask me if Negroes want to win this suit."

Well the mayor told me that all his Negro sharecroppers are so happy you couldn't run them off.

"Let me explain, mister: there are Negroes and then there are Uncle Toms and belly draggers. Nobody fit to bear the name Negro is for segregation. What Negro on a white man's place is satisfied when he's half naked as a jaybird? No use of 'em telling that lie."

Into the store walked a short, dark man who was introduced as the Rev. J. W. Seals.

I understand it was in your church that Negroes held the meeting which led to this case before the supreme court, I said.

"Yes," he said. "Almost immediately, H. B. Betchman, the school superintendent, called me to his office and said that if Negroes didn't stop meeting in my church my job as a teacher at Scott's Branch school was gone.

"I told him that as far as I was concerned he could have my register (list and records of pupils) then. He refused to take it.

"He called me in the next time and asked, 'Are you ready to play ball.' And I said, 'Mr. Betchman, if what I've been playing isn't ball I don't know the game.' He asked for my register."

"Mister, you don't know how tough things got," broke in Mrs. Brown. "Why I'm afraid to take these people's medicine around here. I go over to Utahville and see me a doctor from New York."

"Oh, but we ain't quivering," said Mr. Seals, 54, who was born within six miles of the church he pastors. "They got my teaching job and they fired my wife, too, but we ain't quivering. Take the mayor—he's nothing but a meat man. If he was a man of iron we might be quivering."

"He's right," broke in Mrs. Brown. "I think we've got the dog tied by the neck, as the old saying goes. They're quivering."

"We ain't asking for anything that belongs to these white folks," continued Mr. Seals. "I just mean to get for that little black boy of mine everything that any other South Carolina boy gets. I don't care if he's as white as the drippings of snow.

"We can't stop now just because they've given us a few buildings and school buses."

From over by the pop cooler there came a new voice—that of McCurnel Durant, another farmer:

"He speaks the gospel. I'm not satisfied at all. Even now they don't have enough buses. It hurts my heart to see school let out and the children run like chickens and pigs because the first ones on the buses get the seats."

"Just the other day I counted 82 pupils coming out of a 60-capacity bus," said the Reverend Mr. Seals.

So these were the people behind the starched and polished briefs before the supreme court.

So the "fighting words" and the reports of reprisals were the conditions underlying the court's request that lawyers argue today about whether the court can order a gradual change from segregation to integration in areas such as this.

So this was why many publications which oppose segregation have indicated that they look with fear toward the court's decision. Said Christian Century magazine:

"We regard segregation as both undemocratic and unchristian. We do not believe that equality of education can be provided in segregated schools.

"Nevertheless, we wish this issue had been brought to a head in some other state than South Carolina, where it had probably the least chance—unless in Governor Talmadge's Georgia—of being heard on its merits.

"If the final decision in the case should arouse such resistance in South Carolina and among intransigents elsewhere in the south that it drove southern liberals to take cover on all matter of racial justice, the evolutionary processes which have brought widespread acceptance of the revolutionary social changes resulting from recent supreme court decisions could be tragically slowed up or driven into retreat."

As we walked toward our automobile, ready to leave the county, a hand tapped me on the arm. It was farmer Henry, back to find out what I thought of the courage of Negroes in his county.

I told him that the fighting words on both sides had aroused fear in the court, and among publications such as Christian Century.

"That's kinda strange to me," the farmer said. "Here we been sending American boys across the seas to fight and die for principles that wasn't always easy to understand. But here we got a clear cut American principle of democracy. Don't tell me they gonna let a little talk of riots and bloodshed make 'em weak-kneed and mealy-mouthed.

"You just let 'em know that we Negroes down here are like Gideon's army. A few went down like dogs and lapped the water. The rest were unfit to fight." *See the seventh chapter of Judges, verses 1–7.*

Minneapolis Tribune, November 29–December 8, 1953

Supreme Court, 9–0, Bans Segregation in Schools

by Robert J. Donovan

WASHINGTON, May 17—In a historic decision portending vast social changes throughout the South and in the District of Columbia the United States Supreme Court held unanimously today that racial segregation in public schools is unconstitutional.

The decision read by Chief Justice Earl Warren to a tense courtroom declared that segregation was unlawful under the provision of the Fourteenth Amendment to the Constitution assuring "equal protection of the laws" to all citizens.

The court, however, did not compel an immediate upheaval. Thousands of schools are affected in Washington and in seventeen states where segregation is required, and in four states where the practice is permitted but not required. The court's decision allows for a delay of many months—which may turn out to be a year or more—before issuing decrees enforcing its ruling.

The delay, deliberately decided upon to give states a chance to plan the enormously complex readjustment affecting millions of negro and white school children and their teachers, will be occasioned by the hearing of certain arguments by the court in the fall term. Essentially, the arguments will be on how and when the end of segregation is to be decreed.

Today's decision, which thrilled America's Negro population and promises to give the entire world a new perspective of American democracy, was the most momentous the court has made since the early years of the New Deal. It is regarded as the most important Supreme Court ruling on racial relations since the court held in 1857 that Dred Scott, a Negro slave, was not a citizen. Some of the comment compared the decision to the Emancipation Proclamation.

What the decision means is that it is unconstitutional for

the states and the District of Columbia to maintain some public schools solely for Negro and some solely for white children. The ruling foreshadows the integration of white and Negro children in the same schools in communities which have known nothing but segregation in their entire histories.

The ruling was bitterly received by many Southerners, and some Southern leaders expressed a conviction that the states could find ways to circumvent it. Some Southern states, notably South Carolina and Georgia, had previously threatened, in the event the court held as it did today, to abolish their public school systems. Whether these threats will be carried out remained to be seen.

Some Southerners in Congress said flatly that segregation would continue in the schools of the South regardless of the Supreme Court.

The Supreme Court summarily tossed into the discard the old ruling that segregation was lawful when the states provided separate but equal educational facilities for Negro children.

Speaking for the court, Chief Justice Warren said:

"We conclude that in the field of public education the doctrine of 'separate but equal' has no place. Separate educational facilities are inherently unequal."

The court found that to separate Negro children from white children of similar age and qualifications solely because of their race "generates a feeling of inferiority as to their status in the community that may affect their hearts and minds in a way unlikely ever to be undone."

The Chief Justice, who began reading at 12:52 p.m., said:

"Today education is perhaps the most important function of state and local governments. . . . It is required in the performance of our most basic public responsibilities, even service in the armed forces. It is the very foundation of good citizenship.

"Today it is a principal instrument in awakening the child to cultural values, in preparing him for later professional training and in helping him to adjust normally to his environment. In these days it is doubtful that any child may reasonably be expected to succeed in life if he is denied the opportunity of an education. Such an opportunity, where the state has undertaken to provide it, is a right which must be made available to all on equal terms.

"We come then to the question presented: does segregation of children in public schools solely on the basis of race, even though the physical facilities and other 'tangible' factors may be equal, deprive the children of the minority group of equal educational opportunities? We believe that it does."

In addition to the national capital, these states are affected by the decision: Alabama, Arkansas, Delaware, Florida, Georgia, Kentucky, Louisiana, Maryland, Mississippi, Missouri, North Carolina, Oklahoma, South Carolina, Tennessee, Texas, Virginia and West Virginia.

In these states and in the District of Columbia there are an estimated 9,000,000 white children and 2,260,000 Negro children in public schools.

Four states, not in the South, leave it to local school authorities whether they wish to segregate. They are Arizona, Kansas, New Mexico and Wyoming. Eleven states have no legal provision regarding segregation, and sixteen have specific laws prohibiting it.

In Washington Dr. Hobart M. Corning, Superintendent of Schools, announced that a study of school integration has been in progress, and added: "Now that it is known that the schools will be integrated, the superintendent will continue to do everything possible to prepare the school system for the changes which will now take place."

Washington has 57,716 Negro children in seventy-nine schools staffed with Negro teachers and 43,100 white children in eighty-one schools.

Another promise of compliance "in every particular" came from Attorney General Harold R. Fatzer of Kansas, who said in Topeka he was sure all school administrations in the state would abolish segregation.

Gov. Allan Shivers, of Texas, said his state would comply with the decision.

In Louisiana State Rep. Gilbert Faulk said he thought the Legislature should act immediately to "counteract" the decision, which he called a "blow struck at the vitals of the South."

Gov. James F. Byrnes of South Carolina said he was "shocked" that the Supreme Court "had reversed itself." Gov.

Byrnes had threatened months ago that if the court decision made segregation impossible, South Carolina would abolish the public school system.

In Atlanta Gov. Herman Talmadge of Georgia said the decision "has reduced our Constitution to a mere scrap of paper." He urged "all Georgians to remain calm and resist any attempts to arouse fear or hysteria."

In Georgia, where the Legislature has approved standby laws to abolish the public schools in the event of the decision reached today, State Superintendent of Schools M. D. Collins said he was "not certain" the court's decision applied to Georgia.

Some saw in this statement a clew to the attitude which may be taken by some Southern states as a device for delaying the end of segregation by forcing separate court tests in each case.

Only five cases were before the court today, originating in the District of Columbia, Kansas, South Carolina, Virginia and Delaware. The District of Columbia case differed from the others technically since it concerned the relationship of the Federal Government to its citizens.

The court held that in view of its decision that the Constitution prohibits segregation in the states, "it would be unthinkable that the same Constitution would impose a lesser duty on the Federal government."

In Congress the reaction of many Southerners was sharply hostile to the decision, while members from other sections lauded it.

Sen. Richard B. Russell, D., Ga., called the decision "a clear invasion of the prerogatives of the legislative branch of our government."

"It demonstrates," he said, "that the Supreme Court is becoming a political arm of the executive branch of the government. . . . Ways must be found to check the tendency of the court to disregard the Constitution and decide cases solely on the basis of the personal predilections of some of its members as to political, economic and social questions."

Of the nine court members, Justice Hugo L. Black is from Alabama, Justice Tom C. Clark is from Texas and Justice Stanley F. Reed is from Kentucky.

Rep. John Bell Williams, D., Miss., said the outlawing of segregation will "reverse the gears of orderly process and set the cause of the Negro in the South back 100 years."

Rep. Jamie L. Whitten, D., Mo., predicted that white children in the South would now be sent to private schools causing a "lessening interest" in public schools attended by Negro children. He said, "the Negroes will be the loser."

Sen. Russell B. Long, D., La., warned that the decision "may result in bitter strife and hard feelings which many of us have fought for years to prevent." Sen. Burnet R. Maybank, D., S.C., commented: "In my judgment it was a shameful political rather than judicial decision."

Sen. Harry F. Byrd, D., Va., said that the decision "is the most serious blow that has yet been struck against the rights of the states in a matter vitally affecting their authority and welfare" and "will create problems such as have never confronted us before."

Instead of improving the education of children, Sen. Byrd said, the decision "will have the opposite effect in many areas of the country. . . . In Virginia we are facing now a crisis of the first magnitude."

Rep. Henderson Lanham, D., Ga., said: "I'm sure that the Southern states will so adjust their school system that the races will not be mixed in the schools. I don't anticipate any uprising."

Sen. John J. Sparkman, D., Ala., said there would undoubtedly continue "to be many, many places where segregation by choice has taken place and will continue to take place."

Sen. James O. Eastland, D., Miss., said, "The South will not abide by or obey this legislative decision by a political court. . . . Education cannot thrive in a climate such as would result from the mixture of the races in the public schools."

Said Rep. Thomas G. Abernethy, D., Miss.: "The white and Negro children of my state are not going to school together."

The decision was praised by Northern legislators, including Sen. Herbert H. Lehman, D.-Lib., N.Y., who called the decision "news which all free men throughout the world must hail with joy." He said: "The court has spoken with authority and finality in outlawing the evil and degrading practice of segregation in our schools. The court has found the meaning of the Constitution to be identical with the meaning of moral law."

Rep. Alvin E. O'Konski, R., Wis., said: "The highest court in the land should be complimented for handing down its decision. It is unjust and unfair to segregate Negroes from whites."

Rep. William L. Dawson, D., Ill., a Negro, hailed the decision as "one of the greatest, finest things that has happened since the Declaration of Independence to make a united America and to raise the status of America as a leader in the eyes of all the world."

The National Association for the Advancement of Colored People plans a meeting of the presidents of its state conference later this week—probably Saturday—in Atlanta to study the meaning of the decision.

The decision carries forward by a long step the continuing process going on in recent years of breaking down the barriers of segregation in public transportation, the armed services, theaters, restaurants, hotels and schools. In increasing numbers Negroes have been admitted to colleges and graduate schools in the South.

Thurgood Marshall, special counsel for the N.A.A.C.P., who argued the case against segregation before the court, called the ruling "the most significant decision to date in the field of civil rights." He said he was not worried that Southern states would flout it.

"I don't believe," he said, "that legislatures will buck the Supreme Court or any other government agency. I think Govs. Byrnes and Talmadge are speaking for themselves. The people in the South will follow the law. They are as law-abiding as anybody else."

In general opponents of integration in states such as South Carolina and Georgia advocate that the states turn the public schools over to private interests on the theory that Negroes could then be excluded without violation of the Supreme Court ruling.

The Americans for Democratic Action issued a statement tonight urging Washington and the seventeen states with segregation to abolish it immediately without waiting for argument next fall on the issuance of decrees.

New York *Herald-Tribune*, May 13, 1954

Charge Two with Lynch Death of 14-Year-Old

by Marty Richardson

JACKSON, Miss.—In what is perhaps the shortest time on record in this state in a case where the victim was a Negro, two white men were indicted Tuesday for the lynch-slaying of 14-year-old Emmett Louis Till last Sunday. Emmett's naked body, its head battered and with a bullet hole through, had been weighted with a cotton gin pulley and thrown in the Tallahatchie River.

The men, Roy Bryant, 24, and J. W. Milam, 35, pleaded innocent when arraigned in Sumner, where the crime took place. They were indicted for both kidnapping and murder, and face ten years maximum sentence on the kidnapping and life in the killing.

It was announced that a date for trial will be set this Thursday, and a judge has stated that the trial "will be held during this session of court".

The unprecedentedly swift indictments followed a wave of national outrage which reached a climax Sunday when funeral services were held for the boy in Chicago, his home. He had been in Mississippi visiting relatives.

A number of dramatic anti-climaxes preceded the appearance of the men in court. Feeling had grown so high in Mississippi that they had been moved from the LaFlore County jail to a stronger one at Greenwood in Tallahatchie County. 'Lynch threats' against them had been reported.

National Guardsmen armed with rifles patrolled the space around the jail at one time, whether to prevent a lynching or a possible rescue of the men not having been known.

Another development was a claim by Sheriff H. C. Strider shortly after the arrest of the men that the lynching appeared to him to be 'a frame-up by the NAACP', presumably to 'embarrass' Mississippi.

No other lynching in recent years had aroused the indignation that this crime against a handicapped, 14-year-old boy had. A nationwide check by the CALL & POST Sunday on a half-dozen nationally-famous radio church leaders showed five of them preaching on the lynching, three of them demanding in no uncertain terms that "Something must be done in Mississippi now".

This was the theme expressed at the funeral services in Chicago Sunday by the thousands who viewed the body, dozens of them top Chicago and Illinois leaders and political figures.

Burial had been scheduled for the day before, but the 34-year-old mother of the boy, Mrs. Mamie Bradley, had said "Let the funeral wait so that more people may see my boy".

Young Till was killed after the wife of Roy Bryant had claimed that he 'got fresh' while she was shopping at a small store in Money, Miss. This story of the cause of the lynching was changed when it was learned that the boy had an impediment in his speech and spoke only with difficulty.

Then it was claimed that he 'whistled at her', a story which also broke down when several reputable witnesses brought out that the impediment in speech made the child whistle in pronouncing a number of words.

Much of the outrage expressed in Chicago, and in thousands of letters, wires and telephone messages to President Eisenhower, Attorney-General Herbert Brownell and congressmen from all states, came over the fact that the murder of the boy was the third one since Mississippi first began showing a savage resentment over the Supreme Court ruling on segregated schools and Negroes began a stepped-up voting program.

The one thing which has always handicapped investigations of lynchings in Southern states, the lack of witnesses, did not appear to be likely to come up in the Till boy's lynching.

A number of eye-witnesses, both to the alleged 'incident' in the store and the kidnapping of the boy by the two men later (while the pretty, 21-year-old Mrs. Bryant waited outside in a car) came forward readily and gave their stories.

In the face of the overwhelming evidence against the lynchers, and their own admission that they had kidnapped the boy 'but had turned him loose unharmed', Gov. Hugh White of Mississippi issued a statement in which he said that "Mississippi does not condone such conduct", and that he believed "The courts will do their duty".

Atty. William Henry Huff of the NAACP legal staff did not accept the governor's promise as everything needed in the case. "Unless these men are given death in the gas chamber", he said, "I am going to file a $100,000 damage suit against them in the Mississippi U.S. District Court.

"Even if they are given prison sentences I am going to file the suit", he added.

In Chicago, Emmett's mother, Mrs. Mamie Bradley, said, "I can not think. I just can't think. He didn't do anything to deserve that. Somebody is going to pay for this. The entire State of Mississippi is going to pay for this".

She sobbingly continued: "I can not work. I have nothing left to work for. My whole life is ruined.

"Emmett was a good boy", said Mrs. Bradley. "I know he didn't do anything wrong.

"Emmett was mischievous, but he was not a bad boy", she said. "He's never been in any trouble. He's been my life saver —did the washing, ironing and housework so I could work. He has stood by me like a man. How could anyone do this terrible thing to him?"

Emmett was an eighth grader at the McCosh school. He was born in Chicago and had been in Mississippi only once before on a visit five years ago. His grandfather, Henry Spearman, has been a Chicago resident thirty years and is a plant guard for the Inland Steel Container.

Cleveland Call and Post, September 10, 1955

He Went All the Way

by Murray Kempton

MOSE WRIGHT, making a formation no white man in his county really believed he would dare to make, stood on his tip-toes to the full limit of his sixty-four years and his five feet three inches yesterday, pointed his black, workworn finger straight at the huge and stormy head of J. W. Milam and swore that this was the man who dragged fourteen-year-old Emmett Louis Till out of his cottonfield cabin the night the boy was murdered.

"There he is," said Mose Wright. He was a black pigmy standing up to a white ox. J. W. Milam leaned forward, crooking a cigaret in a hand that seemed as large as Mose Wright's whole chest, and his eyes were coals of hatred.

Mose Wright took all their blast straight in his face, and then, for good measure, turned and pointed that still unshaking finger at Roy Bryant, the man he says joined Milam on the night-ride to seize young Till for the crime of whistling suggestively at Bryant's wife in a store three miles away and three nights before.

"And there's Mr. Bryant," said Mose Wright and sat down hard against the chair-back with a lurch which told better than anything else the cost in strength to him of the thing he had done. He was a field Negro who had dared try to send two white men to the gas chamber for murdering a Negro.

He sat in a court where District Attorney Gerald Chatham, who is on his side, steadily addressed him as Uncle Mose and conversed with him in a kind of pidgin cotton-picker's dialect, saying "axed" for "asked" as Mose Wright did and talking about the "undertaker man."

Once Chatham called him "Old Man Mose," but this was the kindly, contemptuous tolerance of the genteel; after twenty-one minutes of this, Mose Wright was turned over to Defense Counsel Sidney Carlton and now the manner was that of an overseer with a field hand.

214

Sidney Carlton roared at Mose Wright as though he were the defendant, and every time Carlton raised his voice like the lash of a whip, J. W. Milam would permit himself a cold smile.

And then Mose Wright did the bravest thing a Delta Negro can do; he stopped saying "sir." Every time Carlton came back to the attack, Mose Wright pushed himself back against his chair and said "That's right" and the absence of the "sir" was almost like a spit in the eye.

When he had come to the end of the hardest half hour in the hardest life possible for a human being in these United States, Mose Wright's story was shaken; yet he still clutched its foundations. Against Carlton's voice and Milam's eyes and the incredulity of an all-white jury, he sat alone and refused to bow.

If it had not been for him, we would not have had this trial. It will be a miracle if he wins his case; yet it is a kind of miracle that, all on account of Mose Wright, the State of Mississippi is earnestly striving here in this courtroom to convict two white men for murdering a Negro boy so obscure that they do not appear to have even known his name.

He testified yesterday that, as Milam left his house with Emmett Till on the night of August 28, he asked Mose Wright whether he knew anyone in the raiding party. "No, sir, I said I don't know nobody."

Then Milam asked him how old he was, and Mose Wright said sixty-four and Milam said, "If you knew any of us, you won't live to be sixty-five."

And, after the darkened car drove off, with his great-nephew, Mose Wright drove his hysterical wife over to Sumner and put her on the train to Chicago, from which she has written him every day since to cut and run and get out of town. The next day, all by himself, Mose Wright drove into nearby Greenwood and told his story in the sheriff's office.

It was a pathetic errand; it seems a sort of marvel that anything was done at all. Sheriff George Smith drove out to Money around 2 P.M. that afternoon and found Roy Bryant sleeping behind his store. They were good friends and they talked as friends about this little boy whose name Smith himself had not bothered to find out.

Smith reported that Roy had said that he had gone down

the road and taken the little boy out of "Preacher's" cabin, and brought him back to the store and, when his wife said it wasn't the right boy, told him to go home.

Sheriff Smith didn't even take Bryant's statement down. When he testified to it yesterday, the defense interposed the straight-faced objection that this was after all the conversation of two friends and that the state shouldn't embarrass the sheriff by making him repeat it in court. Yet, just the same, Sheriff Smith arrested Roy Bryant for kidnaping that night.

When the body supposed to be Emmett Till's was found in the river, a deputy sheriff drove Mose Wright up to identify it. There was no inquest. Night before last, the prosecution fished up a picture of the body which had been in the Greenwood police files since the night it was brought in, but there was no sign the sheriff knew anything about it, and its discovery was announced as a coup for the state. But, with that apathy and incompetence, Mose Wright almost alone has brought the kidnapers of his nephew to trial.

The country in which he toiled and which he is now resigned to leaving will never be the same for what he has done. Today the state will put on the stand three other field Negroes to tell how they saw Milam and Bryant near the murder scene. They came in scared; one disappeared while the sheriff's deputies were looking for him. They, like Mose Wright, are reluctant heroes; unlike him, they have to be dragged to the test.

They will be belted and flayed as he was yesterday, but they will walk out with the memory of having been human beings for just a little while. Whatever the result, there is a kind of majesty in the spectacle of the State of Mississippi honestly trying to convict two white men on the word of four Negroes.

And we owe that sight to Mose Wright, who was condemned to bow all his life, and had enough left to raise his head and look the enemy in those terrible eyes when he was sixty-four.

from *America Comes of Middle Age:
Columns 1950–1962* (1963)

Justice in Sumner

by Dan Wakefield

Sumner, Mississippi

THE CROWDS are gone and this Delta town is back to its silent, solid life that is based on cotton and the proposition that a whole race of men was created to pick it. Citizens who drink from the "Whites Only" fountain in the courthouse breathe much easier now that the two fair-skinned half brothers, aged twenty-four and thirty-six, have been acquitted of the murder of a fourteen-year-old Negro boy. The streets are quiet, Chicago is once more a mythical name, and everyone here "knows his place."

When the people first heard that there was national, even worldwide, publicity coming to Sumner and the murder trial, they wondered why the incident had caused such a stir. At the lunch recess on the first day of the trial a county health-office worker who had stopped by to watch the excitement asked a visiting reporter where he was from, and shook his head when the answer was New York City.

"New York, Chicago, everywhere," he said. "I never heard of making such a mountain of a molehill."

The feeling that it all was a plot against the South was the most accepted explanation, and when Roy Bryant and J. W. Milam ambled into court September 19 they were armed not only with their wives, baby boys, and cigars, but the challenge of Delta whites to the interference of the outside world. The issue for the local public was not that a visiting Negro boy named Emmett Louis Till had been dragged from his bed and identified later as a body that was pulled from the Tallahatchie River with a seventy-pound cotton-gin fan tied around its neck with barbed wire—that issue was lost when people learned that the world was clamoring to have something done about it. The question of "nigger-killing" was coupled with the threat to the racial traditions of the South, and store-keepers set out jars on their counters for contributions to aid the defense of the accused murderers.

Donations to the fund disqualified several prospective jurors, as prosecutors Gerald Chatham, district attorney, and Robert B. Smith, special assistant attorney general appointed to the case, probed carefully at every candidate for a day and a half before accepting the jury. Judge Curtis Swango, a tall, quietly commanding man, combined order with a maximum of freedom in the court, and when he had Cokes brought in for the jury it seemed as appropriate a courtroom procedure as pounding the gavel.

While the jury selections went on inside, the crowds outside the building grew—and were automatically segregated. Aging, shaggy-cheeked Anglo-Saxons with crumpled straw hats lined a long wooden bench. Negroes gathered across the way at the base of the Confederate statue inscribed to "the cause that never failed." The Negro numbers increased, but not with the Negroes of Sumner. A red-necked deputy whose pearl-handled pistol showed beneath the tail of his sport shirt explained that the "dressed-up" Negroes were strangers. "Ninety-five percent of them's not ours," he said. "Ours is out picking cotton and tending to their own business."

Moses Wright, a Negro locally known as a good man who tends to his business, was the state's first witness. He pressed his back against the witness chair and spoke out loud and clear as he told about the night two white men came to his house and asked for "the boy from Chicago—the one that did the talking at Money"; and how the big, balding man came in with a pistol and a flashlight and left with Emmett Till. Mose fumbled several times under cross-examination but he never lost his straightforward attitude or lowered his head. He still of course was "old man Mose" and "Uncle Mose" to both defense and prosecution, but none of that detracted from the dignity of how he told his story.

The rest of the week he was seen around the courthouse lawn with his pink-banded hat tilted back on his head, his blue pants pulled up high on a clean white shirt by yellow-and-brown suspenders. He walked through the Negro section of the lawn with his hands in his pockets and his chin held up with the air of a man who has done what there was to do and could never be touched by doubt that he should have done anything less than that.

When Mose Wright's niece, Mrs. Mamie Bradley, took the stand it was obvious as soon as she answered a question that she didn't fit the minstrel-show stereotype that most of Mississippi's white folks cherish. Nevertheless, the lawyers of both sides were careful always to address her as "Mamie," which was probably wise for the favor of the jury, since a Clarksdale, Mississippi, radio station referred to her as "Mrs. Bradley" on a news broadcast and spent the next hour answering calls of protest.

J. J. "Si" Breland, dean of the defense attorneys, questioned her while he remained in his seat, occasionally slicing his hands through the air in the quick, rigid motions he moved with throughout the trial. She answered intelligently, steadily, slightly turning her head to one side as she listened to questions, replying with a slow, distinct emphasis. "Beyond the shadow of a doubt," she said, "that was my boy's body."

At lunchtime recess the crowds around the soft-drink and sandwich concession debated her identification of her son, and many were relieved in the afternoon session when Tallahatchie County Sheriff H. C. Strider squeezed his 270 pounds in the witness chair and said the only thing he could tell about the body that had come from the river was that it was human.

Sheriff Strider, who owns 1,500 acres of cotton land, farms it with thirty-five Negro families, has the grocery store and filling station on it, and operates a cotton-dusting concern with three airplanes, is split in his commitments in a way that might qualify him as the Charles E. Wilson of Tallahatchie County. What's good for his feudal plantation is good for the county, and his dual role as law-enforcement officer and witness for the defense evidently didn't seem contradictory to him. His commitments were clear enough that prosecution lawyers once sent two state policemen to search a county jail for one Leroy "Too-Tight" Collins, a key witness for the prosecution who was missing (and never found).

There were still missing witnesses, dark, whispered rumors of fleeing men who saw the crime committed, when Gerald Chatham tugged the sleeves of his shirt and walked over to the jury Friday morning to make the summation of the case for the prosecution. Both he and Smith, who is a former F.B.I. man, had followed every lead and sent state policemen driving through the countryside in search of the Mississippi witnesses, but only two of the four who were named—Willie Reed and Mandy Brandley—were found. The time had come for Chatham to work with what he had.

In a matter of minutes from the time he started talking, the atmosphere of the court was charged with tension as he raised his arm toward the ceiling and shouted that "the first words offered in testimony here were dripping with the blood of Emmett Till." The green plaster walls of the room had grown darker from the clouds of the rain that was coming outside, as Chatham went on with the tones, the gestures, the conviction of an evangelist, asserting that "the guilty flee where no man pursueth," and retelling the story of the boy's abduction in the dark of night.

J. W. Milam, the bald, strapping man who leaned forward in his seat during most of the sessions with his mouth twisted in the start of a smile, was looking at a newspaper. Roy Bryant lit a cigar. With his eyebrows raised and his head tilted back, he might have been a star college fullback smoking in front of the coach during season and asking with his eyes, "So what?"

When Chatham was finished, C. Sidney Carlton, the able attorney for the defense whose large, fleshy face was usually close to where the cameras were clicking, poured a paper cup of water from the green pitcher on the judge's desk, and opened his summation. He spoke well, as usual, but after Chatham's oratory he was doomed to anticlimax. There had been a brief rain and the sun was out with more heat than ever. Defense Attorney J. W. Kellum, speaking briefly after Carlton before the noon recess, had the odds of discomfort against his chances of stirring the jury, but he did his best with the warning that the jurors' forefathers would turn in their graves at a guilty verdict. And then he asked what was undoubtedly the question of the week. If Roy and J. W. are convicted of murder, he said, "where under the shining sun is the land of the free and the home of the brave?"

The question was a fitting prelude to the harangue of John Whitten, the defense's last speaker. The clean-shaven pale young man in a neatly pressed suit and white shirt that defied perspiration announced his faith that "every last Anglo-Saxon one of you men in this jury has the courage to set these men free."

Mr. Whitten went on to declare he had an answer for the state's most convincing evidence—the ring of Emmett Till that was found on the body discovered in the Tallahatchie River. The body really wasn't Emmett Till, Whitten said, and the ring might possibly have been planted on it by the agents of a sinister group that is trying to destroy the social order of the South and "widen the gap which has appeared between the white and colored people in the United States."

He didn't name any group, but the fondly nurtured local rumor that the whole Till affair was a plot on the part of the N.A.A.C.P. made naming unnecessary.

It took the twelve jurors an hour and seven minutes to return the verdict that would evidently help close the gap between the white and colored races in the land of the free and the home of the brave. Tradition, honor, God, and country were preserved in a package deal with the lives of Roy Bryant and J. W. Milam.

Reporters climbed tables and chairs to get a glimpse of the acquitted defendants, and the newspaper, magazine, and television cameras were aimed at the smiles of their wives and families in a flashing, buzzing finale. Then the agents of the outside world disappeared in a rush to make their deadlines, and the stale, cluttered courtroom was finally empty of everything but mashed-out cigarettes, crushed paper cups, and a few of the canvas spectator chairs that the American Legion had sold across the street for two dollars each.

The trial week won't be forgotten here soon, and glimpses of the "foreign" Negroes who don't till cotton fields but hold positions as lawyers, doctors, and Congressmen have surely left a deep and uncomfortable mark on the whites of the Delta. But at least for the present, life is *good* again. Funds are being raised for separate-and-equal school facilities in Tallahatchie County and on Wednesdays at lunchtime four of the five defense attorneys join with the other Rotarians of Sumner in a club song about the glad day "When men are one."

The Nation, October 1, 1955

Respectable Racism

by Dan Wakefield

Jackson, Mississippi
THEIR SHIRTS aren't red and they don't wear sheets—after all, times have changed, and this is 1955. The Citizens Councils that have grown up in the South since the United States Supreme Court decision on school integration are composed of "respectable" gentlemen and ladies (there is now an auxiliary) who are dedicated to depriving the Negro of his civil rights by means of the latest, most up-to-date methods.

The movement, born in Mississippi and copied in Louisiana, Alabama, Texas, Arkansas, Florida, Georgia, and South Carolina (with similar but differently named organizations in Missouri, Tennessee, North Carolina, and Virginia) is a proud, flag-waving challenge to what one council leader labelled the "socialistic doctrine" passed on May 17, 1954. And it is an answer to the call of United States Senator James O. Eastland of Mississippi, who, shortly after the Supreme Court decision was rendered, declared: "We are about to embark on a great crusade. A crusade to restore Americanism, and return the control of our government to the people. . . . Generations of Southerners yet unborn will cherish our memory because they will realize that the fight we now wage will have preserved for them their untainted racial heritage, their culture, and the institutions of the Anglo-Saxon race. We of the South have seen the tides rise before. We know what it is to fight. We will carry the fight to victory."

In the face of the rising tides, fourteen men met together in Sunflower county, Mississippi, in July, 1954, and formed the first Citizens Council. One of those original crusaders, a thirty-two-year-old, red-headed planter from Indianola, Mississippi, who had fought the good fight as captain of Mississippi State's football team not too many years before, is now executive secretary of the state council. The zeal of this man, Robert D. "Tut" Patterson, has been rewarded with a mushrooming of Mississippi membership to more than 60,000. When recently asked what he thought about Mississippi Governor Hugh White's estimate that integration was 100 years away, Mr. Patterson promptly replied, "I say 6,000 years."

"This isn't just a delaying action," he said. "There won't be any integration in Mississippi. Not now, not 100 years from now, maybe not 6,000 years from now—maybe never."

Attorneys, bankers, planters, mayors, former local chamber of commerce presidents, and assorted school officials are among the civic leaders who have joined to help "Tut" Patterson hold back the flood. Just how they are going about it is rather vague, at least in official council announcements. It was first reported that the councils, although definitely opposed to violence, would keep the land pure by "economic pressure." The idea of "economic pressure" drew many bad press clippings, however, and now "Tut" Patterson says there is no such thing.

"We do not recommend economic pressure," he said. "That's false propaganda from the press. But of course, we don't denounce 'freedom of choice' in business arrangements. If employers fire their help, that's their business." When asked what methods are used in the "crusade" if violence and economic pressure are not council weapons, Mr. Patterson laughed and said, "Would Montgomery Ward tell Sears Roebuck how he operates?"

One tool used by the Jackson, Mississippi, council is a mimeographed "confidential communique" mailed to members. "Confidential Communique No. 14," dated August 22, gave information about a Negro named Arrington High who publishes a newspaper urging integration. The "communique" did not suggest any action, but merely reported the situation. Soon after that, Arrington High was asked to remove his money from a local bank, and windows were smashed in his home.

The councilmen assume no responsibility. They grind out the letters on the mimeograph and hope that hate and fear will do the rest. They talk a great deal about the difference between their organization and the Ku Klux Klan, and yet the difference is slight. The klansmen hid their faces with sheets and paraded their deeds in the open. The councilmen hide many of their deeds, or at least many of the deeds their words inspire, behind memos and mimeographs and parade their faces in the open. But whether the means be a memo or a fiery cross, the end is the same—a climate of distrust and fear that breeds unsolved murders and threats of more. Phone calls threatening death are common to the Mississippi Negro leaders, and one National Association for the Advancement of Colored People official in Jackson said shots have been fired into his house.

It can never, of course, be established just which of the incidents that have occurred since the growth of the councils are results, direct or indirect, of council actions. The white front is so united in many Southern towns that the law and civic leaders are often dedicated first to their racial commitments and second to the duties of office. As the Mississippi Citizens Councils' Annual Report puts it in reviewing the year's accomplishments, "The idea of solid and unified backing of circuit clerks, sheriffs, and local and state officials in the proper discharge of their sworn duties was worked out."

This racial priority was evidenced at Sumner, Mississippi, when the prosecutors in the Emmett Till murder case sent state police to search a county jail for a missing prosecution witness. It was seen by a Southern reporter who went to Belzoni, Mississippi, this May to investigate the murder of George Wesley Lee, a Negro minister who had committed the error of trying to vote. The reporter was given the names of four Negro witnesses. When he tried to find them he learned they were all in jail. The sheriff explained they were booked on charges of "stealing" although what they had stolen was strangely unknown.

But all this seems far removed from the chaste room in the Hotel Walthall in downtown Jackson, where much of the business of the Jackson Council and the state Association of Councils is carried on. There a tall, mustachioed man of thirty-nine sits at a long metal office desk with a two-volume "works" of Thomas Jefferson on it and a wrinkled map of Mississippi scotch-taped to the wall above. The man is W. J. "Bill" Simmons, who prepared for the task ahead with a B.A.

at Millsaps College and graduate study at Toule, France, and the Sorbonne. He, like "Tut" Patterson and three office helpers, is a full-time council worker. Recently he volunteered to shoulder another new burden for the cause—editorship of a proposed Citizens Council newspaper that will hopefully "grow into the official organ of all Citizens Councils in the nation."

The office in Room 203 of the Walthall where this and other major plans of strategy are hatched is said to be a rent-free donation from hotel owner E. O. Spencer. Ironically enough, Mr. Spencer is a personal and political friend of Herbert Brownell, and the Attorney General supposedly uses him to dole out what Republican patronage there is in the state of Mississippi. It is a strange connection indeed that joins a patron of the councils with a man who must bear his share of responsibility for the integration decision.

The office in Jackson, like the one in Winona where Patterson himself holds forth, does not hope to bind the hundreds of councils into any hierarchy or strictly defined organization. On the contrary, the looser the network the less the responsibility the leaders need to take. Mr. Simmons emphasized that the state office has no jurisdiction over what local councils may do to help the cause in their own community.

This approach allows the leaders formally to disclaim responsibility for any group's actions—allows, for instance, "Tut" Patterson to say the councils don't use economic pressure, while at Yazoo City, fifty-three Negro signers of a petition for school integration were refused the purchase of food supplies, lost their jobs, and had their credit cut off until all but two of the original petitioners removed their names. Petitions for school integration were filed late this summer in four other Mississippi cities—Clarksdale, Vicksburg, Jackson, and Natchez. Legal technicalities that nullified the petitions were claimed by the school boards, and names of the petitioners were published in local newspapers. No list remains with all of its original signers.

As unwelcome as the petitions are, however, the councils have found that they serve to awaken the whites to the "danger of mongrelization" (a favorite term of council propaganda).

"Our Jackson council started in April with only sixty

members," Bill Simmons said, "and by mid-July we had 300. But after the N.A.A.C.P. petition was filed in late July we went over 1,000 in two weeks' time."

There are, of course, many sections of the South where the process of desegregation is advancing with harmony. In West Virginia, Oklahoma, Maryland, Kentucky, and Delaware, where Negroes have already started to schools with whites in one or more cities, the Association of Citizens Councils claims no foothold. It is areas such as these, proceeding calmly with integration, that are most disturbing to the councils. Wherever they can, council leaders try to monkeywrench this kind of progress. Speakers and organizers from Mississippi councils have traveled through nine other Southern states to promote their cause, and it was council pressure from Mississippi that helped slow the school integration at Hoxie, Arkansas, which had progressed without incident until white-supremacy crusaders came in with propaganda and meetings. These finally culminated in threats to the school superintendent and an early closing of the school's summer term.

Senator Eastland—who jumps to the call of segregation like Pavlov's dog to the sound of a bell—was one of the speakers at a meeting where men from Hoxie were asked to come for council enlightenment. This was the same enterprising Eastland who led a violent one-man Senate internal-security subcommittee investigation of the Southern Conference Educational Fund, which happened to be the only interracial group in the South pressing for desegregation.

Senator Eastland hit another high point in May when he delivered a speech to the Senate "exposing" the Supreme Court decision as a Marxist plot to destroy the government. The court, he said, had been brainwashed by left-wing pressure groups who are "part and parcel of the Communist conspiracy to destroy our country."

The integration issue has submerged other political questions in the Deep South, and in many places election campaigns have been turned into contests among the candidates to surpass each other in promises of maintaining segregation. In last year's gubernatorial election in Georgia, platform planks included pledges to go to jail if the schools were

mixed, and suggestions that a state board of psychiatrists examine any white people who wanted their children to go to
school with Negroes.

The "crusade" is on, sometimes attached to the name of
the councils, sometimes not—but the mimeograph machines
are rolling, and new "confidential communiques" are on the
way. Racial suppression has been made respectable, and those
who doubt it have only to ask how one may join the councils.
A recent advertisement in a Clarksdale, Mississippi, newspaper
urged all the whites of the county to go to "your nearest local bank" and enlist in the cause.

The Nation, October 22, 1955

At Holt Street Baptist Church

by Joe Azbell

As I drove along Cleveland Avenue en route to the Holt Street Baptist Church Monday night, I could see Negroes by the dozens forming a file, almost soldierly, on the sidewalk. They were going to the Rosa Parks protest meeting at the church.

They were silent people, bundled in overcoats, performing what appeared to be a ritual. I parked my automobile a block from the church and noted the time was 6:45. Already cars were strung out for six or seven blocks in each direction.

In fact, the area around the church looked like Cramton Bowl at an Alabama State–Tuskegee football game. Except for one thing: these people were stony silent.

The Negroes eyed me and one inquired if I was a policeman. He turned to his three companions: "He says he ain't the law." I walked up to the steps of the church and two Negro policemen were standing there chatting. Both were courteous when I introduced myself and one went inside and found out about the seating arrangement for the press. Chairs were placed down front for the reporters. The TV cameraman from WSFA-TV and the United Press reporter later took these seats. I stood in the rear of the church during the meeting while Reporter Steve Lesher anchored himself in a chair near the church's pulpit.

The inside of the church is impressive because of its simplicity. The church has the ordinary equipment of the upper middle class white church and there's a large mirror across the back wall.

I observed police squad cars parked two blocks away in each direction from the church and occasionally a police sergeant would drive by and check with the four Negro policemen who were handling the traffic at the church.

I went inside the church and stood at the front for a few minutes. The two rear doors were jammed with people and a long aisle was crammed with human forms like a frozen food package. I went to the rear of the church and it was the same. The Negro policemen pleaded with the Negroes to keep the aisles free so people could get out. In the end the policemen gave up in despair of correcting the safety hazard. Bodies at the front were packed one against the other. It required five minutes for a photographer to move eight feet among these people in trying to leave the building.

The purpose of this meeting was to give "further instructions" on the boycott of city buses which had been started as a protest of the Negroes against the arrest, trial and conviction of Rosa Parks, 42-year-old seamstress, on a charge of violating segregation laws by refusing to give up her seat to a white person and move to the rear of a city bus.

There were four white reporters or photographers at the meeting. Only one other white person attended. He appeared to be a young college student or airman and he came with a Negro and left with a Negro. He sat in the group of Negroes in the balcony.

The meeting was started in a most unusual fashion. A Negro speaker—apparently a minister—came to the microphone. He did not introduce himself but apparently most of the Negroes knew him. He said there were microphones on the outside and in the basement, and there were three times as many people outside as on the inside. There was an anonymity throughout the meeting of the speakers. None of the white reporters could identify the speakers. Most of the Negroes did. The introductions of Fred Daniels and Rosa Parks were clear and brief. Daniels was arrested in the boycott Monday.

The passion that fired the meeting was seen as the thousands of voices joined in singing *Onward, Christian Soldier.* Another hymn followed. The voices thundered through the church.

Then there followed a prayer by a minister. It was a prayer interrupted a hundred times by "yeas" and "uh-huhs" and "that's right." The minister spoke of God as the Master and the brotherhood of man. He repeated in a different way that God would protect the righteous.

As the other speakers came on the platform urging "free-dom and equality" for Negroes "who are Americans and proud of this democracy," the frenzy of the audience mounted. There was a volume of clapping that seemed to boom through the walls. Outside the loudspeakers were blar-ing the message for blocks. White people stopped blocks away and listened to the loudspeakers' messages.

The newspapers were criticized for quoting police authori-ties on reports of intimidation of Negroes who attempted to ride buses and for comparing the Negro boycott with the economic reprisals of White Citizens groups.

The remark which drew the most applause was: "We will not retreat one inch in our fight to secure and hold our American citizenship." Second was a statement: "And the his-tory book will write of us as a race of people who in Mont-gomery County, State of Alabama, Country of the United States, stood up for and fought for their rights as American citizens, as citizens of democracy."

Outside the audience listened as more and more cars con-tinued to arrive. Streets became Dexter traffic snarls. There was hymn singing between speeches. In the end there was the passing of the hats and Negroes dropped in dollar bills, $5 bills and $10 bills. It was not passive giving but active giving. Negroes called to the hat passers outside—"Here, let me give."

When the resolution on continuing the boycott of the bus was read, there came a wild whoop of delight. Many said they would never ride the bus again. Negroes turned to each other and compared past incidents on the buses.

At several points there was an emotionalism that the minis-ters on the platform recognized could get out of control and at various intervals they repeated again and again what "we are seeking is by peaceful means."

"There will be no violence or intimidation. We are seeking things in a democratic way and we are using the weapon of protest," the speakers declared.

I left as the meeting was breaking up. The Negroes made a path for me through the crowd as I went to my car, but the packed group found it uncomfortable to move. A cry of "fire" would have caused a panic that could have resulted in scores of deaths. Negroes on the outside recognized this danger but these people wanted to see and hear what was going on.

There was hymn singing as I drove away. At the first corner where I turned, I nodded at the policemen in a squad car. At the next corner I saw another squad car. And at the next corner where I stopped for a signal light, the driver of another squad car asked if the meeting had ended.

The meeting was much like an old-fashioned revival with loud applause added. It proved beyond any doubt there was a discipline among Negroes that many whites had doubted. It was almost a military discipline combined with emotion.

The Montgomery Advertiser, December 7, 1955

The Shocking Story of Approved Killing in Mississippi

by William Bradford Huie

DISCLOSED here is the true account of the slaying in Mississippi of a Negro youth named Emmett Till.

Last September, in Sumner, Miss., a petit jury found the youth's admitted abductors not guilty of murder. In November, in Greenwood, a grand jury declined to indict them for kidnapping.

Of the murder trial, the Memphis *Commercial Appeal* said: "Evidence necessary for convicting on a murder charge was lacking." But with truth absent, hypocrisy and myth have flourished. Now, hypocrisy can be exposed: myth dispelled. Here are the facts.

Carolyn Holloway Bryant is 21, five feet tall, weighs 103 pounds. An Irish girl, with black hair and black eyes, she is a small-farmer's daughter who, at 17, quit high school at Indianola, Miss., to marry a soldier, Roy Bryant, then 20, now 24. The couple have two boys, three and two; and they operate a store at a dusty crossroads called Money: post office, filling station and three stores clustered around a school and a gin, and set in the vast, lonely cotton patch that is the Mississippi Delta.

Carolyn and Roy Bryant are poor: no car, no TV. They live in the back of the store which Roy's brothers helped set up when he got out of the 82nd Airborne in 1953. They sell "snuff-and-fatback" to Negro field hands on credit; and they earn little because, for one reason, the government has begun giving the Negroes food they formerly bought.

Carolyn and Roy Bryant's social life is visits to their families, to the Baptist church and, whenever they can borrow a car, to a drive-in, with the kids sleeping in the back seat. They call *Shane* the best picture they ever saw.

For extra money, Carolyn tends store when Roy works out-side—like truck driving for a brother. And he has many brothers. His mother had two husbands, 11 children. The first five—all boys—were "Milam children"; the next six—three boys, three girls—were "Bryant children."

This is a lusty and devoted clan. They work, fight, vote and play as a family. The "half" in their fraternity is forgotten. For years, they have operated a chain of cottonfield stores, as well as trucks and mechanical cotton pickers. In relation to the Negroes, they are somewhat like white traders in portions of Africa today; and they are determined to resist the revolt of colored men against white rule.

On Wednesday evening, August 24, 1955, Roy was in Texas, on a brother's truck. He had carted shrimp from New Or-leans to San Antonio, proceeded to Brownsville. Carolyn was alone in the store. But back in the living quarters was her sister-in-law Juanita Milam, 27, with her own two small sons and Carolyn's two. The store was kept open until 9 on week nights, 11 on Saturday.

When her husband was away, Carolyn Bryant never slept in the store, never stayed there alone after dark. Moreover, in the Delta, no white woman or group of white women ever travels country roads after dark unattended by a man.

This meant that during Roy's absences—particularly since he had no car—there was family inconvenience. Each after-noon, a sister-in-law arrived to stay with Carolyn until closing time. Then, the two women, with their children, waited for a brother-in-law to convoy them to his home. Next morning the sister-in-law drove Carolyn back.

Juanita Milam had driven from her home in Glendora. She had parked in front of the store and to the left; and under the front seat of this car was Roy Bryant's pistol, a .38 Colt auto-matic. Carolyn knew it was there. After 9, Juanita's husband, J. W. Milam, would arrive in his pickup to shepherd them to his home for the night.

About 7:30 p.m., eight young Negroes—seven boys and a girl—in a '46 Ford had stopped outside. They included sons, grandsons and a nephew of Moses (Preacher) Wright, 64, a 'cropper. They were between 13 and 19 years old. Four were natives of the Delta, and others, including the nephew, Emmett (Bobo) Till, were visiting from the Chicago area.

Bobo Till was 14 years old; born on July 25, 1941. He was stocky, muscular, weighing about 160, five feet four or five. Preacher later testified: "He looked like a man."

Bobo's party joined a dozen other young Negroes, including two other girls, in front of the store. Bryant had built checkerboards there. Some were playing checkers, others were wrestling and "kiddin' about girls."

Bobo bragged about his white girl. He showed the boys a picture of a white girl in his wallet; and, to their jeers of disbelief, he boasted of his success with her.

"You talkin' mighty big, Bo," one youth said. "There's a pretty little white woman in the store. Since you know how to handle white girls, let's see you go in and get a date with her?"

"You ain't chicken, are yuh, Bo?" another youth taunted him.

Bobo had to fire or fall back. He entered the store, alone, stopped at the candy case. Carolyn was behind the counter; Bobo in front. He asked for two cents' worth of bubble gum. She handed it to him. He squeezed her hand and said: "How about a date, Baby?"

She jerked away and started for Juanita Milam. At the break between counters, Bobo jumped in front of her, perhaps caught her at the waist, and said: "You needn't be afraid o' me, Baby. I been with white girls before."

At this point, a cousin ran in, grabbed Bobo and began pulling him out of the store. Carolyn now ran, not for Juanita, but out the front, and got the pistol from the Milam car.

Outside, with Bobo being ushered off by his cousins, and with Carolyn getting the gun, Bobo executed the "wolf whistle" which gave the case its name:

THE WOLF-WHISTLE MURDER:
A NEGRO "CHILD" OR "BOY" WHISTLED
AT HER AND THEY KILLED HIM.

That was the sum of the facts on which most newspaper readers based an opinion.

The Negroes drove away; and Carolyn, shaken, told Juanita. The two women determined to keep the incident from their "men-folks." They didn't tell J. W. Milam when he came to escort them home.

By Thursday afternoon, Carolyn Bryant could see the story was getting around. She spent Thursday night at the Milams, where at 4 a.m. (Friday) Roy got back from Texas. Since he had slept little for five nights, he went to bed at the Milams' while Carolyn returned to the store.

During Friday afternoon, Roy reached the store, and shortly thereafter a Negro told him what "the talk" was, and told him that the "Chicago boy" was "visitin' Preacher." Carolyn then told Roy what had happened.

Once Roy Bryant knew, in his environment, in the opinion of most white people around him, for him to have done nothing would have marked him a coward and a fool.

On Friday night, he couldn't do anything. He and Carolyn were alone, and he had no car. Saturday was collection day, their busy day in the store. About 10:30 Saturday night, J. W. Milam drove by. Roy took him aside.

"I want you to come over early in the morning," he said. "I need a little transportation."

J. W. protested: "Sunday's the only morning I can sleep. Can't we make it around noon?"

Roy then told him.

"I'll be here," he said. "Early."

J. W. drove to another brother's store at Minter City, where he was working. He closed that store about 12:30 a.m., drove home to Glendora. Juanita was away, visiting her folks at Greenville. J. W. had been thinking. He decided not to go to bed. He pumped the pickup—a half-ton '55 Chevrolet—full of gas and headed for Money.

J. W. "Big Milam" is 36; six feet two, 235 pounds; an extrovert. Short boots accentuate his height; khaki trousers; red sports shirt; sun helmet. Dark-visaged; his lower lip curls when he chuckles; and though bald, his remaining hair is jet-black.

He is slavery's plantation overseer. Today, he rents Negro-driven mechanical cotton pickers to plantation owners. Those who know him say he can handle Negroes better than anybody in the county.

Big Milam soldiered in the Patton manner. With a ninth-grade education, he was commissioned in battle by the 75th Division. He was an expert platoon leader, expert street fighter, expert in night patrol, expert with the "grease gun," with every device for close-range killing. A German bullet tore clear through his chest; his body bears "multiple shrapnel wounds." Of his medals, he cherishes one: combat infantryman's badge.

Big Milam, like many soldiers, brought home his favorite gun: the .45 Colt automatic pistol.

"Best weapon the Army's got," he says. "Either for shootin' or sluggin'."

Two hours after Big Milam got the word—the instant minute he could close the store—he was looking for the Chicago Negro.

Big Milam reached Money a few minutes shy of 2 a.m., Sunday, August 28. The Bryants were asleep; the store was dark but for the all-night light. He rapped at the back door, and when Roy came, he said: "Let's go. Let's make that trip now."

Roy dressed, brought a gun: this one was a .45 Colt. Both men were—and remained—cold sober. Big Milam had drunk a beer at Minter City around 9; Roy had had nothing.

There was no moon as they drove to Preacher's house: 2.8 miles east of Money.

Preacher's house stands 50 feet right of the gravel road, with cedar and persimmon trees in the yard. Big Milam drove the pickup in under the trees. He was bareheaded, carrying a five-cell flashlight in his left hand, the .45 in his right.

Roy Bryant pounded on the door.

Preacher: "Who's that?"

Bryant: "Mr. Bryant, from Money, Preacher."

Preacher: "All right, sir. Just a minute."

Preacher came out on the screened-in porch.

Bryant: "Preacher, you got a boy from Chicago here?"

Preacher: "Yessir."

Bryant: "I want to talk to him."

Preacher: "Yessir. I'll get him."

Preacher led them to a back bedroom where four youths were sleeping in two beds. In one was Bobo Till and Simeon

Wright, Preacher's youngest son. Bryant had told Preacher to turn on the lights; Preacher had said they were out of order. So only the flashlight was used.

The visit was not a complete surprise. Preacher testified that he had heard of the "trouble," that he "sho' had" talked to his nephew about it. Bobo himself had been afraid; he had wanted to go home the day after the incident. The Negro girl in the party had urged that he leave. "They'll kill him," she had warned. But Preacher's wife, Elizabeth Wright, had decided that the danger was being magnified; she had urged Bobo to "finish yo' visit."

"I thought they might say something to him, but I didn't think they'd kill a boy," Preacher said.

Big Milam shined the light in Bobo's face, said: "You the nigger who did the talking?"

"Yeah," Bobo replied.

Milam: "Don't say 'Yeah' to me: I'll blow your head off. Get your clothes on."

Bobo had been sleeping in his shorts. He pulled on a shirt and trousers, then reached for his socks.

"Just the shoes," Milam hurried him.

"I don't wear shoes without socks," Bobo said; and he kept the gun-bearers waiting while he put on his socks, then a pair of canvas shoes with thick crepe soles.

Preacher and his wife tried two arguments in the boy's behalf.

"He ain't got good sense," Preacher begged. "He didn't know what he was doing. Don't take him."

"I'll pay you gentlemen for the damages," Elizabeth Wright said.

"You niggers go back to sleep," Milam replied.

They marched him into the yard, told him to get in the back of the pickup and lie down. He obeyed. They drove toward Money.

Elizabeth Wright rushed to the home of a white neighbor, who got up, looked around, but decided he could do nothing. Then, she and Preacher drove to the home of her brother, Crosby Smith, at Sumner; and Crosby Smith, on Sunday morning, went to the sheriff's office at Greenwood.

The other young Negroes stayed at Preacher's house until

daylight, when Wheeler Parker telephoned his mother in Chicago, who in turn notified Bobo's mother, Mamie Bradley, 33, 6427 S. St. Lawrence.

Had there been any doubt as to the identity of the "Chicago boy who done the talking," Milam and Bryant would have stopped at the store for Carolyn to identify him. But there had been no denial. So they didn't stop at the store. At Money, they crossed the Tallahatchie River and drove west.

Their intention was to "just whip him . . . and scare some sense into him." And for this chore, Big Milam knew "the scariest place in the Delta." He had come upon it last year hunting wild geese. Over close to Rosedale, the Big River bends around under a bluff. "Brother, she's a 100-foot sheer drop, and she's a 100 feet deep after you hit."

Big Milam's idea was to stand him up there on that bluff, "whip" him with the .45, and then shine the light off down there toward that water and make him think you're gonna knock him in.

"Brother, if that won't scare the Chicago ——, hell won't."

Searching for this bluff, they drove close to 75 miles. Through Shellmound, Schlater, Doddsville, Ruleville, Cleveland, to the intersection south of Rosedale. There they turned south on Mississippi No. 1, toward the entrance to Beulah Lake. They tried several dirt and gravel roads, drove along the levee. Finally, they gave up: in the darkness Big Milam couldn't find his bluff.

They drove back to Milam's house at Glendora, and by now it was 5 a.m. They had been driving *nearly three hours*, with Milam and Bryant in the cab and Bobo lying in the back.

At some point when the truck slowed down, why hadn't Bobo jumped and run? He wasn't tied; nobody was holding him. A partial answer is that those Chevrolet pickups have a wraparound rear window the size of a windshield. Bryant could watch him. But the real answer is the remarkable part of the story.

Bobo wasn't afraid of them! He was tough as they were. He didn't think they had the guts to kill him.

Milam: "We never were able to scare him. They had just filled him so full of that poison he was hopeless."

Back of Milam's home is a tool house, with two rooms each about 12 feet square. They took him there and began "whipping" him, first Milam, then Bryant smashing him across the head with those .45's. Pistol-whipping: a court-martial offense in the Army . . . but MP's have been known to do it . . . and Milam got information out of German prisoners this way.

But under these blows Bobo never hollered—and he kept making the perfect speeches to insure martyrdom.

Bobo: "You bastards, I'm not afraid of you. I'm as good as you are. I've 'had' white women. My grandmother was a white woman."

Milam: "Well, what else could we do? He was hopeless. I'm no bully; I never hurt a nigger in my life. I like niggers—in their place—I know how to work 'em. But I just decided it was time a few people got put on notice. As long as I live and can do anything about it, niggers are gonna stay in their place. Niggers ain't gonna vote where I live. If they did, they'd control the government. They ain't gonna go to school with my kids. And when a nigger even gets close to mentioning sex with a white woman, he's tired o' livin'. I'm likely to kill him. Me and my folks fought for this country, and we've got some rights. I stood there in that shed and listened to that nigger throw that poison at me, and I just made up my mind. 'Chicago boy,' I said, 'I'm tired of 'em sending your kind down here to stir up trouble. Goddam you, I'm going to make an example of you—just so everybody can know how me and my folks stand.'"

So big Milam decided to act. He needed a weight. He tried to think where he could get an anvil. Then he remembered a gin which had installed new equipment. He had seen two men lifting a discarded fan, a metal fan three feet high and circular, used in ginning cotton.

Bobo wasn't bleeding much. Pistol-whipping bruises more than it cuts. They ordered him back in the truck and headed west again. They passed through Doddsville, went to the Progressive Ginning Company. This gin is 3.4 miles east of Boyle; Boyle is two miles south of Cleveland. The road to this gin turns left off U.S. 61, after you cross the bayou bridge south of Boyle.

Milam: "When we got to that gin, it was daylight, and I

was worried for the first time. Somebody might see us and accuse us of stealing the fan."

Bryant and Big Milam stood aside while Bobo loaded the fan. Weight: 74 pounds. The youth still thought they were bluffing.

They drove back to Glendora, then north toward Swan Lake and crossed the "new bridge" over the Tallahatchie. At the east end of this bridge, they turned right, along a dirt road which parallels the river. After about two miles, they crossed the property of L. W. Boyce, passing near his house.

About 1.5 miles southeast of the Boyce home is a lonely spot where Big Milam has hunted squirrels. The river bank is steep. The truck stopped 30 yards from the water.

Big Milam ordered Bobo to pick up the fan.

He staggered under its weight . . . carried it to the river bank. They stood silently . . . just hating one another.

Milam: "Take off your clothes."

Slowly, Bobo sat down, pulled off his shoes, his socks. He stood up, unbuttoned his shirt, dropped his pants, his shorts.

He stood there naked.

It was Sunday morning, a little before 7.

Milam: "You still as good as I am?"

Bobo: "Yeah."

Milam: "You've still 'had' white women?"

Bobo: "Yeah."

That big .45 jumped in Big Milam's hand. The youth turned to catch that big, expanding bullet at his right ear. He dropped.

They barb-wired the gin fan to his neck, rolled him into 20 feet of water.

For three hours that morning, there was a fire in Big Milam's back yard: Bobo's crepe-soled shoes were hard to burn.

Seventy-two hours later—eight miles downstream—boys were fishing. They saw feet sticking out of the water. Bobo.

The majority—by no means *all*, but the *majority*—of white people in Mississippi 1) either approve Big Milam's action or else 2) they don't disapprove enough to risk giving their "enemies" the satisfaction of a conviction.

"When the Riots Came"

by Murray Kempton

The Alabama Story

DENNIS HOLT, of Birmingham, is stringy and skinny and wears glasses and is the national debating champion of the United States. He is also president of the student body of the College of Arts and Sciences of the University of Alabama, and, oddly enough for a tall, thin boy, who does not play basketball, is something of a hero on his campus.

Night before last the holy war against one poor, lonely Negro woman (Autherine Lucy) settled down near midnight outside the home of O. C. Carmichael, the beset president of Alabama University. What was left of the rioteers hollered for the head of their president, and Mrs. Carmichael came out to beg them to leave. Dennis Holt stood by the steps of the presidential mansion and watched what happened.

"Somebody called out, 'Let's go get 'em,'" said Dennis Holt last night.

"And three people—two high school boys and a man so drunk he could barely lurch—walked up those steps. And some of us stepped in front of them, and one of us said, 'You're not going anywhere.' You know, they fell back.

"That's all it took—just a little resistance."

But there was no other resistance; the grownups had already capitulated in giving the mob what it wanted. All yesterday Dennis Holt and the rest of the student leaders of Alabama University worked to save their school's honor. They are better than us, their elders, and last night they met and calmly and unanimously resolved that the law must be upheld and justice done and wrong redressed.

All the leaders of Alabama's Student Government Association are Alabama boys and girls. They are, above all other candidates, the elected conscience of their college. Last night, with not one dissenting vote, they voted to accept a Negro as a fellow student rather than bow to the rule of a mob.

Thomas Thigpen, of Greensboro, Alabama, the presiding officer, called them to order and announced that Dennis Holt had a resolution to read. Let us remember these kids who will excite the passion of no headline writer, because, more than sheriffs who do not enforce laws and attorneys-general who do not listen and college presidents who cannot lift their heads, they are the light of the world and whatever hope this sad and tortured territory has.

Dennis Holt stood up to read his resolution. America, he said, has been called to greatness and we, too, have been called. Great segments of the world are watching the student government of the University of Alabama on this seventh day of February, nineteen hundred and fifty-six.

We have a chance, he reminded them, to tell the world that this, our student government, is not run by vandals, goons or thugs. And then they began, these children of the South, to applaud.

Let us say here this evening, said Dennis Holt, that we live by democratic means and democratic methods and that we're opposed to mob violence and mob rule. And then very slowly he recited the terrible events of the last three days:

"An ink bottle—remember that—was thrown at the American flag. An Episcopal minister, a man of God—remember that—was hit in the back with an egg."

Every one of us, said Dennis Holt, has been dealt a blow. The question is not what we may think of integration but what we think of law and order.

And then he looked at them, these students most trusted by the other students of the University of Alabama, and said that he had a thing to tell them. That was his own theory and not necessarily theirs.

"Our university and its trustees may well be famous for all time for running away from a fight. They have acquiesced to the mob. Let us face it: The mob is king on the campus to-day. We must all think a little bit about the fact that the mob won. Let us remember that high school boys were able to sway the board of trustees of a great university."

Let us, he was saying, let us accept our shame and our responsibility.

Dennis Holt's resolution affirmed that the student government hereby resolves that mob violence be denounced at the University of Alabama and that means be found to protect the future personal safety of the students—white or Negro—and the faculty and the reputation of the university.

And then he was finished, and they applauded him for thirty-five seconds, which is too long to be quite proper for sixty people. They seemed to keep it going out of some need to affirm what they had waited so long to hear someone say loud and clear. And when they had shouted their approval, Hartwell Lutz, of Huntsville, Alabama, arose to ask what his resolution meant and how it could help the situation.

"It means," said Dennis Holt, "that we are saying to certain responsible officials of this state that when mob violence occurs, it's time for the law to break it up. We have to convince the state officials that they have the responsibility, not just the students."

Last night, the Student's Christian Association and the International Relations Club passed resolutions like Dennis Holt's; today the law students will follow. Every responsible representative of the opinion of these Deep South students is coming forth to speak for government of law and order. They are better than their elders; we would be lost if they weren't.

All day yesterday, their elders paltered and fumbled. O. C. Carmichael sat in his office and twice announced and twice deferred sessions at which he would be compelled to show his beaten and shamed face to the invading press.

At the end, poor Carmichael could defer no more; and yesterday afternoon he went before a meeting of the university faculty to explain to them why the board of trustees had capitulated and, in Dennis Holt's words, made the mob king of their campus.

He looked with his frightened eyes and his pleading hands —everything about him seemed to cry out, please, no questions—and told them that, if any of them had been confronted with the problem facing the trustees, he was sure that he would have surrendered, too.

Then he said that the hour was growing late and there were many problems to which sensitive troubled men must give their most serious attention, and so didn't they think it was time to adjourn? They thought that it was, most of them. But up stood a very few and spoke with the voice of Dennis Holt.

Charles Farris, of Florida and the Political Science Department, said he thought somebody should ask why the Tuscaloosa police had been so inept in handling the riot. President Carmichael could only answer that he agreed that things might have been done better, but that reality was reality.

Then Charles Farris went to the platform and offered a resolution urging that the university take its Negro students if the law says it has to and ride through any future riots and, if they cannot be quelled, that the university suspend its operations until peace is restored.

At this President Carmichael shrank back with his fluttering hand against the red plush curtain and asked for the ayes and nays. With eyes cast down and heads averted, the majority of the Alabama faculty voted to adjourn and support surrender.

As they walked out, some of them were heard to say that they wished people like Farris wouldn't rock the boat. A few hours later the student leaders met and, without a vote dissenting or a head averted, cast their future behind Dennis Holt.

It is perhaps too much to hope that any of us are as good as our children; we can only thank God that they are better.

The Way It's Got to Be

Autherine Juanita Lucy is not really Autherine Lucy—except to strangers to whom she is a symbol. To her family and to her friends, she has always been Juanita Lucy.

She appears to have been less afraid than most persons in authority were on Monday when a mob seized the campus of the University of Alabama and stoned not just her but, deplorable as it is, two white people as well. The mob was shouting, "Autherine's got to go!" They were shouting about a stranger and not about Juanita Lucy. She may owe some of the glory of her posture to a sense that, when they howled at

Autherine, they were howling at a symbol and not the name of a real woman who is Juanita.

She started on the road which brought her to where she and all the South stand today very casually in the summer of 1952. Polly Myers Hudson, who was her classmate at Alabama's Miles College, called her up and said:

"Juanita, how would you like to go to the University of Alabama?"

"I said I'd like to very much, and we got all the forms and filled them out and went to the university and applied in person—me for library science and her for journalism. We were refused and then we went to court."

In the beginning, she did not tell her family: "They would have opposed it to the nth degree." They believed—who can find a Negro in Alabama who doesn't?—that Negroes should go to State University.

"But they would say and did, 'Why does it have to be you, Juanita?'" Why should she go through this? "My sister still says that. If she were Juanita, she wouldn't be in the University of Alabama."

When she began, Ruby Hurley, the Southern field secretary of the National Association for the Advancement of Colored People, wondered whether she was really a good choice. She seemed, as she seems still, so quiet and reserved that Ruby Hurley was inclined to doubt that she could run her appointed course.

Polly Myers Hudson had been NAACP president at Miles and seemed of stronger cast. Now Polly Myers Hudson has been shunted aside; it was Juanita who went into the bearpit; it was Juanita who was stoned; and it is Juanita—why Juanita of all people?—who has run the course.

She was admitted after the courts gave the university no other choice. The first two days at the school were the lonely days that every new student has, but they were calmer than she expected.

"In the history of education class, I asked a young lady what the name of our professor was and she told me. As I was coming out, a young lady said 'How do you do?' and I answered 'How do you do?'"

The name of the girl who spoke to a lonely student on her

first day in school is not known to any human record, but it must be written somewhere.

"I saw a boy in the bookstore make a funny face at me, but that was all." The first two days were more normal than she could have hoped. Her instructors were especially courteous; there was only one who paid no attention to her at all. He was Charles Farris, who taught her American Government. "He didn't notice me."

She wondered at the time if this was a snub and only found out yesterday that Charles Farris, more than any man on the university faculty, had risen in public to speak for her rights as a student. ("I went to bed," he told his class the next day, "as an employe of the trustees of the University of Alabama and I awake today the employe of a mob.") When she read that, she understood the special courtesy he had shown in simply taking her for granted.

"I guess that is the way it should be." The name of Autherine yesterday brought reporters from London and offers of scholarships from the University of Copenhagen; but the heart of Juanita understood that the only victory would come on that day when she walks unnoticed and taken for granted on the campus of the University of Alabama.

She sat yesterday in Birmingham's colored Masonic building—this is a town where everything is black or white—in a powder blue suit, a mystery to all who came to talk to her. Someone desperately seeking asked her how she would feel if she got into the women's dormitory and was coldly treated. She answered:

"If I go into a dormitory and there are people I cannot reach, I'll just have to remain what you call nonchalant."

He asked her if she was just a young woman who wanted the best education available in the state of Alabama or whether she considered herself a pioneer for her people. And was she proud of her glory, or did she sometimes wonder too why it had to be Juanita?

"I guess," she said almost in apology, "that I do consider myself something of a pioneer. I wish these cameras would go away. I can't be haughty or proud just because everybody seems to know me now." She opened a sheaf of roses from the New York Dress Pressers Union, and rendered by request

of the photographer a pose which conveyed with infinite sub-
tlety how ridiculous this all was. "It just seems that it was put
in my lap."

There were scareheads in the papers outside Birmingham
that she had fled her home in fear of her life. But she spent
Tuesday night in her house as she always has; all night the
telephone rang with obscenities and every time it rang it was
answered.

"Perhaps," she said, "I need a gun but I carry none."

She is the daughter of an Alabama farmer, at twenty-six the
baby of nine children. Her family has dispersed all over America; she has brothers in Detroit and Chicago. She lived a while
in Detroit, and she was very happy there, because it is easier
than Alabama.

"But this is my home and I must stay here. The Negro
must stay in the South because he's needed here. If he must
do something new and different, he must do it here."

And what does she want?

"I have a combination of desires," she said. "I would like to
go to the university in peace and quiet and have friends there."

And when that is over, she would like to be a librarian at
the high school two blocks from her house. That is the wild
dream for which Juanita Lucy reaches: peace with dignity.

When the riots came, she had not felt their terror directly;
and she had been frightened first because the university officials who came to her geography class to protect her had been
so frightened. "I kept asking them what was happening."

The university officials asked afterwards where she could
have found her calm; they assumed that she must have had
training somewhere, and must be paid a great deal; as one of
the girls said, where could she have found those lovely shoes?

Why you of all persons, Juanita? What is this extraordinary
resource of this otherwise unhappy country that it breeds
such dignity in its victims? Why is it, in every great tragedy
there is some poor Negro you can prod and push and never
hear say the wrong thing? Where, as a matter of fact, did
those white students come from who were elected as leaders
of their university and, in their test for which no one could
have trained them, stood up as no grownup did for the dignity of the human person?

This is what William Faulkner was talking about when he said of the Delta Negro that he endured. Through poverty, shame and degradation he endured.

You push and drive Juanita Lucy, tired and holding, so terribly tired and so totally contained, about why of all people she runs her course the way she has and neither of you can answer. This side of God, every observer can only wonder at the resources of the human spirit.

from *America Comes of Middle Age:*
Columns 1950–1962 (1963)

A Brickbat for Education—A Kiss for the Bedroom in Dixie

by Langston Hughes

IF Miss Lucy wanted to go to bed with a white man instead of to college with one, nobody at the University of Alabama would throw stones at her, nor defy the Supreme Court. It is common knowledge in Dixie that some of the Southern politicians who are loudest in defiance of integration keep Negro mistresses, and some have fathered colored families whom they are men enough to support. The millions of mulattoes in the South today are living proof of integration from a long time ago right up to the present.

The "Southern way of life" seems to be a brickbat for education and a kiss for the bedroom—when it comes to whites aiming at Negroes. Miscegenation is an old, old story South of the Mason-Dixon line. If it were not, all of the Negroes down there would be quite dark, African dark, instead of brown, light brown, coffee-and-cream, tan, ivory and white.

Complexions are related to racial heritage, and lots of Negroes in the South are related to white people. Sometimes, as the distinguished Southern author Lillian Smith attests, a man will have a white family and a colored family in the same town —and everybody knows it.

For long standing proof of integration in the deep South, I need go no further than myself. If there were no white blood in my veins, I would not be in color half way between African and Caucasian. On both sides of my family, my white slavery-time great grandparents are clearly remembered.

In my great-uncle's book, "From The Virginia Plantation to the National Capitol" by John Mercer Langston, the white ancestry on my mother's side is recorded in print for anyone to read. Once I was speaking on a Northern campus where all the students were white. One of them was introduced to me

as having the family name Langston. I asked the young man
where he was from. He answered: "Louisa County, Virginia."

I said, "Why, that's where my great-grandparents were
from, too. Perhaps we are related."

The young white man blushed a deep red and, not inclined
to pursue the subject further, disappeared. But I'll bet he was
a distant cousin of mine.

On my father's side, everyone in the family knows that one
of the great-grandfathers who generated my generation was a
white slave trader in Kentucky who became enamoured of
one of my great-grandmothers. Instead of selling her down
the river for profit, he kept her himself—for love. Result,
among others, me! I am not proud of this bastard white
blood in my veins. I had just as leave I did not have it.

But my ancestry is no fault of mine, nor of my African
grandparents living under the ruthless conditions of slavery. I
myself, however, am living proof of integration long before
the Supreme Court ruled upon the subject. Current Southern
hypocrisy in the matter of integration, therefore, makes me
laugh. But the bricks thrown at Miss Lucy make me cry.

Southern white men in slavery time were not the only inte-
grators, however. Some Southern white women went to bed
with their male slaves and loved it, so history records. And a
number of white women married Negroes long before the
Civil War was fought. There were both male and female inte-
grators of the white race way back yonder! Integration is nothing new. Why the white South should raise such a hue and cry
over it today is beyond me. Either white Southerners have lost
their minds, or else they are just Great Pretenders. I don't
know which. Quiet as it is kept, I think they are Pretenders.

Southern gentlemen merely act like they are mad when
they throw bricks at Miss Lucy. The truth of the matter is,
they had rather throw kisses. And, I expect that that alleged
woman in Mississippi over whom the alleged Emmett Till was
allegedly killed might really have wished Emmett had been
just a little older and, instead of allegedly whistling, he had
actually come a little closer to her.

I have known several Southern white women who have followed Negroes out of the South to live with them in wedlock
or in sin in Chicago or Detroit or New York. Integration is a

four-way street—white, black, male, female, vice versa—and has long been a pretty busy thoroughfare in the USA. A few brickbats will hardly make much difference now.

Chicago Defender, March 24, 1956

The Bus Boycott in Montgomery

by L. D. Reddick

MONTGOMERY, ALA.

BEFORE last December, a visitor to Montgomery would have noticed Negroes standing up in the city buses, while there were empty seats right before them. Somebody could then explain that according to local practice, these unoccupied seats were reserved for "whites only." No matter how packed a bus might be with Negro passengers, they were prohibited from sitting in the first 4 seats (which hold about 10 persons). Theoretically, the last 3 back seats (holding about 10 persons) were similarly reserved for Negroes. In fact this was not so. Moreover, if white passengers were already occupying all of their reserved seats and additional white passengers boarded the bus, Negro passengers, sitting in the unreserved section immediately behind the whites, might be asked to get up and "move back" by the bus driver. At times this was done courteously; all-too-often it was an undisguised insult.

Race relations in Montgomery have traditionally been "good" in the sense that Negroes have seldom challenged their state of subordination. The structure of the society was more or less set. Opposition seemed futile. Personal difficulties might be adjusted through some prominent Negro, who would speak with an influential white person. This was the established pattern of paternalism; and it did not disturb the status quo.

But for some reason on Thursday afternoon, December 1, 1955, Mrs. Rosa Parks refused to "move back" when she was ordered to do so by the bus driver. She was *not* sitting in the section reserved for whites (as the *New York Times* mistakenly reported) but in the first seat of the unreserved section. At the time every seat in the bus was taken. So the command for her to "move back" meant that she would have to stand while a white male passenger, who had just taken the bus, would sit. And so she was arrested and for a brief moment jailed.

Mrs. Parks was ideally fitted for her role. She is attractive and quiet, a churchgoer who looks like the symbol of Mother's Day. Her trial was set for the following Monday, December 5. Out of nowhere, it seems, written and mimeographed appeals appeared in the Negro community, saying: ". . . This has to be stopped . . . if Negroes did not ride the buses they could not operate . . . every Negro stay off the buses Monday in protest of this arrest and trial . . ."

Only a fraction of Negro bus riders saw these unsigned appeals but one of the notices did fall into the hands of the local paper, which put it on the front page. Negroes laugh when they tell about this. They say that the newspaper was mostly interested in letting the white folks know what the Negroes were up to. But through this story many Negroes got the news of the Monday plan for the first time. At the Sunday church service, Negro ministers hammered home their endorsement of the projected one-day "protest"—as they consistently called the boycott.

Physically, Montgomery is ideally fitted for a bus boycott. It is just 27.9 square miles in area. Its population, 130,000, is about 40 per cent Negro. Most residents *could* walk to most places in the city.

The judge who tried Mrs. Parks, had he looked into his crystal ball, would have probably dismissed the case. Instead, he found her guilty, fining her $14. She appealed.

All day long on December 5 Negroes stayed off the buses. They did so with such enthusiasm that there was a general feeling that "we ought to continue this."

The Negro ministers had hastily scheduled a mass meeting for Monday evening. Normally, the church holds about 1500 persons. Hours before meeting time, 7:00 p.m., people began filling up the place. By 7 o'clock every seat had been taken and some 3 or 4 thousand standees over-flowed into the street. Outdoor loudspeakers were set up.

Nobody expected such a response. The Negro ministers, rising to the occasion, improvised a declaration of principles. Amid the singing of hymns and some first class oratory—led by Rev. M. L. King Jr.—the audience unanimously adopted the following declaration as read by Rev. Ralph Abernathy: Negroes were not to resume riding the buses until (1) courteous treatment by bus operators was guaranteed; (2) passengers were seated on a first come, first serve basis—Negroes seating from the back of the bus toward the front while whites seat from the front toward the back; (3) Negro bus operators were employed on predominately Negro routes.

Then without the usual money-raising salesmanship, the crowd—inside and outside of the church—filed in and placed dimes, quarters and dollars on the collection table. This was altogether spontaneous.

Since the Negro ministers were cagey about revealing who was directing the movement, that seemed to whet the appetite of the reporters. As a matter of fact, at this point every thing was *ad hoc* and tentative. The emergence of King and Abernathy was almost by chance. No leader was calling the shots. As Abernathy said later, it was never "a one-man-show." The indignation and demands for action by the "common people" swept everyone along like a flood.

II

There had been a long history of abuse by the bus operators. Almost everybody could tell of some unfortunate personal experience that he himself had had or seen. Montgomery Negroes were fed up with the bus service in particular and, like Negroes throughout the South, with race relations in general. The outrage of the Emmett Till murder was alive in everybody's mind. The silence and inaction of the Federal Government, in the face of the daily abuse, beatings and killings of Negro citizens, was maddening. Negroes have no faith at all in Southern law-making and law-enforcing agencies, for these instruments of "justice" are all in the hands of "the brothers of the hoodlums who attack us."

Negroes themselves wanted to get into action. Here and elsewhere they were willing to fight it out—if the fighting was "fair." But Negroes knew on whose side the police and the lily-white militia would be when they came in to "put down disorder." And after that,—there would be the local judges and juries. To remain human, the Negroes simply could not stand by and do nothing. Under the circumstances, the channel into which the Negroes of Montgomery have poured their energies and resentments is the best answer thus far to the question of what to do. Here is organized struggle and group solidarity. It is legal, non-violent and effective.

And so the one-day boycott passed into an indefinite protest that, as of this writing, has run for fourteen weeks.

Both the press and the police expected violence. Early newspaper stories started off in this fashion: "Negro goon squads reportedly have been organized here to intimidate Negroes who ride in violation of a Negro boycott . . ." This was untrue.

The police were equally sure of the image in their minds. Accordingly, they arrested a college student, saying that he had pulled a Negro woman from a bus as she was attempting to get on it. In court it came out that the two were good friends and that they were merrily crossing the street, arm in arm, near a bus. She had told the cops this before the arrest was made but the police believed that there were goons—there had to be—so they saw what they were looking for: "believing is seeing."

The first reaction of the bus company officials was one of arrogance. They pretended that the Negroes were demanding that the company violate the law. This was absurd. The law required segregation, but did not specify the manner of seating so long as it was segregated. The bus company summarily rejected the proposal of the Negroes.

The city commission sided with the bus company, condemning the boycott and declaring that "first come, first serve" would be illegal. And so almost everybody—the bus company, the city commissioners and the white public—expected Negroes to be back on the buses in a few days.

This was only the first of a series of misjudgments on the part of the city fathers. All along they demonstrated that their conception of the Negro was the stereotype of the tired field hand or the witless house servant who could be cajoled or forced to do what the white folks wanted him to do. Even now, after 14 weeks of "education," the commissioners seem not to comprehend the intelligence, resourcefulness and resolve of the people with whom they are dealing.

III

The ex-bus riders soon found themselves face to face with a practical problem: since the buses were taboo, how were the Negroes to get about the city? At first, they called upon the taxis for cheap-rate jitney service. The police stopped this by warning the taxis that by law they must charge a minimum fare of 45 cents. Next, private cars began giving "friends" a lift, along the bus routes. The charge was 15 cents for "gasoline expense." The cops stopped this, too, by insisting that drivers had to have a taxi permit and license.

In reply, the Negroes organized a voluntary motor pool. Almost overnight Montgomery saw a network of private cars spread over the city, picking up and depositing passengers, from dawn until early evening. It was a marvel of quick organization. Even the local press had to concede that the pick-up system moved with "military precision." Some transportation problems that the bus company had grappled with for twenty years were, apparently, solved overnight.

The police searched the books for laws that would dry up the motor pool. One old rule forbade more than three persons to sit on the front seat of an automobile. Lights, brakes, even the position of license tags, were checked by the police frequently. Minor regulations that are seldom invoked in this normally easy-going town were resurrected and severely enforced. Negro taxi drivers really caught it!

The Negro community of Montgomery has neither its own radio station (as does Atlanta, Ga.) nor a widely-read local newspaper. Communication is by word of mouth and through churches mainly. This is probably why frequent mass meetings have proved a necessity. The pattern was established during the first week of the boycott: mass meetings each Monday and Thursday evening. It has been adhered to ever since.

These twice-a-week get-togethers are the soul of the boycott; the Montgomery Improvement Association is the brains. The meetings are rotated from church to church. The speakers, in turn, represent the various denominations. Thus the ground is cut from under any institutional or sectarian jealousy. Rev. King and Rev. Abernathy make it plain by their words and by their sharing of the speakers' platform that they are not self-appointed "leaders" but only "spokesmen" of the movement. Incidentally, the people have "fallen in love" with King, a boyish-looking Ph.D. They look upon Abernathy, also young and an M.A., as a tower of strength. These two men symbolize the poise, the thoughtfulness and the ability of the independent ministers. They are the real and obvious leaders of this mass upsurge. The more vulnerable intellectuals stay discreetly in the background. Rufus Lewis, an ex-football coach and presently a civic-minded business man, is the cool-headed chairman of the motor pool committee.

People come hours ahead of time to get a seat at these mass meetings. A few read papers and books while waiting, but mostly the audiences sing. Hymns such as "Onward Christian Soldiers," "Abide With Me" and "Higher Ground" are moving but the really stirring songs are the lined, camp-meeting tunes, of low pitch and long meter. These seem to recapture the long history of the Negro's suffering and struggle.

IV

By 7 p.m., the time the meeting starts, virtually every inch of space is taken, including standing room. Often as many listeners are outside as inside. Many others do not come at all because they know they cannot get near the church. It is curious that meetings were never scheduled in different parts of the city at different hours on the same night or rotated to different parts of the city on different nights—in order to accomodate the crowds. This suggestion was made but the planning committee never got around to it or concluded that "the people prefer to be together," as several persons had said.

The mass meeting pattern is relatively simple: songs, prayer, latest news and plans, a "pep talk," collection. Often the pastor in whose church the meeting was held would preside or, after preliminary remarks, would turn the meeting over to some official of the Montgomery Improvement Association.

The meetings are serious but thoroughly relaxed. There are quips and jokes—a great deal of genial humor. All classes are present in the audiences but the bulk of the attendants are working class people. It is here that morale is built and sustained. Unity is expressed in words and in the little kindnesses that the people show to each other. The automobile-owning folk, who never rode the buses, and the maids and day-laborers, who depended upon the buses, have come to know each other. The inter-denominational, inter-class integration of the Negro community has called forth much comment. Moreover, the mass meetings have given many persons some place to go; something to think about; something to absorb their energies. There is high purpose these days in the Negro community.

Few whites attend these meetings although they are open to all. Aside from a Lutheran minister who has a Negro congregation, no local white preacher has publicly identified himself with the Negro cause. Many, of course, give assurances privately. A few are in "hot water" for real or suspected sympathies with the boycotters.

But the main force that keeps the people and their leaders together is the idea of the movement itself. These people know that they are fighting a big battle and that it is a vital part of a larger war. Messages and money contributions from many parts of the nation as well as from remote parts of the world have confirmed this belief.

At first, the demands of the boycotters were limited—courtesy, fair play, fair employment. These were all within the segregation laws of the city and state. At one point, the Negroes would have called off the boycott for just the "first come, first serve" arrangement. That day, of course, has long since passed.

Apparently to impress the Negro community with what it could lose, the bus company abruptly stopped all service to Negro neighborhoods. This was supposed to bring Negroes to their knees, crying for the buses. But nobody was impressed. Instead, doubtful would-be bus riders were pushed into the motor pool. The water, they found, was just "fine." On second thought, the bus company decided to re-establish the discontinued lines. So the buses were put back on the routes in the Negro areas. They continued to roll empty.

For about a month negotiations were on and off. Neither side would yield. The boycott held its own. This meant that 75 per cent of the bus riding public was "out," and it cut some $3,000 from each day's revenue. Moreover, fewer whites—probably out of sympathy with the boycott—seemed to be riding.

To counteract this economic squeeze, the mayor called on the white public to support the buses. The so-called White Citizens Council solicited contributions for the poor suffering bus company. No figures were ever given out but the general impression is that very few persons were willing to subsidize the National City Lines, an economic giant that is spread out over the cities and towns of the Middle West and South and has its main office in Chicago. A forced subsidy was made possible by raising the bus fare from 10 to 15 cents. At which point, additional whites stayed off the buses.

V

To break the impasse, the city commission pulled a fast one. On Sunday, January 22, the Negro community was astounded to read in the morning paper that a settlement had been reached. The article said: "The above agreement is concurred in by all three members of the City Commission, as well as by representatives of the bus company and the group representing the Negroes of Montgomery." The terms of the "agreement" were: (1) courtesy to all; (2) white reserve section at the front of the bus, Negro reserve section at rear of bus; (3) special, all-Negro buses during the rush hours. "First come, first serve" would obtain for the unreserved, middle section. The city commission stated that it had nothing to do with the question of employment. The declaration of courtesy carried no machinery for assuring its practice. In short, this latest "agreement" was merely a re-statement of the *status quo ante bellum*. Nevertheless, it sounded like a settlement and many persons who read the story felt that the boycott was over. Some whites were jubilant. Some Negroes were ill. Why had the "leaders" given in?, they asked.

A careful reading of the article raises the question whether it was just poor reporting or something much worse. For example, the names of the "prominent ministers" were not given. Other omissions were equally strange. If this was a release from the city commission, would any newspaper naively print such an important front-page story without first check-ing with the known Negro representatives, who had been ne-gotiating with the bus company and city commission for weeks? Obviously, this announcement was a calculated ma-neuver to get the ex-bus riders back on the buses Sunday morning. Perhaps once the spell of not riding was broken, the boycott would dissolve.

The Negroes foiled this maneuver by a combination of luck and quick action. The story had been sent out Saturday evening by the Associated Press. As it came over the wires into the office of the *Minneapolis Tribune*, the reporter Carl T. Rowan, who had been down to Montgomery to cover the boycott, did what any good reporter would do: he called Rev. M. L. King Jr. to verify the story.

King was amazed. He knew absolutely nothing about any settlement. Rowan then contacted one of the Montgomery commissioners who confirmed the story but refused to give the names of the Negro ministers involved. Under prodding, the commissioner did reveal the denominations of the minis-ters. Rowan then called King again. This clue was enough. King and his colleagues by a process of checking soon identi-fied the "three prominent Negro ministers." It turned out that they were neither prominent nor members of the negoti-ating committee.

It was now late Saturday night. Like minute men, the min-isters of the Montgomery Improvement Association went themselves or sent messages to all of the night clubs and tav-erns in the Negro community, informing the Saturday night revellers of the attempted hoax. Rev. King himself humor-ously stated that he got a chance to see the insides of many a night spot! Result: word got around so well that the next day the buses rolled empty as usual. At the Sunday morning ser-vices, the ministers excoriated the "fake settlement" and re-peated that the "protest" was still on. The commissioners lost face. The Negroes were brought closer together.

By the next day, the "three prominent Negro ministers" had publicly repudiated the commission's press announce-ment. One of the three stated before an open meeting that he had been "tricked" into the conference on the basis of a tele-phone invitation, asking that he join in a discussion of group insurance for the city. This man said that neither he nor the other two Negroes present agreed to any settlement, declaring that they were unauthorized to speak for the ex-bus riders.

Few persons thought that these three Negro ministers would dare challenge the veracity of the city fathers; but they did. This, everybody was sure, would make front page news. But the local press reduced the sensational disclosure to a bare statement of denial that was buried near the end of a long story. When the local dailies did not print his statement, one of the three ministers purchased space for a three-inch ad saying: "The rumor that is out that I agreed with the commissioners on the proposal that they issued is an untrue statement." These words have never been contradicted.

Things now took a turn for the worse. The mayor and the other commissioners embarked upon a "get tough" policy. With a show of anger the mayor denounced the boycott, declared that the white people did not care if another Negro ever rode the buses again, and called upon white employers to stop taking their Negro employees to and from work. He said that white businessmen informed him that they were discharging Negro workers who were participating in the boycott. All three commissioners let it be known that they had joined the White Citizens Council. Even the timid member of the trio mustered up enough bravado to go on television and join the "get tough with Negroes" act. All this, of course, was the traditional, Confederate, flag-waving appeal to white supremacy.

It was to be a field day. The police would "cut the legs off" the boycott by a campaign of arrests for real and imaginary traffic infractions. Negro drivers, who appeared to be in the motor pool, would be questioned about their employment, the balance due on the purchase of their automobiles and the firms with which they had their insurance.

VI

For a moment the protest movement seemed to be wavering. Again, Negroes saw that the very instruments of law and order were being used against them. Surely, a man had the right to give someone a ride in his own automobile. Persons who had not received a traffic ticket in years were booked.

Some ex-bus riders, while waiting to be picked up, were told that there was a law against hitch-hiking; others were accused of "loud talking," walking on lawns and "congregating in white neighborhoods." The daily press printed next to nothing about the wholesale arrests and harassment.

Under such heavy blows the voluntary pick-up system began to weaken. Some drivers were already tired; others disliked "tangling with the law"; still others feared that they could not stand much more provocation without striking back.

The high point of the "get tough" operation was the arrest of Rev. King himself. But if this move was intended to frighten King, it fell flat. He calmly submitted to arrest and jailing. At first, he was not to be let out on bond. The news spread through the Negro community like wildfire. Negroes began rushing down to the jail in such numbers that King was released without having even to sign his own bond.

Meanwhile, a group of Negro business and professional men asked the city for permission to operate a jitney service. This was turned down on the grounds that sufficient transportation was already available. The mayor said, let them ride the buses now rolling empty through the streets. A strange stand for one who didn't care if another Negro ever rode a bus again!

But the city did care. It stood to lose part of the $20,000 in taxes it received from the bus company each year. Downtown merchants cared, too, for some of their businesses were off by as much as a third since the boycott had begun. Most of all, the bus company cared—each day it cared more and more. It let it be known that it would agree to any seating arrangement that the city commissioners would approve.

The worst was yet to come. The inflammatory appeals seemed to give the signal to the violent elements. A stick of dynamite was thrown on the porch of Rev. King's home. The job was amateurish; the damage slight; the intent vicious. Within minutes hundreds of Negroes flocked to King's home; also the police. It was at this moment that non-violent resistance almost faded. Many Negroes wanted to launch a counter-offensive. Rev. King, standing on the front porch of his "bombed" home, pleaded with the angry Negroes: "We are not harmed. Do not get your weapons. Let us not answer hate with hate, violence with violence. But we will continue to stay off the buses." Probably this saved the city from a race riot.

There had been other incidents. Some Negro and white high school students had clashed; one or more cars of white youths had made commando raids on the nearby Negro college, dashing through the campus with lights out, throwing out bags of water, eggs, rocks and a tiny flaming cross. One evening the commandos were ambushed and bombarded with bricks. Another commando car was captured by special police. Another clumsy bomb-thrower hit the fence of E. D. Nixon, the president of the local NAACP chapter.

This flurry of violence had no noticeable effect on the boycott. The leaders were careful but nobody seemed to be at all afraid. On the other hand, it helped convince the patient hopefuls that an all-out fight was the only kind that made any sense.

For two months the Negroes had clung to the hope of a settlement on the basis of their limited demands. But the failure of negotiations and the crude brutality of the "get tough" policy convinced the most conservative ex-bus riders that an attack had to be made upon bus segregation itself. Accordingly, on February 1 a suit was filed in the local federal courts, asking for the end of bus jim crow on the grounds that it is contrary to the 14th Amendment of the Constitution of the United States. Furthermore, the court was asked to stop the city commissioners from violating the civil rights of Negro motorists and pedestrians.

This was a sobering jolt for the city commissioners. The "get tough" policy evaporated overnight. The city fathers, who had been making speeches at the drop of the hat, lapsed into their usual quietude.

VII

Meanwhile, a fresh effort was made to re-open negotiations. This time a white business men's club intervened. Many of them had stores that had been hurt. It is estimated that the boycott has cost Montgomery $1,000,000. The business

men's club met several times, separately, with the city commission and a committee from the Montgomery Improvement Association. Chicago Negroes had thrown a picket line
around the offices of the parent bus company, so it was more
willing than ever to come to terms. The city commissioners,
however, remained adamant. They seem to feel that they can
not afford to yield. So the best that the business men could
offer was little more than the old "fake" settlement that had
been palmed off on the "three prominent Negro ministers."

Some of the drivers in the motor pool were becoming exhausted. Twelve or thirteen weeks of free, voluntary service,
four or five hours per day, is fatiguing. Most of these drivers
have jobs and other obligations. Several of the leaders felt
that maybe the boycott might as well be called off since in the
end the courts would settle the issue. Understandably, people
were becoming battle-weary. For over three months, life had
been like a military operation for the Negro Improvement
Association.

So the leaders, though reluctantly, submitted the proposals
of the business men to the rank and file at one of the mass
meetings. The answer was an almost total rejection. Out of
approximately four thousand persons present, *only two* voted
in favor of calling off the boycott. The morale of the masses,
once again, revived the morale of the leaders.

To date the latest move to break the boycott has been the
indictment of the leaders of the Improvement Association.
This was based on an old anti-labor law of doubtful constitutionality. And again nobody was frightened. Nobody tried to
hide. Many inquired of the sheriff's office: "Is my name on
that Grand Jury list?" If it was, the caller let it be known that
he would come down immediately. Confident, orderly, loyal
to each other, the Negroes again manifested their collective
will and *esprit de corps.*

As for the future, nobody can be sure. The white people of
Montgomery have been amazed by the group discipline of
the Negro community and by the intelligence and organization with which the boycott has been maintained. "I didn't
think they had it in them," is a frequent comment.

Many whites who would like to see the boycott ended and

who feel that the demands of the Negroes are reasonable, are afraid to admit this. They fear that to "give in" on this means that "all" is lost. There are sincere apprehensions that desegregation at any one point will lead to general racial integration—and that means intermarriage! An absurd goblin hovers over every white household. The politicians and White Councils exploit these fears. The chief weakness of the movement for desegregation is that so little is done to remove the unfounded alarms of the thousands who in desperation are flocking to the hate organizations.

The fact is that desegregation has been magnified so greatly in the minds of so many Americans, both Negro and white, that they do not realize how ordinary and natural a non-segregated society is. Non-segregation already prevails in many areas of Southern life—the super markets, for example—with scarcely passing notice. Negroes seem to feel that desegregation will work overnight miracles. Southern whites feel that it will precipitate disaster. They are both wrong. It is neither so glorious nor so dangerous as pictured, even in terms of the values of the opposing groups. A non-segregated society is merely a crude, basic pre-condition for creating a social order in which the higher sensibilities can flourish.

We are all indebted to the Negroes of Montgomery. They say that they are confident of ultimate victory. In a sense, they have already won. They have given us a magnificent case study of the circumstances under which the philosophy of Thoreau and Gandhi can triumph. Moreover, the boycott movement has brought something new into the lives of the Negroes of Montgomery. They would be loath to give it up. Whenever the boycott ends, it will be missed.

March 15, 1956

Dissent, Winter 1956

from

The Negroes of Montgomery

---

by Ted Poston

"No, Sir, I Don't Guess So"

SHE WAS an unlettered woman of about 45, and she had been working as a domestic since her early teens. But she displayed an amazing grasp of economics which should have shamed Mayor W. A. (Tacky) Gayle and Montgomery's other two City Commissioners.

She was the only Negro to whom you had talked who had actually been fired for refusing to ride the Montgomery City Lines buses during the protracted boycott.

"But they hired me back that same night they fired me," she explained. "They had to."

"Because I'm helping them buy that new house they got out in the Mount Meigs section. Because, without me, they couldn't keep that 1955 Buick the Mister insisted on trading the old car in for."

The other six women in the bright red station wagon, which was taking them to their domestic jobs at 6 a.m., chuckled appreciatively. But you found the answer a bit complicated, so you asked her to start at the beginning.

"Well," she said, adjusting her plump body to a more comfortable position, "the Mister ain't such a bad man as white folks go. And until this White Citizens Council thing come along, all of my dealings was with the Missus.

"But after Tacky Gayle, Clyde Sellers and that other Commissioner, Frank W. Parks, got mad at us for not riding them buses, and put it on the television that all three of them had joined the White Citizens Councils, the Mister felt he had to join, too.

"So he comes back home from one of them meetings

where they had made him a sergeant or usher or something the night before. And he walks into my kitchen just as I'm getting ready to put dinner on the table.

"'Sarah,' he said to me (that is not her name). 'Sarah,'" he said, 'you ain't one of them fools that have stopped riding the buses, is you?' And I said, 'Yessuh, I is.'

"And he say: 'I ain't gonna have none of this Communist foolishness in my house, Sarah. Now you're coming to work on that bus tomorrow morning.' And I say: "No, sir. I don't think so.'

"And he say: 'Now don't talk back to me like that, even if you is been here three years.' And before I could say anything else, the Missus calls him in the dining room, and he says to me: 'You just wait a minute, we'll settle this when I come back.'

"I could hear them arguing out there while I put the stuff on the stove to keep it warm, and I could hear him tell the Missus: 'She'll do what I say or get out—'

"So I got my bag together and walked on out the back door while they still was arguing. And in a few minutes, Mrs. Alberta James (driver of the Hutchinson Street Baptist Church station wagon) came whizzing by, and I got on in and went on about my business."

She paused in her long recital, and one of the other women murmured: "Tell him about what happened that night."

"Well," she took up again, "I'm setting home about 10 that night and getting ready to go to bed and there came this knock on the door. I guessed who it was right away, and I went there, and sure enough it was the Mister.

"And before I could even open the screen, he says: 'Sarah, you coming to work tomorrow morning ain't you?' And I said: 'No, sir. I don't guess so; you fired me.'

"And he say: 'Look, ain't no need us losing our heads like this; you come on back to work now.' And I said: 'No, sir; you fired me, and another lady wants me to come to her tomorrow. She said she'd pay me $15 instead of the $12 the Missus pays me.'

"Well, that sort of hit him and he don't say nothing for a minute and I don't say nothing neither. And finally he say: 'If it don't be for the children liking you so much, I wouldn't do it. But you come on back and I'll give you the $15 if I got to.'

"And I say: 'Well, I promised this other lady—' and he said: 'Sarah, you know the children like you; now you come on back to work tomorrow morning.' I don't say nothing and he keeps on talking. He wants to apologize but he can't make himself do it.

"So finally I say: 'I got to ride the bus?' And he say: 'I don't give a damn; you just get there the best way you can. But get there, Sarah; you hear me?'"

The other women couldn't contain their bubbling laughter any longer.

But you ask: "But what is this about you paying for their house and car?"

And the laughter subsides as she answers rather caustically:

"It's just this. I get there at 6:30 every morning. I dress and feed the children and get all three of them off to school while the Mister and Missus both rush out to their work.

"I clean up the upstairs and fix the lunch for the children when they come home for lunch. Then I clean the rest of the house and fix the dinner for the children and the Missus and the Mister. They come home and ain't got nothing to do but set down and eat.

"I admit that she washes up the dinner dishes, for I go home after I serve it, but that is all she does do."

She paused and then continued in a soft, bitter voice:

"Now if I wasn't there to do it, she'd have to do all that herself. And she couldn't do it and go to business too.

"Well, she pays me $12 a week so she can go out and make $52 a week in her job. I know that's what she make, for I seen her payroll stub.

"Now if it wasn't for that $40 a week she makes on me, they couldn't meet the mortgage or the payments on that new car neither. They couldn't make it on his check alone."

"It's the God's truth," one of the other women seconded from the jump seat in the station wagon. "And they ain't the only ones. Practically every one of them young couples and plenty old ones, too, in these new subdivisions can't make it if the women don't work too."

"And if we all was to quit work," another put in, "and the

womens had to stay at home, there'd be more dispossessing than you could shake a stick at, and the instalment people would be taking back everything they owned."

But the original narrator was not through. She was smiling when she concluded her story.

"You know," she said, "I hadn't promised no other lady nothing. And nobody offered me no $15, although I probably could get it somewhere else if I tried.

"But I heard the Missus tell the Mister just that week before that she was getting a $6 raise. And I felt some of that raise belonged to me."

And the general laughter was unrestrained.

You had wanted to recite this little lesson in economics to Mayor Gayle, but he had flatly refused to see you despite the importunings of Grover C. Hall Jr., editor-in-chief of the Montgomery Advertiser.

For it was Mayor Gayle, during the "get-tough-with-the-Negroes" early stage of the boycott, who had publicly appealed to white housewives not to drive their Negro domestics to work as a means of breaking the back of the protest.

"Don't accommodate them," he'd told the white women. "They're laughing at you behind your backs."

The women in the station wagon did indeed laugh uproariously when you mentioned this, and one said:

"He also said on the television that he heard a lot of us was being fired 'cause we wouldn't ride them buses. Who did Tacky think he was kidding?"

But if Mayor Gayle and the other two City Commissioners are unaware of the impact of the six-month-old boycott on the economy of Montgomery as a whole, many other whites are not.

Surely the question was in the mind of a prominent white merchant who went through elaborate negotiations with a Negro business man to have you brought to his home late one night "for a completely off-the-record talk on this mess."

When he first approached the Negro intermediary, he had insisted that you not even be told his name. But he was finally persuaded that the name was unimportant if he couldn't trust a newspaperman anyway.

His original purpose, of course, was to try to enlist your aid in trying to persuade Rev. Martin King, Jr., Rev. Ralph D. Abernathy, Dr. Moses W. Jones, E. D. Nixon and other Negro leaders to call off the bus boycott.

"This thing has already cost Montgomery more than $2,000,000 in money losses alone," he had said. "It's not helping anyone, and surely it won't help the Negroes either if they force half the city into bankruptcy."

You tried to tell him—but he didn't believe you—that neither King nor any of the Negro leaders could really call off the bus boycott.

"They didn't really start it, you know," as he hardly listens. "And they can't end it either. The people, the plain, ordinary Negro people here started this thing and only they can stop it."

And then you tell him of the lesson in economics you'd learned in the station wagon that morning. He seemed impressed, but he was more worried over the mercantile problem.

"Do you realize that we all had the worst Christmas business in the history of Montgomery?" he asked aggrievedly as if you were somehow partly responsible for it.

"I know of at least three credit stores which would have been forced to close down completely if they hadn't had a little pickup at Easter.

"Don't King and that bunch realize that people are losing their jobs over this foolishness? What're they trying to do? Make a ghost town out of Montgomery?"

He mentioned a supermarket which had been forced to let 15 employes out because of a loss of Negro patronage.

"Somebody put out a tale that the owner had contributed to the White Citizens Councils. Well, that's a damned lie and I know it. I asked the man personally. In fact, you won't find any of us business men joining the White Citizens Councils and I hope you let your people know that."

You ask tactfully how many of the fired supermarket salespeople were Negroes and he flushes at your impertinence.

"That's not the point," he said, adding: "I know what you're talking about. I know they've been beefing about having Negroes hired in sales jobs. But if they wreck the stores, then there won't be no jobs for anybody. Can't you tell them that?"

You try to tell him that as far as you have been able to learn there is no organized Negro boycott against the white stores, although many individual Negroes resent the segregated facilities and small discourtesies in some establishments.

"But the main thing," you say, "seems to be that the Negroes don't ride the buses anymore, and the new transportation routes of the car pool operation just don't run through the City Square (which is really a circle).

"If they changed their routes to run through there," you venture, "the police would probably harass their drivers more than they are doing now."

It was not a very satisfactory conference on either side and you saw no reason to tell the merchant that things are going to get worse for him in Montgomery before they get better.

For the boycott movement which has spread in all directions from the bus situation has given the biggest boost yet to Negro business in Montgomery.

You remember the first of the twice-weekly mass meetings you had attended at St. John AME Church, and the quiet, conversational speech by which Rev. King had stirred the crowded auditorium to near bedlam.

Among other things, King had said:

"Until we as a race learn to develop our power, we will get nowhere. We've got to get political power and economic power for our race. For there's never been a moment when the dollar was segregated.

"Let us learn in this struggle that we must patronize Negro business. We've felt too long that if the white man touches something, it is just a little better.

"Let nobody fool themselves. We know at times our own business men fall short, but keep on trading with them anyway until they are strong enough to do better.

"We've got Negro doctors in Montgomery, and they are just as good as the white doctors. I don't see how we can go down to these white Jim-Crow dungeons they set aside for us and keep on being called Mary and Sam or any other first name.

"We've got two Negro lawyers; let's use them. When they arrested me, they said, 'You'd better get you a good white lawyer to get you out of trouble,' and I said: 'Brother, you're talking to the wrong man.'

"We've got Dr. (Richard) Harris down there at Dean's Drug Store. We ought to buy him out and make him have to open a whole chain of drug stores.

"But two things we must gain as a race. We've got to get political power. And we've got to get economic power. So let's get both together."

Later, a manager of one of the five large Negro insurance companies which maintain branch or home offices in Montgomery told you:

"I know it's a terrible thing to say. But sometimes I find myself giving thanks for the White Citizens Councils."

He then produced a mimeographed copy of a handbill which was handed out at a White Citizens Council meeting at the State Coliseum last Feb. 10. Titled "A Preview of the Declaration of Segregation," the handbill said, in part:

"When in the course of human events, it becomes necessary to abolish the Negro race, proper methods should be used. Among these are guns, bows and arrows, sling shots and knives.

"We hold these truths to be self-evident that all whites are created equal with certain rights; among these are life, liberty and the pursuit of dead niggers."

The handbill, after assailing the bus boycott, ended with:

"My friends, it is time we wised up to these black devils. I tell you they are a group of two-legged agitators who persist in walking up and down our streets protruding their black lips. If we don't stop these African flesh eaters, we will soon wake up and find Rev. King in the White House.

The insurance agent said: "Soon after that meeting, the head of one of the white insurance companies here which had been selling inferior policies to Negroes for years announced that he had joined the White Citizens Council.

"So I just mimeographed his statement and made up a few hundred copies of this anti-Negro handbill and gave my agents a copy of each to show their Negro prospects.

"And, man, we've been so rushed with Negroes transferring their old policies to us that we haven't been able to write up new business. And the good thing is that many of these

Negroes who switched are probably getting an honest insurance policy for the first time in their lives.

"I tell you, these White Citizens Councils are a very educational group—in more ways than one."

"They Are No Longer Afraid"

YOU'D been living with it daily for nearly three weeks in Montgomery, but you couldn't quite put your finger on it. Only through the words of others were you finally able to articulate a feeling which had been with you from the beginning.

Mrs. Jo Ann Robinson, dynamic president of the Women's Political Council, had been one of the first to pinpoint it for you.

"Pass the lowliest, the most ignorant one, on the street and you'll see it," she said. "He walks a little straighter, his head is a little higher. He is little more of a man or she a woman because they feel a little more like a man or a woman.

"They no longer lack courage; they're no longer afraid. They're free for the first time in their lives and they know they've won their own freedom. This goes not only for the lowest domestic but for the highest Negro professional also."

J. E. Pierce, Alabama-born economist whom you'd known a decade ago in your native Kentucky, expanded it:

"What you're seeing here is probably the closest approach to a classless society that has ever been created in any community in America. The whites have forced the Montgomery Negro to recognize one thing—that they are Negroes first and then domestics, doctors' wives, scholars or lawyers second.

"But for the first time the Negro is accepting with pride, not shame, the fact that all Negroes look alike to white people. Through their unity, their car pools, their determination to share and share alike, they have found each other—as Negroes . . . Walk a little straighter . . . head a little higher.

"This new dignity is not accidental. And it is no accident that they call each other 'ladies' and 'gentlemen' on every possible occasion. For the first time in their lives they feel like ladies and gentlemen from the bottom to the top."

Dr. Richard Harris of Dean's Drug Store touched on another facet when he cited the sad plight of the huge Negro policeman who daily is assigned to the E. L. Posey parking lot which is the principal transfer point of the highly efficient car pool system organized by the Montgomery Improvement Assn. on McDonough St. near Monroe, and run by its ever-cheerful chief dispatcher, Rev. Joseph H. Cherry.

Pointing out that one of Montgomery's original four Negro cops had been fired for not remaining every minute at the lot, Harris said of the current one:

"Look at the poor fellow. There he stands with the face of the victor, wearing the uniform of the vanquished."

But the ordinary people, the real backbone and rulers of the protest movement, express it even better.

As one jolly young domestic of nearly 300 pounds told you as she settled herself carefully in the center of the back seat of a private car pool pickup—"so I won't unbalance professor's car":

"You just go back up there to New York and tell them we's a happy people. A happy people, that's all."

Nowhere is that happiness, and consciousness of their own power, better expressed than in the incidents, anecdotes—almost a mythology—with which they recount their own experiences and those of others in the six-month boycott.

There was the old woman riding in the bright green station wagon—one of 15 brand new ones which joined 5 private station wagons and a hundred-odd private cars in moving some 20,000 Negroes daily to and from work without any charge at all. She recalled:

"When everybody was getting together last Dec. 5 to get this thing going, I was feeling po'ly. I ain't got no radio, or television, and nobody dropped by that night to tell me what was going on.

"But when I saw nobody at my bus stop that next morning, I knew something was going on. But before I could scout around and ask somebody, that old bus came riding up and stopped—with a policemens right behind it.

"I tried to walk away, but that policemens caught me by the arm and said: 'Go on, Auntie, and get on that bus; ain't nobody gonna harm you.' I tried to say I was waiting for somebody, but he kept on talking and pushing until he pushed me on the bus.

"Wasn't nobody on there but me and the driver, so I knew something was wrong. Well, when we'd went about three blocks, the driver looked back and said sweetly: 'Auntie, you ain't paid your dime fare.'

"And I primped up my face as if in surprise, and asked: 'Didn't that white policemens give you no dime?'

"So he stopped at the next block and put me off like I wanted him to in the first place."

The soft, slurring laughter permeated the whole station wagon.

You never meet, but you hear repeatedly of the Negro janitor whose job is some 15 miles from Montgomery, but who is driven to work each morning by one of the pool cars.

But every day he insists upon being put out a full half-mile from his job. Then he gets on the road and works up a good sweat trudging the rest of the way.

And the boss met him the first morning and asked:

"Frank, you live way over in East Montgomery; how in the name of Christ did you get here?"

And the janitor wiped his wet brow, looked the boss in the eye and said:

"I walked."

"That far?" asked the boss, incredulously. And the janitor retorted:

"Now we never did rightly know from the Bible just how far it was that Christ walked from Bethlehem to Jerusalem, did we?"

The new station wagons—all bright red, green, blue or other shining colors—are a particular source of pride to young and old Negroes alike throughout Montgomery.

You are riding along for a pickup run in the First Baptist station wagon—each of the 15 bears the name of a Negro church and its pastor—when a passing train stops you at the railroad track en route to the Old Field section of Montgomery.

A white man in an ordinary station wagon has also been stopped by the train, and two Negro urchins—the tallest no more than three feet—stand near the white driver and look at his vehicle with ill-concealed contempt.

"That ain't one of OUR station wagons," the eldest one said.

"Naw," rejoined the other. "Ain't *pretty* enough."

Pride in the station wagons has even raised difficulties for the incredible transportation system established by the MIA. As Rev. A. B. Johnson, pastor of Hutchinson St. Baptist Church, pointed out at the twice-weekly mass meeting held one Monday night at the First Baptist Church in sweltering 90-degree heat:

"Now, ladies, we're having a great deal of trouble with people who insist upon waiting for the new station wagons to take them home. Now don't forget the good people who were picking you up and putting you down before you got them station wagons.

"So just take the first car that comes along. Someday we'll probably have enough new station wagons for everybody to ride in.

"And meanwhile, ladies, let's stop looking down our noses at the poor white people we pass trudging along without station wagons. It's not Christian."

The admonition must not have been fully accepted, however, for at the mass meeting the next Thursday at Holt St. Mt. Zion Church. Dr. Moses Jones, MIA vice president, felt constrained to say:

"Now I know we're all so proud of our new station wagons that we want the world to hear about it. But we mustn't give anybody a bad look or needle anybody about it.

"You just go where you're going and let the other fellow go where he's going."

And the loudest "Amen" on your pew came from an elderly woman who had ridden back from the Cloverdale section with you the previous day. She had told you how her employer kept asking her wistfully daily why she didn't ride the buses.

"And I finally told her," she had said, with a twinkle in her eye, "that my arthritis had got so bad that I just couldn't step high enough to get on one of them buses."

Another said her employer had told her:

"Everybody is saying that only Communists refuse to ride the buses."

"And I said, 'I know you got them told, Miss Lucy. 'Cause you wouldn't let no Communist raise your six chillun.'"

And mythology begins when the stories extend beyond the boundaries of Montgomery. You're sitting on one of the cracker boxes outside the E. L. Posey transfer lot—where a constant stream of station wagons are taking only 15 seconds each to unload and reload and be on their way—and you listen idly to two male fertilizer workers enroute home.

"I hear tell that over in Birmingham," one of them is saying with that deadpan expression which telegraphs a coming joke a mile away, "that one of the brothers took a snootful too much one night and then hailed a bus.

"Well, he was so looped that he paid his fare and just dropped down in the first seat he came to. The cracker driver stopped the bus and told him he had to move to the back, but the brother was so stoned that he didn't hear nothing.

"So the driver got out and made a telephone call. Pretty soon, up comes three police cars, an empty bus and the president of the Birmingham bus company. The president climbed on and told the white passengers: 'You all get out of here; there's going to be trouble. So you all just get in that empty bus over there so nobody don't get hurt!'

"So the white folks all piled out and got in the other bus. Then the president whispered to the cracker driver:

"'Now, you wake that nigger up and find out where he wants to go and carry him there. We don't want none of that Montgomery stuff here in Birmingham.'"

Only then does the deadpan expression relax as he joins in the laughter at his own joke.

Or that early morning when you were standing at one of the 32 dispatch stations or 40 pickup stations which are the heart of the car pool operation, and eavesdropped on an old couple discussing Southern customs.

"This stuff about separate but equal has always galled me," the man was saying.

"Reminds me of the time during the first war when they allowed butchers to mix a little horse meat in when they were making rabbit sausage.

"Well, we had a colored butcher out in our section who was getting well on the deal until they grabbed him for putting too much horse meat in the rabbit sausage.

"But when they brought him up before the court, he

pleaded that he was just living up to the principles the white folks had taught him.

"'Jedge,' he told the reb justice of the peace, 'I was just trying to keep everything separate but equal. I never at no time used more than one horse to one rabbit.'"

Again the deadpan dissolved and soft laughter followed.

There were times though when the remarkable young Rev. Martin Luther King, Jr. had to chide his MIA followers for their irrepressible laughter. Like the night the Rev. Ralph D. Abernathy was reading incoming communications at the Thursday night mass meeting at St. John's AME Church.

It appeared that a group of white kindergarten children in a Wisconsin Sunday School had sent their Sunday collection to the Negro bus protesters in Montgomery. And since they were too young to write long letters of sympathy, they had expressed themselves with pictures.

One of the crude little drawings showed an empty bus coming down Dexter Av. (Laughter.) Another showed a church crowded with many people. (Warm chuckles.)

"And another," Abernathy said, "showed a hospital bed with Mr. Bigley in it, and a sentence which read: 'Father, forgive them, they know not what they do.'" (Uproarious laughter.)

(J. H. Bigley, manager of the Montgomery City Lines bus system, had suffered a heart attack when the boycott became effective.)

But King had cut the laughter short by chiding the audience which extended out onto the sidewalk while crowding every seat and aisle in the sweltering church.

"We must not rejoice or laugh to see anybody have a heart attack, not even Mr. Bigley; not even Police Commissioner Sellers or even Sen. Eastland.

"For in our struggle for justice, even Sen. Eastland is a child of God, although at times a straying one. Never let us feel that we must become bitter—even in laughter. Let 16,000,000 children of God inject that thought into American life."

But not even Martin Luther King could remove all bitterness from the voices of the women as they closed the meeting by rising and giving personal testimony to their God.

"Oh, Lawd," one very large and very dark lady moaned as

she looked toward the ceiling as in personal conversation with her Maker, "Oh Lawd, Oh, Lawd, how long?

"They tell me I ain't good enough to sit down with them. They tell me I ain't fit.

"But Lawd," raising her fleshy arms and curling her fingers, "with these black hands, Oh, Lawd, I knead the very bread they put in their mouths.

"With these black breasts," cupping her ample bosom in both hands, "I suckled the children of their loins when their mother was bone dry. My milk, as white as my blood is red, courses through their bodies.

"With these thick lips," protruding them to make them thicker yet, "with these thicks lips, Oh, Lawd, I taste the very food I cook for them to see if it's right.

"Yet, Oh, Lawd, they said I ain't fit to sit beside them on a bus.

"I ask you, Lawd, I ask you. How long?"

No speaker of the evening, including even King, drew such a deep or heartfelt response from the shouting audience.

You faded into the night with 3,000 other Negroes and found yourself muttering too:

"How long, indeed, Lord. How long?"

New York Post, June 15 & 19, 1956

Tallahassee Spirit:
Tired of Being Pushed Around

by Samuel L. Gandy

TALLAHASSEE, Fla.—The citizens of Tallahassee who are engaged in a boycott against the use of the public transit buses are making clear once again that the indigenous nature of the protest is a people's reaction to a deep sense of injustice.

Residents in this western section of upper Florida (familiarly known as southern Georgia) have experienced injustice, violence, and lynchings first-hand. It was in this general section that the widely publicized Live Oaks trial took place.

However, the present reaction differs sharply from a political uprising or a social revolt and has all of the overtones of a spiritual revival. The protesters are on the whole religious people with a commitment to the way of Jesus in social revolution. They sing and pray and testify in evangelical manner, pausing to discuss the problems resulting from the boycott, and then bearing testimony again to their quest for freedom.

I attended two mass meetings in Tallahassee last week (July 6–13) while serving as a consultant at Florida A. and M. University. As I arrived at the already overflowing church sanctuary I could not readily distinguish between the mass meeting as called and what I had known in Virginia as a summer revival session. The audience was forceful in the singing of hymns, spirituals, and prayers that I had heard in my boyhood.

Preparation for the mass meeting always includes a thorough worship period. It is evident that there is no hatred, hostility, nor smoldering bitterness in the protest. It is an issue that the people confront. An issue that calls for morality of higher expression in an immoral situation: of Christian ethics in an un-Christian climate of enforced power. Essentially, it is the world today.

Over and over again members of the inter-Civic Community Council expressed this thought:

"It isn't the matter of buses any longer. It's much deeper than that. It is a matter of the spirit. You just get tired of being pushed around."

Humor is beginning to settle the anxiety that once existed in the tense gathering. Decisions do not come easily, and there are those for whom bus transportation has been the one way of travel all of their lives. Returning to a mass meeting on Wednesday night, I observed a protester raising his hand for the floor. Upon being recognized by the chairman he marched from the rear of the sanctuary to the edge of the rostrum, deposited bits of shredded paper and repeated, "To the buses . . . ashes to ashes . . ."

The packed sanctuary roared with laughter thereby easing the heaviness of debate for the decisions to follow.

Perhaps the most peculiar feeling one receives is the kind of joy which shines in the faces of those who have decided not to ride jim-crow buses anymore. Their down-to-earth confessions of belief in the cause for self-respect and dignity moves one's devotion to truth and liberty.

When one woman who had ridden the buses for 25 years rose to question a proposal by the City Commissioners she prefaced her statement with words of reassurance:

"Now, I am not tired walking. I am willing to continue walking . . ."

All Negro bus passengers are not in accord with the boycott. It is evident that a program of education must be initiated along with the act of protest. There are those who are so thoroughly conditioned that they feel no embarrassment in being denied freedom of movement on the buses. On the whole, these dissenters do not attend the mass meetings.

How to reach them is a problem which the group faces. An acute problem in communication is the daily brainwashing that many domestic workers and unskilled employees confront. Employers are daily trying to convince their employees that the cause is rather futile, certainly cumbersome for them, and that compromise is the least that they can accept—never integration in travel.

The local press and radio stations are mostly unfavorable toward the boycott and twist and distort the news. No effort has been made to refuse anyone admittance to the mass meetings. Reporters are usually present.

The one definite antidote to the problem of dissenters is the fervor generated at the mass meetings. Herein is a kind of fellowship that persuades and restores. As a member testified:

"If we could only get them here. You just can't attend and go back to the buses. You sorta get tied-in to a cause that is right and just."

There is fact in this remark. I was different after the first one I attended. I left the meeting strengthened and heartened in a pull for democracy.

One healthy asset in the social protest is the almost united leadership of ministers. Fashionable and not so fashionable church members and preachers are caught-up together in a common witness and program. All ministers present sit in fellowship fashion on the rostrum and share freely in the thinking of the group.

No one is permitted to hedge from the decision to move forward toward integration in travel. One hard-working woman rose in heated contest with a leader who gave signs of compromising and challenged him to resign from the Executive Committee if "his knees were weakening."

A chorus of voices called for fresh commitment from all leaders. One by one those present rose and endorsed the justice of the cause. When they had finished, the people smiled in broad approval and gave a silent Amen.

There is good cross-community representation of professional workers and non-professional. Class and prestige are forgotten in this effort. There are no big folks and little folks —just folks. Prestige-bearing citizens are learning to drive in the car-pool and snobbish folk just don't attend the meetings.

I believe that Tallahassee folk aren't going to change their minds, even though real pressures are being brought by certain service organizations, the Junior Chamber of Commerce, and others.

The success of the car-pool will determine largely the time-length of an effective boycott of the buses. So far, the car-pool is getting off to a good start. Drivers are being stopped and fined for the least possible traffic infraction and some are being stopped just for pressure-sake.

The immediate need is for station wagons and finance of operation costs. Contributions are raised at each mass meeting but this amount is not sufficient. This effort calls for more than one dollar offerings, unless thousands will give them.

I was invited by a member of the Executive Committee to dinner and discussed with several members present the future of the protest as a movement.

"What are you going to do?" I inquired, as Rev. J. C. Sicele, president of the inter-Civic Community Council listened.

Then he said, "I guess we are going to have to depend on the faith that other citizens all over America have in the justice of our cause and will send contributions to help us win this effort."

As I shook hands with the leaders present, I wondered how long it would take for citizens in Virginia to remember citizens in Tallahassee and catch the fervor of their movement for liberty and send contributions. As the comfortable Gulf Wind train rolled along the shores of the Gulf of Mexico bearing me again to New Orleans, leaving behing a people and a cause, I felt strangely united in spirit with them and determined to tell the story of their struggle for democratic living as if I were still there with them.

Perhaps that is why I must tell it because justice and freedom is everybody's cause, or it is everybody's failure.

Journal and Guide (Norfolk, Va), July 28, 1956

Segregation: The Inner Conflict in the South

by Robert Penn Warren

"I'M GLAD it's you going," my friend, a Southerner, long resident in New York, said, "and not me." But I went back, for going back this time, like all the other times, was a necessary part of my life. I was going back to look at the landscapes and streets I had known—Kentucky, Tennessee, Arkansas, Mississippi, Louisiana—to look at the faces, to hear the voices, to hear, in fact, the voices in my own blood. A girl from Mississippi had said to me: "I feel it's all happening inside of me, every bit of it. It's all there."

I know what she meant.

To the right, the sun, cold and pale, is westering. Far off, a little yellow plane scuttles down a runway, steps awkwardly into the air, then climbs busily, learning grace. Our big plane trundles ponderously forward, feeling its weight like a fat man, hesitates, shudders with an access of sudden, building power; and with a new roar in my ears, I see the ground slide past, then drop away, like a dream. I had not been aware of the instant we had lost that natural contact.

Memphis is behind me, and I cannot see it, but yonder is the river, glittering coldly, and beyond, the tree-sprigged flats of Arkansas. Still climbing, we tilt eastward now, the land pivoting away below us, the tidy toy farms, white houses, silos the size of a spool of white thread, or smaller, the stock ponds bright like little pieces of gum wrapper dropped in brown grass, but that brown grass is really trees, the toy groves with shadows precise and long in the leveling light.

Arkansas has pivoted away. It is Mississippi I now see down there, the land slipping away in the long light, and in my mind I see, idly, the ruined, gaunt, classic clay hills, with the creek bottoms throttled long since in pink sand, or the white houses of Holly Springs, some of them severe and beautiful,

284

or Highway 61 striking south from Memphis, straight as a
knife edge through the sad and baleful beauty of the Delta
country, south toward Vicksburg and the Federal cemeteries,
toward the fantasia of Natchez.

It seems like a thousand years since I first drove that road,
more than twenty-five years ago, a new concrete slab then,
dizzily glittering in the August sun-blaze, driving past the
rows of tenant shacks, Negro shacks set in the infinite cotton
fields, and it seems like a hundred years since I last drove it,
last week, in the rain, then toward sunset the sky clearing a
little, but clouds solid and low on the west like a black range
of mountains frilled upward with an edge of bloody gold
light, quickly extinguished. Last week, I noticed that more of
the shacks were ruinous, apparently abandoned. More, but
not many, had an electric wire running back from the road.
But when I caught a glimpse, in the dusk, of the interior of a
lighted shack, I usually saw the coal-oil lamp. Most shacks
were not lighted. I wondered if it was too early in the
evening. Then it was early no longer. Were that many of the
shacks abandoned?

Then we would pass in the dark some old truck grudging
and clanking down the concrete, and catch, in the split-
second flick of our headlamps, a glimpse of the black faces
and the staring eyes. Or the figure, sudden in our headlight,
would rise from the roadside, dark and shapeless against the
soaked blackness of the cotton land: the man humping along
with the croker sack on his shoulders (containing what?), the
woman with a piece of sacking or paper over her head against
the drizzle now, at her bosom a bundle that must be a small
child, the big children following with the same slow, mud-
lifting stride in the darkness. The light of the car snatches
past, and I think of them behind us in the darkness, moving
up the track beside the concrete, seeing another car light far
yonder toward Memphis, staring at it perhaps, watching it
grow, plunge at them, strike them, flick past. They will move
on, at their pace. Yes, they are still here.

I see a river below us. It must be the Tennessee. I wonder
on which side of us Shiloh is, and guess the right, for we must
have swung far enough north for that. I had two grandfathers
at Shiloh, that morning of April 6, 1862, young men with the

other young men in gray uniforms stepping toward the lethal
spring thickets of dogwood and redbud, to the sound of bird
song. "One hundred and sixty men we took in the first morning, son. Muster the next night, and it was sixteen answered."
They had fallen back on Corinth, into Mississippi.

The man in the seat beside me on the plane is offering me
a newspaper. I see the thumb of the hand clutching the paper.
The nail is nearly as big as a quarter, split at the edges,
grooved and horny, yellowish, with irrevocable coal-black
grime deep under the nail and into the cuticle. I look at the
man. He is a big man, very big, bulging over the seat, bulging
inside his blue serge. He is fiftyish, hair graying. His face is
large and raw-looking, heavy-jowled, thick gray eyebrows
over small, deep-set, appraising eyes. His name, which he tells
me, sounds Russian or Polish, something ending in -ski.

I begin to read the paper, an article about the riots at the
University of Alabama. He notices what I am reading. "Bet
you thought I was from down here," he said. "From the way
I talk. But I ain't. I was born and raised in New York City,
but I been in the scrap business down here ten years. Didn't
you think I was from down here?"

"Yes," I say, for that seems the sociable thing to say.

He twists his bulk in the blue serge and reaches and stabs a
finger at the headline about Alabama. "Folks could be more
gen'rous and fair-thinking," he says. "Like affable, you might
say, and things would work out. If folks get affable and con-
tig'ous, you might say, things sort of get worked out in time,
but you get folks not being affable-like and stirring things up
and it won't work out. Folks on both sides the question."

He asks me if I don't agree, and I say, sure, I agree. Sure,
if folks were just affable-like.

I am thinking of what a taxi driver had said to me in Memphis: "Looks like the Lucy girl wouldn't want to go no place
where people throwed eggs at her and sich. But if they'd jist
let her alone, them Goodrich plant fellers and all, it would
blow over. What few niggers come would not have stayed no
duration. Not when they found she couldn't git the social
stuff, and all."

And what the school superintendent, in middle Tennessee,

had said: "You take a good many people around here that I know, segregationists all right, but when they read about a thousand to one, it sort of makes them sick. It is the unfairness in that way that gets them."

And an organizer of one of the important segregation groups, a lawyer, when I asked him if Autherine Lucy wasn't acting under law, he creaked his swivel chair, moved his shoulders under his coat, and touched a pencil on his desk, before saying: "Yes—yes—but it was just the Federal Court ruled it."

And a taxi driver in Nashville, a back-country man come to the city, a hard, lean, spare face, his lean, strong shoulders humped forward over the wheel so that the clavicles show through the coat: "A black-type person and a white-type person, they ain't alike. Now the black-type person, all they think about is fighting and having a good time and you know what. Now the white-type person is more American-type, he don't mind fighting but he don't fight to kill for fun. It's that cannibal blood you caint git out."

Now, on the plane, my companion observes me scribbling something in a notebook.

"You a writer or something?" he asks. "A newspaper fellow, maybe?"

I say yes.

"You interested in that stuff?" he asks, and points to the article. "Somebody ought to tell 'em not to blame no state, not even Alabam' or Mississippi, for what the bad folks do. Like stuff in New York or Chicago. Folks in Mississippi got good hearts as any place. They always been nice and good-hearted to me, for I go up to a man affable. The folks down here is just in trouble and can't claw out. Don't blame 'em, got good hearts but can't claw out of their trouble. It is hard to claw out from under the past and the past way."

He asks me if I have been talking to a lot of people.

I had been talking to a lot of people.

I had come to the shack at dusk, by the brimming bayou, in the sea of mud where cotton had been. The cold drizzle was still falling. In the shack, on the hickory chair, the yellow girl, thin but well made, wearing a salmon sweater and salmon denim slacks, holds the baby on her knee and leans toward the iron stove. On the table beyond her is an ivory-colored portable radio and a half-full bottle of Castoria. On the other side of the stove are her three other children, the oldest seven. Behind me, in the shadowy background, I know there are faces peering in from the other room of the shack, black faces, the half-grown boys, another girl I had seen on entering. The girl in the salmon sweater is telling how she heard her husband had been killed. "Livin in town then, and my sister, she come that night and tole me he was shot. They had done shot him dead. So I up and taken out fer heah, back to the plantation. Later, my sister got my chillen and brought 'em. I ain't gonna lie, mister. I tell you, I was scairt. No tellin if that man what done it was in jail or no. Even if they had ar-rest him, they might bon' him out and he come and do it to me. Be mad because they 'rest him. You caint never tell. And they try him and 'quit him, doan know as I kin stay heah. Even they convick him, maybe I leave. Some good folks round heah and they helpin me, and I try to appreciate and be a prayin chile, but you git so bore down on and nigh ruint and sort of brain-washed, you don't know what. Things git to goin round in yore head. I could run out or somethin, but you caint leave yore chillen. But look like I might up and leave. He git 'quitted, that man, and maybe I die, but I die goin."

This is the cliché. It is the thing the uninitiate would ex-pect. It is the cliché of fear. It is the cliché come fresh, and alive.

There is another image. It is morning in Nashville. I walk down Union Street, past the Negro barber shops, past the ruinous buildings plastered over with placards of old circuses and rodeos, buildings being wrecked now to make way for progress, going into the square where the big white stone boxlike, ugly and expensive Davidson County Court House now stands on the spot where the old brawling market once was. Otherwise, the square hasn't changed much, the same buildings, wholesale houses, liquor stores, pawn shops, quick lunches, and the same kind of people stand on the corners, countrymen, in khaki pants and mackinaw coats, weathered faces and hard, withdrawn eyes, usually pale eyes, lean-hipped men ("narrow-assted" in the country phrase) like the men who rode with Forrest, the farm wives, young with a baby in arms, or middle-aged and work-worn, with colored cloths over the head, glasses, false teeth, always the shopping bag.

I walk down toward the river, past the Darling Display Distribution show window, where a wax figure stands in skirt and silk blouse, the fingers spread on one uplifted hand, the thin face lifted with lips lightly parted as though in eternal, tubercular expectation of a kiss. I see the power pylons rising above the river mist. A tug is hooting up-river in the mist.

I go on down to the right, First Street, to the replica of Fort Nashborough, the original settlement, which stands on the river bank under the shadow of warehouses. The stockade looks so child-flimsy and jerry-built jammed against the massive, soot-stained warehouses. How could the settlers have ever taken such protection seriously? But it was enough, that and their will and the long rifles and the hunting knives and the bear-dogs they unleashed to help them when they broke the Indians at the Battle of the Bluffs. They took the land, and remain.

I am standing in the middle of the empty stockade when a boy enters and approaches me. He is about fifteen, strongly built, wearing a scruffed and tattered brown leather jacket, blue jeans, a faded blue stocking cap on the back of his head, with a mop of yellow hair hanging over his forehead. He is a fine-looking boy, erect, manly in the face, with a direct, blue-eyed glance. "Mister," he said to me, "is this foh't the way it was, or they done remodeled it?"

I tell him it is a replica, smaller than the original and not on the right spot, exactly.

"I'm glad I seen it, anyway," he says. "I like to go round seeing things that got history, and such. It gives you something to think about. Helps you in a quiz sometimes, too."

I ask him where he goes to school.

"Atlanta," he says. "Just come hitch-hiking up this a-way, looking at things for interest. Like this here foh't."

"You all been having a little trouble down your way," I ask, "haven't you?"

He looks sharply at me, hesitates, then says: "Niggers—you mean niggers?"

"Yes."

"I hate them bastards," he says, with a shuddering, automatic violence, and averts his face and spits through his teeth, a quick, viperish, cut-off expectoration.

I say nothing, and he looks at me, stares into my face with a dawning belligerence, sullen and challenging, and suddenly demands: "Don't you?"

"I can't say that I do," I reply. "I like some and I don't like some others."

He utters the sudden obscenity, and removes himself a couple of paces from me. He stops and looks back over his shoulder. "I'm hitching on back to Atlanta," he declares in a flat voice, "this afternoon," and goes on out of the fort.

This, too, is a cliché. The boy, standing on the ground of history and heroism, his intellect and imagination stirred by the fact, shudders with that other, automatic emotion which my question had evoked. The cliché had come true: the cliché of hate. And somehow the hallowedness of the ground he stood on had vindicated, as it were, that hate.

The boy in the fort was the only person to turn from me, but occasionally there would be a stiffening, a flicker of suspicion, an evasion or momentary refusal of the subject, even in the casual acquaintance of lobby or barroom. At one of the new luxurious motels near Clarksdale (the slick motels and the great power stations and booster stations, silver-glittering by day and jewel-glittering by night, are the most obvious marks of the new boom), a well-dressed young man is talking about a movie being made down near Greenville. The movie is something about cotton, he says, by a fellow named Williams. Anyway, they had burned down a gin in the middle of the night, just for the movie. The woman at the desk (a very good blue dress that had cost money, a precise, respectable middle-aged mouth, pince-nez) speaks up: "Yes, and they say it's the only movie ever made here didn't criticize Mississippi."

"Criticize?" I ask. "Criticize how?"

She turns her head a little, looks at the man with her behind the desk, then back at me. "You know," she says, "just criticize."

I see the eyes of the man behind the desk stray to the license of our car parked just beyond the glass front. It has a Tennessee license, a U-Drive-It from Memphis.

"Criticize?" I try again.

The man had been busy arranging something in the drawer behind the desk. Suddenly, very sharply, not quite slamming, he shoves the drawer shut. "Heck, you know," he says.

"Didn't they make another movie over at Oxford?" I ask.

The man nods, the woman says yes. I ask what that one had been about. Nobody has seen it, not the woman, neither of the men. "It was by that fellow Faulkner," the woman says. "But I never read anything he ever wrote."

"I never did either," the man behind the desk says, "but I know what it's like. It's like that fellow Hemingway. I read some of his writings. Gory and on the seedy side of life. I didn't like it."

"That's exactly right," the woman says, and nods. "On the seedy side of life. That fellow Faulkner, he's lost a lot of friends in Mississippi. Looking at the seedy side."

"Does he criticize?" I ask.

She turns away. The man goes into a door behind the desk. The well-dressed young man has long since become engrossed in a magazine.

My Tennessee license, and Tennessee accent, hadn't been good enough credentials in Clarksdale, Mississippi. But on one occasion, the accent wasn't good enough even in Tennessee, and I remember sitting one evening in the tight, tiny living room (linoleum floor, gas heater, couch, one chair, small table with TV) of an organizer of a new important segregation group (one-time official of the Klan, this by court record) while he harangues me. He is a fat but powerful man, face fat but not flabby, the gray eyes squinty, set deep in the flesh, hard and sly by turns, never genial though the grin tries to be when he has scored a point and leans forward at me, creaking the big overstuffed chair, his big hands crossed on his belly. He is a hill-man, come to town from one of the counties where there aren't too many Negroes, but he's now out to preserve, he says, "what you might name the old Southern way, what we was raised up to."

He is not out for money. ("I just git one dollar ever fellow I sign, the other two goes to Mr. Perkins at headquarters, for expense. Hell, I lose money on hit, on my gasoline.") No, he's not out for money, but something else. He is clearly a man of force, force that somehow has never found its way, and a man of language and leadership among his kind, the angry and ambitious and disoriented and dispossessed. It is language that intoxicates him now. He had been cautious at first, had thought I was from the FBI (yes, he had had a brush with them once, a perjury indictment), but now it seems some grand vista is opening before him and his eyes gleam and the words come.

He is talking too much, tangling himself. All the while his wife (very handsome, almost beautiful, in fact, bobbed, disordered black hair around a compact, smooth-chiseled, tanned face, her body under a flimsy dress tight and compact but gracefully made) has been standing in the deep shadow of the doorway to a room beyond, standing patiently, hands folded but tense, with the fingers secretly moving, standing like the proper hill-wife while the men-folks talk.

"Excuse me," she suddenly says, but addressing me, not the husband, "excuse me, but didn't you say you were born down here, used to live right near here?"

I say yes.

She takes a step forward, coming out of the shadow. "Yes," she says, "yes," leaning at me in vindictive triumph, "but you never said where you're living now!"

And I remember sitting with a group of college students, and one of them, a law student it develops, short but strong-looking, dark-haired and slick-headed, dark bulging eyes in a slick, rather handsome, arrogant—no, bumptious—face, breaks in: "I just want to ask one question before anything starts. I just want to ask where you're from."

Suspicion of the outlander, or of the corrupted native, gets tangled up sometimes with suspicion of the New York press, but this latter suspicion may exist quite separately, on an informed and reasoned basis. For instance, I have seen a Southern newspaper man of high integrity and ability (an integrationist, by the way) suddenly strike down his fist and exclaim: "Well, by God, it's just a fact, it's not in them not to load the dice in a news story!" And another, a man publicly committed to maintaining law and order, publicly on record against the Citizens Councils and all such organizations: "*Life* magazine's editorial on the Till case, that sure fixed it. If Till's father had died a hero's death fighting for liberty, as *Life* said, that would have been as irrelevant as the actual fact that he was executed by the American army for rape-murder. It sure makes it hard."

There is the Baptist minister, an educated and intelligent man, who, when I show him an article in the *Reader's Digest*, an article mentioning that the Southern Baptist Convention had voted overwhelmingly for support of the Supreme Court decision, stiffens and says to me: "Look— look at that title!"

I didn't need to look. I knew what it was: "The Churches Repent."

But there is another suspicion story. A Negro told me this. A man from New Haven called on him, and upon being asked politely to take a chair, said, "Now, please, won't you tell me about the race problem."

To which the Negro replied: "Mister, I can't tell you a thing about that. There's nothing I could tell to you. If you want to find out, you better just move down here and live for a while."

That is the something else—the instinctive fear, on the part of black or white, that the massiveness of experience, the concreteness of life, will be violated; the fear of abstraction. I suppose it is this fear that made one man, a subtle and learned man, say to me: "There's something you can't explain, what being a Southerner is." And when he said that, I remembered a Yankee friend saying to me: "Southerners and Jews, you're exactly alike, you're so damned special."

"Yes," I said, "we're both persecuted minorities."

I had said it for a joke.

But had I?

In the end people talked, even showed an anxiety to talk, to explain something. Even the black Southerners, a persecuted minority, too, would talk, for over and over the moment of some sudden decision would come: "All right—all right—I'll tell it to you straight. All right, there's no use beating around the bush."

But how fully can I read the words offered in the fullest effort of candor?

It is a town in Louisiana, and I am riding in an automobile driven by a Negro, a teacher, a slow, careful man, who puts his words out in that fashion, almost musingly, and drives his car that way, too. He has been showing me the Negro business section, how prosperous some of it is, and earlier he had said he would show me a section where the white men's cars almost line up at night. Now he seems to have forgotten that sardonic notion in the pleasanter, more prideful task. He has fallen silent, seemingly occupied with his important business of driving, and the car moves deliberately down the street. Then, putting his words out that slow way, detachedly as though I weren't there, he says: "You hear some white men say they know Negroes. Understand Negroes. But it's not true. No white man ever born ever understood what a Negro is thinking. What he's feeling."

The car moves on down the empty street, negotiates a left turn with majestic deliberation.

"And half the time that Negro," he continues, "he don't understand, either."

I know that the man beside me had once, long back, had a bright-skinned, pretty wife. She had left him to be set up by a well-off white man (placée is the old word for it). The Negro man beside me does not know that I know this, but I have known it a long time, and now I wonder what this man is thinking as we ride along, silent again.

Just listening to talk as it comes is best, but sometimes it doesn't come, or the man says, "You ask me some questions," and so, bit by bit, a certain pattern of questions emerges, the old obvious questions, I suppose—the questions people respond to or flinch from.

What are the white man's reasons for segregation?

The man I am talking to is a yellow man, about forty years old, shortish, rather fat, with a very smooth, faintly Mongolian face, eyes very shrewd but ready to smile. When the smile really comes, there is a gold tooth showing, to become, in that gold face, part of the sincerity of the smile. His arms seem somewhat short, and as he sits very erect in a straight chair, he folds his hands over his stomach. He gives the impression of a man very much at home in himself, at peace in himself, in his dignity, in his own pleasant, smooth-skinned plumpness, in some sustaining humorousness of things. He owns a small business, a shoe shop with a few employees.

"What does the white man do it for?" he rephrases the question. He pauses, and you can see he is thinking, studying on it, his smooth, yellow face compressing a little. All at once the face relaxes, a sort of humorous ripple, humorous but serious too, in a sort of wry way, before the face settles to its blandness. "You know," he says, "you know, years and years I look at some white feller, and I caint never figure him out. You go long with him, years and years, and all of a sudden he does something. I caint figure out what makes him do the way he does. It is like a mystery, you might say. I have studied on it."

Another Negro, a very black man, small-built and intense, leans forward in his chair. He says it is money, so the white man can have cheap labor, can make the money. He is a bookish man, has been to a Negro college, and though he has never been out of the South, his speech surprises me the way my native ear used to be surprised by the speech of a Negro born and raised, say, in Akron, Ohio. I make some fleeting, tentative association of his speech, his education, his economic interpretation of things; then let the notion slide.

"Yeah, yeah," the yellow man is saying, agreeing, "but—" He stops, shakes his head.

"But what?" I ask.

He hesitates, and I see the thumbs of the hands lightly clasped across his belly begin to move, ever so slowly, round and round each other. "All right," he says, "I might as well say it to you."

"Say what?"

"Mongrelization," he says, "that's what a white man will say. You ask him and he'll say that. He wants to head it off, he says. But—" He grins, the skin crinkles around his eyes, the grin shows the gold tooth. "But," he says, "look at my face. It wasn't any black man hung it on me."

The other man doesn't seem to think this is funny. "Yes," he says, "yes, they claim they don't want mongrelization. But who has done it? They claim Negroes are dirty, diseased, that that's why they want segregation. But they have Negro nurses for their children, they have Negro cooks. They claim Negroes are ignorant. But they won't associate with the smartest and best educated Negro. They claim—" And his voice goes on, winding up the bitter catalogue of paradoxes. I know them all. They are not new.

The smooth-faced, yellow man is listening. But he is thinking, too, the yellow blandness of his face creaming ever so little with his slow, humorous intentness. I ask him what he is thinking.

He grins, with philosophic ruefulness. "I was just studying on it," he says. "It's all true, what Mr. Elmo here says. But there must be something behind it all. Something he don't ever say, that white feller. Maybe—" He pauses, hunting for the formulation. "Maybe it's just pridefulness," he says, "him being white."

Later, I am talking with the hill-man organizer, the one with the handsome wife who asks me where I live now, and he is telling me why he wants segregation. "The Court," he says, "hit caint take no stick and mix folks up like you swivel and swull eggs broke in a bowl. Naw," he says, "you got to raise 'em up, the niggers, not bring the white folks down to nigger level." He illustrates with his pudgy, strong hands in the air before him, one up, one down, changing levels. He watches the hands, with fascination, as though he has just learned to do a complicated trick.

How would you raise the level? I ask.

"Give 'em good schools and things, yeah. But"—and he warms to the topic, leaning at me—"I'd 'bolish common law marriage. I'd put 'em in jail fer hit, and make 'em learn morals. Now a nigger don't know how to treat no wife, not even a nigger wife. He whup her and beat her and maybe carve on her jaw with a pocketknife. When he ought to trick and pet her, and set her on his knee like a white man does his wife."

Then I talk with a Negro grade-school teacher, in the country, in Tennessee. She is a mulatto woman, middle-aged, with a handsome aquiline face, rather Indian-looking. She is sitting in her tiny, pridefully clean house, with a prideful bookcase of books beyond her, talking with slow and detached tones. I know what her story has been, years of domestic service, a painfully acquired education, marriage to a professional man, no children ("It was a cross to bear, but maybe that's why I love 'em so and like to teach 'em not my own").

I ask her why white people want to keep segregation.

"You ought to see the school house I teach in," she says, and pauses, and her lips curl sardonically, "set in the mud and hogs can come under it, and the privies set back in the mud. And see some of the children that come there, out of homes with nothing, worse than the school house, no sanitation or cleanness, with disease and dirt and no manners. You wouldn't blame a white person for not wanting the white child set down beside them." Then with a slow movement of the shoulders, again the curl of the lips: "Why didn't the Federal Government give us money ten years ago for our school? To get ready, to raise us up a little to integrate. It would have made it easier. But now—"

But now? I ask.

"You got to try to be fair," she says.

I am talking with an official of one of the segregation outfits, late at night, in his house, in a fringe subdivision, in a small living room with red velvet drapes at the one window, a TV set, new, on a table, a plastic or plaster bas-relief of a fox hunter hung on the wall, in color, the hunting coat very red and arrogant. My host is seventy-five years old, bald except for a fringe of gray hair, sallow-skinned, very clean and scrubbed-looking, white shirt but no tie, a knife-edge crease to his hard-finish gray trousers. He smokes cigarettes, one after another, with nervous, stained fingers.

He was born in North Kentucky, romantically remembers the tobacco night riders ("Yeah, it was tight, nobody talked tobacco much, you might get shot"), remembers the Civil War veterans ("even the GAR's") sitting round, talking to the kids ("Yeah, they talked their war, they had something to remember and be proud of, not like these veterans we got nowadays, nothing to be proud of"), started out to be a lawyer ("But Blackstone got too dry, but history now, that's different, you always get something out of it to think about"), but wound up doing lots of things, finally, for years, a fraternal organizer.

Yes, he is definitely a pro, and when he talks of Gerald L. K. Smith he bursts out, eyes a-gleam: "Lord, that man's mailing list would be worth a million dollars!" He is not the rabble-rouser, the crusader, but the persuader, the debater, the man who gives the reasons. He is, in fact, a very American type, the old-fashioned, self-made, back-country intellectual —the type that finds apotheosis in Mark Twain and Abraham Lincoln. If he is neither of them, if he says "gondorea" and "enviro-mental" and "ethnolology," if something went wrong, if nothing ever came out quite right for him along the long way, you can still sense the old, unappeased hungers, the old drives of a nameless ambition. And he is sadly contemptuous of his organizers, who "aren't up to it," who "just aren't posted on history and ethnolology," who just haven't got "the old gray matter."

I ask him why the white man wants segregation.

"He'll say one thing and another," he says, "he knows in his bones it ain't right to have mixing. But you got to give him the reasons, explain it to him. It is the ethnolology of it you got to give. You got to explain how no *Negroes*"—he pronounces it with the elaborate polemical correctness, but not for polemics, just to set himself off intellectually, I suppose, from the people who might say *nigger*—"explain how no Negroes ever created a civilization. They are parasites. They haven't got the stuff up here." And he taps his forehead. "And explain how there is just two races, white and black, and—"

"What about the Bible," I ask, "doesn't the Bible say three?"

"Yes, but you know, between you and me, I don't reckon you have to take much stock in the Bible in this business. I don't take much stock in Darwin in some ways, either. He is too enviromental, he don't think enough about the blood. Yes, sir, I'll tell you, it's hard to come by good books on ethnolology these days. Got a good one from California the other day, though. But just one copy. Been out of print a long time. But like I was saying, the point is there's just two races, black and white, and the rest of them is a kind of mixing. You always get a mess when the mixing starts. Take India. They are a pure white people like you and me, and they had a pretty good civilization, too. Till they got to shipping on a little Negro blood. It don't take much to do the damage. Look at 'em now."

That is his argument. It is much the same argument given me by another official of another segregation group, whom I sit with a week later in another state, a lawyer, forty-five or -six, of strong middle height, sandy blond, hands strong with pale hairs and square-cut, scrubbed-looking nails. He is cagey at first, then suddenly warm, in an expanding, sincere, appealing way. He really wants to explain himself, wants to be regarded as an honest man, wants to be liked. I do like him, as he tells about himself, how he had gone to college, the hard way I gather, had prepared to be a teacher of history in high school, had given that up, had tried business in one way or another, had given that up, had studied law. "You ought to know my politics, too," he says. He was New Deal till the Court-packing plan. "That disgusted me," he says, and you believe him. Then he was for Willkie, then for Dewey, then Dixiecrat, then for Eisenhower. (I remember another lawyer, hired by another group: "Hell, all Southerners are Republicans at heart, conservative, and just don't know they're Republican.")

But Eisenhower doesn't satisfy my friend now. "We'll elect our own President. Our organization isn't just Southern. We're going national. Plenty of people in Chicago and other places feel like we do. And afraid of a big central government, too. We'll elect our own President and see how Chief Justice Warren's decision comes out."

I ask if the main point is the matter of States Rights, of local integrity.

"Yes, in a way," he says, "but you got to fight on something you can rouse people up about, on segregation. There's the constitutional argument, but your basic feeling, that's what you've got to trust—what you feel, not your reasons for it. But we've got argument, reasons."

He hesitates, thumps the desk top in a quick tattoo of his strong, scrubbed-looking fingers (he isn't a nervous man in the ordinary sense, but there are these sudden bursts), twists

300 ROBERT PENN WARREN

himself in his chair, then abruptly leans forward, jerks a drawer open (literally jerks it), and thrusts an envelope at me. "Heck, you might as well see it," he says.

I look at it. The stuff is not new. I have seen it before, elsewhere. It was used in the last gubernatorial campaign in Tennessee, it was used in the march on the Capitol at Nashville a few weeks ago. There are the handbills showing "Harlem Negro and White Wife," lying abed, showing "Crooner Roy Hamilton & Teenage Fans," who are white girls, showing a school yard in Baltimore with Negro and white children, "the new look in education." On the back of one of the handbills is a crudely drawn valentine-like heart, in it the head of a white woman who (with feelings not indicated by the artist) is about to be kissed by a black man of the most primitive physiognomy. On the heart two vultures perch. Beneath it is the caption: "The Kiss of Death."

Below are the "reasons": "While Russia makes laws to protect her own race she continues to prod us to accept 14,000,000 Negroes as social equals and we are doing everything possible to please her. . . . Segregation is the law of God, not man. . . . Continue to rob the white race in order to bribe the Asiatic and Negro and these people will overwhelm the white race and destroy all progress, religion, invention, art, and return us to the jungle. . . . Negro blood destroyed the civilization of Egypt, India, Phoenicia, Carthage, Greece, and it will destroy America!"

I put the literature into my pocket, to join the other samples. "If there's trouble," I ask, "where will it begin?"

"We don't condone violence," he says.

"But if—just suppose," I say.

He doesn't hesitate. "The red-neck," he says, "that's what you call 'em around here. Those fellows—and I'm one of them myself, just a red-neck that got educated—are the ones who will feel the rub. He is the one on the underside of the plank with nothing between him and the bare black ground. He's got to have something to give him pride. Just to be better than something."

To be better than something: so we are back to the pridefulness the yellow man had talked about. But no, there is more, something else.

There is the minister, a Baptist, an intellectual-looking man, a man whose face indicates conscience and thoughtfulness, pastor of a good church in a good district in a thriving city. "It is simple," he says. "It is a matter of God's will and revelation. I refer you to Acts 17—I don't remember the verse. This is the passage the integrationists are always quoting to prove that integration is Christian. But they won't quote it all. It's the end that counts."

I looked it up: *And hath made of one blood all nations of men for to dwell on all the face of the earth, and hath determined the times before appointed, and the bounds of their habitation.*

There is the very handsome lady of forty-five, charming and witty and gay, full of dramatic mimicry, a wonderful range of phrase, a quick sympathy, a totally captivating talker of the kind you still occasionally find among women of the Deep South, but never now in a woman under forty. She is sitting before the fire in the fine room, her brother, big and handsome but barefoot and rigid drunk, opposite her. But she gaily overrides that small difficulty ("Oh, don't mind him, he's just had a whole bottle of brandy. Been on a high-lonesome all by himself. But poor Jack, he feels better now"). She has been talking about the Negroes on her plantation, and at last, about integration, but that only in one phrase, tossed off as gaily and casually as any other of the evening, so casual as to permit no discussion: "But of course we have to keep the white race intact."

But the husband, much her senior, who has said almost nothing all evening, lifts his strong, grizzled old face, and in a kind of *sotto voce* growl, not to her, not to me, not to anybody, utters: "In power—in power—you mean the white race in power."

And I think of another Southerner, an integrationist, saying to me: "You simply have to recognize a fact. In no county where the Negroes are two to one is the white man going to surrender political power, not with the Negroes in those counties in their present condition. It's not a question of being Southern. You put the same number of Yankee liberals in the same county and in a week they'd be behaving the same way. Living with something and talking about it are two very different things, and living with something is always the slow way."

And another, not an integrationist, from a black county, saying: "Yeah, let 'em take over and in six months you'd be paying the taxes but a black sheriff would be collecting 'em. You couldn't walk down the sidewalk. You'd be communized, all right."

But is it power. Merely power? Or any of the other things suggested thus far?

I think of a college professor in a section where about half the population is Negro. The college has no Negro students, but— "The heat is on," he says. "But listen, brother," he says, "lots of our boys don't like it a bit. Not a bit."

I ask would it be like the University of Alabama.

"It would be something, brother. I'll tell you that, brother. One of our boys—been fooling around with an organization uptown—he came to me and asked me to be sure to let him know when a nigger was coming, he and some friends would stop that clock. But I didn't want to hear student talk. I said, son, just don't tell me."

I asked what the faculty would do.

"Hide out, brother, hide out. And brother, I would, too."

Yes, he was a segregationist. I didn't have to ask him. Or ask his reasons, for he was talking on, in his rather nasal voice —leaning happily back in his chair in the handsome office, a spare, fiftyish man, dark-suited, rather dressy, sharp-nosed, with some fringe-remnants of sandy hair on an elongated, slightly freckled skull, rimless glasses on pale eyes: "Yeah, brother, back in my county there was a long ridge running through the county, and one side the ridge was good land, river bottom, and folks put on airs there and held niggers, but on the other side of the ridge the ground so pore you couldn't grow peas and nothing but pore white trash. So when the Civil War came, the pore white trash, as the folks who put on airs called them, just picked down the old rifle off the deer horns over the fireplace and joined the Federals coming down, just because they hated those fellows across the ridge. But don't get me wrong, brother. They didn't want any truck with niggers, either. To this day they vote Republican and hate niggers. It is just they hate niggers."

Yes, they hate niggers, but I am in another room, the library of a plantation house, in Mississippi, and the planter is
talking to me, leaning his length back at ease, speaking deliberately from his high-nosed, commanding face, the very
figure of a Wade Hampton or Kirby Smith, only the gray uniform and cavalry boots not there, saying: "No, I don't hate
Negroes. I never had a minute's trouble with one in my life,
and never intend to. I don't believe in getting lathered up,
and I don't intend to get lathered up. I simply don't discuss
the question with anybody. But I'll tell you what I feel. I
came out of the university with a lot of ideals and humanitar-
ianism, and I stayed by it as long as I could. But I tell you
now what has come out of thirty years of experience and careful consideration. I have a deep contempt for the Negro race
as it exists here. It is not so much a matter of ability as of
character. Character."

He repeats the word. He is a man of character, it could
never be denied. Of character and force. He is also a man of
fine intelligence and good education. He reads Roman history. He collects books on the American West. He is widely
traveled. He is unusually successful as a planter and businessman. He is a man of human warmth and generosity, and eminent justice. I overhear his wife, at this moment, talking to a
Negro from the place, asking him if she can save some more
money for him, to add to the hundred dollars she holds, trying to persuade him.

The husband goes on: "It's not so much the hands on
my place, as the lawyers and doctors and teachers and insurance men and undertakers—oh, yes, I've had dealings all
around, or my hands have. The character just breaks down.
It is not dependable. They pay lip service to the white
man's ideals of conduct. They say, yes, I believe in honesty
and truth and morality. But it is just lip service. Most of the
time. I don't intend to get lathered up. This is just my private opinion. I believe in segregation, but I can always protect myself and my family. I dine at my club and my land is
my own, and when I travel, the places I frequent have few
if any Negroes. Not that I'd ever walk out of a restaurant,
for I'm no professional Southerner. And I'd never give a
nickel to the Citizens Council or anything like that. Nor

have any of my friends, that I know of. That's townpeople stuff, anyway."

Later on, he says: "For years, I thought I loved Negroes. And I loved their humor and other qualities. My father—he was a firster around here, first man to put glass windows in for them, first to give them a written monthly statement, first to do a lot to help them toward financial independence—well, my father, he used to look at me and say how it would be. He said, son, they will knock it out of you. Well, they did. I learned the grimness and the sadness."

And later, as we ride down the long row of the houses of the hands, he points to shreds of screening at windows, or here and there a broken screen door. "One of my last experiments," he says, dourly. "Three months, and they poked it out of the kitchen window so they could throw slops on the bare ground. They broke down the front door so they could spit tobacco juice out on the porch floor."

We ride on. We pass a nicely painted house, with a fenced dooryard, with flower beds, and flower boxes on the porch, and good, bright-painted porch furniture. I ask who lives there. "One of the hands," he says, "but he's got some energy and character. Look at his house. And he loves flowers. Has only three children, but when there's work he gets it done fast, and then finds some more to do. Makes $4,500 to $5,000 a year." Some old pride, or something from the lost days of idealism, comes back into his tone.

I ask what the other people on the place think of the tenant with the nice house.

"They think he's just lucky." And he mimics, a little bitterly, without any humor: "Boss, looks lak Jefferson's chillen, they jes picks faster'n mine. Caint he'p it, Boss."

I ask what Jefferson's color is.

"A real black man, a real Negro, all right. But he's got character."

I look down the interminable row of dingy houses, over the interminable flat of black earth toward the river.

Now and then, I encounter a man whose argument for segregation, in the present context, has nothing to do with the Negro at all. At its simplest level its spokesman says: "I don't give a durn about the niggers, they never bother me one way or another. But I don't like being forced. Ain't no man ever forced me."

But the law always carries force, you say.

"Not this law. It's different. It ain't our law."

At another level, the spokesman will say it is a matter of constitutionality, pure and simple. He may even be an integrationist. But this decision, he will say, carries us one more step toward the power state, a cunningly calculated step, for this decision carries a moral issue and the objector to the decision is automatically put in the role of the enemy of righteousness. "But wait till the next decision," he will say. "This will be the precedent for it, and the next one won't have the moral façade."

Precedent for what? you ask.

"For government by sociology, not law," he will say.

"Is it government by law," one man asks me, "when certain members of the Supreme Court want to write a minority decision, and the great conciliator conciliates them out of it, saying that the thing is going to be controversial enough without the Court splitting? Damn it, the Court should split, if that's the honest reading of the law. We want the reading of the law, not conciliation by sociology. Even if we don't happen to like the kind of law it turns out to be in a particular case."

And another man: "Yes, government by sociology not law is a two-edged business. The next guy who gets in the saddle just picks another brand of sociology. And nothing to stop him, for the very notion of law is gone."

Pridefulness, money, level of intelligence, race, God's will, filth and disease, power, hate, contempt, legality—perhaps these are not all the words that get mentioned. There is another thing, whatever the word for it. An eminent Negro scholar is, I suppose, saying something about that other thing. "One thing," he says, "is that a lot of people down here just don't like change. It's not merely desegregation they're against so much, it's just the fact of any change. They feel some emotional tie to the way things are. A change is disorienting, especially if you're pretty disoriented already."

Yes, a lot of them are disoriented enough already, uprooted, driven from the land, drawn from the land, befuddled by new opportunities, new ambitions, new obligations. They have entered the great anonymity of the new world.

And I hear a college student in the Deep South: "You know, it's just that people don't like to feel like they're spitting on their grandfather's grave. They feel some connection they don't want to break. Something would bother them if they broke it."

The young man is, I gather, an integrationist. He adds: "And sometimes something bothers them if they don't break it."

Let us give a name now to whatever it is that the eminent Negro scholar and the young white college boy were talking about. Let us, without meaning to be ironical, call it piety.

What does the Negro want?

The plump yellow man, with his hands folded calmly over his belly, the man who said it is the white man's "pridefulness," thinks, and answers the new question. "Opportunity," he says. "It's opportunity a man wants."

For what? I ask.

"Just to get along and make out. You know, like anybody."

"About education, now. If you got good schools, as good as anybody's, would that satisfy you?"

"Well," the yellow man begins, but the black, intense-faced man breaks in. "We never had them, we'd never have them!"

"You might get them now," I say, "under this pressure."

"Maybe," the yellow man agrees, "maybe. And it might have satisfied once. But"—and he shakes his head—"not now. That doctrine won't grip now."

"Not now," the intense-faced man says. "Not after the Supreme Court decision. We want the law."

"But when?" I ask. "Right now? Tomorrow morning?"

"The Supreme Court decision says—" And he stops.

"It says deliberate speed," I say, "or something like that."

"If a Negro wants to study medicine, he can't study it. If he wants to study law, he can't study it. There isn't any way in this state for him to study it."

"Suppose," I say, "suppose professional and graduate schools got opened. To really qualified applicants, no funny business either way. Then they began some sort of staggered system, a grade or two at a time, from either top or bottom. Would something like that satisfy you? Perhaps not all over the state at the same time, some place serving as a sort of pilot for others where the going would be rougher."

The yellow man nods. The intense-faced man looks down at his new and newly polished good black shoes. He looks across at the wall. Not looking at me, he says, "Yes, if it was in good faith. If you could depend on it. Yes."

He hates to say it. At least, I think he hates to say it. It is a wrench, grudging.

I sit in another room, in another city, in the Deep South, with several men, two of them Negroes. One Negro is the local NAACP secretary, a man in build, color and quality strangely like the black, intense-faced man. I am asking again what will satisfy the Negroes. Only this time the intense-faced man does not as readily say, yes, a staggered system would be satisfactory. In fact, he doesn't say it at all. I ask him what his philosophy of social change is, in a democracy. He begins to refer to the law, to the Court, but one of the white men breaks in.

This white man is of the Deep South, born, bred and educated there. He is a middle-aged man, tall, rather spare but not angular, the impression of the lack of angularity coming, I suppose, from a great deliberation in voice and movement, a great calmness in voice and face. The face is an intellectual's face, a calm, dedicated face, but not a zealot's. His career, I know, has been identified with various causes of social reform. He has sat on many committees, has signed many things, some of them things I personally take to be nonsense. What he says now, in his serene voice, the words and voice being really all that I know of him, is this: "I know that Mr. Cranford here"—and he nods toward this black, intense-faced man —"doesn't want any change by violence. He knows—we know—that change will take time. He wants a change in a Christian way that won't aggravate to violence. We have all got to live together. It will take time."

Nobody says anything. After a moment I go back to my question about the philosophy of social change. Wearily the intense-faced man says something, something not very relevant, not evasive, just not relevant. I let the matter drop. He sits with his head propped on his right hand, brow furrowed. He is not interested in abstractions. Why should he be?

Again, it is the Deep South, another town, another room, the bright, new-sparkling living room of the house of a Negro businessman, new furniture, new TV, new everything. There are several white men present, two journalists, myself (I've just come along to watch, I'm not involved), some technicians, and about ten Negroes, all in Sunday best, at ease but slightly formal, as though just before going in to a church service. Some of the Negroes, I have heard, are in the NAACP.

The technicians are rigging up their stuff, lights and cameras, etc., moving arrogantly in their own world superior to human concerns. In the background, in the dining room, the wife of our host, a plump, fortyish mulatto, an agreeable-looking woman wearing a new black dress with a discreet white design in it, stands watching a big new electric percolator on a silver tray. Another silver tray holds a bottle of Canadian whisky, a good whisky, and glasses. When someone comes out of the kitchen, I catch a glimpse of a gray-haired Negro woman, wearing a maid's uniform.

It is a bright, sunny, crisp day outside. The coffee is bubbling cheerfully. Out the window I see a little Negro girl, about ten years old, with a pink bow in her hair, an enormous bow, come out of a small pink house with aquamarine trim and shutters, and a dull blue roof. She stands a moment with the pink bow against the aquamarine door, then moves through the opening in the clipped privet hedge, a very tidy, persnickety hedge, and picks her way down the muddy street, where there is no sidewalk.

One of the journalists is instructing a Negro who is to be interviewed, a tall, well-set-up, jut-nosed, good-looking dark brown man in a blue suit. He has a good way of holding his head. "Now you're supposed to tell them," the journalist is saying, "what a lot of hogwash this separate but equal stuff is. What you said to me last night."

Pedagogical and irritable, one of the technicians says: "Quiet, quiet!"

They take a voice level. The dark brown man is very much at ease, saying: "Now is the time for all good men to come to the aid of their country."

The interview begins. The dark brown man, still very much at ease, is saying: "—and we're not disturbed. The only people disturbed are those who have not taken an unbiased look. We who have taken our decision, we aren't disturbed." He goes on to say the Negroes want an interracial discussion on the "how" of desegregation—but with the background understanding that the Court decision is law.

The journalist cuts in: "Make it simple and direct. Lay it on the line."

The tall brown man is unruffled. There is sweat on his face now, but from the lamps. He wipes his face, and patiently, condescendingly, smiles at the journalist. "Listen," he says, "you all are going back to New York City. But we stay here. We aren't afraid, but we live here. They know what we think, but it's a way of putting it we got to think about."

He says it is going to take some time to work things out, he knows that, but there is a chorus from the Negroes crowded back out of range of the camera: "Don't put no time limit—don't put any time on it—no ten or fifteen years!"

The dark brown man doesn't put any time on it. He says all they want is to recognize the law and to sit down in a law-abiding way to work out the "how" and the "when."

"That's good, that's all right!" the chorus decides.

Leave the "how" in detail up to the specialists in education. As for the "when"—the dark brown, jut-nosed man hesitates a second: "Well, Negroes are patient. We can wait a little while longer."

The dark brown man gets up to his considerable height, wipes the sweat off his face, asks the journalist: "You got your playback?"

The chorus laughs. It is indulgent laughter of human vanity and such. Sure, any man would like to hear his voice played back, hear himself talking.

There is no playback. Not now, anyway.

The dark brown man is receiving the handshakes, the shoulder-slaps, of his friends. They think he did well. He did do well. He looks back over his shoulder at the white men, grins. "When I got to leave," he says, "who's going to give me that job as chauffeur? I see that nice Cadillac sitting out front there."

There are the quick, deep-throated giggles.

I turn to a Negro beside me. "Ten years ago," I ask, "would this have been possible?"

"No," he says.

Then there is another house, the tangle of wires, the jumble of rig and lights, and another Negro being arranged for an interview. There is no air of decorous festivity here, just a businesslike bustle, with the Negro waiting. This one will be knocked off quick. It's getting on to lunch.

This one, one of the journalists told me, is supposed to be the Uncle Tom. He is a middle-aged man, fair-sized, tallish, medium brown, with a balding, rather high forehead. He is wearing a good dark suit. His manner is dignified, slow, a little sad. I have known him before, know something about him. He had begun life as waterboy on a plantation, back in the times when "some folks didn't think a thing of bloodying a Negro's head, just for nothing, and I have seen their heads bloodied." But a white man on the plantation had helped him ("Noticed I was sort of quick and took an interest in things, trying to learn"), and now he is a preacher. For a voice level he does not say, "Now is the time for all good men to come to the aid of their country." He says: "Jesus wept, Jesus wept, Jesus wept."

The journalist tells him he is supposed to say some good things for segregation.

The Negro doesn't answer directly to that. "If you have some opinions of your own," he says, "your own people sometimes call you a son-of-a-gun, and sometimes the white people call you a son-of-a-gun."

Your own people. And I remember that the men at the last house had said: "Don't tell him you've seen us, don't tell him that or you won't get him to talk."

Is integration a good thing, the journalist asks him, and he says: "Till Negro people get as intelligent and self-sustaining they can't mix." But he flares up about discrimination along with segregation: "That's what makes Negroes bitter, wage differentials, no good jobs, that and the ballot." As for the Court decision, he says: "It's something for people to strive for, to ascertain their best."

I break in—I don't think the machinery is going yet—and ask about humiliation as a bar to Negro fulfilment.

"Segregation did one thing," he says. "No other race but the Negroes could build up as much will to go on and do things. To get their goals."

What goals? I ask.

"Just what anybody wants, just everything people can want to be a citizen," he says.

This isn't what the journalist has come for.

Things aren't promising too well. Uncle Tom is doing a disappearing act, Old Black Joe is evaporating, the handker-chief-head, most inconveniently, isn't there. The genie has got out of the bottle clearly labeled: *Negro* segregationist.

But maybe the genie can be coaxed back into the bottle. The sad-mannered man is, the journalist suggests, a pro-segregationist in that he thinks segregation built a will to achieve something.

The machinery gets going, the mike is lifted on its rod, the slow, sad voice speaks: "For segregation has test steel into the Negro race and this is one valuable point of segregation—seg-regation has proven that Negroes in the South, where it's practiced most, have done a fine job in building an economic strength beyond that of many other sections in the United States of America. Negroes own more farm land in Mississippi than any other state in the United States that is engaged in agriculture."

He goes along, he says, "with the idea you should have a moderate approach. You will never be able to integrate chil-dren on the school campus, the mothers holding a lot of bit-terness in their hearts against each other white and colored."

It will take time, he says: "It is absurd otherwise, it's just foolish thinking for people to believe you can get the South to do in four or five years what they have been doing in the North for one hundred years. These people are emotional about their tradition, and you've got to have an educational program to change their way of thinking and this will be a slow process."

Yes, the genie is safely back in the labeled bottle. Or is he?

For the slow, sad voice is saying: "—has got to out-think the white man, has got to outlive the white man—"

Is saying: "—no need of saying the South won't ever integrate—"

Is saying: "—not ultimate goal just to go to white schools and travel with white people on conveyances over the country. No, the Negro, he is a growing people and he will strive for all the equalities belonging to any American citizen. He is a growing people."

Yes, Uncle Tom is gone again, and gone for good. Too bad for the program. I wondered if they got this last part on tape.

The Negro turns to the journalist and asks if he has interviewed other people around.

"Yes, saw Mr. So-and-so of the Citizens Council."

Had we interviewed any other Negroes?

"Oh, some," after a shade of hesitation.

Had we seen So-and-so and So-and-so?

"No—why, no. Well, we want to thank you—"

We leave the sad-mannered, slow man and we know that he knows. He isn't a big enough fool not to know. White men have lied to him before. What is one more time after all the years?

Besides, what if you do tell him a lie?

There are, as a matter of fact, in Arkansas, Negroes who go from door to door collecting money to fight integration. There *are* Uncle Toms.

So it all evens out.

I ask my question of the eminent Negro scholar. His reply is immediate: "It's not so much what the Negro wants as what he doesn't want. The main point is not that he has poor facilities. It is that he must endure a constant assault on his ego. He is denied human dignity."

And I think of the yellow girl wearing the salmon sweater and slacks, in the shack in the sea of mud, at dusk, the girl whose husband has been shot, and she says: "It's how yore feelings git tore up all the time. The way folks talk, sometimes. It ain't what they say sometimes, if they'd jes say it kind."

She had gone to a store, in another town, for some dress goods, and had requested a receipt for the minister who manages the fund raised in her behalf. By the receipt the saleswoman identifies her and asks if "that man up yonder is still in jail for killing a nigger."

"Well," the girl had said, "if you want to put it that a-way."

"They can't do anything to a man for something he does drunk," the saleswoman has said.

The girl has laid the package down on the counter. "If you want it that a-way," she has said, "you kin take back yore dress goods. They's other places to buy."

She tells me the story.

And I think of another woman, up in Tennessee, middle-aged, precise, the kind of woman who knows her own competent mind, a school inspector for county schools, a Negro. "We don't want to socialize. That's not what we want. We do everything the white folks do already, even if we don't spend as much money doing it. And we have more fun. But I don't want to be insulted. If somebody has to tell you something, about some regulation or other, they could say it in a low, kind voice, not yell it out at you. And when I go to a place to buy something, and have that dollar bill in my hand, I want to be treated right. And I won't ride on a bus. I won't go to a restaurant in a town where there's just one. I'll go hungry. I won't be insulted at the front door and then crawl around to the back. You've got to try to keep some respect."

And in Tennessee again, the Negro at the biracial committee meeting says: "My boy is happy in the Negro school where he goes. I don't want him to go to the white school and sit by your boy's side. But I'd die fighting for his right to go."

"We don't want to socialize," the woman in Tennessee says.

The college student, a Negro, in Tennessee, says: "The Negro doesn't want social equality. My wife is my color. I'm above wanting to mix things up. That's low class. Low class of both races."

The Negro man in Mississippi says: "Take a Negro man wanting a white woman. A man tends to want his own kind, now. But the white folks make such an awful fuss about it. They make it seem so awful special-like. Maybe that's what makes it sort of prey on some folks' mind."

And I remember the gang rape by four Negroes of a white

woman near Memphis last fall, shortly after the Till killing. "One of our boys was killed down in Mississippi the other day and we're liable to kill you," one of the Negroes said as they bludgeoned the man who was with the woman and told him to get going.

This is a question for Negroes only. *Is there any difference between what the Negro feels at the exclusions of segregation, and what a white man feels at the exclusions which he, any man, must always face at some point?*

"Yes, it's different," the Negro college administrator says, "when your fate is on your face. Just that. It's the unchange-ableness. Now a white man, even if he knows he can't be President, even if he knows the chances for his son are one in many millions—long odds—still there's an idea there."

And the Negro lawyer: "Yes, it's different. But it's not easy to name it. Take how some unions come in and make some plant build nice rest rooms, one for white, one for Negroes, but same tile, same fixtures and all. But off the white ones, there's a little lounge for smoking. To make 'em feel superior to somebody. You see what I mean, how it's different?"

He thinks some more. "Yes," he says, "I got my dreams and hopes and aspirations, but me, I have to think what is sort of possible in the possibilities and probabilities. Some things I know I can't think on because of the circumstances of my birth."

And he thinks again, looking out the window, over Beale Street. "Yes, there's a difference," he says. "A Negro, he doesn't really know some things, but he just goes walking pregnant with worries, not knowing their name. It's he's lost his purpose, somewhere. He goes wandering and wondering, and no purpose."

I look out the window, too, over Beale Street. It is late afternoon. I hear the pullulation of life, the stir and new tempo toward evening, the babble of voices, a snatch of laughter. I hear the remorseless juke boxes. They shake the air.

What's coming?

"Whatever it is," the college student in the Deep South says, "I'd like to put all the Citizens Council and all the

NAACP in one room and give every man a baseball bat and lock 'em in till it was over. Then maybe some sensible people could work out something."

What's coming? I say it to the country grade-school superintendent. He is a part-time farmer, too, and now he is really in his role as farmer, not teacher, as we stand, at night, under the naked light of a flyspecked 200-watt bulb hanging from the shed roof, and he oversees two Negroes loading sacks of fertilizer on a truck. "I know folks round here," he says, and seeing his hard, aquiline, weathered face, with the flat, pale, hard eyes, I believe him.

"They aren't raised up to it," he says. "Back in the summer now, I went by a lady's house to ask about her children starting to school. Well, she was a real old-timey gal, a gantheaded, barefoot, snuff-dipping, bonnet-wearing, hard-ankled old gal standing out in the tobacco patch, leaning on her hoe, and she leaned at me and said, 'Done hear'd tell 'bout niggers gonna come in,' and before I could say anything, she said, 'Not with none of my young 'uns,' and let out a stream of ambeer."

"Would you hire a Negro teacher?" I asked.

"I personally would, but folks wouldn't stand for it, not now, mostly those who never went much to school themselves. Unless I could prove I couldn't get white." He paused. "And it's getting damned hard to get white, I tell you," he says.

I ask if integration will come.

"Sure," he says, "in fifty years. Every time the tobacco crop is reduced, we lose just that many white sharecroppers and Negroes. That eases the pain."

What's coming? And the Methodist minister, riding with me in the dusk, in the drizzle, by the flooded bayou, says: "It'll come, desegregation and the vote and all that. But it will be twenty-five, thirty years, a generation. You can preach love and justice, but it's a slow pull till you get the education." He waves a hand toward the drowned black cotton fields, stretching on forever, toward the rows of shacks marshaled off into the darkening distance, toward the far cypresses where dusk is tangled. "You can see," he says. "Just look, you can see."

What's coming? I ask the young lawyer in a mid-South city, a lawyer retained by one of the segregation outfits. "It's coming that we got to fight this bogus law," he says, "or we'll have a lot of social dis-tensions. The bogus law is based on social stuff and progress and just creates dis-tension. But we're gaining ground. Some upper-class people, I mean a real rich man, is coming out for us. And we get rolling, a Southern President could repack the court. But it's got so a man can't respect the Supreme Court. All this share-the-wealth and Communist stuff and progress. You can't depend on law any more."

What can you depend on? I ask.

"Nothing but the people. Like the Civil War."

I suggest that whatever the constitutional rights and wrongs of the Civil War were, we had got a new Constitution out of it.

"No," he said, "just a different type of dog saying what it is."

I ask if, in the end, the appeal would be to violence.

"No, I don't believe in violence. I told Mr. Perkins, when we had our mass meeting, to keep the in-ci-dents down. But you get a lot of folks and there's always going to be in-ci-dents."

I ask if at Tuscaloosa the mob hadn't dictated public policy.

"Not dictate exactly." And he smiles his handsome smile. "But it was a lot of people."

He has used the word *progress*, over and over, to damn what he does not like. It is peculiar how he uses this laudatory word—I can imagine how he would say it in other contexts, on public occasions, rolling it on his tongue—as the word now for what he hates most. I wonder how deep a cleavage the use of that word indicates.

What's coming? I ask the handsome, aristocratic, big gray-haired man, sitting in his rich office, high over the city, an ornament of the vestry, of boards of directors, of club committees, a man of exquisite simplicity and charm, and a member of a segregation group.

"We shall exhaust all the legal possibilities," he says.

I ask if he thinks his side will win. The legal fight, that is.

He rolls a cigarette fastidiously between strong, white, waxy forefinger and thumb. "No," he says. "But it is just something you have to do." He rolls the cigarette, looking out the window over the city, a city getting rich now, "filthy rich," as somebody has said to me. There is the undertone and unceasing susurrus of traffic in the silence of his thoughts.

"Well," he says at last, "to speak truth, I think the whole jig is up. We'll have desegregation right down the line. And you know why?"

I shake my head.

"Well, I'll tell you. You see those girls in my office outside, those young men. Come from good lower-middle-class homes, went to college a lot of them. Well, a girl comes in here and says to me a gentleman is waiting. She shows him in. He is as black as the ace of spades. It just never crossed that girl's mind, what she was saying, when she said a gentleman was waiting." He pauses. "Yes, sir," he says, "I just don't know why I'm doing it."

I am thinking of walking down Canal Street, in New Orleans, and a man is saying to me: "Do you know how many millions a year the Negroes spend up and down this street?"

No, I had said, I didn't know.

He tells me the figure, then says: "You get the logic of that, don't you?"

What's coming? And the college student says: "I'll tell you one thing that's coming, there's not going to be any academic freedom or any other kind around here if we don't watch out. Now I'm a segregationist, that is, the way things are here right now, but I don't want anybody saying I can't listen to somebody talk about something. I can make up my own mind."

What's coming? And a state official says: "Integration sure and slow. A creeping process. If the NAACP has got bat sense, not deliberately provoking things as in the University of Alabama deal. They could have got that girl in quiet and easy, but that wouldn't satisfy them. No, they wanted the bang. As for things in general, grade schools and high schools, it'll be the creeping process. The soft places first, and then one county will play football or basketball with Negroes on the team. You know how it'll be. A creeping process. There'll be lots of court actions, but don't let court actions fool you. I bet you half the superintendents over in Tennessee will secretly welcome a court action in their county. Half of 'em are worried morally and half financially, and a court action just gets 'em off the hook. They didn't initiate it, they can always claim, but it gets them off the hook. That's the way I would feel, I know."

What's coming? I ask the taxi driver in Memphis. And he says: "Lots of dead niggers round here, that's what's coming. Look at Detroit, lots of dead niggers been in the Detroit River, but it won't be a patch on the Ole Mississippi. But hell, it won't stop nothing. Fifty years from now everybody will be gray anyway, Jews and Germans and French and Chinese and niggers, and who'll give a durn?"

The cab has drawn to my destination. I step out into the rain and darkness. "Don't get yourself drownded now," he says. "You have a good time now. I hope you do."

What's coming? And a man in Arkansas says: "We'll ride it out. But it looked like bad trouble one time. Too many outsiders. Mississippians and all. They come back here again, somebody's butt will be busted."

And another man: "Sure, they aim for violence, coming in here. When a man gets up before a crowd and plays what purports to be a recording of an NAACP official, an inflammatory sex thing, and then boasts of having been in on a lynching himself, what do you call it? Well, they got him on the witness stand, under oath, and he had to admit he got the record from Patterson, of the Citizens Council, and admitted under oath the lynching statement. He also admitted under oath some other interesting facts—that he had once been indicted for criminal libel but pleaded guilty to simple libel, that he has done sixty days for contempt of court on charges of violating an injunction having to do with liquor. Yeah, he used to run a paper called *The Rub Down*—that's what got him into the libel business. What's going to happen if a guy like that runs things? I ask you."

What's coming? And the planter leans back with the glass in his hand. "I'm not going to get lathered up," he says, "because it's no use. Why is the country so lathered up to force the issue one way or the other? Democracy—democracy has

just come to be a name for what you like. It has lost responsibility, no local integrity left, it has been bought off. We've
got the power state coming on, and communism or socialism,
whatever you choose to call it. Race amalgamation is inevitable. I can't say I like any of it. I am out of step with the
times."

What's coming? I ask the Episcopal rector, in the Deep
South, a large handsome man, almost the twin of my friend
sitting in the fine office overlooking the rich city. He has just
told me that when he first came down from the North, a generation back, his bishop had explained it all to him, how the
Negroes' skull capacity was limited. But as he has said, brain
power isn't everything, there's justice, and not a member of
his congregation wasn't for conviction in the Till case.

"But the Negro has to be improved before integration," he
says. "Take their morals, we are gradually improving the standard of morality and decency."

The conversation veers, we take a longer view. "Well, an-
thropologically speaking," he says, "the solution will be ab-
sorption, the Negro will disappear."

I ask how this is happening.

"Low-class people, immoral people, libertines, wastrels,
prostitutes and such," he says.

I ask if, in that case, the raising of the moral level of the
Negro does not prevent, or delay, what he says is the solution.

The conversation goes into a blur.

What's coming? And the young man from Mississippi says:
"Even without integration, even with separate but pretty
good facilities for the Negro, the Negro would be improving
himself. He would be making himself more intellectually and
socially acceptable. Therefore, as segregationists, if we're logical, we ought to deny any good facilities to them. Now I'm
a segregationist, but I can't be that logical."

What's coming? And the officer of the Citizens Council
chapter says: "Desegregation, integration, amalgamation—
none of it will come here. To say it will come is defeatism. It
won't come if we stand firm."

And the old man in north Tennessee, a burly, full-blooded,
red-faced, raucous old man, says: "Hell, son, it's easy to solve.

Just blend 'em. Fifteen years and they'll all be blended in. And by God, I'm doing my part!"

Out of Memphis, I lean back in my seat on the plane, and watch the darkness slide by. I know what the Southerner feels going out of the South, the relief, the expanding vistas. Now, to the sound of the powerful, magnanimous engines bearing me through the night, I think of that, thinking of the new libel laws in Mississippi, of the academic pressures, of academic resignations, of the Negro facing the shotgun blast, of the white man with a nice little, hard-built business being boycotted, of the college boy who said: "I'll just tell you, everybody is *scairt*."

I feel the surge of relief. But I know what the relief really is. It is the relief from responsibility.

Now you may eat the bread of the Pharisee and read in the morning paper, with only a trace of irony, how out of an ultimate misery of rejection some Puerto Rican school boys—or is it Jews or Negroes or Italians?—who call themselves something grand, The Red Eagles or the Silver Avengers, have stabbed another boy to death, or raped a girl, or trampled an old man into a bloody mire. If you can afford it, you will, according to the local mores, send your child to a private school, where there will be, of course, a couple of Negro children on exhibit. And that delightful little Chinese girl who is so good at dramatics. Or is it finger painting?

Yes, you know what the relief is. It is the flight from the reality you were born to.

But what is that reality you have fled from?

It is the fact of self-division. I do not mean division between man and man in society. That division is, of course, there, and it is important. Take, for example, the killing of Clinton Melton, in Glendora, Mississippi, in the Delta, by a man named Elmer Kimbell, a close friend of Milam (who had been acquitted of the murder of Till, whose car was being used by Kimbell at the time of the killing of Melton, and to whose house Kimbell returned after the deed).

Two days after the event, twenty-one men—storekeepers, planters, railroad men, school teachers, preacher, bookkeepers

—sent money to the widow for funeral expenses, with the note: "Knowing that he was outstanding in his race, we the people of this town are deeply hurt and donate as follows." When the Lions Club met three days after the event, a resolution was drawn and signed by all members present: "We consider the taking of the life of Clinton Melton an outrage against him, against all the people of Glendora, against the people of Mississippi as well as against the entire human family. . . . We humbly confess in repentance for having so lived as a community that such an evil occurrence could happen here, and we offer ourselves to be used in bringing to pass a better realization of the justice, righteousness and peace which is the will of God for human society."

And the town began to raise a fund to realize the ambition of the dead man, to send his children to college, the doctor of Glendora offered employment in his clinic to the widow, and the owner of the plantation where she had been raised offered to build for her and her children a three-room house.

But, in that division between man and man, the jury that tried Elmer Kimbell acquitted him.

But, in that same division between man and man, when the newspaper of Clarksdale, Mississippi, in the heart of the Delta, ran a front-page story of the acquittal, that story was bracketed with a front-page editorial saying that there had been some extenuation for acquittal in the Till case, with confusion of evidence and outside pressures, but that in the Melton case there had been no pressure and "we were alone with ourselves and we flunked it."

Such division between man and man is important. As one editor in Tennessee said to me: "There's a fifth column of decency here, and it will, in the end, betray the extremists, when the politicians get through." But such a division between man and man is not as important in the long run as the division within the individual man.

Within the individual there are, or may be, many lines of fracture. It may be between his own social idealism and his anger at Yankee Phariseeism. (Oh, yes, he remembers that in the days when Federal bayonets supported the black Reconstruction state governments in the South, not a single Negro held elective office in any Northern state.) It may be between his social views and his fear of the power state. It may be between his social views and his clan sense. It may be between his allegiance to organized labor and his racism—for status or blood purity. It may be between his Christianity and his social prejudice. It may be between his sense of democracy and his ingrained attitudes toward the Negro. It may be between his own local views and his concern for the figure America cuts in the international picture. It may be between his practical concern at the money loss to society caused by the Negro's depressed condition and his own personal gain or personal prejudice. It may be, and disastrously, between his sense of the inevitable and his emotional need to act against the inevitable.

There are almost an infinite number of permutations and combinations, but they all amount to the same thing, a deep intellectual rub, a moral rub, anger at the irremediable self-division, a deep exacerbation at some failure to find identity. That is the reality.

It expresses itself in many ways. I sit for an afternoon with an old friend, a big, weather-faced, squarish man, a farmer, an intelligent man, a man of good education, of travel and experience, and I ask him questions. I ask if he thinks we can afford, in the present world picture, to alienate Asia by segregation here at home. He hates the question. "I hate to think about it," he says. "It's too deep for me," he says, and moves heavily in his chair. We talk about Christianity—he is a church-going man—and he says: "Oh, I know what the Bible says, and Christianity, but I just can't think about it. My mind just shuts up."

My old friend is an honest man. He will face his own discomfort. He will not try to ease it by passing libel laws to stop discussion or by firing professors.

There are other people whose eyes brighten at the thought of the new unity in the South, the new solidarity of resistance. These men are idealists, and they dream of preserving the traditional American values of individualism and localism against the anonymity, irresponsibility and materialism of the power state, against the philosophy of the ad-man, the morality of the Kinsey report, and the gospel of the bitch-goddess. *To be Southern again:* to recreate a habitation for the values they would preserve, to achieve in unity some clarity of spirit, to envisage some healed image of their own identity.

Some of these men are segregationists. Some are desegregationists, but these, in opposing what they take to be the power-state implications of the Court decision, find themselves caught, too, in the defense of segregation. And defending segregation, both groups are caught in a paradox: in seeking to preserve individualism by taking refuge in the vision of a South redeemed in unity and antique virtue, they are fleeing from the burden of their own individuality—the intellectual rub, the moral rub. To state the matter in another way, by using the argument of *mere* social continuity and the justification by mere *mores*, they think of a world in which circumstances and values are frozen; but the essence of individuality is the willingness to accept the rub which the flux of things provokes, to accept one's fate in time. What heroes would these idealists enshrine to take the place of Jefferson and Lee, those heroes who took the risk of their fate?

Even among these people some are in discomfort, discomfort because the new unity, the new solidarity, once it descends from the bright world of Idea, means unity with some quite concrete persons and specific actions. They say: "Yes—yes, we've got to unify." And then: "But we've got to purge certain elements."

But who will purge whom? And what part of yourself will purge another part?

"Yes, it's our own fault," the rich businessman, active in segregation, says. "If we'd ever managed to bring ourselves to do what we ought to have done for the Negro, it would be different now, if we'd managed to educate them, get them decent housing, decent jobs."

So I tell him what a Southern Negro professor had said to me. He had said that the future now would be different, would be hopeful, if there could just be "one gesture of graciousness" from the white man—even if the white man didn't like the Supreme Court decision, he might try to understand the Negro's view, not heap insult on him.

And the segregationist, who is a gracious man, seizes on the word. "Graciousness," he says, "that's it, if we could just have managed some graciousness to the race. Sure, some of us, a lot of us, could manage some graciousness to individual Negroes, some of us were grateful to individuals for being gracious to us. But you know, we couldn't manage it for the race." He thinks a moment, then says: "There's a Negro woman buried in the family burial place. We loved her."

I believe him when he says it. And he sinks into silence, feeling the rub, for the moment anyway, between the man who can talk in terms of graciousness, in whatever terms that notion may present itself to him, and the man who is a power for segregation.

This is the same man who has said to me, earlier, that he knows integration to be inevitable, doesn't know why he is fighting it. But such a man is happier, perhaps, than those men, destined by birth and personal qualities to action and leadership, who in the face of what they take to be inevitable feel cut off from all action. "I am out of step with the times," one such man says to me, and his wife says, "You know, if we feel the way we do, we ought to do something about it," and he, in some deep, inward, unproclaimed bitterness, says, "No, I'm not going to get lathered up about anything."

Yes, there are many kinds of rub, but I suppose that the commonest one is the moral one—the Christian one, in fact, for the South is still a land of faith. There is, of course, the old joke that after the Saturday night lynching, the congregation generally turns up a little late for church, and the sardonic remark a man made to me about the pro-integration resolution of the Southern Baptist Convention: "They were just a little bit exalted. When they got back with the home folks a lot of 'em wondered how they did it."

But meanwhile, there are the pastors at Glendora and Hoxie and Oxford and other nameless places. And I remember a pastor, in Tennessee, a Southerner born and bred, saying to me: "Yes, I think the Court decision may have set back race equality—it was coming fast, faster than anybody could guess, because so quiet. But now some people get so put out with the idea of Negroes in church, they stop me on the street and say if I ever let one in they won't come to church. So I ask about Heaven, what will they do in Heaven?

"'Well,' one woman said, 'I'll just let God segregate us.'

"'You'll *let* God segregate you?' I said, and she flounced off. But I ask, where is Christianity if people can't worship together? There's only one thing to try to preach, and that is

Christ. And there's only one question to ask, and that is what would Christ do?"

Will they go with him, I ask.

"They are good Christian people, most of them," he says. "It may be slow, but they are Christians."

And in a town in south Kentucky, in a "black county," a Confederate county, where desegregation is now imminent in the high schools, the superintendent says to me: "The people here are good Christian people, trying to do right. When this thing first came up, the whole board said they'd walk out. But the ministers got to preaching, and the lawyers to talking on it, and they came around."

I asked how many were influenced by moral, how many by legal, considerations.

About half and half, he reckons, then adds: "I'm a Rebel myself, and I don't deny it, but I'm an American and a law-abiding citizen. A man can hate an idea but know it's right, and it takes a lot of thinking and praying to bring yourself around. You just have to uncover the unrecognized sympathy in the white man for the Negro humiliation."

Fifty miles away I shall sit in a living room and hear some tale of a Negro coming to somebody's front door—another house—and being admitted by a Negro servant and being found by the master of the house, who says: "I don't care if Susie did let you in. I don't care if Jesus Christ let you in. No black son-of-a-bitch is coming to my front door."

After the tale, there is silence. All present are segregationist, or I think they are.

Then one woman says: "Maybe he did take a lot on himself, coming to the front door. But I can't stand it. He's human."

And another woman: "I think it's a moral question, and I suffer, but I can't feel the same way about a Negro as a white person. It's born in me. But I pray I'll change."

The successful businessman in Louisiana says to me: "I have felt the moral question. It will be more moral when we get rid of segregation. But I'm human enough—I guess it's human to be split up—to want things just postponed till my children are out of school. But I can't lift my finger to delay things."

But this man, privately admitting his division of feeling,

having no intention of public action on either side, is the sort of man who can be trapped, accidentally, into action.

There is the man who got the letter in the morning mail, asking him to serve as chairman of a citizens committee to study plans for desegregation in his county. "I was sick," he says, "and I mean literally sick. I felt sick all day. I didn't see how I could get into something like that. But next morning, you know, I did it."

That county now has its schedule for desegregation.

There is another man, a lawyer, who has been deeply involved in a desegregation action. "I never had much feeling of prejudice, but hell, I didn't have any theories either, and I now and then paid some lip service to segregation. I didn't want to get mixed up in the business. But one night a telephone call came. I told the man I'd let him know next day. You know, I was sick. I walked on back in the living room and my wife looked at me. She must have guessed what it was. 'You going to do it?' she asked me. I said, hell, I didn't know, and went out. I was plain sick. But next day I did it. Well," he says, and grins, and leans back under the shelves of law books, "and I'm stuck with it. But you know, I'm getting damned tired of the paranoiacs and illiterates I'm up against."

Another man, with a small business in a poor county, "back in the shelf country," he calls it, a short, strong-looking, ovoidal kind of man with his belt cutting into his belly when he leans back in his office chair. He is telling me what he has been through. "I wouldn't tell you a lie," he says. "I'm Southern through and through, and I guess I got every prejudice a man can have, and I certainly never would have got mixed up in this business if it hadn't been for the Court decision. I wouldn't be out in front. I was just trying to do my duty. Trying to save some money for the county. I never expected any trouble. And we might not have had any if it hadn't been for outsiders, one kind and another.

"But what nobody understands is how a man can get cut up inside. You try to live like a Christian with your fellow man, and suddenly you find out it is all mixed up. You put in twenty-five years trying to build up a nice little business and raise up a family and it looks like it will all be ruined. You get word somebody will dynamite your house and you in it. You go to lawyers and they say they sympathize, but nobody'll take your case. But the worst is, things just go round and round in your head. Then they won't come a-tall, and you lay there in the night. You might say, it's the psychology of it you can't stand. Getting all split up. Then, all of a sudden, somebody stops you on the street and calls you something, a so-and-so nigger-lover. And you know, I got so mad not a thing mattered any more. I just felt like I was all put back together again."

He said he wished he could write it down, how awful it is for a man to be split up.

Negroes, they must be split up, too, I think. They are human, too. There must be many ways for them to be split up. I remember asking a Negro school teacher if she thought Negro resentment would be a bar to integration. "Some of us try to teach love," she says, "as well as we can. But some of us teach hate. I guess we can't help it."

Love and hate, but more than that, the necessity of confronting your own motives: *Do we really want to try to work out a way to live with the white people or do we just want to show them, pay off something, show them up, rub their noses in it?*

And I can imagine the grinding anger, the sense of outrage of a Negro crying out within himself: *After all the patience, after all the humility, after learning and living those virtues, do I have to learn magnanimity, too?*

Yes, I can imagine the outrage, the outrage as some deep, inner self tells him, yes, he must.

I am glad that white people have no problem as hard as that.

The taxi drew up in front of the apartment house, and I got out, but the driver and I talked on for a moment. I stood there in the rain, then paid him, and ran for the door. It wasn't that I wanted to get out of the rain. I had an umbrella. I wanted to get in and write down what he had said.

He was a local man, born near Nashville, up near Goodlettsville, "raised up with niggers." He had been in the army, with lots of fighting, Africa, Sicily, Italy, but a lot of time bossing work gangs. In Africa, at first, it had been Arabs, but Arabs weren't "worth a durn." Then they got Negro work battalions.

But here are the notes:

Niggers a lot better than Arabs, but they didn't hurt them-selves—didn't any of 'em git a hernia for Uncle Sam—race prejudice—but it ain't our hate, it's the hate hung on us by the old folks dead and gone. Not I mean to criticize the old folks, they done the best they knew, but that hate, we don't know how to shuck it. We got that God-damn hate stuck in our craw and can't puke it up. If white folks quit shoving the nigger down and calling him a nigger he could maybe get to be a asset to the South and the country. But how stop shoving?

We are the prisoners of our history.

Or are we?

There is one more interview I wish to put on record. I shall enter it by question and answer.

Q. You're a Southerner, aren't you?

A. Yes.

Q. Are you afraid of the power state?

A. Yes.

Q. Do you think the Northern press sometimes distorts Southern news?

A. Yes.

Q. Assuming that they do, why do they do it?

A. They like to feel good.

Q. What do you think the South ought to do about that distortion?

A. Nothing.

Q. Nothing? What do you mean, nothing?

A. The distortion—that's the Yankees' problem, not ours.

Q. You mean they ought to let the South work out a way to live with the Negro?

A. I don't think the problem is to learn to live with the Negro.

Q. What is it then?

A. It is to learn to live with ourselves.

Q. What do you mean?

A. I don't think you can live with yourself when you are hu-miliating the man next to you.

Q. Don't you think the races have made out pretty well, considering?

A. Yes. By some sort of human decency and charity, God knows how. But there was always an image of something else.

Q. An image?

A. Well, I knew an old lady who grew up in a black county, but a county where relations had been, as they say, good. She had a fine farm and a good brick house, and when she got old she sort of retired from the world. The hottest summer weather and she would lock all the doors and windows at night, and lie there in the airless dark. But sometimes she'd telephone to town in the middle of the night. She would telephone that somebody was burning the Negroes out there on her place. She could hear their screams. Something was going on in her old head which in another place and time would not have been going on in her old head. She had never, I should think, seen an act of violence in her life. But something was going on in her head.

Q. Do you think it is chiefly the red-neck who causes violence?

A. No. He is only the cutting edge. He, too, is a victim. Responsibility is a seamless garment. And the northern boundary of that garment is not the Ohio River.

Q. Are you for desegregation?

A. *Yes.*

Q. When will it come?

A. Not soon.

Q. When?

A. When enough people, in a particular place, a particular county or state, cannot live with themselves any more. Or realize they don't have to.

Q. What do you mean, don't have to?

A. When they realize that desegregation is just one small episode in the long effort for justice. It seems to me that that perspective, suddenly seeing the business as little, is a liberating one. It liberates you from yourself.

Q. Then you think it is a moral problem?

A. Yes, but no moral problem gets solved abstractly. It has to be solved in a context for possible solution.

Q. Can contexts be changed?

A. Sure. We might even try to change them the right way.

Q. Aren't you concerned about possible racial amalgamation?

A. I don't even think about it. We have to deal with the problem our historical moment proposes, the burden of our time. We all live with a thousand unsolved problems of justice all the time. We don't even recognize a lot of them. We have to deal only with those which the moment proposes to us. Anyway, we can't legislate for posterity. All we can do for posterity is to try to plug along in a way to make them think we —the old folks—did the best we could for justice, as we could understand it.

Q. Are you a gradualist on the matter of segregation?

A. If by gradualist you mean a person who would create delay for the sake of delay, then no. If by gradualist you mean a person who thinks it will take time, not time as such, but time for an educational process, preferably a calculated one, then yes. I mean a process of mutual education for whites and blacks. And part of this education should be in the actual beginning of the process of desegregation. It's a silly question, anyway, to ask if somebody is a gradualist. Gradualism is all you'll get. History, like nature, knows no jumps. Except the jump backward, maybe.

Q. Has the South any contribution to make to the national life?

A. It has made its share. It may again.

Q. How?

A. If the South is really able to face up to itself and its situation, it may achieve identity, moral identity. Then in a country where moral identity is hard to come by, the South, because it has had to deal concretely with a moral problem, may offer some leadership. And we need any we can get. If we are to break out of the national rhythm, the rhythm between complacency and panic.

This is, of course, an interview with myself.

Segregation: The Inner Conflict in the South (1956)

"If You Got the Guts . . ."

by Murray Kempton

ON the Wednesday after Labor Day, the Kentucky National Guard lumbered into Sturgis to bring peace to nine Negro children who had entered their hometown high school.

The guard brought the clatter and the tumult of history, and ten-year-old James Gordon sat on the floor of his white house back in the hills of the worn-out mine four miles from here and thirteen miles from Sturgis and heard the radio talking about it.

He listened all the way through, and then he looked up at his mother and said:

"Mommy, if they can go to the school in Sturgis, why can't we go to the school in Clay?"

Louise Gordon said she began then to really think about it for the first time. And then she answered:

"If you got the guts to go, I got the guts to take ye."

"Every summer for the last three years there's rumors back here that the children are going to school in Clay in the fall. Of course there's nobody you could ask about it. And then the bus comes back here in September and picks up the children and takes them down the road to Providence and the school they've always gone to.

"And then James asks me this question, and him a little boy and me twenty-eight years old and I'd never even thought of it."

She drove down to Clay on Thursday and up the hill to the white school and talked to Mrs. Irene Powell, its principal. Irene Powell said Clay Consolidated was terribly crowded and Louise Gordon answered that it wasn't as crowded as the school in Providence. Irene Powell said that James and his little sister Theresa couldn't meet the school standards and would probably have to be put back a year. Louise Gordon said that she and they could bear that.

331

"So I went back and called the principal at Providence. She said, 'Mrs. Gordon, your children are qualified to go into the grade they're in here in any school in the United States.'"

William Lloyd Garrison said, "I am in earnest and I will not equivocate and I will be heard." Ulysses S. Grant said he would fight it out on this line if it took all summer. A Marine sergeant whose name no one remembers said, "Come on, you bastards, do you want to live forever?" Those are the lines of the American legend; they are in the books and engraved on the plaques.

Set beside them Louise Gordon saying to her little boy in her house on a coal bed: "If you got the guts to go, I got the guts to take ye."

The words that will make up the American legend of our lifetime are not spoken by generals or by candidates for the Presidency of the United States. They are spoken in a bedroom by a woman who is a stranger to us all, a thin, wonderfully sassy woman named Louise Gordon.

Last Friday, she got in her car with James and Theresa and drove to the Clay Consolidated School to take them in and a group of citizens met her at the entrance and told her to go home. They knew her only, they still know her only, as Louise who used to work in the kitchen of their short-order café. That night the Reverend Minvill Clark, as representative of the Anglo-Saxon God of Clay, came out to persuade her not to come back.

"He asked me, 'Louise, could you promise that one of your children wouldn't end up marrying one of our children?'

"I said I couldn't promise anything. My kids will come home with somebody, and I got a son and a daughter and I can't help it. But I must say I wouldn't mind seeing it legal for a change."

She was obviously a hard case.

Her sister, Mattie Smith, cooked for Herman Clark, the Mayor of Clay. On the morning Louise Gordon was turned back first, Mayor Clark led the defending army. Mattie Smith was standing on his porch and watched him, and then went back to the kitchen and hung up her apron and went home for good.

But, by now, Louise Gordon was almost done. Most of the

Negroes who lived around her in the patch began to fall away; they were not hostile, but they were confused and frightened. The Reverend Mr. Clark's missionaries went to see her husband, James, over at the garage where he works in Sturgis; James stopped talking about how he felt. "I don't know about James," she said, "I can't seem to get through to him. I don't know what he really thinks." And there came into her voice the edge of sadness at thinking about somebody who had to bear the load she carries so casually without understanding why he bears it.

She talked a long time to two visitors yesterday morning, lying on the bed at the house of one of her neighbors, casual talk most of it, leading nowhere much, wondering as her visitors wondered what were the roots of her lonely pilgrimage.

"What are the roots, do you suppose?" she said. "I wish somebody would ask me that, instead of this stuff about my long-range plans and all this silly publicity, because where the roots are is really the thing I'd like to think about."

She'd given up reading the papers and she does not seem more than politely interested in her television schedule, because the Louise Gordon she sees and reads about obviously does not seem to her the Louise Gordon she knows.

She was sitting up on the bed when she began talking about her loneliness.

"I think of my people working over there"—she waved her hand at Clay—"Somebody ought to beat their butts for them. God knows, I need a job"—her feet came down on the floor—"but to go over there to work and cook and scrub"— she was on her knees now, her face down to the floor in a pantomime of the ancient posture of subjection—"and prostrate myself and humble myself for three dollars a day? That Mayor didn't even know my sister Mattie's last name."

And then, as she got up, Louis Lomax, a Hearst reporter who happens to be a Negro, said with the infinite, tolerant wisdom of his Southern childhood:

"Oh, heck, Louise, next fall all your neighbors will have their kids in that school and they'll be sitting here telling you how they won the fight." And Louise Gordon smiled and said she supposed they would.

"And now I think everybody ought to go home; the

National Guard, you all, yes, me too, and leave those kids in school to make their way. My children will make their way; the white children will make their way too. Let them work it out together."

She smiled and thanked her visitors for passing the time with her.

There's no running water back on the patch; one man who delivers her water bottled from Clay refused to go on selling it to her three days ago. She found a new supply, but it did not seem to her a very important issue.

"The way things go, if I can't buy water any more, I figure God will make it rain for four days. There's springs back in those hills. What's water, anyway?"

It seemed, walking away down the road that will probably not be paved in Louise Gordon's lifetime, somehow silly to believe in cause and effect; history is a series of divine and beautiful accidents like the moment of truth that happened at the same time to a little boy and his mother when she looked at him and said that together they would charge the guns. It is a little hard to think that now I am coming home and I am condemned before the week is out to have some smug party who has never seen Clay or Louise Gordon explain to me exactly what made her do what she did.

The story of the South is the most beautiful and important story on earth today, because it is the frontier of an old, heroic American tradition. These are great people—great Americans—and they are the heritage, not of some race or other, but of all Americans. Each is different, but, with all of them, the mystery of someone like Louise Gordon, who can live in the shadows all her life and then be ready with precisely the right word abides to taunt and tease us and touch our sense of awe. The story is quite simply that a terrible beauty sleeps and waits down here.

from *America Comes of Middle Age:*
Columns 1950–1962 (1963)

The Ordeal of Bobby Cain

by George McMillan

Clinton, Tennessee

THERE is an ironic inevitability in the location of Clinton High School. It sits smack at the foot of Foley Hill, Clinton's Negro community. You can't come off the hill to go downtown—to go anyplace—without passing the school.

Most of Clinton's Negro children have been passing it every day of their lives—and then, if they were of high-school age, have traveled 17 more miles to go to *their* school, a Negro school in Knoxville.

Until last August. Up on Foley Hill on the night of Sunday, August 26th, at 434 Jarnigan Street, a sixteen-year-old boy named Bobby Cain lay sleepless, frightened by the knowledge that the next morning he would have to enter that school at the foot of the hill. He did not want to go down that hill in the morning. Overnight, Clinton High had changed, in Bobby's eyes, from an accustomed landmark to the focus of an agonizing personal dilemma.

He either had to go to Clinton High, down that hill, just two tenths of a mile, or never go to school again.

For, by a quirk of history, the federal court ruling that made it possible for Bobby to go to Clinton High made it impossible for him to go back to Austin High in Knoxville. Anderson County would now no longer pay Bobby's tuition at Austin nor the cost of transporting him to Knoxville.

And it had become plain to Bobby, that Sunday for the first time, that to go to Clinton High might be an act of physical courage. All day long the sensitive intelligence network of mothers and sisters who worked as domestics "downtown" had been bringing home news of trouble. A white man had turned up down there, was calling on people, showing them pictures of a Negro man kissing a white girl. He was stirring people up.

Bobby had never wanted to go to Clinton if there "was going to be a disturbance about it." In the world within a world of Foley Hill, Bobby was known as quiet, serious and "a good boy." Now he was worried by the talk. At 7:00 P.M. he switched on the TV set in the living room of the small concrete-block Cain home to hear the news. The news was that a stranger named John Kasper had come to Clinton to fight integration at Clinton High School, and he threatened to have a protest picket line in front of the school the next morning.

Bobby did not want to go through a picket line. But he did not say so then. Instead, he dressed to go to the Sunday-evening service at Mount Sinai Church with his mother. He is meticulously clean and keeps a looking-glass shine on his shoes. His mother, Mrs. Robert Cain, a stocky, heavy-set woman, had to hurry him. "Bobby, you come on!" he heard her call from the porch.

He went, for it is part of the favorable repute in which Bobby is held that he is a dutiful son.

The service turned out to be a prayer for peace, come morning. "Help us to love our enemies," said the Reverend O. W. Willis, "and send our children down the hill with peace in their hearts." Bobby stood outside, talking with other youngsters, two of whom had already failed to enroll because they were going to "wait and see what happened."

On the way home, along the narrow, curbless dim-lighted lanes of Foley Hill, Bobby finally spoke to Mrs. Cain. "Mama," he said, "I want to get an education, but I don't want to go down there in the morning."

"You can't pay any attention to what they say to you," she said in a characteristic tone of hers, half harsh, half tender.

"I know there are people who hate me," said Bobby.

"Then you've got to take it," she answered.

"I'd rather go back to Austin High," said Bobby.

"No, no," she said, her voice rising. "From now on, you're going down the hill to school. Nobody can afford to send you back to Austin." Mrs. Cain is a household servant, and Mr. Cain is an odd-jobs carpenter.

There was no use. When Bobby got home, he went to his room, undressed, and got down on his knees and prayed. He asked "the Lord to watch over me during the day."

He had decided to go to Clinton High. But it was a decision that kept him awake that Sunday night.

He was scared.

It is useless to ask a man who has somehow gone beyond what he thought was his limit of courage to tell you where he found his unexpected resource. He very seldom knows. This was exactly Bobby Cain's plight the day I first talked with him, on September 14th, the Friday afternoon that marked the end of his third week in Clinton High.

During those weeks, this quiet adolescent who wanted to avoid any "disturbance" had been the victim of some of the most angry racial vituperation in recent American history. Afraid though he was to go to school because there might be a picket line, he had continued to go after the school was besieged by an uncontrolled mob.

But he had trouble explaining why. It was still too soon, for one thing. As we talked, drops of sweat gathered on his forehead and began to run down his cheek. He pressed his palms together nervously. He reminded me of the men I had interviewed when I served as a Marine combat correspondent in World War II. It is impossible for men who have really "had it" to talk about their experience until their memories have had an interval in which to reject the intolerable.

When I asked him, for example, what names he had been called when he ran the gantlet of segregationists who crowded around the sidewalks of Clinton High, he looked away, and answered in a voice so low I could barely hear him.

"Coon . . ." he said, his voice trailing off. He insisted he could not remember any others.

And Bobby, like most true combat veterans, knew very little about the shape of the larger events of which he was a part. He remembered that the first day of school had been relatively uneventful (of the more than 800 enrolled students only about 25 had failed to report) and that there wasn't much trouble the second morning, only a few pickets. But by the time school was out, there was a large crowd around the building, muttering ugly things to him as he came out. He did not know that that same day a hearing had been held on charges made earlier against Kasper, the outsider who was leading the opposition to integration, and that Kasper had been freed in the morning, and had announced thereupon that he was not leaving town until the Negroes had withdrawn from school, or until the whole school board resigned. Bobby knew there was to be a meeting "downtown" that night.

When he got home, he sat down in the living room, and "just kind of trembled for a little while." Later, he tried to do homework, but the atmosphere was not exactly serene. That night Foley Hill began to stir in fear. It was a small community, about 200 Negroes in a town of 4,000, with nothing in its history to prepare it for racial violence.

East Tennessee was not Mississippi; indeed, America's first abolitionist newspaper was published in the area, and the region had voted against joining the Confederacy. But if the Negroes could, as one of them said, "go almost anywhere in East Tennessee," it was still a region with another pertinent tradition. Clinton was within an area where it was part of the code to settle disputes without help from the law. The danger, as some of the adults on Foley Hill saw it, was not so much from racial hatred, as that any open argument might be settled with gunfire.

It is hard to say exactly what happened on Foley Hill that night, and on the successive nights until the National Guard arrived in Clinton. A leading Negro newspaper has said that Foley Hill became an arsenal. A rumor was circulated that the men of Foley Hill at one time took up tactical positions, covering the roads that led up to it.

Bobby stayed around the house. Mrs. Cain says that he began to "act different and strange with his brothers and sisters. They got on his nerves, and he asked me to keep them quiet."

When bedtime came, Bobby took two aspirins, prayed, and again lay sleepless for hours.

Things had got so bad at Clinton High by Wednesday morning that "they took us in the side door," Bobby said. A newspaper account says that "a milling mob of approximately 1,000 gathered at the school." An elderly Negro woman was tripped and struck in the face by a white man.

By then, Bobby had begun to think of "inside the school"

as his sanctuary. The white students were not unfriendly. "They didn't make any cracks, and one teacher came up to me in the hall that day and apologized," Bobby recalls.

"We're sorry you have to go through this," she said to Bobby.

But outside the school, the mutterings were turning into an ugly and menacing rumble. The mob would not leave the school. Some of the angriest were a handful of students; "the same group who were troublemakers inside the school were the troublemakers outside," a teacher observed.

The sheriff of Anderson County arrived at school and "temporarily withdrew" the 12 Negro students, Bobby among them. When he got home this time, on Wednesday, Bobby "sat and trembled for a long time." He was preparing himself for another talk with his mother, a serious one.

"I had decided I wasn't going back," he said.

After supper, there was another of those improvised Foley Hill councils of war, and Bobby attended with his mother. The sheriff turned up. "He told us if we'd only send our children back to Austin High," Mrs. Cain recalls, "he'd drive them down himself every day." His offer was refused.

While this handful of parents and children were meeting, Kasper was speaking at the courthouse to "a crowd estimated at from 1,000 to 3,000 cheering and howling persons," according to a report. Photographers and reporters were pushed around. Kasper was delivering an "ultimatum" to officials to "get those Negroes out of Clinton High."

When Bobby and his mother got home, he put it to her, as strongly as a boy like him might dare.

"I can't go back down there," he told her.

Mrs. Cain "just sat Bobby down in a chair," she recalls. Then she told him: "I had to scuffle to get what little education I got. I'm as worried about that mob as you are. But what about the others in there asleep? Where are your brothers and sisters going to school if you don't stick?"

Mr. Cain was there. "I wouldn't be so worried," he told his wife, "if Bobby was a girl. I don't think they'd hurt a girl."

But Mrs. Cain ignored him. "Bobby," she said, "you'll never feel right with yourself if you don't go back."

Bobby took his aspirin, went off to bed, got down on his knees, and "prayed to the Lord to help me get through that line in the morning."

When Bobby Cain went to school on Thursday morning he had with him a little pocketknife of the kind boys often carry. "I wasn't mad," he says. "I could take the names they called me. But I was gonna protect myself."

As Bobby went into school, a woman stepped out of the crowd and whacked him on the shoulder with a stick. "You nigger!" she yelled. Bobby kept walking, head down. "I didn't want to see her face," he says.

The Negro students had not been using the school cafeteria—they were not sure they were supposed to—and as they walked at lunchtime to a drive-in custard spot three blocks away to eat, a crowd followed. Bobby and another boy were pushed off the sidewalk, into the street.

"There were just these two little colored boys against 200 white men," an eyewitness told a reporter from a Knoxville paper.

A heckler stepped forward and grabbed at Bobby. Bobby drew his little pocketknife, just as the police arrived. The official police account says that Bobby "tried to defend himself with a knife." He was taken into protective custody, and held at the jail until an older brother could come for him.

That was a turning point. Bobby can talk about what happened on Thursday reflectively, as he cannot talk about the earlier events.

"After that day," he says, "I found a little courage of my own. I won't say I wasn't afraid after that. But it came to me for the first time that I had a right to go to school. I realized that it was those other people who were breaking the law, not me. That night I determined to stick it out for Bobby Cain, and not for anybody else."

After that day, he never again had so much trouble getting to sleep, although Foley Hill was still as tense as ever. At last, on Saturday night, 100 state troopers dramatically arrived in Clinton and restored order. They were followed the next day, Sunday, by the National Guard. Kasper was convicted of contempt and sentenced to a year in jail. He is now out on bond.

Bobby did not stop trembling at home until well into the second week, long after the National Guard had taken over. What helped him most was the attitude of the white student body at Clinton High.

They grew more and more friendly. "They'd ask me about my homework, did I have it done, things like that," Bobby recalls with obvious pleasure. One of his teachers observed that the members of Clinton High's football team ("they're the elite at this time of the school year," she said) went out of their way to talk with Bobby.

Although he had been an above-average student at Austin High, he did not settle down to his homework until the third week of school, at the same time that it became possible for him to make the two-tenths-mile trip to Clinton High unescorted.

He scored his first scholastic triumph the day I interviewed him, on Friday, September 14th. The day before, his history teacher, Mrs. Don Byerly, had asked his class to memorize the Declaration of Independence as the next day's assignment. When it came time to recite, Mrs. Byerly asked Bobby to come to the front of the room.

"I knew it," Bobby said. "When I finished, she said to me, "That's very good, Bobby, very good.'"

Collier's, November 23, 1956

A Sequel to Segregation

by Richard B. Stolley

ON Sept. 21, 1956 subscribers and newsstand dealers in Choctaw County, Ala. received an issue of LIFE containing a story of special interest to them. "The Restraints: Open and Hidden," the fourth instalment of LIFE's series on segregation, showed among other things how Willie and Allie Lee Causey, a Negro couple, lived and worked in the 95% Negro community of Shady Grove, Ala. Choctaw County is a poor "piney woods" section of the deep South. The nearest town to Shady Grove is Silas (pop. 400).

The story told how Willie Causey earned a good livelihood as a woodcutter and farmer, running a small but successful business with a truck, power tools and his own work crew. It also told how Allie Lee Causey taught school in a ramshackle building and it quoted her opinion on the Negro problem in the following words: "Integration is the only way through which Negroes will receive justice. We cannot get it as a separate people. If we can get justice on our jobs, and equal pay, then we'll be able to afford better homes and good education."

On Tuesday, Sept. 25, four days after the story appeared, Willie Causey, a vigorous man of 55, rose at dawn, did some chores around the farm and got ready for a day's woodcutting. The gas gauge of his truck, a two-ton 1954 Chevrolet in which he carried newly cut logs to the woodyard in Silas, registered almost empty. After breakfast he told his 23-year-old son "L.C." to drive the truck in to one of the two McPhearson service stations in Silas and get the tank filled up with gas.

At McPhearson's station L.C. parked the truck and went inside to pay the previous week's gas bill. While he was inside, a white man named Hilton Roberts jumped in the truck and drove it a few hundred yards down the road, parking it in the front yard of his home. Roberts was an employe of a prosperous pulpwood dealer, E. L. ("Mike") Dempsey, who had been buying the wood that Willie Causey cut. (Willie later learned that Dempsey had ordered the truck confiscated.)

Frightened and bewildered by the removal of the truck, L.C. hitched a ride back home and told his father what had happened. Willie Causey drove into Silas in his 1955 Chevrolet sedan and went to Hilton Roberts' house. The truck was still parked in the yard but there was no one home. Causey decided he had better go to see Mike Dempsey, but Dempsey was at his office 35 miles away in the upper part of the county. Needing gas for the trip, Causey drove to McPhearson's station and pulled up to the pump. The operator, Pete McIlwain, made no move toward the car for almost 10 minutes. Then at last he came over and said, "Willie, I got orders not to sell you any more gas."

"Sir?"

"I got orders to sell you no more gas, and nothing else either."

Causey thought it was a joke. He grinned and said, "Mister Pete, I been buying gas here for 15 years. What have I done that you can't sell me gas?"

"Do you take LIFE magazine, Willie?" McIlwain asked.

"No, sir."

"Well, you go get yourself a LIFE magazine and you'll know why I can't sell you gas."

No one in the Causey family had yet seen the LIFE story. The photographs had been taken two months previously, the Causeys did not know when the story would appear and they had almost forgotten about it. Mrs. Causey had heard other Negro teachers talking about the article during a teachers' meeting the day after the issue appeared, but she had not seen a copy of the magazine herself.

Puzzled, Willie Causey was getting ready to drive away from the gas station. Just then Mrs. Rosie McPhearson, the owner of this and another gas station in Silas, drove by. She saw Causey, stopped in the middle of the road, jumped out of her car and walked over. She did not speak to Causey, as she usually did, and he thought she looked very upset about something.

Mrs. McPhearson, a handsome, spirited widow whose wealth and family background have made her one of the leading

344 RICHARD B. STOLLEY

figures of Choctaw County, was more than upset. She was angry. She had previously left an order concerning Causey at both her stations and was making sure now that it would be followed: "If he comes around, don't sell him another gallon of gas."

Later, explaining her attitude toward the LIFE story and toward Causey, Mrs. McPhearson said, "People in the north don't understand what we're up against down here. Willie said he owned all those things—why, Mr. Dempsey owned that truck."

She was also angry because her son, John McPhearson, had sold Causey a power saw on time and Willie had turned the saw in on a new one he had bought from someone else, John said, without completing the payments. "Talk about restraints," Mrs. McPhearson went on, "if he thinks he had restraints before, I'd like to know what he thinks he's got now. It's the burrheads like him that are causing us trouble. We ought to ship every one of them back to Africa. You're going to have to change the pigment of their skin . . . and until you do that none of my grandchildren are going to school with them. The people up north think they're going to cram it down our throats, but they're not."

When Mrs. McPhearson walked past him at the gas station, Willie Causey realized that whatever trouble he was in was bad trouble. He drove away and stopped at the second McPhearson station. The attendant came out and said, "Willie, I got orders not to sell you gas."

"What's the matter?" Causey pleaded. "I been raised here in Silas and lived here all my life. What did I do?"

"That magazine," the attendant said. "That's the awfulest thing I've ever seen."

"Captain," Causey said, "I don't know what this is about any magazine. All I know is that everybody is fussing at me. You white folks are the law. Will you speak a good word for me, Captain?"

"Willie," the attendant said, "I don't know a good word to speak for you."

At this point Willie Causey was so perturbed that he gave up trying to see Dempsey and instead went directly to Shady

Grove school where his wife taught. After listening to his story she told him to return to the farm and not to leave.

That week the Causeys found that no merchant they approached in Silas would sell them anything. Willie Causey slaughtered a calf and dug vegetables from the garden to provide food for his family.

Writing to her brother in Nashville about their situation, Allie Lee Causey said, "Here is a mean place, Silas. The story they did on us is true. The pictures are true, the school is true. The work is true, the home is true. But these people are very, very mad."

With his truck gone Willie Causey could not work, but his wife continued to teach, fearful each day that she would lose her job. On Friday morning, Sept. 28, she and another teacher drove into Butler, the county seat. Both teachers wanted an advance on their salaries, which were not due to be paid until the 10th of the following month. Mrs. Causey did not want to face the superintendent of schools, Wiley C. Allen, whose permission would be required for an advance, and so the other teacher went into the courthouse alone. In a few minutes she was back. The board of education was in session in Mr. Allen's office, she reported, and they wanted to see Allie Lee Causey immediately.

Mrs. Causey spent an hour and a half being questioned by the board. How did LIFE find her for the story? How many people from LIFE came to Choctaw County? How often did they come? Where did they come from? One board member said incredulously, "The white folks around here would like to know how this all got started. We never knew any of our colored people to get in LIFE magazine." Mrs. Causey explained that she had not asked LIFE to come but that the magazine had got in touch with her family through a brother in another part of Alabama.

The board's questioning dealt with Mrs. Causey's statement on integration. Superintendent Allen read her own words to her from the magazine, then leaned back in his chair and said, "Now, Allie Lee, suppose you tell us just what you meant by those remarks."

Mrs. Causey hedged: "Those are not my exact words."

"If that's so," said Allen, "it seems to me that you have a pretty good case against LIFE." (This was the first of many times that a white person in Choctaw County would urge Mrs. Causey to sue.)

The board of education voiced strong objections to Mrs. Causey's advocacy of integration. As Superintendent Allen says, "We're not used to hearing the word 'integration' mentioned in this county." Last spring Mrs. Causey and the 101 other Negro teachers in Choctaw had been expressly forbidden to discuss it in their classes. But Mrs. Causey had felt free to talk to LIFE's reporter and photographer on the story because both of them are Negroes.

The board members had other complaints. They charged Mrs. Causey with stating that Negro teachers are paid less than white teachers, when in fact their salaries are the same if their education and experience are the same. Mrs. Causey made no such statement in the story, but the board inferred it from her general remarks about "justice" and "equal pay" for the whole Negro race.

Board member Claude G. Wimberley, a soft-spoken general-store owner in Silas, told her he was angry and disappointed because the article made it sound as if the whites had constantly harassed the Causeys. The truth was just the opposite, he said. For example, a year or so earlier Causey's logging truck had been rammed by a white man driving a pickup truck. The highway patrol said Causey's lights were defective, threatened to impound his truck and to put him in jail. Wimberley had rescued him with a $300 loan, which he said Willie had not repaid.

"I know I have helped Willie, and I know others have helped him," Wimberley told Mrs. Causey. "But that wasn't in the magazine." Other board members agreed: Willie Causey was an inveterate borrower. As Wimberley put it, "Willie's credit was regarded as good, but he was always exercising it." When the article came out, "we felt as if we had been slapped in the face."

After the school board's cross-examination Mrs. Causey was excused from the meeting and was granted permission to draw a $260 advance on her salary. She thought she had won an acquittal. Over the weekend she tried to cheer up her husband. As long as she had a job, she said, they would get along. Things would work out.

On Monday, Oct. 1, Mrs. Causey got a letter from Superintendent Allen. It read:

"This is to give notice to you that you are hereby suspended as a teacher in the Choctaw County school system until you can give proof to me and the members of the Board of Education that you did not make the statement as was quoted by you in the September 24, 1956 issue of LIFE magazine. Your suspension starts on October 1, 1956. (signed) Wiley C. Allen, Superintendent of Schools."

The situation now looked bleak for the Causeys. Next morning they left home with the six children who still live with them and drove to Mobile to stay with Mrs. Causey's parents. Mrs. Causey still had most of the $260 advance but she had no savings. The savings had been spent on her summer school work at Alabama State College for Negroes where she had completed work on her bachelor of science degree in elementary education. Willie Causey had earned no money for a week. Monthly payments on the car and furniture were due.

In Mobile they worried about their farm back in Choctaw County. They talked about their problem and tried to think what they could do to make peace with the white people of Choctaw County. Mrs. Causey was afraid that no matter what they did she would not get her job back. Willie Causey was afraid to ask for his truck until the white men sent for him. He paced the floor restlessly, saying, "I never been out of work this long before in my whole life." His wife wrote to a friend: "I have had a hard time all my life but I won't give up. I want to help my people, the Negroes."

After four days the Causeys made their decision. Leaving their children in Mobile, they would return to Silas to find out just how strong the antagonism was and to try to get support from some of their white neighbors. Mrs. Causey's family worried about the decision but the Causeys thought they could go back and assess the situation without stirring up any additional trouble.

On Sunday, Oct. 7, Willie and Allie Lee Causey returned to Choctaw County, driving in by a back road so as to miss the town of Silas. For advice and encouragement they brought with them Mrs. Causey's 82-year-old father, Albert Thornton. He had lived in Choctaw County for many years and was remembered with fondness and respect by many white people. The Causeys hoped he would be able to plead his daughter's case.

The first man they went to see was J. T. Allen (a distant relative of School Superintendent Wiley Allen), owner of a general store and cotton gin in the town of Cromwell and, more important to the Causeys, president for more than 30 years of the county board of education. He is a ruddy-faced, genial man of considerable influence in Choctaw County.

J. T. Allen had not been present at the school board meeting when Mrs. Causey was questioned, but he knew what had happened and he had concurred in the suspension, though he had warned the board that Mrs. Causey could probably go to court and win back her job. He told her all this when she and her father met him in his general store.

"I hope we can settle this peaceably," Allen said, "without a law suit against the board. You might get your job back here, but there isn't another county in Alabama that would hire you."

So far as Allen was concerned, the issue was settled. If she could furnish proof, such as a statement from LIFE that she was misquoted and misrepresented, perhaps he could call a meeting of the board, but otherwise, "I don't see what can be done."

J. T. Allen has since explained his stand on the Causey case to LIFE. "These southern Negroes," he says, "are different from yours up north. We think we're good to them and know how to handle them. We try to help them, look after them, see that they get enough to eat, have a job, get along all right. They don't expect equality and wouldn't know what to do if they had it. The only time we have trouble is when it's stirred up by people like the schoolteacher. There wasn't a white man in this county that approved of that story." Then, in a more jocular tone, "If you Yam Dankees will leave us alone, we'll handle everything all right."

Allen believes that the white people of Choctaw County went out of their way to help Willie Causey and that he has now forfeited any right to their sympathy. "The best thing to do with this matter is not to stir it up any further," Allen says. "It's all straightened out."

After the discouraging talk with J. T. Allen the Causeys and Mr. Thornton went back to see Superintendent Allen. The superintendent criticized Mrs. Causey for her "attitude" at the earlier board meeting and again suggested that she sue LIFE. Mrs. Causey refused and with that refusal her teaching career in Choctaw County ended.

That same afternoon Willie Causey set out to find where he stood with the loggers of the county. About 15 years ago he had given up day-labor work and gone into the wood-producing business. He worked for pulpwood dealers and occasionally for private landowners who let him cut wood on their timber tracts for a share of the price of each cord. This share, called "stumpage," usually came to about $5 a cord (not $2 a cord as LIFE erroneously reported). In a good week Causey could gross more than $300, and after paying stumpage, gasoline bills and crew wages he sometimes netted as much as $100.

Willie Causey's economic future depended on Mike Dempsey, whose seizure of Causey's truck had made it impossible for Willie to transport wood. A Negro friend went with Causey to Dempsey's tiny brick office on the edge of the pine forest near Cromwell. The friend went in alone and asked Dempsey to see Causey. Dempsey said he would.

As soon as Causey entered the office, Dempsey pulled out a copy of the magazine, slammed his hand against it and said, "Willie, this has got you into a lot of trouble."

Dempsey seemed to Causey angrier than he had ever seen him. He said he would get into trouble with the federal government over the picture in the article that showed Causey's 16-year-old son cutting wood. It is against the U.S. child labor law to employ a person under 18 in a hazardous industry like logging, and a pulpwood dealer caught in a violation might have his wood confiscated.

Dempsey went on, reading aloud: "He owns his own equipment for woodcutting, including power tools and a truck, and can compete successfully with white men in the same line of work." That, said Dempsey, was an outright lie.

Causey owed money on the truck and the power saw and was indebted also to a garage owner in Silas and to various other white men. Dempsey said the total amount owed by Willie Causey came to nearly $800.

As Causey recalls the conversation, Dempsey went on to say, "We set you up in business, Willie. We bought you a truck and a saw, we gave you wood to cut and we paid you the same as everybody else gets. And then this comes out."

The story should have made clear, Dempsey later insisted to LIFE representatives, that white men held mortgages on Willie Causey's equipment and that they tried to help him, not hinder him. Causey did not "own" the equipment, Dempsey claimed, even though he used it daily and kept it at his home and was making regular payments on it.

It is impossible for Willie Causey to say conclusively how much he owes and to whom. He is an unlettered man whose finances have usually been handled by his wife. While she was away at college this summer Willie allowed his affairs to become tangled. He borrowed money and did not tell Allie Lee until weeks later. While convalescing from an infected foot he had allowed time payments to lapse. Before Mrs. Causey had had time to straighten things out the trouble over the article began.

Dempsey accused Causey of owing him money for the truck. Causey bought the truck originally from another pulpwood dealer for whom he used to work. The dealer allowed him to use the truck and pay for it on time. Shortly after Causey began selling wood to Dempsey in 1955 the latter took over the balance due on the truck, which he says stood then at $563.50. Causey later bought some truck tires from Dempsey, increasing the amount he owed him. Causey thinks he has paid in full and more. But he says he has never received a statement on his payments. The best his wife can do is add up the amounts Dempsey deducted from Causey's checks for wood. According to her the sum is larger than all debts to Dempsey that she knows anything about. John McPhearson insists Willie still owes him for the power saw which was traded in on a new one. A lumber dealer in Silas says that he has not yet been fully paid for the lumber which Willie Causey purchased from him to build the three additional new rooms on the back of the Causey home. And a Silas garage owner, Lockwood Livingston, says Causey owes him for a motor job on his truck.

As Mike Dempsey continued to criticize him, Willie Causey says he realized that he could expect no help. Twice, he says, Dempsey's anger reached such peaks that he half rose from behind his desk. Finally Willie says he told him, "Willie, you were a good hand. You put on more wood for a small crew than anybody else I had. But that magazine has knocked you right out of a job. We all came to an agreement. Nobody is going to sell you any more stumpage, and you'll never get another job from me."

At that moment Willie Causey decided that he had to move out of Choctaw County. Over and over Negro friends reported to him and his wife that white people were demanding that the Causeys get out. John McPhearson, who had sold Willie Causey the power saw, sent word through a Negro friend: whatever you do, don't ever come back to Silas.

It had been 17 days since the article appeared. This was longer than some people expected the Causeys to stay around. As Don Blount, editor of the *Choctaw Advocate*, told a LIFE editor, "When I read that in LIFE, I figured that man must have his bags packed." The Causeys returned to Mobile.

After making arrangements for a moving van to pick up their belongings, they went back to the farm on Friday, Oct. 12 to pack and get ready for the movers. Mrs. Causey slaughtered her flock of 19 chickens, plucked them and stored in the freezer. Willie Causey brought in wagonloads of corn and dug two bushels of potatoes. He puttered around three new uncompleted rooms which the family had never lived in and never would live in. The hilltop on which the house stood was unusually quiet, for the younger children had been left in Mobile. Only the mockingbirds whistled loudly and swooped low over the yard to pick up stray seeds and insects.

There was some difficulty about getting the freezer and bedroom suite out of the county. Mrs. Causey had bought them on the instalment plan from G. W. Allen, a furniture and appliance dealer (and no relation to the other Allens previously mentioned), and she had not yet finished paying for them. When he heard the Causeys were planning to move,

Allen sent out a truck to pick up both the freezer and the furniture. Mrs. Causey begged the truck drive not to take the
freezer as this would spoil hundreds of dollars worth of beef,
pork, poultry and vegetables.

Willie Causey drove to Allen's store and asked for time to
raise money and pay off the bill. Allen agreed. But Allen
warned the Causeys not to move either the freezer or the
bedroom set until they had paid him in full. "You think
you're in trouble now," he told them, "but if you move that
furniture you'll be in the jailhouse." From friends and relatives the Causeys raised nearly $400 to take care of Allen's
bill.

The Causeys had hoped to stay on the farm until the moving van arrived on Monday, but by late Saturday afternoon
they were frightened by reports from neighbors that some
white people were stirred up about their return and intended
to come out looking for trouble. Once again the family left
hurriedly for Mobile.

On Monday, Willie Causey rode out to Choctaw County in
the moving van with the driver and his helper, both Negroes.
On the way Causey explained what had happened to him and
told the two men about the rumors. One rumor was that if
they tried to move the furniture, white men would hide
alongside the road and attack the truck. Arriving at the farm,
the Negroes loaded the van quickly. Just as they were getting
ready to leave they glanced across the road and saw three
white men standing in the woods, staring silently at them.
The driver put Causey in the middle of the front seat between
himself and his helper, explaining, "If they get you, they'll
have to get us too." All three were scared as they drove off,
but the white men never moved.

Mike Dempsey, Causey's former employer, has told an editor of LIFE that he expected to hear talk of violence to the
family, but he says that he never heard any.

Willie Causey made one more trip back to Choctaw
County. He needed his truck before he could look for a new
job as a woodcutter. He called Dempsey on the phone and
asked if he could have it back. Yes he could, Dempsey said, if
he paid off his debt. Dempsey's accountant, Melvin Pritchard,
said the debt was $301.79. Willie Causey asked no questions.

He told Pritchard that if he would take the truck the next day to the woodyard outside Silas, Causey's son L.C. would meet him there with the money.

Pritchard never showed up. The truck was still in Hilton Roberts' front yard the following day, its back wheel securely chained. Dempsey now says that he intends to sell the truck—"legally, of course."

When Pritchard failed to deliver the truck at the appointed time, Willie Causey left Choctaw County for good.

The Causeys have now left Alabama and moved to another southern city, hoping to patch up their lives. In the weeks since Allie Lee Causey was suspended by the board of education, she has thought a lot about the things she said in LIFE. "I told the truth in the magazine," she says. "Justice and integration, that's what I want. Look at that picture of my school. Is that justice? A dozen of my first-graders didn't have books. Is that justice?"

In Choctaw County no colored school has indoor toilets. Only one has running water inside the building. There are only two lunchrooms in all 33 Negro schools.

In many other places in the South an equalization program, designed to make Negro schools as good as white schools, has been in progress since the late 1940s, and especially since the 1954 Supreme Court decision against school segregation. But not in Choctaw County.

Some members of the school board acknowledge the disparity in the school systems but say they can do nothing about it. The big problem is, of course, money. Last year a $700,000 budget had to be stretched to cover the two school systems, and 95% of it, Superintendent Allen estimates, went for teachers' salaries and school buses.

"I feel we have done no wrong," Mrs. Causey wrote in a letter. "Justice is that political virtue which renders every man his due. Justice also consists of the principles of honest dealing with each other and a fixed purpose to do no one wrong or injury. I wouldn't have lost my job if justice had been in the education board."

Today all that remains of Willie and Allie Lee Causey in Choctaw County is their empty house on the hill. Its littered rooms testify to the haste in which its owners left. On the front stoop lies a discarded brown-skinned doll staring vacantly into the empty yard. The garden is untidy. Its vegetables rot in the ground. On a bare bedroom wall between two windows hangs a calendar, still turned to the month of September. No one thought to turn it to October. It is a month the Causeys hope someday to forget.

Life, December 10, 1956

Montgomery Morning

by Wilma Dykeman and James Stokely

Montgomery, Alabama

IN the still hours just before daylight on the morning of December 21, fog hung heavy over the dome of Alabama's gleaming white state capitol building. The shrouded streets which stretched away from it through the city of Montgomery were silent. It was easy, in those small hours, to unloose the imagination and wonder if some of the ghosts of 1861 might not be lurking in the "Cradle of the Confederacy" on this morning which was to make Southern history. For if it is true that the hand that rocks the cradle is the hand that rules the world, with a slightly different meaning of words this cradle was presently to be rocked to its foundations.

As daylight came, warm and springlike, Court Square—at the opposite end of the wide main street leading up to the capitol—began to waken. Around the dry fountain, with its tiers of figurines, plump pigeons strutted on the wet pavement. Traffic began to pick up. The giant wreaths of Christmas lights strung across the street became more visible. And the city buses began to roll in and out of the square, loading and unloading passengers. In the doorways of the dress shops, the men's ready-to-wear and hardware stores, the newsstands and the offices and drugstores, people stood watching the buses. This was the morning when a year-old boycott and a generations-old tradition were to end.

Negroes and whites sat or stood at the central segregated bus stop—watching; people drove by slowly, peering from their cars to see what was happening on the buses; and men leaning against the parking meters and standing on the street corners in their shirt sleeves, watched. This was the morning that segregation on the city buses of Montgomery gasped its last and integration breathed its first, and there was tension implied in both the birth and the death.

The morning went quietly. A couple of cars filled with watchful white men in leather jackets parked on two sides of Court Square for the first hour, then slowly moved away. Groups of well-dressed Negro leaders stood at the central bus stop and rode several of the runs. The Rev. Martin Luther King, Jr., who has become the public symbol of the Negro cause, entered a bus and took a seat near the front. The day's pattern developed—most of the buses were only partially filled, but the Negroes rode, for the most part, in the middle seats, a few at the very front, a few at the rear; and the whites rode almost together far to the front. A few whites who were eager for the day to have full meaning rode on the back seat; at least one or two sat by Negroes. By late afternoon the word had gone out over town that "Everything's O.K.; nothing happening."

It was the very calmness of the day that was the great news here. People who said nothing had happened meant nothing violent, to make headlines. Actually a great deal had happened which might make news for years to come. Before a new year can begin, an old year must end. Before a new era of human dignity can be born, old indignities must die. On December 21, an era as well as a year came to an end in Montgomery. It was important that Alabamans and Americans alike should realize that what was disappearing was as meaningful as what was developing.

For one thing, the familiar cardboard signs spelling out segregation were gone from the buses. Gone too was the custom that had compelled Negroes to pay their fares at the front door and then often get off the bus and climb back on at the rear door. And the abusive language of some of the drivers calling their passengers "black apes" and "damned niggers" was stilled. Most apparent of all, perhaps, the stream of walking women had almost disappeared.

"The real power of the boycott was the Negro women," a housewife in one of the white residential areas told us. "Every morning they came by our door here. It was like watching a brook to look out and see them going by steadily for an hour or so every morning and an hour or so every afternoon. And this morning they weren't there. The brook had dried up."

Other things, less tangible but not a whit less real, have gone from Montgomery too. Their essence might be summed up in the words of one Negro: "Now there isn't any more hang-dog looking at a white man. We face him. We got a proud look."

On a street in one of the newer residential areas, as we walked along in the pleasant morning between the rows of green lawns and lush pyracantha bushes heavy with clusters of flaming berries, we saw a carload of young schoolboys slow down just past us and shout something before they roared away. We turned and asked a Negro woman walking behind us what they had hollered. Small and lively as a sparrow in her brown coat and brown head-scarf and brown skin, she smiled at us. "They was just meddlin' me. They have to act theyself up. I don't pay them no mind, when they get through actin' theyself up, everything be all right." She had no resentment —against the cruel boys in the present or the bus drivers in the past. "They wasn't all bad. Jus' a few real low mean. My bus driver I hadn' seen in a year welcome me back this mornin'. Like my family I work for: they told me to stay off the buses, they didn' blame us for what we's doin'."

We talked with a Negro man who summed up the remarkable self-control his people had shown in this great victory of their boycott. "We don't use the word 'victory,'" he assured us firmly. "We don't want to even have the attitude of the word. Like Reverend King told us at one of our meetings, the attitude of 'victory' wouldn't be worthy of us, and it would be a barrier to the growth we hope for in others."

The conduct and accomplishments of the Negroes during the past year have obviously shaken some of the firmest convictions held by the whites. In the beginning of the boycott it was often said that Negroes "can't organize anything but a crap game," and if they did, they "can't hold out." But they did organize, 50,000 strong, and they didn't develop into an army and they didn't degenerate into a mob. They remained individuals united by a vision. In a region where patience on the long haul is considered a somewhat less colorful personal asset than pride in the instant's dramatic gesture, one of the most astonishing features of this boycott, to white residents, was the daily plodding persistence with which the Negroes moved toward their goal.

Then, of course, the white people began to admit the Negroes were organized, but "outsiders" had done it: Communists, "NAACPs," "some of Brownell's gang," "troublemakers" in general. And, of course, the Negroes would submit to the old pressures anyway: a few arrests, some bullying, a few bed-sheets.

"For a while there, the police would stop your car, maybe two or three times a day," one Negro leader said. "'Get out, nigger.' You'd show your driving license and they'd ask you all the questions already filled out on it. Or they'd book you for going twenty-five miles an hour in a twenty-mile speed zone."

But the spirit didn't break and the Negroes were never provoked into retaliation.

"Then white boys would throw water on us, or a Coca-Cola bottle from a car. Or once in awhile they'd spit on us. Even in the last few weeks over twenty cars have had acid thrown on them."

Mass arrest of the famous ninety was the whites' real panzer effort at group intimidation that failed and backfired. "For the first time," a professor at a local Negro college told us, "it became honorable to go to jail. Everybody whose name wasn't on that list felt sort of slighted, like he hadn't done his share." Those who had always been so scared of the police and jail now were clamoring to take the part of the punished.

The final test came when the Ku Klux Klan announced, on the night the Supreme Court handed down its last decision, that it would stage a demonstration in the Negro part of town. Before such a threat the Negro would once have cowered behind closed doors and darkened windows. But this time the Negro community greeted them almost as it would any other parade. As the estimated forty carloads of Ku Kluxers drove by, lights stayed on, doors were ajar, men, women and children watched openly, in silence. It took enormous courage to face this robed and ancient enemy with such nonchalance. In the end it was the Klan that weakened first. Their parade turned into a side street and disappeared. The Kluxers themselves had set the final seal of solidarity and emancipation on the Negro citizens.

Physical intimidation failed—and so did economic threats.

For if one fact has emerged clearly to both white and Negro community in this crisis it is the intertwining of their economy. As one person put it: "Our schools may not be integrated, but our dollars sure are." Early in the boycott when the Mayor asked the women of Montgomery not to go after their maids and, if the maid wouldn't walk to work, to fire her, one housewife said, "The Mayor can do his own cooking if he wants to. I'm going after my cook." The Negro women knew their employers well enough, too, to be aware of their general distaste for mops and ironing boards. They knew instinctively that these people might tolerate injustice but never inconvenience.

"They talked about firing all the Negroes in the boycott from their jobs," a Negro man told us. "But then I guess they got to thinking about all those white folks' houses we rent. No payroll, no rent. What would those poor white widows living on their husbands' estates do? And what about all those refrigerators and cars and furniture we owed payments on? The storekeepers didn't want that stuff back. They wanted the money. No, after a little thinking there was very few of us fired from work."

Perhaps the most insidious enemy the Negro of Montgomery faced was his attitude toward himself. Indoctrinated for generations by assurances of his inferiority, in many cases he was uncertain as to his own power to sustain this movement. One will tell you now: "I wasn't sure how well we'd stick together or how long we'd last. But the people were way out ahead of the leaders at first. Then we all went together and there wasn't any doubt we'd go on as long as necessary."

Under these pressures and doubts, the Negroes have discovered the power of their dollars, the strength of their religion and the hidden resources within themselves. And one of the sorest problems facing Negroes everywhere was met and solved: the bridging of that great gap between the really learned and the desperately illiterate. A white woman in Montgomery who had taken part in interracial group meetings said, "You met time and again with the Negro leaders but somehow you felt that you weren't ever touching the real core—couldn't reach that vast group of Negroes to even know what they were thinking. Even their leaders were isolated from them." But those the Rev. King calls "the Ph.D.'s and the D.s" were brought together by the boycott.

This was true because from first to last the movement worked through the churches. "The only way you can reach the great mass of Southern Negroes today is through their churches," one club woman said, "and the churches were the great power behind the success of this Montgomery boycott. It had religious meaning from the beginning."

If there have been improvements in the Negro community of a Sunday, perhaps even more important is the change in the Saturday night world. That cuttings, stabbings and drunkenness have decreased is attested by all the Negroes and admitted by most of the whites. As the pressures of despair and frustration have been partially supplanted by the pressures of self-respect and hopefulness, some of the destructiveness has been supplanted by better citizenship.

As the first days of bus integration passed without notable incident (a Negro woman reported she was slapped and shoved by a white man as she left the bus, and a white woman on another bus reported that a Negro man winked at her), some of the white community still were far from reconciled. We saw two young men sitting at the bus stop—wild, blue-eyed boys with sun-hardened skins. "Well, Buck, what we gonna do with these damned niggers?" And one of the leaders of the White Citizens' Council assured us, "The bus situation here is far, far from settled. It can erupt any time. We're doing our best to keep down any violence, but this is a highly charged situation. Some of these boys mean business."

A bulky taxi driver analyzed developments: "It's all looked all right so far. And it may go on quiet enough, if don't nobody get radical. But this thing's touchy. Could be set off any minute. Then who knows what'll happen?"

Another said simply, "The South will always remain the South."

When a shotgun blast was fired at the Rev. King's home on December 23, the pastor did not notify the police. But he mentioned the incident quietly to his congregation during church services. "Even if my attackers 'get' me," he said, "they will still have to 'get' 50,000 other Negroes in Montgomery." He reminded his motionless visitors that "some of us may have to die," but urged his congregation never to falter in the belief that whatever else changed, God's love for all men would continue. "The glory to God that puts man in his place will make brothers of us all," he said. Such calm in the presence of violence must give the whole city pause.

A tentative proposal has been made to start a white bus boycott and organize a white car pool. The illogic of this, in view of the fact that the Negro car pool was ruled illegal a few weeks ago, seems not to have occurred to the proposers. With characteristic Southern humor someone suggested that the Negroes should run an ad in the local paper: "FOR SALE—Slightly used old station wagons for new car pools."!

No matter what may happen tomorrow in Montgomery, the fact remains that the Negro here will never be the same again. What one of the leaders, a tall, dark, articulate man, told us is obviously true: "On December 5 last year, the Negro in Montgomery grew from a boy to a man. He'll never be the same again. A white man had always said before, 'Boy, go do this,' 'Boy, do that,' and the Negro jumped and did it. Now he says, 'I don't believe I will,' or he does it, but up straight, looking at the white man. Not a boy any more. He grew up."

The image of the frontiersman has always been vivid in the American mind and memory. One of our frequent laments today is for the disappearing frontier which has been so much a part of American history. To a visitor in Montgomery there is the suggestion of a new frontiersman. His weapons are those of Thoreau and Gandhi rather than Crockett and Boone, but the wilderness he faces is no less terrifying. Working on the frontiers of a faith and freedom whose meanings and dynamics have been too little explored before this, these new frontiersmen, black and white, may lead us—and some of the colored and white millions of the world—into a new experience of democracy.

The Nation, January 5, 1957

Martin Luther King: Where Does He Go from Here?

by Ted Poston

Montgomery, Ala.

THE BUSES of Montgomery are no longer segregated. The bombings of Negro churches and homes have, for the moment at least, ceased. And the leader of the historic non-violent struggle here has received international acclaim as a young man of unusual ability.

But where, at 28, does Martin Luther King Jr. go from here?

The youthful minister pondered the question the other day in his comfortable home here, and his brooding gaze went far beyond the walls of the tastefully furnished living room.

He had returned only the day before from Washington, where he, Roy Wilkins of the NAACP, and A. Philip Randolph, AFL-CIO vice president, had conferred with scores of the most influential Negro leaders in America to plan a May 17 "Pilgrimage of Prayer" to the nation's capital.

His slanted eyes were almost closed as he considered his answers. And then he said:

"Frankly, I don't know."

A pause, and then:

"There's so much remaining to be done here in Montgomery and I feel I have a responsibility to stay and help get things done. I feel that whatever your job is, you should do it as well as if you thought it was to be your last job. But when you are as young as I am—"

His voice trailed off for the moment. But it was not a new thought for King. Just a year ago, when he had first been firmly catapulted into the headlines, he discussed the problem with Rev. J. Pius Barbour, his friend and mentor at Crozier Theological Seminary.

Barbour teased him about his nationwide publicity, and King said:

"Frankly, I'm worried to death. A man who hits the peak at 27 has a tough job ahead. People will be expecting me to pull rabbits out of the hat for the rest of my life. If I don't or there are no rabbits to be pulled, then they'll say I'm no good."

He reverted to the theme of early success as he discussed his future the other day.

"One of the frustrations of any young man is to approach the heights at such an early age," he said. "The average man reaches this point maybe in his late forties or early fifties.

"But when you reach it so young, your life becomes a kind of decrescendo. You feel yourself fading from the screen at a time you should just be starting to work toward your goal.

"And no one knows better than I that no crowds will be waiting outside churches to greet me two years from now when some one invites me to speak."

The question of Martin Luther King's future is not a theoretical one. For he has been receiving offers of jobs and positions across the country.

There has been widespread discussion, for instance, of offering him the presidency of Fisk University in Nashville, to fill the post left vacant by the recent death of Dr. Charles Johnson, one of the country's most responsible Negro spokesmen.

King had heard of the discussion and felt flattered when he was unofficially "sounded out" on the proposal. But he gave little indication the other day that he might accept such a position.

"I feel a responsibility for continuing my work in the field of civil rights," he said, "and the church offers me more freedom to continue that work.

"When I first entered the ministry, I thought I might like to teach or be an educator like Dr. Benjamin Mays at Morehouse College, who so greatly influenced my life, but I have learned to love the pastorate now and I don't think I would like to leave it.

"I don't think I could have the same kind of freedom I have now if I were a college president. After all, colleges have boards of trustees, and many of the white trustees in the South might feel—and with justification—that my activities might hurt the institution economically."

He paused again and idly fingered the hair of his active little 17-month-old daughter, Yolande Denise ("Yoki"), who had halted her destructive course around the living room to come to rest at his knee. And he rephrased the point.

"I do have a great desire to serve humanity," he said, "but at this particular point, the pulpit gives me an opportunity and a freedom that I wouldn't have in any other sphere of activity."

Although he probably is the only man who hasn't, King said he had not heard of increasing suggestions that he become a national executive of the NAACP and help direct the national fight for civil rights. But he immediately rejected the idea.

"They've got some of the ablest men in the country directing the NAACP right now," he said, "there would be no need of my services there.

"And I feel that it is the duty and responsibility of the clergy to supplement the work of the NAACP. That is why I insisted that every member of my congregation join the local chapter here long before the bus protest began.

"For the NAACP is a vital weapon in our fight for freedom. We must continue our struggle in the courts. Our major victories there have come through the work of the NAACP.

"One thing the gradualists don't seem to understand is that we are not trying to make people love us when we go to court, we are trying to keep them from killing us.

"At the same time, we must support organizations like the NAACP that are trying to mold public opinion. Legislation changes man's external relations with other men; education changes them internally."

His own mention of "trying to keep them from killing us" brought King back to the original question of where does he go from here. For he recalled the two attempts to bomb his own home and the danger faced by Yolande and Mrs. Coretta Scott King.

"If ever I get around to thinking about my future," he said, "I must also think of my family. I've got to think of what's best for them also. It is not pleasant to live under the threat of death even if Coretta and I reject such threats personally. But I do have a responsibility to my family, and that must always be a consideration."

The young minister feels deeply about his obligation to Montgomery and is aware of the magnitude of the obstacles still facing Negroes here in their quest for full citizenship. And much of his immediate local activity may be devoted to efforts to establish a bridge of communication between the Negro and white communities here.

"Since Time magazine published a cover story on our movement recently," he said, "I think I have observed a lessening of the tensions and feelings against me and the movement itself."

But this means no slackening, of course, of King's Montgomery Improvement Assn.'s efforts to gain full citizenship for all Montgomerians. That was quite evident last Monday night when the still-weekly mass meeting of the former bus boycotters was held in King's Dexter Av. Baptist Church.

Speaker after speaker, King included, stressed the MIA's next local project—the matter of Negro registration and voting. The MIA has long been conducting classes on registration for prospective Negro voters, but now they conduct tests to see how the "students" are progressing.

As Rev. S. S. Seay told the cheering throng Monday night (a throng not as large but as enthusiastic as any which attended the twice-weekly bus boycott meetings for a full year):

"We're going to test you ourselves before you go down there to the board of registrars. And if you pass our test and don't pass theirs, we'll have good reason to go down there and find out why you don't pass. Knowledge is knowledge and the white folks don't have no corner on it, and we'll find out why you didn't pass just as sure as you are born to die."

Both Seay and the Rev. H. H. Hubbard, another older minister, twitted King that they were making their first appearance in his pulpit since he came to Montgomery in 1954. And both pointed out that Dexter Av. Baptist is an "uppity" Negro church where the shout "Amen" is frowned on.

But James Pierce, the Alabama State College economist and long-time Dexter member, defended his church by saying:

"Dexter Av. may be one of those sophisticated churches, but I'm here to testify that Rev. King has ruined more faces with crying than anybody else I know. Because I almost broke out crying myself yesterday when he preached on his recent trip to the birth of Ghana."

Inferentially, both sides were referring to King's original aversion to the ministry because of his suspicion of the "emotionalism" in religion in Negro churches.

But King no longer fears or rejects that shouting, amen-ing emotionalism. He knows that without it—displayed twice weekly—in different Negro churches here for a full year, the bus boycott movement would never have been a success.

In fact, King's ability to hold all Montgomery's varied Negro factions together for the long 12-month struggle was cemented in the near-worship of the elderly, emotional domestics who form the mass backbone of the Montgomery Improvement Assn.

In Martin Luther King Jr., at 28, they see the son they never had or would like to have had. As one old lady explained to this writer:

"He makes up to me for all my two boys didn't do. You know, my boys is the biggest whisky-drinkers in Montgomery. But he at least brought them half the way to salvation. During the whole bus protest, they never rode the buses—even if they did save the bus fare to buy more whisky."

And no one is more aware than King that the die-hards have by no means given up their fight against equal rights for Negroes in Montgomery, even if the arrest of a half dozen suspected arsonists and bombers has outlawed violence momentarily in large sections of the white community.

Just last week, hundreds of Montgomery Negroes received in the mail copies of a four-page tabloid called "The Truth: a Newspaper Devoted to the Rights of All Races." And it purported to be a Negro newspaper edited by one "Jim White" (as opposed to Jim Crow) with a Post Office Box No. 471 in Wetumpka, Ala.

But even Time magazine apparently has been unable to convince the die-hards of the basic intelligence of Negroes in Montgomery. For the badly edited sheet used every non-profane expression which is repugnant to Negroes while pretending to be a Negro publication.

Practically the whole four pages were devoted to heavy-handed attacks on King. Of his recent trip to Ghana, one story said:

"Members of his congregation have been assessed $25.00 each (they weren't, although some contributed $25.00 for this purpose) to defray his expenses. Some have balked and refused to give anything, others have readily agreed to donate $25.00 to be rid of him for at least a while. There is speculation among many in his congregation that once he is in Africa, a fund will be raised to keep him there."

But the particular gem in The Truth was a front-page centered box which was headed: "King Not at Communist Meeting."

The short box story said simply:

"Despite rumors to the contrary, Rev. Martin Luther King was not at the recent meeting of the Communist Party in Chicago. He has been so busy that he cannot attend all meetings."

And this sheet was mailed straight-faced to Negroes exactly 16 months after the first mass meeting at which they voted unanimously to boycott the buses until segregated seating was abolished.

And where does Martin Luther King Jr. go from here?

Nowhere immediately. There's still much to be done in Montgomery.

New York Post, April 14, 1957

A Rabbi in Montgomery

by Harry L. Golden

RABBI Seymour Atlas replaced the telephone and knew at once that the inevitable decision had been made for him. He had served the congregation Agudath Israel of Montgomery, Alabama for close to ten years. His contract would not expire until September, 1958, but this latest telephone call in a series of many such communications convinced him that he could no longer serve as a rabbi in Montgomery.

Through the open door of the study the Negro janitor was watching the rabbi. He was keenly aware of what had been going on between the rabbi and his board of trustees, because of a special "interest" in the matter; in his spare time he was one of the "directors of transportation" in the Montgomery bus strike against racial segregation. The janitor could now tell from the rabbi's expression that the distressing business had finally reached a climax. He put his broom aside, went into the study and told him: "Rabbi, when you leave, I leave."

It all began on the eve of Brotherhood Week, 1956. The Negro radio station in Montgomery had arranged for a special program: "an interfaith trio" which included a Roman Catholic priest, Rabbi Atlas, and a Protestant, the Negro clergyman Rev. Ralph Abernathy. But that very morning Abernathy, along with twenty-five others, had been arrested on an old "inciting to boycott" statute, because of their leadership in the bus strike. The interfaith program was saved, however, when one of the national news services bailed out Rev. Abernathy and drove him direct from the jail to the broadcasting studio with not a moment to spare to give his talk on "Brotherhood." *Life* magazine wrote up the story with a photo of the three clergymen, reviewing as well the progress of the bus strike.

The board of trustees of the synagogue were chagrined at

this publicity. They were angry at *Life*, at Rev. Abernathy, at the bus strike; but they were particularly angry at their Rabbi Atlas. They ordered him to demand a "retraction" from *Life*. He was to explain that the Brotherhood Week had been purely coincidental; that it had nothing to do with Negroes, Rev. Abernathy, Supreme Court decisions, or with the Montgomery bus strike. The rabbi of course refused to be a party to any such nonsense; and the trustees were in for yet another shock at the very next Sabbath service during which Rabbi Atlas offered up a prayer for the success of the bus strike against racial segregation. The trustees realized now that they had a serious matter on their hands and decided to meet as often as possible in order "to keep the situation under control."

One of the important trustees happened also to be the membership chairman of the Montgomery White Citizens Council, and he came to offer "some sound advice." He recalled to Rabbi Atlas the incident of some years before when "Rabbi Goldstein was given twenty-four hours to get out of town" because of a sermon condemning the conviction of the Scottsboro boys. The trustee further urged the rabbi to join the White Citizens Council—"and you can remain in Montgomery as long as you care to stay here." Rabbi Atlas told the trustee that he had made an evil proposal that violated every tenet of the Jewish faith. The issue was joined. From now on it was to be a "war of attrition" between the rabbi and the trustees of Agudath Israel, who immediately ordered the rabbi to "make no further speeches or statements outside the synagogue" and to give up inviting Negro clergymen to the weekly Hebrew class: "We want you to disassociate yourself from the Negroes completely while you are the rabbi here."

Of the twenty-seven trustees, the rabbi had only one supporter, who of course was completely overwhelmed at every meeting. In the meantime the rabbi was being subjected to the "silent treatment." Except for necessary communication during the conduct of the services or the business of the synagogue, no one spoke to him; they literally turned their backs as he passed them in the synagogue or on the street. No one visited his home; he felt himself completely alone. Four years earlier he had brought a refugee from Poland and installed him as the *shochet*, and now even the refugee severed all personal relations; he, too, thought that the trustees were right.

Less than half of the trustees were Southern-born, to say nothing of the refugee *shochet*; and so the humor of the situation was not lost on the beleaguered Rabbi Seymour Atlas, who was born, raised, and educated in the Faulkner country way down around Greenville, Mississippi. A Southern boy, he had never been in any other part of the country except Mississippi and Louisiana until he went off to Brooklyn, New York—first to the Mesifta Torah Vodaath and then to the Rabbinical Seminary for his ordination as an orthodox rabbi. The rabbi's father had been cantor and *shochet* in three or four Southern cities and was now living in retirement in Shreveport, Louisiana.

At this stage of the controversy Rabbi Atlas urged the trustees to put the issue before a full congregational meeting. For nine and a half years the rabbi had taught their children in his Hebrew School, arranged the bar-mitzvahs and the educational and recreational programs. He had ample reason to feel that he had made many friends among the 225 families of Agudath Israel. But the trustees refused to call such a meeting, explaining that "it would excite the people too much and make matters much worse."

At this point in the story it is well to let Rabbi Atlas make an observation in answer to one of my questions: "Rabbi, you went through all of this; what was it that made these people so frightened?" To this he replied:

"I searched long and thoroughly. I did not see or hear of a single event or act which could have been construed as being a threat to the Jewish community or to any individual among us. For instance, I was Master of the Montgomery Scottish Rite lodge, and in my continued activities in Masonry I did not detect the slightest change in the kindly and respectful attitude toward me from my fellow Masons, all 'white' upper middle class Gentiles; and this at a time when my own trustees refused to speak to me."

I would like to supplement the rabbi's statement with an observation of my own based on years of study of the Jews of the South. I believe the fear which exists in some of the Jewish communities of the deep South is part of an overall (and wholly unwarranted) "sense of insecurity" and is not particularly related to the Negro problem. Rather it is the "constant" fear of Gentile "anger," irrespective of the "object" of that anger. The Jew feels himself helpless when the "anger" is the result of the failure of the cotton crop, for instance, or because of an economic depression; but in this case he feels that he can finally do something about it. He can join the White Citizens Council and pretend that he's angry, too.

And now the drama was drawing to its close. In accordance with his usual procedure the rabbi published the title of his weekly sermon in the daily press. And the forthcoming sermon was to be on "Social Integration." The trustees were beside themselves with rage, but they knew that they could say nothing that would make the rabbi change his mind on any of these matters. The synagogue was filled to overflowing. Fear was clearly evident on the faces of most of the congregation, especially the members of the White Citizens Council. A trustee told the rabbi that members of the Ku Klux Klan were in the audience as the rabbi went into his sermon on "the successful integration of the Arab minority with the Jews in Israel." The audience was taken aback.

By this time the trustees had had enough. Their nerves were worn to a frazzle and the following day came that final telephone call from the chairman: "Rabbi, you are hereby ordered to submit all sermons to the trustees two or three days before printing or making delivery of same." Of course the rabbi knew that he could no longer serve the congregation Agudath Israel of Montgomery. The trustees accepted his resignation and voted unanimously that the next rabbi must sign a pledge not to discuss Negroes or the segregation issue "in any manner, shape or form whatsoever."

Rabbi Atlas went on to the B'nai Sholom Congregation of Bristol, Va.-Tenn. The congregation includes the small Jewish communities of Johnson City, Kingsport, and Elizabeth, in Tennessee; and Gate City, Pennington Gap, Abingdon, Marion, and Pulaski in Virginia; in addition to Bristol, which is both in Virginia and Tennessee. He conducts Hebrew classes for the children and an adult study class in each of these towns, in addition to the other duties of a spiritual leader.

Rabbi Atlas is thirty-five years old, and married to a girl who had come from Lithuania in recent years. They have three children, two daughters, seven and five, and a son, two years old.

Congress Weekly, May 13, 1957

Violence at Central High

by Relman Morin

LITTLE ROCK, Ark., Sept. 23 (AP)—A howling, shrieking crowd of men and women outside Central High School, and disorderly students inside, forced authorities to withdraw eight Negro students from the school Monday, three and one-half hours after they entered it.

At noon, Mayor Woodrow Wilson Mann radioed police officers on the scene, telling them to tell the crowd: "The Negro students have been withdrawn."

Almost immediately, the three Negro boys and five girls left the school under heavy police escort. The officers took them away in police cars.

Crowds clustered at both ends of the school set up a storm of fierce howling and surged toward the lines of police and state troopers. They were beaten back.

The explosive climax came, after the school had been under siege since 8:45 a.m., when the Negroes walked quietly through the doors. Police, armed with riot guns and tear gas, had kept the crowd under control.

Inside, meanwhile, students reported seeing Negroes with blood on their clothes. And some whites who came out—in protest against integration—pictured wild disorder, with policemen chasing white students through the halls, and attacks on Negroes in the building.

The break came shortly before noon.

Virgil Blossom, school superintendent, said he asked Gene Smith, assistant chief of police at the scene, if he thought it would be best to pull out the Negroes. Smith said he did.

Mann's announcement, ordering the police to notify the crowd, came minutes afterward.

Three newspapermen were beaten by the crowd before the sudden turn in the situation. They were Paul Welch, a reporter, and Gray Villette and Francis Miller, photographers.

All three are employed by *Life* magazine. A man smashed Miller in the face while he was carrying an armful of camera equipment. Miller fell, bleeding profusely.

Even after the Negroes left the school, the crowds remained. Teen-agers in two automobiles cruised the outskirts yelling, "Which way did the niggers go?"

During the hours while the Negroes were in school an estimated 30 to 50 white students left. The crowd yelled, cheered, and clapped each time a white student left the school. "Don't stay in there with the niggers," people yelled.

Four Negroes were beaten and some arrests were made before the eight students went into the school.

The initial violence outside the school was a frightening sight. Women burst into tears and a man, hoisted up on a wooden barricade, roared, "Who's going through?"

"We all are," the crowd shouted. But they didn't.

The drama-packed climax of three weeks of integration struggle in Little Rock came just after the buzzer sounded inside the 2,000-pupil high school at 8:45, signaling the start of classes.

Suddenly, on a street leading toward the school the crowd spotted four Negro adults, marching in twos, down the center of the street. A man yelled, "Look, here come the niggers!"

They were not the students. One appeared to be a newspaperman. He had a card in his hat and was bearing a camera.

I jumped into a glass-windowed telephone booth on the corner to dictate the story. As the crowd surged toward the four Negroes they broke and ran.

They were caught on the lawn of a home nearby. Whites jumped the man with the camera from behind and rode him to the ground, kicking and beating him. They smashed the camera.

This, obviously, was a planned diversionary movement to draw the crowd's attention away from the school. While I was dictating, someone yelled, "Look! They're going into the school!"

At that instant, the eight Negroes—the three boys and five girls—were crossing the schoolyard toward a side door at the south end of the school. The girls were in bobby sox and the boys were dressed in shirts open at the neck. All were carrying books.

They were not running, not even walking fast. They simply strolled toward the steps, went up and were inside before all but a few of the two hundred people at that end of the street knew it.

"They're going in," a man roared. "Oh, God, the niggers are in the school."

A woman screamed, "Did they get in? Did you see them go in?"

"They're in now," some other men yelled.

"Oh, my God," the woman screamed. She burst into tears and tore at her hair. Hysteria swept the crowd. Other women began weeping and screaming.

At that moment a tall, gray-haired man in a brown hunting shirt jumped on the barricade. He yelled, waving his arms: "Who's going through?"

"We all are," the people shouted.

They broke over and around the wooden barricades, rushing the policemen. Almost a dozen police were at that corner of the street. They raised their billy clubs.

Some grabbed men and women and hurled them back. Two chased a dark-haired man who slipped through their line, like a football player. They caught him in the schoolyard, whipped his coat down his arms, pinning them, and hustled him out of the yard.

Another man, wearing a construction worker's hat, suddenly raised his hands high in front of a policeman. It was only a dozen yards or so in front of the phone booth.

I couldn't see whether the officer had a gun in the man's stomach, but he stopped running abruptly and went back. Two men were arrested.

Meanwhile, a cavalcade of cars carrying state troopers, in their broad-brimmed campaign hats and Sam Browne belts, wheeled into the street from both ends. They came inside the barricades, and order was restored for a moment. The weeping and screaming went on among the women. A man said, "I'm going in there and get my kid out."

An officer said, "You're not going anywhere."

Suddenly another roar—and cheering and clapping—came

from the crowd. A white student, carrying his books, came down from the steps. He was followed by two girls wearing bobby sox. In the next few minutes, other students came out. Between 15 and 20 left the school within the next half hour.

Each time they appeared, the people clapped and cheered. "Come on out," they yelled. "Don't stay in there with the niggers. Go back and tell all of them to come out."

Inside, it was reported, the eight Negro students were in the office of the principal. A moment later, two policemen suddenly raced into the building through the north door. When they came out, they were holding a girl by both arms, rushing her forcibly toward a police prisoners' wagon.

For an instant it looked as though the crowd would try to break the police lines again and try to rescue her. But the police put her in the car and drove swiftly down the street. Screams, catcalls, and more yelling broke out as the car raced down the street. A man, distraught, came sprinting after it. "That's my kid there," he yelled. "Help me get my kid out."

But the car was gone. Soon afterwards four white students ran down the steps of the school and across the street. Policemen were chasing them.

One of the boys said they had caught a Negro boy outside the principal's office in the school. "We walked him half a length of the building and we were going to get him out of there," they said. They refused to give their names.

Meanwhile, on the streets, at both ends of the school, clusters of troopers took up their stations, reinforcing the police. The crowds heckled them, hurling insults and some obscenity.

"How you going to feel tonight when you face your neighbors?" a man shouted.

The people called the police "nigger lovers" and insulted them. The officers stood, poker-faced, making no response.

Then the crowd, lacking any other object, turned on the newspapermen and photographers. A boy jumped up, caught the telephone wire leading from one of the three booths to the main wire and swung on it, trying to break it. The booth swayed and nearly toppled to the street.

Someone said, "We ought to wipe up the street with these Yankee reporters."

"Let's do it right now," another replied.

But it was only words. Nothing happened. The same woman who had first burst into tears buttonholed a reporter and said, "Why don't you tell the truth about us? Why don't you tell them we are a peaceful people who won't stand to have our kids sitting next to niggers?"

People in the crowd reported gleefully—and shouted it at the other officers—that one policeman had torn off his badge and thrown it on the ground.

"There's one white man on the police force," a burly slick-haired youth in a T-shirt yelled at the policeman in front of him. Sporadic tussles broke out, from time to time, when men tried to pass the police and trooper lines. The police wrestled one man to the street and then, taking him by the hands and arms, hauled him into the squad car and drove off.

A number of plainclothesmen—some reported to be FBI agents—kept circulating up and down in front of the school.

Inside there was no sign that this was different from any other school day. Students who came out at the 10:30 recess said that, in one class of 30 students, only one stayed in the classroom when a Negro entered.

AP wire copy, September 23, 1957

"We Were Kicked, Beaten"

by James L. Hicks

Little Rock, Ark.

THIS REPORTER and three other Negro newsmen were kicked, beaten and chased away from the Little Rock Central High School here Monday at the exact time that nine Negro children slipped into the school under the very nose of the mob. The three who were beaten along with the writer were L. A. Wilson, editor of The Tri-State Journal in Memphis, Tennessee; Moses Newson of the Afro-American newspaper; and Earl Davy, photographer of the Arkansas State Press, a Negro paper in Little Rock. None of us were seriously injured.

Davy, whose camera was taken and smashed by the mob, received six gashes in his right leg where he was kicked by the mob as he lay on the ground. The beating which we received from the hands of the mob was witnessed by two FBI agents who questioned us immediately after. We had outrun the mob to a point about four blocks from the school. Although it was not planned, the four newsmen actually served as the decoy which got the nine Negro children into the school.

It happened this way:

No white persons and few Negroes except the Negro reporters and Mrs. L. C. Bates, NAACP leader, knew that the Negro children were going to attempt to go to school Monday morning. Sunday night's radio had quoted Mrs. Bates as saying that the Negroes would not go to school. This was all according to plan, to keep the mob down as small as possible.

But as the radio was giving out this report, this reporter and the other Negro newsmen were even then making the rounds of the children's homes where they were given instructions to be at Mrs. Bates' home at 8 a.m. Monday prepared to go to school. Monday morning at 7, this reporter went alone to the school where already a mob of about 100 white persons had formed. I then went to Mrs. Bates' home where the nine Negro children had gathered by.

By arrangement the children were to stay at the Bates' home until they received a call from the Deputy Police Chief notifying them that it was safe to come to the school. At about 8:35 the call came. Mrs. Bates, hoping to slip the children into the school, asked the Negro newsmen not to go along for fear that their cameras would tip the mob off as to what was happening.

We then agreed to accept the plan on the condition that we be given a few minutes head start to get to the school before the kids arrived. Accordingly, we hopped into the car of L. A. Wilson and headed for the school. We parked the car two blocks from the school and began walking to the school.

As we walked along 16th Street, approaching the school which is located on Park Street, we began to pass groups of whites heading for the school. They were sullen towards us but none spoke.

At Park Street we came face to face with a mob of about 100 whites standing on the corner. When they saw us, they rushed toward us yelling "Here come the niggers." We stopped and the mob rushed upon us. Wilson was in front with Newson. I was a step behind on the narrow sidewalk with Davy. As the crowd rushed upon us, a man whom I will always remember said: "We are not going to let you niggers pass. This is our school. Go back where you came from."

I stepped up and said: "We are not trying to go to school, we are reporters." The mob leader said: "We don't care, you're niggers and we are not going to let you go any further." Someone then yelled "kill 'em" and the mob rushed upon us.

A man threw a punch at Wilson, another kicked Newson and a one-armed man slugged me beside my right ear. We turned to run and found ourselves trapped by the crowds whom we had passed as we walked up the street to the school. In the mob we became separated. Davy at one point was running down the sidewalk beside me. As we met a group of five men the mob yelled "stop them," "kill them" and one of them stuck out his foot and tripped Davy as he ran.

As he went down he began to crawl up the side of the slope of a vacant lot. I started over toward the lot and saw about five men drag him down from the slope into the sidewalk again, then ran in the middle of the street. By this time, I saw Newson run into the street also.

We made it to the other side of the street and as we reached the next corner, with the mob on our heels, a motorcycle cop came out of a side street. We turned to get near the cop who we thought would help us, but he simply got off his motorcycle and yelled: "Leave that boy alone." By that time a man rushed up to Newson who was standing a few feet away from the cop's motorcycle and kicked him.

Meanwhile, my one-arm friend came rushing at me again with about 15 others. Newson and I then cut across a lawn and turned the corner into a side street. We looked back and no one was coming after us then, but the one-armed man who had outdistanced the others. When we saw he was alone we stopped. Then he stopped.

He ran back to the corner and yelled: "Here are two of them down here. Come on down and help me get them." But nobody from the mob came around the corner to join him. He then shook his fist at us and went back to join the mob. We stood there on the sidewalk three blocks away from the school and presently Wilson and Davy joined us.

Wilson's suit was covered with dirt and mud where he had been knocked down and kicked. Davy's camera had been wrenched from his hands and his legs were bleeding and battered with gashes.

As we stood there in the white neighborhood trying to decide what to do, two policemen in a radio car came up. We told them what had happened and asked them if they would escort us back up to the mob. They told us that while we had been beaten by the mob, the Negro children had slipped into the school. We asked them if they could take us back up there so we could get Davy's camera. They told us they would not give us any escort and suggested that we stay away from the school.

As we stood there, two FBI agents came up and identified themselves. They told us out of the sides of their mouths to walk four blocks down the street and wait for them there. It was obvious that they didn't wish the mob to see them talk-ing to us. We went to the appointed place and they took our names and told us they had seen what happened.

I certainly can identify the one-armed who slugged me. As this is being written, the children are now in the school, so the white children are walking out and the mob is howling around the school demanding that police let them get the Negroes.

After we were safely out of the mob area, reports came over the radio that we had been sent to the school as "decoys" to the mob so that they would not notice the Negro children when they slipped in.

This is actually what happened but it certainly was not in our plan.

New York Amsterdam News, September 28, 1957

President Sends Troops to Little Rock, Federalizes Arkansas National Guard; Tells Nation He Acted To Avoid Anarchy

by Anthony Lewis

WASHINGTON, Sept. 24—President Eisenhower sent Federal troops to Little Rock, Ark., today to open the way for the admission of nine Negro pupils to Central High School.

Earlier, the President federalized the Arkansas National Guard and authorized calling the Guard and regular Federal forces to remove obstructions to justice in Little Rock school integration.

His history-making action was based on a formal finding that his "cease and desist" proclamation, issued last night, had not been obeyed. Mobs of pro-segregationists still gathered in the vicinity of Central High School this morning.

Tonight, from the White House, President Eisenhower told the nation in a speech for radio and television that he had acted to prevent "mob rule" and "anarchy."

The President's decision to send troops to Little Rock was reached at his vacation headquarters in Newport, R.I. It was one of historic importance politically, socially, constitutionally. For the first time since the Reconstruction days that followed the Civil War, the Federal Government was using its ultimate power to compel equal treatment of the Negro in the South.

He said violent defiance of Federal Court orders in Little Rock had done grave harm to "the prestige and influence, and indeed to the safety, of our nation and the world." He called on the people of Arkansas and the South to "preserve and respect the law even when they disagree with it."

Action quickly followed the President's orders. During the day and night 1,000 members of the 101st Airborne Division were flown to Little Rock. Charles E. Wilson, Secretary of the

Defense, ordered into Federal service all 10,000 members of the Arkansas National Guard.

Today's events were the climax of three weeks of skirmishing between the Federal Government and Gov. Orval E. Faubus of Arkansas. It was three weeks ago this morning that the Governor first ordered National Guard troops to Central High School to preserve order. The nine Negro students were prevented from entering the school.

The Guardsmen were gone yesterday, withdrawn by Governor Faubus as the result of a Federal Court order. But a shrieking mob compelled the nine children to withdraw from the school.

President Eisenhower yesterday cleared the way for full use of his powers with a proclamation commanding the mob in Little Rock to "disperse."

At 12:22 P.M. today in Newport the President signed a second proclamation. It said first that yesterday's command had "not been obeyed and willful obstruction of said court orders exists and threatens to continue."

The proclamation then directed Charles E. Wilson, Secretary of Defense, to take all necessary steps to enforce the court orders for admission of the Negro children, including the call of any or all Arkansas Guardsmen under Federal command and the use of the armed forces of the United States.

Later in the afternoon the President flew from Newport to Washington, arriving at the National Airport at 4:50 o'clock.

He began his broadcast speech with this explanation of the flight:

"I could have spoken from Rhode Island, but I felt that in speaking from the house of Lincoln, of Jackson and of Wilson, my words would more clearly convey both the sadness I feel in the action I was compelled to take and the firmness with which I intend to pursue this course.***"

It was a firm address, with some language unusually strong for President Eisenhower.

"Under the leadership of demagogic extremists," the President said, "disorderly mobs have deliberately prevented the carrying out of proper orders from a Federal court. Local authorities have not eliminated that violent opposition."

The President traced the course of the integration dispute in Little Rock. He noted especially that the Federal Court there had rejected what he called an "abrupt change" in segregated schooling and had adopted a "gradual" plan.

"Proper and sensible observance of the law," the President said, "then demanded the respectful obedience which the nation has a right to expect from all the people. This, unfortunately, has not been the case at Little Rock.

"Certain misguided persons, many of them imported into Little Rock by agitators, have insisted upon defying the law and have sought to bring it into disrepute. The orders of the court have thus been frustrated."

The reference to "imported" members of the mob was seen as a sign that the Federal Bureau of Investigation had information, obtained through agents in Little Rock, on the organization of yesterday's violence.

The President tried to make it plain that he had not sought the use of Federal power in Little Rock, nor welcomed it. Rather he suggested that as Chief Executive he had no choice.

"The President's responsibility is inescapable," he said at one point. At another he said that when the decrees of a Federal court were obstructed, "the law and the national interest demanded that the President take action."

"The very basis of our individual rights and freedoms," he said, "is the certainty that the President and the Executive Branch of Government will support and insure the carrying out of the decisions of the Federal Courts, even, when necessary, with all the means at the President's command.

"Unless the President did so, anarchy would result.

"There would be no security for any except that which each one of us could provide for himself.

"The interest of the nation in the proper fulfillment of the law's requirements cannot yield to opposition and demonstrations by some few persons.

"Mob rule cannot be allowed to override the decisions of the courts."

The President appeared fit and vigorous when he stepped into his White House office tonight to face a battery of news and television cameras.

His face showed the ruddiness of the outdoors exercise he has been enjoying on the golf links.

The President, who wore a gray single-breasted suit with blue shirt and tie, spoke calmly and his voice, after setting a steady deliberate pace, rose only occasionally as he sought emphasis for certain words and phrases.

It rose on the word "firmness" when he spoke of his course in this grave situation, and "mob" when he referred to the perpetrators of the Little Rock violence, and "agitators" he said were brought in from the outside.

On the wall on either side of him as he spoke hung portraits of the four leaders whom the President had stated he regards as the greatest American heroes—Benjamin Franklin, George Washington, Abraham Lincoln and Robert E. Lee.

But in his thirteen-minute address tonight, General Eisenhower mentioned only Lincoln.

The New York Times, September 25, 1957

from

We Went South

"A Man Has To Take a Stand"

by James N. Rhea

MEET the boss man.

I call him that because I don't want to use his name. I don't want to get him in trouble with the police down in New Orleans.

Somehow, though, I wouldn't worry too much if the police should learn about him. The boss knows how to handle himself all right.

You'll need a little background to understand the boss man.

Louisiana has laws forbidding white people and Negroes from meeting or mingling in any social milieu.

The races are not supposed to eat in the same restaurants. They are not supposed to ride in the same taxis. When Ben Bagdikian and I were in New Orleans doing research for this assignment, for a while we had visions of going from the same place to the same place in separate cabs.

But Negro cab drivers would have none of this. They took us together wherever we wanted to go, although now and then one would show some reluctance. In general, their attitude reflected a philosophy which one driver expressed this way:

"I don't make them segregation laws and I don't like them segregation laws and I sneak and break one ever' once in awhile just to keep my soul alive."

I have forgotten how much I tipped that man.

Well, primarily because Bagdikian turned out to have a surprising taste for breaking the law, we got to wondering how far Negroes would go to accept us in areas forbidden to white people by law.

386

The philosophical cab driver, whom we had adopted temporarily, said that he thought some Negroes customarily ignored those laws. (He did himself.) He had seen white people in some Negro restaurants around town. He knew a little jazz spot that we could visit and see what happened.

("Ain't much good jazz in New Orleans any more, now Pops. Seems like all the good ones got to do like Old Satch and cut out for the North.")

He took us to the little club. We got out of the cab and walked single file toward the door. The brown doorman waved the cab driver through, then he waved me through, then he waved Ben away from the door.

"Got to challenge this man," he said.

"Why?" I asked.

"He's white, ain't he?"

"He says he is."

"Got to see the boss man about him," the doorman said, shaking his head sadly. "Ain't me, it's the law."

"Take us to your leader," Bagdikian said.

The doorman led us down a narrow corridor to a closed door, then hurried away. You'd have thought he was afraid of the boss man. We knocked on the door. A heavy voice drawled:

"Walk in, whoever you are."

We opened the door and stepped inside the small office. On a plushly upholstered lounge chair, with his bare feet resting on a footstool, sat the boss man, watching television in air-conditioned comfort. He was a big man, as trim as Ezzard Charles, whom he resembled slightly. Of course he had not expected to see a white man step into his office then, but he didn't bat an eye.

His behavior was that of a man who had faced many a demanding situation and faced it well. He did not rise from his chair. He raised his eyebrows a little, and said:

"Well, fellows?"

We told him we were reporters working together, and that we were trying to learn something about the pattern of segregation in New Orleans because we knew Negroes there had petitioned the court for integration in schools.

The boss man laughed, and invited us to sit down. Then he told us that ever since the integration decision, Louisiana has been cracking down harder and harder on Negroes and whites who try to establish lines of communication.

"For instance, you guys being in my place—that white man there, could get me fined a hundred dollars and much worse it could get my license lifted. What would I do out of the club business?"

We chatted for about an hour. He gave us much helpful information about the city. Then abruptly he got up and said:

"Come on, fellows, let's go in and have a drink and hear some music."

We argued that we didn't want him to risk anything to be nice to us. He refused to listen. It was on to the bands for us, he insisted. He held the door open for us. Ben passed through first. As I started out, the boss man whispered:

"A white man who thinks like him is worth a hundred dollars to me these days."

I stepped back inside for a moment.

"How about the license?" I asked.

He frowned as if in pain, and then laughed.

"Sometimes a man has to take a stand on a awfully small issue," he said. "The Constitution is the law. Segregation laws ain't really law. Maybe they'll nab me. Well, 'bout time I went to the wire for the cause!"

We went in and heard the music and the boss man picked up the check. He got away with the check. He also got away with the fact of having served us.

Whoever wants to understand what is happening in the South these days ought to understand why the boss man was willing to lay his business on the line for "a awfully small issue." From talking with him, you can see that the boss man has been caught up in the movement, the same one in which Negro mothers are sending their small children into hostile white schools.

He is what some writers like to call the New Southern Negro. He isn't new. There are just more like him today. All around the South, Ben and I saw him, and wherever he could he tried to help us out.

As a rule, I am no more uncomfortable in the South than I am in the North; for in the South I move mostly in a world of Negroes, entering the world of the whites only when necessary.

But Ben and I, in order to work together, had to keep searching for the points at which those worlds overlapped, and sometimes we had to force the overlapping. In general a pattern for our work was established in Nashville, the first city we visited.

We had known that we could not share the same hotels, and that I would not be permitted to visit Ben at his hotel to work. For this reason, Ben went by my hotel with me on our first night in Nashville to see how things would be there.

"Now," I began to the Negro clerk, "I am a newspaper reporter and I—."

The clerk was a remarkable man.

"Sir," he said, "I am not at all interested in what profession you may be practicing, I am interested in accommodating you the best I can."

I told him to hold his horses, that I had been about to ask him if it would be all right for my white co-worker to visit me at the hotel.

Righteous indignation distorted that man's face.

"Sir," he said, "are you suggesting that we here are as bigoted and arrogant as those people who are trying to keep our kids out of their schools? If you have a friend who happens to be white, red, green or an Eskimo, when he visits you is your business and his. All I want is the rent money."

And that was all there was to that. Ben and I met at dinner there regularly to talk over our work. The Negroes around accepted Ben almost as easily as they accepted me because they could see that he accepted them.

White taxi drivers and other white persons seemed to be perplexed by us at times—but, as Bagdikian says, that could have been for any number of very good reasons that had nothing at all to do with race.

In Nashville and Little Rock the airports were certainly common grounds for us. Not even the toilet, that most segregated of all Southern facilities, was separate.

Only in New Orleans did a white person in an official capacity seem to go out of the way to make things tough for me.

I went into the Dryades Market Branch of the National

Bank of Commerce on Dryades Street to cash some travelers checks. A white woman watched closely while I countersigned 20 checks for a total of $200 and then said:

"Those signatures do not match."

"Why didn't you stop me after the first one or two, then?" I asked.

"I wanted to study them further."

"Every one is the same."

"Some places you close the 'e' and others you don't. The same is true of the loops in your capital r's."

This was patent nonsense. I have been cashing travelers checks for years. She called the manager over, and he asked if I had any document with my signature on it. I told him I did, but that it was the same as that on the checks, and walked out.

I went straight to the American Express Company office on Canal Street and explained my plight. They were reluctant to cash the checks there, too. But they seemed impressed by the fact that I called someone at the Monteleone Hotel (white) to discuss my situation. Just before Ben came from that hotel to join in my protest, they relented and cashed my checks.

At first I was very angry.

Then I got to thinking about those children up in Little Rock, and suddenly I had no problems at all.

"You Can't Legislate Human Relations"

by Ben H. Bagdikian

I AM a criminal in the state of Louisiana.

The crimes I hereby confess to are punishable by 10 years in jail and fines of $10,000.

The crimes are as follows:

On Sept. 22 and 23 in New Orleans, on at least 10 separate occasions I ate meals with a friend and fellow worker. I talked with him in his hotel room, I listened to some music with him and I rode with him in a taxicab.

My friend and fellow criminal is James Rhea, also a reporter for these newspapers. We were committing crimes when we ate together, talked together and rode cabs together because he is Negro and I am white, and it is against the law for Negroes and whites to do these things together in the State of Louisiana.

These are no "old traditional" laws. They were passed July 16, 1956.

They are representative of wild racist laws passed by Deep South legislatures under pressure from the White Citizens Councils. They are part of a last-ditch gesture to stave off congressional civil rights laws and federal court decisions. The constitutionality of such state laws is dubious indeed, but in the meantime they control human relations more rigidly than in any place else in the world, except possibly in the Belgian Congo and Union of South Africa.

On a strictly constitutional basis these laws would seem to deny the right of peaceable assembly and freedom of expression and association, since we were both otherwise law-abiding, we were associating for legitimate purposes and the premises we met on were public places, whose proprietors had no objections to our meeting.

Something akin to thought control has been instituted. Up until recently public school teachers and faculty members of state colleges could be removed for "immorality" and "wilful neglect" and "incompetency." On July 8, 1956, the governor of Louisiana signed a new state law, Act No. 252, providing loss of job for another reason:—"advocating or in any manner performing any act toward bringing about the integration of the races within the public school system or any public institution of higher learning of the state of Louisiana."

Presumably this means that any teacher or state college professor who advocates compliance with the Constitution of the United States and its interpretations by the Supreme Court is risking dismissal.

The effect on the community is something immediate and noticeable. Educators fear to talk and even to teach freely. Many jazz bands no longer play in New Orleans because they have both Negro and white players.

These new laws are so untypical of even Louisiana that the state's tourist pamphlets have been made obsolete and almost illegal. For example, an official information booth handed this reporter a pamphlet entitled, "Louisiana," published by the Louisiana Department of Commerce and Industry. It bears illustrations of Negro and white musicians and says:

". . . only in New Orleans—birthplace of jazz—does one capture the true rhythm of this form of musical expression . . . many of the veteran jazzmen are still blowing hot licks in jazz orchestras in New Orleans' Vieux Carre and else-where. . . ."

The great jazz bands of today have Negro and white musicians playing together—Louis Armstrong, Duke Ellington, Benny Goodman, George Shearing. But not in The Home of Jazz.

Some of the city's great sports events are ended, like the Tulane-Army game, because the Army team is desegregated.

Community choral groups which used both Negro and white choirs have stopped giving concerts.

Where they try to continue they are forced into absurd sub-terfuges, as in the case of the Invisible Piano.

Roy Hamilton is a popular Negro singer. Enthusiasts of this balladeer also know his piano accompanist, Graham Forbes. On Aug. 4, Mr. Hamilton gave two performances at the big Municipal Auditorium in New Orleans. Posters and advertise-ments billed Roy Hamilton as singing, with Graham Forbes, accompanist. It was a successful stand. Thousands of listeners heard the Hamilton-Forbes combination. But they didn't see Mr. Forbes or see his piano. He was playing the piano behind a curtain which had been arranged to keep him from view of the audience. The piano accompaniment came disembodied from behind the drapes. Because Mr. Forbes is white.

The law which kept Mr. Forbes behind the curtain and which presumably made Jim Rhea and me outlaws is a Louisiana constitutional amendment, Act 579 of the Regular Session of the 1956 Louisiana legislature, reading:

"An Act to prohibit all interracial dancing, social functions, entertainments, athletic training, games, sports, or contests and other such activities; to provide for separate seating and other facilities for white and negroes. (The lawbooks in the state spell Negro with a small 'n.')

"Section 1. That all persons, firms and corporations are prohibited from sponsoring, arranging, participating in or permitting on premises under their control . . . such activities involving personal and social contact in which the participants are members of the white and negro races. . . .

"Section 3. That white persons are prohibited from sitting in or using any part of seating arrangements and sitting in or using any part of eating arrangements and sanitary or other facilities set apart for members of the negro race. That negro persons are prohibited from sitting in or using any part of seating arrangements and sanitary or other facilities set apart for white persons.

"Section 4. Any persons, firm or corporation violating the provisions of this Act shall be guilty of a misdemeanor and upon conviction shall be fined not less than $100 or more than $1,000 and imprisoned for not less than 60 days or more than one year."

It was approved and signed by Gov. Earl Long July 16, 1956, and went into effect Oct. 15, 1956.

An old New Orleanian, a Negro, was asked if there had been race trouble before passage of the law. He said:

"Race trouble? Why down in the French Quarter apartments, Negro and white families have been living side by side for years, for couple of centuries I guess. And this used to be a pretty good town. Now it gets worse every month. I think if they would just let colored go where they want, and let whites go where they want, it would work itself out. But this? It's not like America."

Another worried Louisianian, a white, said:

"You know, we've always had Jim Crow laws and laws against intermarriage, and I think that because of that it was easier for the White Citizens Council to get these new laws across. Why, it's not so different from Nazi laws when you think about it."

Hitler's racist Nuremberg Laws, denounced by the entire civilized world in 1935, said it was "for the protection . . . and purity of the German blood" and held that "marriage between Jews and subjects of Germany or kindred blood are forbidden . . . extramarital relations between Jews and subjects of Germany or kindred blood are forbidden" and provided penalty of "penal servitude."

Article 740-79 of the Louisiana Criminal Code reads:

"Miscegenation is the marriage or habitual cohabitation with knowledge of their difference in race between a person of the Caucasian or white race and a person of the colored or negro race. Whoever commits the crime of miscegenation shall be imprisoned with or without hard labor for not more than five years."

Such laws forbidding marriage between white and non-white citizens have been on the law books for a long time. Louisiana is not the only state with them. Twenty-three states, including all the Southern ones, have some kind of racial marriage law. Section 360 of Alabama's laws, Title 14, reads:

"This section manifests a public policy to prevent race amalgamation and to safeguard the racial integrity of the white and negro peoples. . . ."

But while Hitler's 1935 Nuremberg marriage laws defined "a Jew" as "anyone who is descended from at least three grandparents who were racially Jews . . ." the racial laws of some Southern states make the Nuremberg edict sound like wild liberalism. In Alabama, a "negro" is defined as "a person of mixed blood descended on the part of the father or mother from negro ancestry without reference to or limit of time or number of generations removed."

A note to this Alabama codification adds:

"Prior to this amendment only persons descended from negroes through the third generation were classed as negroes, but now one drop of negro blood seems to be sufficient to create the offense of miscegenation. . . . Proof that defendant's grandfather had kinky hair . . . and questions involving nose and other features of grandfather were properly admitted."

It adds that ". . . proof of a man's race may be made by his admission either verbally or by conduct in associating with negroes, attending negro churches, sending children to negro schools and otherwise voluntarily living on terms of social equality with them."

Thus, legislatures in the Deep South have extended their old racial marriage laws to sports, music, school, eating, talking, and almost every area of normal social behaviour. Some of these same legislators are the ones who have attacked the Supreme Court school integration decision and Civil Rights laws with the Southern battle cry:

"You can't legislate human relations."

The Providence Journal and Evening Bulletin,
October 20 & 22, 1957

The 19-Day Ordeal of Minnie Jean Brown

by Ted Poston

THIS is the ordeal that Minnie Jean Brown, 16, was forced to endure for the 19 school days since her reinstatement in Little Rock's integrated Central H.S. last Jan. 13.

By orders of Principal Jess W. Matthews, she was not to "retaliate, verbally or physically, to any harassment" which might be heaped upon her by any white student in the school.

So for 19 days, they spat on her, called her "Nigger" and "Nigger bitch," twice threw hot soup down her neck in the school cafeteria and kicked her to the campus ground in the presence of her mother.

And Thursday, one white girl, Frankie Gregg, 17, who had been following her from class to class all week yelling "Nigger" and "Nigger bitch, I hate your guts," finally pushed Minnie Jean beyond endurance.

"I haven't bothered you. So you let me alone, white trash," Minnie Jean retorted.

The white girl then swung her pocketbook, striking Minnie Jean's head.

So Matthews telephoned Mrs. W. B. Brown early Friday morning to tell her that her daughter had again been suspended.

"Why was she suspended?" the mother asked. "The white girl called Minnie Jean names, struck her over the head—"

"She was suspended for talking back to a white girl," said the Principal. "I've sent you a letter to that effect."

"But the girl struck Minnie Jean, called her unprintable names—" Mrs. Brown protested. And Matthews said:

"Minnie Jean had no right to retaliate. She broke her probation by talking back."

As Mrs. Brown was attempting to get to see Superintendent of Schools Virgil Blossom, Matthews' letter arrived.

The note, marked "Suspension Notice," said succinctly:

"It has become my duty to inform you that Minnie Jean Brown has been suspended from Central HS for the following reasons:

"Reinstated on probation Jan. 13, 1958, with the agreement that she would not retaliate verbally or physically, to any harassment but would leave the matter to the school authorities to handle:

"After provocation of girl student, called the girl 'white trash,' after which the girl threw her purse at Minnie Jean."

(Signed) Jess W. Matthews, principal."

But Minnie Jean was still recalling what happened right after the girl struck her.

"They took us both into the office of Mrs. Elizabeth Huckleby, vice principal for girls, and she said we ought to apologize to each other. Frankie wouldn't do it, so Mrs. Huckleby told her:

"'Frankie, you think this over. Now, we are not going to suspend or expel you for this. But you just think it over.'"

Blossom confirmed she had not been suspended and said: "Frankie has a good citizenship record."

Suspensions automatically run for three days, but Blossom said no date had been set for a conference with Minnie Jean and her parents, as required before a suspension is lifted.

Blossom announced that a white boy, Lester Judkins Jr., who had dumped soup on Minnie Jean Thursday after the purse-throwing incident, also was suspended.

Blossom said that normal studies had been maintained for 98 per cent of the students during the five months of integration.

He said the incidents that have occurred were "certainly part of a program of harassment" by a small group of persons opposed to integration.

But, without elaborating, he said both sides were to blame.

New York Post, February 9, 1958

The Book

by Murray Kempton

THERE is a picture of Ernest Green in its proper order as a member of the class of 1958 in *Tix*, the yearbook of Central High School, and the notation that jazz is his hobby and that he was a transfer from Horace Mann, the Negro school.

There is in addition a panel of pictures of soldiers, but no other suggestion of the events for which this year at Central High is unlikely to be forgotten. *Tix* is otherwise what every high school yearbook, however increased by substance and imagination, ends up being, the portraits of the homecoming queen and the football players and the reserve cheerleaders and the members of the societies in this particularly complex civilization.

But Ernest Green's yearbook is different from all others, because in it are written the good-bys of fourteen of his 601 fellow graduates to this boy, a Negro, younger than the average among them, whose name has engraved their class in history.

"You know how it is in high school," said Ernest Green yesterday. "Kids ask you to write in their books and then they ask to write something back in yours."

Some of them began, unconscious of any need to celebrate this moment with rhetoric: "Man, this English is rough" . . . or "Enjoyed having you in solid" . . . or "This government course is for the birds" and like expressions of solidarity against the oppressor. But they all ended up expressing some of the same soul's cry:

"I have found you a real nice fellow."

"I want to take the opportunity to tell you that I think you have displayed remarkable courage in your struggle to prove your rights as an American."

"I have admired your courage this year, and I'm glad you made it through all right."

"I have enjoyed having home room with you this year.

398

Your friendship has meant a lot to me. I want to wish you all the luck possible in the future, for you deserve it. May God bless you richly."

"May you always have the best during the future. Things have turned out for the best no matter how one feels personally. You've stood the test and passed it. May you always have this much courage."

"I know it has been a hard year for you."

"I have really admired you for your courage through all the year. I hope you can always remain so."

"I know you're a real nice guy and best wishes."

"I know it has been real tough for you over here. But now that it is all over, I know that you and I are happy."

"It has been a sincere pleasure to have been your friend. May God always guide you and keep you safe."

"I really admire you, Ernest. I doubt if I could have done half so well had the circumstances been reversed. May you achieve all your goals, and they be the best."

The last was written across the portrait of a girl especially marked by her classmates for honor for her qualities. And most of them had been written by those seniors most admired by the rest of the class, by Student Council members and by belles, which, of course, figures, because pretty girls feel no need to assert their place in a master race. They were, these fourteen souvenirs of Ernest Green's, from the leaders of the school.

No one who has ever tried to do his best and failed could read them without taking note of their uniform sense of envy of Ernest Green for having done what they doubted they could have done. This sense seems to have occurred to Ernest Green, who, having done what he did, of course does not find it especially brave.

"I don't know what it would do, if you ran their names," he said. They are that hope out of all our troubles, the historic best of the white South, the silent South.

Ernest Green closed the book and talked about how it felt to be graduated.

"You know for me," he said, "there'll never be a graduation like this again. I've been looking forward to it for twelve years."

It may seem odd, but he was not talking about being the first Negro to be graduated with white children from a high school in Arkansas. He was talking only about what it was like just to be graduated from high school.

He sat among his records, Errol Garner, Art Blakey, the Modern Jazz Quartet; there is a marvelous process of cultural diffusion among those who know, wherever they are.

"I got a record," he said, "one of my friends borrowed. I like it more than anything the Modern Jazz Quartet has ever done. It's that Variation Number 1 on 'God Rest Ye Merry, Gentlemen.' That John Lewis . . ."

It seemed a little beside the point, looking at the jacket of the MJQ record, those four familiars of Padua bearded like pards, three of them Southerners, to ask of this Southerner how it had felt to walk across the grass carrying his diploma. For this, at the end, is simply a kid who owes money at the record store and hasn't had much time this year for the tenor saxophone.

"I don't know," he said, about the moment he walked under the lights and waited for the boos that never came. "It was kind of like a bomb that was a dud."

There remains the book with its notes of homage; there remain the crowd in the stands and the wonder that lay behind its silence, a silence of respect and envy. That silence seemed to say that this is a Southerner, this is our child and this our product; we made him and we salute him. He is better than we are; he has done something we would not have the guts to do, and we salute him with our silence. The South made him, and he is its better, most of all because he does not boast or brag or in any way indicate he knows it.

from *America Comes of Middle Age:*
Columns 1950–1962 (1963)

How To Solve the Segregation Problem

by Harry L. Golden

How to Solve the Segregation Problem

THOSE who love North Carolina will jump at the chance to share in the great responsibility now confronting our Governor and the State Legislature. The Special Session of the Legislature, scheduled to open in a few days, will be asked to pass a series of amendments to the State Constitution. These proposals submitted by the Governor and his Advisory Education Committee, include the following—(A) The elimination of the compulsory attendance law, "to prevent any child from being forced to attend a school with a child of another race." (B) The establishment of "Education Expense Grants" for education in a private school, "in the case of a child assigned to a public school attended by a child of another race." (C) A "uniform system of local option" whereby a majority of the folks in a school district may suspend or close a school if the situation becomes "intolerable."

But suppose a Negro child applies for this "Education Expense Grant" and says he wants to go to the private school too? There are fourteen Supreme Court decisions involving the use of public funds; there are only two "decisions" involving the elimination of racial discrimination in the public schools.

The Governor has said that critics of these proposals have not offered any constructive advice or alternatives. Permit me therefore to offer an idea for the consideration of the members of the Special Session. A careful study of my plan, I believe, will show that it will save millions of dollars in tax funds and eliminate forever the danger to our public education system. Before I outline my plan, I would like to give you a little background.

One of the factors involved in our tremendous industrial growth and economic prosperity has been due to the fact that the South, voluntarily, has all but eliminated VERTICAL

SEGREGATION. The tremendous buying power of the twelve million Negroes in the South has been based wholly on the *absence of racial segregation*. The white and Negro stand at the same grocery and super-market counters; deposit money at the same bank-teller's window; pay phone and light bills to the same clerk; walk through the same dime and department stores, and stand at the same drug-store counters. It is only when the Negro *"sets"* that the fur begins to fly. Now since we are not even thinking about restoring VERTICAL SEGRE-GATION, I think my plan would not only comply with the Supreme Court decisions, but would maintain *"sitting down"* segregation. Now here is the GOLDEN VERTICAL NE-GRO PLAN. Instead of all those complicated proposals, all the Special Session need to do is pass one small amendment which would provide ONLY desks in all the public schools of our State; NO SEATS. The desks should be those standing-up jobs, like the old-fashioned bookkeeping desk. Since no one in the South pays the slightest attention to a VERTICAL NE-GRO, this will completely solve our problem. And it is not such a terrible inconvenience for young people to stand up during their class-room studies. In fact this may be a blessing in disguise. They are not learning to read sitting down, any-way; maybe "standing up" will help. This will save more MIL-LIONS of dollars in the cost of our "Remedial English" course when the kids enter college. In whatever direction you look with the GOLDEN VERTICAL NEGRO PLAN, you save MILLIONS of dollars, to say nothing of eliminating for-ever any danger to our public education system upon which rests the destiny, hopes, and happiness of this society.

How To Solve the Segregation Problem:
The White Baby Plan

The VERTICAL NEGRO PLAN is actually being imple-mented to some extent in Atlanta, Georgia. The Negroes buy their bus and railroad tickets and proceed immediately to the platform where they are free to walk up and down unsegre-gated. The waiting rooms with all the concessions and bever-age coin boxes, etc., are empty.

Now this new WHITE BABY PLAN offers another possi-ble solution.

Here is an actual case history of the "White Baby Plan to End Racial Segregation." Some months ago there was a revival of the Lawrence Olivier movie, "Hamlet," and several Negro school teachers were anxious to see it. One Saturday afternoon they asked some "white" friends to loan them two of their little children, a 3-year-old girl, and a 6-year-old boy, and holding these white children by the hands, they obtained tickets from the movie-house cashier without a moment's hesitation. They were in like Flynn.

This would also solve the baby-sitting problem for thousands and thousands of "white" working mothers. There can be a mutual exchange of references, then the people can sort of pool their children at a central point in each neighborhood, and every time a Negro wants to go to the movies all she need do is pick up a white child—and go.

Eventually the Negro community can set up a factory and manufacture white babies made of plastic, and when they want to go to the opera or to a concert, all they need do is carry that plastic doll in their arms. The dolls of course should all have blond curls and blue eyes, which would go even further; it would give the Negro woman and her husband priority over the "whites" for the very best seats in the house.

The Golden Vertical Negro Plan in Operation

Four "Dime" stores, in as many great Southern cities have put the Golden Vertical Negro Plan into operation, as an effective means of ending racial segregation. This is being accomplished without the slightest trouble or even the hint of controversy. In each of these stores they had never served Negroes at their snack bars; but when they read of the Golden Vertical Negro Plan, they removed their stools, and now the "whites" and the Negroes stand up at the bars, eating and drinking like mad and everybody's happy about the whole thing.

And one follows the other. Take for instance High Point, North Carolina. There, Woolworth's does not serve Negroes at the snack counter, whereas Kress' does. The reason of course is that Kress' took out the stools. Some folks have sent a petition to Woolworth's urging them to take out the stools so that folks can come and go as free citizens in a happy city.

The interesting thing about the Golden Vertical Negro Plan is that it works just as well in Atlanta as it does in High Point.

The stools of course will come back—gradually. Maybe at first the Negroes can just lean against the seat in a sort of half-standing position; and by such easy stages finally get to a forty-five-degree angle without stirring up anything.

The Golden Carry-the-Books Plan

This may help toward the final solution of the "integration" problem of the South, implementing the several Supreme Court decisions to end racial segregation in the public schools.

There is no vertical segregation. But neither is there "45-degree-angle" segregation if the "sitting" or "leaning" Negro is a servant, a domestic, or a chore-boy of some kind.

Therefore the Negro parents of the South should make this proposition to their local school boards: that they will allow their children to carry the books for their "white" class mates. A system can easily be worked out whereby the Negro boy, (going to an integrated school), can meet a "white" classmate at a convenient corner, a block or so away from the school, and carry the "white" boy's books into the school building. And if there are sixteen Negro students in a school of four hundred "whites", an alternating system can be worked out so that by the end of the semester, each "white" boy will have had his books carried into the school building by a Negro student, at least once.

The Negro girls would not have to participate in this "Golden Carry-the-Books-Plan". The girls should wear a sort of miniature apron over their street dresses, and this would settle everything once and for all. Everybody would be satisfied. Eventually, I suspect, the "white" girls may even adopt those cute little aprons themselves, but they will have served their purpose.

I know I am calling on the Negroes to make a considerable sacrifice, but it is worth it because this would settle the matter even for the most outspoken "white supremacists". If it became known throughout the South that the Negro boys were toting books for the "whites", and that Negro girls were wearing aprons to school, all the school kids could go on with their work without any further disturbance from segregation-ist mobs, National Guardsmen, or Federal troops.

Golden Out-of-Order Plan in Operation

One of the great retail chain stores has put the Golden "Out-of-Order Plan" into operation and with considerable success. They placed an "Out-of-Order" sign on the "white" drinking fountain in most of their stores in the "Upper" south. Within six weeks everybody was drinking the "colored" water without any bad effects, physical or emotional; and all the signs came off, "Out-of-Order," "white" and "colored." There is a problem however. In most of these stores they made this experiment in the "Basement," and naturally they could not put an "Out-of-Order" sign simultaneously on the other floors. The whole idea would have been given away and made matters worse. I understand they intend to stagger the "Out-of-Order" signs from now on. They'll put them up on the second and fourth floors and then double back to the main and third floors. This thing has to be done—gradually.

You throw a tiny pebble into a stream and you never really know the extent of the ripples.

In a seminar on education in Tennessee I suggested to the Negro parents to make sure that their children study French immediately upon entering high school. We know of course, that there is no vertical segregation, but if the vertical Negro suddenly begins to talk French, he can even sit down without creating any serious emotion among the "whites." I had a fellow try this out on the cashier's line at the A&P store. He suddenly asked the cashier about some product in French, and the "white" folks ahead of him actually broke ranks to give him priority.

Of course there could be too much of a good thing. If the Negroes of the South follow my suggestion it is possible that within twenty years they'll all be talking French; it would no longer be a novelty. But by that time there may not be need for any more "Golden Plans."

The Carolina Israelite,
May–June, 1956—May–June, 1958

Ordeal in Levittown

by David B. Bittan

DOGWOOD HOLLOW was like any other mass-produced sub-urb on August 11 of last summer—hot, humid and saturated with boredom. Some residents were pushing power mowers. Others, like William E. and Daisy Myers at 43 Deepgreen Lane, were at work indoors. Myers was painting the kitchen woodwork. His wife was busy with a mop.

Dozens of people saw the couple that day and the next. No one paid any attention. Just a painter and a maid, they thought. For, unlike the 60,000 residents of Dogwood Hollow and the other sections of Levittown, in Bucks County, Pa., the Myerses were Negroes. During its first five years, Levittown has assimilated yellow-skinned and red-skinned Americans—but no Negroes.

At 11 a.m. on August 13, Dogwood Hollow housewives began to gather outside the Myers home. Questioning of their mailman had confirmed that Negroes had moved in. By seven, cars were bumper to bumper on Deepgreen Lane. By 10, hundreds of persons spilled over the sidewalk, screaming curses and insults. At midnight, two stones shattered the picture window of the Myers home—and builder William J. Levitt's dream of the "perfectly planned community."

Myers, 34, and his wife, 33, both college-educated, had bought the Levittown house from its owner for $12,150. They had moved from a nearby community that was, in fact, bordered on several sides by expanding Levittown. Friends in Levittown had encouraged them. "We expected some trouble," said Myers, "but nothing like this."

For eight straight nights, the mob ruled Dogwood Hollow. It defied township police and state troopers sent by Gov. George M. Leader. Then a stone felled a local policeman. State troopers charged with flailing riot sticks. The mob dispersed. But the ordeal of Bill and Daisy Myers had just begun.

This writer, who lives in Dogwood Hollow and covered the violence as a newspaperman, then saw the harassment take a new form. A flaming cross blazed on the lawn of Myers's friend and next-door neighbor, Lewis Wechsler. Another cross was burned outside a friendly Quaker's house. Levittowners shuffled down Deepgreen Lane, clapping hands and walking dogs they called "Nigger." Vile threats were whispered over Myers's telephone. His fire insurance was canceled as a "bad risk." A druggist refused to deliver medicine because his driver was "scared." Tradesmen lost customers for "serving the niggers." Despite a round-the-clock state-police guard, a foot-high "KKK" was painted in red on Wechsler's house.

While Myers went to work as an $85-a-week equipment tester in a nearby factory, white friends had to stand guard over Mrs. Myers, six-week-old Lynda and their sons, Billy, five, and Stevie, three. Myers's firm resolve to remain in Levittown was shaken only when a vacant house directly behind theirs became a "clubhouse" for the anti-Negro forces. A Confederate flag flew from its rooftop, and a phonograph blared *Old Man River* at all hours. Finally, Myers appealed to State Attorney General Thomas D. McBride.

Moving decisively, McBride ended the war of nerves. He obtained a court order charging eight Levittowners with an "evil conspiracy." (The charge against one was later dropped.) The Bucks County Court was asked to stop them—and anyone else—from harassing the Myerses or their friends. An injunction granted October 23 still is in effect. Since then, not a single incident has been reported. But life is far from perfect for the Myerses. Though more people are friendly, their relations with most of their neighbors are superficial.

How did a vocal minority, a tiny segment of the population, succeed in throwing a peaceful community into turmoil? Observers say it was due in part to the prevailing feeling in the new developments that they can remain white islands; here, homeowners feel, is a step up on the social ladder, not to be shared with Negroes.

The rallying point for the anti-Negro forces was the hastily organized Levittown Betterment Committee. Its executive committee, whose chairman is James E. Newell, a native of Durham, N.C., voted to contact the Ku Klux Klan for help. A week later, it reversed the vote. Newell was one of those named in the injunction. So was the ex-vice-chairman, who was fined for his part in a cross burning.

Opposing this group was the new Citizens' Committee for Levittown. The Rev. Ray L. Harwick, a 32-year-old Evangelical and Reformed minister, accepted leadership of the committee because of his church's policy on integration and because, he says, "I couldn't look the other way." His committee filled the vacuum of leadership left by the town's established institutions. Only a handful of churchmen spoke up, politicians were singularly silent, and the police were unable to handle the situation.

Because of his stand, Harwick received three a.m. telephone calls, threats signed "KKK" and criticism from some of his congregation. The Quakers and the Jewish community, because they spoke up for the Myerses, were accused of engineering the move-in. The National Association for the Advancement of Colored People was said to have put up the money. The long-established Levittown Civic Association investigated and found the charges were false.

Criticism was directed by others against Levittown's founder for keeping Negroes out in the first place. Levitt's answer has been: ". . . Most whites prefer not to live in mixed communities. . . . The responsibility [for this] is society's. . . . It is not reasonable to expect that any one builder should or could undertake to absorb the entire risk and burden of conducting such a vast social experiment."

In the original Levittown on Long Island, several Negro families have owned homes, which they bought second-hand. However, the New Jersey Division Against Discrimination is investigating complaints that Levitt is violating a state law in refusing to sell to Negroes in his newest project, near Burlington, N.J.

Levittown, Pa., a year after the Myerses' arrival, has learned that it can live with Negroes. Its worst fears have not been realized. If housing values are down, it is because of the recession. There has been no mass exodus of whites, no influx of

Negroes. A second Negro family moved in without incident late in June.

Organized opposition to the Myerses has collapsed. Some members of the Betterment Committee recently joined in a losing campaign against fluoridation of Levittown's water. Others of this group participated in a losing fight to keep a new high school from being named after J. Robert Oppenheimer. Newell was defeated by a 2–1 margin when he ran for Dogwood Hollow committeeman in May.

Last year's violence has left its mark on Bill and Daisy Myers. But their memories have begun to fade as, more and more, they become a part of Levittown. "Sooner or later," Myers says, "I know we will be accepted for what we are—for ourselves."

Look, August 19, 1958

from
Black Like Me

by John Howard Griffin

In the bus station lobby, I looked for signs indicating a colored waiting room, but saw none. I walked up to the ticket counter. When the lady ticket-seller saw me, her otherwise attractive face turned sour, violently so. This look was so unexpected and so unprovoked I was taken aback.

"What do you want?" she snapped.

Taking care to pitch my voice to politeness, I asked about the next bus to Hattiesburg.

She answered rudely and glared at me with such loathing I knew I was receiving what the Negroes call "the hate stare." It was my first experience with it. It is far more than the look of disapproval one occasionally gets. This was so exaggeratedly hateful I would have been amused if I had not been so surprised.

I framed the words in my mind: "Pardon me, but have I done something to offend you?" But I realized I had done nothing—my color offended her.

"I'd like a one-way ticket to Hattiesburg, please," I said and placed a ten-dollar bill on the counter.

"I can't change that big a bill," she said abruptly and turned away, as though the matter were closed. I remained at the window, feeling strangely abandoned but not knowing what else to do. In a while she flew back at me, her face flushed, and fairly shouted: "I *told* you—I can't change that big a bill."

"Surely," I said stiffly, "in the entire Greyhound system there must be some means of changing a ten-dollar bill. Perhaps the manager—"

She jerked the bill furiously from my hand and stepped away from the window. In a moment she reappeared to hurl my change and the ticket on the counter with such force most

410

of it fell on the floor at my feet. I was truly dumfounded by this deep fury that possessed her whenever she looked at me. Her performance was so venomous, I felt sorry for her. It must have shown in my expression, for her face congested to high pink. She undoubtedly considered it a supreme insolence for a Negro to dare to feel sorry for her.

I stooped to pick up my change and ticket from the floor. I wondered how she would feel if she learned that the Negro before whom she had behaved in such an unlady-like manner was habitually a white man.

With almost an hour before bus departure, I turned away and looked for a place to sit. The large, handsome room was almost empty. No other Negro was there, and I dared not take a seat unless I saw some other Negro also seated.

Once again a "hate stare" drew my attention like a magnet. It came from a middle-aged, heavy-set, well-dressed white man. He sat a few yards away, fixing his eyes on me. Nothing can describe the withering horror of this. You feel lost, sick at heart before such unmasked hatred, not so much because it threatens you as because it shows humans in such an inhuman light. You see a kind of insanity, something so obscene the very obscenity of it (rather than its threat) terrifies you. It was so new I could not take my eyes from the man's face. I felt like saying: "What in God's name are you doing to yourself?"

A Negro porter sidled over to me. I glimpsed his white coat and turned to him. His glance met mine and communicated the sorrow, the understanding.

"Where am I supposed to go?" I asked him.

He touched my arm in that mute and reassuring way of men who share a moment of crisis. "Go outside and around the corner of the building. You'll find the room."

The white man continued to stare, his mouth twisted with loathing as he turned his head to watch me move away.

In the colored waiting room, which was not labeled as such, but rather as COLORED CAFÉ, presumably because of interstate travel regulations, I took the last empty seat. The room was crowded with glum faces, faces dead to all enthusiasm, faces of people waiting.

The books I had bought from the Catholic Book Store

weighed heavily in my pocket. I pulled one of them out and, without looking at the title, let it fall open in my lap. I read:

". . . it is by justice that we can authentically measure man's value or his nullity . . . the absence of justice is the absence of what makes him man." Plato.

I have heard it said another way, as a dictum: *"He who is less than just is less than man."*

I copied the passage in a little pocket notebook. A Negro woman, her face expressionless, flat, highlighted with sweat, watched me write. When I turned in my seat to put the notebook in my hip pocket, I detected the faintest smile at the corners of her mouth.

They called the bus. We filed out into the high-roofed garage and stood in line, the Negroes to the rear, the whites to the front. Buses idled their motors, filling the air with a stifling odor of exhaust fumes. An army officer hurried to get at the rear of the white line. I stepped back to let him get in front. He refused and went to the end of the colored portion of the line. Every Negro craned his head to look at the phenomenon. I have learned that men in uniform, particularly officers, rarely descend to show discrimination, perhaps because of the integration of the armed forces.

We sweated through our clothes and I was ready to leave and try for a later bus when they allowed us to board. Though nominally segregation is not permitted on interstate buses, no Negro would be fool enough to try to sit anywhere except at the rear on one going into Mississippi. I occupied a seat to myself not far from the back. Muffled conversations sprang up around me.

"Well, here we go into Mississippi—the most lied-about state in the union—that's what they claim," a man behind me said.

"It's the truth, too," another said. "Only it's Mississippi that does all the lying."

We drove through New Orleans under an overcast sky. Air conditioning in the bus cooled us comfortably. As we crossed the bridge, the water of Lake Pontchartrain reflected the sky's gray tone, with whitecaps on its disturbed surface.

The bus stopped at the outskirts of town to take on more passengers. Among them was a striking Negro man, tall, slender, elegantly dressed—the "Valentino" type. He wore a mustache and a neatly trimmed Van Dyke beard. He walked toward the rear, giving the whites a fawning, almost tender look. His expression twisted to a sneer when he reached the back and surveyed the Negroes.

He sat sidewise in an empty seat across the aisle from me and began to harangue two brothers behind him. "This place stinks. Damned punk niggers. Look at all of them—bunch of dirty punks—don't know how to dress. You don't deserve anything better. *Mein Kampf!* Do you speak German? No. You're ignorant. You make me sick."

He proceeded to denounce his race venomously. He spoke fragments of French, Spanish and Japanese.

I averted my head to the window and watched the country fly past as we traveled through an area of sunlight. I did not want to become involved in any discussion with this strange man. He was soon in violent argument with one of the brothers. They quarreled to the point of rage over whether Juárez was in Old Mexico or New Mexico.

The elegant one shouted, "You can't lie to Christophe. Christophe's got brains. No ignorant punk like you can fool him. You never been to Juárez!"

He jumped abruptly to his feet. Fearing violence, I turned toward him. He stood poised, ready to strike the other, his eyes narrowed to slits of hatred.

"If you hit me, you'll just be hitting me in the wrong," the poorly dressed Negro said, looking calmly up at Christophe. His seat companion added with a gentle smile, "He's my brother. I'd have to take his part."

"You threatening me?" Christophe whispered.

"No, now look," the brother placated. "Why don't you two agree just not to talk."

"He won't say another word to me? You promise?" Christophe said. He lowered his fist, but his face did not relax.

"No, he won't—will you?"

The poorly dressed one shrugged his shoulders pleasantly. "I guess——"

"Don't speak! Don't speak!" Christophe shouted into his face.

"Okay . . . Okay . . ." he said, glancing toward me as though to say the elegant Christophe must be insane.

Christophe glared at him for some time before moving over into the seat next to me. His presence set my nerves on edge. He was cunning and apparently vicious and I did not know what kind of scene he might start. I stared out the window, turning so far he could see only the back of my head.

He slouched far down in the seat and, working his hands wildly in the air as though he were playing a guitar, he began to sing the blues, softly, mournfully, lowering his voice at the obscene words. A strange sweetish odor detached from him. I supposed it to be marijuana, but it was only a guess.

I felt his elbow dig into my ribs. "How you like that, pappy?"

I nodded, trying to be both polite and noncommittal. He had pulled his hat down over his eyes. He lighted a cigarette and let it dangle from his lips. I turned back to the window, hoping he would leave me alone.

He nudged me again and I looked around. He bent his head far back to gaze at me under his lowered hat brim. "You don't dig the blues, do you, daddy?"

"I don't know," I said.

He studied me with narrowed eyes. Then, as though he had found some answer, he flashed me a magnificent smile, leaned hard against me and whispered. "I bet you dig this, daddy."

He punched his hat back, concentrated, stiffened his hands, palms upward, in a supplicating gesture and began softly to chant *Tantum ergo sacramentum, Veneremur cernui* in as beautiful Latin as I have ever heard. I stared at him dumfounded as he chanted the Gregorian version of this famous text.

He glanced at me tenderly, his face soft as though he were on the verge of tears. "That got you, didn't it, dad?"

"Yes," I said.

He made a huge sign of the cross, lowered his head and recited, again with perfect Latin diction, the *Confiteor*. When it was over, he remained still, in profound introspection. Above the hum of the bus's wheels on the pavement, silence surrounded us. No one spoke. Doubtless those nearest us who had witnessed the strange scene were perplexed.

"You were an altar boy, I guess," I said.

"I was," he said, not raising his head. "I wanted to be a priest." His mobile face revealed every emotion. His eyes darkened with regret.

The man across the aisle grinned and said: "Better not believe anything he tells you."

Christophe's handsome face congealed instantly to hatred.

"I told you not to talk to me!"

The man's brother intervened. "He just forgot." Then to the poorly dressed one, "Don't say *anything* to him. He can't stand you."

"I was talking to the other fellow, the one in the dark glasses," he said.

"Shut up!" Christophe shouted. "You were talking *about* me—and I don't even want you to do that."

"Just be quiet," the man's brother said. "He's going to be mad at you anything you say."

"Goddamn, it's a free sonofabitching country," the other said feebly, the smile remaining unchanged on his face. "I'm not afraid of him."

"Well, just hush—no need in you talking to him," his brother pleaded.

"You keep him quiet—or else," Christophe said haughtily.

My stomach contracted with uneasiness, certain there would be a fight. I was astonished to see Christophe cut his eyes around to me and wink, as though secretly he were amused. He glared his "enemy" down for some time before turning back to me. "I came to sit by you because you're the only one here that looks like he's got enough sense to carry on an intelligent conversation."

"Thank you," I said.

"I'm not pure Negro," he said proudly. "My mother was French, my father Indian."

"I see. . . ."

"She was Portuguese, my mother—a lovely woman," Christophe sighed.

"I see. . . ."

The man across the aisle smiled broadly at the obvious admission of a lie from Christophe. I gave him a warning glance and he did not challenge our friend's French-Portuguese-Indian background.

"Let's see," Christophe said, eying me speculatively. "What blood have you got? Give me a minute. Christophe never makes a mistake. I can always tell what kind of blood a man's got in him." He took my face between his hands and examined me closely. I waited, certain this strange man would expose me. Finally, he nodded gravely to indicate he had deciphered my blood background. "I have it now." His eyes glowed and he hesitated before making his dramatic announcement to the world. I cringed, preparing explanations, and then decided to try to stop him from exposing me.

"Wait—let me——"

"Florida Navaho," he interrupted triumphantly. "Your mother was part Florida Navaho, wasn't she?"

I felt like laughing, first with relief and then at the thought of my Dutch-Irish mother being anything so exotic as Florida Navaho. At the same time, I felt vaguely disappointed to find Christophe no brighter than the rest of us.

He waited for my answer.

"You're pretty sharp," I said.

"Ha! I never miss." Instantly, his expression degenerated to viciousness. "I hate us, Father."

"I'm not a Father."

"Ah, you can't fool Christophe. I know you're a priest even if you are dressed in civilian clothes. Look at these punks, Father. Dumb, ignorant bastards. They don't know the score. I'm getting out of this country."

His anger vanished. He leaned to whisper in my ear, his voice suddenly abject. "I'll tell you the truth, Father. I'm just out of the pen—four years. I'm on my way to see my wife. She's waiting with a new car for me in Slidell. And God . . . what a reunion we're going to have!"

His face crumpled and his head fell against my chest. Silently he wept.

"Don't cry," I whispered. "It's all right. Don't cry."

He raised his head and rolled his eyes upward in agony. His face bathed in tears, all of his arrogant defenses gone, he said: "Sometime, Father, when you say Mass, will you take the white Host for Christophe?"

"You're wrong to believe I'm a priest," I said. "But I'll remember you the next time I go to Mass."

"Ah, that's the only peace," he sighed. "That's the peace my soul longs for. I wish I could come back home to it, but I can't—I haven't been inside a church in seventeen years."

"You can always go back."

"Nah," he snorted. "I've got to shoot up a couple of guys."

My surprise must have shown. A smile of glee lighted his face. "Don't worry, Daddy. I'm going to watch out. Why don't you get off with me and let's shoot up this town together."

I told him I could not. The bus slowed into Slidell. Christophe got to his feet, straightened his tie, stared furiously at the man across the aisle for a moment, bowed to me and got off. We were relieved to have him gone, though I could not help wondering what his life might be were he not torn with the frustrations of his Negro-ness.

At Slidell we changed into another Greyhound bus with a new driver—a middle-aged man, large-bellied with a heavy, jowled face filigreed with tiny red blood vessels near the surface of his cheeks.

A stockily built young Negro, who introduced himself as Bill Williams, asked if I minded having him sit beside me.

Now that Christophe was gone, the tensions disappeared in our Negro section. Everyone knew, from having heard our conversation, that I was a stranger in the area. Talk flowed easily and they surrounded me with warmth.

"People come down here and say Mississippi is the worst place in the world," Bill said. "But we can't all live in the North."

"Of course not. And it looks like beautiful country," I said, glancing out at giant pine trees.

Seeing that I was friendly, he offered advice. "If you're not used to things in Mississippi, you'll have to watch yourself pretty close till you catch on," he said.

The others, hearing, nodded agreement.

I told him I did not know what to watch out for.

"Well, you know you don't want to even look at a white woman. In fact, you look down at the ground or the other way."

A large, pleasant Negro woman smiled at me across the aisle. "They're awful touchy on that here. You may not even know you're looking in a white woman's direction, but they'll try to make something out of it," she said.

"If you pass by a picture show, and they've got women on the posters outside, don't look at them either."

"Is it that bad?"

He assured me it was. Another man said: "Somebody's sure to say, 'Hey, boy—what are you looking at that white gal like *that* for?'"

I remembered the woman on the bus in New Orleans using almost the same expression.

"And you dress pretty well," Bill continued, his heavy black face frowning in concentration. "If you walk past an alley, walk out in the middle of the street. Plenty of people here, white and colored, would knock you in the head if they thought you had money on you. If white boys holler at you, just keep walking. Don't let them stop you and start asking you questions."

I told him I appreciated his warning.

"Can you all think of anything else?" he asked the others.

"That about covers it," one of them said.

I thanked him for telling me these things.

"Well, if I was to come to your part of the country, I'd want somebody to tell me," Bill said.

He told me he was a truck driver, working out of Hattiesburg. He had taken a load to New Orleans, where he had left his truck for repairs and caught the bus back to Hattiesburg. He asked if I had made arrangements for a place to stay. I told him no. He said the best thing would be for me to contact a certain important person who would put me in touch with someone reliable who would find me a decent and safe place.

It was late dusk when the bus pulled into some little town for a stop. "We get about ten minutes here," Bill said. "Let's get off and stretch our legs. They've got a men's room here if you need to go."

The driver stood up and faced the passengers. "Ten-minute rest stop," he announced.

The whites rose and ambled off. Bill and I led the Negroes toward the door. As soon as he saw us, the driver blocked our way. Bill slipped under his arm and walked toward the dim-lit shed building.

"Hey, boy, where you going?" the driver shouted to Bill while he stretched his arms across the opening to prevent my stepping down. "Hey, you, boy, I'm talking to you." Bill's footsteps crunched unhurriedly across the gravel.

I stood on the bottom step, waiting. The driver turned back to me.

"Where do you think you're going?" he asked, his heavy cheeks quivering with each word.

"I'd like to go to the rest room." I smiled and moved to step down.

He tightened his grip on the door facings and shouldered in close to block me. "Does your ticket say for you to get off here?" he asked.

"No sir, but the others——"

"Then you get your ass back in your seat and don't you move till we get to Hattiesburg," he commanded.

"You mean I can't go to the——"

"I mean get your ass back there like I told you," he said, his voice rising. "I can't be bothered rounding up all you people when we get ready to go."

"You announced a rest stop. The whites all got off," I said, unable to believe he really meant to deprive us of rest-room privileges.

He stood on his toes and put his face up close to mine. His nose flared. Footlights caught silver glints from the hairs that curled out of his nostrils. He spoke slowly, threateningly: "Are you arguing with me?"

"No sir . . ." I sighed.

"Then you do like I say."

We turned like a small herd of cattle and drifted back to our seats. The others grumbled about how unfair it was. The large woman was apologetic, as though it embarrassed her for a stranger to see Mississippi's dirty linen.

"There's no call for him to act like that," she said. "They usually let us off."

I sat in the monochrome gloom of dusk, scarcely believing that in this year of freedom any man could deprive another of anything so basic as the need to quench thirst or use the rest room. There was nothing of the feel of America here. It was rather some strange country suspended in ugliness. Tension hung in the air, a continual threat, even though you could not put your finger on it.

"Well," I heard a man behind me say softly but firmly, "if I can't go in there, then I'm going in here. I'm not going to sit here and bust."

I glanced back and saw it was the same poorly dressed man who had so outraged Christophe. He walked in a half crouch to a place behind the last seat, where he urinated loudly on the floor. Indistinguishable sounds of approval rose around me—quiet laughter, clearing throats, whispers.

"Let's all do it," a man said.

"Yeah, flood this bus and end all this damned foolishness."

Bitterness dissolved in our delight to give the bus driver and the bus as good as they deserved.

The move was on, but it was quelled by another voice: "No, let's don't. It'll just give them something else to hold against us," an older man said. A woman agreed. All of us could see the picture. The whites would start claiming that we were unfit, that Negroes did not even know enough to go to the rest room—they just did it in the back of the bus; never mentioning, of course, that the driver would not let us off.

The driver's bullish voice attracted our attention.

"Didn't you hear me call you?" he asked as Bill climbed the steps.

"I sure didn't," Bill said pleasantly.

"You deaf?"

"No sir."

"You mean to stand there and say you didn't hear me call you?"

"Oh, were you calling me?" Bill asked innocently. "I heard you yelling 'Boy,' but that's not my name, so I didn't know you meant me."

Bill returned and sat beside me, surrounded by the approval of his people. In the immense tug-of-war, such an act of defiance turned him into a hero.

As we drove more deeply into Mississippi, I noted that the Negro comforted and sought comfort from his own. Whereas in New Orleans he paid little attention to his brother, in Mississippi everyone who boarded the bus at the various little towns had a smile and a greeting for everyone else. We felt strongly the need to establish friendship as a buffer against the invisible threat. Like shipwrecked people, we huddled together in a warmth and courtesy that was pure and pathetic.

The threat grew as we penetrated deeper toward the center of the state. The distance between the whites and the blacks grew tangibly greater, even though we saw only the backs of their heads and shoulders, their hats and the cigarette smoke rising from them as night fell and bus lights were switched on. They said nothing, did not look back, but hostility emanated from them in an unmistakable manner.

We tried to counter it by being warm and kind to one another, far more than strangers usually are. Women discussed where they lived and promised to visit one another, though all knew that such visits would never take place.

As we neared Poplarville, agitation swept through the bus. Everyone's mind was on the Parker youth's lynching and the jury's refusal to consider the FBI evidence against his lynchers.

"Do you know about Poplarville?" Bill whispered.

"Yes."

Some of the whites looked back. Animated Negro faces turned stony.

Bill pointed out places in a quiet, expressionless voice. "That's the jail where they snatched him. They went up to his cell—the bastards—and grabbed his feet and dragged him down so his head bumped against each stairstep. They found blood on them, and blood at the bottom landing. He must've known what they were going to do to him. He must've been scared shitless."

The bus circled through the streets of a small Southern town, a gracious town in appearance. I looked about me. It was too real for my companions, too vivid. Their faces were pinched, their expressions indrawn as though they felt themselves being dragged down the jail stairway, felt their own heads bumping against the steps, experiencing the terror . . .

Bill's voice cut through, sourly: "That's the courthouse where they made that decision." He looked at me to see if I understood what decision he meant. I nodded.

"That's where they as much as told the whites, 'You go ahead and lynch those niggers, we'll see you don't get in any trouble.'"

I wondered what the whites in front were thinking. The lynching and the callous decision of the Pearl River County Grand Jury were surely on all their minds. Perhaps the injustice was as nightmarish to them as it was to those surrounding me.

We drove through wooded countryside into the night. Bill dozed beside me, his snores adjusted to the hum of the tires. No one talked. After a while Bill roused himself and pointed out the window. "That's where they fished his body out of the creek," he said. I cupped my hands to the window but could see only black masses of foliage against a dark sky.

We arrived at Hattiesburg around eighty thirty. Most of the Negroes hurried to the rest rooms. Bill gave me instructions with such solicitude that I was alarmed. Why, unless there was real danger, would he be so careful to help me avoid it? I wondered. He told me where I should go first, and whom I should request to see.

"What's the best way to get there?" I asked.

"Have you got some money?"

"Yes."

"Take a cab."

"Where do I catch one?"

"Any of those cabs out there," he said pointing to a string of parked cabs driven by white men.

"You mean a white driver'll take a Negro passenger?" I asked.

"Yeah."

"They wouldn't in New Orleans . . . they said they weren't allowed to."

"They're allowed to do anything to get your dime here," he said. We walked to one of the cabs.

"Yessir, where can I take you?" the driver said. I looked through the window to see a pleasant young man who showed no hint of animosity. Bill told him the address where he should deliver me.

"Wait just a second, will you?" Bill told the driver. He grabbed my arm and walked away.

"I'll find out where you're staying. I'll come around about noon tomorrow and check on you to see you're all right."

Again I was overwhelmed that strangers should go to such trouble for me.

I thanked him. He hesitated, as though uncertain and then said. "I'm not buttin' into your business, but if you're planning on getting a girl—you don't want to get one that'll burn you."

"I sure don't." I thought of La Fontaine's *Les deux amis*, where the friend offers to help rid the hero of his sadness, even to procuring a girl for him. I detected no hint of lasciviousness in Bill's voice or manner, certainly no element of pimping; no, he was simply trying to protect me.

"If you do plan on getting one, you better let me help you find a clean one."

"I'm worn out, Bill," I said. "I guess I'll by-pass it tonight."

"That's fine . . . I just didn't want you to go getting yourself messed up."

"I appreciate it."

The cab driver delivered me to an address on Mobile Street, the main street of the Negro quarter. It was narrow, cluttered, lined by stores, cafés, bars. He was completely civil, and in such an authentic way, I felt it was his real nature and not just a veneer to please the customer—the way I had seen it in the stores in New Orleans.

"Looks awful wild down here," I said as I paid him. I had to speak loudly to make him hear me above the shouts and the amplified wails of juke-box rock-and-roll music.

"If you don't know the quarter, you'd better get inside somewhere as soon as you can," he said.

My contact inside referred me to another person in the quarter. As I walked down Mobile Street, a car full of white men and boys sped past. They yelled obscenities at me. A satsuma (tangerine) flew past my head and broke against a building. The street was loud and raw, with tension as thick as fog.

I felt the insane terror of it. When I entered the store of my second contact, we talked in low voices, though he made no effort to be guarded or cautious in expressing his contempt for the brutes who made forays into the area.

"The sonsabitches beat one boy to a pulp. He was alone on a stretch of walk. They jumped out of the car, tore him up and were gone before anyone knew what was happening," he said. "They framed another on a trumped-up charge of carrying whisky in his car. He's one of the finest boys in town. Never drinks."

His bitterness was so great I knew I would be thought a spy for the whites if I divulged my identity.

Another car roared down the street, and the street was suddenly deserted, but the Negroes appeared again shortly. I sought refuge in a Negro drugstore and drank milkshakes as an excuse to stay there.

A well-dressed man approached and asked if I were Mr. Griffin. I told him I was. He said there was a room for me and I could go to it whenever I got ready.

I walked through the street again, through the darkness that was alive with lights and humanity. Blues boomed from a tavern across the street. It was a sort of infernal circus, smelling of barbecue and kerosene.

My room was upstairs in a wooden shanty structure that had never known paint. It was decrepit, but the Negro leaders assured me it was safe and that they would keep a close watch on me. Without turning on my light, I went over and sat on the bed. Lights from the street cast a yellowish glow over the room.

From the tavern below a man improvised a ballad about "poor Mack Parker . . . overcome with passion . . . his body in the creek."

"Oh Lord," a woman said in the quiet that followed, her voice full of sadness and awe.

"Lordy . . . Lordy . . ." a man said in a hushed voice, as though there were nothing more he could say.

Canned jazz blared through the street with a monstrous high-strutting rhythm that pulled at the viscera. The board floor squeaked under my footsteps. I switched on the light and looked into a cracked piece of mirror bradded with bent nails to the wall. The bald Negro stared back at me from its mottled sheen. I knew I was in hell. Hell could be no more lonely or hopeless, no more agonizingly estranged from the world of order and harmony.

I heard my voice, as though it belonged to someone else, hollow in the empty room, detached, say: "Nigger, what you standing up there crying for?"

I saw tears slick on his cheeks in the yellow light.

Then I heard myself say what I have heard them say so many times. "It's not right. It's just not right."

Then the onrush of revulsion, the momentary flash of blind hatred against the whites who were somehow responsible for all of this, the old bewilderment of wondering, "Why do they do it? Why do they keep us like this? What are they gaining? What evil has taken them?" (The Negroes say, "What sickness has taken them?") My revulsion turned to grief that my own people could give the hate stare, could shrivel men's souls, could deprive humans of rights they unhesitatingly accord their livestock.

I turned away from the mirror. A burned-out light globe lay on the plank floor in the corner. Its unfrosted glass held the reflection of the overhead bulb, a speck of brightness. A half-dozen film negatives curled up around it like dead leaves. I picked them up and held them before the light with strange excitement, curious to see the image that some prior occupant of this room had photographed.

Each negative was blank.

I imagined him going to the drugstore to pick up the package of photos and hurrying to this squalid room to warm himself with the view of his wife, his children, his parents, his girl friend—who knows? He had sat here holding blank negatives, masterpieces of human ingenuity wasted.

I flicked the negatives, as he must have done, toward the corner, heard them scratch dryly against the wall and flap to the floor. One struck the dead globe, causing it to sing its strange filamental music of the spheres, fragile and high-pitched above the outside noises.

Music from the juke box, a grinding rhythm, ricocheted down the street.

> *hangity*
> *hangity   hangity   oomp*
> *Harangity   oomp   oomp*

The aroma of barbecue tormented my empty insides, but I did not want to leave the room to go back into the mainstream of hell.

I took out my notebook, lay across the bed on my stomach and attempted to write—anything to escape the death dance

out there in the Mississippi night. But the intimate content-
ment would not come. I tried to write my wife—I needed to
write to her, to give her my news—but I found I could tell
her nothing. No words would come. She had nothing to do
with this life, nothing to do with the room in Hattiesburg or
with its Negro inhabitant. It was maddening. All my instincts
struggled against the estrangement. I began to understand
Lionel Trilling's remark that culture—learned behavior patterns so deeply engrained they produce unconscious, involun-
tary reactions—is a prison. My conditioning as a Negro, and
the immense sexual implications with which the racists in our
culture bombard us, cut me off, even in my most intimate
self, from any connection with my wife.

I stared at the letter and saw written: *Hattiesburg, November 14. My darling*, followed by a blank page.

The visual barrier imposed itself. The observing self saw the
Negro, surrounded by the sounds and smells of the ghetto,
write "Darling" to a white woman. The chains of my blackness would not allow me to go on. Though I understood and
could analyze what was happening, I could not break through.

Never look at a white woman—look down or the other way.

*What do you mean, calling a white woman "darling" like
that, boy?*

I went out to find some barbecue, down the outside steps,
my hand on the cool weathered railing, past a man leaning
forward with his head cushioned on his arm against a wall,
leaking into the shadows; and on into a door somewhere.
There were dim lights and signs: NO OBSENETY ALLOWED and
HOT LINKS 25¢.

A roundfaced woman, her cheeks slicked yellow with sweat,
handed me a barbecued beef sandwich. My black hands took
it from her black hands. The imprint of her thumb remained
in the bread's soft pores. Standing so close, odors of her body
rose up to me from her white uniform, a mingling of hickory-
smoked flesh, gardenia talcum and sweat. The expression on
her full face cut into me. Her eyes said with unmistakable
clarity, "God . . . isn't it awful?" She took the money and
stepped back into the open kitchen. I watched her lift the
giant lid of the pit and fork out a great chunk of meat. White
smoke billowed up, hazing her face to gray.

The meat warmed through the bread in my hand. I carried the sandwich outside and sat on the back steps leading up to my room to eat it. A streak of light from the front flowed past me, illuminating dusty weeds, debris and outbuildings some distance to the rear. The night, the hoots and shouts surrounded me even in this semi-hiding place.

hangity

hangity   *hangity*

Harangity   . . .

The music consumed in its blatant rhythm all other rhythms, even that of the heartbeat. I wondered how all of this would look to the casual observer, or to the whites in their homes. "The niggers are whooping it up over on Mobile Street tonight," they might say. "They're happy." Or, as one scholar put it, "Despite their lowly status, they are capable of living jubilantly." Would they see the immense melancholy that hung over the quarter, so oppressive that men had to dull their sensibilities in noise or wine or sex or gluttony in order to escape it? The laughter had to be gross or it would turn to sobs, and to sob would be to realize, and to realize would be to despair. So the noise poured forth like a jazzed-up fugue, louder and louder to cover the whisper in every man's soul, "You are black. You are condemned." This is what the white man mistook for "jubilant living" and called "whooping it up." This is how the white man can say, "They live like dogs," never realizing why they must, to save themselves, shout, get drunk, shake the hip, pour pleasures into bellies deprived of happiness. Otherwise, the sounds from the quarter would lose order and rhythm and become wails.

I felt disaster. Somewhere in the night's future the tensions would explode into violence. The white boys would race through too fast. They would see a man or a boy or a woman alone somewhere along the street and the lust to beat or to kill would flood into them. Some frightful thing had to climax this accelerating madness.

Words of the state song hummed through my memory:

Way down South in Mississippi, Cotton blossoms white in the sun,

We all love our Mississippi, Here we'll stay where livin' is fun.
The evening stars shine brighter, And glad is every dewy morn,
For way down South in Mississippi, Folks are happy they have been born.

Scenes from books and movies came back—the laces, the shaded white-columned veranda with mint juleps served by an elegantly uniformed "darky," the honor, the magnolia fragrance, the cotton fields where "darkies, happy and contented," labored in the day and then gathered at the manse to serenade their beloved white folks with spirituals in the evening after supper . . . until the time when they could escape to freedom.

Here, tonight, it was the wood plank beneath my seat, the barbecue grease on my lips, the need to hide from white eyes degenerate with contempt . . . even in the land "where livin' is fun."

And God is loved in Mississippi, Home and church her people hold dear.

I rose stiffly to my feet. Suddenly I knew I could not go back up to that room with its mottled mirror, its dead light bulb and its blank negatives.

I knew of one white man in Hattiesburg to whom I might turn for help—a newspaperman, P. D. East. But I hesitated to call him. He has been so persecuted for seeking justice in race relations I was afraid my presence anywhere near him might further jeopardize him.

I washed my hands and mouth under an outside faucet and walked around into the street to a phone.

P. D. was not at home, but I explained the situation to his wife, Billie. She said she was long ago inured to shocks, and insisted on having P. D. rescue me.

"Not if it's going to cause you people more trouble," I said. "I'm scared to death, but I'd rather stay here than get you in any deeper."

"It's late," she said. "I'll contact P. D. He can bring you here without your being seen. Stand in front of the drugstore.

He'll pick you up. Only one thing. You're not to do any of your investigating around this area—okay?"

"Of course not," I said.

"I mean, that would really get us in a jam . . ."

"Of course—I wouldn't think of it."

I waited in front of the lighted drugstore which was closed down for the night. My nerves tightened each time a car passed. I expected another satsuma to be thrown or another oath to be hurled. Other Negroes stood in other doorways, watching me as though they thought I was insane to stand there in the bright light. A sensible man would wait in the darkness.

Moments later a station wagon passed slowly and parked a few yards down the street. I was certain it must be P. D. and wondered at his foolishness in parking where he would have to walk along a sidewalk toward me, past a gantlet of Negroes who might not recognize him and who had good cause that night to resent any white man.

He got out and walked easily toward me, huge in the dim light. I could not speak. He shook my Negro hand in full view of everyone on the street. Then in his soft and cultivated voice he said: "Are you ready to go?"

I nodded and we returned to his car. He held the door for me to get in and then drove off.

"It's amazing," he said, after an uncomfortable silence.

We drove through the darkened streets to his home, talking in a strangely stilted manner. I wondered why, and then realized that I had grown so accustomed to being a Negro, to being shown contempt, that I could not rid myself of the cautions. I was embarrassed to ride in the front seat of the car with a white man, especially on our way to his home. It was breaking the "Southern rule" somehow. Too, in this particular atmosphere my "escape" was an emotional thing felt by both of us.

I repeated my plea that he not take me home if it meant any embarrassment or danger for his wife and child. He ignored this.

When we drove into his carport, his wife stood in the shadows beside the house.

"Well, hello, Uncle Tom," she said.

Once again the terrible truth struck me. Here in America,

in this day, the simple act of whites receiving a Negro had to be a night thing and its aura of uneasiness had to be countered by gallows humor.

What did we fear? I could not say exactly. It was unlikely the Klan would come riding down on us. We merely fell into the fear that hangs over the state, a nameless and awful thing. It reminded me of the nagging, focusless terror we felt in Europe when Hitler began his marches, the terror of talking with Jews (and our deep shame of it). For the Negro, at least, this fear is ever-present in the South, and the same is doubtlessly true of many decent whites who watch and wait, and feel the deep shame of it.

from *Black Like Me* (1961)

Students Hit Woolworth's for Lunch Service

by Albert L. Rozier Jr.

FOUR freshman students of this institution started Monday afternoon what they termed a "passive demand for service" at the lunch counter of a downtown five and dime store.

According to Ezell Blair, leader of the group, he and three other students—Franklin McCain, David Richmond, and Joseph McNeill—went into the store at approximately 4:30 p.m. on Monday, purchased small articles from a counter near the lunch bar and took seats at the lunch counter.

Following is a dialogue of the initial conversation between Blair and the waitress behind the lunch counter:

Blair: "I'd like a cup of coffee, please."

Waitress: "I'm sorry. We don't serve colored here."

Blair: "I beg to disagree with you. You just finished serving me at a counter only two feet from here."

Waitress: "Negroes eat on the other end."

Blair: "What do you mean? This is a public place, isn't it? If it isn't, then why don't you sell membership cards? If you do that, then I'll understand that this is a private concern."

Waitress: "Well you won't get any service here!"

After this conversation, said Blair, the waitress left them and went to the other end of the counter.

Immediately following this conversation, however, he stated that a Negro girl, a helper on the counter, confronted them, saying, "You are stupid, ignorant! You're dumb! That's why we can't get anywhere today. You know you are supposed to eat at the other end."

After this brief encounter, the students said they were completely ignored. When they asked questions, they were not answered.

"I told the waitress we'd sit there until we were served," said McNeill. She said nothing. Policemen came in and stared at us and walked up and down the aisle, but said nothing to us. We figured it was an effort on their part to frighten us away, but we stayed until 5:30, when the store closed," he continued.

The group said they tried to talk to the manager of the lunch counter and when they were refused audience, asked to speak with the manager of the store, but were denied this, too. They said that during the entire time they have been there, they have not so much as seen the manager.

The next morning, Tuesday, February 3, a group of approximately twenty students—including the freshman initiators of the demonstration—returned and took seats at the counter.

They entered the store at 10:30 a.m. and remained throughout the day. They were not served, the waitress stating that "it's a store regulation—a custom."

Blair stated that the demonstration was originally planned for two or three weeks; but that now, "We are preparing to continue to sit for as long as is necessary—until we're served."

The Register (North Carolina A & T), February 5, 1960

A. Philip Randolph,
New York, October 1942.

Schomburg Center for Research in Black Culture, New York Public Library

Members of CORE (*l. to r.*: Worth Randle, Wallace Nelson, Ernest Bromley, James Peck, Igal Roodenko, Bayard Rustin, James Felmet, George Houser, and Andrew Johnson) about to embark on a trip to test interstate bus segregation, 1947.

Courtesy Swarthmore College Peace Collection

Atlanta Constitution editor Ralph McGill at the White House, October 1945.
AP/Wide World Photos

Roi Ottley, 1943.
Alexander Alland, courtesy Schomburg Center for Research in Black Culture, New York Public Library

Thomas Sancton of *The New Republic*, May 1944.
AP/Wide World Photos

A. Philip Randolph, ca. 1948.
James C. Campbell, courtesy Schomburg Center for Research in Black Culture, New York Public Library

Charles H. Loeb at the
Cleveland *Call and Post*.
Left: Loeb's press badge.
Courtesy Stella Loeb-Munson

Langston Hughes.

Carl Rowan in the offices of the *Minneapolis Tribune*, January 1963.

Lillian Smith, 1945.
AP/Wide World Photos

Ted Poston of *The New York Post*.
Courtesy Kathleen A. Hauke

Relman Morin outside Little Rock's Central High School, September 1957.
AP/Wide World Photos

Wilma Dykeman and James Stokely.
Courtesy Wilma Dykeman

James N. Rhea and Ben H. Bagdikian on the cover of a collection of their articles published in 1957.
Courtesy Ben Bagdikian and the Providence Journal Company

Pauli Murray, 1941.
Schlesinger Library, Radcliffe Institute, Harvard University

John Howard Griffin (*r.*), a white writer who underwent medical treatments to darken his skin. New Orleans, 1959.
© *Don Rutledge*

Richard Stolley (r.) and *Life* editor Hugh Moffett on the steps of a Shady Grove, Alabama, home abandoned by an African-American family in the wake of *Life*'s series, "Segregation," November 1956.

Harry Golden (*c.*) at Carver College, Charlotte, North Carolina, August 1958.
Grey Villet, courtesy TimePix

George Collins (*l.*) and Cliff MacKay of the Baltimore *Afro-American*.
Courtesy Baltimore Afro-American

Bayard Rustin (*l.*) and A. Philip Randolph (*interviewed at r.*) during a news conference at the headquarters of the March on Washington Committee, August 3, 1963.
AP/Wide World Photos

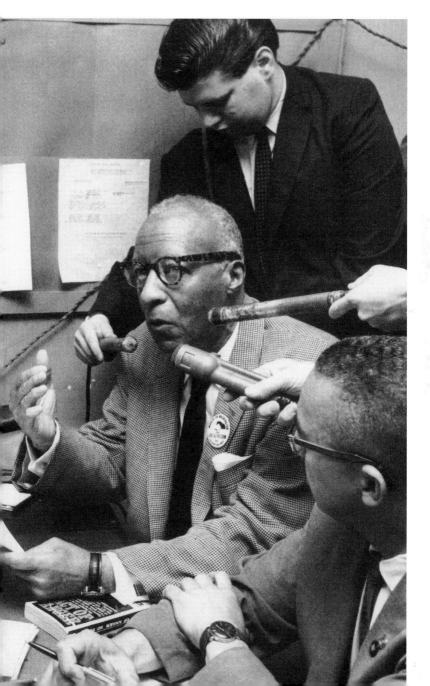

Ralph Ellison speaks at a Senate subcommittee hearing on racial problems in big cities, August 1966.
AP/Wide World Photos

John Herbers (*seated*) in the Mississippi office of United Press International, 1962.
Courtesy John Herbers

L. D. Reddick, 1949.

George Schuyler (*r.*) and Malcolm X in
the Harlem studios of WLIB, July 1964.

Hedrick Smith (*standing, 2nd from r.*) takes notes as an interracial group prays in front of the Albany, Georgia, city hall, July 30, 1962. Members of the group were later jailed for refusing to move on.

James Baldwin on the cover of *Time*, May 17, 1963.

Norman Podhoretz, 1961.
Gert Berliner

Harrison Salisbury with
Robert Kennedy.
*Harrison Salisbury Papers, Butler Library,
Columbia University*

On the steps of the Capitol in Montgomery, Alabama, after the Selma-to-Montgomery march (*c. to r., middle row*): James Baldwin, Bayard Rustin, A. Philip Randolph, and John Lewis.

Opposite page: Jeremiah X,
Julian Bond, John Lewis, and
Amsterdam News reporter
Jimmy Hicks (*l. to r.*) across
the street from the Sixteenth
Street Baptist Church in
Montgomery after it was
bombed, September 1963.
Danny Lyon / Magnum Photos

Claude Sitton of *The New York
Times*, May 1968.
New York Times

Michael Dorman (*l.*) talking with James Meredith after his first classes at the
University of Mississippi, October 2, 1962.
Courtesy Michael Dorman

June E. Johnson.

Annell Ponder.
© Danny Lyon / Magnum Photos

Relman Morin (*l.*) interviews Senator John Kennedy, April 1960.
AP/Wide World Photos

Opposite page: Tom Hayden (*l.*) being attacked by Carl Hayes, a local electrician
in McComb, Mississippi, October 1961

Charlayne Hunter and Hamilton Holmes are escorted away after completing registration at the University of Georgia, January 1961.

AP/Wide World Photos

Julian Mayfield, 1959.
*Schomburg Center for Research in Black Culture,
New York Public Library*

Stetson Kennedy, Marion Palfi, and
Langston Hughes, Atlanta, 1947.
Griffith J. Davis, courtesy Stetson Kennedy

Tom Dent, New Orleans, June 1966.
Dennis J. Cipnic, courtesy Monica Cipnic

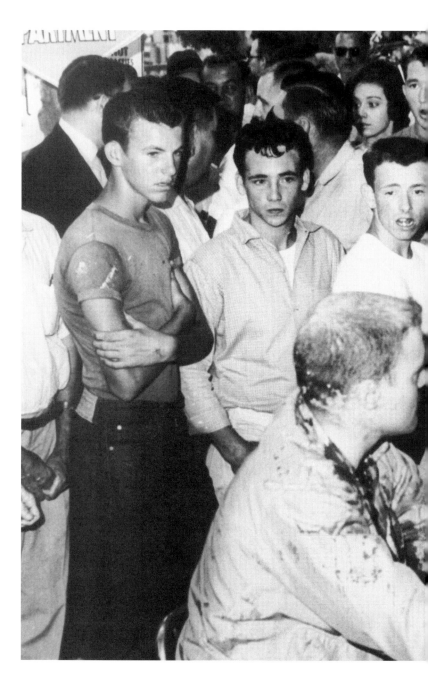

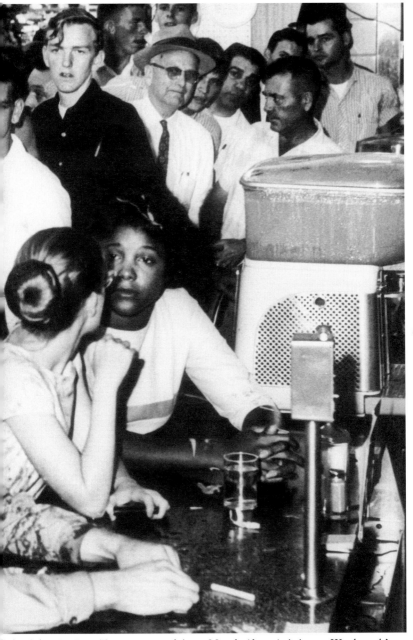

John Salter Jr., Joan Trumpauer, and Anne Moody (*l. to r.*) sit-in at a Woolworth's lunch counter in Jackson, Mississippi, May 1963.

Above: Robert Penn Warren at work, April 1956.
Leonard McCombe, courtesy TimePix

Negro Sitdowns Stir Fear of Wider Unrest in South

by Claude Sitton

CHARLOTTE, N.C., Feb. 14—Negro student demonstrations against segregated eating facilities have raised grave questions in the South over the future of the region's race relations. A sounding of opinion in the affected areas showed that much more might be involved than the matter of the Negro's right to sit at a lunch counter for a coffee break.

The demonstrations were generally dismissed at first as another college fad of the "panty-raid" variety. This opinion lost adherents, however, as the movement spread from North Carolina to Virginia, Florida, South Carolina and Tennessee and involved fifteen cities.

Some whites wrote off the episodes as the work of "outside agitators." But even they conceded that the seeds of dissent had fallen in fertile soil.

Appeals from white leaders to leaders in the Negro community to halt the demonstrations bore little fruit. Instead of the hoped-for statements of disapproval, many Negro professionals expressed support for the demonstrators.

A handful of white students joined the protests. And several state organizations endorsed it. Among them were the North Carolina Council on Human Relations, an inter-racial group, and the Unitarian Fellowship for Social Justice, which currently has an all-white membership.

Students of race relations in the area contended that the movement reflected growing dissatisfaction over the slow pace of desegregation in schools and other public facilities.

It demonstrated, they said, a determination to wipe out the last vestiges of segregation.

Moreover, these persons saw a shift of leadership to younger, more militant Negroes. This, they said, is likely to bring increasing use of passive resistance. The technique was conceived by Mohandas K. Gandhi of India and popularized among Southern Negroes by the Rev. Dr. Martin Luther King Jr. He led the bus boycott in Montgomery, Ala. He now heads the Southern Christian Leadership Conference, a Negro ministers' group, which seeks to end discrimination.

Negro leaders said that this assessment was correct. They disputed the argument heard among some whites that there was no broad support for the demonstrations outside such organizations as the National Association for the Advancement of Colored People.

There was general agreement on all sides that a sustained attempt to achieve desegregation now, particularly in the Deep South, might breed racial conflict that the region's expanding economy could ill afford.

The spark that touched off the protests was provided by four freshmen at North Carolina Agricultural and Technical College in Greensboro. Even Negroes class Greensboro as one of the most progressive cities in the South in terms of race relations.

On Sunday night, Jan. 31, one of the students sat thinking about discrimination.

"Segregation makes me feel that I'm unwanted," McNeil A. Joseph said later in an interview. "I don't want my children exposed to it."

The 17-year-old student from Wilmington, N.C., said that he approached three of his classmates the next morning and found them enthusiastic over a proposal that they demand service at the lunch counter of a downtown variety store.

About 4:45 P.M. they entered the F. W. Woolworth Company store on North Elm Street in the heart of Greensboro. Mr. Joseph said he bought a tube of toothpaste and the others made similar purchases. Then they sat down at the lunch counter.

A Negro woman kitchen helper walked up, according to the students, and told them, "You know you're not supposed to be in here." She later called them "ignorant" and a "disgrace" to their race.

The students then asked a white waitress for coffee.

"I'm sorry but we don't serve colored here," they quoted her.

"I beg your pardon," said Franklin McCain, 18, of Washington, "you just served me at a counter two feet away. Why is it that you serve me at one counter and deny me at another. Why not stop serving me at all the counters."

The four students sat, coffeeless, until the store closed at 5:30 P.M. Then, hearing that they might be prosecuted, they went to the executive committee of the Greensboro N.A.A.C.P. to ask advice.

"This was our first knowledge of the demonstration," said Dr. George C. Simkins, who is president of the organization. He said that he had then written to the New York headquarters of the Congress of Racial Equality, which is known as CORE. He requested assistance for the demonstrators, who numbered in the hundreds during the following days.

Dr. Simkins, a dentist, explained that he had heard of a successful attempt, led by CORE, to desegregate a Baltimore restaurant and had read one of the organization's pamphlets.

CORE's field secretary, Gordon R. Carey, arrived from New York on Feb. 7. He said that he had assisted Negro students in some North Carolina cities after they had initiated the protests.

The Greensboro demonstrations and the others that it triggered were spontaneous, according to Mr. Carey. All of the Negroes questioned agreed on this.

The movement's chief targets were two national variety chains, S. H. Kress & Co. and the F. W. Woolworth Company. Other chains were affected. In some cities the students demonstrated at local stores.

The protests generally followed similar patterns. Young men and women and, in one case, high school boys and girls, walked into the stores and requested food service. Met with refusals in all cases, they remained at the lunch counters in silent protest.

The reaction of store managers in those instances was to close down the lunch counters and, when trouble developed or bomb threats were received, the entire store.

Hastily painted signs, posted on the counters, read: "Temporarily Closed," "Closed for Repairs," "Closed in the Interest of Public Safety," "No Trespassing," and "We Reserve The Right to Service the Public as We See Fit."

After a number of establishments had shut down in High Point, N.C., the S. H. Kress & Co. store remained open, its lunch counter desegregated. The secret? No stools.

Asked how long the store had been serving all comers on a stand-up basis, the manager replied:

"I don't know. I just got transferred from Mississippi."

The demonstrations attracted crowds of whites. At first the hecklers were youths with duck-tailed haircuts. Some carried small Confederate battle flags. Later they were joined by older men in faded khakis and overalls.

The Negro youths were challenged to step outside and fight. Some of the remarks to the girls were jesting in nature, such as, "How about a date when we integrate?" Other remarks were not.

In a few cases the Negroes were elbowed, jostled and shoved. Itching powder was sprinkled on them and they were spattered with eggs.

At Rock Hill, S.C., a Negro youth was knocked from a stool by a white beside whom he sat. A bottle of ammonia was hurled through the door of a drug store there. The fumes brought tears to the eyes of the demonstrators.

The only arrests reported involved forty-three of the demonstrators. They were seized on a sidewalk outside a Woolworth store at a Raleigh shopping center. Charged with trespassing, they posted $50 bonds and were released.

The management of the shopping center contended that the sidewalk was private property.

In most cases, the demonstrators sat or stood at store counters talking in low voices, studying or staring impassively at their tormentors. There was little joking or smiling. Now and then a girl giggled nervously. Some carried bibles.

Those at Rock Hill were described by the local newspaper, The Evening Herald, as "orderly, polite, well-dressed and quiet."

Questions to their leaders about the reasons for the demonstrations drew such replies as:

"We feel if we can spend our money on other goods we should be able to eat in the same establishments," "All I want is to come in and place my order and be served and leave a tip if I feel like it," and "This is definitely our purpose: integrated seating facilities with no isolated spots, no certain seats, but to sit wherever there is a vacancy."

Some newspapers noted the embarrassing position in which the variety chains found themselves. The News and Observer of Raleigh remarked editorially that in these stores the Negro was a guest, who was cordially invited to the house but definitely not to the table. "And to say the least, this was complicated hospitality."

The newspaper said that to serve the Negroes might offend Southern whites while to do otherwise might result in the loss of the Negro trade.

"This business," it went on, "is causing headaches in New York and irritations in North Carolina. And somehow it revolves around the old saying that you can't have your chocolate cake and eat it too."

The Greensboro Daily News advocated that the lunch counters be closed or else opened on a desegregated basis.

North Carolina's Attorney General, Malcolm B. Seawell, asserted that the students were causing "irreparable harm" to relations between whites and Negroes.

Mayor William G. Enloe of Raleigh termed it "regrettable that some of our young Negro students would risk endangering these relations by seeking to change a long-standing custom in a manner that is all but destined to fail."

Some North Carolinians found it incomprehensible that the demonstrations were taking place in their state. They pointed to the progress made here toward desegregation of public facilities. A number of the larger cities in the Piedmont region, among them Greensboro, voluntarily accepted token desegregation of their schools after the Supreme Court's 1954 decisions.

But across the state there were indications that the Negro had weighed token desegregation and found it wanting.

When commenting on the subject, the Rev. F. L. Shuttlesworth of Birmingham, Ala., drew a chorus of "amens" from a packed N.A.A.C.P. meeting in a Greensboro church. "We don't want token freedom," he declared. "We want full freedom. What would a token dollar be worth?"

Warming to the subject, he shouted:

"You educated us. You taught us to look up, white man. And we're looking up!"

Praising the demonstrators, he urged his listeners to be ready "to go to jail with Jesus" if necessary to "remove the dead albatross of segregation that makes America stink in the eyes of the world."

John H. Wheeler, a Negro lawyer who heads a Durham bank, said that the only difference among Negroes concerned the "when" and "how" of the attack on segregation.

He contended that the question was whether the South would grant the minority race full citizenship status or commit economic suicide by refusing to do so.

The Durham Committee on Negro Affairs, which includes persons from many economic levels, pointed out in a statement that white officials had asked Negro leaders to stop the student demonstrations.

"It is our opinion," the statement said, "that instead of expressing disapproval, we have an obligation to support any peaceful movement which seeks to remove from the customs of our beloved Southland those unfair practices based upon race and color which have for so long a time been recognized as a stigma on our way of life and stumbling block to social and economic progress of the region."

It then asserted:

"It is reasonable to expect that our state officials will recognize their responsibility for helping North Carolina live up to its reputation of being the enlightened, liberal and progressive state, which our industry hunters have been representing it to be."

The outlook for not only this state but also for the entire region is for increasing Negro resistance to segregation, according to Harold C. Fleming, executive director of the Southern Regional Council. The council is an interracial group of Southern leaders with headquarters in Atlanta. Its stated aim is the improvement of race relations.

"The lunch-counter 'sit-in'," Mr. Fleming commented, "demonstrates something that the white community has been reluctant to face: the mounting determination of Negroes to be rid of all segregated barriers.

"Those who hoped that token legal adjustments to school desegregation would dispose of the racial issues are on notice to the contrary. We may expect more, not less, protests of this kind against enforced segregation in public facilities and services of all types."

The New York Times, February 15, 1960

"A Good City Gone Ugly"

by David Halberstam

NASHVILLE

THIS is the city whose integration plan has been called a model for other Southern cities; where white mobs were quickly and cleanly handled during school openings, where Negroes have voted and enjoyed justice in the courts, where bus segregation was ended by quiet agreement between city and Negro leaders, where the racist demagogue John Kasper is now meditating in the county jail.

It is a good city. Yet early this month, in the words of a photographer who had just watched white hoodlums stuff cigarette butts down the collars of Negro college students, it was "a good city gone ugly." For the sit-in demonstrations of Negro students at a lunch counter have turned Nashville into one of the South's most explosive racial areas.

As I write this, a special biracial citizens' committee is trying to solve the dilemma, and a temporary ceasefire has been announced. But the damage is already staggering: city court trials have been a farce; seventy-seven Negro and three white college students were convicted and fined fifty dollars each for (non-violent) disorderly conduct; sixty-three more will soon be tried; the original eighty have been rearrested on state charges; mass meeting of Negroes follows mass meeting; rumor follows bomb threat. And the end is not in sight.

For the Negroes have announced their determination not to pay any fines. According to Earl Mays, a student leader at Fisk University: "If they don't let us in down there at the counters, then they better have enough cells. They better have a lot of cells."

"Can you imagine what will happen if 150 or more Negroes spend thirty-three days in jail?" asked the Reverend Will

440

Campbell, a trouble shooter for a national church group. "Can you imagine what it will do to this city?"

Nashville is not Little Rock. The struggles over integration in schools and busses were settled years ago. Ironically, however, that may be part of the trouble now. The battle, in the view of the white community, was over. Discussion stopped; white consciences were cleansed. Four months ago, when a group of Negroes requested a meeting about the lunch-counter problem, no one paid the slightest attention to them; a few weeks ago, when the sit-ins started, very few people really took them seriously.

The Reverend James Lawson, a thirty-one-year-old Negro leader of the sit-ins who became a storm center when he was dismissed as a student from Vanderbilt University Divinity School for his part in them, believes that "Nashville was ripe for this. Sure, the people of Nashville thought they were making good progress. But to a lot of us, to the young Negroes, this talk of good progress is sheer hypocrisy. The Supreme Court decision hasn't even touched other areas where serious injustices are overlooked.

"Progress has come," said Lawson, who spent three years in India and is a firm believer in passive resistance, "but it hasn't begun to touch some of the commonplaces of life that affect the Negro deeply, the normal but subtle things that bite at his internal life, that he feels make him subhuman." For an example, Lawson mentioned a time when he and his fiancée were downtown shopping and wanted a cup of tea about four o'clock. "It was such a normal thing to do," he said, "and then we realized it was impossible. That's why the Negroes were ready for this." The Negroes, Lawson went on, "are tired of middle-class methods of seeking our rights. The legal redress, the civil-rights redress, are far too slow for the demands of the time. The sit-in is a break with the accepted tradition of change, of legislation and the courts. It is the use of a dramatic act to gain redress." The Negro demonstrators carried printed reminders with them: "Remember the teachings of Jesus Christ, Mahatma Gandhi, and Martin Luther King . . . remember love and nonviolence."

This, then, was the feeling. But the feeling had been there a long time. It was the sudden expression of it that became significant. I remember a policeman who stood cursing all Negroes and Communists as fifty-six Negroes were arrested in the bus depot. Even as the last one was arrested, forty new ones arrived at the back door. "It ain't really them!" he moaned. "Where do they all come from? I thought we just got them all."

Whether the Negroes win or lose—here, in Montgomery, throughout the South—and regardless of how many are arrested and how many are beaten, the significant thing about the sit-ins is the emergence of young Negroes as active participants. For nearly six years, starting with the Supreme Court decision, little was heard from young Negroes in the South. Was it possible that the race question was a bigger issue on the Northern and Eastern campuses than it was on the campuses of Southern Negro colleges?

The Negro, according to the Southern myth, is content. Even the young ones. The myth has exploded with the sit-ins. For a week I have watched the Negroes at their meetings, watched them growing more determined and confident all the time, surprised by their own strength. On the Saturday when eighty were arrested, they came in waves: the police would arrest the first wave, expecting to put a stop to it, and then came the second wave, and then the third. The idea that the demonstrating Negroes were like the Kasper mobs and could be handled with the same tactics (arrest a few, get a leader) proved a major miscalculation. While the first eighty were being tried in city court, hundreds of other Negroes gathered at the First Baptist Church to plan further strategy. What if the students at Tennessee State were expelled for their part in the sit-ins? "Then we'll close the school," said Willie Stewart, one of the leaders. "We'll all go out together. If we all stick together they can't stop us no matter what is handed down from whom."

Earl Mays, one of the original sit-in demonstrators, told me that the sit-ins marked the end of the young Negroes' passive attitude toward civil rights. "It's true we've been passive up to now," he said. "Up to now. But we are all dissatisfied with this slow legal maneuvering." Mays, twenty-three now, was eighteen when the Supreme Court made its decision. "I was in high school when that decision came out and I was like a lot of other young people: it came at a very important time, you know. I was very impressionable and I had a lot of faith. It seemed so very important. It said to me that this democracy works and that the things I knew were wrong really were wrong. And so I waited for them to change. But then there was all this dodging and skuldugging and hiding and then the young Negroes got the idea that it wasn't going to happen— or at least that it wasn't going to be done for us. That feeling has been there, but this is the first time we've shown it. This will mushroom. When the eighty went to trial there were 2,500 Negroes at the courthouse. We didn't have any rally, any pep talk, to get them out—they just came. We've got nothing to lose and we realize this is our problem."

City officials had calculated that the demonstrations would collapse because of the fear of arrest. But the Negro students, as Earl Mays said, have little to lose: no jobs, no position, no social fear of arrest. Thus they can stand up to the police. When the eighty were arrested, older Negroes tried to post bond. The students refused. "It was a revelation to us," said Z. Alexander Looby, a veteran attorney and patriarch among Negro leaders here. "Those kids didn't want to get out of jail. They didn't want to make their bond. They felt their cause and wanted to prove it. A revelation." The students, however, were finally persuaded to post bond pending appeal of their cases, but they have sworn they will never pay the fines.

This in part illustrates some of the difference in generations. "The older Negro looked only to the courts for help," said Rodney Powell, a student here. "While this community, at first, felt the sit-in was too radical and kept its hands off, once we got into it and they saw how we felt they supported us whole-heartedly. It is no longer just a student movement. It is a community movement." Because of this there was some protest in the Negro community over the fact that both Negro representatives were college presidents. The feeling was that having one Negro minister would have been more representative.

If the students were a revelation to their elders, they must also have been a revelation to themselves when they ran into organized harassment from white hoodlums at the counter that Saturday of the arrests. The scene was Woolworth's, and it was an almost unbelievable study in hate. The police were outside the store at the request of the management. Inside were almost 350 people, all watching the counter like spectators at a boxing match. To the side of the counter, on the stairs leading to the mezzanine, was a press gallery of reporters and photographers. At the counter were the Negroes, not talking to each other, just sitting quietly and looking straight ahead. Behind them were the punks.

For more than an hour the hate kept building up, the hoodlums becoming increasingly bold. The crowd watched appreciatively: "Here comes old green hat," referring to one of its favorite hoods. "Looks like it'll go this time." The Negroes never moved. First it was the usual name calling, then spitting, then cuffing; now bolder, punching, banging their heads against the counter, hitting them, stuffing cigarette butts down the backs of their collars. The slow build-up of hate was somehow worse than the actual violence. The violence came quickly enough, however—two or three white boys finally pulled three Negro boys from the counter and started beating them. The three Negroes did not fight back, but stumbled and ran out of the store; the whites, their faces red with anger, screamed at them to stop and fight, to please goddam stop and fight. None of the other Negroes at the counter ever looked around. It was over in a minute.

The police did not arrest the whites. Some say it was Woolworth's fault for not calling the police into the store, but the incident obviously reflected the uncertainty of the city administration and the curious position of Mayor Ben West. West, even more than Estes Kefauver, has been identified as a friend of the Negroes. Over the past six years he has carefully cultivated the Negroes and his reward is that in nearly any election within the city limits he or his candidate is unbeatable; the opposition didn't even run a candidate against him in the last election. But the sit-in demonstration put West on the spot and revealed one of the curious anomalies of factional politics in the South. For although West has strong Negro and labor support, he is also a tough machine politician with the factional support of wealthy Nashville businessmen and the Dixiecrat Nashville *Banner*. With the more liberal Nashville *Tennessean*'s opposition, West could be through if the *Banner* drops him.

"Ben really got caught in this one," a politician told me. "It was a real showdown of conflicting interests. Here he had the Negroes pushing hard and expecting him to deliver on one side; and on the other he had the *Banner* and the money-bags pushing just as hard. I mean he was in a tough one—why, suppose Estes got caught in a dispute between labor and the Negroes. It's the same thing."

The store owners went to see West and asked him to stop the Negroes from even entering the stores. West refused. But he did back up the lunch-counter arrests. For the benefit of the Negroes he invoked his past support, his Kasper record (in which they are no longer interested), and his own belief in civil rights. To a direct question he said that he personally did not think it was fair to refuse a man a twenty-five-cent sandwich after that person had spent money in the store. While he and his aides continued to call for law and order, West, usually a confident politician who leaves few decisions to subordinates, welcomed the citizens' committee to get the monkey off his back.

Like the *Tennessean* and other liberal white interests in Nashville, the mayor was reluctant to commit himself on the final question at issue: were the Negroes right? The far-reaching as well as the immediate implications of the lunch-counter question make it tricky. Besides the obvious conflict with individual property rights, it brings up several other problems. "I don't think many fair-minded people really object to the Negroes eating at the lunch counters," said one white businessman. "But this thing is touchy. If they eat at the lunch counter at Cain-Sloan, why can't they eat at the fine dining room there, and if they can eat at that dining room, why can't they eat at the B & W Cafeteria or any other restaurant in town? This thing goes pretty deep.

"Then you take this downtown area. We had to fight like the devil to keep it alive. Well, after all this fuss, if these rural people from out in the country think they're going to eat with Negroes, they may not come here to shop. They'll stay in their own towns and try some of these new shopping centers." He cursed lightly. "Damn those dime-store owners. If they'd only had the sense and the guts to give those Negro kids a ham sandwich that first day, then all this never would have happened. There wouldn't be this demonstration, not too many Negroes would insist on the right, and the country people wouldn't know it had happened."

But it's not that simple. If the Negroes had gotten the ham sandwich it would have been something else next: a movie theater, a baseball game, a playground. A continuing pressure seems inevitable. Not only have they fought hard here, but it has become obvious that they have become stronger day by day, surprised by their own ability to stand up. In the establishment of the biracial committee they have won their first victory: it is exactly what they requested originally. In learning what they can do in this crisis, they have readied themselves for others. At one of the student meetings, Willie Stewart told the other students: "We are like someone swimming this fifty-mile lake and we are exactly twenty-five miles out. We can either swim back twenty-five miles and be exactly where we were, or we can work just as hard and swim ahead those twenty-five miles."

The Reporter, March 31, 1960

Fear and Hatred Grip Birmingham

by Harrison E. Salisbury

BIRMINGHAM, Ala., April 8—From Red Mountain, where a cast-iron Vulcan looks down 500 feet to the sprawling city, Birmingham seems veiled in the poisonous fumes of distant battles.

On a fine April day, however, it is only the haze of acid fog belched from the stacks of the Tennessee Coal and Iron Company's Fairfield and Ensley works that lies over the city.

But more than a few citizens, both white and Negro, harbor growing fear that the hour will strike when the smoke of civil strife will mingle with that of the hearths and forges.

It is not accidental that the Negro sit-in movement protesting lunch-counter segregation has only lightly touched brooding Birmingham. But even those light touches have sent convulsive tremors through the delicately balanced power structure of the community.

The reaction has been new manifestations of fear, force and terror punctuated by striking acts of courage.

No New Yorker can readily measure the climate of Birmingham today.

Whites and blacks still walk the same streets. But the streets, the water supply and the sewer system are about the only public facilities they share. Ball parks and taxicabs are segregated. So are libraries. A book featuring black rabbits and white rabbits was banned. A drive is on to forbid "Negro music" on "white" radio stations.

Every channel of communication, every medium of mutual interest, every reasoned approach, every inch of middle ground has been fragmented by the emotional dynamite of racism, reinforced by the whip, the razor, the gun, the bomb, the torch, the club, the knife, the mob, the police and many branches of the state's apparatus.

In Birmingham neither blacks nor whites talk freely. A

pastor carefully closes the door before he speaks. A Negro keeps an eye on the sidewalk outside his house. A lawyer talks in the language of conspiracy.

Telephones are tapped, or there is fear of tapping. Mail has been intercepted and opened. Sometimes it does not reach its destination. The eavesdropper, the informer, the spy have become a fact of life.

Volunteer watchmen stand guard twenty-four hours a day over some Negro churches. Jewish synagogues have floodlights for the night and caretakers. Dynamite attempts have been made against the two principal Jewish temples in the last eighteen months. In eleven years there have been twenty-two reported bombings of Negro churches and homes. A number were never reported officially.

Birmingham's whites and blacks share a community of fear. Some Negroes have nicknamed Birmingham the Johannesburg of America.

"The difference between Johannesburg and Birmingham," said a Negro who came South recently from the Middle West, "is that here they have not yet opened fire with the tanks and big guns.

"I have lived in Alabama all my life," said a newspaperman. "Birmingham is going to blow one of these days. And when that happens that's one story I don't want to be around to cover."

"Remember," a business man said, "Birmingham is no place for irresponsible reporting. Be careful of what you say and who you mention. Lives are at stake."

"I'm ashamed to have to talk to you off the record," said an educator. "It is not for myself. But these are not ordinary times. The dangers are very real and people up North must realize that."

"Excuse me," an educated Negro woman said. "But I just don't understand the white people around here. They seem to act so crazy. It doesn't make any sense. Don't they know there is a limit to what people will stand?"

"If you sow hate, you reap hate," said a Negro pastor.

The Birmingham of another era, that of the happy-go-lucky, ignorant Negro, the serio-comic dramas of Eighteenth Street (the Harlem of Birmingham), and the setting of

Octavus Roy Cohen and his Florian Slappey stories, has vanished. Gone with it is Birmingham's fabulous Judge Abernathy, who let Negro prisoners determine the length of their stay in the Birmingham jail with a roll of the dice.

When the Negro student sit-in movement reached Birmingham ten days ago it set in motion a sequence of events almost reflexive in character.

Birmingham had been quiet during the early phases of the student protests. Two months ago a dozen Negro students went to a public park and began a brief "prayer for freedom." It was curtailed when the police arrested the students on a charge of public disorder.

Then on Thursday, April 2, ten Negro students went two by two into five downtown Birmingham stores. They made small purchases and sat at the lunch counters. All were arrested immediately on charges of trespassing. They were held eighteen hours before being able to make bond.

The next seventy-two hours were busy ones for the Birmingham police. They arrested three Negro ministers, the Rev. F. L. Shuttlesworth, the Rev. Charles Billups and the Rev. C. Herbert Oliver. Mr. Shuttlesworth was arrested twice on successive days.

The police also arrested Thomas Reeves, a 21-year-old white student at Birmingham-Southern College and part-time preacher, and Jessie Walker, a Negro student from Daniel Payne University.

Each of those arrested was charged with "vagrancy." In addition, Mr. Reeves and Mr. Oliver, who was hauled barefooted and in his bathrobe from his home, were charged with "intimidating a witness."

By Birmingham custom, persons charged with vagrancy are not admitted to bail. They are held incommunicado for three days. In actual practice, such a prisoner is sometimes permitted to make one telephone call. But not always. A person arrested on a vagrancy warrant simply disappears for three days. His friends and family may not know what has happened to him.

This is a favorite technique of Birmingham's Police Commissioner, Eugene Connor. Mr. Connor is a former sports broadcaster known as "Bull" because of the timbre of his

voice. He served as Birmingham Police Commissioner for sixteen years in the late Nineteen Thirties and Nineteen Forties.
His administration was a stormy one.

He went into eclipse for several years but made a comeback
in 1958, running on a platform of race hate.

"Bull is the law in Birmingham, like it or not," a business
man said.

Mr. Connor is the author of many widely quoted apho-
risms. He once said:

"Damn the law—down here we make our own law."

On another occasion he declared:

"White and Negro are not to segregate together."

"Only legitimate hold-ups will be investigated," he announced after evidence had been uncovered that some Birmingham robberies were inside jobs.

Mr. Shuttlesworth has been a frequent target of Mr. Connor's men. He has three cases on appeal. His church has been
bombed twice. In one bombing his home was destroyed.
Both he and his wife were injured and a white pastor was
badly manhandled by a Birmingham mob when the three of
them sought to use the white waiting room of the local bus
depot.

A test of the forces symbolized by Mr. Connor is now in
the making—a product of the seismic Birmingham reaction to
the Negro student sit-ins.

It centers on young Reeves. He is a slight youngster weighing about 137 pounds and standing five feet eight inches. He
wears horn-rimmed glasses, suffers from asthma and is notice-
ably shy and diffident.

He has been charged by the police with "intimidating a
witness." The witness presumably was one of the ten Negro
students arrested for sit-ins.

The parents of young Reeves have received threats of
death. The youth has been restricted to the campus of Birmingham-Southern, technically on administrative probation.
Actually, the step is for his physical protection.

A cross was burned on the Birmingham-Southern campus,
possibly because of the Reeves case, possibly because ninety-
seven Birmingham-Southern students had signed a petition to
Gov. John Patterson protesting his action in forcing Alabama

College to expel Negro sit-in demonstrators. The petition did not protest segregation. It protested political interference with the academic process.

Dr. Henry King Stanford, president of Birmingham-Southern, has been subjected to extraordinary pressures. But he has not buckled under. He supported the right of his students to send their petition to Governor Patterson on the ground of academic freedom. When he was confronted with threats and demands that young Reeves be expelled he again stood his ground. He declined to prejudge the case.

In Birmingham this kind of courage does not come cheaply. Dr. Stanford has been told that the college's position in the Reeves case will cost it a minimum of $1,500,000. This is the amount that the college had hoped to raise in a drive for badly needed building funds this year.

But as one Birmingham citizen said, "You weigh the situation. You take the counsels of caution. You listen to the voices which say don't rock the boat. But finally the time comes when a man has to stand up and be counted."

If fear and terror are common in the streets of Birmingham, the atmosphere in Bessemer, the adjacent steel suburb, is even worse.

On the night the Birmingham police arrested Mr. Shuttlesworth a band of floggers went to work in Bessemer.

The victim was a white woman, Barbara Espy, 19 years old, a former WAC. She was seized by four or five men, dragged into a car, beaten until she signed a confession that she had been "dating" Negroes.

She has since sworn out warrants charging that she was abducted and beaten by a sheriff's deputy, an alderman and three other persons.

The sheriff repeatedly refused to entertain charges against his deputy. The Federal Bureau of Investigation has been asked to look into the case for possible violations of civil rights.

One of the students who participated in the "prayer for freedom" lived in Bessemer. An evening or two later seven carloads of hooded men roared into the street where the youngster lives with his mother and sister.

Armed with iron pipes, clubs and leather blackjacks into

which razor blades were sunk the men attacked the boy and his mother and sister. The mother and sister protected the boy with their bodies. The men broke a leg of the mother, smashed open her scalp and crushed her hands.

Forty-five minutes after the alarm had been given, the police arrived, but the band had fled. The next day two deputies visited the mother in the hospital. She recoiled in horror. They were two of those who had beaten her, she said. No charges were lodged.

"She is afraid to say anything," a man familiar with the case declared.

A year ago a Negro girl and a white girl, both elementary pupils, quarreled on the way to school. A white man emerged from a near-by house with a bull whip and flogged the Negro girl. The police failed to respond to a call from the Negro school principal.

For weeks Negro children had to go to school an hour early and were held in school an hour late so they would not come into contact with white children.

The list of beatings, intimidations and violence could be continued almost indefinitely.

But not everything goes according to plan.

At the height of the last week's tension the Harvard debating team came to town. It met in an open and publicly announced contest with the debate squad of Miles College, a Birmingham Negro school.

Whites and blacks talked from the same platform. Whites sat with blacks in the audience in violation of one of Birmingham's most cherished ordinances. No policemen appeared. It could not have been more normal or peaceful had the contest been held in Cambridge, Mass.

The New York Times, April 12, 1960

Eye of the Storm

by Dan Wakefield

We're just not gonna do it.—*Don Hallmark, program chairman, Montgomery, Ala. White Citizens Council*

Nothing can stop us.—*Billy Smith, Negro student sit-in demonstrator, Greensboro, N.C.*

Montgomery

Beneath the gold draperies that canopy the long, high-ceilinged stage of the Montgomery, Alabama, City Hall sat the officers of the local White Citizens Council and their honored guests—the top officials of the city, county and state police forces. Montgomery Safety Commissioner L. B. Sullivan, who heads the police and fire departments of this city of roughly 70,000 white and 50,000 Negro citizens, stood at the rostrum and told his appreciative public audience:

Since the infamous Supreme Court decision rendered in 1954, we in Montgomery and the South have been put to a severe test by those who seek to destroy our time-honored customs. . . . I think I speak for all the law-enforcement agencies when I say we will use all the peaceful means at our disposal to maintain our cherished traditions.

So stand the police of Alabama—on the side of law, order and the cherished traditions of the white citizens. Indeed, the topic of this particular meeting was "A Salute to Law and Order." I attended it with a young man and woman who live in Montgomery, and we sat throughout the proceedings in silence, neither clapping nor rising from our seats during the several standing ovations. Throughout the speeches I was taking notes, and this, along with our failure to rise and applaud at appropriate moments, was evidently enough to brand us as

453

"outsiders." When we walked toward the door at the end of the meeting a middle-aged man in a brown business suit followed along beside us and began to shout at me, "Did you get enough information? I hope you got all the information you wanted!"

I said yes, thanks, I had all the information I wanted. He continued to follow, shouting and pointing at us, and other people began to stop and stare. He yelled out, "I know who you are! I know who all three of you are!"

By the tone of his voice and the look on his face, he seemed to be under the impression that we were, at the very least, three of the Four Horsemen of the Apocalypse. I extended my hand and told him my name, but he drew back and shouted, "Never mind, I know who you are! You're not welcome here!"

We walked on out of the door, and when we got to the street, several young sport-shirted men and one elderly white citizen fell in behind us. We walked on in silence to the car, which was parked around the corner from the City Hall, across the street from the fire station. Not looking back, we seated the girl in the car. I got in next to her by the door, and the other young man walked around to get in the driver's seat. Before he got in, my door was yanked open and two of the men who had followed us were grabbing at me, cursing and trying to pull me out of the car. They grabbed for my arms, legs and the notebook and papers I carried, tearing at my clothes and ripping my jacket.

The young man who had come to the meeting with me quickly hustled the girl out of the car. She ran across the street to the fire station, where four or five Montgomery city firemen were standing outside and watching us. She yelled "Help" as she ran toward them, and they hurried inside, retreating into a back room of the fire station, and refusing to answer when the girl pounded on the door.

My own yells by now had become quite loud and quite sincere, and the zealous citizens, who still hadn't managed to pull me out of the car, finally ran off down the street and out of sight. My two friends got back into the car, and just before we drove away the firemen appeared again outside the fire station across the street. They were smiling at us. Evidently they, too, were unmoved by, or unaware of, the doctrine of the uses of "peaceful means" in preserving tradition that their boss, Safety Commissioner Sullivan, had espoused in behalf of himself and his men at the meeting a few minutes earlier.

In fairness to the inspired citizens who attacked us, however, it ought to be explained that the Citizens Council "Salute to Law and Order" program was not exactly a Gandhian conference on the merits of love and non-violence, and L. B. Sullivan's text was far from being The Sermon on the Mount. One of the significant and dangerous features of the respectable racism practiced by the White Citizens Councils is that although their leaders and orators never fail to mouth a firm dedication to law and order at every public gathering, they also stir the passions of their crowds with provocative and outraged attacks on all those who oppose their principles, and deliver soul-searing declamations on the sacred cause of white supremacy. If zealots leave these meetings and vent their passionate dedication to the cause by violent means, the Citizens Council officials can, of course, deny responsibility by citing their statements upholding "legal, peaceful means" of action.

Safety Commissioner Sullivan, for instance, could disclaim any incitement to violence in his speech by pointing to his clearly stated belief in "peaceful means" of preserving the threatened white traditions. But after that affirmation (a not too radical stand for a city police chief), he got down to more alarming matters. The City of Montgomery, he explained to his audience, was selected long ago as "a site for racial agitators and troublemakers to attack our cherished way of life." The pressure had increased of late, he said, because of the efforts of civil-rights groups to influence politicians in Congress and in the coming Presidential elections. The rabble-rousers had so far met with little success, he reported, but there were dangers ahead:

Not since Reconstruction have our customs been in such jeopardy. . . . We can, will and must resist outside forces hell-bent on our destruction. . . .

As if this weren't enough to inflame the breast of any loyal white citizen, Mr. Sullivan went on to state: "We want these outside meddlers to leave us alone"; then, in a slow, mean-ingful tone of irony: *"If they do otherwise, we'll do our best to 'accommodate' them here in Montgomery."*

And who could say that the citizens who shortly afterwards attacked us were not just doing their best to "accommodate" some "outside meddlers"?

The audience had also been informed that outsiders were the real cause of the attempted Negro prayer march to the steps of the state Capitol on March 6, which barely was pre-vented from turning into a riot when an angry mob of 5,000 whites assembled to stop the demonstration. Program chair-man Don Hallmark of the Montgomery White Citizens Council told the meeting that "The people who sponsored this demonstration were disappointed—they had a lot of money in it."

The Citizens Council "Salute to Law and Order" was held to honor the law-enforcement officials for their work in dis-pelling the mob and preventing violence at that demonstra-tion. But one of the important groups that took an active part in controlling that explosive situation was not represented on the platform along with the city, county and state police offi-cials feted by the Council. This was the group of armed horsemen whose appearance on the scene marked a new ad-dition to the law-enforcement procedures of the South. The band of mounted "deputies," led by Sheriff Mac Sims Butler, was composed of wealthy cattlemen from the surrounding area who now are on call for emergencies, and have several times come into town with their horses in trailer trucks for "civil defense" drills. During the prayer-march demonstration, they roughed up and threatened three press photographers, two from Alabama papers and one from Magnum of New York. One of the photographers was arrested for refusing to obey an officer (deputy) who told him to move back. These non-uniformed mounties are unknown by face or name for public record, and have been especially vigilant in preventing any pictures being taken of them.

Reasons of secrecy no doubt prevented them from appear-ing on the Citizens Council platform to share the honors with the city, county and state police, but perhaps that was all for the best. The volunteer horsemen might well have been disappointed at the public's appreciation of their efforts. An estimated 5,000 of their fellow white citizens had turned up to form the mob that they helped to hold in tow on March 6, but not more than fifty sat scattered in Montgomery's large City Hall on "Law and Order" night. When Don Hallmark stepped to the front of the stage to open the meeting, he looked around the nearly vacant auditorium and asked: "Where is everybody?"

The only answer was an uneasy shifting as necks craned around at empty rows, and Mr. Hallmark, after asking those scattered at the back and the sides to come on down front and center, attempted to dispel the momentary gloom with a hopeful appraisal that "We think we make up for numbers in quality here. . . ."

It is easier to assemble larger numbers of white citizens for a mob than for a meeting. But that is not hard to understand —a mob at least offers excitement, but even the most ardent white supremacist must at this stage be weary of the ceremonies of the Citizens Councils. It is now six years since the conception of the W.C.C. sprang full-blown from the forehead of Robert "Tut" Patterson in Sunflower County, Mississippi, and with occasional and usually minor variations, the meetings of these defenders of the faith throughout the South remain as unchanged in rhetoric and style as high school graduation ceremonies.

As is the usual custom at these proceedings, chairman Hallmark harangued the conscience of his audience on the need for financial as well as moral support of their principles (last year Alabama's white citizens coughed up only $4,000 for the cause, while their brothers in Mississippi gave $160,000). In the same familiar formulas, Mr. Hallmark reaffirmed the organization's principles ("states' rights," segregation, "preservation of our cherished customs") and its unbending allegiance to them ("despite federal prisons or anything else, no force can make us integrate").

It was Safety Commissioner Sullivan who provided the only new notes in the evening's incantations. If there were any skeptics present who had doubted the feelings of the police about their role in quelling the mob at the prayer-march, Mr. Sullivan soothed their minds. He complimented the mob for

its "cooperation" with the law-enforcement officials by finally
dispersing without drawing blood, and made it clear that the
police had not only been there to preserve the peace, but to
preserve the white traditions as well. "Spring is here, and
birds are singing," Mr. Sullivan said, "but with the help of
our law-enforcement people, the *blackbirds* aren't gonna sing
on the Capitol steps."

The white citizens laughed, and rose to a standing ovation.

The segregationist politicians and Citizens Council orators
constantly compare the current threat to "Southern customs"
with the crisis of Reconstruction; and indeed the rhetoric and
attitudes of that era have been revived by the whites who are
fighting to preserve segregation. In describing the atmosphere of the South in Reconstruction, W. J. Cash (in his brilliant book, *The Mind of the South*) wrote a passage that
perfectly fits the situation today in die-hard Dixie areas, especially in Alabama and Mississippi:

> Criticism, analysis, detachment, all those activities and attitudes so
> necessary to the healthy development of any civilization, every one
> of them took on the aspect of high and aggravated treason.

The cry of "treason" from a small band of anti-Semitic,
anti-Negro bigots in Montgomery, plus intimidation by the
local Ku Klux Klan, have effectively wrecked what few groups
there were in the city which mildly promoted a less than
Dixie-dedicated approach to the race question. The unaffili-
ated bigot group, composed of both men and women (female
suffrage seems to be its main difference from the Klan) is centered on Rear Admiral John G. Crommelin (Ret.), a former
chairman of the Millions for McCarthy Committee, and a
weekly newspaper called the Montgomery *Home News*. The
paper is indistinguishable in its ideology from *Common Sense*,
The National Defender and similar bigot-sheets which have
long been published in the country. But the difference is that
this is a "home-town hate paper." You buy it on the newsstand, or in the hotel lobby. The degree of its acceptability in
the community can be seen in the fact that in its April 7 issue,
eighteen candidates for political office in the city, county and
state advertised in its pages. Most of them allude to their dedication to the cherished local customs, and John Crommelin,

"the Whiteman's Candidate to the U.S. Senate," is if possible even more explicit:

> As your Senator, I will ATTACK and EXPOSE the Anti-Defamation league of B'nai B'rith (ADL); the malarial-mosquito of integration and REAL HIDDEN ENEMY of White Christian Alabamians. THIS MUST BE DONE. The ADL (all jew) is the mosquito; the NAACP (jew controlled Negro) is the germ.

The message that the whole campaign against segregation is part of the "Communist-Jewish" conspiracy is also brought to the citizens of Montgomery by Mr. Crommelin on the local television station.

In the search for traitors, the Jew is an ideal target for the white Southern racist. As the threat to local racial customs grows, the embattled white-Protestant zealot finds in the Jew a ready-made "outsider" living in his midst, and the results are a rise in anti-Semitic feeling which is likely to end in incidents like the bombing of synagogues (the most recent of which took place in Gadsen, Alabama, this spring). This current rise in anti-Semitism in the South is, like the rest of the current rhetoric of hate, nothing new, and its roots were well explained by W. J. Cash:

> The Jew . . . is everywhere the eternal alien [writes Mr. Cash] and in the South, where any difference had always stood out with great vividness, he was especially so. Hence it was perfectly natural that, in the general withdrawal upon the old heritage, the rising insistence on conformity to it, he should come in for renewed denunciations; should, as he passed in the street, stand in the eyes of the people as a sort of evil harbinger and incarnation of all the menaces they feared and hated—external and internal, real and imaginary.

The White Citizens Councils, which claim to be clean of prejudice of any kind, are fond of pointing to their acceptance of Jewish members. Indeed, the Jew in the South may often join his local Citizens Council with genuine dedication—not so much in the desire to protect the tradition of white supremacy as to protect himself and his family. This reasoning was well explained in an anonymous letter from a Jewish member of the Mississippi Citizens Council which was published in the April edition of the Montgomery Citizens Council newspaper under the heading, "A Jewish View":

Because I have always manifested such respect for my own religion, my fellow members of my local Citizens Council would not for one moment entertain thoughts of turning the Citizens Councils' activities into anti-Semitic channels. This pattern is, I am confident, being repeated in all the towns and cities where respected and self-respecting Jewish Southerners have felt as I feel—that segregation must be maintained and that membership in the Citizens Council will help to maintain it. I speak from first-hand knowledge when I say that there are many Jewish members of Citizens Councils both here and in Alabama . . . the Jew who attempts to be neutral is much like the ostrich. And he has no right to be surprised or amazed when the target he so readily presents is fired upon.

But the target of the Jew is fired upon anyway, if not by the White Citizens Council he has joined, then by the Klan and the local white-Protestant hate groups that won't allow him to join. The Jews, however, are few in number in the South, and not everyone who stands outside the firm boundaries of white supremacy can be labeled a Jew; these others, then, are labeled Communists. The enemies of Southern white tradition are "atheists, socialists, communists, red republicans, jacobins . . ."; this list was not composed by John G. Crommelin, who carries on the crusade today, but by Dr. J. H. Thornwell, speaking in 1850, the year before he assumed the presidency of the College of South Carolina. The two evil specters conjured up by the racists as the current enemies of Southern white tradition are not new inventions, but old ghosts brought down again from the attic of the past.

The Montgomery patriots who dedicate themselves to rooting out the Communist-Jewish conspiracy have been successful in breaking up any groups of "traitors" in town who do not adhere to the Southern segregation stand. An interracial prayer group of local church women, many of them wives of well-known Montgomery business and religious leaders, had been meeting for four or five years to sing hymns, pray and have coffee together, but this treasonous conspiracy was wrecked in September of 1958 when the local segregation patriots took down license numbers of the attending ladies, took pictures of them as they came out of the church where they had met, and published their names and the names of their husbands' businesses in the *Home News*. The ladies began to

receive threatening and obscene phone calls, husbands publicly denied approval of their wives' treachery (some took ads
in the Montgomery *Advertiser*, disassociating themselves
from their wives' guilty activities) and the group has not met
since.

An even more subtle conspiracy was uncovered recently by
the zealous followers of the *Home News* and the K.K.K. This
was the establishment of a branch of the Mental Health Society in Montgomery. Its meetings at first were quite well attended, but then the Klan and its Crommelin friends turned
out to picket and distribute literature explaining that "mental
health" was only another aspect of the Communist-Jewish
conspiracy. The aim of the Mental Health Society was to
"brainwash" good Southerners into accepting integration. It
was further revealed that these "mental health" people had a
secret hospital in Alaska where Southerners were taken to
have lobotomies performed on them which changed them
once and for all into accepting communism and integration.
To further prove their case against mental health (if there indeed could be any doubts left), the "patriots" pointed out
that most psychiatrists are Jews.

The people who had been attending the mental-health
meetings may not have been convinced of the logic of the
attack on their society, but they were genuinely frightened
at the K.K.K. picket lines which greeted them before and
after the meetings. Attendance dropped off until the society
decided not to hold any more public meetings; their last gathering was held under the auspices of another local organization not tarnished by the stigma of "mental health."

The local patriots of segregation are actually wise in seeing
"mental health" as a threat to all they hold dear, for the current segregation pattern of Montgomery is one of the most
intricate pieces of insanity on exhibit in the Western world. Its
complex absurdity can perhaps be glimpsed by the following
illustration: physicians' offices in Montgomery have separate,
segregated waiting rooms, but many doctors have colored receptionists; lawyers' offices have single, "integrated" waiting
rooms, but only white receptionists.

The growing hysteria surrounding the protection of the
complicated local traditions of segregation not only makes

any criticism of them by native whites a sign of treason, but any violation of them by outsiders, however unintentional, a hostile and probably conspiratorial act of aggression and/or subversion. A group of undergraduate students from Mac-Murray College in Illinois, who stopped in Montgomery several weeks ago in the course of a sociology field trip through the South, were found guilty of such "subversion." They had been to a cattle ranch one morning and came into Montgomery that afternoon, where they met for lunch with some of the local Negro students and ministers in a private room of the Regal Café, a small restaurant in the Negro section. Someone saw the white students entering the café with Negro students, and the police were notified. Several police cars came, a TV reporter and camera man followed, and the Mac-Murray students were arrested and charged with disturbing the peace. The evidence rested on the fact that after the police cars and camera man arrived, a crowd began to gather. The judge found the defendants guilty, and they must return to Montgomery to stand trial for their crime—eating lunch with Negro ministers and students.

They were apprehended under a new city statute that makes any action "calculated" to disturb the peace a crime; of course the arresting officers and the judge and jury decide what type of action is so "calculated." This statute is the new weapon the city has devised to help maintain its complex customs of segregation. Before this, the city had passed a series of statutes outlawing a number of specific types of race-mixing—for instance, the playing of checkers or dominoes by Negroes and whites—but revoked them this year in the fear that they would be found unconstitutional by higher courts. It is felt that the new statute on action "calculated" to disturb the peace can cover such threats to the safety of the city as interracial domino games, and at the same time have a better chance of standing up if challenged constitutionally, for it makes no specific mention of race.

So another piece of chewing gum is stuck in the dike that holds back the threatening tide. The segregationist may now sleep easier, knowing that a white man who sits down to have a ham sandwich with a Negro can be arrested and sent to jail for disturbing the peace. But isn't there any reason for alarm, even for the white segregationist, as he sees the walls between the races rise higher? Montgomery is a city of 70,000 whites and 50,000 Negroes; a city whose recent years have been scarred by bombings, and recently threatened by a mob, and whose Negro leaders have pledged their continuing fight for an equality whose realization stirs many whites to violence. Isn't it only practical to establish some form of communication between the races? I went with that question to Carl Bear, a leading Montgomery businessman and an official of the Chamber of Commerce.

Mr. Bear is a middle-aged man whose hair is turning to a distinguished steel-gray, and whose broad shoulders, firm jaw and thin, straight-set mouth, combine with his deliberate manner to convey an impression of rocklike solidity. Mr. Bear looks like the kind of a man who, if he ever played fullback, would not even bother to look for holes in the line when he carried the ball. I began to ask him some questions, and before answering he told me to put my notebook and pencil away. He said that after we talked I could write out some questions if I wished and he would write out the answers and send them to my hotel. The essence of his stand—and that of so many of his fellow white businessmen and community leaders—is most clearly summed up in the written statement he subsequently sent me:

The relationship presently existing between the white and negro races is substantially attributable to the breakdown of communications between the races which occurred approximately four years ago following the bus-boycott incident. Since that incident the only voices which have been heard concerning our social problems have been those of the extremists, or professional agitators, of both races who in neither case represent a majority of the white or negro community. I believe that essentially most of us, of whatever race, are men of good will and earnestly desire to get along with one another. However, there is a crucial need for the more emotionally mature and substantial citizens of both races to assert the leadership which good stewardship requires of them. In my opinion, most negroes of this community do not want integration; they do want equality, but they believe that equality can be had while the races remain segregated. They also realize that equality is a status in society which must be earned and cannot be accomplished by force, nor can it be conferred by judicial decree or legislative enactment. They know that this earned equality will require much more education, extending over a period of many years.

(signed) Carl H. Bear

The exhausting revelation of this statement is that "communication" between the races means much more than sitting down at a table together. The heart of the problem is not that the white man refuses to sit down at the table, but rather that when he does, he refuses to see the real face of the man he is sitting across from. His whole life has prepared him to believe that the man across the table is good ol' Preacher Brown; and who can blame his blind refusal to see that it is Martin Luther King instead?

The main streets of downtown Montgomery come together in a quiet, sun-swept intersection that carries an aura of charm and well-being. A fountain sprays in the warm spring light, soothing music streams from public Muzak-boxes attached to light-poles, and the wide main street stretches gracefully upward to the alabaster columns and dome of the state Capitol, handsome against a sky of perfect postcard blue. In this peaceful scene stand the landmarks of conflict, past and present, whose turbulence seems so foreign to the setting. It was in this Capitol that Jefferson Davis took the oath of office as President of the Confederate States on February 18, 1861; a little below the Capitol's dome is the small frame building that served as "the White House of the Confederacy." It was here, just a block down the street in the Dexter Avenue Baptist church, built by Negroes during Reconstruction, that a young minister named Martin Luther King, Jr., took over the pulpit on September 1, 1954. And it was here, in this same church, that several hundred Negroes assembled March 6 for their prayer march to the Capitol and emerged to find a mob of 5,000 angry whites. Montgomery is already known as "the Cradle of the Confederacy"; it is also the cradle of the Negroes' non-violence movement against segregation which started here five years ago with the bus boycott and now is shaking the South.

Surely the white people of Montgomery, who watched that movement begin, lived with it, and saw its success, should understand better than any other Southern whites what it's all about. But they refuse even to believe it. Five years after the beginning of the bus boycott, and less than a month after the Negro student sit-in demonstrations in public eating places throughout the city, Carl Bear can sit at his desk and write that "In my opinion, most negroes of this community do not want integration. . . ."

Martin Luther King, Jr., wrote in his book that, after the boycott was over, the Montgomery whites had a new respect for the Negro citizens. It is certainly true that the Negroes gained great dignity from what they did, and that by all rational standards the white people should have gained a greater respect for them. But the feelings involved in this conflict have little or nothing to do with rationality. Judging from the whites I talked to recently in Montgomery, the successful boycott did not increase their respect for the Negroes who carried it out, but rather increased the mistrust and hatred of them.

The sentiments of the majority of local whites toward the Reverend King and the leaders of the boycott are probably reflected with accuracy in the outrage vented on them by the press. To *The Alabama Journal*, Mr. King is a "despicable character." In denouncing the recent sit-in demonstrations, the Montgomery *Advertiser* had this to say about the Reverend Ralph Abernathy, who is now the head of the Montgomery Improvement Association (the Negro group formed by King to carry out the bus boycott):

> Instead of diplomas and teacher certificates, they [the Negro student sit-in demonstrators] can mount in a frame upon the wall a picture of Dr. Abernathy jazzing around in his Gandhi impersonation for the TV and *Life* Magazine cameras, using them as potted palms in his act of aggrandizement.

Negro leaders like King and Abernathy are especially despised and ridiculed, for they are not the Negroes who fit the image of the shuffling old Uncle Toms—the image which the white so tenaciously holds on to because it gives meaning to his whole rationale that the Negro isn't yet ready for equality, and is in fact genetically and educationally (or both) incapable of assuming the responsibilities of full citizenship. Part of the insistence by Southern whites that the movement for Negro rights is a plot engineered by outsiders (Jews and Communists) is based on the reasoning that the Negro is unable to carry it out himself. The emergence of Southern Negro leaders like King and Abernathy confounds the old comfortable theories—but does not disprove them to the segregationist.

Even today, the Southern white can say with conviction, along with Carl Bear, that the majority of Negroes do not want integration. How do they know? Why, they *asked*. I have never yet been in a city in the South in which at least one white person didn't explain to me that Negroes didn't really want integration; they had been assured of this only the other day when they asked their maid, or their yard man, who had been with them all these years and surely wouldn't lie. Perhaps the example that best explains the irony of these reports is one told by a white citizen of Montgomery who was present when the family maid was asked what she thought about the bus boycott. "Oh, my folks don't want to have anything to do with that kind of trouble," the maid had assured her employers. "Me, I walk to work, and my brother Jim, he drives and picks up some other folks and takes 'em to work, and we just stay away from those buses—we don't want to have anything to do with that boycott."

Much is made of the genuine love that Southern whites feel for the Negroes, and such love indeed exists, as long as the Negro stays "in his place"—which is out in the cottonfield, mindin' his business and hummin' a tune. A recent editorial in the *Alabama Journal* tells us how warm the feelings are for those Negroes who stick to their cotton pickin':

One of the pleasant items in the day's news was a report made by the Negro county agent to the Montgomery County Board of Revenue. . . . Among specific individual reports was the fact that Minnie Guice of Mt. Meigs produced the first bale of cotton in the county in 1959. . . .

Outsiders are hard to convince that white citizens of Montgomery take pride in such achievements by Negroes who conduct successful farming operations and who are not led astray by the visiting agitators who come into the county to make trouble.

Farm stories about our Negroes such as these reported by the county agent show how pleasant are the racial relations here when our natives are left alone by the troublemakers.

There are loving words for Minnie Guice, who produced the first bale of cotton in the county; but stones for Autherine Lucy, who tried to enter Alabama University. Despite the editorials of the *Alabama Journal*, however, Autherine Lucy is not going back to bailing cotton; but it well may be that Minnie Guice's daughter will try to enter Alabama University. That is the awful truth that the whites refuse to face, for it means nothing less than that the past they are trying to preserve is already lost.

The stubborn attempt to preserve the myth of the old, dependent Negro who likes things just as they are—the myth which is so essential to the rationale of segregation—has many complex and powerful roots. Certainly the whole area of sexual guilt and fear, which Cash explains so well, is a primary factor in the present violent attempt of the whites to preserve the *status quo* of segregation. But besides the unconscious motivations, there are also some practical considerations involved in the fight to preserve white supremacy in the South. I mean considerations of the pocketbook.

An Alabama labor leader told me that he was convinced "that one of the aims of the Citizens Councils, and the more extreme hate campaigners, is the opposition to the economic policy of the AFL-CIO and the weakening of the labor movement in the South."

The threat that unions will mean integration has always been one of the major weapons of Southern management in keeping their workers from organizing, and thereby keeping down wages of both white and Negro workers. "Management can't go in and tell the white worker that they'll have to pay *him* more if Negro wages go up—so they feed him this social stuff instead—tell him that if he joins a union it means he'll have 'nigger officers.'

"The leadership of the Citizens Councils comes from the Chambers of Commerce, the landowners, the businessmen. This is partly an economic war for them. They need cheap labor—which means Negroes; any time there's a threat of an increase in industrial wages, there's a threat to their labor supply. Some of the leaders of the Citizens Council in Montgomery are contractors who wouldn't work a union man on a job. Most all their labor is Negroes."

When asked if the propaganda of the Citizens Councils had made organizing more difficult, the union leader said, "Oh, Christ, yes. In fact, it makes it more difficult to hold what you have."

There have been abortive efforts to form a white "Southern Federation of Trade Unions," but lately the talk of that has given way to intensive and often successful efforts of Klan and Citizens Council union members to take over AFL-CIO locals. "I've seen cases where they turned local union meetings into Citizens Council meetings," the labor official said.

The Klan and the rabid, less "respectable" Citizens Councils draw much of their support from the white laboring class (Elston Edwards, Imperial Wizard of the K.K.K., is a paint-sprayer in the Atlanta Chevrolet plant and a member of the U.A.W. local there) and in many places in the South they have turned union locals almost into "branches" of the segregation groups. Efforts of the international unions to remedy the situation have been of little or no avail. And most of the skilled-craft unions in the deep Southern states—particularly in the building trades—are exclusively white. The Carpenters Union in Montgomery, for instance, is all white.

The continuance of cheap labor in the South, which rests so heavily on the system of segregation, is one of the major lures used to bring in Northern industry. And the absentee Northern owners—who control most of the industry in Alabama as well as in other Southern states—ask no questions about labor practices and make no attempt to interfere in the "local customs" of segregation. As the Alabama labor official summed up their position: "They sit in their ivory towers in the North and their hands are clean."

Harold Fleming, director of the Southern Regional Council with headquarters in Atlanta, affirmed that the Northern corporations which are going into the South "have it within their power to make a tremendous impact" on the pattern of segregation.

For instance, Douglas Aircraft recently opened a plant in Charlotte, N.C., and went in with the understanding from local leaders that they would hire on a non-discriminatory basis. Few cities are likely to refuse the promise of a new industry that makes such a stipulation. But the Douglas example is

one of a very few such cases. "For the most part," Mr. Fleming said, "the corporations that come down here are interested only in avoiding conflict."

That is an understandable desire, but even the business
strategy for avoiding areas of racial conflict is often based on
a naive view of the situation, Mr. Fleming said. Businessmen
tend to pick spots where "everything is quiet," without seeming to realize that today's "quiet spot" may be tomorrow's
explosion. A business might have chosen to set up a branch in
Mississippi, for instance, rather than in Little Rock during the
school trouble, on the grounds that all was quiet in Mississippi. No new businesses came to Little Rock during the
school crisis; now that it is over, the Little Rock Chamber of
Commerce leaders are trying to attract new business with the
line that "We've already had it here; this is a safe spot to
come."

It is sad that more Northern corporations have not attempted to take fair-employment practices with them when
they open branches in the South, for they are among the few
"outsiders" who could make any dent in the local Southern
segregation patterns. With the exception of labor unions in
some areas (this year, for instance, the North Carolina State
Labor Council not only ruled against segregation in its locals,
but made a public statement supporting the Negro student
sit-in demonstrations), the involvement and the influence of
outside forces in the Southern crisis has been pitifully small.
Yet the "Southern crisis" is, in the end, the American crisis.

In many places, especially Alabama and Mississippi, the die-
hard segregationists have seceded again, at least intellectually,
from the rest of the country, and the attempt of national organizations of which they are a part to influence their actions
on segregation has usually met with rebuff and withdrawal.
This has been the case with the churches in almost every instance. The formation of Methodist "Laymen's Leagues" in
the South has been one kind of withdrawal by whites from
the influence of their national church group. Another typical
example of the church situation occurred while I was in Alabama. The National Council of the Episcopal Church sent
out an "advisory statement" urging support of the Negro sit-
in demonstrations. The Rev. C. C. J. Carpenter, Bishop of

Alabama, quickly issued a statement saying that Episcopalians in the diocese of Alabama should "ignore" the Council's advice.

In the same week, the national board of the YWCA came out in support of the sit-ins; the Montgomery YWCA quickly met and issued their own statement, deploring the national stand. The local branch is now studying the possibility of breaking off relations with the national organization.

There is a tragic irony in the fact that, as the Southern whites increase their own segregation from the outside world, the Southern Negroes become much more involved in the life beyond their own communities. At the same time that the Bishop of Alabama was telling his flock to ignore the words of the National Episcopal Council, and the white girls of the Montgomery "Y" were considering cutting off relations with the national organization, the Reverend Ralph Abernathy was in Ghana, attending a conference on non-violent action, and Mrs. A. W. West had just returned from Washington to report to the Negro's Montgomery Improvement Association on the recent White House Conference on Children and Youth.

"Don't worry about the Negroes here," one white Montgomery resident told me. "They're doing fine. It's the whites you ought to worry about."

Atlanta

Once during every session of the Georgia legislature, the state's two U.S. Senators return from the battle in Washington to give of their wisdom and inspiration to the troops at home, and in turn be duly honored for their latest forays against the federal menace. This occasion is usually—and especially in recent years—a time of solemn rejoicing and rededication to the common cause of states' rights, segregation and the preservation of the cherished Southern traditions. Standing ovations from the state legislators, as well as from the grateful citizens packed in the gallery, are a customary part of the tribute accorded the Senators. But this year it was different. When Senators Richard Russell and Herman Talmadge made their appearance at the last session of the legislature, the politicians rose and cheered as usual, but the gallery was seated and silent. It was filled with mothers who carried signs that said "Save Our Schools."

The mothers were members of an organization called HOPE (Help Our Public Education), which was formed here a year and a half ago and has spread throughout the state. Its purpose is to keep the public schools open in compliance with a federal court order for the beginning of integration in Atlanta schools this September. Until two mothers of Atlanta school children got together in November, 1958, "to do something" about the possible shutdown of public education in the face of court integration orders, there had been no public discussion of the issue locally beyond the usual political oratory promising that "It can't happen here."

The mothers who organized HOPE held public meetings, circulated literature, sent speakers to talk on the issue before any group throughout the state, and for the first time brought the subject into the open. Their work has been much like that of the mothers' group formed to try to open the schools in Little Rock—except that HOPE began *before* a crisis came. Mrs. Donald Green, one of the mothers on the HOPE board, said recently: "Since we started a year and a half before the 'shock' of the actual court order, we hope we'll be able to save the day. We've gotten help from the mothers in the Little Rock group, and mothers' groups in other states have asked us for help. There's a real feeling of fellowship among these groups in the South."

The debate on school integration in Georgia, begun by HOPE, has come into almost daily headline prominence in recent weeks with the deliberations of the Sibley Commission, a study group appointed by the state legislature at the end of its last session to hold public hearings and then make a report and possible recommendations on the school question by May 1. This was a week before the federal ruling is expected on whether or not the Atlanta school board must put its court-accepted pupil placement plan (beginning with the 12th grade and working down a grade each year) into operation this September.

It is still possible that the Atlanta schools will close, at least temporarily (though Atlanta Mayor Hartsfield says they won't close for a single day because "we're too busy making progress here"). Governor Ernest Vandiver was elected on the promise of total segregation, but the new force of public opinion on the side of keeping the schools open may give him an excuse to retreat. Some political observers in the state believe that the Governor will try to wait until Negroes are ordered into the schools, so the federal court—rather than the state legislators—will have to knock out Georgia's segregation laws, thus leaving him and the other politicians "officially" free from the blame.

Whatever tactical stalls may occur, the work of HOPE and the Sibley hearings have changed the whole climate of the conflict. In Atlanta, eighty-five of 114 witnesses told the Sibley Commission they favored keeping the schools open in compliance with the court integration order. In every one of the ten counties where hearings were held, even in the most die-hard segregation spots in south Georgia, HOPE had witnesses to support its stand. Even the most optimistic observers were surprised and encouraged by the fact that not only Atlanta, but a total of five of the ten districts where hearings were held had a majority of witnesses in favor of maintaining public education even if it meant integration. "A lot of us," one HOPE mother said, "never dreamed that the state was even split on the issue."

The results of the hearings, and the popular support of HOPE (which recently presented a petition signed by 10,000 voters supporting open schools) does not mean that there is a great wave of sentiment for integration in Georgia. HOPE does not take any stand for or against integration, but presents the issue purely as a matter of schools or no schools. The Klan and the Citizens Council elements are powerful here, too, and the ladies of HOPE are subjected to obscene and threatening phone calls from outraged segregationists. Georgia, like Alabama and Mississippi, is one of the states that Martin Luther King called "the South of Resistance," but the difference is that in Georgia there is now an open debate, at least on the issue of school integration. Where there is a public dialogue, bringing the issues and arguments into the open, there is hope. In Alabama and Mississippi there is none.

Raleigh

A constant theme of Southern segregationist orators, waving the banner of states' rights, is that basic changes in local customs and traditions cannot be lastingly imposed from the outside. They are perfectly right; Reconstruction proved the point. But they, as well as we observers in the North, forget that when we speak of "the South" (e.g., "the South Says Never!," "the South Spurns the Court"), we really mean the *white* South. This mistake in terminology allows us to overlook the fact that the South means Martin Luther King as well as Richard Russell, and that the greatest pressure for change in the South today is not being "imposed from the outside" but is coming from within. It is the pressure of Southern Negroes to do away with segregation in all its forms, and its most dramatic and significant expression is the movement that has grown from the Negro student sit-in demonstrations.

Harold Fleming, who, as head of the Southern Regional Council, has probably been in closer touch than anyone else with all aspects of the racial conflict in the South in the past decade, told me in Atlanta:

"Just as the Supreme Court decision was the legal turning point, the sit-ins are the psychological turning point in race relations in the South. This is the first step to real change— when the whites realize that the Negroes just aren't having it any more."

The leaders and representatives of the new generation of Southern Negroes who have shown that in spite of jeers, threats, jails or mobs "they just aren't having it any more" assembled Easter weekend at Shaw University in Raleigh, N.C., and affirmed that the movement they began with the lunch-counter demonstrations was only the beginning of their struggle for full equality.

If there had been any possibility that the spirit of protest born in the student sit-ins that have broken out in every state in the South would peter out as a passing fad, there was no such possibility after this conference. The meeting, which was sponsored by the Southern Christian Leadership Conference (a new organization led by the Rev. Martin Luther King, Jr., and other young Southern Negro ministers) established goals, strategy and lines of communication for the future in a series of discussions and workshops held by the students. Up to this point, the student demonstrations have been spontaneous; in the future they will not be. The students now have their own organization, which will work with, but not be led by, adult groups such as the Southern Christian Leadership Conference, CORE (Congress on Racial Equality) and the NAACP, as well as local church and civic groups.

The question of the role of adults in the student movement was a ticklish one, for in a sense the movement is a protest not only against segregation practices, but against the older Negro leaders. Where many sit-ins have taken place, older Negroes have been skeptical and fearful of the results, feeling that the students were "going too far" at the present time. At a recent meeting of the Montgomery Improvement Association, the organization which carried out the Negro bus boycott, the Rev. S. S. Seay chided his fellow elders by saying that "A lot of our people don't seem to understand what the young people are doing—they say they don't agree with them. Well, that just means they aren't catching the significance of events—it's a case of intellectual sluggishness."

The conflict on tactics has actually been going on for some time throughout the South. In Atlanta, for instance, the local NAACP lawyer who had led the Negro community's battle for civil rights for several decades opposed a group of younger Negroes, in their late twenties and early thirties, when they wanted to boycott the city's segregated trolley cars several years ago. The elders felt that it wasn't the right time, but the "Young Turks" won out, the boycott was successful, and the younger men emerged as the more influential leaders in the Negro community.

The sit-ins have brought the students' feeling of protest over the adults' "slow" tactics into the open, and after some initial reluctance, most of the adults have gotten behind the movement with moral, legal and financial help. The student action has, in fact, become a great source of pride and new morale for their elders, who have been in the battle so long.

Miss Ella J. Baker, executive director of the Southern

Christian Leadership Conference, told the adults at the rally that "The younger generation is challenging you and me— they are asking us to forget our laziness and doubt and fear, and follow our dedication to the truth to the bitter end."

And King, in the evening's main speech, hit hard at the same theme, saying that the student movement "is also a re-volt against the apathy and complacency of adults in the Negro community; against Negroes in the middle class who indulge in buying cars and homes instead of taking on the great cause that will really solve their problems; against those who have become so afraid they have yielded to the system."

Already, many Negroes who have known nothing else but subservience to segregation all their lives have found new hope and courage in the students' example. Harold Bar-donille, a junior at South Carolina State College in Orange-burg, S.C., was telling several students at the Raleigh conference how the old Negroes from surrounding farms had come to the college to offer their help when they heard that police had broken up a prayer march by turning fire hoses on the students and had made mass arrests.

"When they heard about it, a group of tenant farmers came up to the campus," Bardonille explained. "And I mean these were real *tenant* farmers—*dirt* farmers. You know? They went up to one of the profs and said, 'What're you gonna do about all those chillun that got hosed?' They said they wanted to help, and they'd do anything they could. They don't know what they can do, but they look to us for leadership. They're eager to be a part of this."

Harold Bardonille told the story with a kind of awe, which was only appropriate. Those tenant farmers in the depths of South Carolina are the kind of Negroes whom King describes with the lines of the Blues that say, "Been down so long that 'down' don't bother me." But now even they are looking up because a new generation has shown them it is possible. To the students, in fact, it is not only possible but necessary.

Camus wrote in his novel *The Plague* that the people who risked their lives to join the "sanitary squads" that fought the disease did so not out of any sense of heroics, but because "they knew it was the only thing to do, and the unthinkable thing would then have been not to have brought themselves to do it." That is the spirit in which the Negro students seem to have taken up their fight against the "plague" of segregation. It seems so luminously obvious to them that what they are doing "is the only thing to do." Those students who came from every state in the South to the conference, at Raleigh went about their business with a quiet determination and a minimum of oratory; to look at the small groups of students scattered on the grass of the campus in the afternoon workshop sessions, or seated in the humid classrooms in the earnest discussion periods, you might imagine you had stumbled into an ordinary spring day of study at any small college. In the "breaks" between sessions the students smoked and talked, exchanging news of what was going on in their own school and city. Billy Smith, a student at A & T College in Greensboro, was telling a Nashville student how he and his friends had been training the high school kids in the town to take over the sit-ins when the college term ended for summer vacation.

"They'll carry it right on till we get back in the fall," he said. "We can't let it stop just because of vacation. We're ready to keep on going for five or six years, or whatever it takes. This is no fad—this is it."

And "it" does not mean merely the end of segregation at lunch counters. As Harold Bardonille put it, "We're trying to eradicate the whole stigma of being inferior." The lunch-counter protest is only a symbol of the students' expression that "they aren't having it any more." Already students in many of the cities have broadened their work to include help in voting registration and preparation of economic boycotts among the adult community. Billy Smith said when he got to Greensboro that he and his fellow students would be starting a "door-to-door knock" in the Negro community to "inform them about 'selective buying.'"

The reports of the ten workshops that studied the major phases of the movement from "the Philosophy of Non-Violence" to "Jail *vs.* Bail" revealed the scope and commitment of the students' ideas. The young girl from the "Jail *vs.* Bail" committee reported quietly that her group's recommendations were that the students arrested in demonstrations receive no bail and pay no fines; that all persons arrested stay in jail. "This," she explained, "will show that arrest will not deter us."

One group of students studied the role of college adminis-trations, and decided that Negro college presidents and ad-ministrators should back the students' action (at least to the extent of not allowing them to be expelled) and should be willing to do this at the risk of their own jobs. Most of the Negro colleges in the South are state-controlled, and have white boards of directors. Thus, many Negro college admin-istrators who have expressed private sympathy with the stu-dent movement have had to maintain public silence—and, in the case of Alabama State, allow some of the student demon-stration leaders to be expelled. The students at the conference expressed their belief that the college administrators should put the movement for equality above their own careers—as the students indeed have put it above their own education.

The workshop that studied the "interracial" nature of the movement (there were about a dozen white students at the conference from colleges in both the North and the South) recommended that "this shouldn't just be a movement for Negroes but for all people who are against injustice." The representative of the "Preparations for Non-Violence" com-mittee stressed that only those who are certain they can meet the threats and violence with passive resistance should take part in the demonstrations, but that "for those who can't take intimidation, find something else for them to do—even if it's licking stamps."

The commitment to non-violence is a keystone of the movement, and the Negroes have learned its power and im-portance. At the Raleigh mass meeting, King preached the difficult text of this doctrine he has given them to use as their weapon against the ugly mobs they have faced already and will face even more often in the coming months and years. He said:

"Do to us what you will and we will still love you. We will meet your physical force with soul force. You may bomb our homes and spit on our children and we will still love you. But be assured that we will wear you down with our capacity to suffer. . . ."

That is the road they have set upon, and they have already passed the point of no return.

The Nation, May 7, 1960

They Can't Turn Back

by James Baldwin

I AM the only Negro passenger at Tallahassee's shambles of an airport. It is an oppressively sunny day. A black chauffeur, leading a small dog on a leash, is meeting his white employer. He is attentive to the dog, covertly very aware of me and respectful of her in a curiously watchful, waiting way. She is middle-aged, beaming and powdery-faced, delighted to see both the beings who make her life agreeable. I am sure that it has never occurred to her that either of them has the ability to judge her or would judge her harshly. She might almost, as she goes toward her chauffeur, be greeting a friend. No friend could make her face brighter. If she were smiling at me that way I would expect to shake her hand. But if I should put out my hand, panic, bafflement, and horror would then overtake that face, the atmosphere would darken, and danger, even the threat of death, would immediately fill the air.

On such small signs and symbols does the Southern cabala depend, and that is why I find the South so eerie and exhausting. This system of signs and nuances covers the mined terrain of the unspoken—the forever unspeakable—and everyone in the region knows his way across this field. This knowledge that a gesture can blow up a town is what the South refers to when it speaks of its "folkways." The fact that the gesture is not made is what the South calls "excellent race relations." It is impossible for any Northern Negro to become an adept of this mystery, not because the South's racial attitudes are not found in the North but because it has never been the North's necessity to construct an entire way of life on the legend of the Negro's inferiority. That is why the battle of Negro students for freedom here is really an attempt to free the entire region from the irrational terror that has ruled it for so long.

Of course, there are two points of view about the position

of the Negro in the South and in this country, and what we have mainly heard for all these years has been the viewpoint of the white majority. The great significance of the present student generation is that it is through them that the point of view of the subjugated is finally and inexorably being expressed. What students are demanding is nothing less than a total revision of the ways in which Americans see the Negro, and this can only mean a total revision of the ways in which Americans see themselves.

The only other black man at the airport is one of the shapeless, shambling ones who seem always to be at Southern airports for the express purpose of making sure that I get my bags into the right taxicab—the right cab being the one that will take me. And he performs this function in the usual, headdown way. There is an alcove here with "Colored Waiting Room" printed above it. This makes me realize that a study of Federal directives regarding interstate travel would have been helpful only if I had come South to be a test case —that is, if I had come to *be* a story as opposed merely to writing one. As an interstate passenger, both I and the airport would be breaking the Federal law if I were to go into a colored waiting room.

I tell my taxi driver that I am going to the university. There is no need to specify which of the city's two universities I mean, and he tells me that there are people going out there all the time. *Oh, you people have caused a lot of talk*, he seems to be saying. He is a pallid, reddish type, around forty, I suppose, quite good-natured and utterly passive. There seems to be no point in asking what he thinks of the situation here. Even to mention it is to mark oneself as a troublemaker, which my typewriter, accent, and presence have already sufficiently done. Yet I have the feeling that he would love to say something about it—but perhaps if he did he would also be marked as a troublemaker. I volunteer a few comments about the landscape, in the faint hope of opening him up. The South *is* very beautiful but its beauty makes one sad because the lives that people live, and have lived here, are so ugly that now they cannot even speak to one another. It does not demand much reflection to be appalled at the inevitable state of mind achieved by people who dare not speak freely about those things which most disturb them.

The cab driver answers me pleasantly enough, taking his tone and also, alas, the limits of the conversation from me. We reach the campus of the Florida Agricultural and Mechanical University. It is a land-grant college. When it was founded, in 1887, "by constitutional provision and legislative enactment," it was the State Normal College for Colored. Later on it became the Florida A. & M. College for Negroes. After the Second World War—possibly, by this time, it had become redundant—the "for Negroes" was dropped.

It is a very attractive campus, about a mile outside of town, on the highest of Tallahassee's seven hills. My driver seems very proud of the State of Florida for having brought it into being. It is clear that he intends to disarm any criticism I may have by his boasts about the dairy farm, the football field, the guesthouse, the science buildings, the dormitories. He is particularly vocal about the football team, which seems to be, here as on less beleaguered campuses, the most universally respected of the university's achievements. F.A.M.U. turns out, in fact, to be just as poor a center of learning as almost any other university in this country. It is very nearly impossible, after all, to become an educated person in a country so distrustful of the independent mind. The fact that F.A.M.U. is a Negro university merely serves to demonstrate this American principle more clearly; and the pressure now being placed on the Negro administration and faculty by the white Florida State Board of Control further hampers the university's effectiveness as a training ground for future citizens. In fact, if the Florida State Board of Control has its way, Florida will no longer produce citizens, only black and white sheep. I do not think or, more accurately, I refuse to think that it *will* have its way but, at the moment, all that prevents this are the sorely menaced students and a handful of even more sorely menaced teachers and preachers.

My driver impresses upon me the newness of most of the campus buildings. Later on I found out that these buildings date from 1956, just two years after the Supreme Court declared the separate-but-equal statute to be invalid. The old buildings, however, are dreadfully old and some of the faculty live in barracks abandoned by the Air Force after the Second World War. These too were "renovated" after the separate-but-equal statute had been outlawed. During the time that "separate-but-equal" was legal it did not matter how unequal facilities for Negroes were. But now that the decree is illegal the South is trying to make Negro facilities equal in order to keep them separate. From this it may not be unfair to conclude that a building, a campus or a system is considered renovated when it has merely been disguised. But I do not say any of this to my driver.

The university guesthouse is not expecting me; this frightens and angers me, and we drive to a motel outside of town. The driver and the Negro woman who runs the motel know each other in a casual, friendly way. I have only large bills and the driver has no change; but the woman tells him she will take the money I owe him out of my room rent and pay him when he comes again. They speak together exactly as though they were old friends, yet with this eerie distance between them. It is impossible to guess what they really think of each other.

Some students I met in New York had told me about Richard Haley. I had written him and he now arrives and places himself, shortly, as my ally and my guide. He and another member of F.A.M.U.'s staff had come to the airport earlier to meet me but had arrived too late. I tell him that I had concluded, from the fact that I was not met, that the F.A.M.U. people had not wanted me to come and had taken this way to let me know. Haley is a tall man in his early forties, who, shortly after I left Tallahassee, was dismissed from his position in the Music Department because he backed the student protest movement. He looked grave as I spoke, said he appreciated my bluntness and agreed that I might find hostility on the part of many of the people I was likely to meet. The events of the last few months had created great divisions in the Negro world. The F.A.M.U. president, for example, would not be glad to see me, for he and his supporters were hoping that the entire problem would somehow go away. These men are in an impossible position because their entire usefulness to the State of Florida depends on their ability to influence and control their students. But the students do not trust them, and this means the death of their influence and their usefulness alike. These men are as unable as is the State of Florida to find anything that will divert the students from their present course.

Until now the Negro college president's usefulness to the students, to the Negro community and to the state was determined by the number of alternatives to equality that he could produce out of the Southern hat. The docility of the students was the tacit price agreed upon for more funds, new buildings, more land. And these were tangible alternatives, for these things were hideously needed. As for curricular expansion, it usually came about in order to contain the discontent of Negro students. For example, at one time the state made no provision for the study of law at its Negro university. Students then applied, with every intention of testing the legality of the state's position, for instruction in white colleges. To prevent such testing, law was added to the Negro university curriculum. And what has happened is that precisely those dormitories, chemistry labs, and classrooms for which Negro presidents formerly bargained are now being built by the South in a doomed attempt to blunt the force of the Supreme Court decision against segregation. Therefore, the Negro college president has literally nothing more whatever to offer his students—except his support; if he gives this, of course, he promptly ceases to be a Negro college president. This is the death rattle of the Negro school system in the South. It is easy to judge those Negroes who, in order to keep their jobs, are willing to do everything in their power to subvert the student movement. But it is more interesting to consider what the present crisis reveals about the system under which they have worked so long.

For the segregated school system in the South has always been used by the Southern states as a means of controlling Negroes. When one considers the lengths to which the South has gone to prevent the Negro from ever becoming, or even feeling like, an equal, it is clear that the Southern states could not have used schools in any other way. This is one of the reasons, deliberate or not, that facilities were never equal. The demoralizing Southern school system also says a great deal about the indifference and irresponsibility of the North. The Negro presidents, principals and teachers would not be nearly so frightened of losing their jobs if the possibility of working in Northern schools were not almost totally closed to them.

Richard Haley found a room for me in town and introduced me to the Tallahassee Inter-Civic Council, an organization that makes no secret of its intention to remain in business exactly as long as segregation does. It was called into existence by a bus boycott in 1956. The Tallahassee boycott began five months after the boycott in Montgomery, and in a similar way, with the arrest of two Negro coeds who refused in a crowded bus to surrender their seats to whites on the motorman's order. The boycott ran the same course, from cross-burning, fury and intransigence on the part of the city and bus officials, along with almost total and unexpected unanimity among the Negroes, to reprisal, intimidation and near-bankruptcy of the bus company, which took its buses off the streets for a month.

The Reverend C. K. Steele, president of the ICC, remembers that "those were rough days. Every time I drove my car into the garage, I expected a bullet to come whizzing by my head." He was not being fanciful: there are still bullet holes in his living room window. The Reverend Daniel Speed, a heavy, rough-looking man who might be completely terrifying if he did not love to laugh and who owns a grocery store in Tallahassee, organized the boycott motor pool, with the result that all the windows were blown out of his store. The Speed and Steele children are among the state's troublesome students. And Speed and Steele, along with Haley, are the people whom the students most trust. Speed's support of the students is particularly surprising in view of his extreme vulnerability as a Negro businessman. "There has been," he told me, "much reprisal," but he preferred that I remain silent about the details.

Haley drove me to the hotel that he had found for me in one of the two Negro sections of Tallahassee. This section seems to be the more disreputable of the two, judging at least from its long, unpaved streets, the gangs of loud, shabby men and women, boys and girls, in front of the barbershops, the poolroom, the Coffee House, the El Dorado Café and the Chicken Shack. It is to this part of town that the F.A.M.U. students come to find whisky—this is a dry county, which means that whisky is plentiful and drunkards numerous—and women who may or may not be wild but who are indisputably available. My hotel is that hotel found in all small Southern towns—all small Southern towns, in any case, in which a hotel for Negroes exists. It is really only a rather large frame house, run by a widow who also teaches school in Quincy, a town not far away. It is doomed, of course, to be a very curious place, since everyone from N.A.A.C.P. lawyers, visiting church women and unfrocked preachers to traveling pimps and the simply, aimlessly, transiently amorous cannot possibly stay anywhere else. The widow knows this, which makes it impossible for her—since she is good-natured and also needs the money—to turn anyone away. My room is designed for sleeping—possibly—but not for work.

I type with my door open, because of the heat, and presently someone knocks, asking to borrow a pencil. But he does not really want a pencil, he is merely curious about who would be sitting at a typewriter so late at night—especially in this hotel. So I meet J., an F.A.M.U. student who is visiting a friend and also, somewhat improbably, studying for an exam. He is nineteen, very tall and slender, very dark, with extraordinarily intelligent and vivid brown eyes. It is, no doubt, only his youth and the curious combination of expectancy and vulnerability, which are among the attributes of youth, that cause me to think at once of my younger brothers when they were about his age.

He borrows the pencil and stands in the door a moment, being much more direct and curious about me than I am able to be about him. Nevertheless I learn that he is from a Florida town not very far away, has a sister but is the only son of very modestly situated people, is studying here on a scholarship and intends to become a bacteriologist. There is also about him something extremely difficult to describe because, while all of us have been there, no one wishes to remember it: the really agonizing privacy of the very young. They are only beginning to realize that the world is difficult and dangerous, that they are, themselves, tormentingly complex and that the years that stretch before them promise to be more dangerous than the years that are behind. And they always seem to be wrestling, in a private chamber to which no grownup has access, with monumental decisions.

Everyone laughs at himself once he has come through this storm, but it is borne in on me, suddenly, that it *is* a storm, a storm, moreover, that not everyone survives and through which no one comes unscathed. Decisions made at this time always seem and, in fact, nearly always turn out to be decisions that determine the course and quality of a life. I wonder for the first time what it can be like to be making, in the adolescent dark, such decisions as this generation of students has made. They are in battle with more things than can be named. Not only must they summon up the force to face the law and the lawless—who are not, right now in Tallahassee, easily distinguishable—or the prospect of jail or the possibility of being maimed or killed; they are also dealing with problems yet more real, more dangerous and more personal than these: who they are, what they want, how they are to achieve what they want and how they are to reconcile their responsibilities to their parents with their responsibilities to themselves. Add to this exams; the peculiar difficulty of studying at all in so electric a situation; the curious demoralization that can occur in a youngster who is unable to respect his college president; and the enormous questions that, however dealt with or suppressed, must live in the mind of a student who is already, legally, a convict and is on a year's probation. These are all very serious matters, made the more serious by the fact that the students have so few models to emulate. The young grow up by watching and imitating their elders—it is their universal need to be able to revere them; but I submit that in this country today it is quite impossible for a young person to be speeded toward his maturity in this way. (This impossibility contains the key to what has been called "the beat generation.") What the elders have that they can offer the young is evidence, in their own flesh, of defeats endured, disasters passed and triumphs won. This is their moral authority, which, however mystical it may sound, is the only authority that endures; and it is through dealing with this authority that the young catch their first glimpse of what has been called the historical perspective. But this does not, and cannot exist, either privately or publicly, in a country that has told itself so many lies about its history, that, in sober fact, has yet to excavate its history from the rubble of romance. Nowhere is this clearer than in the South today, for if the tissue of myths that has for so long been propagated as Southern history had any actual validity, the white people of the South would be far less tormented people and the present generation of Negro students could never have been produced. And this is certainly one of the reasons that the example of Martin Luther King, Jr., means so much to these young people, even to those who know nothing about Gandhi and are not religious and ask hard questions about nonviolence. King is a serious man because the doctrine that he preaches is reflected in the life he leads. It is this acid test to which the young unfailingly put the old, this test, indeed, to which it is presently putting the country.

I suggest to J. that perhaps he and his friend would like a drink and we carry my half-bottle of bourbon down the hall. His friend turns out to be really his distant cousin and a gospel singer, and I begin to realize that J. himself is very religious in much the same way I remember myself as being. But once I myself had left the church I suppose I thought all young people had, forever. We talk, I somewhat lamely, about the religious standards J.'s family expects him to maintain. I can see, though I do not know if he can—yet—that he talks about these standards because he is beginning to wonder about his lifelong ability to live up to them. And this leads us, slowly, as the bourbon diminishes and the exam begins to be forgotten, to the incipient war between himself and his family and to his strange position on the F.A.M.U. campus. J. is one of those youngsters whose reality one tends to forget, who really believe in the Ten Commandments, for whom such words as "honor" and "truth" conjure up realities more real than the daily bread. From him I get my first picture of the campus, a picture that turns out to be quite accurate. The actively dissident students are a minority, though they have the tacit, potentially active support of the entire student body. J. is not one of the active students because he is going to school on a scholarship and is afraid of hurting his family by being thrown out of school. He himself confesses that the fact that he can be deterred by such a consideration means that he is "not ready for action yet." But it is very clear that this unreadiness troubles him greatly. "I don't know," he keeps saying, "I don't know what's the right thing to do." But he is also extremely unhappy on the campus because he is part of that minority of students who actually study. "You know," he says, with that rather bewildering abruptness of a youngster who has decided to talk, "the dean called me in one day and asked me why I didn't have any friends. He said: 'I notice you don't go out much for athletics.' I told him I didn't come to college to be an athlete, and anyway I walk all the time and I've got all the friends I need, everybody respects me and they leave me alone. I don't want to hang out with those kids. They come over here"—the section of town in which we were sitting—"every night. Well, I wasn't raised that way." And he looks defiant; he also looks bewildered. "I got the impression that he would like me better if I was more like all the other kids." And now he looks indignant. "Can you imagine that?"

I do not tell him how easily I can imagine that, and he gets around to saying that he would rather be in some other college—"farther north, in a bigger town. I don't like Tallahassee." But his parents want him to remain nearby. "But they're worried about my being here now, too, on account of the student sit-ins, so maybe—" He frowns. I get a glimpse of his parents, reading the newspapers, listening to the radio, burning up the long-distance wires each time Tallahassee is in the news. He tells me about the twelfth of March, 1960, when a thousand marching students were dispersed by tear gas bombs and thirty-five of them were arrested. "I was on the campus—of course I knew about it, the march, I mean. A girl came running back to campus, she was crying. It seemed the longest time before I could make any sense out of what she was saying and, Lord, I thought there was murder in that town." But he is most impressed by this fact: "I came over here that night and maybe you don't know it, but this part of town is always wide open but that night—" he gestures— "boy, nobody was in the streets. It was quiet. It was dark. It was like everybody'd died. I couldn't believe it—*nothing!*"

He is silent. "I guess they were afraid." Then he looks at me quickly. "I don't blame them." I think that he means that he has no right to blame them. "I've got to make some kind of decision soon," he says.

I tell him that I am coming to the campus the next day, and this elicits from him the names of students he wants me to meet, and also the names of Reverend Steele, Reverend Speed and Mr. Haley. I think it is safe to say that these three, along with one other person whom I cannot, for the person's sake, name—and it strikes me as horrendous that such a consideration should be necessary in this country—were the four Negro adults most respected by the students. This fact alone, since they are four utterly dedicated and intransigent people, ought to cause the municipality to reflect.

The next day I meet and briefly talk to A., lean, light-colored, taciturn, nineteen, from Ohio, a sociology major, who has been arrested for his part in the sit-ins and is on a year's probation. He is very matter-of-fact and quiet, very pleasant and respectful, and absolutely tense with the effort this costs him. Or perhaps I exaggerate, but I am always terribly struck by the abnormal self-containment of such young people. A. speaks about the possibility of transferring to another college. Somehow I do not get the impression that this possibility is very real to him, and then I realize that part of his tension is due to worry about his exams.

I also talk to V., eighteen, from Georgia, the skinniest child I have ever seen, who is also on a year's probation. He is rather bitter about the failure of the Negro community to respond as he had expected it to. "*I* haven't got to live with it," he tells me—somewhat unrealistically since, as it later turns out, his relatives are determined to keep him in Tallahassee and he will certainly be living with the problem for the next couple of years. "I did it for them. Looks like they don't appreciate it." He was appalled that the Negroes of Frenchtown—the section of town in which I am staying—should have vanished on the evening of March 12. I got the impression that he had rather expected them to meet the students in the street with trumpets, drums and banners.

During the sit-ins of February the students had attempted, without success, to see the mayor and had spoken, without results, to the managers of the local Woolworth and McCrory dime stores. (As of this writing, the mayor of Tallahassee, who, I was told, uses the word "nigger" freely, has seen the students of his city only at lunch counters and in court.) It was to break the official and managerial silence that the sit-in of March 12 was organized. It was on this occasion that members of the White Citizens' Council, along with friends, sympathizers and people who "just happened to be in from the country for the day," met the students with baseball bats and knives. The good people of Tallahassee were not in the streets that day, of course; there were only the students, the police and the mob; and from this, which has now become a pattern in the South, I think it is safe to suggest that the convictions of the good people have less reality than the venom and panic of the worst. The police did not arrest any members of the mob but dispersed the students with tear gas and arrested, in all, thirty-five of them, twenty-nine Negroes and six whites.

Tallahassee has been quiet since March 12. The students felt that this time they themselves had been too quiet. Students from Tallahassee's two universities—Florida State, set up for whites, and Florida A. & M. for Negroes—are not allowed to visit each other's campuses. And so, on a Monday night during my May visit, they met in a church to make plans for a prayer meeting on the steps of the Capitol to remind the town that the students had no intention of giving up their struggle. There were about twenty students, in a ratio of about two Negroes to one white. It was a CORE meeting (the Congress of Racial Equality is an organization dedicated to bringing about change by passive resistance to social injustice), and Haley, Steele and the warrior to whom I can give no name were present as the Adult Leadership.

The prayer meeting had originally been the brain storm of R., a white student, foreign-born, very measured in speech, very direct in manner. There was first some uncertainty as to whether the prayer meeting should be held at all because of the pressure of exams and the homegoing plans of students, many of whom would have departed by Thursday.

There had also been the hope originally, since CORE is by now a dirty word in Tallahassee, of getting broader community support by asking the ministers of all faiths to give the news to their congregations and urge them to join the students. It was possible to gauge the depth of official hostility and community apathy by the discussion this suggestion precipitated.

One of the Negro students suggested that not all the ministers were to be trusted; one of them would surely feel it his duty to warn the police. A white coed student protested this vehemently, it being her view that there was no possible harm in an open prayer meeting—"It's just a y'all-come *prayer* meeting!"—and refused to believe that the police would not protect such spectacular piety. And this brought up the whole question of strategy: If the police were not warned, then the prayer meeting would have to be described as spontaneous. "But you can't," said a Negro coed, "*decide* to have a *spontaneous* prayer meeting. Especially not on the steps of the Capitol on Thursday at one o'clock." "Oh, it'll be spontaneous enough," said another student—my notes do not indicate his color—"by the time we start praying." D., a white coed, was against informing the police: "We love them dearly," she said with rather heavy sarcasm, "but I don't want them to get the impression that I'm asking their permission to do *anything*." "We're not asking their permission," said another white student. "We have every right to have a prayer meeting and we're just informing them of it." "There's no reason," said the girl who felt that the police would not possibly do anything to peacefully praying people, "for them not to treat us just like they'd treat any other group of citizens."

This led to rather cynical laughter and someone, looking around the room, offered to name "oh, about twenty-five multicolored reasons." In all this there was no question of fear of the police; there was simply no belief whatever that they would act impartially or "that they might turn out," as Reverend Steele unconvincingly suggested, "to protect us." It is significant, I think, that none of the students, except for one lone girl—who turned out to be the daughter of a segregationist and who was therefore in a way defending her father against the imputation of villainy—believed that they could call on the police for protection. It was for this reason that it was decided not to ask the city's ministers to invite their congregations. "If too many people know, they'll just have time to call in all those people from the country and State troopers, and it'll be a mess," someone said. And this left open the great question of how, precisely, to handle the police. Was it, strategically speaking, better to inform them or better to give them no warning. "If you tell the police," said one Negro student, "it's just as good as telling the White Citizens' Council." Again it is significant that no one, white or black, contested this statement. It was finally decided not to inform the police and to arrive at the steps of the Capitol singly or in pairs. "That way they won't have time to get their boys together."

Now the prayer meeting, in fact, did not take place. Phones began ringing early in the morning of the scheduled day, warning that news of the plans had somehow leaked out and the students could expect great trouble if they tried to get to the Capitol.

A day later I talk with Haley and ask him what, in his judgment, is the attitude of most white people in the South. I confess myself baffled. Haley doesn't answer my question directly.

"What we're trying to do," he tells me, "is to sting their consciences a little. They don't want to think about it. Well, we must make them think about it.

"When they come home from work," Haley continues, "and turn on the TV sets and there *you* are—" he means *you the Negro*—"on your way to jail again, and they know, at the bottom of their hearts, that it's not because you've done anything wrong—something happens in them, something's got to happen in them. They're human beings, too, you know," and he smiles. We are standing in the hall of the university's music building.

It is near the end of the day and he is about to go and give an exam. I have heard him say what he has just told me more than once to some embittered and caustic student, trying with all his might to inculcate in the student that charity without which—and how this country proves it!—social change is meaningless. Haley always speaks very quietly. "We have to wake up all those people in the middle," he says. "Most white people in the South don't especially like the idea of integration, but they'll go along with it. By and by they'll get used to it."

And all this, I think to myself, will only be a page in history. I cannot help wondering what kind of page it will be, whether we are hourly, in this country now, recording our salvation or our doom.

I can tell from the way Haley looks at me that he knows that *I* am feeling rather caustic and embittered today. I wonder how *he* feels. I know that he is afraid of losing his job. I admire him much more than I can say for playing so quietly a chips-down game.

Haley goes off to give his exam and I walk outside, waiting for my taxi and watching the students. Only a decade and a half divide us, but what changes have occurred in those fifteen years! The world into which I was born must seem as remote to them as the flood. I watch them. Their walk, talk, laughter are as familiar to me as my skin, and yet there is something new about them. They remind me of all the Negro boys and girls I have ever known and they remind me of myself; but, really, I was never like these students. It took many years of vomiting up all the filth I'd been taught about myself, and half-believed, before I was able to walk on the earth as though I had a right to be here.

Well, they didn't have to come the way I came. This is what I've heard Negro parents say, with a kind of indescribable pride and relief, when one of their children graduated or won an award or sailed for Europe: began, in short, to move into the world as a free person. The society into which American Negro children are born has always presented a particular challenge to Negro parents. This society makes it necessary that they establish in the child a force that will cause him to *know* that the world's definition of his place and the means used by the world to make this definition binding are not for a moment to be respected. This means that the parent must prove daily, in his own person, how little the force of the world avails against the force of a person who is determined to be free. Now, this is a cruel challenge, for the force of the world is immense. That is why the vow *My children won't come like I came* is nothing less than a declaration of war, a declaration that has led to innumerable casualties. Generations of Negro children have said, as all the students here have said: "My Daddy taught me never to bow my head to nobody."

But sometimes Daddy's head was bowed: frequently Daddy was destroyed.

These students were born at the very moment at which Europe's domination of Africa was ending. I remember, for example, the invasion of Ethiopia and Haile Selassie's vain appeal to the League of Nations, but they remember the Bandung Conference and the establishment of the Republic of Ghana.

Americans keep wondering what has "got into" the students. What has "got into" them is their history in this country. They are not the first Negroes to face mobs: they are merely the first Negroes to frighten the mob more than the mob frightens them. Many Americans may have forgotten, for example, the reign of terror in the 1920's that drove Negroes out of the South. Five hundred thousand moved North in one year. Some of the people who got to the North barely in time to be born are the parents of the students now going to school. This was forty years ago, and not enough has happened—not enough freedom has happened. But these young people are determined to make it happen and make it happen now. They cannot be diverted. It seems to me that they are the only people in this country now who really believe in freedom. Insofar as they can make it real for themselves, they will make it real for all of us. The question with which they present the nation is whether or not we really want to be free. It is because these students remain so closely related to their past that they are able to face with such authority a population ignorant of its history and enslaved by a myth. And by this population I do not mean merely the unhappy people who make up the Southern mobs. I have in mind nearly all Americans.

These students prove unmistakably what most people in this country have yet to discover: that time is real.

Mademoiselle, August 1960

The Negro Revolt Against "The Negro Leaders"

by Louis E. Lomax

As Pastor Kelly Miller Smith walked to the lectern to begin his Sunday sermon, he knew his parishioners wanted and needed more than just another spiritual message. The congregation—most of them middle-class Americans, many of them university students and faculty members—sat before him waiting, tense: for Nashville, like some thirty-odd other Southern college towns, on that first Sunday in March of this year, was taut with racial tension in the wake of widespread student demonstrations against lunch-counter discrimination in department stores.

Among the worshipers in Pastor Smith's First Baptist Church were some of the eighty-five students from Fisk and from Tennessee Agricultural and Industrial University who had been arrested and charged with conspiracy to obstruct trade and commerce because they staged protests in several of Nashville's segregated eating places. Just two days before, Nashville police had invaded Mr. Smith's church—which also served as headquarters for the demonstrators—and arrested one of their number, James Lawson, Jr., a Negro senior theological student at predominantly white Vanderbilt University, on the same charge.

The adult members of the congregation were deeply troubled. They knew, as did Negroes all over America, that the spontaneous and uncorrelated student demonstrations were more than an attack on segregation: they were proof that the Negro leadership class, epitomized by the National Association for the Advancement of Colored People, was no longer the prime mover of the Negro's social revolt.

Each protest had a character of its own, tailored to the local goals it sought to achieve. Neither the advice nor the aid of recognized Negro leaders was sought until after the students had set the policy, engaged the enemy, and joined the issue. Despite the probability that the demonstrations would be met with violence, the students took direct action, something Negro leadership organizations consistently counseled against. By forcing these organizations not only to come to their aid but to do their bidding, these militant young people completely reversed the power flow within the Negro community.

"Father forgive them," Mr. Smith began, *"for they know not what they do."* And for the next half-hour, the Crucifixion of Christ carried this meaning as he spoke:

"The students sat at the lunch counters alone to eat and, when refused service, to wait and pray. And as they sat there on that southern Mount of Olives, the Roman soldiers, garbed in the uniforms of Nashville policemen and wielding night sticks, came and led the praying children away. As they walked down the streets, through a red light, and toward Golgotha, the segregationist mob shouted jeers, pushed and shoved them, and spat in their faces, but the suffering students never said a mumbling word. Once the martyr mounts the Cross, wears the crown of thorns, and feels the pierce of the sword in his side there is no turning back.

"And there is no turning back for those who follow in the martyr's steps," the minister continued. *"All we can do is to hold fast to what we believe, suffer what we must suffer if we would win, and as we face our enemy let us say, 'Father, forgive them, for they know not what they do'."*

This new gospel of the American Negro is rooted in the theology of desegregation; its major prophets are Christ, Thoreau, Gandhi, and Martin Luther King. But its missionaries are several thousand Negro students who—like Paul, Silas, and Peter of the early Christian era—are braving incalculable dangers and employing new techniques to spread the faith. It is not an easy faith, for it names the conservative Negro leadership class as sinners along with the segregationists. Yet, this new gospel is being preached by clergymen and laymen alike wherever Negroes gather.

Negro businessman John Brooks temporarily deserted his place in a picket line around Thalhimers department store, in Richmond, to make this comment to newsmen:

"The Bible says, 'A little child shall lead them,' but it didn't say these children should have to drag us. We should willingly follow these young people's example. I am suggesting that mothers picket one day, ministers the next, doctors the next, and so on until we bring segregation to its knees."

And all over the South the Negro masses said, "Amen." So ran the litany as the once reluctant elders walked and shouted in cadence behind their offspring. Without doubt, the students had delivered a telling blow against the centralization of Negro leadership.

The demonstrators have shifted the desegregation battle from the courtroom to the market place, and have shifted the main issue to one of individual dignity, rather than civil rights. Not that civil rights are unimportant—but, as these students believe, once the dignity of the Negro individual is admitted, the debate over his right to vote, attend public schools, or hold a job for which he is qualified becomes academic.

Thus, the Negro question, as Tocqueville called it, comes full circle, back to where it started late in the seventeenth century when Christian and puritan America, supported by a good deal of spurious scholarship, downgraded the Negro from villenage (a state he shared with the entire servant class of that era) to slavery, by arguing the inferiority of the Negro as a human being—a soul to be saved, most certainly, but a being somewhat lower than the white Christian with respect to the angels. This concept endured during Reconstruction in the South after the Civil War and formed the foundation upon which the complex and sometimes contradictory structure of segregation was built.

Negro leaders spent seventy-five years remodeling that structure, trying to make it more livable by removing such horrible reminders of the past as lynchings, denial of the ballot, restrictive covenants in housing, and inequalities of public facilities. Only after the intractable Deep South emasculated every move toward equalization did the Negro leadership class sue for school integration. Even then it was a segmented, room-by-room assault. But these student demonstrators have —in effect—put dynamite at the cornerstone of segregation and lit the fuse.

This revolt, swelling under ground for the past two

decades, means the end of the traditional Negro leadership class. Local organization leaders were caught flat-footed by the demonstrations: the parade had moved off without them. In a series of almost frantic moves this spring, they lunged to the front and shouted loud, but they were scarcely more than a cheering section—leaders no more. The students completed their bold maneuver by jabbing the leadership class in its most vulnerable spot: the Southern schoolteachers. Many of these, as the Norfolk *Journal and Guide* put it, "were ordered to stop the demonstrations or else!" Most Negro school administrators kept silent on the matter: a few of them, largely heads of private colleges, supported the students; while others —notably Dr. H. C. Trenholm of Alabama State College— were forced by white politicians to take action against the students. As a Negro reporter from New York, I talked with scores of Southern Negro leaders and they admitted without exception that the local leadership class was in dire difficulty.

National leadership organizations fared only slightly better. The NAACP rushed its national youth secretary, Herbert Wright, into the area to conduct "strategy and procedure" conferences for the students.* Lester Granger, the executive director of the Urban League, issued a statement saying the demonstrations were "therapeutic for those engaged in them and a solemn warning to the nation at large"—this despite the fact that, in Mr. Granger's words, "the League does not function in the area of public demonstrations."

The NAACP does not always move with such swiftness when local groups, some of them laced with NAACP members, set off independent attacks on racial abuse. The Montgomery bus boycott is a classic case in point. But the impact of these new student demonstrations was such that the NAACP was forced to support the students or face a revolt by its Southern rank and file. This does not impeach the NAACP's motives for entering the demonstrations—its motives and

---

*The NAACP was not the first organization to offer aid to the students. At the invitation of Dr. George Simkins, president of the Greensboro, North Carolina, NAACP branch, the Congress of Racial Equality (CORE) sent field workers to the scene several days before the NAACP moved into action. An unimpeachable source told me that Dr. Simkins has been severely criticized by NAACP officials for this.

work have the greatest merit—but it does illustrate the reversal of the power flow within the Negro community.

"The demonstrations are not something we planned," NAACP public-relations director Henry Moon told me. "The students moved on their own. We didn't know what was going on until it happened. However, it should be kept in mind that many of the students involved are NAACP people."

The NAACP's frank admission that it had no part in planning a demonstration against segregation that resulted in upwards of a thousand Negroes being jailed—coupled with its prompt defense of the demonstrators—marks the end of the great era of the Negro leadership class: a half-century of fiercely guarded glory, climaxed by the historic school desegregation decision of 1954, during which the NAACP by dint of sheer militancy, brains, and a strong moral cause became the undisputed commander-in-chief of the Negro's drive for equality. These demonstrations also ended a two-century-long *modus vivendi* based on the myth of the Negro leader.

The phrase "Negro leadership class" pops up, Minerva-like, in most histories and essays about the Negro. White writers generally take its validity for granted, but Negro writers, of late, when they speak analytically of the Negro leader, do so with contempt.

The myth of a Black Moses, the notion that Negroes had or needed a leader, began to take shape in the early years of the nation when a troubled America viewed the Negro as an amorphous mass undulating in the wilderness of ignorance rather than as individuals, each to be dealt with purely on merit. When the myth took on flesh, the Negro leader had the provincial outlook of the white community that fashioned him: in the pre-Civil War North, Frederick Douglass, leading his people out of slavery; in the South, the plantation preacher.

Had Emancipation meant that the Negro would become just another of the racial strains to be absorbed into the American melting pot, the myth of the Negro leader would have evaporated. But as Abraham Lincoln so clearly stated, this is precisely what Emancipation did not mean. Consequently, the myth not only continued but took on even greater significance.

There were three chief prerequisites for becoming a Negro leader: (1) approbation of the white community, (2) literacy (real or assumed), and (3) some influence over the Negro masses. Each community spawned an array of "professors," "doctors" (not medical men), "preachers," "bishops," "spokesmen" who sat down at the segregated arbitration table and conducted business in the name of the Negro masses.

These leaders received their credentials and power both from the white community and from the Negro masses, who stood humble before their white-appointed leaders. This status was heady stuff for the early twentieth-century Negro elite, many of whom could remember the snap of the master's whip, and they began to function as a social class. As a result, three generations of educated Negroes dreamed of an equal but separate America in which white power spoke only to black power and black power spoke only to God, if even to Him.

But the Negro leadership class has produced some practical and positive results: the concept provided America with an easy way of doing business with a people it had wronged and did not understand; it provided a platform for talented Negroes—many of whom were dedicated to the interests of the masses. During the last three decades, however, Negro leadership organizations, based in the North and with a national approach to the Negro's problem, eclipsed the local leaders. The heads of these organizations assumed the general title of "Leader of Leaders."

The NAACP rose in power during the decade of the 'forties by winning a series of court victories which broke down restrictive covenants and ordered Southern states to equalize the salaries of Negro and white schoolteachers and the facilities of Negro and white public schools. Its position was further strengthened when the Urban League fell into disfavor, as far as Negroes were concerned, because of its reluctance to give aid to Negro labor unionists. Then, in 1949, two of the Negro members of the League's board of directors resigned, claiming that white real-estate operators controlled the League.

The NAACP, on the other hand, saw the sign in the sky and was more definite in its support of the Negro labor unionists. As a result, the NAACP also eclipsed A. Philip Randolph and his Pullman porters' union—the third of the "Big Three" Negro leadership organizations—and at mid-century it stood atop the heap.

But the NAACP's main ally was the upsurge of freedom that swept the world in the wake of Nazism and in the face of Communism. Far-reaching social change was in the air. It *could* happen here. Who would bring it? How? The NAACP had the center of the stage; its position was based on solid performance; Negroes—smarting under the charge that they forever fight among themselves—closed ranks around "Twenty West Fortieth Street," the New York headquarters of the NAACP.

And so a curtain was lowered between the opponents and the advocates of a broader desegregation. It was a sham curtain, to be sure, for there was no unity on either side. But for the Negro, as has been true so often in the past, the well-reasoned lie worked. Negro writers, clergymen, schoolteachers, lawyers, social workers—all who commanded a public platform—agreed without conspiring that we would not disagree in public with the NAACP. Many of us felt that the NAACP was too committed to legalism: not committed enough to direct action by local people. There was an endless parade in and out of the NAACP's national office of Negroes who felt that the desegregation fight should take on a broader base. But until the spring of 1958, four years after the school desegregation decision, not a single desegregation-minded Negro engaged in serious open debate with the NAACP. Even then, unfortunately, the debate came in terms of personalities rather than policy.

The decade of the 'fifties was an incredible era for the Negro leadership class, particularly for the NAACP. That the NAACP hung together at all is a monument to its vitality as well as to the effectiveness of its muffling curtain.

First off, by suing for school integration the NAACP immobilized the majority of the Negro leadership class. The entire structure of the Negro community was designed to function in a separate but equal America. Negro newspapers, in addition to being protest organs, were the social Bibles of Negro society. They had their "400" and a list of the year's best-dressed women. The Negro church was ofttimes more Negro than church. Negro businesses depended upon the concept of a Negro community for survival (as late as 1958 Negro businessmen in Detroit criticized the NAACP for holding its annual convention at a "white" downtown hotel, which meant that local Negro merchants failed to benefit from the gathering). The dilemma of the Negro teacher was even more agonizing. If Negroes really meant business about integration, then it was obvious that the Negro leadership class could remain leaders only by working to put themselves out of business.

To this one must add the internal problems of the NAACP itself. In 1948–49, Walter White, then the executive secretary of the NAACP, divorced his Negro wife and married Poppy Cannon, a white woman. This brought on an organizational crisis that might have resulted in ruin if the board of directors had not given Mr. White a year's leave of absence. Nobody expected Mr. White to return to his post and Roy Wilkins, who had been Mr. White's loyal assistant for almost twenty years, turned in an excellent performance as acting executive secretary. But the following spring Mr. White did return. Another organizational crisis was averted by making him secretary of external affairs and Mr. Wilkins secretary of internal affairs. Things remained that way until 1955, when Mr. White died. Nor was that the only separatist movement going on within the NAACP. Since 1939 the entity known to the public as the NAACP has actually been two organizations: the NAACP, headed by the late Walter White and now by Roy Wilkins, and the NAACP Legal Defense and Education Fund, headed by Thurgood Marshall.

The initial reason for the separation was to provide tax relief for contributors to the Legal Defense and Education Fund, which functions solely as a legal redress organization. The NAACP, on the other hand, maintains a lobby in Washington and so its contributors are not entitled to tax exemptions. For fifteen years, however, the two organizations

maintained quarters in the same building and shared an interlocking directorate. In 1952 the Legal Defense and Education
Fund moved to separate quarters and in 1955 the interlocking
directorate was ended. The tax matter aside, the cleavage
came about as a result of deep internal troubling, the details
of which are still in the domain of "no comment." In the
midst of all this, Mrs. Franklin D. Roosevelt left the NAACP
board for reasons that have never been fully disclosed.

The lynching of Emmett Till in Mississippi produced yet
another crisis for the Negro leadership class. Mrs. Mamie
Bradley, Till's mother, became a *cause célèbre* and Negro leadership organizations became locked in a bitter struggle over
just where Mrs. Bradley would speak and under whose auspices. But even before Mrs. Bradley started her speaking tour
there was the famous Chicago wash-pot incident. Till's body
lay in state in a Chicago funeral home: somehow—nobody,
including the funeral director, knows just how—a wash pot
covered with fine chicken wire was placed at the head of the
bier. Thousands of Negroes filed by to see the grim remains,
and as they passed they dropped money in the wash pot. How
many times the pot was filled and emptied, nobody knows:
nobody knows where the money went. I was among the
newsmen who went to check the wash-pot story but when we
got there the pot, complete with chicken wire and money,
had vanished.

After the funeral, Mrs. Bradley embarked on an NAACP-
sponsored speaking tour, traveling by air, with secretary. Bitter disputes about money raised during her appearances came
from all sections and her tour finally petered out.

Nevertheless, these were glamorous years for successful
Negroes; almost all got the title of Negro leader. Their
names and faces appeared on ads endorsing soap, cigarettes,
whiskeys, and ladies' personal items. Adam Clayton Powell
endured in Congress, always reminding his flock that, some
ten years earlier, he was the first Negro to call the late Senator
Theodore Bilbo, of Mississippi, a "cesspool"; Paul Robeson
called a press conference and announced that Negroes would
not fight with America against Russia; Jackie Robinson took a
day off from the Brooklyn Dodgers to assure the House Un-
American Activities Committee that Mr. Robeson was wrong.

Indeed we would fight. Joe Louis, who had dispelled doubts during the dark days of Dunkirk by proclaiming, "America will win 'cause God is on our side," made an all-expense-paid visit to a Washington, D.C., courtroom and embraced the defendant, James Hoffa, in full view of the jury, peppered with Negroes. Father Divine announced that he brought about integration, and he had a white wife to prove it!

These incidents—some humorous, some tragic, but all of them significant—had a grave impact on the Negro leadership class; a less stout-hearted group would have exploded from so much internal combustion. But it was the tense drama of school integration that provided the bailing wire for a show of unity.

I was there and it was a moving and unforgettable experience to see Negro students at Clinton, Sturgis, Clay, and Little Rock dodge bricks as they raced to and from school under armed guard. It was a magnificent hour for these fortuitously elite youngsters, many of whom became international heroes. But few of us lost sight of the Negro masses in these cities. They were still called "Jim," "Mary," "Aunt Harriet," and "Uncle Job"; they had to buy clothes they were not allowed to try on; their homes were searched by police without warrants; their heads were bloodied, their jobs threatened if they dared protest. They darted in and out of drug and department stores where they dared not sit down. They were denied free access to the polls, and if they received a just day in court it was usually when all parties concerned were Negroes.

Despite the march of well-scrubbed, carefully selected Negro students into previously all-white schools, it was crystal clear that the fundamental question of the Negro's dignity as an individual had not been resolved. The glory was the NAACP's and nobody begrudged it. Yet, there was a widespread doubt that a nationally directed battle of attrition that took so long and cost so much to bring so little to so few would ever get to the heart of the issue.

There were many local heroes during the decade of the 'fifties: they all had a brief hour, were clasped to the breasts of national leadership organizations, but when their public-relations and fund-raising value slipped they fell into disuse.

Mrs. Daisy Bates, president of the Arkansas State NAACP and the undisputed moving spirit behind the integration of Little Rock's Central High School, affords an example of life behind the monolithic curtain.

The Spingarn Medal of 1958, voted annually by the NAACP to the person or persons who have contributed most to racial advancement during the previous year, was awarded to the Little Rock Nine. When the students received notice of the award and realized that it did not include Mrs. Bates—whose home had been bombed, her business destroyed—they rejected the citation. The powers-that-be at Twenty West Fortieth Street reversed themselves and Mrs. Bates was included in the award, which she and the students accepted with full smiles, amid thunderous ovations. The Negro press reported the Bates case in great detail and interpreted the incident as overt evidence of the covert pressure the NAACP had been exerting on local Negro leaders for some time.

The curtain had begun to lift; it had achieved a great good, for it had produced a façade of unity; yet it had cloaked some terrible wrongs, including the smothering of home-grown, local Negro leaders who, even then, sensed the restlessness of the masses. The Reverend Dr. Martin Luther King, Jr., was the lone successful exception, and even he came into international prominence mainly because the NAACP refused to help the Montgomery bus boycotters when they at first demanded something less than full integration.

Acting on pleas from Negroes in other Southern communities, Dr. King organized the Southern Christian Leadership Council (the organization has undergone several name changes but this is the current one) to instigate non-violent protests in Southern cities. The NAACP has a most active program all through the South and a clash between the two organizations—that is to say, Dr. King and Mr. Wilkins—seemed inevitable. To end rumors of a power struggle between them, Dr. King flew to New York and made a public show of purchasing life memberships in the NAACP for himself and his Montgomery Improvement Association. Dr. King and Mr. Wilkins then embarked on a series of infrequent private talks that may go down in history as the Negro leadership class's great and final hour.

The King-Wilkins talks of 1957–58 undoubtedly covered the issue of just who would do what and where, but central in the discussion was the common knowledge that many NAACP members were disenchanted with Wilkins' leadership. The two men came out from the talks as one, each co-sponsoring the activities of the other's organization.

Dr. King and Mr. Wilkins joined also with A. Philip Randolph to sponsor the highly successful Washington Prayer Pilgrimage of 1957, during which Dr. King emerged, to quote editor James Hicks, of the *Amsterdam News*, "as the number-one Negro leader." But the following year King and Wilkins ignored the sentiments of some five hundred Negro spokesmen, representing three hundred leadership organizations, at the Summit Meeting of Negro Leadership and gave their reluctant endorsement to the Senate's watered-down civil-rights proposal. The Negro press reacted with shock.

The criticism was even worse when, a few months later, King, Wilkins, and Randolph met with President Eisenhower to explain why Negroes were displeased with the first civil-rights bill to be passed in eighty-three years. The *Afro-American*'s Louis Lautier wrote: "Ike charmed the Negro leaders and neither of them uttered a word of criticism."

Little Rock kept the NAACP in the foreground, while a near-fatal stiletto wound at the hands of a crazed Harlem woman—and internal difficulties with his own Montgomery Association—rendered Dr. King almost inactive for some eighteen months. But this year, Dr. King moved to Atlanta and began to give the lion's share of his time to the Southern Christian Leadership Council. Mr. Wilkins was on hand and the NAACP appeared as co-sponsor when the Council launched a South-wide voting drive on behalf of the Negro masses.

In one sense it was 1958 all over again. Congress was locked in a civil-rights debate that we all knew would culminate in some kind of legislation. Both Dr. King and Mr. Wilkins were on hand backstage as liberal Congressmen planned their moves. But in another, perhaps more significant, sense the early months of this year were unlike 1958. Negroes, particularly the youth, were restless: they were tired of compromises, piecemeal legislation, and token integration which, as Martin Luther

King phrased it, "is a new form of discrimination covered up with certain niceties and complexities." A small but growing segment of the Negro population had joined a Muslim faith that preaches the superiority of the black man and the imminent destruction of the white man. Then there is the matter of Africa: hardly a week passes that that awakening giant's cries for "Free DOOM" don't ring out over the radio and television into the ears of American Negroes—ashamed, as they most certainly are, that they are still oppressed. The law, particularly in the South, was against them; but for the militant young people this was the time for all good Negroes to be in jail.

Meanwhile the Negro leadership class—itself often guilty of rank, class, and color discrimination—was continuing to operate under a concept that begged the question of the dignity of the Negro individual. The literature of Negro progress is littered with such terms as "the talented tenth," "the exceptional Negro," "the new Negro," "the break-through Negro," and in recent years "the accepted" and "the assimilated Negro." Sharing the outlook of the white liberals who finance them, and sincerely so, Negro leadership organizations have focused their attention, by and large, on matters that are of interest to the talented Negro rather than the Negro masses. By so doing the Negro leadership class ignored the basic problem of human dignity in favor of themselves and their white peers—a distinction which the segregationists refused to accept. Thus an impassable void has separated the leaders of both sides for the past decade; and the ordinary Negro has been in the no man's land between.

The lunch-counter demonstrations moved to the center of the void, and menaced both principals: the recalcitrant South, by striking closer to the heart of segregation than any other widespread local movements have ever struck before; the Negro leadership class by exposing its impotence.

The Negro leadership class, still torn by jealousy, dissension, and power struggles, rushed to the aid of the students and their mass supporters, and attempted to make complete recovery by "correlating" and "co-ordinating" the movements. But as one Southern NAACP branch president said to me, "how can I correlate something when I don't know where and when it's going to happen?"

I found that established leaders don't have the same fire in their stomachs that the students and the rallying Negro masses have. As the Southern Regional Council interim report on the demonstrations reflects, Southern leaders, Negro and white, are saying, "Before this happened we could have integrated lunch counters. Now it is almost impossible." What the report does not explain is why the lunch counters were not already integrated. This, again, is black power talking to white power about something neither fully understands.

When I talked to the students and their mass supporters I heard them quote the *Wall Street Journal*, of all things, to show that they had hit the segregationists in the pocket-book. I also discovered that in March five Southern cities had already yielded to the demands of the demonstrators and were serving Negroes at lunch counters without incident. Eighteen other cities had interracial committees working to resolve the matter. In each case the students have made it plain that they will not accept segregation in any form.

But neither the students nor their real supporters dwelt unduly on such practical results. For them, individually and as a group, the victory came when they mustered the courage to look the segregationists in the face and say, "I'm no longer afraid!"

The genius of the demonstrations lies in their spirituality; in their ability to enlist every Negro, from the laborer to the leader, and inspire him to seek suffering as a badge of honor. By employing such valid symbols as singing, praying, reading Gandhi, quoting Thoreau, remembering Martin Luther King, preaching Christ, but most of all by suffering themselves—being hit by baseball bats, kicked, and sent to jail—the students set off an old-fashioned revival that has made integration an article of faith with the Negro masses who, like other masses, are apathetic toward voting and education.

Now the cook, the maid, the butler, and the chauffeur are on fire with the new faith. For the first time since slavery the South is facing a mass revolt against segregation. There is no total explanation for what has happened. All I know is that as I talked with the participants I realized that people were weary of the very fact of segregation. They were no longer content "to let the NAACP do it"; they wanted to get into the fight and they chose the market place, the great center of American egalitarianism, not because it had any overwhelming significance for them but because it was there—accessible and segregated. Tomorrow—and they all believe there will be a tomorrow—their target will be something else.

Few of the masses who have come to the support of these students realize that in attacking segregation under the banner of idealism they are fighting a battle they refused for five years to enter in the name of legalism. But there is a twinkle in the Southern Negro's eye. One gets the feeling that he is proud, now that he has come to full stature and has struck out with one blow against both segregation and the stifling control of Negro leaders.

In all truth, the Negro masses have never been flattered by the presence of these leaders, many of whom—justifiably or not—they suspected were Judas goats. The Negro masses will name leaders and will give them power and responsibility. But there will never again be another class of white-oriented leaders such as the one that has prevailed since 1900.

For the Negro masses this is the laying down of a heavy burden. As the deep South is slowly learning, it faces a race of Negro *individuals*—any of whom, acting out of deep religious faith, may at any moment choose the most available evidence of segregation and stage a protest. And when he does the entire Negro community will close ranks about him.

If Negro leadership organizations accept this verdict of change gracefully they can find a continuing usefulness as a reservoir of trained personnel to aid the local Negro in pressure techniques and legal battles. Indeed, within four weeks after the lunch-counter demonstrations began, just such a pattern was established. I have investigated the mechanics of the demonstrations in twenty-six cities and in each instance I found that the students and their local supporters moved first on their own; CORE came in by invitation and provided classes in techniques of non-violence; and the NAACP provided lawyers and bondsmen for those who were arrested. If Negro leadership organizations don't accept this state of affairs, they will be replaced, as they were in Montgomery.

Thurgood Marshall and the NAACP Legal Defense and Education Fund have already set an excellent pattern which other leadership organizations will do well to study. As a symbol, Mr. Marshall inspires local citizens to act; when they do act, and at their request, Marshall brings the skill of his organization to their defense. Thurgood Marshall's role as the inspiring servant of the masses accounts for much of what has been accomplished to date in and for the United States—including his appearance in London as counsel to the Kenya natives.

Negro leadership organizations know what the revolt means and are about reconciled to being servants rather than catalysts—at least I think so. I cannot say the same for the Negro leadership class as a whole. My month-long investigation unearthed a good deal of foot-dragging by moneyed Negroes in high places. They are not too pleased to see young Negro students sit down at the conference table with Southern white city officials. Some Negro college presidents are set to execute strange maneuvers. I would not be surprised, for example, if some of the student demonstrators who are studying under grants from foundations suddenly find their scholarships have been canceled on recommendation from their college presidents . . . for "poor scholarship." But nobody noticed their scholarship until they sat down at a previously all-white lunch counter.

The student demonstrators have no illusions. They know the segregationists are not their only enemies. But the students told me they are not prejudiced—they are willing to stand up to their enemies, Negro and white alike.

It is not premature, then, to write this epitaph to the Negro leader while at the same time announcing the birth of the Negro individual. The christening has already begun; the funeral is yet a few days off. This is as it should be, America being committed, as it most certainly is, to orderly social transition. But there is no reason whatsoever to doubt that both events will come off on schedule.

Harper's, June 1960

Fifth Avenue, Uptown:
A Letter from Harlem

by James Baldwin

THERE is a housing project standing now where the house in which we grew up once stood, and one of those stunted city trees is snarling where our doorway used to be. This is on the rehabilitated side of the avenue. The other side of the avenue —for progress takes time—has not been rehabilitated yet and it looks exactly as it looked in the days when we sat with our noses pressed against the windowpane, longing to be allowed to go "across the street." The grocery store which gave us credit is still there, and there can be no doubt that it is still giving credit. The people in the project certainly need it—far more, indeed, than they ever needed the project. The last time I passed by, the Jewish proprietor was still standing among his shelves, looking sadder and heavier but scarcely any older. Farther down the block stands the shoe-repair store in which our shoes were repaired until reparation became impossible and in which, then, we bought all our "new" ones. The Negro proprietor is still in the window, head down, working at the leather.

These two, I imagine, could tell a long tale if they would (perhaps they would be glad to if they could), having watched so many, for so long, struggling in the fishhooks, the barbed wire, of this avenue.

The avenue is elsewhere the renowned and elegant Fifth. The area I am describing, which, in today's gang parlance, would be called "the turf," is bounded by Lenox Avenue on the west, the Harlem River on the east, 135th Street on the north, and 130th Street on the south. We never lived beyond these boundaries; this is where we grew up. Walking along 145th Street—for example—familiar as it is, and similar, does not have the same impact because I do not know any of the people on the block. But when I turn east on 131st Street and

Lenox Avenue, there is first a soda-pop joint, then a shoeshine "parlor," then a grocery store, then a dry cleaners', then the houses. All along the street there are people who watched me grow up, people who grew up with me, people I watched grow up along with my brothers and sisters; and, sometimes in my arms, sometimes underfoot, sometimes at my shoulder—or on it—their children, a riot, a forest of children, who include my nieces and nephews.

When we reach the end of this long block, we find ourselves on wide, filthy, hostile Fifth Avenue, facing that project which hangs over the avenue like a monument to the folly, and the cowardice, of good intentions. All along the block, for anyone who knows it, are immense human gaps, like craters. These gaps are not created merely by those who have moved away, inevitably into some other ghetto; or by those who have risen, almost always into a greater capacity for self-loathing and self-delusion; or yet by those who, by whatever means—War II, the Korean war, a policeman's gun or billy, a gang war, a brawl, madness, an overdose of heroin, or, simply, unnatural exhaustion—are dead. I am talking about those who are left, and I am talking principally about the young. What are they doing? Well, some, a minority, are fanatical churchgoers, members of the more extreme of the Holy Roller sects. Many, many more are "moslems," by affiliation or sympathy, that is to say that they are united by nothing more—and nothing less—than a hatred of the white world and all its works. They are present, for example, at every Buy Black street-corner meeting—meetings in which the speaker urges his hearers to cease trading with white men and establish a separate economy. Neither the speaker nor his hearers can possibly do this, of course, since Negroes do not own General Motors or RCA or the A & P, nor, indeed, do they own more than a wholly insufficient fraction of anything else in Harlem (those who *do* own anything are more interested in their profits than in their fellows). But these meetings nevertheless keep alive in the participators a certain pride of bitterness without which, however futile this bitterness may be, they could scarcely remain alive at all. Many have given up. They stay home and watch the TV screen, living on the earnings of their parents, cousins, brothers, or uncles, and only leave the house to go to the movies or to the nearest bar. "How're you making it?" one may ask, running into them along the block, or in the bar. "Oh, I'm TV-ing it"; with the saddest, sweetest, most shamefaced of smiles, and from a great distance. This distance one is compelled to respect; anyone who has traveled so far will not easily be dragged again into the world. There are further retreats, of course, than the TV screen or the bar. There are those who are simply sitting on their stoops, "stoned," animated for a moment only, and hideously, by the approach of someone who may lend them the money for a "fix." Or by the approach of someone from whom they can purchase it, one of the shrewd ones, on the way to prison or just coming out.

And the others, who have avoided all of these deaths, get up in the morning and go downtown to meet "the man." They work in the white man's world all day and come home in the evening to this fetid block. They struggle to instill in their children some private sense of honor or dignity which will help the child to survive. This means, of course, that they must struggle, stolidly, incessantly, to keep this sense alive in themselves, in spite of the insults, the indifference, and the cruelty they are certain to encounter in their working day. They patiently browbeat the landlord into fixing the heat, the plaster, the plumbing; this demands prodigious patience; nor is patience usually enough. In trying to make their hovels habitable, they are perpetually throwing good money after bad. Such frustration, so long endured, is driving many strong, admirable men and women whose only crime is color to the very gates of paranoia.

One remembers them from another time—playing handball in the playground, going to church, wondering if they were going to be promoted at school.One remembers them going off to war—gladly, to escape this block. One remembers their return. Perhaps one remembers their wedding day. And one sees where the girl is now—vainly looking for salvation from some other embittered, trussed, and struggling boy—and sees the all-but-abandoned children in the streets.

Now I am perfectly aware that there are other slums in which white men are fighting for their lives, and mainly losing. I know that blood is also flowing through those streets and that the human damage there is incalculable. People are continually pointing out to me the wretchedness of white people in order to console me for the wretchedness of blacks. But an itemized account of the American failure does not console me and it should not console anyone else. That hundreds of thousands of white people are living, in effect, no better than the "niggers" is not a fact to be regarded with complacency. The social and moral bankruptcy suggested by this fact is of the bitterest, most terrifying kind.

The people, however, who believe that this democratic anguish has some consoling value are always pointing out that So-and-So, white, and So-and-So, black, rose from the slums into the big time. The existence—the public existence—of, say, Frank Sinatra and Sammy Davis, Jr., proves to them that America is still the land of opportunity and that inequalities vanish before the determined will. It proves nothing of the sort. The determined will is rare—at the moment, in this country, it is unspeakably rare—and the inequalities suffered by the many are in no way justified by the rise of a few. A few have always risen— in every country, every era, and in the teeth of regimes which can by no stretch of the imagination be thought of as free. Not all of these people, it is worth remembering, left the world better than they found it. The determined will is rare, but it is not invariably benevolent. Furthermore, the American equation of success with the big times reveals an awful disrespect for human life and human achievement. This equation has placed our cities among the most dangerous in the world and has placed our youth among the most empty and most bewildered. The situation of our youth is not mysterious. Children have never been very good at listening to their elders, but they have never failed to imitate them. They must, they have no other models. That is exactly what our children are doing. They are imitating our immorality, our disrespect for the pain of others.

All other slum dwellers, when the bank account permits it, can move out of the slum and vanish altogether from the eye of persecution. No Negro in this country has ever made that much money and it will be a long time before any Negro does. The Negroes in Harlem, who have no money, spend what they have on such gimcracks as they are sold. These include "wider" TV screens, more "faithful" hi-fi sets, more "powerful" cars, all of which, of course, are obsolete long before they are paid for. Anyone who has ever struggled with poverty knows how extremely expensive it is to be poor; and if one is a member of a captive population, economically speaking, one's feet have simply been placed on the treadmill forever. One is victimized, economically, in a thousand ways —rent, for example, or car insurance. Go shopping one day in Harlem—for anything—and compare Harlem prices and quality with those downtown.

The people who have managed to get off this block have only got as far as a more respectable ghetto. This respectable ghetto does not even have the advantages of the disreputable one—friends, neighbors, a familiar church, and friendly tradesmen; and it is not, moreover, in the nature of any ghetto to remain respectable long. Every Sunday, people who have left the block take the lonely ride back, dragging their increasingly discontented children with them. They spend the day talking, not always with words, about the trouble they've seen and the trouble—one must watch their eyes as they watch their children—they are only too likely to see. For children do not like ghettos. It takes them nearly no time to discover exactly why they are there.

The projects in Harlem are hated. They are hated almost as much as policemen, and this is saying a great deal. And they are hated for the same reason: both reveal, unbearably, the real attitude of the white world, no matter how many liberal speeches are made, no matter how many lofty editorials are written, no matter how many civil-rights commissions are set up.

The projects are hideous, of course, there being a law, apparently respected throughout the world, that popular housing shall be as cheerless as a prison. They are lumped all over Harlem, colorless, bleak, high, and revolting. The wide windows look out on Harlem's invincible and indescribable squalor; the Park Avenue railroad tracks, around which, about forty years ago, the present dark community began; the unrehabilitated houses, bowed down, it would seem, under the great weight of frustration and bitterness they contain; the dark, the ominous schoolhouses from which the child may emerge maimed, blinded, hooked, or enraged for life; and the churches, churches, block upon block of churches, niched in the walls like cannon in the walls of a fortress. Even if the administration of the projects were not so insanely humiliating (for example: one must report raises in salary to the management, which will then eat up the profit by raising one's rent; the management has the right to know who is staying in your apartment; the management can ask you to leave, at their discretion), the projects would still be hated because they are an insult to the meanest intelligence.

Harlem got its first private project, Riverton*—which is now, naturally, a slum—about twelve years ago because at that time Negroes were not allowed to live in Stuyvesant Town. Harlem watched Riverton go up, therefore, in the most violent bitterness of spirit, and hated it long before the builders arrived. They began hating it at about the time people began moving out of their condemned houses to make room for this additional proof of how thoroughly the white world despised them. And they had scarcely moved in, naturally, before they began smashing windows, defacing walls, urinating in the elevators, and fornicating in the playgrounds. Liberals, both white and black, were appalled at the spectacle. I was appalled by the liberal innocence—or cynicism, which comes out in practice as much the same thing. Other people were delighted to be able to point to proof positive that nothing could be done to better the lot of the colored people. They were, and are, right in one respect: that nothing can be done as long as they are treated like colored people. The people in Harlem know they are living there because white people do not think they are good enough to live anywhere else. No amount of "improvement" can sweeten this fact. Whatever money is now

*The inhabitants of Riverton were much embittered by this description; they have, apparently, forgotten how their project came into being; and have repeatedly informed me that I cannot possibly be referring to Riverton, but to another housing project which is directly across the street. It is quite clear, I think, that I have no interest in accusing any individuals or families of the depredations herein described: but neither can I deny the evidence of my own eyes. Nor do I blame anyone in Harlem for making the best of a dreadful bargain. But anyone who lives in Harlem and imagines that he has *not* struck this bargain, or that what he takes to be his status (in whose eyes?) protects him against the common pain, demoralization, and danger, is simply self-deluded.

being earmarked to improve this, or any other ghetto, might as well be burnt. A ghetto can be improved in one way only: out of existence.

Similarly, the only way to police a ghetto is to be oppressive. None of the Police Commissioner's men, even with the best will in the world, have any way of understanding the lives led by the people they swagger about in twos and threes controlling. Their very presence is an insult, and it would be, even if they spent their entire day feeding gumdrops to children. They represent the force of the white world, and that world's real intentions are, simply, for that world's criminal profit and ease, to keep the black man corraled up here, in his place. The badge, the gun in the holster, and the swinging club make vivid what will happen should his rebellion become overt. Rare, indeed, is the Harlem citizen, from the most circumspect church member to the most shiftless adolescent, who does not have a long tale to tell of police incompetence, injustice, or brutality. I myself have witnessed and endured it more than once. The businessmen and racketeers also have a story. And so do the prostitutes. (And this is not, perhaps, the place to discuss Harlem's very complex attitude toward black policemen, nor the reasons, according to Harlem, that they are nearly all downtown.)

It is hard, on the other hand, to blame the policeman, blank, good-natured, thoughtless, and insuperably innocent, for being such a perfect representative of the people he serves. He, too, believes in good intentions and is astounded and offended when they are not taken for the deed. He has never, himself, done anything for which to be hated—which of us has?—and yet he is facing, daily and nightly, people who would gladly see him dead, and he knows it. There is no way for him not to know it: there are few things under heaven more unnerving than the silent, accumulating contempt and hatred of a people. He moves through Harlem, therefore, like an occupying soldier in a bitterly hostile country; which is precisely what, and where, he is, and is the reason he walks in twos and threes. And he is not the only one who knows why he is always in company: the people who are watching him know why, too. Any street meeting, sacred or secular, which he and his colleagues uneasily cover has as its explicit or im-

plicit burden the cruelty and injustice of the white domination. And these days, of course, in terms increasingly vivid
and jubilant, it speaks of the end of that domination. The
white policeman standing on a Harlem street corner finds
himself at the very center of the revolution now occurring in
the world. He is not prepared for it—naturally, nobody is—
and, what is possibly much more to the point, he is exposed,
as few white people are, to the anguish of the black people
around him. Even if he is gifted with the merest mustard
grain of imagination, something must seep in. He cannot
avoid observing that some of the children, in spite of their
color, remind him of children he has known and loved, perhaps even of his own children. He knows that he certainly
does not want *his* children living this way. He can retreat from
his uneasiness in only one direction: into a callousness which
very shortly becomes second nature. He becomes more callous, the population becomes more hostile, the situation
grows more tense, and the police force is increased. One day,
to everyone's astonishment, someone drops a match in the
powder keg and everything blows up. Before the dust has settled or the blood congealed, editorials, speeches, and civil-
rights commissions are loud in the land, demanding to know
what happened. What happened is that Negroes want to be
treated like men.

Negroes want to be treated like men: a perfectly straightforward statement, containing only seven words. People who
have mastered Kant, Hegel, Shakespeare, Marx, Freud, and
the Bible find this statement utterly impenetrable. The idea
seems to threaten profound, barely conscious assumptions. A
kind of panic paralyzes their features, as though they found
themselves trapped on the edge of a steep place. I once tried
to describe to a very well-known American intellectual the
conditions among Negroes in the South. My recital disturbed
him and made him indignant; and he asked me in perfect innocence, "Why don't all the Negroes in the South move
North?" I tried to explain what *has* happened, unfailingly,
whenever a significant body of Negroes move North. They do
not escape Jim Crow: they merely encounter another, not-
less-deadly variety. They do not move to Chicago, they move
to the South Side; they do not move to New York, they move

to Harlem. The pressure within the ghetto causes the ghetto walls to expand, and this expansion is always violent. White people hold the line as long as they can, and in as many ways as they can, from verbal intimidation to physical violence. But inevitably the border which has divided the ghetto from the rest of the world falls into the hands of the ghetto. The white people fall back bitterly before the black horde; the landlords make a tidy profit by raising the rent, chopping up the rooms, and all but dispensing with the upkeep; and what has once been a neighborhood turns into a "turf." This is precisely what happened when the Puerto Ricans arrived in their thousands—and the bitterness thus caused is, as I write, being fought out all up and down those streets.

Northerners indulge in an extremely dangerous luxury. They seem to feel that because they fought on the right side during the Civil War, and won, they have earned the right merely to deplore what is going on in the South, without taking any responsibility for it; and that they can ignore what is happening in Northern cities because what is happening in Little Rock or Birmingham is worse. Well, in the first place, it is not possible for anyone who has not endured both to know which is "worse." I know Negroes who prefer the South and white Southerners, because "At least there, you haven't got to play any guessing games!" The guessing games referred to have driven more than one Negro into the narcotics ward, the madhouse, or the river. I know another Negro, a man very dear to me, who says, with conviction and with truth, "The spirit of the South is the spirit of America." He was born in the North and did his military training in the South. He did not, as far as I can gather, find the South "worse"; he found it, if anything, all too familiar. In the second place, though, even if Birmingham *is* worse, no doubt Johannesburg, South Africa, beats it by several miles, and Buchenwald was one of the worst things that ever happened in the entire history of the world. The world has never lacked for horrifying examples; but I do not believe that these examples are meant to be used as justification for our own crimes. This perpetual justification empties the heart of all human feeling. The emptier our hearts become, the greater will be our crimes. Thirdly, the South is not merely an embarrassingly backward region, but a part of this country, and what happens there concerns every one of us.

As far as the color problem is concerned, there is but one great difference between the Southern white and the Northerner: the Southerner remembers, historically and in his own psyche, a kind of Eden in which he loved black people and they loved him. Historically, the flaming sword laid across this Eden is the Civil War. Personally, it is the Southerner's sexual coming of age, when, without any warning, unbreakable taboos are set up between himself and his past. Everything, thereafter, is permitted him except the love he remembers and has never ceased to need. The resulting, indescribable torment affects every Southern mind and is the basis of the Southern hysteria.

None of this is true for the Northerner. Negroes represent nothing to him personally, except, perhaps, the dangers of carnality. He never sees Negroes. Southerners see them all the time. Northerners never think about them whereas Southerners are never really thinking of anything else. Negroes are, therefore, ignored in the North and are under surveillance in the South, and suffer hideously in both places. Neither the Southerner nor the Northerner is able to look on the Negro simply as a man. It seems to be indispensable to the national self-esteem that the Negro be considered either as a kind of ward (in which case we are told how many Negroes, comparatively, bought Cadillacs last year and how few, comparatively, were lynched), or as a victim (in which case we are promised that he will never vote in our assemblies or go to school with our kids). They are two sides of the same coin and the South will not change—*cannot* change—until the North changes. The country will not change until it re-examines itself and discovers what it really means by freedom. In the meantime, generations keep being born, bitterness is increased by incompetence, pride, and folly, and the world shrinks around us.

It is a terrible, an inexorable, law that one cannot deny the humanity of another without diminishing one's own: in the face of one's victim, one sees oneself. Walk through the streets of Harlem and see what we, this nation, have become.

from *Nobody Knows My Name* (1961)

Finishing School for Pickets

by Howard Zinn

Atlanta, Ga.

ONE quiet afternoon some weeks ago, with the dogwood on the Spelman College campus newly bloomed and the grass close-cropped and fragrant, an attractive, tawny-skinned girl crossed the lawn to her dormitory to put a notice on the bulletin board. It read: Young Ladies Who Can Picket Please Sign Below.

The notice revealed, in its own quaint language, that within the dramatic revolt of Negro college students in the South today another phenomenon has been developing. This is the upsurge of the young, educated Negro woman against the generations-old advice of her elders: be nice, be well-mannered and ladylike, don't speak loudly, and don't get into trouble. On the campus of the nation's leading college for Negro young women—pious, sedate, encrusted with the traditions of gentility and moderation—these exhortations, for the first time, are being firmly rejected.

Spelman College girls are still "nice," but not enough to keep them from walking up and down, carrying picket signs, in front of two supermarkets in the heart of Atlanta. They are well-mannered, but this is somewhat tempered by a recent declaration that they will use every method short of violence to end segregation. As for staying out of trouble, they were doing fine until this spring, when fourteen of them were arrested and jailed by Atlanta police. The staid New England women missionaries who helped found Spelman College back in the 1880s would probably be distressed at this turn of events, and present-day conservatives in the administration and faculty are rather upset. But respectability is no longer respectable among young Negro women attending college today.

"You can always tell a Spelman girl," alumni and friends of the college have boasted for years. The "Spelman girl" walked gracefully, talked properly, went to church every Sunday, poured tea elegantly and, in general, had all the attributes of the product of a fine finishing school. If intellect and talent and social consciousness happened to develop also, they were, to an alarming extent, by-products.

This is changing. It would be an exaggeration to say: "You can always tell a Spelman girl—she's under arrest." But the statement has a measure of truth. Spelman girls have participated strongly in all of the major actions undertaken by students of the Atlanta University Center* in recent months. They have also added a few touches of their own and made white Atlanta, long proud that its nice Negro college girls were staying "in their place," take startled notice. A few weeks ago a Spelman student, riding downtown on the bus, took a seat up front. (This is still a daring maneuver, for in spite of a court decision desegregating the buses, most Negroes stay in the rear.) The bus driver muttered something unpleasant, and a white woman sitting nearby waved her hand and said, "Oh, she's prob'ly goin' downtown to start another one o' them demonstrations."

The reputedly sweet and gentle Spelman girls were causing trouble even before the recent wave of sit-ins cracked the wall of legalism in the structure of desegregation strategy. Three years ago, they aroused the somnolent Georgia Legislature into near-panic by attempting to sit in the white section of the gallery. They were finally shunted into the colored area, but returned for the next legislative session. This time they refused to sit segregated and remained on their feet, in a pioneering show of non-violent resistance, until ordered out of the chamber.

The massive, twelve-foot stone wall, barbed-wire fence and magnolia trees that encircle the Spelman campus have always formed a kind of chastity belt around the student body, not only confining young women to a semi-monastic life in order

---

*The Atlanta University Center is a loose federation of six privately supported Negro colleges in Atlanta: Morehouse College for men, Spelman College for women, Clark College, Morris College, Atlanta University (the graduate school), and the Interdenominational Theological Center. Spelman gets its name from the mother-in-law of John D. Rockefeller. The older Rockefeller's money put Spelman on its feet.

to uphold the ruling matriarchs' conception of Christian morality, but "protecting" the students from contact with the cruel outside world of segregation. Inside the domain of the Atlanta University Center, with its interracial faculty, occasional white students and frequent white visitors, there flourished a microcosm of the future, where racial barriers did not exist and one could almost forget this was the deep South. But this insulation, while protecting the University Center's island of integration, also kept the city of Atlanta for many years from feeling the barbed resentment of Negro students against segregation. Spelman girls, more sheltered than women at the other colleges, were among the first to leave the island and to begin causing little flurries of alarm in the segregated world outside.

Even before bus segregation in the city was declared illegal, some Spelman girls rode up front and withstood the glares and threats of fellow passengers and the abuse of the bus driver. Once, a white man pulled a knife from his pocket and waved it at a Spelman sophomore sitting opposite him in a front seat. She continued to sit there until she came to her stop, and then got off. Spelman students, along with others, showed up in the main Atlanta library in sufficient numbers last year to worry the city administration into a decision to admit Negroes there. The girls spent hours between classes at the county courthouse, urging Negroes to register for voting. They made a survey of the Atlanta airport in connection with a suit to desegregate the airport restaurant, and a Spelman student took the witness stand at the trial to help win the case.

Such activities may bring bewilderment to the conservative matriarchy which has played a dominant role in the college's history, but they are nothing short of infuriating to the officialdom of the State of Georgia, ensconced inside the gold-domed Capitol just a few minutes' drive from the Negro colleges of the Atlanta University Center. Georgia's bespectacled but still near-sighted Governor Vandiver, who resembles a pleasant and studious junior executive until he begins to speak, began his current burst of hysteria when student leaders at the six Negro colleges put their heads together and produced a remarkable document which was placed as a full-page ad in the Atlanta newspapers on March 9 (and reprinted by *The Nation* on April 2). The document, entitled "An Appeal for Human Rights," catalogued Negro grievances with irritating specificity and promised to "use every legal and nonviolent means at our disposal" to end segregation. Vandiver's reaction was immediate: the appeal was "anti-American" and "obviously not written by students." Furthermore, the Governor said: "It did not sound like it was prepared in any Georgia school or college; nor, in fact, did it read like it was written in this country." Actually, a Spelman student had written the first rough draft, and student leaders from the other five colleges collaborated in preparing the finished product.

On the sixth day after publication of the appeal, at 11:30 on a Tuesday morning, several hundred students from the Atlanta University Center staged one of the South's most carefully planned and efficiently executed sit-in demonstrations at ten different eating places, including restaurants in the State Capitol, the county courthouse and City Hall. Among the demonstrators were several carloads of Spelman students, riding into town that morning without the knowledge of deans or presidents or faculty, to participate in the sit-ins, tangle with the police and end up in prison.

Of the seventy-seven students arrested, fourteen were Spelmanites; and all but one of the fourteen were girls from the deep South, from places like Bennettsville, South Carolina; Bainbridge, Georgia; Ocala, Florida—the Faulknerian small towns of traditional Negro submissiveness.

The Atlanta *Constitution* and the *Journal* noted the remarkable discipline and orderliness of the demonstration. Perhaps their training came in handy; in prison, Spelman girls were perfect ladies. A Spelman honor student sat behind bars quietly reading C. S. Lewis' *The Screwtape Letters*, while flashbulbs popped around her.

The State of Georgia, however, reacted with a special vindictiveness. To the seventy-seven sit-inners, the Fulton County prosecutor has added the names of the six students who wrote and signed "An Appeal for Human Rights." All eighty-three are facing triple charges of breaching the peace, intimidating restaurant owners and refusing to leave the premises, the penalties for which add up to nine years in prison and $6,000 in fines. The use of "conspiracy" charges to tie all eighty-three students to each of the ten eating places creates a theoretical possibility of ninety-year sentences. Nothing is fantastic in this state.

On May 17, to commemorate the 1954 Supreme Court decision, over a thousand students marched through downtown Atlanta to a mass meeting at the Wheat Street Baptist Church, while a hundred hastily summoned state troopers guarded the Capitol a few blocks away with guns, billy clubs and tear gas. The students were heavily armed with books and songs, and when they were assembled in the church sang, "That Old Ne-gro, He Ain't What He Used to Be!"

What is the source of this new spirit which has angered the state administration and unsettled the old guardians of genteel passivity? There is something fundamental at work which is setting free for the first time the anger pent up in generations of quiet, well-bred Negro college women, not only at Spelman College, but at Fisk, Bennett, Alabama State and other institutions throughout the South. The same warm currents which are loosening the ice-blocks of the *status quo* throughout the world are drifting into the South and mingling with local eddies of discontent. What has been called a global "revolution in expectations" rises also in the hearts and minds of Southern Negroes.

Expanding international contacts are reaching even into small Southern colleges. The arrested Spelman girl from Bennettsville, South Carolina, spent last year in Geneva studying international relations, and spent the summer in Soviet Russia. The Atlanta student who helped draft the appeal had just returned from a year of studying music in Paris. Last September, two young African women, under the auspices of the militant Tom Mboya, flew in from Kenya to enroll at Spelman. The tame-sounding phrase "cultural exchange" may have revolutionary political implications.

Like many Negro campuses in the South, Spelman is losing its provincial air. This spring, the first white students came— five girls from Midwestern colleges who are the advance guard of a long-term exchange program. In the past few months there has been a sudden burgeoning of contact, both intellectual and social, with students from the half-dozen white colleges in Atlanta. Liberal Southern whites have joined the faculties of Spelman and Morehouse colleges. This growing interracial contact is helping to break down the mixture of awe-suspicion-hostility with which deep-South Negroes generally regard whites. And for Spelman, unexpressed but obvious pressure to adopt the manners and courtesies of white middle-class society breaks down as Spelman girls get a close look at how whites really behave.

The new Spelman girl is having an effect on faculty and administrators. Many who were distressed and critical when they first learned their sweet young things were sitting behind bars, later joined in the applause of the Negro community and the nation at large. Spelman's President Albert Manley, who inherited the traditions of conservatism and moderation when he took the helm seven years ago, has responded with cautious but increasing encouragement to the boldness of his young women. At the college commencement exercises this year, Manley startled the audience by departing from the printed program and the parade of parting platitudes with a vigorous statement of congratulations to the senior class for breaking the "docile generation" label with its sit-ins, demonstrations and picketing.

Four years ago, a girl in my Western Civilization course spoke candidly and bitterly about her situation and that of her classmates. "When I was little," she said, "my mother told me: remember, you've got two strikes against you—you're colored, and you're a woman; one more strike and you're out—so be careful." The student continued: "That's the trouble with all these Spelman girls. They're careful. They hardly utter a peep. They do everything right, and obey the rules, and they'll be fine ladies some day. But I don't want to be that kind of a lady. I'm leaving at the end of the semester and going back up North."

I don't know where that student is today. She would have graduated with this class on Commencement Day, with students who marched and picketed and sat-in and were arrested, and will soon come up for trial. I wish she had stayed to see.

The Nation, August 6, 1960

"Ain't Those Cheerleaders Something"

by John Steinbeck

W‍HILE I was still in Texas, late in 1960, the incident most reported and pictured in the newspapers was the matriculation of a couple of tiny Negro children in a New Orleans school. Behind these small dark mites were the law's majesty and the law's power to enforce—both the scales and the sword were allied with the infants—while against them were three hundred years of fear and anger and terror of change in a changing world. I had seen photographs in the papers every day and motion pictures on the television screen. What made the newsmen love the story was a group of stout middle-aged women who, by some curious definition of the word "mother," gathered every day to scream invectives at children. Further, a small group of them had become so expert that they were known as the Cheerleaders, and a crowd gathered every day to enjoy and to applaud their performance.

This strange drama seemed so improbable that I felt I had to see it. It had the same draw as a five-legged calf or a two-headed foetus at a sideshow, a distortion of normal life we have always found so interesting that we will pay to see it, perhaps to prove to ourselves that we have the proper number of legs or heads. In the New Orleans show, I felt all the amusement of the improbable abnormal, but also a kind of horror that it could be so.

At this time the winter which had been following my track ever since I left home suddenly struck with a black norther. It brought ice and freezing sleet and sheeted the highways with dark ice. I gathered Charley from the good doctor. He looked half his age and felt wonderful, and to prove it he ran and jumped and rolled and laughed and gave little yips of pure joy. It felt very good to have him with me again, sitting up right in the seat beside me, peering ahead at the unrolling road, or curling up to sleep with his head in my lap and his silly ears available for fondling. That dog can sleep through any amount of judicious caresses.

Now we stopped dawdling and laid our wheels to the road and went. We could not go fast because of the ice, but we drove relentlessly, hardly glancing at the passing of Texas beside us. And Texas was achingly endless—Sweetwater and Balinger and Austin. We bypassed Houston. We stopped for gasoline and coffee and slabs of pie. Charley had his meals and his walks in gas stations. Night did not stop us, and when my eyes ached and burned from peering too long and my shoulders were side hills of pain, I pulled into a turnout and crawled like a mole into my bed, only to see the highway writhe along behind my closed lids. No more than two hours could I sleep, and then out into the bitter cold night and on and on. Water beside the road was frozen solid, and people moved about with shawls and sweaters wrapped around their ears.

Other times I have come to Beaumont dripping with sweat and lusting for ice and air-conditioning. Now Beaumont with all its glare of neon signs was what they called froze up. I went through Beaumont at night, or rather in the dark well after midnight. The blue-fingered man who filled my gas tank looked in at Charley and said, "Hey, it's a dog! I thought you had a nigger in there." And he laughed delightedly. It was the first of many repetitions. At least twenty times I heard it—"Thought you had a nigger in there." It was an unusual joke—always fresh—and never Negro or even Nigra, always Nigger or rather Niggah. That word seemed terribly important, a kind of safety word to cling to lest some structure collapse.

And then I was in Louisiana, with Lake Charles away to the side in the dark, but my lights glittered on ice and glinted on diamond frost, and those people who forever trudge the roads at night were mounded over with cloth against the cold. I dogged it on through La Fayette and Morgan City and came in the early dawn to Houma, which is pronounced Homer and is in my memory one of the pleasantest places in the world. There lives my old friend Doctor St. Martin, a gentle, learned man, a Cajun who has lifted babies and cured colic among the shell-heap Cajuns for miles around. I guess he knows more about Cajuns than anyone living, but I remembered with longing other gifts of Doctor St. Martin. He makes the best and most subtle martini in the world by a process approximating magic. The only part of his formula I know is that he uses distilled water for his ice and distills it himself to be sure. I have eaten black duck at his table—two St. Martin martinis and a brace of black duck with a burgundy delivered from the bottle as a baby might be delivered, and this in a darkened house where the shades have been closed at dawn and the cool night air preserved. At that table with its silver soft and dull, shining as pewter, I remember the raised glass of the grape's holy blood, the stem caressed by the doctor's strong artist fingers, and even now I can hear the sweet little health and welcome in the singing language of Acadia which once was French and now is itself. This picture filled my frosty windshield, and if there had been traffic would have made me a dangerous driver. But it was pale yellow frozen dawn in Houma and I knew that if I stopped to pay my respects, my will and my determination would drift away on the particular lotus St. Martin purveys and we would be speaking of timeless matters when the evening came, and another evening. And so I only bowed in the direction of my friend and scudded on toward New Orleans, for I wanted to catch a show of the Cheerleaders.

Even I know better than to drive a car near trouble, particularly Rocinante, with New York license plates. Only yesterday a reporter had been beaten and his camera smashed, for even convinced voters are reluctant to have their moment of history recorded and preserved.

So, well on the edge of town I drove into a parking lot. The attendant came to my window. "Man, oh man, I thought you had a nigger in there. Man, oh man, it's a dog. I see that big old black face and I think it's a big old nigger."

"His face is blue-gray when he's clean," I said coldly.

"Well I see some blue-gray niggers and they wasn't clean. New York, eh?"

It seemed to me a chill like the morning air came into his voice. "Just driving through," I said. "I want to park for a couple of hours. Think you can get me a taxi?"

"Tell you what I bet. I bet you're going to see the Cheer-leaders."

"That's right."

"Well, I hope you're not one of those trouble-makers or reporters."

"I just want to see it."

"Man, oh man, you going to see something. Ain't those Cheerleaders something? Man, oh man, you never heard nothing like it when they get going."

I locked Charley in Rocinante's house after giving the attendant a tour of the premises, a drink of whisky, and a dollar. "Be kind of careful about opening the door when I'm away," I said. "Charley takes his job pretty seriously. You might lose a hand." This was an outrageous lie, of course, but the man said, "Yes, sir. You don't catch me fooling around with no strange dog."

The taxi driver, a sallow, yellowish man, shriveled like a chickpea with the cold, said, "I wouldn't take you more than a couple of blocks near. I don't go to have my cab wrecked."

"Is it that bad?"

"It ain't is it. It's can it get. And it can get that bad."

"When do they get going?"

He looked at his watch. "Except it's cold, they been coming in since dawn. It's quarter to. You get along and you won't miss nothing except it's cold."

I had camouflaged myself in an old blue jacket and my British navy cap on the supposition that in a seaport no one ever looks at a sailor any more than a waiter is inspected in a restaurant. In his natural haunts a sailor has no face and certainly no plans beyond getting drunk and maybe in jail for fighting. At least that's the general feeling about sailors. I've tested it. The most that happens is a kindly voice of authority saying, "Why don't you go back to your ship, sailor? You wouldn't want to sit in the tank and miss your tide, now would you, sailor?" And the speaker wouldn't recognize you five minutes later. And the Lion and Unicorn on my cap made me even more anonymous. But I must warn anyone testing my theory, never try it away from a shipping port.

"Where you from?" the driver asked with a complete lack of interest.

"Liverpool."

"Limey, huh? Well, you'll be all right. It's the goddamn New York Jews cause all the trouble."

I found myself with a British inflection and by no means one of Liverpool. "Jews—what? How do they cause trouble?"

"Why, hell, mister. We know how to take care of this. Everybody's happy and getting along fine. Why, I *like* niggers. And them goddamn New York Jews come in and stir the niggers up. They just stay in New York there wouldn't be no trouble. Ought to take them out."

"You mean lynch them?"

"I don't mean nothing else, mister."

He let me out and I started to walk away. "Don't try to get too close, mister," he called after me. "Just you enjoy it but don't mix in."

"Thanks," I said, and killed the "awfully" that came to my tongue.

As I walked toward the school I was in a stream of people all white and all going in my direction. They walked intently like people going to a fire after it has been burning for some time. They beat their hands against their hips or hugged them under coats, and many men had scarves under their hats and covering their ears.

Across the street from the school the police had set up wooden barriers to keep the crowd back, and they paraded back and forth, ignoring the jokes called to them. The front of the school was deserted but along the curb United States marshals were spaced, not in uniform but wearing armbands to identify them. Their guns bulged decently under their coats but their eyes darted about nervously, inspecting faces. It seemed to me that they inspected me to see if I was a regular, and then abandoned me as unimportant.

It was apparent where the Cheerleaders were, because people shoved forward to try to get near them. They had a favored place at the barricade directly across from the school entrance, and in that area a concentration of police stamped their feet and slapped their hands together in unaccustomed gloves.

Suddenly I was pushed violently and a cry went up: "Here she comes. Let her through. . . . Come on, move back. Let her through. Where you been? You're late for school. Where you been, Nellie?"

The name was not Nellie. I forget what it was. But she shoved through the dense crowd quite near enough to me so that I could see her coat of imitation fleece and her gold earrings. She was not tall, but her body was ample and full-busted. I judge she was about fifty. She was heavily powdered, which made the line of her double chin look very dark.

She wore a ferocious smile and pushed her way through the milling people, holding a fistful of clippings high in her hand to keep them from being crushed. Since it was her left hand I looked particularly for a wedding ring, and saw that there was none. I slipped in behind her to get carried along by her wave, but the crush was dense and I was given a warning too. "Watch it, sailor. Everybody wants to hear."

Nellie was received with shouts of greeting. I don't know how many Cheerleaders there were. There was no fixed line between the Cheerleaders and the crowd behind them. What I could see was that a group was passing newspaper clippings back and forth and reading them aloud with little squeals of delight.

Now the crowd grew restless, as an audience does when the clock goes past curtain time. Men all around me looked at their watches. I looked at mine. It was three minutes to nine.

The show opened on time. Sound of sirens. Motorcycle cops. Then two big black cars filled with big men in blond felt hats pulled up in front of the school. The crowd seemed to hold its breath. Four big marshals got out of each car and from somewhere in the automobiles they extracted the littlest Negro girl you ever saw, dressed in shining starchy white, with new white shoes on feet so little they were almost round. Her face and little legs were very black against the white.

The big marshals stood her on the curb and a jangle of jeering shrieks went up from behind the barricades. The little girl did not look at the howling crowd but from the side the whites of her eyes showed like those of a frightened fawn. The men turned her around like a doll, and then the strange procession moved up the broad walk toward the school, and the child was even more a mite because the men were so big. Then the girl made a curious hop, and I think I know what it

was. I think in her whole life she had not gone ten steps without skipping, but now in the middle of her first skip the
weight bore her down and her little round feet took measured, reluctant steps between the tall guards. Slowly they
climbed the steps and entered the school.

The papers had printed that the jibes and jeers were cruel
and sometimes obscene, and so they were, but this was not
the big show. The crowd was waiting for the white man who
dared to bring his white child to school. And here he came
along the guarded walk, a tall man dressed in light gray, leading his frightened child by the hand. His body was tensed as
a strong leaf spring drawn to the breaking strain; his face was
grave and gray, and his eyes were on the ground immediately
ahead of him. The muscles of his cheeks stood out from
clenched jaws, a man afraid who by his will held his fears in
check as a great rider directs a panicked horse.

A shrill, grating voice rang out. The yelling was not in chorus. Each took a turn and at the end of each the crowd broke
into howls and roars and whistles of applause. This is what
they had come to see and hear.

No newspaper had printed the words these women
shouted. It was indicated that they were indelicate, some even
said obscene. On television the sound track was made to blur
or had crowd noises cut in to cover. But now I heard the
words, bestial and filthy and degenerate. In a long and unprotected life I have seen and heard the vomitings of demo-
niac humans before. Why then did these screams fill me with
a shocked and sickened sorrow?

The words written down are dirty, carefully and selectedly
filthy. But there was something far worse here than dirt, a
kind of frightening witches' Sabbath. Here was no spontaneous cry of anger, of insane rage.

Perhaps that is what made me sick with weary nausea. Here
was no principle good or bad, no direction. These blowzy
women with their little hats and their clippings hungered for
attention. They wanted to be admired. They simpered in
happy, almost innocent triumph when they were applauded.
Their was the demented cruelty of egocentric children, and
somehow this made their insensate beastliness much more

heartbreaking. These were not mothers, not even women. They were crazy actors playing to a crazy audience.

The crowd behind the barrier roared and cheered and pounded one another with joy. The nervous strolling police watched for any break over the barrier. Their lips were tight but a few of them smiled and quickly unsmiled. Across the street the U.S. marshals stood unmoving. The gray-clothed man's legs had speeded for a second, but he reined them down with his will and walked up the school pavement.

The crowd quieted and the next cheer lady had her turn. Her voice was the bellow of a bull, a deep and powerful shout with flat edges like a circus barker's voice. There is no need to set down her words. The pattern was the same; only the rhythm and tonal quality were different. Anyone who has been near the theater would know that these speeches were not spontaneous. They were tried and memorized and carefully rehearsed. This was theater. I watched the intent faces of the listening crowd and they were the faces of an audience. When there was applause, it was for a performer.

My body churned with weary nausea, but I could not let an illness blind me after I had come so far to look and to hear. And suddenly I knew something was wrong and distorted and out of drawing. I knew New Orleans, I have over the years had many friends there, thoughtful, gentle people, with a tradition of kindness and courtesy. I remembered Lyle Saxon, a huge man of soft laughter. How many days I have spent with Roark Bradford, who took Louisiana sounds and sights and created God and the Green Pastures to which He leadeth us. I looked in the crowd for such faces of such people and they were not there. I've seen this kind bellow for blood at a prize fight, have orgasms when a man is gored in the bull ring, stare with vicarious lust at a highway accident, stand patiently in line for the privilege of watching any pain or any agony. But where were the others—the ones who would be proud they were of a species with the gray man—the ones whose arms would ache to gather up the small, scared black mite?

I don't know where they were. Perhaps they felt as helpless as I did, but they left New Orleans misrepresented to the world. The crowd, no doubt, rushed home to see themselves on television, and what they saw went out all over the world, unchallenged by the other things I know are there.

from *Travels with Charley:*
In Search of America (1962)

"Good Jelly's" Last Stand

by David Halberstam

NASHVILLE

THE other day the local police raided a Negro barbecue and beer joint and arrested nine people. The raid and the arrests came as something of a shock to the owner. "I don't know why they're bothering me," said Henry ("Good Jelly") Jones, restaurateur, bootlegger, and politician. "It ain't election time." But bother him they did, and because Good Jelly (or just "Jelly" to his friends) is something of a local celebrity these days, there was a sizable press section on hand for his trial.

The reporters were not disappointed. Good Jelly's wife, when asked whether a gallon jug was the same jug found during the raid, answered, "I don't know. Jugs don't have no names." Later the white prosecuting attorney asked her why she found it so easy to answer defense questions and so hard to understand his. "Mr. City Attorney," said Robert Lilliard, her Negro attorney, "she's a little confused by all your high-class words. You just talk like we talk down at Good Jelly's and we'll be all right." "High-class words," snorted the city attorney. "What's so high-class about the words 'white corn'?"

The case came out as everyone knew it would: the charges against Good Jelly and his friends were dismissed. For if Good Jelly has a striking ability to get into trouble, he has an even more remarkable ability to get out of it. Fifteen times he has been called before the bar of justice in recent years, fourteen times he has been set free. The explanation of this enviable batting average lies deep in the structure of Southern politics, the Negro's role in it, and the specific power structure of Nashville. Henry Jones, with his golfer's cap, big flashing smile, and long police record, is a power. He is among the last of the ward heelers. Very simply, he controls the votes of a large number of unbelievably poor people, and for a minimum of service, protection, and financial reward, he delivers these same votes without the slightest concern for ideology.

In Nashville, he is the Negro whom many Negroes like least to think about; he is the Negro whom many whites like most to think about. In his own blunt word, he is a "nigger"; what is worse, that is all he wants to be. Respectable Negro society shuns him, yet to some of the Negro poor he is perhaps the only truly big man in their lives.

Good Jelly first became interested in politics at an early age. Because he was an uneducated Negro there were distinct limitations to the ambitions he might reasonably entertain and yet many people who govern his city and who dedicate schools and other buildings in the highest of ideals are perfectly willing to deal with him. "Call him a backdoor Negro," said one white leader; "they won't have their picture taken with him, and they won't pose with him, even at Negro functions. But they know how to get hold of him." When a white man once complained about Jelly's police record and about his bootlegging and the fact that he has many friends among politicians, a Negro answered: "That's the way you people really want him."

It is hardly surprising, then, that the complexities of playing the system at both ends have produced two Jellies. They are separate but equal Jellies. There is a Jelly for whites and a Jelly for Negroes. The whites' Jelly is an ingratiating Uncle Tom, laughing, smiling, hiding from any slightly serious question or threat behind the big smile and a joke (in which old Jelly is always the butt). The Negroes' Jelly is something different. He is kind: he has clothed many of his people, housed more, and fed them all. If he calls one and gives him the key to the big black Cadillac and says it's time to move the Caddy, the man is honored by the assignment; if he calls eight of them together and says that the newspaper wants their picture and that he, Jelly, approves of the idea, then a picture of eight smiling faces is taken; if he tells them to vote this way or that, they vote this way or that.

"I carry a lot of weight around here," Jelly admits. "'Bout half the people in this precinct I control. Two hundred, three hundred people. They're my people."

Good Jelly is a dark, stocky man of about fifty, whose use of minstrel-show techniques in front of whites is a legitimate heritage. As a young man he left his Nashville home and joined the cast of the Mandy Green from New Orleans Minstrel Show (the poor man's version of the famous Silas Green show). For Mandy Green he traveled the South as what he calls "one of those black-face comedians, and I was pretty good." Then he returned to Nashville, where he became associated with the then ruling Negro ward heeler, "Pie" Hardison. "I was Pie's chauffeur. He thought I was a pretty good fellow, and I was a good driver and a good talker, and so he got me into politics. One time Pie said I ought to be in there pitching for the mayor, and I said: 'If you want the mayor, then I'm pitching one hundred per cent,' and so I got him the votes."

Pie Hardison is gone now and his heir does his pitching from a small hut off a dark alley deep in the Negro slums. In a small half-masonry, half-wooden café, he cooks, bootlegs, and politicks. There is one small sign over the door—it is upside down—and it says "BEST." Jelly says this is not the name of the café, that the name is "Jones Barbecue." It is a small café and there are no menus, only signs on the walls. At one end of the café white beans cost twenty-five cents, at the other they cost twenty-one cents. There, with regular violations of local whiskey laws ("We have some whiskey but we don't have no beer—we have to send out for the beer"), he operates his machine: the restaurant is essential to his success as a politician.

For Good Jelly's machine has been described by one reporter as "the lame, the sick, the poor, and a few of the penniless." Good Jelly himself says: "Down in this part folks don't have but a little money and so they come over here when they have a little and we feed them, and they come over here when they don't have any money and we still feed them. I don't turn them down. I always feed them and I get them a place to sleep, most times right here, and get them to a hospital, and even a job sometimes. They get what I got, these folks, and they don't forget."

If the voters don't forget, neither does Good Jelly. He keeps a thorough file on each of his debtors: name, favors granted, address—or frequently the address of someone who will know where to find the debtor. Before election day Good Jelly will make sure all his friends are registered; he will also send out cards reminding them of their civic responsibility. Come election day and Good Jelly takes out his big Cadillac and herds his people to the polls. He likes to start early; it gives him more time later in the day for rounding up slackers. "I'll tell you why Good Jelly has got so many friends," said Robert Lilliard, the Negro attorney who is also a city councilman. "A lot of these politicians just like him: you can really count on Jelly. If he's for you, why you can check his precinct the next day and his votes will be there. If you treated him right."

Good Jelly himself says that he asks little for his interest in politics. "I'm for any man that's a good man," he is fond of saying. How does he tell who's a good man? "I read about this man, see, and I can tell if he's for me. I want to know all the issues."

Is that all? What issues? "A lot of these men, they want to be politicians and so they come and see Jelly and I see how friendly they are, and they're pretty friendly. They're good men. We talk about these issues. All of these issues." He repeated emphatically: "I'm for any man that's a good man."

Other interpretations of Good Jelly's political motivations have been offered from time to time. "I'd say he gets an average of about $300 for an election," one white politician told me. "It depends. On a close local election with a lot at stake I expect he's gotten $500 or more. Maybe a thousand."

"How much money did you get for the sheriff's race," I asked him point-blank.

"Money? Money? I wouldn't do none of that," he said. "The man, he come down here and he was a good man and he said how he wanted to do right . . ."

It is not without a touch of regret that many white politicians, worried by the new power of the sit-in leaders and the young Negro ministers, foresee the demise of Good Jelly and his kind. "You make the deal with Jelly," one politician said, "and that's it. You don't have to worry about him coming downtown with a bunch of his damn people and sitting down at some nice restaurant, or calling the damn newspapers and announcing he's going to picket some company for better jobs. Jelly's all right. Take care of him on the drunk and disorderly and that kind of thing, and that's it."

"He comes through?" I asked.

"We take care of him and he takes care of us," the man answered.

It was, of course, inevitable, given a one-party electorate in which factions outweigh issues in local elections, that more than one faction would sooner or later make demands on Good Jelly's talents. Thus for the past two years he has been caught right in the middle of the factional fight between the forces of the mayor and the forces of the city judge, who might one day like to run for mayor.

In the past, Good Jelly usually swung with the judge. But as a student of local politics (you never know who will be your next ally and similarly your next enemy), he steadfastly refuses to burn his bridges. "I been a deeply strong supporter of the mayor. I'm not mad at him. He knows ol' Good Jelly." Similarly, as a student of the science of local law enforcement, Good Jelly is hesitant about turning on the police. "The police," he says, "they see I'm a pretty good fella, and like I'm trying to do the right thing and they're all right. I like the police."

A showdown between the two factions came during last year's election for sheriff. The mayor's forces favored the incumbent; the other forces, including the city judge, favored his opponent. Police and sheriff's deputies swarmed over Good Jelly's café all week long. Several times Jelly was threatened with arrest. He placed signs for the incumbent in his café, but the policemen couldn't watch everywhere: while they sat and talked with Good Jelly in the front of the café, Mrs. Good Jelly slipped out the back and voted the Jelly machine for the opponent—who carried that precinct five to one.

Jelly's lack of concern about civil rights galls many young Negroes in Nashville. "If John Kasper were running against Thurgood Marshall and it was a local race and the right people went to see Jelly for Kasper, that's all it would take," said one Negro bitterly. Jelly himself has said: "My folks, they're not the integration type. They're not interested in all that. All

they want is a little food." Attorney Robert Lilliard has explained Jelly's continuing popularity in just about the same
terms: "Those folks, they aren't going to eat at Woolworth's
or Grant's or anything like that. But they got to eat. Jelly's
the only thing those people have, and he looks mighty good
to them."

But even Lilliard concedes that sooner or later other political leaders will supplant Good Jelly Jones and his kind among
the Negroes. "You take this city, growing all the time, and the
city limits going out, and the Negro making a little more
money all the time—a thing like Jelly got, it's getting to be
less and less important all the time. Five, ten years from now
there probably won't be any Good Jelly. Pretty soon both
sides too busy worrying about this middle-class vote to pay
for Jelly. That's where the next battle will be."

The Reporter, January 19, 1960

The Evicted

by Fred Travis

"No person, whether acting under color of law or otherwise, shall intimidate, coerce, or attempt to intimidate, threaten, or coerce any other person for the purpose of interfering with the right of such other person to vote or to vote as he may choose for, or not to vote for, any candidate for the office of President, Vice President, Presidential elector, member of the Senate, or member of the House of Representatives, delegates or commissioners from the territories or possessions, at any general, special or primary election held solely or in part for the purpose of selecting or electing any such candidate."

—*Section 131, Civil Rights Act of 1957,*
Federal Statutes.

Mrs. Georgia Mae Turner grubbed at a shallow trench with a cotton hoe, trying to drain a puddle of water in front of her tent in a camp called "Freedom Village" three miles south of Somerville, Tennessee. The fifty-eight-year-old widow and three of her five children were among a growing number of Negroes being forced off the land because they registered and voted in Fayette County, where Negroes outnumber whites by more than two to one.

"I been on that farm for thirty-eight year," Mrs. Turner said, pausing to wipe from her face the cold rain that beat down incessantly. "I worked for Mr. McNamee, and when he died I stay on an' work for his widow. I always done what that woman say. I never disobey my boss lady, and I ain' holdin' nothin' ag'in her now. I'll let the Lord settle with her.

"I worked shares," Mrs. Turner continued. "Sometimes Mrs. McNamee say I owe her as much as fo' or five thousan' dollar, an' I work it all off. I don't owe her nothin' when I lef'. In good years, I sometimes use t' make fifty or hun'red dollar. I don' know. She al'ays kep' the 'counts.

"Last summer I wen' down to Somerville an' register to vote and she say she seen my pi'ture in th' paper. She say, 'I got you pi'ture,' and I don' know what she mean at fust. Then she tell me las' fall I got to get offn her farm. She say she don' want me there no mo'. I say I get off at th' end o' th' year. Now this tent my home but it about as good as that house I had."

"I register to vote in September," said William Trotter, who moved into the tent camp with his wife and six children. "In October, my landlord came down to th' cotton fiel' 'n' say, 'Willie, you'll have t' get out. I'm gonna fix up th' house.'"

These are some of the results of the Federal government's first attempt to enforce the right of Negroes to vote in Deep South counties where they outnumber the white man but are heavily dependent upon him for economic survival. On the outcome of this effort will hinge the chances for Negroes in Mississippi, Alabama, Georgia, and South Carolina to participate freely in future elections, and perhaps determine the course of new civil rights legislation in Congress.

For the Fayette and Haywood County cases in Tennessee have produced a conflict between the Negro's civil rights and the white man's property rights which ultimately must be resolved by the United States Supreme Court. Before that happens, however, there may be an explosion of racial violence more intense than any the South has experienced in the desegregation of public schools. Emotions are running high on both sides, with threats and accusations and even occasional gun-fire being exchanged. If the government's case fails, more than 700 Negro families may be ordered out of the farm tenant and sharecropper shacks which have been their only homes most of their lives. Ignorant and unskilled, they are incapable of earning a living except by raising cotton, corn, and soybeans, and maybe a few chickens and hogs.

Negroes work the land under many arrangements. A few tenants lease the land and work it with their own equipment. But most are sharecroppers and are furnished a house, food, equipment, seed, fertilizer, medicine, and other supplies on credit. When the harvest is in, the sharecropper's part is usually about a half to a third of the crop, out of which he must pay for items advanced him. The net profit on the five to twenty acre plots may range from $50 to $300 a year, though it is just as liable to turn out to be a loss of that much or more.

Fayette and Haywood Counties, thirty miles east of Memphis, in the West Tennessee cotton country, are part of the Old South. Their broad fields stretch on each side of the Nashville-to-Memphis highways, and sharecropper and tenant shacks stand out against the flatlands. Aside from the few sawmills, cotton gins, and soybean oil mills, there is practically no industry.

Fayette County, on the Mississippi state border, has 24,577 residents, but the number has been dropping steadily since 1940 as both whites and Negroes seek opportunities elsewhere. Seventy per cent of the population is Negro, and they own about ten per cent of the land. The white people were so exercised over the Democratic Party's civil rights position that they voted for the States' Rights ticket in 1948 and 1956 and, in 1960, voted Republican for the first time.

Before last August, a few Negroes had been permitted to vote in Federal and state elections, but they always were excluded from the county Democratic primary in which local officials are named. The county primary, financed by qualifying fees imposed upon the candidates and without sanction in state law, is regarded as a private affair for the white people, though the nominations are equivalent to election to local offices.

Haywood County to the north has a population of 23,393, of which sixty per cent is Negro. Until last August, no Negro had ever voted in that county unless he did so during the Reconstruction.

The policy in these two counties was in sharp contrast to most of Tennessee, which is a border state and has adopted generally what is by Southern standards a moderate policy in handling racial problems. Negroes long have been permitted to vote in other counties and are even encouraged to do so by politicians in the metropolitan areas. Voting qualifications have been so lax that Negroes in some cities were not even required to be alive to have their names on the registration books.

Trouble started in Haywood and Fayette Counties in 1959 when the Negroes, with some outside help, organized Civic and Welfare Leagues. Groups of them went to the old courthouse in the middle of the Brownsville public square to register but found the Haywood County election commission had just resigned.

In Fayette County, when Negroes began showing up in groups at the election commission office, they were told they could not register. The Federal government's Commission on Civil Rights sent in agents to investigate, and the Federal district court at Memphis issued an injunction prohibiting local officials from blocking the registrations.

"As long as just a few of us were registered and voted, the white folks didn't pay no attention to us," said Scott Franklin, who runs a little store in the Moscow community down near the Mississippi line. He is president of the Fayette County Civic and Welfare League.

"After we got out this injunction, I heard some white people say, 'We can beat them.' Then we didn't know what it was. Now we know they was going to run us out of the county."

Franklin and other Negro merchants, like John McFerren, who runs a pint-sized "supermarket" just outside Somerville, the seat of Fayette County, were among the first to feel the economic pressure. Their credit and deliveries from local wholesalers were cut off. An oil distributor removed the gasoline pumps from in front of Franklin's store. Salesmen for distributors in Memphis and Jackson, Tennessee, said they would have to stop supplying the Negro merchants or lose their white customers. What little the Negroes could get to sell they had to haul from Memphis.

When Negroes went into white stores to make purchases, the clerks checked their names against lists of registered voters or Welfare League members before making the sale. Credit and even gasoline for farm tractors were refused those who had registered.

As word of the Negroes' plight spread, assistance arrived in the form of food packages from Memphis, Nashville, New York, Chicago, and other cities. Roy Wilkins, chairman of the Leadership Conference on Civil Rights, reported the situation to the Democratic Platform Committee at Los Angeles a few days before the party's nominating convention opened last July.

"Today as we talk here," he said, "Negro farmers in Fayette County who persisted and finally registered to vote are being refused gasoline for their tractors, trucks, and other farm machinery. Distributors of four nationally-known oil companies have joined in this punishment of men who sought merely to exercise their American right to vote." Negro leaders in the registration drive, he continued, had been "blacklisted by local merchants and cannot buy food and clothing."

"I trust the Justice Department will do something about this," he added. "Meanwhile, people cannot eat and cannot make their crops."

Agents of the Federal Bureau of Investigation joined those of the Civil Rights Commission in an investigation. They reported merchants checking lists of Negroes who had registered or were members of the Welfare Leagues and refusing sales to them.

James A. Kurts, a clerk in the Economy Store in Brownsville, was quoted by an FBI agent as having said he was told by the store owners "not to extend credit to names that appear on a list" of members of the Haywood County Civic and Welfare League.

Notice of tenant lease and sharecropper contract termination began shortly after Tennessee's August Democratic primary to nominate Federal and state officials. Negroes voted in the primary in both counties, and some of them claim lists of names were compiled at the polls for use in the campaign for economic retaliation. Others registered later in preparation for the November general election and found their names were added to the lists.

Last December, the Justice Department went into the Federal court at Memphis and asked a temporary injunction restraining landowners from evicting Negroes who had registered. John Doar, the government attorney, called the planned evictions "the most cruel step people could take against citizens of this country in telling them to get off the land. The United States government says this is wrong."

Nine of the white defendants called by the government as witnesses clammed up, claiming Fifth Amendment protection against self-incrimination. An exception was one white woman, Mrs. Esther Green, who testified she had refused to sign a petition pledging economic action against Negroes who registered; she explained, "I think for myself." She recalled a 1959 visit by Shelby Dixon, a cotton ginner in the Stanton community, to her farm "way up in the hills in Haywood County." Dixon, she said, asked her to sign a promise not to help any member of the National Association for the Advancement of Colored People, the Haywood County Civic and Welfare League, "or anyone else that the central committee does not approve of."

"That was too broad," Mrs. Green said. "I told him it didn't sound right to me, and I didn't want to sign."

Isaac Smith Carter, a white tenant on another farm, testified his landlord had refused to have anything to do with him after he refused to join in the campaign to hamper Negro registration.

The defense denied that Negroes were being evicted in reprisal for voting and insisted that the dismissals resulted from the inefficiency of tenants and mechanization of farming. One landowner, Montezuma Carter, Jr., said he was shifting to machines and had "no earthly need" for the ten Negro tenant families on his property.

Federal Judge Marion S. Boyd of Memphis refused to grant the government's request to halt the evictions. "The Civil Rights Act is intended to protect the right to register and vote and provide injunctive relief against such interference and coercion," he said. "That's all it does, I believe . . . I don't believe this court has any right to enjoin the evictions or enjoin the altering of leases."

A few days later, he was overruled by the Sixth United States Circuit Court of Appeals, which held that the Negroes could not be evicted as an interference with their right to vote. The Appeals Court left it to Judge Boyd to decide how its finding should be enforced. Boyd then told landlords they could not evict Negro tenants without proving in his court that the eviction was not an attempt to interfere with the Negroes' voting rights. Boyd's decision places the burden of proof on the landlord, but it also leaves a door open for evictions in connection with a normal rearrangement of agricultural practices. The action of the courts to date has been a temporary holding action aimed at maintaining the status quo while the issue is being litigated. Further hearings were ordered before a final decision, and there is no doubt the case ultimately will reach the United States Supreme Court.

Meanwhile, bitterness hangs heavily over the land. The tent camp set up on the 200-acre farm of Shepherd Towles, one of the few Negroes with substantial landholdings in the area, was denounced by whites as a publicity stunt to attract sympathy and relief for the Negroes.

"It's just a propaganda stunt," declared Mayor I. P. Yancy of Somerville. "I don't know of any need around here."

White landowners and businessmen, on the advice of their lawyers, who include practically the entire bar associations of both counties, decline to discuss the situation with strangers.

"Don't quote me and don't mention my name," said one farmer. "I'm a defendant in that Federal court case. We defendants refer to ourselves as the 'Honor Roll' and laugh about it, but it's a mighty dry laugh, I'll tell you. Those niggers go down there to those government lawyers and swear out those false affidavits. Of course, they are all lies, but you've got to hire yourself a lawyer and defend yourself just the same. It's mostly the work of some of those Northern agitators. They came down here and got the niggers all stirred up and told them they ought to go register and vote," he continued.

"We've known this was coming for a long time, and we've been trying to reduce our nigger population. Of course, we are mechanizing our farms. We've got to stay in business. Why, we've got sixty or seventy mechanical cotton pickers in this county already, and each one of them can do the work of seventy-five niggers. We got plenty of corn-picking machines, and a lot of farmers are turning to raising livestock. You don't need many farm hands for livestock."

He cited the national trend toward mechanized farming and the consolidation of farms into bigger units. In the 1,223 square miles of Fayette and Haywood Counties, the number of farm units dropped by 1,815 between 1954 and 1959 and the number of farm tenants declined by 1,586.

"We just don't have any need for so many niggers any more," said another landowner, who was equally emphatic in his demands for anonymity. "I'm not a defendant in one of those Federal court cases yet, and I don't want to be. I'm trying to get the niggers off my land before they enjoin me. I'm going to machines."

The whites called attention to the fact that Negroes have declined tenant and sharecropper offers from Arkansas and other Tennessee counties where their race is in a minority and farm hands are badly needed. The Somerville weekly newspaper, *The Fayette County Falcon*, carried a number of advertisements offering places in Phillips County, Arkansas, and Lauderdale County, Tennessee.

But the Negroes were deeply suspicious of the offers, seeing them as a further part of the campaign to get them out of the county so the white man can remain firmly in control of the ballot box.

"Man come out here and say he want ten tenant families fo' his farm somewheres over 'bount Nashful," said Mrs. Turner. "He say he got eighty acres of land. What he go'n do wit' ten tenant fam'lies on a farm no bigger'n that?"

John McFerren, who was busy directing the operation of "Freedom Village," said: "The sheriff told us we could go to other counties without being shot at and intimidated. A landowner over in Lauderdale County say he want two families to work for wages but he won't say how much wages."

McFerren, whose "supermarket" is plastered inside with signs like "PLEASE DON'T DISCUSS POLITICS IN HERE UNLESS YOU ARE REGISTERED TO VOTE," reported he had checked out two of the job offers and rejected them. "They couldn't answer details on assurances of making a living on the farms," he said. He disputed the claim that the machine could replace the Negro and predicted that a lot of landowners would go broke trying to use machines on the small, sometimes hilly farms.

Whites claim McFerren has found a profitable operation in handling the relief packages for the displaced tenants, but the Negro leader denies this.

When a shot was fired into the tent city, wounding slightly a Negro man sleeping there with his wife and four children, McFerren said: "I expected they'd try to get me, but I didn't think they would shoot into the tents while people were asleep in them." He warned of possible further violence: "The white people started the shooting. I'm a non-violence man myself, but I can't always control my people. Some of these people are getting pretty desperate.

"We need government help to get relief from this pressure," he continued, "and we need relief from this boycott the white folks have put on us. We need medical help, too. We don't have a Negro doctor in this county, and the Negroes can't get any help from the white clinics. We have to go to Memphis to get a doctor, and that's nearly forty miles away."

McFerren declined to identify the organizations which are providing assistance in the form of food, clothing, and money; he said he was afraid he might omit one from the list and offend someone. One organization which has contributed substantially is the Southern Conference Education Fund, a favorite target of Mississippi's Senator James Eastland, who likes to call it a Leftist organization or worse.

"This is just a sample of what is going to happen in Mississippi when the Negroes try to vote down there," said the Reverend Kelly Miller Smith of Nashville, a leader in the Reverend Martin Luther King's Southern Christian Leadership Conference. "If we don't win the fight for the vote in Fayette County, we won't have a chance in other areas of the South."

If the government wins its fight, the Negroes may get the right to free use of the ballot in Fayette and Haywood Counties, but there may not be many of them around to enjoy it. Meanwhile, conditions in the West Tennessee cotton country are likely to get a lot worse before there is any improvement.

The Progressive, February 1961

Challenge to Negro Leadership: The Case of Robert Williams

by Julian Mayfield

There is one, and only one, issue in the Robert Williams case. That single issue is: Shall the National Association for the Advancement of Colored People endorse the advocacy by a local NAACP officer of stopping "lynching with lynching" or "meeting violence with violence"?

> —from *The Single Issue*, a pamphlet distributed at the NAACP national convention in New York, July 1959.

For some time now it has been apparent that the traditional leadership of the American Negro community—a leadership which has been largely middle class in origin and orientation —is in danger of losing its claim to speak for the masses of Negroes. This group is being challenged by the pressure of events to produce more substantial and immediate results in the field of civil rights or renounce the position it has long held. The dramatic Tuskegee and Montgomery boycotts, the rash of student sit-ins—none was inspired by the National Association for the Advancement of Colored People, the Urban League, or the established Negro church denominations, but it is to their credit that they hurriedly gave the boycotts and sit-ins their blessing and, as with the NAACP, much needed financial help. They were thereby able to present a united front to their common enemy, the system of white supremacy.

But the challenge to middle-class Negro leaders—including the newer type like Martin Luther King—remains. It is inherent in the rapid growth of the militant, white-hating Muslim movement among working-class Negroes. It can be heard in the conversations of black intellectuals and students from the South who regard the efforts of the NAACP, the Urban League, and most religious and civic leaders with either disdain or despair, in the belief that they are doing too little, too timidly and too late.

Probably nothing more clearly illustrates this challenge, however, than the case of *Wilkins vs. Williams*. Robert F. Williams is the president of the Union County, North Carolina, branch of the NAACP. *Wilkins vs. Williams* was a hearing before the board of directors of the NAACP in New York City, which grew out of three criminal cases that were disposed of in one day by the Superior Court in Monroe, the seat of Union County.

Before this court on May 5, 1959, stood James Mobley, B. F. Shaw, and Louis Medlin. Mobley, a mentally retarded colored man, was charged with assault with intent to commit rape on a white woman. (He admitted he had caught her wrist during an argument.) Shaw, a white man, was charged with assault on a Negro chambermaid who claimed he had kicked her down a flight of stairs in the hotel where she worked. The case of the other white defendant, Medlin, was the most inflammatory. He was accused of having entered the home of a Negro woman, eight months pregnant, of attempting to rape her, and, when she resisted and tried to flee across a field, of brutally assaulting her and her six-year-old son. A white woman neighbor had witnessed the assault and summoned the police.

The Union County branch of the NAACP is the only one of its kind now in existence. Its members and supporters, who are mostly workers and displaced farmers, constitute a well-armed and disciplined fighting unit. Union County Negroes have had more than their share of ugly race relations, and by 1959, their experience—which we shall examine in detail later —had taught them to rely on their own resources in their dealings with the white community. After Medlin was arrested, their first impulse was to mount an assault against the Monroe jail, seize the prisoner, and kill him. It was Robert Williams who restrained them. He pointed out that murdering Medlin would place them in the position of the white men who, shortly before, had dragged Mack Charles Parker from a jail in Poplarville, Mississippi, and lynched him. Besides, Williams argued, so much national and international attention was focused on Monroe that the judge and juries would be forced to punish the white men.

But Williams was wrong. Impervious to world opinion, the court freed both Shaw and Medlin, and committed the mentally retarded Negro to prison for two years. (Only the last-minute discovery by his attorney of a technicality, which reduced the charge from rape to assault, prevented the judge from handing down a thirty-year sentence.) On the steps of the courthouse, Williams issued an angry statement to a UPI reporter:

> We cannot take these people who do us injustice to the court and it becomes necessary to punish them ourselves. In the future we are going to have to try and convict them on the spot. We cannot rely on the law. We can get no justice under the present system. If we feel that injustice is done, we must right then and there, on the spot, be prepared to inflict punishment on the people.
>
> Since the federal government will not bring a halt to lynching in the South, and since the so-called courts lynch our people legally, if it's necessary to stop lynching with lynching, then we must be willing to resort to that method.

Roy Wilkins, executive secretary of the NAACP, called Williams from New York to ask about the statement. Williams confirmed it as his and said he intended to repeat it that afternoon for several radio and television stations eager to interview him. He would make it clear, he assured Wilkins, that he was not speaking for the NAACP but for himself, though he would stress that his views represented the prevailing feeling of the colored people in Union County. Wilkins replied that it would be virtually impossible for the general public to separate Williams's statement from the policies of the NAACP since he would be identified as an officer of the organization. Williams then made his scheduled appearances, and the next day, May 7, Wilkins sent a telegram directing him to suspend his activities as a local officer pending consideration of his status at a meeting of the Association's board of directors. Williams answered that he would attend the meeting with counsel.

Thus the stage was set for a contest between a highly respected leader of a distinguished national organization and a relatively unknown young Southerner capable of issuing rash statements on the steps of a courthouse. *Wilkins vs. Williams* aroused heated discussions in nearly every Negro community in the country, but it was obvious from the beginning that Williams was bound to lose. At a closed hearing in June, before the Committee on Branches, Williams, represented by Conrad Lynn, a veteran civil-rights attorney, asserted that his statement had been made under emotional duress, and that he had not meant to imply that Negroes should exercise anything more than their legal right to self-defense and the right to come to the defense of another party against criminal attack. The committee upheld the action of its executive secretary and suspended Williams for six months. A few weeks later, the delegates to the Association's fiftieth annual convention voted 764 to 14 against Williams and in favor of suspension.

The one-sided vote should have settled the matter, with Williams returning to obscurity. But the questions raised by *Wilkins vs. Williams* are profound, and still far from settled. A close examination of relevant documents and newspaper files, and interviews with some of the principals involved, leads one to conclude that the real issue was never raised, and that Williams was slapped on the wrist for having stated publicly what many of his fellow Negroes, even those on the board of directors of the NAACP, felt but did not think it politic to express. Indeed, a statement issued by Roy Wilkins on May 6, 1959, deploring Williams's statement might well have been written by Williams himself.

. . . At the same time it must be recognized that the mood of Negro citizens from one end of the nation to the other is one of bitterness and anger over the lynching [of Mack Parker] in Poplarville, Miss., April 25, and over numerous instances of injustice meted out to Negroes by the courts in certain sections of the South. They see Negroes lynched or sentenced to death for the same crimes for which white defendants are given suspended sentences or set free. They are no longer willing to accept this double standard of justice.

If Negroes were no longer willing to accept the double standard of justice, *what were they to do about it?* Wilkins did not say, but one paragraph in the brief Williams submitted to the Committee on Branches provides the answer which he has been expounding ever since and which daily finds wider and wider acceptance:

He [Williams] believes the message of armed self-reliance should

be spread among Negroes of the South. He is convinced that a somnolent national government will only take action when it is made
aware that individual Negroes are no longer facing the mobs in isolation but are acquiring the habit of coming to the aid of their menaced brothers.

But this was precisely the position which the NAACP could
not publicly support. The organization was already being subjected to constant harassment by the Southern states. And to
have advocated Williams's position would have exposed the
NAACP to widespread criticism from many of the people
who now warmly support it, those who, for the most part,
prefer the legalistic or pacifist approach to American race relations. Moreover, the possible resulting violence could have
shaken the nation to its very foundation, and caused it intense
embarrassment in the conduct of its diplomacy with a largely
non-white world. But the situation in the South that provoked Williams's statement and the ensuing controversy remains unchanged. The NAACP's rejection of Williams's
position only postponed the crisis facing Negro leadership; it
did not eliminate it. Because it seems probable that Williams
—and other young men and women like him—will play an increasingly vocal role in the social maelstrom that is the American Southland, a closer look at him, his views, and the
environment that produced him, may be revealing.

I first met Robert Williams at the center of a revolution,
and I am certain that this has colored my attitude toward
him. It was in Havana in the summer of 1960. Relations between the Eisenhower administration and the Castro government had deteriorated almost to the breaking point. White
and black leaders in the United States had already denounced
Fidel Castro's efforts to win friends and sympathy among
American Negroes. Adam Clayton Powell, once a warm supporter, had disavowed the Cuban leader. Joe Louis's public
relations firm, under strong public pressure, had been forced
to drop its Cuban account, and Jackie Robinson had taken
Castro to task in his New York *Post* column. The prominent
Negroes who had flocked to Havana soon after the revolution
succeeded had gone home and not returned.

Yet there at the Hotel Presidente, a guest of the Casa de las

Americas, a Cuban cultural agency, was Robert Williams, a tall man in his middle thirties, of massive shoulders and thick girth. In Havana he wore the wide-brimmed hat of the *gua-jiro* (peasant) and a beard that would have been impressive anywhere else but in the land of Fidel Castro and his comrades. This was Williams's second visit to the island since the revolution, and he was a celebrity, applauded wherever he went. In personal appearances, and in magazine and newspaper articles, Williams had been excoriating the United States, his main charge being that America talks freedom abroad while denying it to its black citizens at home. Williams and Castro had frequently appeared together on television and a warm friendship had developed between them. The relationship had mutual advantages: the Cuban leader was furnished with a gold mine of propaganda material to use in his clash with the Eisenhower administration, and Williams had a platform from which he could speak and be heard around the world. His attacks on the United States nearly involved him in a fist fight with an American newspaperman who angrily accused him of unpatriotic behavior in airing an embarrassing domestic problem in a country that was hostile to the United States. Unwittingly the reporter had touched on one of the keystones of Williams's strategy.

"What some people don't understand," he told me one evening, "is that in the South we're fighting for our lives." He was referring to the broad economic offensive white officials and businessmen have mounted against militant Negroes throughout the South. "I'm in this struggle to win, and I'll win it any way I can. If somebody gets embarrassed, that's too bad."

An opportunity to test the effectiveness of his approach had arisen on his first trip to Cuba. A telephone call from Monroe informed him that his wife and children were receiving threats from the Ku Klux Klan. Furious, he stormed down to the United States embassy, stopping only to pick up a correspondent friend from *Prensa Latina*, the Cuban News Service. He demanded and received an audience with Ambassador Philip Bonsal with whom he lodged a vigorous protest. The harassed diplomat no doubt realized the potentially explosive propaganda material that could fall into Castro's hands. He agreed to submit Williams's written protest to Washington, and within a few hours Mrs. Williams and her children had a guard of several police cars.

Williams believes that the white supremacist system of the South could not survive very long without the support, or the tacit consent, of various agencies of the federal government. At the same time, he is convinced that the federal government offers the only real hope the Negro has of winning any large measure of his civil rights. But Washington will act only under strong pressure, and this the Negro people must create by a more militant assertion of their rights—including "meeting violence with violence." The white South, through its traditional alliance with conservative Republicans, subjects the federal government to an enormous amount of pressure and wins appreciable results. Consequently, it has been able to defy the Supreme Court's school desegregation order for seven years with little federal intervention. Williams concedes that the Negro cannot match the South's great resources in either money or Congressional influence, despite the best intentions of Northern liberals and even a liberal President. But the Negro does have a formidable weapon in his sensitive position in international affairs. Without the cold war and the competition between the colossi of West and East, it seems doubtful that the many African nations could have gained independence so rapidly. Certainly the history of U.S. intervention in Latin America indicates that the Cuban revolution would not have been permitted to swing so far to the left if not for the extreme degree of United States sensitivity to world opinion today. For the same reason (though he knows it is possible to exaggerate the similarities), Williams believes the American Negro has been presented with the finest opportunity history is likely to offer him to obtain full participation in our national life.

Thus, when President Eisenhower was in India championing the rights of Asians to better housing, Williams wired him in care of Prime Minister Nehru (also an NAACP member) to protest a housing redevelopment scheme, largely financed by federal funds, that Union County officials had designed to destroy the best Negro neighborhood in

Monroe. Eisenhower acted with unusual haste, and the project has been stalled ever since.

Nowhere was Williams's method of subjecting every racial incident to world exposure more effectively demonstrated than in the "Kissing Case." On October 28, 1958, two Monroe colored boys, James Hanover Thompson and David "Fuzzy" Sampson, eight and nine years old, were arrested and charged with assault on a white female. Earlier that afternoon, in a game with some white children, James had either kissed or been kissed by a seven-year-old white girl. The boys were held incommunicado three days before Williams knew they were under arrest. Ironically, according to Williams, his first intelligence came from the mayor of Monroe who telephoned because he said he knew Williams was a "troublemaker" and he wanted to know if Williams had any ideas about how to handle the case. (The mayor denies he made the call.) It seemed to Williams that the boys required immediate legal aid which was not available in Union County. He submitted a request to the national office of the NAACP; but meanwhile, on the sixth day after their arrest, in a closed hearing, without defense counsel, Judge J. Hamilton Price heard the case and committed the boys to indeterminate terms in reform school.

Williams, through an intermediary, was responsible for Ted Poston's breaking the story in the New York *Post*, and from there, it spread around the world with lightning-like rapidity. Demonstrations were staged against American embassies in Europe, outstanding intellectuals protested to the State Department, and Canon L. John Collins of London's St. Paul's Cathedral became involved in a lively transatlantic feud with Luther H. Hodges, then governor of North Carolina. (The governor, to his embarrassment, was first informed of the "Kissing Case" by a reporter while in the middle of a television interview in Philadelphia.) Eventually the boys were released from the reform school and allowed to go back to live with their mothers who had been forced to move out of Union County. "Without the pressure of world opinion," Williams insists, "those boys would still be in custody."

These stories, which I later verified, were related to me during long nightly conversations in Havana. One evening I asked Williams a question I thought he might not answer. What truth was there in the rumor that had been circulated during the NAACP convention that his men were not only armed (in the South, after all, a surprisingly large number of people keep guns) but that they were in fact a small army, drilled and disciplined, with access to an arsenal?

He laughed. "Hell, man, that's no secret, and I don't know why it should frighten the board of directors of the NAACP. Everybody in Monroe knows what we have, that we know how to use it, and that we are willing to use it. The Mayor and the Chief of Police know, and so does the Klan. Come to Monroe when you get back to the States and see for yourself." This was the same kind of invitation that had taken me to Cuba and two months later I was in Monroe, North Carolina.

Some Southern towns are lovely, with great old houses that slumber on broad streets beneath spreading, ancient trees. In such towns even a Negro writer on a hurried visit can perceive that, although *his* ancestors only supplied the labor under the ante-bellum system of caste and privilege, at least there was a comprehensive society in which everyone had a place; and, dimly, he can understand why the Southern aristocracy fought so desperately to retain the cruel and dehumanizing system that was slavery. Here, at least, social relations had a symmetry wherein the dark, ugly things were hidden away, in the slave quarter or on the backstairs of the big house.

But Monroe is not such a town. It is ugly. There is little distinction in the architecture of its finest houses; and although it is built on hills, there is a dreary flatness about it. Worse, it is a composite town. Unpainted one-room Negro shacks, which rent for an inflated ten dollars a month, sit within a stone's throw of the tiny, neat, unimaginative bungalows of the white middle class. One can drive three blocks in any direction and see the graphic reality of race relations in Union County. The Northern visitor, keenly aware that violence always simmers beneath the seeming tranquility, wonders that anybody, black or white, would want to fight over this place.

In the days of the steam engine Monroe was a prosperous railroad maintenance town. A generation ago Robert Williams's father, along with a significant number of Monroe's colored men, serviced the trains and earned a steady living at it. They bought their own homes in the colored section called Newtown, sent their children to the colored school most of the year, and saw in their youngsters the hope of a better future. If they were not a genuine middle class, they were better off than the tenant farmers and sharecroppers in the county's rural population. But the Diesel engine supplanted steam, and the depression and mechanization displaced most of the tenant farmers and sharecroppers; and, though Monroe did not die, it was left severely crippled.

By the time Williams had grown to adolescence, unemployment was a chronic problem in Newtown. He served a hitch in the army, somehow squeezed in three years of college at West Virginia State and Johnson C. Smith College in nearby Charlotte, and then enlisted in the Marine Corps for a tour of duty. On returning to Monroe, he entered the lists of the letters-to-the-editor columns of the Charlotte newspapers and seems to have spent most of his time incensing the local whites by debunking their notions of white supremacy. During this period he married Miss Mable Robinson, a sturdy, tall, attractive woman with whom he has had two children. He worked at his trade of machinist while he wrote his provocative letters to the newspapers. It is possible that no one outside of North Carolina would ever have heard of Williams if the Supreme Court had not ordered school desegregation in 1954.

It is still difficult to imagine the impact of the Court's decision on small Southern towns. Intercourse between the races—that is, social intercourse during the Southern day which, as James Baldwin has pointed out, is quite different from the guilt-ridden, integrated Southern night—was the function of the local white officials and businessmen, and colored ministers and other self-appointed spokesmen who purported to represent the views of their fellow Negroes. White lawyers in Monroe often defended Negroes who were in trouble (not too vigorously, to be sure) and were paid by the NAACP chapter. There was an understanding, a working relationship, between the whites who ran the town and the colored ministers. The whites would try to control their extremists, and in return, the black men of God helped to keep the black population in its place.

But suddenly, one Monday in 1954, a long held tradition was struck a death-blow. The NAACP, which had never claimed to be anything but a moderate organization, became the ogre of the Southland. Acknowledged membership in it could mean the loss of job, credit, and physical security. Negro doctors, lawyers, undertakers—whoever had to be licensed by the state—promptly withdrew from membership. When the Union County chapter was apparently in its last throes (with only six members), Robert Williams was drafted for the presidency. ("You're the only fool left," said one of those who urged him to accept the position.) Somewhat innocently, Williams set about trying to recruit members among the respectable middle class, and, needless to say, he failed absolutely. In desperation he turned to the lower class of the Negro community. He likes to tell of the day he walked into a pool parlor and asked if anyone there wanted to join the NAACP. The players looked at him in astonishment: "Man, do you mean *we* can belong to that organization?" From that time on, Williams has had as many members as he could manage, sometimes more. He says of that period, "I made an important discovery. The woman earning ten, fifteen dollars a week as a domestic, the sharecropper, the ditch-digger—they were more loyal to the NAACP than the Negroes who were much better off. They would stick under pressure, probably because they had less to lose and we were the only fighting organization they had."

As the Union County branch of the NAACP grew, so did the Ku Klux Klan, which had renewed its activity soon after the Supreme Court decision. Most of the Klan's wrath was directed against Dr. A. E. Perry, one of the six who had remained in the chapter when Williams assumed leadership. The popular young physician, who was fairly prosperous, had built an attractive, ranch-style home overlooking a new highway. The Klan considered the house an affront, and it believed that Perry contributed large sums of money to the NAACP chapter. It publicly announced its intention of running him out of the county.

"When we heard over the radio," Williams says, "that a Klan meeting had drawn 8,000 people, we figured it was time to take a stand. You see, there are only 13,000 people in the county." (Klansmen from surrounding counties were swelling the attendance.) The colored men of Monroe armed themselves with the heaviest weapons available, and set up an alarm system that would summon them instantly to the scene of any trouble. A regular night guard was established around Dr. Perry's home. Trenches were dug, Molotov cocktails prepared, and gas masks and helmets were distributed. At one point during this troubled period the police attempted to seize the weapons, but desisted when Williams and Perry threatened a law suit. (Nothing in the laws of North Carolina and of most Southern states restricts or contravenes the constitutional right "to keep and bear arms, and be secure in one's person.")

A Klan motorcade, sixty cars strong, invaded Newtown on the evening of October 5, 1957. As was their custom, the robed Klansmen fired at the homes of the Negroes as they drove past. Near Dr. Perry's home they were confronted with the sustained fire of several scores of men who had been instructed by Williams not to injure anyone if it could be helped. At the first sign of resistance the Klan motorcade dissolved into chaos. Panicky Klansmen fled in every direction, some of them wrecking their automobiles. There have been no Klan motorcades in Monroe since.*

It is interesting to speculate on why this significant event received so little publicity. Monroe Chief of Police Mauney admitted to the Associated Press the next day that there had been a motorcade—he knew because it had included several police cars—but he denied that there had been an exchange of gunfire. Williams invited the press to Newtown to view the bullet-scarred houses and the wrecked automobiles whose owners did not care to come to claim them. Nevertheless, few people outside the state knew that the clash had taken place, and that the Klan had sustained a decisive defeat. Compare

---

*Dr. Perry has been driven out of Union County. The county's leading Catholic layman, he was arrested in 1958 and indicted on charges of performing an abortion on a white woman. Sole evidence submitted against him was her uncorroborated statement. He was convicted, sent to prison, and barred from Union County. Denied the right to practice medicine, he now works as an assistant to an undertaker in Durham.

this with the nationwide news coverage and wide applause given the Indians in nearby Lumberton County, when they routed a Klan meeting with gunfire a few weeks later. About this Williams says, "It's as if they were afraid to let other Negroes know what we have done here. We have proved that a hooded man who thinks a white life is superior to a black life is not so ready to risk his white life when a black man stands up to him." He recalls proudly that in Monroe they have had their sit-ins and wade-ins, but none of their boys and girls has been the victim of violence from racist hoodlums. "They know, don't you see, that we are not passive resisters."

The morale of the Negroes in Union County is high. They carry themselves with a dignity I have seen in no other Southern community. Largely vanished are the slouching posture, the scratching of head, and the indirect, mumbled speech that used to characterize the Negro male in the presence of whites. It is as if, in facing up to their enemies, they have finally confronted a terrible reality and found it not so terrible after all.

But they have had to pay a price for their new self-respect. Paternalism has been destroyed in Union County. The leftover food that the colored maid could once carry home is now consigned instead to the garbage pail, and the old clothes that found their way to the colored section are now either sold or burned. The intimate communication that used to pass from mistress to maid, master to workman (seldom in the reverse direction) has largely disappeared. Negroes suspected of belonging to the NAACP are told "Let Williams feed you!" and "Let Williams find you a place to live!" as they are fired from their jobs and evicted from their homes. Northern owners of the new factories, by agreement with the city fathers, hire no Negroes but import white workers from Charlotte, twenty-five miles away. It would almost appear that the rulers of Monroe society had determined to strengthen the Union County NAACP and Williams's influence on the colored community; and, in fact, that is what they have done.

But what role is Williams likely to play in the future? Although he has shown great personal courage and demonstrated effective leadership ability in Monroe, he can claim no large following outside his own county. True, he has a scattering of fervent supporters in the United States, Europe, and Latin America, who subscribe to *The Crusader*, the weekly newsletter in which he flays not only white supremacists but Negro moderates who accommodate themselves to the system. But he is in danger of being driven out of Monroe where his standard of living is close to penury. (No one will employ him in any capacity in Union or nearby counties.) Certainly the present national leadership of the NAACP does not fear that Williams will undermine their position in the near future. The organization is still the most effective civil rights force in the country, and few of its members have shown any inclination to abandon it.

But sooner than anyone now supposes, three factors may create a social climate in the South in which a Robert Williams will play a leading role. They are the growing militancy of Negro students; the intransigence of the Southern white oligarchy; and the depressed Negro working class and peasantry. The students and the white ruling groups of the South are locked in a struggle that has greater ramifications than perhaps even they realize. At stake is not whether a black child shall sit beside a white child in a schoolroom or at a lunch counter; it is not even whether a black *boy* sits beside a white *girl* and one day marries her. At stake is the very existence of the Southern oligarchy, its entrenched power and traditional privileges which rest on a non-democratic political system and an economy based on a plentiful supply of cheap, unorganized labor. Ultimately the struggle in the South will determine who will represent the states and the Congressional districts in Washington, who will sit in the legislatures, the city halls, and the courts, who will operate the industries and the arable land. As the real issue becomes more apparent, two developments seem certain. First, those who now wield power will refuse to yield beyond a minimum of token desegregation and will retaliate, often violently and in defiance of federal law; and second, the students will abandon the technique of passive resistance as it proves ineffectual in seriously disturbing the power structure of Southern society.

The most decisive factor in the conflict will probably be the Negro laboring class, heretofore unheard from. These are the great masses of the unskilled, who belong to no labor unions or civic organizations, whose churches are more concerned with leading their flocks to heaven than to a fuller share of democracy on earth, whose only fraternity is that of the millions of neglected and untrained who have nothing to barter in the labor market but their willingness to work. Only yesterday the man of this class could pick the cotton, run the elevator, pack the crate, but now the machine can do it better and displaces him. Government statistics hardly suggest how great his number is, much less what he is feeling and thinking, but we know he is everywhere. (The industrialization programs of the South almost always exclude him. Fourteen per cent of the black labor force is now unemployed as opposed to 7 per cent for the nation as a whole.) A casual walk through any colored section of a Southern town or city will reveal him, standing on the corner, lounging near the bar, slouched on the doorstep, staring into the uncertainty that is his future. The "they" in his life, those who make decisions that vitally affect him, are not only the governments, federal, state, and local, the captains of industry and finance, but even the Negro middle class and the striking students, all of whom seem to be going someplace without him. It is not *his* children that all of the school desegregation furor is about; he is lucky if he can keep them in the colored school. No one can presently claim to speak for this man, not church, union, nor NAACP; and just as he does not yet clearly understand the social forces arrayed against him, neither do *they* understand *him* or the various stimuli to which he is likely to respond.

Predictions are risky at best, but it seems safe to say that as these forces come into sharper conflict in what is essentially an attempt to overthrow an entrenched political and economic power, the Negro leadership class will be faced with a crisis, for its purely legalistic (or passive resistance) approach will clearly not be able to control the dynamics of the Negro struggle. Then to the fore may come Robert Williams, and other young men and women like him, who have concluded that the only way to win a revolution is to be a revolutionary.

Commentary, April 1961

The Not-Buying Power of Philadelphia's Negroes

by Hannah Lees

PHILADELPHIA

W$_{\text{HEN}}$ four hundred ministers in one city advise their congregations not to buy something, a lot of whatever that something may be goes unbought and the company that makes it is quickly aware of the fact. For a month and a half, starting March 19, the congregations of four hundred Negro churches in Philadelphia have not bought Sunoco gas or oil for their cars and trucks or Sun fuel oil to heat their homes. Last January for exactly one week they were not buying Gulf gas or oil. Last October for two weeks they were not drinking Pepsi-Cola. And last summer for two months they were not eating any cakes or pies made by the Tasty Baking Company.

These periods of mass inaction have been the result of a joint decision reached last May by the pastors of those four hundred churches. They call it their Selective Patronage Program and their purpose is simple and forthright: to persuade —they reject words like "force" or "demand"—one company after another in Philadelphia to employ more Negroes in prestige jobs.

Their method is equally simple and forthright. A delegation of ministers, sometimes five, usually four, calls on whatever company the group has decided to investigate and politely inquires how many Negroes it employs and in what jobs. The companies have given this information willingly so far, and they might as well; the ministers usually already know, unofficially. The first meeting is always exploratory, but a second meeting is then requested a week or two later. At this meeting the ministers, though still quiet, still polite, are specific about what they want. At first it wasn't very much. Lately, as with the present Sun boycott, it has become a good deal. Whether they are now asking too much only time will tell.

565

With the Tasty Baking Company, the second firm they visited and the first one where they encountered opposition, the ministers asked the company to hire two Negro driver-salesmen, two Negro clerical workers, and three or four Negro girls in the icing department, where the workers had traditionally been all-white. They were not interested in the fact that the Tasty Baking Company already had hundreds of Negro employees. What they are interested in is placing Negro workers in positions of dignity and responsibility. Their aim is to change the public image of Negro workers. The Tasty Baking Company did not have any Negroes driving trucks or working in its office.

When Mr. Pass, the personnel manager of the company, and Mr. Kaiser, the president, pointed out that they had no need, just then, for more driver-salesmen or clerical workers, the ministers said politely but firmly that they still hoped these people could be hired within two weeks. If not, the four hundred ministers they represented would have to advise their congregations on the Sunday following not to buy any Tasty cakes or pies until they were hired.

Mr. Kaiser understandably felt pushed and resistant. The Negro driver-salesmen and clerks and icers were not hired within the two weeks, and the ministers did tell their congregations not to buy any Tasty cakes or pies until further notice. Printed advertisements to this effect mysteriously appeared in bars, beauty parlors, and barbershops. Nobody knows how many thousand dollars' worth of sales the Tasty Baking Company lost during those summer months, but there are 700,000 Negroes in Philadelphia and a large proportion have some connection with those four hundred churches. When the boycott was officially called off two months later from four hundred pulpits, the Tasty Baking Company had in its employ two Negro driver-salesmen, two Negro clerical workers, and some half-dozen Negro icers.

The Pepsi-Cola Company, which was called on last September, was also resistant to the ministers' requests. On October 2, a boycott was called from four hundred pulpits. Two days later the spokesman of the delegation received a telegram saying that Pepsi-Cola had hired the requested personnel. But the boycott lasted two weeks, because it is a policy of the ministers not to call a boycott off until the new employees are actually at work.

Gulf Oil, which was approached last winter at the height of the heating season, showed no interest in meeting with the ministers. When three weeks had gone by without an appointment being arranged, a boycott of Gulf products was called the next Sunday. The day after that the switchboards at Gulf were jammed with calls canceling oil contracts. Gulf then moved so quickly to meet the ministers' demands that the boycott lasted only a week. But here a new factor entered: the union. One of the ministers' stipulations, that the new Negro employees must not be the first to be laid off, conflicts with seniority provisions in Gulf's union contract. Union officials met with the ministers and explained that they were sympathetic with their aims, but not when they collided with union bargaining. Three Negro truck drivers had been hired and after thirty days joined the union. All has been serene, but seasonal layoffs have begun by now. If drivers with seniority are laid off first, the union is not likely to take it lying down. The ministers may decide to finesse that one.

Bond Bread, Freihofer Bread, Coca-Cola, and Seven-Up all seem to have found the ministers' requests reasonable when they were called on. So, apparently, have Esso, Cities Service, Atlantic, and Mobil. None of these companies has had to cope with a boycott. Atlantic, which already had some Negroes in clerical and executive jobs before the ministers came to call, says it now has twenty-five Negroes in white-collar jobs, including a chemist, a psychologist, and a former football hero in sales promotion. They say that they are well pleased with the quality of work these employees do and with the general office morale. The ministers mention Atlantic frequently as an example of how smoothly their project goes when everyone co-operates.

The origin and operation of the Selective Patronage Program are somewhat shrouded in mystery. It acknowledges no leaders, and no one will say who called the first meeting. "Some of us just got together," they say, "and decided we could not in good moral conscience remain silent while our congregations patronized companies that were discriminating against Negroes." The names of the ministers who have called on the various companies are on public record, but there is a different delegation for each company and a different spokesman. The Reverend Alfred G. Dunston, pastor of the Wesley A.M.E. Zion Church, has been the spokesman with Sun Oil. The Reverend Leon Sullivan of the Zion Baptist Church was the spokesman with the Tasty Baking Company. The Reverend Joshua E. Licorish, of Zion Methodist Church, was the spokesman with Gulf and with the union.

The Philadelphia Commission on Human Relations, which investigated the Tasty boycott at the request of the Chamber of Commerce—and found no illegal discrimination but no evidence of positive integration either—mentions Dr. Noah Moore, a bishop in the Methodist Church, the Reverend Lorenzo Shepard, pastor of the Mount Olivet Baptist Tabernacle, and the Reverend Leon Sullivan as prominent in the campaign. But no one will say who makes up the priority committee, which meets—always at a different place—to decide on the next target and what they will ask for. They have, they say, no officers, no by-laws, no minutes, no dues, and no treasury.

"But it is the best-organized unorganized program you ever saw in action," one of them said to me. "We can call a boycott of a quarter of a million people within twenty-four hours and call it off within twenty-four hours." A quarter of a million is probably not too high. Lined up solidly behind the ministers are fraternal organizations, social clubs, insurance agents, bartenders, beauticians, the N.A.A.C.P., and the Negro newspapers. Even local dealers whose sales have been hurt by the various boycotts seem to go along with the program.

Highhanded and arbitrary as the Selective Patronage Program may seem, it is hard to find anything illegal or even really unethical in it. The ministers are simply exercising their democratic right to "advise" their friends what to buy and what not to buy. They are, of course, using their buying power to pressure these companies to hire employees they may not need at the moment, but their position is that if they waited for any of these companies to *need* that many Negro employees they would wait a long time. "We have waited too long already," one of them said.

A consistent complaint of both liberals and conservatives has been that Negroes did not do enough for themselves, did not exercise enough leadership in solving their own problems. These Negro ministers are exercising leadership and, so far, with impunity. The Tasty Baking Company consulted both the Chamber of Commerce and their own lawyers to see if any counteraction were possible. The conclusion seemed to be that it would be pretty hard to take a group of unorganized ministers to court, and even if they could it would not help Tasty's position much.

The ministers point out that some three thousand Negro boys and girls graduate from Philadelphia high schools every year and usually end by taking the jobs that nobody else wants because they are the last to be chosen. Many of them, the ministers admit, are not as highly qualified as they should be, but even the qualified ones have to fight the preconceived idea that they are not qualified. This, essentially, is the battle the ministers are trying to fight for them.

There are some new elements to the Sun Oil boycott now in progress. The ministers are feeling their strength and pushing harder than ever before. They may be pushing too hard, but perhaps they have to, to find out how far and how fast they can move. They phoned Sun at the end of January and requested a meeting. Sun arranged a meeting for February 3 in a very relaxed mood. A year ago Sun had asked the Reverend Leon Sullivan and Dr. Jerome Holland, president of Hampton Institute, to advise it in setting up a program of increased Negro employment in white-collar jobs. At that time it had hired two Negro clerks. It had records of hundreds of Negro employees at its Marcus Hook refinery, some in responsible supervisory jobs. It had just decided to include three Negro colleges in its yearly talent search. Sun felt it was in the clear.

The ministers didn't agree. They weren't interested in the number of Negroes working in the refinery. Negroes had always held jobs like that. "You hired two Negro clerks a year ago, but none since," they said. "Two in an office force of fifteen hundred isn't much, is it? And you have no Negroes driving trucks. And even though you plan to include Negroes in your talent search, you haven't actually hired any."

Sun said business had fallen off. They had had to move more slowly than they planned, but were now going ahead as fast as they could.

At the second meeting, two weeks later, the ministers quietly dropped what must have seemed to Sun a bombshell. They wanted Sun to hire twenty-four Negro employees: nineteen additional office workers, three permanent truck drivers, and a motor-products salesman. When? Within the next month.

Sun said that wasn't possible, not within a month. There would not be anywhere near nineteen new job openings in the office in that time. And how could it hire three new truck drivers when they were just about to lay off thirty-five as the heating season ended?

It may be a coincidence that what the ministers have asked for at Sun is just about equivalent to the number of white-collar Negroes now employed by Atlantic. Philadelphia is the home office of both Sun and Atlantic. Each of them has about fifteen hundred people working in its home office. The ministers say that twenty-five Negroes in an office force of that size is not much to ask; that they can be found and will have to be if Sun wants any Negro customers around Philadelphia. The Urban League could supply them, say the ministers; they themselves could supply them if asked.

Sun has not, so far, asked the ministers to recruit for them, but it has been in touch with the Urban League. By March 16, the last meeting before the boycott deadline of Sunday, March 19, Sun had interviewed nineteen Negro applicants for clerical work, and had hired one of them. The others, they said, did not have the necessary qualifications. Sun had also hired one Negro salesman and upgraded one man from mechanic to truck driver. The ministers had accepted Sun's stand that it could not take on new truck drivers while about to lay off old ones and said they would settle for upgrading to truck driver three of their men who were already employed by Sun.

The boycott was called on March 19 and is still in progress. As of late April, Sun had hired about half the workers requested by the ministers. There were seven more Negro girls in the home office, there were two Negro salesmen, and three drivers had been upgraded from work in the garage and the refinery. Sun says that from now on it will hire people as needed, interviewing both white and Negro applicants without discrimination. When asked about the loss in business, spokesmen for the firm shrug and say it is hard to estimate. They seem unruffled and without resentment, but say flatly that they cannot do more. And there is no reason why they should if they can get along without Negro customers. The ministers estimate, however, that Sun is losing some $7,000 a week. And the number of Negro customers Sun may have to get along without seems to be increasing.

Those four hundred unorganized ministers now plan to spread their boycott progressively, first across the state and then, they say, across the country if necessary. On Sunday, April 9, they began the first part of what they call the second phase of their program. All the Negro Masonic lodges across the state announced a boycott of Sun products. Their members number 25,000 and they claim to be able to influence several times that many. Perhaps they can. If Sun has still not hired the requested twenty-four Negro workers in another couple of weeks, the ministers say the boycott will spread to all the churches across Pennsylvania, and after that to all the men's and women's clubs. And after that they will go beyond Pennsylvania.

Wouldn't it have been more logical, I asked, to start with all the churches in Pennsylvania?

"A boycott of the Masons is easier to control," I was told, "and easier to call off in a hurry if Sun fills its quota. We could easily call on a boycott of all the churches, but it might take a while to call it off. We don't want to hurt Sun. We aren't mad at anybody. We just want to see our boys and girls in decent jobs."

Do the ministers have this much power? They probably don't know themselves yet. They must feel there is a certain poetic justice in big business feeling pushed by its traditionally most subservient employees. They may feel there is a special poetic justice that Sun Oil, owned by the Pews who for years controlled the Negro vote in Philadelphia by dropping money where it would do the most good, should now be having to negotiate with the new Negroes. But this proposed state-wide and possibly nation-wide boycott which originated with four hundred unorganized ministers is loaded with dangerous possibilities. George Schermer, executive director of the Philadelphia Commission on Human Relations, has been glad to see these Negro ministers exercising leadership. As long as they can function in this amorphous state, he is all for them, he says, but if they can make good on this spreading boycott, it may be hard not to develop an overt organization with leaders and factions and ultimate corruption. At the very least, any real organization could sooner or later run into some sort of conspiracy suit. These are the dangers ahead of the crusading ministers.

"Power corrupts, you know the old saying," I reminded one of the ministers. "Aren't you afraid that all this mushrooming power may land you in trouble?" He smiled gently. "No, honey," he said, "because we haven't any heroes to feed on that power, we haven't any leaders or bosses. And we aren't going to have any. As long as we can make out without them, we'll do fine." As long as they can, he is probably right.

The Reporter, May 11, 1961

Reporter Tails "Freedom" Bus, Caught in Riot

by Stuart H. Loory

MONTGOMERY, Ala., May 20.—A wild mob of men and women, uncontrolled by police, pounced on newsmen and then on a group of nineteen Negro and white students who alighted today at the Greyhound bus terminal here after a ride from Birmingham to test segregated intrastate bus practices.

I trailed the bus from Birmingham to Montgomery in a car and was on the bus platform in the middle of the violence but escaped injury.

The small group of men and women was attacked by a mob of 100 at first. But the mob rapidly grew into the thousands.

"Get those niggers" one dark-haired woman, primly clad in a yellow dress, shouted.

The mob had first pummeled three National Broadcasting Co. newsmen and several other photographers, smashing their equipment. Then it turned to vent its unsatisfied fury on the band of students who stood quietly on the bus platform, apparently not knowing what to do after completing the ride from Birmingham.

Using metal pipes, baseball bats, sticks and fists, the mob surged on the small group of Freedom Riders, clubbing, punching, chasing and beating both whites and Negroes. When some of the bus riders began to run, the mob went after them, caught them and threw them to the ground. The attackers stomped on at least two of them. One of the mobsters carried an open knife but didn't use it.

In two hours it was over, after the police used tear gas. The toll was twenty-two injured with five of them in the hospital. Of the injured, eight were white—four newsmen, two girls from the bus, a male student and John Seigenthaler, thirty-two, administrative assistant to United States Attorney General Robert F. Kennedy.

One woman was among the nine persons arrested—all of them white. Some were booked on charges of disorderly conduct and refusing to obey an officer. Two were held on drunk charges.

After the rioting came to an end in the terminal, two negroes were attacked in front of the building. They were slapped, punched, knocked down and stomped on.

Then, in the intersection of Adams and Court Sts., a half block from the terminal, a mob of whites put upon a group of negroes. A white threw a bottle at a negro. The negroes, all townspeople, retaliated with rocks. Then a white poured an inflammable liquid over a negro and set his clothes on fire. The police and mounted sheriff's deputies broke the riot up with tear gas and the crowd dispersed for the day.

Gov. John Patterson in a statement said: "I have no sympathy for law violators whether they be agitators from outside Alabama or inside-the-state troublemakers."

An hour after the police broke up the mob, Gov. Patterson said:

"It is our duty to maintain the law and I will not allow any group to take the law into their hands. The good name of our state and our people is at stake, and I can state frankly that violence of any type will not be tolerated.

"The highways of Alabama are safe and state patrolmen will do all in their power to enforce law and order at all times. We have the men, the equipment and the will to keep the public peace, and we use no help—from the Federal government, from 'interested citizens' or anyone else.

"While we will do our utmost to keep the public highways clear and to guard against all disorder, we cannot escort busloads or carloads of rabble-rousers about our state from city to city for the avowed purpose of disobeying our laws, flaunting (sic) our customs and traditions and creating racial incidents. Such unlawful acts serve only to further enrage our population. I have no use for these agitators or their kind."

From the time the split-level St. Petersburg Express pulled out of the Greyhound terminal in Birmingham at 8:30 a.m. Central Standard Time, until it arrived at the terminal here at 10:23 a.m., the ride went without incident. It was escorted by Birmingham motorcycle police, their sirens screaming, to the city limits and then picked up by the state highway patrol, which brought it almost to the city limits of Montgomery. One unmarked police car, carrying two plain-clothesmen, stayed behind the road cruiser constantly as it barreled down the highway at speeds up to eighty-seven miles an hour.

Overhead, a highway patrol airplane circled continuously, looking for potential danger on the seven-minute ride from the Montgomery city limits to the terminal. Two Montgomery detectives followed the bus in an unmarked car. Police cars were seen all along the route.

But when the bus pulled into the terminal, there was not a policeman in sight. The mob gathered quickly on the platform.

The students, somber and quiet, stepped off the bus. Newsmen, including the television men with cameras and microphones, approached them for an interview.

John Lewis, twenty-one, of Troy, Ala., a student at the American Baptist Seminary in Nashville, Tenn., acted as spokesman for the group. He was asked the purpose of the trip.

"We just got out of Birmingham. We got to Montgomery. . . ." he said and then his words trailed off as his gaze fixed over the shoulder of this reporter.

Mr. Lewis had spotted the mob approaching. The group of students and newsmen started to give way down the platform to the advancing crowd.

One of the mob hit Moe Levy of NBC across the face. That was the first blow. The mob surrounded the cameramen, grabbed their equipment and flung it against the pavement until microphone, recording equipment and cameras were broken shambles. Meanwhile, a "Life" magazine cameraman was attacked.

Then the mob turned to the students—sixteen Negroes, two white girls and a white man.

"Get those niggers!" the mob shouted.

The group was standing with their backs to a metal tube fence atop a ten-foot retaining wall. Below the wall was a post office parking lot and driveway. A white spectator was heard explaining what happened to a late coming friend this way:

"They just took those niggers and threw them over that fence. They didn't push them, they didn't shove them, they threw them over that rail."

His description was only a little exaggerated. Some of the students were indeed thrown, others jumped, some were pushed. All landed atop cars parked next to the wall. They scampered down from the cars and ran onto the post office loading platform. No asylum was granted.

Now it was five minutes after the outbreak started. There were still no police in sight. The fighting had spread to streets surrounding the terminal and the post office driveway.

The mob began hurling the baggage after the students. The suitcases landed on the cars and on the ground, spilling out their contents—here a black bow tie, there a religious picture postcard, somewhere else a purple nightgown and a bible.

Then, ten minutes after the first slap, a squad of police arrived under the command of Public Safety Commissioner L. B. Sullivan.

"I really don't know what happened," Mr. Sullivan told this reporter. "When I got here all I saw were three men lying in the street. There was two niggers and a white man.

"We called an ambulance for the white man but it was broken down and couldn't come, so two policemen took him to the hospital. I don't know what happened to the niggers."

The one white man this reporter saw with severe head injuries—his face was covered with blood, his lips and eyes were swollen, his blond hair caked with matted blood and dirt—was identified by Mr. Lewis as James M. Zwerg, twenty-one, an exchange student from the University of Wisconsin attending Fisk University in Nashville this year.

Before the bus left Birmingham, Mr. Zwerg and two white girls had sat with the Negroes for eighteen hours waiting to board a bus to Montgomery. Two hours before the bus pulled out, they gathered on the platform and sang Negro spirituals and hymns. Mr. Zwerg sang a solo part in "Oh Lord, keep your eyes on the prize."

Now his beating was over. He stood between Mr. Lewis, who was also beaten, and William Barbee, nineteen, another Nashville Seminary student. All three were bleeding.

Police made no effort to render first aid.

"The niggers will have to get out of here in a nigger taxi. The white boy will have to go in a white taxi," one officer said.

Dazed, Mr. Zwerg was led to a green Chevrolet, carrying the markings of Lane's Taxi at the terminal. He sat there. The taxi driver would not come near the car.

While policemen refused to interfere, two teen-agers from the mob poked their heads through the cab's open windows.

Mr. Zwerg's eyes were open but expressionless. He hardly moved. The bleeding had stopped.

Softly, one of his tormentors said:

"You're a rotten son of a bitch. Your mother is a dog. You are a dog. You know that? You ride with the niggers."

Mr. Zwerg shook his head in agreement.

"Can't you do something to get him out of here," Mr. Lewis asked this reporter, who witnessed the exchange.

I turned to a detective and said, "Excuse me, I don't want to butt in, but can't you do something to get him out of here," pointing to Mr. Zwerg.

The detective, nattily dressed in brown suit, conservative tie and straw hat, a diamond Masonic sword in his lapel, said: "He's free to go."

"But can't you get the driver of this taxi to take him away?"

"We ain't arranging transportation for these people. We didn't arrange their transportation here and we ain't going to take them away."

I explained the situation to Mr. Zwerg.

"You can't get me out of here. I don't even know where I am or how I got here," Mr. Zwerg said.

An hour later, he was still sitting in the cab.

One eyewitness to Mr. Zwerg's beating said he was the first of the students struck. Dan O. Dowe, state editor of "The Alabama Journal," said:

"Mr. Zwerg was hit with his own suitcase in the face. Then he was knocked down and a group pummeled him. Then one of the mob members picked him up and put his (Mr. Zwerg's) head between his (the mob member's) knees. Then the others took turns hitting him."

While all this was happening, I was standing next to a young father and his blonde, red-faced daughter who was about three.

"Daddy, what are they doing?"

The father didn't answer.

"Daddy, what's happening?"

"Well, they're really carrying on," the father said as he watched the mob.

A short-order cook joined the father. "Those niggers are getting what for today," he said, smiling. The father didn't smile.

"Daddy, what are they doing?"

I saw a reporter and photographer from "The Birmingham News" run for their car. The photographer had had his 35-mm. camera with expensive lens smashed by the crowd.

"Where are you going?" I asked.

"Take your tie off and get in this car. If anybody asks you, you're a Ku Kluxer, remember that."

I removed my tie. We drove around the block. I got out of the car and went back to the terminal.

Joe C. Morgan, president of Local 1314, Amalgamated Street, Electric Railway and Motor Coach Employees of America, A.F.L.-C.I.O., along with J. T. Duncan, chief Greyhound dispatcher in Birmingham, had ridden with the students.

"We were told we would have protection all the way," Mr. Morgan said. "We had it right up to the terminal and then it disappeared."

"Would you have allowed the bus to come if you knew there would be no police here?" I asked.

"No sir," he answered.

The driver of the bus was Joe Caverno, a stocky, powerful man who had first refused to take the bus out. At 6:05 a.m., he came to the bus, waiting at the platform with the would-be passengers at the door.

He went to the bus and said:

"I'm supposed to drive this bus to Dothan, Ala., through Montgomery, but I understand there is a big convoy down the road and I don't have but one life to give and I don't in-tend to give it to CORE of the N double A C P, and that's all I have to say."

Mr. Caverno disappeared back into a room marked "drivers only." Shortly before 8:30, he emerged after Birmingham Po-lice Commissioner Eugene Connor arrived and apparently played a part in arranging the escort.

On Wednesday, Mr. Connor had escorted seven of the students to the Tennessee border, asking them to get out of the state to save themselves and Alabama "a lot of trouble."

The students returned with fourteen others yesterday. During the night they waited and tried, unsuccessfully, to board three buses for Montgomery. Intrastate bus transportation (but not local buses in Birmingham and Montgomery) is still segregated.

The students sat in the waiting room marked "white waiting room for intrastate passengers." They tested the men's room and the white ticket counters and were served. Mr. Zwerg was refused service at the lunch counter in the Negro waiting room and was removed by police.

Last night a crowd of 3,000 gathered and heaped abuse on the students, throwing soda pop in their faces and stepping on their feet as they sat.

Finally, Mr. Connor ordered barricades set up a block away from the terminal in each direction and the crowd thinned. Less than a hundred spectators and almost as many police saw the bus off.

New York *Herald-Tribune*, May 21, 1961

Tear Gas and Hymns

by Murray Kempton

"Bless those cowards outside and our stupid Governor."

Montgomery is a legend written by cooks, janitors and country preachers. They came last night, as they have come so often to their First Baptist Church, this time to greet their children, twelve of the Nashville students whose test of segregated bus facilities had ignited their city the day before.

They came through unaccustomed attention, past clusters of white teenagers, standing in couples in the park across the street, silent, untrustworthy. John F. Kennedy's United States marshals, looking as if their hands were already blistering from the tense and unfamiliar grip of the billy, seemed a home guard of family men suddenly called up for an invasion.

In moments involving urgency, the average marshal was puffing after he had lumbered so much as ten feet. There were seventy of these gallant but unskilled conscripts; and going up the steps no wise man would have bet on them to hold off a minority of dedicated hoods—no more than fifty—who dared to aggress against them.

The national honor was being defended by men who looked overmatched even wearing six-shooters. The mob was pushing them back and back until the pavement before the church had become a postage stamp beachhead. The marshals experimented with tear gas and it floated back up the steps. The Negroes came out through the church doors coughing and wiping their eyes.

Inside, little pockets of tear gas floated about the rear of the church. The cooks and janitors and country preachers had every reason to believe—knowing themselves under siege—that the mob outside was bombarding them. They sat waving the fans donated by the Ross Clayton Funeral Home and they sang "Love Lifted Me." The chorus was thin, the melody sad and without pulse.

Somehow they seemed to have come not to lift themselves and those fortunate strangers privileged to watch them, but only to sit together and endure what might fall upon them.

The Reverend S. S. Seay, their chairman, stopped them from the rostrum. "Nobody is singing as if he believes," he said, "I want everybody to believe."

They began again louder and with more effort and spirit. It still seemed as if the years have brought them, more than any other sadness, a terrible loss of hope in a white South.

The bus riders, looking like children, were lined up in the second row of steel chairs. None of them sang and half of them held their hands over their eyes in the prayer gesture. The Attorney General of Alabama had haggled over them all afternoon; they are subject to arrest for contempt of a state injunction. There are restraints on arresting sinners like these in church, but they had no reason to believe that they would not be taken away some time that night. They are the best kind of protestants, the ones who will go to jail if they have to but do not exult at the prospect.

Downstairs before the meeting they'd quite suddenly put their hands together and one of them had said, "We've gone this far through hell; we can go a little farther."

The windows had been closed one by one against the gas and the high old room had begun to stifle, and the thunder outside was silent. The Reverend B. D. Lambert, who has a dancer's soul in a short clumsy body, began the prayer chant: "This is a great moment in history. We thank Thee, Lord, for the protection Thou hast given us. You have blessed us in so many ways that we have not the words to describe them. You are too wise to make a mistake and too powerful to fail. Bless our enemy and we thank Our Father for these fine young people."

One of the children in the second row felt the white bandage on the back of his head and looked embarrassed at this compliment from a grownup. "You, God, have been with us since 1955."

An outrider came back to whisper a report of a car burned and rocks hurled and even the fire trucks called out to hold the patch of pavement, and then stopped in mid-passage as the cadence of the Reverend Mr. Lambert began to move the church into a world of hope and prayer somewhere beyond battles' menaces.

"Bless all those cowards standin' outside that can't fight unless they have a mob to come with them. Bless that stupid Governor of ours."

The riot car went by outside screaming through the windows. "He holds us in the hollow of His hand." The Reverend Mr. Lambert beat on. "We don't know whether we will get home or not. But we are with Him in His house."

Somewhere in those few moments in the house when all pain and menace were forgotten, the police and the marshals and the sheriff's men cleared the streets outside.

By now there was not a breath of air in the room. The Reverend Ralph Abernathy arose to say: "We don't have to sweat here. The United States marshals are supposed to be out there to protect us." And then, in his shirt sleeves, Martin Luther King walked onto the platform and said: "We aren't going to become panicky. We're going to stand up for what we know is right.

"I just talked to Attorney General Kennedy."

His tone was matter of fact; the fans went on futilely beating before faces unsurprised. A Montgomery cook takes it for granted that while she sits under siege, Martin King can call the Attorney General of the United States on a Princess phone in the basement downstairs.

"He says he will stay in his office all night. He had been promised that no mob would be allowed to assemble. But they are at that door. Fear not. We have gone too far to turn back."

King and Abernathy went outside to talk to the marshals. They were met by a state trooper who said, "All right, are you going in or out?" In Montgomery, whatever the freaks of circumstance, a Negro minister is to be yelled at, a white thug to be cajoled.

The various choirs sang; the room settled down to a quiet where the sounds of the fans struggling through the air was loudest of all. There had fallen the long silence of endurance. There was a collection. The Reverend Fred Shuttlesworth, the merriest agitator of them all, had won them back to laughing at the Governor when he stopped in the middle to listen to a whisper in his ear and announced:

"The city is now under martial law and troops are on their way here."

There was a sudden great cheer. These people ask so little. The windows began to open to an unexpectedly quiet outside world; the damp, cool air came in; the fans slowed down; the cooks and janitors seemed to feel themselves solid protected citizens, waiting for the United States Army. They got John Patterson's National Guard, blinking against the television camera lights, lining up with jittery bayonets at the ready, perhaps one hundred scrawny boys who looked like the kids who had been standing in the park earlier and perhaps were those kids and thus to be commended for getting home and into their uniforms so quickly after their dispersal.

A Birmingham girl who had driven downtown for Coca-Colas came back with her car windows smashed by a rock. The First Baptist Church seemed to be the only place of peace in town. In the church, Martin King was speaking. On the pavement outside, Police Commissioner L. L. Sullivan was arguing that the meeting should break up now and the congregation go home. He was soft and soothing and without a note in his voice a stranger would trust.

By now, they had been there more than three hours. Little children were sleeping on the red plush back of the altar, like Italian paintings of the little St. John drowsing at the Last Supper. By now, the lights from their windows shone only on the bayonets of the National Guard in otherwise empty streets.

They began singing the "Battle Hymn of the Republic." The face of Fred Shuttlesworth seemed suddenly gray with weariness. At twenty of twelve there appeared on the rostrum State Adjutant General Henry V. Graham and State Public Safety Director Floyd Mann. Mann, almost by himself, had broken up the Greyhound mob the day before.

The Reverend Mr. Seay said that he had been asked to introduce the Adjutant General but first he would like to introduce a friend. "I choose my words when I talk about white folks, but there is a Christian soul in Mr. Mann. I think we ought to stand on our feet and thank him."

And everyone in the room stood up, and the mother in front awoke her child so he could stand up too and thank a white public servant who had done his duty.

And then arose the Adjutant General, a tall straight man, and said, "Fellow Citizens of Alabama," and then read Governor Patterson's proclamation of martial law, a horrid, pompus mash blaming the victims for the crime.

General Graham read this affront through right down to the words "so that the great seal of Alabama" and said that for their safety, the well-being of the city and the good of the state he was ordering them to stay there until morning.

And they rose, these gracious patient people, having again been insulted according to the habit of their state, and applauded General Graham too.

The Reverend Mr. Seay's misty glasses were heavy with reproach. "I don't think," he said, "that was a document for cheering. I want to be respectful to our leaders and to the government of Alabama but if John Patterson hadn't been playing cheap politics we wouldn't be here now. I think you ought to take those cheers back."

The repentant heads nodded and they began singing that they would overcome and sat down for the dawn watch. Out on the pavement, hemmed in by the National Guard, a woman was wondering how she would be able to call her boss. These are proud, brave and faithful people and some of them even found time to worry about the wives of pillars of the White Citizens Councils who were in danger of having to cook their own breakfasts this morning.

That danger was lifted three and a half hours later, when this message was transmitted over the Montgomery police radio:

"We understand that at 3 A.M. the National Guard turned those niggers loose from that church. Look for them, and if you find any see them safely home."

from *America Comes of Middle Age:*
Columns 1950–1962 (1963)

2 Mob Victims Ready To Die for Integration

by Bob Duke

Two adamant "Freedom Riders"—battered and bruised from beatings administered by a white mob—vowed Saturday afternoon to sacrifice their lives if necessary to break down racial barriers in the South.

They were beaten into insensibility by the mob who attacked 22 integrationists after they debarked from a bus here Saturday morning.

The two smiled wryly from their hospital beds in St. Jude's Hospital, refusing to halt a crusade against Dixie segregation laws which has brought them to the brink of death.

One of the patients is black and the other is white. But they have one thing in common: a hatred of segregation and a pledge to destroy it.

The duo are James W. Zwerg, 21, a white exchange student at Fisk University in Nashville; and William F. H. Barbee, 19, a student at American Baptist Theological Seminary in Nashville. Both are members of the Southern Christian Leadership Conference, headed by the Rev. Martin Luther King.

Zwerg, a native of Appleton, Wis., is a slim, blond man who maintains that "equality should be the goal of all Americans." He was the second person assaulted by the mob.

When he arrived in Montgomery, he was in good shape, both mentally and physically. When the mob finished with him, he was in bad shape all-around.

Zwerg sustained several cracked teeth, cuts about the face and head and bruises of the body during the unprovoked assault.

After the beating, he remained in a Negro taxi cab for about 30 minutes before a Highway Patrol car took him to the hospital. He sat in the front seat of the vehicle with blood streaming from his face, his eyes staring straight ahead as if in a hypnotic trance.

From his hospital bed Zwerg recounted to an Advertiser reporter events occurring before and after the brutal beating.

"We expected violence when we got off the bus and failed to see any policemen around," he said, emitting a groan from his mashed, blood-caked lips.

"They (the mob) assaulted a cameraman first, and then turned on me. One of them knocked me to the pavement, calling me a dirty nigger-lover.

"At this point, all of them pounced on me, stomping me, kicking me, and swearing they were going to kill me. That's all I remember until I awakened in the Negro cab.

"I remained groggy for a long time, wondering in my semiconscious state why I wasn't being taken to a hospital.

"I understand your police commissioner said he didn't send for an ambulance because I hadn't requested one. I'd like to know how I could request one in my dazed condition. I suppose a person has to be dead before anyone will call an ambulance in Montgomery.

"You may inform the people in Montgomery and the rest of the Deep South states that we intend to continue our 'freedom rides' until the last vestige of segregation disappears from bus stations.

"We took a vow when we left Nashville that we would give our lives if necessary to abolish discrimination in the South. We knew that many Southerners would hate us at first, but we prefer to believe that this hatred will someday change to love and we can all live together in peace and harmony."

Zwerg said Negroes and whites will continue their campaign against segregation, declaring that more groups were prepared to take the place of the one halted in Montgomery.

"We're not doing this just for ourselves, but for all Americans," he said. "How can we meet the Communist threat, win the allegiance of African and Asian nations, as long as there is injustice against minority groups in this country?" he asked.

He pooh-poohed the prevailing Southern belief that Negroes and liberals were trying to mongrelize the Negro and white races in America. "Negroes, like whites, prefer to marry within their own race," he contended.

Zwerg constantly expressed the opinion that there would be a change of feeling among Southerners on the racial issue.

Asked what he thought would happen if such a reversal doesn't take place, he replied: "There'll be a change. God and love will take care of that."

Barbee was in worse condition than Zwerg. His face was puffed and swollen and his voice was barely perceptible as he related the vicious beating he received.

He was the Negro who was pulled by members of the mob from a taxi while a group of Freedom Riders were fleeing from the bus station area.

Barbee was almost in the cab when two white men grabbed him, pushing and shoving him to the entrance of the station. He escaped from the men but was captured again when he ran to the rear of the station.

The Negro youth gave this account of the incident:

"After I got away from the first two men, about six or seven more grabbed me near the loading platform. I pleaded with them to let me go, but they knocked me down and started stomping me.

"I don't know what happened then because I was unconscious. While they were beating and cursing me, I had the uneasy feeling they intended to murder me. I awakened at the hospital."

Barbee was saved by Alabama Public Safety Director Floyd Mann, who pulled his pistol on the white assailants and threatened to shoot them unless they moved away from the unconscious Negro.

He was unaware that Mann had saved his life at the time. But he praised the public safety director when he was informed of Mann's act.

Like Zwerg, Barbee vowed to continue his moves against Southern segregation, saying he is willing to "surrender my life for the cause of justice."

"We knew they would probably beat us before we got here," he stated. "We were willing to give our all so men of every race, creed and color may be equal before the law."

Both Zwerg and Barbee disclaimed any hatred toward the mob of whites who assaulted them.

Barbee ended the interview on a defiant note. "We'll batter your segregation institutions until they crumble to dust," he said with emotion.

The two bruised and battered Freedom Riders fell asleep as the reporter was leaving. With all the trouble in Birmingham, they hadn't slept in three days, they said.

The Montgomery Advertiser, May 21, 1961

A Walk Through a Georgia Corridor

by Charlayne Hunter

ON one hot day early in July of 1959, Hamp (Hamilton Holmes) and I went down to the Court House in Atlanta to have our application forms certified, a routine but necessary step in our attempt to enroll as students in the University of Georgia. We went to one judge and presented the papers. Though the papers were in order he flatly refused to sign and waved us away, saying, "You people are just trying to start something." Finally, the Clerk of the Superior Court signed the forms which certified our status as residents of the State of Georgia, but he said, "This doesn't mean that you are going to get in." As an afterthought, he added, "Course it doesn't mean you won't get in either."

All this talk made little sense to me. After all, I had gone to school with white students before. My family and I had lived in Alaska while my father was stationed there.

I recalled the first day I walked into class there. I was the only Negro student in the eighth grade, and except for a few smaller students in the first or second grades, the only Negro in the entire school. I thought about my first day in class in Alaska a long time after the clerk had left. The first person in the class to speak to me that day had been a 16-year-old girl from Alabama. We became close friends from that day on. There was a boy in the class, too, a Texan, who eagerly jumped at any opportunity to sing the praises of his native state and of Sam Rayburn, Speaker of the House—and, of course, a Texan.

The two years between the time when Hamp and I first applied and our eventual admittance to the campus at Athens were filled with official excuses and delays, legal hearings and conferences, rumors and counter rumors in the press and elsewhere. The net result always seemed to be to push us further from our goal.

So I had enrolled at Wayne State in Detroit to begin work-ing toward the Journalism major which the University of Georgia still denied me. Hamp enrolled at Morehouse and began his pre-med work there. As the lawyers argued back and forth and we became "temporary" students on our own respective campuses, there were times when I myself began to doubt that I would ever get my degree from Georgia rather than Wayne.

So it was on that afternoon of January 6, 1961, when I rushed into the dormitory at Wayne, grabbed my mail and ran up to my room on the second floor, my only concern was getting into something comfortable before going to sorority meeting at 5 o'clock.

I had not been in my room ten minutes before I was called to answer the phone out in the hall. Expecting to hear one of my friends on the other end I was surprised to hear instead, an unfamiliar voice saying, "Congratulations!"

"For what?" I asked, completely in the dark.

The woman on the other end identified herself as a reporter for a New York paper. She told me that news had just come over the wires that Federal Judge Bottle had ordered Hamp and me admitted to the University of Georgia.

By the time she managed to read the entire release to me, both of us were between laughter and tears. My caller brought both of us back to reality by pointing out that she had a story to write.

From that moment on there was no possibility of a mo-ment of calm and quiet in which I could think about what was ahead. Downstairs the switchboard operator was soon swamped by calls. I grew even more confused as reporters seemed to be arriving by the carload.

In a way it was a relief to break away and rush off to soror-ity meeting. I arrived, bubbling over with elation, and began eagerly sharing the long-awaited news with my Delta sisters. But I found their reaction rather puzzling. Instead of sharing in my jubilation, they became quiet and solemn.

It was not until 36 hours later, as I sat on the plane to Atlanta that I began to realize what they had already seen. As I looked around the plane, wishing for someone with whom I could share my happiness, all the faces I saw were cold and unfamiliar. Gradually I began to realize what I had left behind, what might be ahead.

It was several days before the full impact of my friends' unspoken fears struck home. Hamp and I, struggling through throngs of reporters, photographers and hostile or curious onlookers, managed to get registered for classes. Though not before we had been temporarily brought to a halt by a last-ditch injunction granted the lawyers for the state. We had begun to learn how to hear and not to hear harsh names, the threats, the jeering laughter, while being silently grateful for the occasional friendly greetings of a small minority and the fair-minded treatment of most of the University officials and faculty members.

It was uncomfortable to have to attend classes under guard, but we were already hopeful that this would soon be unnecessary. There had been crowds outside my dormitory on Tuesday night after my first full day of classes, but the fire-crackers and the taunts had not prevented my going to sleep. After my classes on Wednesday, January 16, I came back to the dormitory prepared for more of the same, but almost totally unprepared for what was actually to happen.

It was about 2 p.m. when the detectives brought me back to my ground-floor room at Center Myers. There were crowds outside, but then there had been crowds since the first moment I arrived on campus. The lobby of the dormitory was almost empty, but after I had gone to my room many of the girls came down as they had the day before—to welcome, observe, inspect. Mrs. Porter, the housemother, came down and told the girls not to stay too long because I was tired. She had advised me earlier that it would be best to have my dinner in my room that night. This again, seemed only a normal precaution considering the circumstances.

It began getting dark around six o'clock. After the last of the girls had gone, everything became amazingly quiet inside the dorm. I picked up a book and tried to study, but then the firecrackers began popping outside as they had the night before. I decided there was nothing to do but go to bed, despite the racket outside. Mrs. Porter came in again to see if I had eaten and to ask how I was feeling. She suggested that I keep

the blinds closed and stay away from the windows. "We expect some trouble," she said.

Later, as I went out into the hall for a drink of water, I
caught a glimpse of the faculty members the students had
nicknamed "The Baby-Sitting Crew." It seemed to me the
group was larger than it had been the night before. I returned
to my room. After a while the noise outside gradually grew
louder and uglier.

Though I did not know it at the time, a hotly-disputed basketball team last-minute defeat at the hands of Georgia Tech
had helped to create anything but a mood of sweet reasonableness in the crowd that had marched from the gym to the
dormitory.

Reading or sleeping was out of the question. I was in the
first room of the duplex apartment. Suddenly there was a
loud crash from the bedroom. Not stopping to think, I
rushed in, only to be stopped in my tracks by another crash as
a Coca Cola bottle followed the brick which had ripped
through the window a moment before. Jagged splinters of
window glass and fragments of the bottle had spattered across
my dress, slippers and the skirts and blouses I had not yet had
time to unpack.

Strangely enough I was not at all afraid at this moment. Instead I found myself thinking as I stood there in the middle
of the wreckage, *So this is how it is.*

At this time I did not know that all of the lights in the dormitory had been turned out. With the rest of the building in
darkness the three brightly-lit windows of my apartment must
have made a most inviting target for the mob out on the
lawn.

I heard the Dean's voice in the hall and called out to him,
but he did not hear me. I met a campus patrolman in the hall
and told him what had happened. As he went into my room
to investigate I continued down the hall to the counselor's
office a couple of doors away. There in the darkness I went to
the window and looked out. All I could see was a moving
mass, not a face that could be recognized as that of a separate
person. Even the voices seemed to run together in one confusion of shouts and jeers.

Turning from the window, I saw that the partition between

the counselor's room and the lobby was open. The crashing of glass and the screams of one girl on the floor above, who had been struck by a brick as she looked out of her window, had brought most of the girls into the lobby. Some of them passed back and forth, looking in to see how I was reacting to all this.

I realized it was nearing time for the 11 o'clock news and that my mother in Atlanta would be waiting up for it. I called her and told her that I was all right. Though I knew she could hear the noise in the background, she seemed relatively calm. But I could not get her to promise that she would go to bed at once, without waiting to look at the television news program.

After I hung up, one of the most genuine persons it has been my good luck to meet came down and began talking to me. Though it was clear that she herself was nervous, she did all she could under the circumstances to take my mind off what was going on.

This was anything but easy, since by now the hostility from outside was being echoed by some of those inside the dorm. Perhaps it was partially out of hysteria, or partially out of a re-action to the fact that the girl upstairs had been hurt. At any rate, a group of girls began tramping in a continuous circle, yelling insults first at me and then at the schoolmate who had come in to befriend me.

It was hard to sit there and listen to some of the things that were said about me without being able to answer. I was told I was about to become "a black martyr, getting 50 dollars a day for this,"—a piece of news that would have considerably surprised my family.

The city police outside, after having waited in vain for the state patrol, finally resorted to tear gas and the crowd outside began to break up. The gas fumes began seeping into the dorm and the girls were told to change the linen on their beds. This prompted deliberately loud offers of a dime or a quarter to "Charlayne" for changing the sheets of these same residents who professed to believe I was already being paid at a rate of over six dollars an hour, if figured on the basis of an eight-hour day.

My little friend was beginning to get drowsy, though she

tried not to show it, and I suggested that she go to bed, assuring her that I would be all right. After she had left I wondered how many people, myself included, would have had the courage to do what she had done.

The House-Mother came in, looking worn from the ordeal of trying to console 150 overwrought girls. She gave me an orange. "It's a sweet orange," she said. "I think you might enjoy it."

Mrs. Porter left again as I began peeling the orange. Before I had finished, she was back again. This time she was serious and unsmiling.

Slowly, sympathetically, she told me that the Dean had said I would have to leave. I was to be taken to Atlanta so that I would be safe—and so that the other girls in the building would also be safe.

I don't think I heard the rest of what she said. I suddenly felt totally sick and miserable. All I could think was *I've failed, I've failed*. I began to cry and, hard though I tried, I couldn't stop. Mrs. Porter reassuringly patted me on the arm and told me not to cry and not to worry. "Everything will be all right," she said. But, needless to say, I could not really believe this.

I packed quickly, not even bothering to remove the pieces of glass from my suitcase. Dean Williams came to my room and repeated what Mrs. Porter had said. Feeling totally empty inside I followed him out of the room, stopping only to pick up my Madonna from the table beside the bed. Afterwards it bothered me to think that people looking at the pictures might mistakenly think I was crying because of fear. But at that moment I was too sick to care.

The girls were all quiet now. They were huddled together in the lobby as I came by. A few of them started to hiss, but they were immediately shushed into silence by the others.

The state troopers had finally arrived. As we came out into the chilly night air I saw the gray patrol cars parked at the curb. The husky, red-faced troopers in their gray uniforms and broad-brimmed hats were impassive and coolly official in speech and manner.

We stopped to pick up the Dean of Women at her residence. I remember saying something about being sorry to inconvenience her at that hour, to which she answered that she couldn't sleep from worrying about what was going on. When we arrived at the home at which Hamp was living, he was on the telephone, talking to Attorney Hollowell in Atlanta. Hamp wanted to drive his car home. I realized how near hysteria I was when I found myself insisting almost wildly that he leave his car and ride back with me in the patrol car.

As we sped along the often bumpy highway toward home, Hamp and I had little to say. Neither of us could get used to the idea that we had been "suspended." Yet what could we say or do about it?

I remember almost nothing of the trip itself. Before I knew it we were in Atlanta, turning into my block and pulling up in front of the porch where the man had stood so many long months ago telling me that I should give up the idea of trying to go to the University of Georgia.

The news of our coming had preceded us and a few close friends had gathered at the house. Most reassuring of all, my mother, her hair done up in braids, came out with open arms to welcome both Hamp and me and to take some of the sting out of our forced homecoming.

That night is behind me now, no more troublesome than any other bad dream remembered once in a while. What I prefer remembering now are the court rulings that readmitted us, the decision not to close the University, the Legislature's dropping of the state's segregation laws. But most of all I appreciate the courage of those faculty members, students, and citizens of Georgia who spoke out against mob rule and stood up for our right to attend classes in peace. It was because of all these things that there was no disturbance when I went into the cafeteria with three classmates the other day for my first meal in a University dining room.

Today as I walked from class, I met many students who nodded, or smiled, or greeted me in one way or another. I had watched one student as she approached from quite a distance. We smiled—and so did the little kitten she was carrying in the pocket of her sweater.

Later that day, back in the dorm, the House-Mother came

down to bring me a letter which had a "postage due" on it.
In her own sweet way, and with a charming smile, she inquired as to how my day had gone. Before long she was called
to help one of "her girls" make a costume for a ball she was
to attend that night. Assured that I was all right and not
lonely, the dear lady went off to perform another of her thou-
sand-and-one duties as mother to over 150 girls.

Just about that time there was a knock at the door and a
tall, blonde, rather attractive girl came in with a bag of groceries in her arms. "Hi," she said, smiling. "Let's cook dinner.
I'm starved."

Whatever sadness I felt was forgotten as we made a tossed
salad. I began washing the lettuce, and she and another girl
who had come along began slicing tomatoes and all sorts of
vegetables that go to make up a tossed salad. We fried ham-
burgers too.

Dishes washed, food eaten, company gone, I was alone
again. A little sad still, a little lonely. Perhaps. But at least I
knew that I would not always be lonely. My friends at Wayne
would always be my friends—though they'll graduate and go
their various ways . . .

The room was a little too warm—it gets warm early in
Georgia. So I went over and opened the window. New
screens had replaced the ones through which the brick and
coke bottle ripped that night. There were no mobs on the
lawn outside. No tear gas was in the air, nor patrol cars at the
curb. Only beautifully landscaped grounds, green shrubbery
and, across the street, a lovely modernistic church whose steps
—once crowded with on-lookers, demonstrators and cameramen—were deserted in the shadows of late afternoon. A couple strolled past, hand in hand, completely absorbed in each
other.

Maybe I am poorly qualified to predict what tomorrow will
be like—a tomorrow made up of days which may be weeks,
months and even years in coming . . . when Charlayne
Hunter and Hamilton Holmes will be forgotten except by
those who have come to know them as classmates or as
friends.

But tomorrow, when some of the "problems" which complicate living together for human beings in Georgia, and the nation, have faded far into the background, not one, not two, but many Negro students will be able to walk through a Georgia corridor unnoticed except for their abilities or the impact of their individual personalities.

The Urbanite, June 1961

Travel Notes from a Deep South Tourist

by Frank Holloway

THE Sunday after the mob violence in Montgomery, Ala., Harold Andrews, an Atlanta college student, and I decided to go to Montgomery to join the Freedom Riders. We didn't have the money, and most of the Southern Christian Leadership Conference people and the Student Non-Violent Coordinating Committee were already in Montgomery so we couldn't get travel funds from them. We ran all over town after money, and finally borrowed some from a neighbor. He told us that his only regret was that he didn't have more to give us.

We bought our tickets at the Greyhound Bus Station, and went to the station cafeteria which had never served Negroes. We were served without any trouble, the first Negroes to eat there, and we felt pretty good that this was settled. However, there were heavy detachments of plainclothes policemen on the scene. I don't know how they got there so fast but there they were. After a piece of pie and about three cups of coffee, we went to the loading dock to board the bus. The plainclothesmen were right behind us, trying to be inconspicuous. We got on the bus and sat in the first and second seats on the left side. I think this sort of shook the bus driver up. He kept looking at us and then got off the bus and talked to a couple of the policemen, pointing in our direction. The other passengers were mumbling and I could sense they were talking about us.

"It looks like the Freedom Ride is starting right here," I said to Harold. After about ten minutes the driver got back on the bus, and we were on our way. A police car followed us until we reached the city limits.

When we pulled into the LaGrange, Ga., station, the driver told us we had a 15-minute rest stop. Harold and I got off the bus and went into the so-called "white" waiting room. We

were met by a man who called himself the manager or something like that. He told us the "colored" waiting room was
around in back. We smiled slightly and kept on walking into
the white waiting room. He said, "Get out of the —— white
waiting room and go where you belong." We still didn't say
anything to him. About this time up pops a policeman telling
us to "get your —— outa here or else." I asked the policeman
where was the rest room. He pulled his night stick or blackjack, swung wildly at us. We backed off, but he did hit us a
little. Then the manager and two or three other men pushed,
hit and kicked us right on out of the waiting room.

People were beginning to gather on the outside. The bus
was about to leave, so we got back on and sat in front as before. Outside we noticed two of the "agitators," telephoning.
We believe they passed the word on that two Freedom Riders
were en route to Montgomery.

One thing that made us feel rather good happened at
Tuskegee when the bus picked up some Negro passengers,
who went to the rear. A couple of minutes later a Negro man
came up and sat by Harold. He told Harold that he noticed us
sitting in the front when he got on and that he had never seen
this before in Alabama. Then he said it came to him we were
Freedom Riders, and that he felt an obligation to us and himself to join us in the front, although he was afraid to. He also
said he didn't exactly go along with the non-violence jive the
students were practicing. So for the remainder of the trip we
talked to him about non-violence in opposition to violence.

We arrived in Montgomery about 9 p.m. The city seemed
to be going crazy. There were masses of people out on the
streets with police cars, state troopers and federal marshals,
and the noise of sirens. Our bus was escorted from the city
limits to the Greyhound station by two carloads of marshals.
In the heart of town, mobs of people waved their fists and
yelled at us. At the station we met a mob estimated to be
1,500 strong. We sat in the bus for a few minutes and then got
off. The marshals held the mob off and some 20 of them surrounded us to protect us. One of them told me that the news
had gotten to Montgomery that two more Freedom Riders
(us) were arriving that night, hence the mob's welcome party.
Anyway, we went into the "white" waiting room and tried to

phone for help, while the marshals were holding back the crowd on the outside. We couldn't contact the Montgomery Negro leaders, so we decided to get some sort of transportation to one of their houses. But the cab drivers refused to take us and the Negroes were afraid to come anywhere near the bus station. So there we were, stranded, not knowing anyone and with no place to go, and no way to get there. Negroes outside of the waiting room were afraid to help us. They said some Negro cars had been burned by the mob and they feared it might happen again. We had no choice but to try to walk away. One Negro told us there was a large mass meeting at the First Baptist Church, where Rev. Ralph Abernathy is pastor, and that Dr. King and all the Freedom Riders were there.

We left on foot, not knowing what direction to take. Before we got 50 feet from the station we were stopped by the police and federal marshals, who made us go back into the bus station for our own protection. We went into the "white" waiting room, and Montgomery police came in and told us we would have to go to the "Negro" side, because the mob outside was angry and they didn't want to have "any trouble like we had yesterday."

We didn't say anything, but just continued telephoning, trying to reach some Montgomery Negro leaders. Again, they asked us to move, this time more firmly. The federal marshals came up to us and stood by us silently. The police asked us to move a third time and when we didn't they put us under arrest. We were charged with refusing to obey an officer.

About an hour after our arrest we were freed. Two sergeants escorted us back to the bus station. They refused to tell us why we were freed or where we were going. In fact, they told me to "shut your —— mouth or else we'll take matters into our own hands." So I shut up. At the bus station we still had the problem of making contact with the Negro community. It seemed that everything and everybody was working against us, and we didn't know what to do or where to go.

Finally a brave young Negro cab driver came by to help us. Well, we were glad to see that cat. For one solid hour or more we rode through Montgomery streets, trying to get to the church, but the streets to the church were blocked off by Alabama Guards. We ran into several road blocks and were searched five times, but we finally made it to the church.

Two or three hundred National Guardsmen surrounded the church. Inside were three or four times as many people as the church was supposed to hold, and it was very hot and uncomfortable. Some people were trying to sleep, but there was hardly room for anybody to turn around. Dr. King, other leaders and the Freedom Riders were circulating through the church talking to people and trying to keep their spirits up.

But it was a relief and like a haven to be among friends. Anyway, they kept us in the church overnight until about six a.m. when everybody left. We Freedom Riders went to Negro homes.

We stayed there three days, during which time we had several workshops on non-violence. We couldn't move around the city, being guarded by the National Guard. In the meantime, several other Freedom Riders joined us.

About 7:30 a.m. Wednesday, the first busload of Freedom Riders left for Jackson, beginning our invasion of the Sovereign State of Mississippi and its rigid segregation.

I left on another bus at 11 a.m. First, we ate integrated in the "white" room without any trouble, guarded by about 50 National Guardsmen. We were also escorted on our ride by troopers and Guardsmen, about 10 cars in front of us and maybe 15 behind us. Ahead of the parade were some 20 Montgomery motorcycle police, who left us at the city limits.

We had several reporters and National Guardsmen on our bus. The Guards sat both behind and in front of us, with their commanding officer standing in front, looking as if he would shoot us if we made the slightest move. So we didn't make the slightest move.

The newsmen interviewed us and other times we looked out of the window at the pretty scenery and talked about what we would eat at Jackson. Some of us slept and some read.

The Alabama troopers and National Guardsmen left us at the state line, and more hostile Mississippi troopers and Guardsmen picked us up. The bus didn't make any regularly scheduled stops, but we did stop at a Negro cafe on the road with five minutes for whatever we had to do. After a five-hour ride, this was hardly time enough for all of us, but we were more fortunate than the first bus, which didn't stop any place. We made several requests to the driver for rest stops, but he had orders not to stop. At the outskirts of small Mississippi towns, people outside their houses and stores shook their fists and threw rocks at us. I thought it was rather amusing, because the trip had gotten so dull and tiresome.

At Jackson the city police met us and escorted us to the bus station. Behind all these escorts I felt like the President of the United States touring Russia or something. Outside the bus a sort of tunnel of guards led from the bus to the "white" waiting room. In fact, they had blocked the way to the "Negro" waiting room, so that if some of us had changed our minds we couldn't have used the "Negro" rest room anyway.

We got off the bus and walked through the "tunnel" of troopers, guardsmen, city police and reporters. At the door of the waiting room a policeman stood there like the doorman of the Waldorf Astoria and opened the door for us. There were more police inside. I guess the crooks in the city had a field day because all the Jackson police were at the bus station making tunnels and opening doors for us.

We tried to make our way through the crowded cafeteria but never did get there. I still wonder what do they serve in that cafeteria, since they guard it as if it was Fort Knox or America's security weapon. Anyway, a policeman in blue pants and lots of white, shiny buttons pinned on his shirt, by the name of Captain Ray, came over and said, "You people must leave, keep moving," etc. I kept moving because it was so crowded I was pushed all over the place. Captain Ray ordered again, "You people move on." His boys then began picking out the black people and placing them under arrest. Being black, I was arrested.

There was one white fellow and a very fair Negro who had a hard time getting arrested. The white fellow had to tell a policeman that he was with the Freedom Riders. Then they took us out to the paddy wagon.

We got in and immediately began to sing our student songs. I heard one white spectator say to another, "What in

the —— those niggers singing about?" and the other one answered, "I don't know, but they'll change their tune soon as
they get their head beaten in a couple of times." "You're
right," the first one said. "The police aren't going to take any
—— from those niggers like the other places did."

We sang until we reached the jail. Inside, the captain told
us to stop singing. They took us to a room to be booked, and
here we received unusually kind treatment. "What is your
name, sir?" a policeman who was booking me asked. "My
name is Frank Holloway," I replied. "Excuse me, sir," he said,
"You mean your name is *Mister* Frank Holloway."

I could tell it was nearly killing them to be kind and polite,
and that they were just following orders they didn't like and
throwing some sarcasm in to make it easier on them.

After dinner they took us to our cells which were fairly
clean; the beds were hard and uncomfortable but sleepable.
About 12 of us were in one two-room cell.

We stayed in the city jail for two days, singing, discussing
the news, telling jokes, etc. Time passed pretty fast because
we had a lot to talk about and were becoming better acquainted with each other. The food wasn't too hot, but staying hungry most of the time made it taste pretty good. They
gave us clean linen, soap, toilet articles, which I thought was
very accommodating. That day we were allowed to shave,
which they told me is very uncommon in Mississippi.

Then they took us to a room where we met the other Freedom Riders and our lawyer, so we could decide what to do at
the hearing. We decided right away to plead not guilty (of
breach of the peace), and to take any sentence given to us.

There were many reporters and few spectators in the courtroom. This was the largest crowd they had ever had in this
courtroom, I was told. The judge showed little interest in our
attorney's and the city attorney's arguments. As soon as they
concluded, the judge ruled guilty and gave us two months
suspended sentences and $200 fines, or 67 days time to serve.

Found guilty of breach of the public peace, for trying to use
facilities of the Trailways Bus Station, for which we had bought
tickets with good American money, we went back to the city
jail to wait for transfer to the county jail. We were taken to the
Hinds County jail right across the street from the city jail.

When we went in we were met by some of the meanest looking, tobacco-chewing lawmen I have ever seen. They ordered us around like a bunch of dogs, and I really began to feel like I was in a Mississippi jail. Our cell was nasty and the beds were harder than the city jail beds, hardly sleepable, but the eight of us in our cell had to lie down somewhere. It was very cold during the night because the window was broken, and we didn't have enough cover.

We struggled through a horrible breakfast the next morning. I had slipped in a couple of bars of soap from the city jail and decided to take a shower, but the shower didn't work properly, and the sink didn't either. We didn't have much to do but wait and see if lunch would be as bad as breakfast. After lunch we wrote letters we couldn't mail because we had sealed them up. We talked about the Freedom Rides, the Student Movement in general, and our commitment to non-violence. Dinner was worse than breakfast or lunch, although I hadn't thought that was possible. We read a little literature we had smuggled in, and then lay down on those things they called beds, and had a very chilly and unrestful sleep.

After breakfast next day, we began to sing Student Movement songs. A jailer came into our ward and told us to "cut out that —— noise." We kept on singing. He told us we were "a bunch of smart —— and we got ways of taking care of black —— niggers who get out of their place." We kept on singing, and we couldn't hear all of the cussing and name-calling.

The jailer left and came back with somebody of higher authority, and we had two Mississippi experts cussing us out. We kept on singing, and they threatened to put us in the sweat box or solitary. They took three of us and told us they were going to put all of us in the sweat box if we didn't shut up. We kept on singing, and they took a few more of us to the sweat box and threatened to beat the rest of us over the head with a stick.

Later, when they realized we were not going to stop singing regardless of what they did to us, they brought those they had locked up in the sweat box back to the cell. One jailer told me they could get rid of a nigger in Mississippi, and nobody could do anything about it. The first thing that came into my mind was the Charlie Parker case.*

After several days they ordered us to pack up and get ready to move. Later a bunch of armed guards escorted us to two station wagons, which took us to the Hinds County penal farm. When we got there we met several men in ten-gallon hats, looking like something out of an old Western, with rifles in their hands, staring at us as if we were desperate killers about to escape. This tickled me, and I had to smile. Here we were, non-violent Freedom Riders, who had come to jail to stay there, and they led us through a tunnel of men holding rifles to prevent our escape. They locked us up in the farm jail. Soon they took us out to a room, boys on one side and girls on the other. One by one, they took us into another room for questioning before they gave us our black and white stripes.

There were about eight guards with sticks in their hands in the second room, and the Freedom Rider being questioned was surrounded by these men. Outside we could hear the questions, and the thumps and whacks, and sometimes a quick groan or a cry, when their questions weren't answered to their satisfaction. They beat several Riders who didn't say, "Yes sir," but none of them would Uncle-Tom the guards.

Rev. C. T. Vivian of Chattanooga was beaten pretty bad. When he came out he had blood streaming from his head. They took him to the penal farm doctor, who apparently patched him up so he looked like he had not been beaten when we saw him again.

We could hear somebody slap a girl Freedom Rider, and her quick, little scream—I guess it was knocked out of her. She was about five feet tall and wore glasses, and they beat her because she wouldn't Uncle-Tom them or behave in a subservient manner.

I wasn't beaten myself, but they did call me all the dirty names they seemed able to think of. I was about the 15th man

---

*Charles Parker, a Negro charged with rape, was abducted from the Mississippi jail and murdered by a mob in 1959. His body was found in a river. After investigation, the FBI offered its extensive report to a grand jury, which returned no indictments.

to go in there, and the prison doctor must have warned them about beating us after Reverend Mr. Vivian's injuries.

So, after being guarded by men with guns big enough to kill an elephant, called nasty and unbelievable names, beaten until blood ran down some of our faces, we were ordered to work in the fields in 100-degree weather from sunup until sundown. I didn't get a chance to work too long and get too hot, because I was soon released.

My friend Harold Andrews and I got out on a $500 appeal bond to go back to Montgomery as witnesses in a case against the city of Montgomery and its police department because of our unlawful arrest in Montgomery.

Guards rushed us back to Jackson, sirens clearing the way, being, I suppose, so glad to get rid of a couple of Freedom Riders. We told our lawyer about the brutality inflicted on the Freedom Riders, and that if something weren't done, someone might be killed at that farm. Our lawyers notified the FBI and the Negro Freedom Riders were transferred back to the Hinds County jail, where they were at least safe from guards at the isolated penal farm.

This experience of Freedom Riding and being locked up in Mississippi is something I will never forget. But I wouldn't trade it for anything. I am glad I was a witness undergoing the suffering which Negroes endure in Mississippi and helping in the big push for freedom all over the South. I feel also that the Freedom Riders are bringing about a new life for the Negro community in Mississippi. I would willingly go through the whole ordeal again.

New South, July/August 1961

Everybody Eats But Americans

by George Collins

SOMETIMES it's hard to be colored in Maryland.

This was proven Tuesday when a team of AFRO reporters, posing as non-existent African diplomats, from a non-existent African country, were served by three restaurants, heretofore closed to persons of color.

Although they were refused service at two others, the restaurant officials concerned, either apologized or attempted to give the fake dignitaries assistance in getting food.

It all started last week when we got the idea that an entourage of "home-grown" Africans should visit several restaurants known to bar persons of color and see what would happen.

For no particular reason, we decided that reporter Herbert Mangrum, would be the central character in this African fantasy and would be accompanied by a staff of aides, including an aide-de-camp, an attache, official photographer and chauffeur.

Herb was given the name of Orfa Adwiba, and dubbed the finance minister from Goban, a small African country on the East Coast of Africa.

No such country or person exists.

Herb's first name, Orfa, in reality is AFRO spelled backwards. The Adwiba bit, just as it sounds, was nothing more than ad libbing.

We picked Goban as the name of our country because it almost sounds like a genuine country.

However, we took care of this bit of similarity by juggling the spelling and literally moving our country clean across Africa.

The real Gabon is on the west coast of Africa and borders the Congo Republic.

We located our country, of Goban, on the east coast of Africa and said it was known for its "betel" nut.

Mangrum, it was understood, came to this country seeking financial assistance to develop the betel nut in an effort to strengthen our economy.

In a costume befitting his status, Mangrum was a picture of regal splendor in his maroon robe, trimmed in blue and gold. Beneath this he wore another one of blue cotton-like material.

His crowning piece was a leopard-skin covered crown, emblazoned with multi-colored stones.

The aide-de-camp, in real life, was associate editor Rufus Wells. The part of the attache and spokesman for the delegation fell to the lot of yours truly.

Wells and I wore official diplomatic morning attire,—tie, tails, hickory striped pants, crowned with top hats.

Adding further touches of reality, I carried a leather portfolio, crammed with a batch of papers which meant absolutely nothing.

In case the need for names arose—and it did—Wells' name was Dula Okoro and I answered to the tag of Loua Aklulu, and spoke mangled English, with drippings of an Oxford accent.

Official photographer, as expected, was none other than AFRO lensman I. Henry Phillips, and the air-conditioned, glittering, 1961 Cadillac limousine was driven by David Phillips, no relation to our man.

The car came from Arlington S. Phillips, funeral director.

Assuming an air of dignified importance—which wasn't easy under the circumstances, the entourage emerged from the main entrance of the AFRO building.

We were the target of incredible stares from both pedestrians and motorists as we posed for photographs just before entering the sleek limousine.

After the picture taking, David, a former Morgan student, gave the sparkling Cadillac the gun.

It's 10 a.m. and we head east on Route 40, selecting what restaurants we'll hit on the return trip. During the 45-mile drive to Northeast, Md., where the caravan turned around, we were the object of endless stares.

At Northeast, we see an impressive looking restaurant and decided there's no better place to launch our 125-mile tour than here at the "Madison House."

The chauffeur eased the limousine to the curb, a few feet away from the main entrance of the restaurant.

Using his best manners David Phillips alighted from the car and took up his position at the rear door of the limousine.

The door swung open and Dulah Okoro (Wells) stepped out first. Wells preceded Minister Adwiba only because it was a bit clumsy for His Highness to climb over him from his seat, where he was sandwiched between his attache and the aide-de-camp.

Looking as if he were the most important man in the world, the minister headed for the restaurant entrance, followed closely by Wells and me.

As planned, Herb paused at the door, allowing me to step forward and open it. Again taking the lead, the "African official" walked through the door.

Inside, a pleasant faced woman, smilingly greeted us:

"Good morning, how many is in your party?" she asked keeping her eyes glued to Mangrum's flowing garb.

"Three," I said in my best Africanese.

We were then shown to the main dining room amidst stares from diners already having lunch.

Without delay, a smiling waitress sauntered to our table, bearing three huge menus.

With a clipped "thank you" and a slight nod of the head, I accepted the menus and turned my attention to Mangrum.

Wanting to leave no doubt that Minister Adwiba must be catered to, I leaned over and read off the menu in a low-pitched voice befitting that of a highly trained African.

After getting the okay from Herb, I asked the waitress, pointing to the menu as I did so, to bring us three orders of the day's special—veal cutlets, mashed potatoes, green peas, rolls, butter and coffee.

The waitress took our order, but not before asking me if we understood the menu.

"Yes, yes," I replied in smothered English, "I know a bit of English and we were making out okay."

After the waitress left, the woman hostess came to our table and asked if we needed any help with the menu.

"No, thank you, we are doing fine," I said with a flourish, confident that we were a smash hit.

Then aide-de-camp Okoro dreamed up a bit that was not in the original script.

"We should go to the restroom and wash our hands," Wells (Okoro) said while we held a whispered conference, replete with endless nodding of the heads.

As I had done when we were seated, I got up and stood at the back of Mangrum's chair, moving it back as he stood up.

Taking our places, in back, we trailed the phony minister to the restroom, where I again showed utmost respect by opening the door, bowing in the process.

Back at the table, a glance around the attractive dining room revealed that all eyes were trained on our party.

Soon the smiling waitress returned, carrying a tray loaded with the golden brown cutlets and all the trimmings.

Just as we had hoped, that waitress got the message that Mangrum was top dog. Without being told, she walked past me and served the finance minister first.

Completing the service, the waitress checked the table periodically to make sure His Highness and his aides were satisfied.

"Is everything all right? Can I get something else for you?" she asked on each visit to the table.

Then came the incident which nearly floored the "diplomats." The hostess came over and asked:

"Is everything all right?" she wanted to know.

"Yes, yes, just fine," I replied.

"Can I have his (indicating Mangrum) autograph?" the hostess asked, displaying the eagerness of a teenager seeking the signature of her rock 'n' roll idol.

Taking the extended picture post card, "He will be glad to as soon as he finishes lunch," I assured her.

More garbled English, hand-waving, head nodding conference followed as I presumably explained the request to the finance minister.

Finally, and in English, yet, Herb wrote:

"On behalf of my staff and myself, thanks for a wonderful lunch." The card was signed:

"Orfa Adwiba, minister of finance, Goban."

As I handed the autographed card to the hostess, she almost melted with gratitude and said:

"Oh thank you, thank you very much," she repeated, glancing at Mangrum with what came close to revered awe.

She then retreated to what appeared to be an office, only to return moments later to bid the party farewell.

"I hope you enjoyed your lunch. And I wish you an enjoyable visit," the hostess said, glowing with smiles.

"If you are in this area again, we'll be glad to have you stop in," she said as I paid the $3.40 check. More smiles and gratitude were forthcoming when I, with a flourish, handed her a dollar and requested:

"Will you please see that the charming waitress gets this?"

I then joined Minister Adwiba and Okoro outside where photographer Phillips was firing away. He had entered the dining room moments before and photographed the dignitaries.

Phillips was also asked if he wanted to be served with the main party or at a separate table.

He graciously declined, explaining that he only wanted to get pictures of the party. He had to leave in a hurry after watching the trio talk quietly while eating lunch.

"I had to get the h—— out of there before I cracked up," I. Henry said, once safely in the luxurious confines of the limousine.

Only after we were safely out of the immediate surroundings did we drop the dignity, seriousness, pomp and ceremony.

Stop number two was the Redwood Inn, in the heart of Aberdeen.

With the usual amount of protocol, and solemnity, we alighted at the yellow painted section of the curb, at the entrance of the restaurant.

"Who are you and where are you from?" the sullen man at the counter near the door barked, as the party entered.

"We are from Africa, and we are en route to Washington," I said, really leaning on the by now polished African dialogue.

"Go over there," the man ordered, as he pointed to an empty dining room on the west side of the building, adjacent to the kitchen. In the east side dining room several white customers were having a lunch.

With a slight bow, I pulled out the chair for Mangrum, then took a seat only after he was comfortably seated.

Although the spacious dining room was empty, we still had an audience.

Several colored employees in the kitchen really gave us the star-gazing treatment. Soon a waitress bounced over to the table and distributed menus.

"What will you have?" she asked, after making sure we could read the menu.

"His Highness only wants something light," I replied, adding: "pie and coffee perhaps."

"What kind, please?" the waitress said, speaking deliberately slow, to make sure I understood her.

At a brief huddle with His Highness, I informed the waitress that we would have one slice of cherry, and two of apple pie, with coffee.

She retreated to the kitchen, where the group of watching workers took temporary leave of their observation positions.

Although our hearts were not in it, because we were about to pop from the full course meal a few minutes earlier, we dug in, using the best of table manners.

While eating and softly chatting, a voice floated from the kitchen over to our table.

"They are from the state department," one of the workers told his colleagues.

I asked for our check and again the big voiced man came into the picture.

"Who did you say he was?" the man asked me as I presented him the check.

"Oh, that is His Highness Minister Orfa Adwiba, of Goban," I began my spiel which was almost perfected by now.

"Goban," the man repeated, giving me a stony stare.

"Yes, yes, Goban," I began, giving life to a phantom country. "It is on the east coast of Africa, you see, and is known for the betel nut," I began laying it on. "Do you understand?" I concluded.

"Yeah, yeah," the man said in a voice that just could have easily said "you are lying to your teeth."

Clutching my portfolio, I joined the others outside and posed for more photographs.

Inquiring as to why Phillips the photographer, hadn't joined us, I uncovered a new bit of intelligence from the official photographer. Phil gave this account of an exchange between him and two men, both of whom identified themselves as managers of the restaurant.

"When I started to go in the man halted me at the door and told me no pictures inside the restaurant."

"You are not going to make an example of my place," I. Henry quoted the man as saying.

Deserting the east end of Route 40, the entourage then headed for the west end and the Double T. Diner, in Catonsville where the night before student sitdowners had been thrown in the jail for trying to eat.

Diamond T. also was the source of a new, but weird bit of intelligence.

"Let me see your credentials," the little man roared as he blocked the path of the party making its way to a table.

"Credentials?" I repeated with fake astonishment.

"Yeah, let me see your credentials," the man restated in a stronger voice.

"We only want food, why credentials?" I asked, really leaning on the accent.

"His Highness is not accustomed to showing credentials before he gets food," I continued.

The exchange was temporarily halted as I huddled with the finance minister, conveying the man's statement.

Nodding his head and shrugging his shoulders, Herb indicated that he would not permit his dignity to be insulted and turned and walked out of the restaurant to the porch.

Following His Highness, I suddenly turned and beckoned to the man.

He beckoned me back and I re-entered the door.

"His Highness doesn't understand, will you please explain?" was my diplomatic plea.

"It's a state law. You see people like you have to show your credentials before you can be served."

"State law?" I asked with amazement.

"You see, over here (America) we have what you call private enterprise. In private enterprise, we can do what we want to."

"Enterprise?" I repeated, showing complete bewilderment.

"Private enterprise is our business, our domain and we can do anything we feel is good for the business."

"I see," I told the man and started to leave.

"You don't have to leave. I only want to see your credentials. I'm sorry you are leaving, but you don't have to," he said, giving the entourage a long hard look.

As the touring diplomats piled into the car hardly a soul around Route 40 and Rolling Rd. moved as their eyes were glued to the caravan.

To further check the treatment accorded visiting Africans by highway restaurants, we picked the Bantam Restaurant, just across the street from the Hi-Way Diner.

By an amazing "coincidence," Hi-Way is the restaurant which had three Philadelphians thrown in jail when they tried to get service.

A woman, who had taken up a position at the door when the entourage pulled up, greeted us:

"I'm sorry, but we're closed. You see we close between 2 and 5 p.m.," in a voice oozing with niceness.

"I understand," I told her and added:

"We have just come from your capital and are en route to New York. His Highness is a mite hungry, perhaps you can direct us to a nearby restaurant?" I asked.

"Oh, let me see. Are you going into the city?" she wanted to know.

"No, no, we are going through the ah . . . how do you say . . . the tunnel," I told her.

"Well, I don't know too much about Pulaski highway but there is a Howard Johnson restaurant there and I'm sure they will be glad to serve you," trying to be helpful to the diplomats.

"That apparently is some distance, and His Highness would like something to eat as soon as possible," I explained, adding, "could you tell me if the one across the street (the Hi-Way) is open this time of day?"

"Yes, but he (Minister Adwiba) wouldn't want to eat there. It is for truckers," the woman declared.

Although a few customers were seated in the Bantam, and a couple left while we were reloading, the workers did appear to be getting the place ready for the dinner hour.

David Phillips again gunned the Cadillac and we deserted Ritchie Highway for the city.

Wanting to add a new twist to the thus-far highly triumphant tour, we wanted to test Miller's Restaurant at Fayette and Hanover Sts., to see how they treat "foreigners" of color.

Easing through heavy downtown traffic, the sleek black limousine came to a halt at the Fayette St. entrance of the restaurant.

Amidst stares more likely to be found in a small town rather than a sprawling metropolitan city, we alighted with the usual amount of aplomb.

Entering the door, we saw a sign which said: "Use west dining room."

At the door we were met by a short man who said:

"I'm sorry, but I can't serve you."

Facing what proved to be our last hurdle, I relayed the message to Mangrum, using shoulders, hands, and head to demonstrate my point.

Signaling that he understood, Herb whispered something in mangled English.

As I turned to face the short man, I was told again, "I can't serve you, I'm sorry, you'll have to see the manager."

"The manager, please," I said. The waiter disappeared and moments later a taller man, identifying himself as the manager, and not the head waiter, as has been reported in the daily press, greeted us. This was the same man I had talked to on numerous occasions when the students were staging sit-ins at Millers.

"We are from Africa, and are enroute from your capital to New York," I began with what was rapidly becoming an old line. (Just how old, I found out a short while later.)

Continuing, I told the man, "His Highness is hungry, but your representative said he can not serve us."

"That's unfortunate," the taller man said, furrowing his brow. "We certainly don't want to embarrass you; will you come with me?" he asked.

For the first time during the whole trip, I preceded our finance minister in the east dining room, which was empty and had no lights.

While we took seats, the manager turned on the lights and sent a waiter to our table.

Armed with massive menus, the waiter, whose English was little improved over mine, arrived at the table.

"What will you have?" he asked, making ready to write the orders.

After whispering a whole lot of nothing to the finance minister, using my hands and head to make the point, I told the manager we wanted cocktails before ordering.

"We want . . . how do you say it . . . two scotches with water and one bourbon with water," I managed to get out.

Then came time for ordering food, and again found it necessary to get "something light." There were two reasons for this "light eating," but I only gave the waiter one of them.

"You see His Highness is en route to New York for a meeting and dinner engagement. He doesn't want to spoil his appetite, just something to tide him over, you see," the waiter was told.

He apparently was impressed because he took the orders for three cups of chicken noodle soup, with no apparent afterthought. Although he had already loaded the table with bread of all descriptions, light, brown and dark.

However the other reason we were eating light was because the area is a regular stomping ground for daily reporters assigned to the downtown beat.

Many of them, covering Criminal Court, City Hall, Police Headquarters, know Mangrum and me.

"To run into one of these fellows now," we thought would blow a perfect day.

So, as leisurely as we could under the circumstances, we sipped the drinks and got rid of the soup, keeping a wary eye on the door at the same time.

It paid off, too, but I'm a little ahead of the story. While we were eating, the manager who had interceded in our behalf, came to the table and began a friendly chat.

"Where are you from?" he asked with apparent genuine interest.

"We are from Goban (not Gabon) and the purpose of Minister Orfa Adwiba's visit here is to seek financial aid in developing the betel nut," I began.

"You see, His Highness hopes to strengthen our economy by developing the great potentials of this nut," I rambled on.

"I see," the man said. "That is interesting. You know, I read the National Geographical Magazine and it carries a lot about Africa.

"Do you get it?" he asked.

"No, no, but perhaps other members of my government do," I said, beginning to squirm with the thought that maybe we just might be stuck with an authority on such matters.

Then the very thing we were apprehensive about happened.

As I was getting the check from the waiter, Mangrum spied a Sunpapers reporter, Richard Pollack, entering the restaurant.

I have talked to Pollack several times in the past.

For the first time during the 125-mile, five and three quarter hour ride, we did violence to protocol.

After tipping the waiter a dollar, I moved to the cashier's cage, but I wasn't paying the cashier much attention. My eyes were on Mangrum as he, flowing robe and all, rushed to the door, yanked it open and made a beeline to the limousine.

Thank goodness, it was parked at the curb. Otherwise, we would have been trapped.

As the cashier, an elderly woman, gave me what was left of a five-dollar bill, I headed for the door. But who was standing there as big as life? That's right. One Richard Pollack, the reporter with a nose for a story.

"I'm Dick Pollack, reporter for the Sunpapers," he began. He didn't recognize me.

"Oh, I see," I replied, "but I'm in a terribly big hurry; you see the minister is en route to New York for an appointment and we are far behind schedule," I told the newsman.

"I see, sir," he said politely, "but can you give me the name of the Prime Minister?"

Really laying it on, I replied:

"He is the minister of finance."

"What country does he represent?" Pollack asked.

"He is from Goban, off the east coast of Africa," said I, spelling it out—G-o-b-a-n—to make sure he got it right.

"Oh, that's where Dr. Sweitzer is, isn't it?"

"Yes, yes," I told him in my best African dialect.

"Will you spell the minister's name, please?" he asked, further delaying my getaway.

"Orfa (not Sorfa as Dick printed) Adwiba," I spelled in a slow but camouflaged tone.

As he did with the country, Pollack wrote the minister's name exactly as I spelled it, using an edition of the Sunpaper as copy paper.

Further questions were met with a polite, but firm:

"You'll have to excuse me, please, but the minister is very late and I must leave," I told him and hopped in the car just as David zipped away from the curb, but not before photographer Phillips had recorded the sidewalk interview.

The Afro-American (Baltimore), September 2, 1961

from
Revolution in Mississippi

by Tom Hayden

The Project Begins

SNCC, in its attempt to ignite a mass non-violent movement, designated the formidable and sovereign state of Mississippi as the site of its pilot project. Moses moved to McComb, a city of 13,000. He found a number of local adults, high school students, and non-student youth eager to assist him. They provided contacts, housing, some transportation, and (particularly the students) began canvassing the surrounding area, determining the numbers of registered and unregistered voters, informing the citizens of the SNCC program and inviting them to participate. By the end of the first week, John Hardy, Nashville, and Reggie Robinson, Baltimore, had arrived as SNCC field representatives to help in the project.

On August 7, 1961, the SNCC Voter Registration School opened in Burglundtown in a combination cinder block-and-paintless wood frame two-story structure which houses a grocery below and a Masonic meeting hall above. A typical voter registration (or citizenship) class involved a study of the Mississippi State Constitution, filling out of sample application forms, description of the typical habits of the Southern registrar—whose discretionary powers are enormous—and primarily attempted the morale building, encouragement and consequent group identification which might inspire the exploited to attempt registration.

On the first day of the school, four persons went down to the registrar's office in nearby Magnolia, the county seat of Pike; three of them registered successfully. Three went down on August 9th; two were registered. Nine went down on August 10th; one was registered. By this time, articles in the local press, the (McComb) *Enterprise-Journal*, had increased awareness of the project, stirring a few Negroes from Walthall and Amite to come to the McComb classes. However, the thrust of the movement was somewhat blunted on the evening of August 10th when one of the Negroes who had attempted to register was shot at by a white. (It is now clear that the shooting had nothing to do with the attempted registration that day. However, in the minds of the Negro community, for whom the vote is intimately connected with intimidation and violence, the association was made between the two events.) Attendance at the Voter Registration School quickly diminished.

Moses and the others began to rebuild. People were talked to; nights were spent in the most remote areas; days were spent canvassing all around. Then on August 15th, the first of a still continuing series of "incidents" occurred. On that day, Moses drove to Liberty (yes, it is ironic), the county seat of Amite, with three Negroes (Ernest Isaac, Bertha Lee Hughes and Matilda Schoby) who wished to register. Moses was asked to leave the registrar's office while the three attempted to fill out the registration forms. The three claim that while they were so engaged the registrar assisted a white female in answering several of the questions. Upon completing the test, the applicants were told by the registrar that their attempts were inadequate. The registrar then placed the papers in his desk and asked the three not to return for at least six months, at which time presumably they might try further. (I have been told by a reliable Federal source that the tests were not of a quality character.)

Leaving Liberty, driving toward McComb, the group was followed by a highway patrolman, Marshall Carwyle Bates of Liberty, who flagged them over to the side of the road. Bates asked the driver, Isaac, to step out of his car and get inside of the police car in the rear. Isaac complied. Then Moses left the car and walked back to the police car to inquire about the nature of the pull-over. Bates ordered Moses back to the car and shoved him. Thereupon, Moses began to write the Marshall's name on a pad of paper, and was shoved into the car. Moses, incidentally, was referred to as the "nigger who's come to tell the niggers how to register." Finally, the contingent of four Negroes was ordered to drive to the Justice of the Peace's office in McComb, where Moses was eventually charged with impeding an officer in the discharge of his duties, fined $50 and given a suspended sentence. Moses phoned the Justice Department, collect, from the station, which alerted the police to his significance. (The local paper called collect the next day, was refused by the Justice Department, and asked editorially why Moses was so privileged.) The fine was paid by the NAACP in order to appeal the case, and Moses did go to jail for a period of two days, during which he did not eat.

On the same day several other SNCC persons entered Pike County: Gwendolyn Green, Washington; Travis Britt, New York; William Mitchell, Atlanta; Ruby Doris Smith, Atlanta; James Travis, Jackson; and MacArthur Cotton, Jackson. Responsibilities were divided and the canvassing increased.

Registration, Sit-Ins, and Violence

During this same time there had been requests from Negroes in Walthall county to set up a school there. A site for the school and living quarters were offered. John Hardy was selected to go to the area. Along with several others, he established the school on August 18th. About 30 persons attended the first session. Eighty percent of the Negroes in Walthall are farmers, and 60 percent own their own land The heavy schedule imposed on the farmers at this time of year required that classes be scheduled so as not to conflict with the workday schedule. School was held at the Mt. Moriah Baptist Church and at private homes. Moses came into Amite several days later and remained for nearly a week, teaching and visiting "out the dirt roads." On August 22nd, four Negroes tried to register in Liberty; none succeeded; no incident occurred. By this time, however, dramatic events were occurring in Pike County.

On August 18th, Marion Barry from Nashville, a SNCC field representative particularly concerned with initiating direct action, arrived in McComb. Those students too young to vote, many of whom had canvassed regularly, were eager to participate actively. The Pike County Non-Violent Movement was formed; workshops in the theory and practice of nonviolence were held. On August 26th two of the youths, Elmer Hayes and Hollis Watkins (both 18), sat-in at the lunch counter of the local Woolworth's, the first direct action incident in the history of the county. The two were arrested and

remained in jail 30 days. The charge: breach of peace. Their
arrest set the stage for a mass meeting in McComb on August
29th. The Reverend James Bevel, of Jackson, spoke to a
crowd of nearly 200. The paper of the following day carried
the story lead, in large type, and the local columnist warned
the citizens that the Negroes were not engaged in a mere
passing fad, but were serious in intention.

On August 30th, a sit-in occurred at the lunch counter of
the local bus station. Isaac Lewis, 20, Robert Talbert, 19, and
Brenda Lewis, 16, were arrested on charges of breach of peace
and failure to move on. They remained in jail for 28 days. By
now, a current of protest had been generated throughout the
counties. Subsequent events intensified the feeling. On August 29th, Bob Moses took two persons to the registrar's office in Liberty. They were met by Billy Jack Caston (cousin of
the sheriff and son-in-law of State Representative Eugene
Hurst) who was accompanied by another cousin and the son
of the sheriff. (Should this seem peculiar, read Faulkner.) Caston smashed Moses across the head and dropped him to the
street. The other Negroes were not harmed. Moses' cuts required eight stitches. Moses filed assault and battery charges
against Caston, perhaps the first time in the history of Amite
that a Negro has legally contested the right of a white man to
mutilate him at fancy. Approximately 150 whites attended the
trial on August 31st. Among other questions, Caston's attorney asked Moses if he had participated in the riots in San
Francisco or Japan; Moses replied that he had not. Upon the
suggestion of law officials, Moses left the trial, at which he
was the plaintiff, before the "not guilty" verdict in order to
escape mass assault.

Meanwhile in Walthall, the first attempt to register Negroes
since the Justice Department suit of the Spring of 1961 was
made. Five persons went to Tylertown, the county seat, with
John Hardy. As all businesses close at noon on Thursdays,
only two of the five had time to take the test. One was a
teacher, the other a senior political science major at Jackson
State College (Negro). Both failed. On the same day Hardy,
in an interview with the editor of the *Tylertown Times*, made
a remark which was interpreted as an endorsement of atheism.
This was to "mark" Hardy, if he had not already been

marked. On the following evening a mass "encouragement" meeting was held in rural Tylertown; about 80 attended. Again, a mass meeting was held on September 4th to emphasize the significance of the vote and of citizenship.

On September 5th, three Negroes waited two hours in Tylertown, then were informed that the registrar had to attend a meeting and would not be able to register them. The following day another Negro appeared at the registrar's office, and was told to return at a time more convenient for the registrar.

Back in Liberty (Amite county seat), on August 31st, Travis Britt had appeared at the registrar's office with several Negroes. He was told by the registrar to get out of the office. As he stood outside, Bob Moses approached with two witnesses of his August 29th beating to prepare affadavits against Caston. Suddenly two shots were fired outside. Two of the three Negroes attempting to register interrupted their work to rush out, thinking Moses and Britt were in jeopardy. A crowd of whites had gathered, as had police, but the source of the shooting was unclear. At any rate, the office was scheduled to close at noon, which prevented the three from finishing the test. They report that they had been told by the registrar that they could return whenever ready. No incidents occurred outside when they all left, although the white group remained.

On September 5th, fear became terror throughout the region as a result of the beating of Travis Britt in Liberty. He and Moses accompanied four Negroes to the registrar's office. Let Britt's words tell the story: "There was a clerk directly across the hall who came rushing out while we were waiting, and ordered us to leave the hallway. He said he didn't want a bunch of people congregating in the hall. So we left and walked around the building to the court house, near the registrar's window. By the time we reached the back of the building a group of white men had filed into the hall, in about the same spot we'd been 'congregating' in. They were talking belligerently. Finally one of the white men came to the end of the hall as if looking for someone. He asked us if we knew Mr. Brown. We said no. He said, You boys must not be from around here. We said he was correct. This conversation was interrupted by another white who approached Bob Moses and started preaching to him: how he should be

ashamed coming down here from New York stirring up trouble, causing poor innocent people to lose their homes and
jobs, and how he (Bob) was lower than dirt on the ground
for doing such a thing, and how he should get down on his
knees and ask God forgiveness for every sin of his lifetime.
Bob asked him why the people should lose their homes just
because they wanted to register and vote. The white gentleman did not answer the question, but continued to preach.
He said that the Negro men were raping the white women up
North, and that he didn't want and wouldn't allow such a
thing to start down here in Mississippi. He went on to say
that the Negro in New York was not allowed to own homes
or establish businesses so why didn't we go the hell back
home and straighten out New York instead of trying to
straighten out Mississippi. At this point Bob turned away and
sat on the stoop of the court house porch, and the man talking to him took a squatting position. Nobody was saying anything. I reached in my pocket and took out a cigarette. A tall
white man, about middle-aged, wearing a khaki shirt and
pants stepped up to me and asked 'Boy, what's your business?'
at which point I knew I was in trouble. (Recall: Moses had already been beaten earlier, had filed charges, had called Washington, and was much less 'open game' than Britt at this
point. T.H.) The clerk from the hallway came to the back
door leading to the courthouse with a smile on his face and
called to the white man, 'Wait a minute; wait a minute!' At
this point, the white man, whom they called Bryant, hit me in
my right eye. Then I saw this clerk motion his head as if to
call the rest of the whites. They came and all circled around
me, and this fellow that was called Bryant hit me on my jaw,
then on my chin. Then he slammed me down; instead of
falling, I stumbled onto the court house lawn. The crowd
(about 15, I think) followed, making comments. He was holding me so tight around the collar, I put my hands on the collar to ease the choking. The clerk hollered 'Why don't you hit
him back?' This set off a reaction of punches from this fellow
they called Bryant; I counted fifteen; he just kept hitting and
shouting, 'Yes, why don't you hit me, nigger? Yes, why don't
you hit me, nigger?' I was beaten into a semi-conscious state.
My vision was blurred by the punch in the eye. I heard Bob

tell me to cover my head to avoid any further blows to the face. I told Bryant if he was through beating me, I was ready to go. The clerk said, yes, I should go. Then this guy they called Bryant yelled, 'Brothers, shall we kill him here?' I was extremely frightened by the sincere way he said it. No one in the crowd answered the question, and Bryant (I found out his last name was Jones) released me. Moses then took me by the arm and took me to the street, walking cautiously to avoid any further kicks or blows. The Negro fellow that had been taking the registration test gave up in the excitement, and we saw him in his truck. The white men advised him to get the hell out of town, saying they were surprised that he was associating with our kind." Charges were not pressed.

On September 7th, John Hardy accompanied two persons to the registrar's office at Tylertown. The two were informed by the registrar that he didn't want to have anything to do with them because he was already involved in a suit with the Federal government. Says Hardy: "I entered the office to ask why. The registrar, John Woods, had seen me on one other occasion, the 30th. After telling him my name, he came out very insultingly and boisterously questioning my motives and reasons for being in Mississippi and said I had no right to mess in the niggers' business and why didn't I go back where I came from. He reached into his desk drawer and ordered me out at gunpoint. As I turned to leave he struck me over the head with the pistol. I left his office and walked about a block. I decided to go to the sheriff's office to report the assault and possibly make charges. But this was not necessary because the sheriff found me. He told me to come with him or he would beat me 'within an inch of your life.' After being put in jail (the charge was resisting arrest and inciting a riot, and later disorderly conduct) I was interrogated at length by a city attorney and later by the district attorney. About 7:30 I was taken to Magnolia jail for 'your own protection.' I was in jail until the following night."

The Hardy case deserves more than outrage. It holds the possibility of legal response which might form a precedent against the state's using its official machinery to interfere with civil rights. John Doar of the U.S. Justice Department, Civil Rights Division, charged that if Hardy were tried and convicted, Negroes would be discouraged from attempting to vote (an action constituting a violation of the Civil Rights Act), and irreparable damage would be done the nation. Subsequently, the Federal government has been striving to prevent Hardy's trial. On September 20th, the Justice Department, filing its complaint before U.S. District Judge Harold Cox in Meridian, Mississippi, asked for court orders forbidding intimidation or coercion of Negroes seeking to vote in Walthall and appealed for prevention of the Hardy trial.

On September 21st, Judge Cox declined to stop the state court trial. Among his remarks, as quoted by the Associated Press: "It is difficult to conceive how the United States can possibly be irreparably damaged by this criminal case down in Walthall County, Mississippi." "While it must be presumed that John Hardy is guilty of everything with which he is charged, it must likewise be presumed that justice will be done in the trial of the case." "This incident occurred September 7th and the government waited until September 20th to ask for instant relief. It looks like the government has a self-made emergency." "(It would be improper) for me to permit a clash of the sovereignty of the state and Federal governments on such a case."

The Federal government announced it would next appeal to the 5th Circuit Court of Appeals, in Montgomery, Alabama. On October 4th, Assistant Attorney General Burke Marshall argued before the Montgomery Court that Walthall is a place of "near lawlessness." He accused Mississippi of a "trumped-up charge" in the Hardy case, which was "an attempt to intimidate them to prevent them from registering to vote." A Mississippi assistant attorney general, Edward Cates, responded (according to A.P.) that the Federal government is seeking to "condemn a whole state without evidence," that Federal lawyers have presented no proof that Negroes in Walthall are afraid to try to register following Hardy's arrest. A three member tribunal is presently (October 13th) considering the case, with no outcome yet announced. (ED. NOTE: The Justice Department suit has been successful.)

from *Revolution in Mississippi* (1962)

Dixie's Race Signs "Gone With the Wind"

by William Kennedy

JACKSONVILLE, Fla.—Thinking the time was ripe to do a picture story on those sales counters which long have offered a selection of such signs as "For Sale," "Keep Out," "Bad Dog," "Colored," "White," "White Only," "Colored Entrance," "Colored Service Window" and the like, this Courier correspondent set out on a shopping tour of local dime, department, and hardware stores.

In the bad old days (only yester-year), such signs could be had for 10¢ on cardboard, or 45¢ on metal. Best sellers were the catch-all plain race labels, which could be tacked on any door.

My first stop happened to be Grant's. They had everything else but segregation signs. Maybe they keep them on a segregated counter these days, instead of integrated with other signs, I thought.

"Don't you have any 'White' and 'Colored' signs?" I asked a salesgirl.

"We have white cardboard signs with blue letters, and black metal signs with luminous orange letters," she said helpfully.

"I mean with the words 'White' and 'Colored' written on them," I explained, wondering how dumb a damnyankee can get.

"Oh, no!" she said, looking frightened.

Sold out, I figured.

"When are you expecting more in?" I inquired.

"We're not," she said. "It's a discontinued item. We sent all the ones we had back."

Dazed, I staggered down the street to Kress. No soap. Same story. And so across to Woolworth's. Nothing doing. Feeling rather like I was trying to buy a bottle out of season, I approach a gentleman clerk and put the question.

"Those things are against the law now!" he exclaimed

righteously, looking at me as though I must be an arch-criminal or FBI agent. I didn't argue, thinking it far better to leave him in blissful ignorance.

All this seemed too good to be true. Perhaps the down-town department stores, upon integrating their lunch counters last Spring, had decided the best way to win back their Negro customers was to get those signs off their sales counters as well as off their walls.

"I'll bet those signs are still easy to get out in the lily white suburbs," I said to myself.

Across the river and into the trees of Jax' South Side I went, straight to a Woolworth branch. No luck. I tried the hardware next door. Ditto.

There was no doubt about it—segregation signs were not to be had in our town for love or money!

Thoroughly excited now, I jumped into my Hupmobile and raced 39.7 miles farther South, down U.S. 1, until I came to St. Augustine. Woolworth, Western Auto, the hardware store—they no more had jim crow signs for sale than dodo birds.

In fact, the clerks all looked at me as if to say, "Doesn't this guy read the papers?" or "Wonder what swamp he's been hiding in?"

Of course, I can't vouch for all the Lynchburgs of the South, but for all I know the enlightenment has reached them too.

Who deserves the credit for this veritable revolution?

Perhaps there is a sign-making monopoly, and some nice guy got hold of it and stopped making segregation signs, big business though it was. But no—a check revealed that there are lots of sign-making companies, in lots of places.

Somehow they all seem to have gotten the idea that jim crow signs are un-nice, unlawful, or out-of-date.

Not being able to get ready-made, store-boughten segregation signs is going to make things mighty hard on Mr. Charlie.

The Pittsburgh Courier, December 9, 1961

Over 500 Negro Arrests in Albany

by Trezzvant W. Anderson

ALBANY, Ga.—With more than 500 Negroes, (youth and adults) having been arrested by the middle of last week, the Southwide fight against racial discrimination was in full force on this new front, a middle-sized city which has produced more than its share of outstanding Negroes.

The anti-segregation attack, here, a really massive one, is aimed at a variety of areas and is being led by the Albany movement, headed by Dr. W. G. Anderson, president of the Albany NAACP Branch.

It is composed of the NAACP, the Student Non-Violent Coordinating Committee, CORE and other groups.

Historically, Albany is a city which, by all standards, ought to have non-discrimination. It is the home of a number of the nation's outstanding Negroes in many fields.

For example, Albany is the home of Cong. William L. Dawson (D.-Ill.), whose home still stands on Newton Road. It is the home of ex-Ambassador to Liberia, Richard E. Jones, who rose to the rank of brigadier-general in Illinois; it is the home of Ray Charles, jazz singer; also, it can claim Roy Hamilton, jazz star, from near-by Leesburg.

It is home of famed Sam Solomon, who led Florida Negroes into political emancipation during the 30's; it is the home of pretty Dr. Jean Noble, president of Delta Sigma Theta Sorority, and a teacher at a New York City university, and it is the home of Judge Henderson, boss of the longshoremen, from Charleston, S.C., to New Orleans. Also, Albany is the home of Henry Wynn, Atlanta business tycoon; it is the home of the fabulous C. W. King and his seven sons, who include Clennon King, Slater King, leader of the Wednesday march, and Atty. C. B. King and the others who have gained national recognition.

Should any of them return here under present conditions,

they would have to accept jim-crow status. Thus the current blitzkrieg is more than timely. Also, it is long over-due.

This, too, is the home of rabid race-hater James Gray, publisher of the Albany Herald, and owner of a radio and TV station. He is chairman of the Georgia Democratic State Committee.

Congressman Dawson is vice chairman of the Democratic National Committee. Mr. Gray is a transplanted Northerner, from Massachusetts.

The Albany Movement is asking for non-discriminatory use of the railroad and bus stations, city library, city parks, hospitals and buses. Also, it asks for the employment of negro policemen, better jobs on the city payroll, representation on juries and better jobs in private facilities, which cater to Negro trade, such as stores and shops.

Lunch counter desegregation is a goal, also.

The movement sprang into life in November, after five Negroes were arrested when they tried to eat in the dining room of the Trailways Bus station, here. This effort came shortly after city police had shot and killed a Negro at the bus station, and tempers were strained.

The bus station adjoins the main Negro business district in which are located offices of doctors, dentists, insurance firms, a theatre, the office of Atty. C. B. King and other businesses.

Three of the arrested persons were members of the Albany NAACP Youth Council, Evelyn Toney, Eddie Wilson and Julian Carswell. They were joined by two adults.

Last Sunday, the movement went into high gear when 11 "Freedom Riders" of the Student Non-Violent Coordinating Committee (seven Negroes and four whites) rode a Central of Georgia train non-segregated, from Atlanta into the Albany railroad station. Then, they sought to use the waiting room and restaurant and were all arrested by Police Chief Laurie Pritchett.

The charge was disorderly conduct, obstructing traffic and failure to obey an officer, who ordered them to move on.

Their trial, last Monday, Tuesday and Wednesday, triggered the massive effort when students at Albany State College, to the number of some 400, marched around the City Hall where the trials were being held. The city police moved in and made mass arrests. Tuesday, many adults joined the youth marchers and they, too, were arrested and put in jail.

Among the arrested adults was Mrs. W. G. Anderson, wife of the head of the Albany Movement. Most of the adults chose to post bond, but most of the students preferred to remain in jail. The triggering mass detention of the "Freedom Riders" group Sunday saw the entire 11 (whites and Negroes) going to jail.

Among them were: James Forman, 32, Chicago, Ill., who had a part in the Fayette County (Tenn.) "Tent City" episode, as an aide to John McFerren and, later, was arrested in Monroe, N.C., in the Union County uprisings, headed there by Robert Williams, NAACP figure now believed to be in Cuba; Miss Lenore Taitt, an Atlanta student movement leader; Joseph Charles Jones, Charlotte, N.C., who headed the successful student demonstrations of the Johnson C. Smith University students in February, 1960, and Bernard S. Lee, youth director of Dr. M. L. King Jr.'s Southern Christian Leadership Conference, who was student body head at Alabama State College, Montgomery, in 1960, when he and eight others were expelled for student demonstrations, there.

There were two Albany Negroes among the 11 arrested "Freedom Riders": Willie Mae Jones and Bertha Gober. The first to go on trial was Per Larson, 25, of New York City, a Dane.

It was during his trial that the initial group of Albany State College students moved to the City Hall, and began parading and singing. Wednesday morning, an additional 80-odd Negroes were arrested when they staged a prayer meeting at the City Hall.

At a mass meeting, held at a church, Tuesday night, the Movement voted to continue its efforts to get first-class treatment in Albany, regardless of the cost.

The Movement is a well-coordinated one, and has gained the support of the majority of Negro citizens, both top leaders and rank-and-filers.

For four days, prior to the Sunday train ride, Georgia NAACP Field Secretary Vernon E. Jordan of Atlanta, was in Albany firming up plans.

When the riders and students were arrested, the NAACP

furnished its brilliant legal chief in Georgia Atty. Donald L. Hollowell, as defense counsel. He was assisted by Atty. C. B. King of this city, who has been associated with him in several cases.

The leaders of the movement plan to continue until "something gives," they told The Courier, and a united Negro citizenry is behind them.

Whether Georgia officials will react against the students of the state-supported college, as certain other Dixie states did, and expel them, remained to be seen, at mid-week. No students had been on trial, up to that time.

The Pittsburgh Courier, December 23, 1961

A Negro Tourist in Dixie

by Bettye Rice Hughes

IT WAS mostly curiosity that caused me to set out from Los Angeles on a tour of the South by bus last November, just twelve days after the Interstate Commerce Commission's order went into effect forbidding separation by races in interstate busses and terminals. My trip lasted six weeks and carried me through Oklahoma, Arkansas, Tennessee, the Carolinas, Florida, Georgia, Alabama, and part of Mississippi.

The purpose of my tour was twofold: I wanted to see at first hand how many Southern states were complying with the ICC ruling; and I also wanted to see if a female Negro tourist traveling alone—unheralded and unprepared for—would receive a different reception from that which had greeted the Freedom Riders.

The trip began uneventfully. I traveled straight across the middle of Arkansas and saw no "White" or "Colored" signs on the rest rooms or waiting rooms. I was certainly not welcomed with open arms and I could sense the hostility brought on by my presence in some towns, but I was served without incident.

In Memphis I encountered the first separate waiting rooms. There were stares from other passengers when I went into the main waiting rooms, but nothing more. I was served in the restaurant. In Monteagle, Tennessee, I saw the first evidence that the "Colored" and "White" signs had recently been removed. After a while I began to look for the different methods used in covering over these signs. In no case were new ones installed. Above the doors of rest rooms the color designations were often painted out or covered with metal strips, leaving an off-centered "Men" and "Women." But there were still four rooms, their racial backgrounds identifiable by location and by the length of the covered-up area on the signs.

I realize now that my naïveté about Southern customs was a protective cloak. Even when white people appeared to ignore me, my actions often drew stares from Negro passengers. I was subjected to my first real attempt at discrimination in Florence, South Carolina. I had transferred from Trailways to Greyhound. The bus was an express from New York City and was crowded with passengers going home for Thanksgiving. Florence was the first stop in South Carolina. I had not intended at first to go inside the terminal. I wasn't particularly hungry and I was a little short of money anyway. But a Negro girl sitting next to me, a native South Carolinian, said she wished she had a Coke and a hot dog and I thought I might as well join her. I asked her to go in with me, but she refused and asked me to bring her a sandwich.

There were no signs, so I went in the waiting room in front of me and on through to the restaurant just as I had been doing in other cities. As I walked into the restaurant the cashier looked up, turned red, and started pointing and yelling, "There's another one just across the waiting room!" Since she was looking everywhere but directly at me, I wasn't entirely sure at first that she was talking to me. I thought she might be talking to an elderly white man in front of me. (So did the poor old man, who turned and went out.)

Then I noticed a young Negro fellow who had been following me stop abruptly and leave the restaurant. There was no mistake about whom she meant. Stalling for time, I feigned innocence and asked her, "What's the difference? This one's fine, thank you." The cashier gave me a look that was anything but cordial but turned away from me to attend to her cash register. As soon as I moved toward the counter, a tall white counterman followed, and all the myths, half-truths, exaggerations, and facts concerning treatment of Negroes in the South swarmed through my mind. He kept repeating, "There's another one for you over there, through that door."

"What's the difference?" I asked him. "All I want is a sandwich."

"Just go on over to the other restaurant and you'll find out the difference," he said. He began to get redder and I got scared. "I don't want to stand here and argue. Just go on over to the other restaurant where you belong."

"I'm not arguing," I insisted, "but one's as good as another with me."

At this point he stalked off and I felt sure he was going to get the police or the White Citizens Council or the Ku Klux Klan—maybe all three. To my surprise, all he did was go back behind the lunch counter.

By now most of the white passengers were pointedly staring at their food. No one uttered a word and only a few even glanced at me. A customer got up from the counter and I sat down. I had no idea what was going to happen. I was sure I would not get service, but I did not intend to leave and give the counterman the satisfaction of saying that I went because of his threats. So I sat.

Just before the end of the lunch break, a waitress came over and took my order. My bravado had paid off. Nevertheless, when I returned to the bus I was no longer optimistic about what might lie ahead as we moved farther South, and I dreaded the next bus stop.

And yet at Charleston and Savannah, much farther South, I received service in restaurants and went into the main waiting rooms and rest rooms without incident. The other Negro passengers, who went to the waiting rooms formerly designated as "Colored," had started watching to see what I was going to do at the rest and lunch stops. Several of them asked me, "Are you riding for us?" I said that in a sense I was. But no one offered to go into the main waiting area with me.

Throughout Florida all "Colored" and "White" signs had been removed, and at the terminals that had separate waiting rooms I received service along with the other passengers. My courage had returned somewhat, so once again I was not prepared for trouble. When I entered the main restaurant in Tallahassee, a white man yelled back to the kitchen, "Tell Roy to come here!" Roy came out of the kitchen with his dishwasher's apron on. We were both black. So Roy could serve me, the ICC ruling would be obeyed, and the management could save face. Very neat. I had read of this happening to other Negro travelers in the South, but when I was faced with a real live instance I didn't know whether to laugh or cry. Roy came over, very nervous, and asked for my order. I smiled at him and said, "What are they doing? Making you the scapegoat?" No answer. So I put on a sober face and gave him my order.

My first stop in Alabama was at Dothan. I had been worry-ing about Alabama all night. When we got to the terminal, I saw no "White" or "Colored" signs, and when the other Ne-gro passengers went into the once segregated waiting room I went into the main waiting room and then into the restau-rant. As I sat down I noticed the ICC ruling against discrimi-nation on the wall and I must say it made me feel much better. The waitress took my order while a Negro cook stared through the service door from the kitchen. After she had brought my coffee, I heard the waitress say to a white woman sitting at the counter, "I know how you feel. I don't like it either but there ain't nothing we can do about it." The white woman got up and walked out.

But after I had sat over my coffee about five minutes, the waitress came over, smiled at me, and asked me where I was from. She stayed and talked. How did I like the South? Where was I going? As I was paying my check, she called after me, "I hope you have a nice trip."

From Dothan I traveled northeast into Georgia. At the ma-jor stops in that state—Atlanta, Macon, Savannah—I saw the separate waiting rooms but no "White" or "Colored" signs in the terminals. I went into the main waiting rooms and ad-joining rest rooms and ate in the main restaurants. But at the smaller towns where the interstate express busses do not stop, the signs were still up, and all along the highway I noticed that Negroes and whites were still using separate waiting rooms. Discrimination is still rigidly enforced for passengers traveling within the state of Georgia. Only the interstate Ne-gro passengers would sit in the middle or to the front of the bus. All other Negro passengers moved as far back as they could even though posted at the bus entrance was a sign stat-ing that according to the ICC ruling, passengers were to be seated without regard to race, color, creed, or national origin. In Georgia and also in Alabama I often saw white passengers stand up in the aisles for miles rather than sit down beside a Negro passenger. I also saw a Negro woman stand for two hours rather than take an empty seat beside a white passenger.

At Winfield, Alabama, a white man had been holding the

door of the restaurant open for the bus passengers. But he took one look at me and slammed the door in my face. Nothing was said by the driver, by me, or by the bus passengers following. I just opened the door and went into the restaurant. As soon as I had sat down, the waitress was in front of me to take my order. I smiled to myself: this sort of hospitality was nearly as hard to bear as more direct forms of hostility. But I was given service.

Of all the towns I stopped in, I was most apprehensive about Anniston, Alabama. It had made international headlines six months previously when a bus carrying Freedom Riders had been burned. There were stares and an oppressive silence as I sat and drank my buttermilk. Negro passengers who had gone into the "Colored" waiting room would glance in at me. But I was served.

When the Greyhound express bus to Los Angeles reached Mississippi, it took what seemed to me a curious route. It certainly would have been faster to go from Alabama straight through the middle of Mississippi and then down to El Paso —the main transfer point for all Southern routes. Instead, we took a sharp turn northward, went across the northeastern tip of Mississippi, and without making a rest stop ended back "up north" in Memphis before we turned back down to El Paso. In other words, interstate passengers going from east to the west by Greyhound bus over the southern route never set foot on Mississippi soil.

On the return trip through Arkansas and Texas, I was given service in all the restaurants. At Dallas there were separate waiting rooms, but both Negro and white passengers as well as Indians and Mexicans were in the main one. There were, however, no Negroes eating in the main cafeteria during the time I was there.

Frankly, I do not know whether the treatment I received was due to the fact that I was traveling in the wake of the Freedom Riders or whether it was because I was traveling alone and without publicity. It may have been a combination of both. I felt that the threat of violence was always there— particularly in South Carolina, Georgia, and Alabama—but somehow it never erupted.

My own feeling, as one who is naturally interested in the

securing of full rights for all members of my race, is that the advances that have been won through group action may now be reinforced by individual action. I believe that what must happen next is for Southern white people to get used to seeing Negroes in waiting rooms, rest rooms, and cafeterias. And it is just as necessary, it seems to me, for Southern Negroes to get used to seeing other Negroes bypassing the segregated areas so that they may take courage and insist on the best facilities and service available for their money.

The Reporter, April 26, 1962

The Reporter in the Deep South

---

by John Herbers

In *Absalom, Absalom!*, one of William Faulkner's great Gothic novels of Yoknapatawpha County, Quentin Compson goes to Harvard and is questioned endlessly by his Canadian roommate and others: *"Tell about the South. What's it like there? Why do they live there? Why do they live at all?"* Young Compson has some trouble describing the incredible state of affairs back home.

That was 1910. Today, Yoknapatawpha county, after being left alone for more than 50 years, is undergoing rather drastic, externally wrought changes. Telling about it can be fraught with difficulty, if not for the novelist, for the journalist who must live there.

I have found some curiosity among newspapermen about how racial news is covered in the Deep South. Implied in the questioning is this: what strange set of circumstances shapes news coming from the South, and how do we know some of it is not being suppressed?

It would be no overstatement to say the Deep South is a unique region and the reporter responsible for writing about it for both local and external consumption undergoes a unique experience. Circumstances do shape his copy but usually not in the way the uninitiated might suspect.

My purpose here is to explain some of the problems involved and the framework in which the reporter must function. To do so, I must confine myself to Mississippi, still the hard core of the Deep South, and to my point of view as a wire service reporter. In doing so, however, the problems—shared to some degree by all reporters in the region—can be presented in acute form.

It is necessary first to give a brief description of social and political conditions. There is running through the South what is commonly called the black belt. Its characteristics include

639

an agrarian economy, a large Negro population and ultra conservative opinion in economic and social matters on the part
of its white leadership. Virtually the same climate of opinion
exists in all black belt counties whether they be in North Carolina, Tennessee or Alabama.

The difference in Mississippi is that these counties cover almost the entire state and there is no large urban area or extensive coastline to mitigate the black belt influence such as
exists in, say, Louisiana or Georgia. Black belt thinking has
permeated all facets of public life and it dominates the civic
and business leadership of Jackson, the capital and largest city,
as well as most other larger communities in the state.

Neither the federal government nor civil rights organizations such as the National Association for the Advancement of
Colored People chose to press for equal rights for Negroes in
the hard core areas of segregation until changes had been
made in the border states. For six years following the
Supreme Court's 1954 desegregation decision, Mississippi was
an anxious spectator while the federal courts slowly brought
about integration in some areas of life in surrounding states.
With each decision and with each racial incident white opposition to any change in the status of the Negro hardened. The
moderates were neutralized.

Thus, in 1961, when the civil rights front moved into Mississippi in the form of freedom rides, Justice Department intervention in voting, numerous federal court lawsuits and
demonstrations by local Negroes, the resistance was something like dragging an angry tom cat by his tail across a thick
carpet.

It would take several columns to describe adequately the
climate of opinion existing in the white community at this
time. It will do here to state that news reporters are not the
most popular people around. The least of the problems for
the reporter, however, are the threat of being mauled in
places like McComb and procedural difficulties. A few examples will suffice.

We cover Mississippi from Jackson with a five-man UPI
bureau. It is customary to maintain part-time correspondents
in most areas of the state to protect us on breaking news.
Usually these people work for newspapers or radio stations

and are an integral part of their community. The average community is engaged in an all-out drive for industry to stem population losses and bring in much-needed prosperity. More than almost anything else its Chamber of Commerce does not want the name of the town associated with racial strife. As a result we are not likely to be tipped on a story with a racial angle by anyone in the community. (This is not true, generally, in counties where a daily newspaper is published, but they are few and far between.)

Instead, it is likely to come from a Negro leader and usually it has come to him by a devious route. One day last summer an NAACP leader in Jackson called in a report that a plantation hand in a remote county had been lynched by his landlord and his sheriff. He said the report had come from Chicago from a relative of the victim. John Garcia, a staff reporter, spent several hours on the telephone trying to find out what had happened, but no one would claim any knowledge of the alleged incident. The sheriff went so far as to say he had seen the youth who was reported dead "hanging around town" that very morning. But when he was pressed for more information he spouted profanity and ungrammatical denials. Garcia moved a brief story on the basis of what the NAACP leader and the sheriff had said. In it, he cleaned up the sheriff's speech except for one phrase with bad grammar, perhaps to retain some degree of realism. This prompted a call from a client editor who complained that he knew the sheriff to be a college graduate and we were slanting the news by making him appear illiterate.

It was not until later in the day that we found out what the story really was. We sent a staff reporter, Ted Smith, to the scene, 100 miles away. He found that the young man in question was in jail and had been there for three days charged with assault and battery on his landlord.

The defendant's mother told Smith she saw her son severely beaten, without provocation, by the sheriff and the landlord and he had been taken to a hospital for treatment before being jailed. At the jail, Smith found the youth had been questioned by an FBI agent. But the sheriff would not let Smith interview him and sent Smith away from the jail. By this time people around town were beginning to grumble about UPI "stirring up trouble" and Smith left town under threat.

The FBI reported it found no ground for entering the case and its findings were not disclosed. The story probably rated no more than two paragraphs on the national wires, although we carried the details locally. One news bureau was spent and frustrated.

Southern police usually are cordial to newspapermen. Jackson police were during the freedom rides last summer. Recently, they used police dogs to break up a crowd of Negroes who were protesting segregation of the state fair. Several were chased for blocks, and one bystander, who had nothing to do with the demonstration, was bitten on the leg. A reporter went to the hospital to interview him. Everything was fine, it seemed. The city had bought him a new pair of pants and the mayor, Allen Thompson, had sent his apologies. This seemed nice of the mayor and it was included in the story.

But it had no sooner appeared than the telephone started ringing. One call was from Chief Detective M. B. Pierce to Bureau Manager Cliff Sessions. He said the mayor was upset by the story. He had offered no apologies and owed none. The man should have moved if he did not want to be bitten. We stood accused of irresponsible reporting.

When the Interstate Commerce Commission order against segregated travel facilities went into effect Nov. 1, UPI checked several cities to see what they would do about it. Most planned to continue segregation but the mayors of Winona and Grenada said they would comply with the ICC order. But they had not reckoned with Citizens Council leaders who leaped into action as soon as the story appeared. The mayor of Winona explained he thought he had been talking to an ICC agent rather than to a reporter. The mayor of Grenada said in a formal statement he was misquoted, and the Chamber of Commerce and city council adopted resolutions condemning "false" news reports, all of which were carried in full in the Grenada *Sentinel-Star* without explanation. I wrote a personal letter to Publisher Joe Lee:

"It was perfectly clear that when the Citizens Council people put the screws on your mayor, then came the statements of denial, reso-

lutions, etc. It doesn't matter to us what they do about the bus stations in Grenada, but it is news that has to be covered. And I sure
resent being used as a scapegoat for a public official who is forced to
back down from his prearranged plan.

Lee agreed and printed the letter in full on page one. We
never heard from the mayor.

Usually we don't come out smelling as sweet. In one city
we were harassed by the newspaper and both radio stations
for reporting some behind-the-scenes developments that did
not fit the official version of what happened.

These are not isolated incidents. Everyone is emotionally
involved. Persons who never before paid attention to news
coverage have suddenly become experts on how the delicate
subject should be handled. For a long time we were told that
the activities and statements of integration leaders were not
news because they did not have enough following to give
them substance. That is seldom heard now. Most complaints
concern the way the news is worded. For example, when
Memphis integrated three schools we relayed this abbreviated
version on the state radio wire:

(Memphis, Tennessee)—Thirteen children ended more than a
century of school segregation in Memphis today.

They romped and played with their white classmates then left for
home half an hour early.

The children were accompanied from the schools by their parents
and whisked away in automobiles about 2:30 this afternoon. The
white students were dismissed at the regular 3 o'clock time.

A policeman reported earlier that he saw two Negro girls skipping
rope with some white youngsters at one of the three schools integrated. A Negro boy was seen running hand in hand with a new-
found white friend at another school.

The whites and Negroes ate at the same tables in the cafeteria and
put away their dirty dishes together.

There was none of the bloodshed and violence that erupted at
Little Rock and New Orleans when schools were integrated."

This prompted an "official protest" from a subscriber.
"Why can't you report the facts without romancing the Negro
race?"

The reporter begins to feel he is in a strait jacket. While he may not acknowledge criticism as being justified, he may find himself writing without direction. He is inclined to turn out dead-pan copy when interpretive reporting may be in order.

Newspapers, by and large, understand the problems involved and the reporter's need for freedom. There is considerable sensitivity to the fact that newspapers outside the South frequently play down racial strife in their own cities and play it up under a Southern dateline. There is a feeling that every incident is played nationally. Actually, the great bulk of that reported never goes beyond the state wires. There simply is not room, and probably no demand, for all of it on the trunk wires.

This leads to another problem. We feel a responsibility to report this type of news in some detail. It is used by subscribers, and it is felt that justice is more apt to prevail in the light of publicity. In doing so, however, we load our wires with it and the energy of the news staff is consumed in tracking it down. Taken in large doses it can be pretty dreary stuff. Some days more than half the stories on the wire pertain either directly or indirectly to the race issue.

Dealing with the subject day in and day out the reporter may acquire a strange sense of imbalance. He may become preoccupied by this one issue and find himself a stranger to the larger, more important events in the world today, a provincial fellow.

There is, I believe, a need for a new approach in reporting the kind of social change that is going on in the South today. Certainly dead-pan rendering of facts is not helping to bridge the gap of misunderstanding that exists between races and groups involved. Why does the Main Street banker persist in thinking all integration leaders are wild-eyed Godless radicals saturated by Communism, when many of them are deeply religious and in many ways conservative; why do some liberals always categorize all white segregationists as irresponsible, insensitive lawbreakers, when frequently they are acting in conviction out of a lifetime of conditioning to their "way of life?" Why, unless there has been some breakdown in communications, whether through mass media or otherwise. It cannot all be attributed to blind prejudice.

Obviously, there is a limit to what wire services can do under the most favorable circumstances. Most newspapers seem content to continue under the old formulas. Last summer, during trial of a lawsuit for admission of a Negro to the University of Mississippi, an unusual opportunity presented itself for conveying some of the deeper meaning involved. The trial was conducted in a federal courtroom under a giant mural painted in the 1930's by a WPA artist. It was meant to depict rebuilding of the South but within the stereotyped framework of the Old South—forward-looking whites working and planning in front of a large columned building with magnolia trees and a steamboat in the background, while Negroes, segregated, pick cotton or strum a banjo.

The scene below was different—a well-dressed Negro youth on the stand asking for admission to Ole Miss, an outrageous request if placed in juxtaposition with the mural, and vice versa; a dark-skinned woman lawyer with a Grecian profile demanding, and getting, a court instruction on the correct pronunciation of "Negro" for benefit of the white attorneys; a gesticulating state attorney with a Tidewater Virginia accent deploying an array of dilatory tactics.

Those two scenes told a lot about the way things are and the way people think they are, about the past and about the future. We moved a story on it. It wasn't a great piece but it was a fresh approach, and it told more than any story of the trite testimony in the trial. It drew compliments from other journalists, but that was as far as it got. I had a hard time finding it in print.

Most newspapers from outside the region have played the Southern integration story from the point of view that it—the court-ordered change—is morally right, the law of the land and inevitable. Obviously, the wire services cannot do this and they should not be asked to any more than they should be asked to write from the point of view of the Main Street banker who looks on freedom riders as the lawbreakers, considers state segregation laws superior to U.S. Supreme Court rulings, and looks forward to the day when the courts will return to William Graham and *Plessy vs. Ferguson*. Wire services can and should maintain a vigilant watch for any violation of individual or group freedoms guaranteed to all citizens of the United States and report the truth as nearly as it can be ascertained. Finding and reporting the truth has become a

good deal more difficult than it used to be, and it probably
will become worse before it's better. There is a need, as never
before, for highly competent, skeptical reporters who can, if
nothing else, keep the record straight.

Nieman Reports, April 1962

Sheriff Harasses Negroes at Voting Rally in Georgia

by Claude Sitton

SASSER, Ga., July 26—"We want our colored people to go on living like they have for the last hundred years," said Sheriff Z. T. Mathews of Terrell County. Then he turned and glanced disapprovingly at the thirty-eight Negroes and two whites gathered in the Mount Olive Baptist Church here last night for a voter-registration rally.

"I tell you, cap'n, we're a little fed up with this registration business," he went on.

As the 70-year-old peace officer spoke, his nephew and chief deputy, M. E. Mathews, swaggered back and forth fingering a hand-tooled black leather cartridge belt and a .38-caliber revolver. Another deputy, R. M. Dunaway, slapped a five-cell flashlight against his left palm again and again.

The three officers took turns badgering the participants and warning of what "disturbed white citizens" might do if this and other rallies continued.

Sheriff Fred D. Chappell of adjacent Sumter County, other law enforcement officials and a number of the disturbed white citizens clustered at the back of the sanctuary. Outside in the black night, angry voices drowned out the singing of the crickets as men milled around the cars parked in front of the little church on the eastern edge of this hamlet in southwestern Georgia.

On the wall was an "All-American Calendar" advertising a local funeral home. It displayed pictures of President Kennedy and past Presidents.

The concern of Sheriff Zeke Mathews, "twenty years in office without opposition," is perhaps understandable.

Terrell County has 8,209 Negro residents and only 4,533 whites. While 2,894 of the whites are registered to vote, only

647

fifty-one Negroes are on the rolls, according to the Secretary of State's office.

On Sept. 13, 1960, Federal District Judge William A. Bootle handed down the first decision under the Civil Rights Acts of 1957 and 1960, which guarantee Negro voting rights.

The judge enjoined the Terrell County Board of Voter Registrars from making distinctions on the basis of race or color, illegally denying Negroes their rights under state and Federal laws and administering different qualification tests for the two races.

Judge Bootle refused a request from the Justice Department that he appoint a voter referee to oversee the registration. But he retained jurisdiction in case further court directives might become necessary.

Nevertheless, Negroes contended that because of fear and intimidation, subtle and not so subtle harassment and delaying tactics, they still found it difficult to register. Many of them are illiterate. This presents a further barrier since they are required by state law to pass a difficult qualification test.

Another source of the sheriff's concern is the fact that field secretaries for the Student Non-Violent Coordinating Committee, an Atlanta-based civil rights organization, began a voter registration drive in the county last October.

Sheriff Mathews said the racial crisis in near-by Albany also had aroused local whites and had brought the "agitators" to Sasser.

Two workers of the student committee active in Terrell County were present as the meeting opened with a hymn, "Pass Me Not, Oh Gentle Saviour."

They are Charles Sherrod, 25, from Petersburg, Va., a Negro, who took part in the sit-in demonstrations in 1960 against lunch-counter segregation, and Ralph Allen, 22, a white student at Trinity College, from Melrose, Mass.

Some of the participants said they had driven here from adjoining Lee and Daugherty counties to encourage others by their presence. Among them were two other workers, in the student committee, Miss Penelope Patch, 18, of Englewood, N.J., a white student at Swarthmore College, and Joseph Charles Jones, 24, a Negro from Charlotte, N.C.

After the hymn, Mr. Sherrod, standing at the pine pulpit on

the rostrum, led the Lord's Prayer. The audience repeated each line after him.

Overhead, swarms of gnats circled the three light globes and now and then one of the audience would look up from the pine floor to steal a fearful glance at the door.

Mr. Sherrod then read from the Scriptures, pausing after completing a passage to say:

"I'm going to read it again for they're standing on the outside."

The sound of voices around the automobiles parked beside the church could be heard as license numbers were called out. And the faces of the audience stiffened with fear.

A group of thirteen law officers and roughly dressed whites clumped through the door at this point. One pointed his arm at three newspaper reporters sitting at the front and said:

"There they are."

"If God be for us, who can be against us," read Mr. Sherrod. "We are counted as sheep for the slaughter."

With the exception of Deputy Dunaway, who stood smoking a cigarette at the rear, the whites withdrew to confer among themselves.

Mr. Sherrod began another prayer.

"Give us the wisdom to try to understand this world. Oh, Lord God, we've been abused so long; we've been down so long; oh, Lord, all we want is for our white brothers to understand that in Thy sight we are all equal.

"We're praying for the courage to withstand the brutality of our brethren."

And, in this country where Negroes have frequently fallen under the club, the blackjack and the bullet, no one appeared to doubt that the brutality of which he spoke would not be long in coming.

Nevertheless, the audience swung into a hymn with gusto, singing "We Are Climbing Jacob's Ladder." The deputy in the doorway swung his flashlight against his palm and looked on through narrowed eyes.

Lucius Holloway, Terrell County chairman of the voter registration drive, stood up.

"Everybody is welcome," he said. "This is a voter registration meeting."

Sheriff Mathews trailed by Deputy Dunaway burst into the sanctuary and strode to the front. Standing before the reporters, but looking away from them, he began to address the audience.

"I have the greatest respect for any religious organization but my people is getting disturbed about these secret meetings," he said.

"I don't think there is any colored people down here who are afraid. After last night the people are disturbed. They had a lot of violence in Albany last night."

The sheriff and chief deputy introduced themselves to the reporters and shook hands. Negroes had said they had been warned that the rally would be broken up, but the law officers seemed taken aback by the presence of the newsmen.

Sheriff Mathews then turned to the Negroes, saying that none of them was dissatisfied with life in the county. He asked all from Terrell to stand.

"Are any of you disturbed?"

The reply was a muffled "Yes."

"Can you vote if you are qualified?"

"No."

"Do you need people to come down and tell you what to do?"

"Yes."

"Haven't you been getting along well for a hundred years?"

"No."

The sheriff then said he could not control the local whites and that he wanted to prevent violence.

"Terrell County has had too much publicity," he said. "We're not looking for violence."

Chief Deputy Mathews then expressed his viewpoint.

"There's not a nigger in Terrell County who wants to make application to vote who has to have someone from Massachusetts or Ohio or New York to come down here and carry them up there to vote," he said.

The sheriff turned to Ralph Allen.

"Ralph," he said, "I'm going to have to ask you to stay out of this county until this thing quiets off.

"I don't appreciate outside agitators coming in here and stirring up trouble and it's causing us a lot of trouble. I've helped more colored people than any man in the South, I reckon.

"Would you mind telling me who pays you?" he asked Mr. Allen.

The student replied that he received a subsistence allowance from the committee.

"They give you your orders?"

"They place me."

The chief deputy took over the questioning.

"Then you got Terrell County—that's your project, huh?"

A long exchange of forceful questions followed. After that, Deputy Mathews turned to the others and told them:

"There is a prohibit to register between now and December."

Under Georgia law, registration goes on throughout the year, although only those registered at various specified times prior to the primaries and elections may vote in them.

Sheriff Mathews then pointed to the crowd of whites at the back of the sanctuary.

"Gentlemen," he said to the reporters, "those are all of them.

"The people have lost faith and respect in the coordinating bunch. They don't have to have it, Cap'n. They don't have to have it."

Deputy Mathews informed the Negroes that it would not be "to your interest" to continue the meeting.

"You don't have to have nobody from Massachusetts to come down here and help you the way to the court house," he said.

In another reference to Mr. Allen, he commented:

"I don't think he's got any business down here, to tell you the damn truth."

Deputy Mathews turned to Deputy Dunaway and ordered him to take the names of all those present.

"I just want to find out how many here in Terrell County are dissatisfied," explained Sheriff Mathews.

Turning to a local Negro and pointing at Mr. Allen, the Chief Deputy then said:

"He's going to be gone in two weeks, but you'll still be here."

As the names were collected, Deputy Mathews began pressing questions on Mr. Sherrod and interrupting him sarcastically as the Negro tried to reply.

He turned to Mr. Allen again. Shaking a finger in his face, he said:

"You couldn't get a white person to walk down the street with you."

When Deputy Dunaway asked the names of five Negro youths sitting on a bench with Miss Patch, they refused to give them.

"I wouldn't either," said Deputy Mathews.

As the Sheriff walked away, he said to reporters:

"Some of these niggers down here would just as soon vote for Castro and Khrushchev."

The Negroes began humming a song of protest popularized during the sit-in demonstrations, "We Shall Overcome." And as the law officers withdrew to the outside, the song swelled to a crescendo.

The business meeting then got under way. Miss Patch reported on her work in Lee County. Mr. Allen told of having been knocked down twice last Saturday, beaten and threatened with death by white men in Dawson, the county seat.

Charles Jones asked Mr. Holloway if anything had been heard from the Justice Department regarding an investigation into the dismissal of a Negro teacher.

"No," replied the chairman.

Shortly after 10 o'clock, the Negroes rose and joined hands in a circle. Swaying in rhythm, they again sang, "We Shall Overcome." Their voices had a strident note as though they were building up their courage to go out into the night, where the whites waited.

Lucius Holloway prayed.

"Our concern is not to destroy," he said. "Our concern is not to displace or to fight, but to build a community in which all our children can live and grow up in dignity."

The Negroes then filed out the front door past the group of law officers.

"I know you," said one officer to a Negro. "We're going to get some of you."

Flashlight beams slashed through the darkness to spotlight

the face of Miss Patch as the white student climbed into an automobile with some Negroes from Lee County. The whites standing by cursed but made no move toward the car.

Miss Patch and her companions pulled out behind the station wagon in which the newsmen were riding. But the air had been let out of the right front tire of the wagon, forcing it to stop close to the church. The other car stopped, too.

Carloads of whites roared past again and again while the tire was being changed. A deputy stopped and said with mock solicitude, "Help you, cap'n?" He drove away grinning.

Five whites in an automobile trailed the station wagon and the car in which Miss Patch was riding to Albany, eighteen miles away. Newsmen stopped to take the license number but the plate had been bent over to conceal it. The whites swerved into a side street and sped away.

A mechanic who examined the station wagon today found that quantities of sand had been poured into the gasoline tank, causing untold damage to the engine. He found no evidence of a puncture on the tire, only a knife mark on the valve where the air had been released.

The New York Times, July 27, 1962

The Hostile Witness

by Murray Kempton

THE City of Albany wound up its case Friday against Martin Luther King and dozens of unknown Southern children for littering the streets and praying in places of public passage and otherwise disturbing its way of life.

The final witness for the city was Charles Jones, field secretary of the Southern Non-Violent Coordinating Committee, who is in jail for disturbing the peace and who was therefore a hostile witness. Charles Jones is twenty-three and of Charlotte, North Carolina, and that state's colored college. He has been in jail ten times or more, the longest on the Rock Hill, South Carolina, chain gang.

It was the assignment of Grady Rawls, Albany's City Attorney, to set Charles Jones before Federal Judge Robert Elliott, who wants very obviously to hate and fear him as a vagrant, a disturber and an enemy of concord.

Grady Rawls is a fat man, and an unexpected embodiment of the tense and disturbed white South, because he almost falls asleep on his feet and frequently falls asleep in his chair. Charles Jones is young and thin, his hands and feet moving all the time, a live one with a body going places. Grady Rawls confronted Charles Jones with the assurance that no Negro could do anything but make a fool of himself when confronted by a distinguished white attorney. And Charley Jones was scared; he wanted terribly not to make a mistake. He sat on the stand, and in the long intervals between the questions, he shook almost with the ague. But when he came to answer, he went very fast.

"Are you paid a salary?" Grady Rawls asked. "How do you subsist?"

Charles Jones rubbed his hands and smiled, "At times I wonder."

Grady Rawls asked him if there were Communists in the

movement. Charles Jones answered, "No." Grady Rawls
handed up a leaflet labeled "Remember This Week" and asked
Charles Jones whether he had had a part in preparing it.

"I didn't," said Charley Jones, "have a part in preparing it.
But I do remember that week. I remember Martin Luther
King being arrested, and Bill Hansen being arrested, and
C. B. King being struck by the sheriff."

Grady Rawls rocked back and forth, almost asleep, his belly
brushing now and again against the counsel's table, and put
the next question:

"Have you encouraged juveniles to sit-in?"

Charley Jones looked at his hands. "I don't check ages,"
he answered. "I have informed people what I intended to
do, and that anything they did was their personal commitment. If they felt they should, they should make up their
minds."

Charles Jones is an anarchist and a proud one.

"Do you," asked Grady Rawls, "regard the city ordinance
to regulate parades and mass demonstrations as illegal?"

Charles Jones looked up straight in Grady Rawls's eye.

"I don't think there's an ordinance against a mass meeting
yet. And I've never considered what I've done a parade. On the
legality of the legislation, I am not qualified to judge. But in its
application, I have definitely felt that it has been unjustly used
to deny Negroes the right of assembly to redress grievances."

"And why," Grady Rawls asked, "don't you exercise your
legal right to resort to the courts?"

Charles Jones shook a little and framed his answer.

"I don't know any legal proceedings that would require the
City Commissioners to sit down on our grievances. Many
grievances cannot be settled by legal proceedings. I think that
is why the Constitution provides for freedom of assembly so
that people can bring their grievances before government and
bring them to a peaceful, democratic result."

And those, by one of those accidents which make the South
enchanting, were the last words spoken for the plaintiff in this
case. They were, of course, the point. Albany now has to go
to the Court of Appeals and try to prove that the exercise of
free assembly is a nuisance. And Charley Jones had closed the
question. Grady Rawls, still unconscious—he had only been

cross-examining a colored boy, after all—turned and began putting irrelevant documents into the record.

I don't think anyone understands what has happened to the South in the last ten years. Negroes have come up who sit on the stand and confound white lawyers.

Charley Jones was so weary when he finished that he left the courtroom and shook by himself for a terribly long while. Then he came back to the recess. A visitor said to him that it was too bad that the South knew at last what it was doing and, without violence, is containing him and the children who listen to him. This, of course, seems to be defeat; to Charley Jones, who has been to Southern jails, it seems like victory.

He looked at the wall across the way. "And, you don't think," he wondered, "that we have come a long way when they don't hit us any more?"

from *America Comes of Middle Age:*
Columns 1950–1962 (1963)

Meredith Blocked at Ole Miss

by W. F. Minor

OXFORD, Miss. —Gov. Ross Barnett, personally acting as registrar, Thursday flouted the federal courts and denied Negro James Meredith admission to the University of Mississippi.

But the justice department, moving quickly Thursday night, ignored Barnett and moved to cite Ole Miss Chancellor J. D. Williams and two other university officials for contempt of three federal court orders to register the Negro.

Barnett read to Meredith the proclamation of interposition which he had invoked last week and told Meredith under its powers he refused to recognize the federal court order for Meredith's admission to the 114-year-old all-white university.

The slightly built 29-year-old Negro, the first of his race to win court ordered admission to a white state education institution in Mississippi, then drove off with two federal marshals and a department of justice attorney who had accompanied him to the campus.

During the tense closed-door face-to-face conference between Barnett and Meredith, Barnett reportedly threw down a copy of the interposition resolution in front of the Negro student and told him "you will not be registered."

Sources said the justice department attorney told Barnett "you realize you are in contempt, don't you?"

Barnett, a source in the conference said, declared: "Who are you to say that I am in contempt?"

The governor reportedly added that it would be up to the courts to decide on the issue of contempt.

As Meredith stepped into the waiting automobile to leave, one student lunged towards him but was restrained by a highway patrolman and didn't get within reach of the Negro.

Neither he nor the federal marshals made any comment as they drove from the campus and headed for a highway in the direction of Memphis. Meredith and the marshals had driven to Oxford from Memphis Thursday afternoon.

Barnett, who came to the campus in midafternoon with Lieut. Gov. Paul Johnson and assistant Atty. Gen. Dugas Shands, awaited Meredith's arrival in the continuation study center on the Ole Miss campus.

About an hour before Meredith's arrival, the board of trustees of institutions of higher learning, meeting in Jackson, had clothed Barnett with all powers to act as registrar in Meredith's case.

The college board had agonized over what course to take for the past five days under pressure by Barnett to defy three federal court injunctions to register Meredith even if it meant going to jail.

The marshals arrived at the continuation study center accompanied by highway patrol cars at 4:30 p.m., and the Negro Air Force veteran, wearing glasses, emerged from the car and after a moment's silence students who had gathered outside a cordon of state highway patrolmen in front of the building booed Meredith but launched no disturbance.

Twenty minutes later when Meredith emerged the crowd had grown substantially. The boos rang out in louder crescendo as Meredith entered an automobile with the marshals and drove away.

The crowd included several adults from off the campus who had been identified with active pro-segregationist movements. At one point, the students launched into a chant "We want Ross" and also gave a resounding Ole Miss cheer, traditionally called "hotty toddy."

A line of 100 patrolmen ringed the driveway outside the conference room and reporters along with the crowd of students were held back about 75 feet from the entrance to the building.

Barnett emerged from the continuation study center two minutes after Meredith's departure and made a brief talk to the students before stepping into a state highway car to drive to the airport, waving his hand triumphantly.

A man who came out of the alumni building with Barnett, and said he sat in on the meeting of the governor with Meredith, gave this account of the brief interview:

Meredith appeared calm and said little.

Robert Ellis, the university registrar, quietly read a copy of the federal court order demanding that Meredith be admitted. Meredith had brought along the copy.

Then Ellis excused himself and left the room.

Barnett told Meredith that he was denying his application for enrollment.

In Washington, a justice department spokesman said Atty. Gen. Robert F. Kennedy and Barnett held a telephone conversation after the governor's arrival at Oxford.

The spokesman said the conversation was "very friendly" but indicated there was no change in the position of either official.

Kennedy earlier had summed up his position:

"We are going to make sure that the court orders are followed."

The state college board, meeting at Jackson, placed the matter in the hands of Gov. Ross Barnett at almost the same hour the governor was arriving on the campus here.

Thomas J. Tubb, chairman of the board, said the resolution made Barnett, in effect, the Ole Miss registrar as far as the Meredith case is concerned.

"Whatever he does is our action," said Tubb.

Tubb said the board members were announcing their resolution only after Meredith failed to appear before them at Jackson at 3 p.m., as he had been instructed to do in a letter from the board.

This was the first indication that the board had sought to bring Meredith to Jackson instead of the campus at Oxford.

Earlier a federal court in Meridian barred the state from arresting Meredith on his conviction of false voter registration.

At the same time, the two-judge court left in effect a state court judge's order prohibiting the University of Mississippi from enrolling Meredith.

The order was signed by U.S. District Judges Harold Cox and Sidney Mize.

The two federal judges also set a hearing for Monday on a request that the state be enjoined from enforcing its new law prohibiting the university from enrolling anyone with a criminal record or a "moral turpitude" charge against him.

Later—at Hattiesburg, a three-judge panel of the U.S. Fifth

circuit court of appeals gave the justice department the order it wanted to override the state court injunction against Meredith's enrollment.

Meredith was convicted Thursday morning in a 10-minute trial without his presence on the charge of giving false information in applying for voter registration.

The order signed by the federal judges covered three aspects of the case:

1. It restrained any state law enforcement officer from arresting Meredith in connection with the conviction.

2. It restrained any state officers from arresting him on any charge growing out of a new law prohibiting the university from enrolling anyone with a criminal record or a charge of "moral turpitude" against him. The bill was issued by the Legislature Wednesday night and signed into law early Thursday by Gov. Ross Barnett.

3. It refused to stay a state court judge's injunction prohibiting the university from enrolling Meredith—in effect, leaving the state and federal courts at loggerheads on the issue.

The Times-Picayune (New Orleans),
September 21, 1962

On the Mississippi Warfront: Oxford's a Town All Shook Up

by James L. Hicks

(Editor's Note: This dispatch was written before James Meredith was enrolled last Monday.)

OXFORD, Miss.—If you think Nikita Khruschev "shook up" New York City when he paid a surprise visit to the United Nations you should have been here last Thursday and seen what James H. Meredith did to Oxford, Mississippi.

Meredith literally rocked and rolled this town out of its senses and he never even came to town—he just held a press conference and said he was coming!

I've never seen such chaos and bedlam in all my life.

This is how it was:

Meredith swooped into town by Border Patrol plane on Wednesday and literally stunned everyone here including the state troopers by having the nerve to come here at all.

He caught Governor Ross Barnett flatfooted by arriving while the governor was still 30 miles away racing to beat him here. But the Lt. Governor recovered himself sufficiently to risk contempt of the Federal Courts and turned Meredith away as the town heaved a sigh of relief.

But Meredith left with a promise that he would be back and as soon as he left, the State of Mississippi, from the governor on down, immediately set about putting on a show of strength to convince themselves (and they hoped Meredith too) that he wouldn't have a chance if he returned again.

In order to do this they massed every law officer the state of Mississippi could produce and poured them into little Oxford. There were so many state troopers and sheriffs and peace officers present that they completely filled up the National Guard Armory and had to rent room for the troopers from private rooming houses.

They borrowed gas masks from the National Guard and the

Jackson, Mississippi city police (200 miles away) rushed here with their private police dogs which they tied up on the Ole Miss campus.

By Thursday morning the little city of Oxford assembled a regional combat zone with every red blooded white man in the city standing at the ready.

Let's face it—it was a terrific show of strength and the local newspapers and the radio stations began to proudly boast about the "ring of protection" around the city and to point out that Meredith and the handful of marshalls would hear about the "ring" and give up any plans they might have to try again.

And then it happened!

Meredith announced from Memphis that he was "coming in."

I don't know how it was when Caesar "cast the die" and notified Rome that he was going to cross the Rubicon.

But I'm sure that the Romans could not have dropped their togas in more utter confusion than did the "armed ring" around Oxford, Miss. last Thursday.

The town was stunned with disbelief.

How could he dare? Was he crazy? Hadn't he heard the radio reports of all these troopers and peace officers massed around the town. Didn't he know that unlike the day before when the governor got lost, didn't he know that today both the Governor and the Lt. Gov. were on hand. Was this Negro actually fearless?

"He can't possibly be coming—is he coming?"

Everybody in Oxford glued their ears to a radio—and the radio didn't let them down as it crackled:

"Meredith has been spotted traveling in this direction, 30 miles from Oxford."

The state troopers panicked. Chief Birdsong, in charge of all the troopers, suddenly flashed an order over the car radios for all troopers to report immediately to the National Guard Armory.

You can imagine what that did to this town of 6,500.

All of a sudden about 1,000 troopers stationed on all sides of the town are told to rush to one point.

They rushed—right smack dab into the middle of town and

into one of the worst traffic jams Oxford has ever seen. It looked like Times Square on New Year's Eve.

Some made it to the armory—others just couldn't do it. The chief had them all take off their badges and name plates and sent them rushing back out to their posts on the highways and around the city.

Then the townspeople got into the act. Students from Ole Miss—1,000 strong—rushed from their classes and took up positions with the troopers around the main gate of the University. Half the folks in town hopped into their cars and went out on the highway leading from Memphis from which Meredith was supposed to be coming.

Then a radio report came saying that Meredith was coming in by plane. The other half of the city then hopped into their cars and rushed to the airport.

That created another mess.

In fact by this time the whole town was in a mess.

I don't know what they were expecting.

But they acted as if this lone young Negro youth was a man from Mars who would descend upon the town spouting brimstone and fire from his mouth while raining thunder, lightning and destruction from both nostrils.

Since I still am not permitted (because of my race,) to stand at the main gate of Ole Miss, I jumped into my U-Drive-It car and headed out on the highway with the rest of the excited yokels.

I was aware that I was the only Negro on the streets and I didn't relish the idea of getting swept up in a mob of white people out to destroy, or watch a lone Negro destroyed.

But I figured that if Meredith did come in by convoy I might be lucky enough to sandwich my car into the convoy with him.

I knew I had no friends in the mob so I reasoned that if I were able to get into his convoy I would at least be riding with the North when the Second Civil War began.

About a mile out of town, however, I came upon a spot where the road from Memphis intersects the road from the airport and this, of course, was an ideal spot to wait, inasmuch as I could catch him there whether he came by air or land.

The only thing wrong with this was that half the people in town also realized this and were already there so when I pulled off into a picnic grove and parked I parked with rebels to the right and left, in front and behind me. I was well aware that for me this could be the zero hour whether Meredith came or not.

But these people were so excited by this time that they had no eyes for an ordinary Negro—they were looking for a man from outer space named Meredith.

And then it happened again. The local radio crackled: "We have a report that Meredith is definitely coming by air—" and at that very moment a small plane flew overhead.

Someone looked up and yelled, "There he is!"

And God is my witness, someone else yelled:

"Stop him!"

And then there in that picnic grove of trees everybody started their car at the same time and everybody moved forward or backward with about a third of the cars either ramming into, or backing into, one another, or into a tree!

I saw at least five fenders smashed and one car almost climbed a tree. I sat in my car and didn't move a finger.

I would have shook with laughter if I had not been surrounded by people who wouldn't appreciate my laughter.

So I satisfied myself with the thought that superman Meredith had really shook up the town.

Five minutes later a radio report said Meredith was still in Memphis and not thinking about coming to Oxford.

Everybody went home!

New York Amsterdam News, October 6, 1962

"It Was War—and Marshals Were Losing"

by Rick Tuttle

OXFORD, Miss.—The U.S. marshal lay on the tile floor bleeding from an artery in the neck. He was hit by a shotgun pellet and was in danger of bleeding to death.

"Somebody get a doctor in here."

"What is it? What is it?"

"They have a shotgun now. By God, they've got a shotgun."

We were inside Ole Miss' administration building. Outside, in the darkness, the mob howled. And the shotgun roared from beyond the screen of tear gas set down by white-helmeted marshals who hid behind parked autos.

I have never been shot at before. It isn't pleasant.

Inside, three men worked on Marshal Graham Same, trying to stop the flow of blood.

"Where the hell's a doctor?"

"We're trying to get one."

"Try hell, this man's dying!"

Same didn't die. He was removed from our fortress a half hour later in critical condition.

Other marshals stumbled in from the outside, blood dripping from small pellet nicks on their faces and ears. Their helmets were gashed from bricks and bottles.

In a telephone booth, Assistant Attorney General Dean Markham was talking to the White House, where President Kennedy and Attorney General Robert Kennedy made the big decisions.

"Listen, they're shooting now. Send those troops."

But for hours the troops did not come.

More gas masks did arrive and I got one. I had been momentarily blinded earlier by the penetrating irritant and could not go outside without one.

I dodged out the front door and hid behind a huge column.

"Bam-bam-bam."

665

The slugs plunked against the brick building above my head and buried themselves in the door frames.

"That was a .22 automatic," said a marshal lying on the porch beside me.

"Blam." Glass crashed off to the left.

"That was bigger," he said.

"Must be .30 caliber. Sounds like a carbine."

The marshals did not return the fire. They couldn't. They could only see the charging lines of howling rebels in the blackness—not the snipers.

I adjusted my mask and got a whiff of teargas. I scrambled back into the building.

The doors burst open behind me and a rebel was thrown to the floor. His head was split open.

"He had a bulldozer. He was charging us," a gasping marshal said. The marshal, Albert Taylor of Chula Vista, Calif., collapsed in a fit of nausea. He had ripped off his mask to pull the driver off his tractor.

Two marshals wrapped the dozer driver's head in bandages, but the blood soaked through immediately and ran down his neck in a thin line. When he was wrapped up, a marshal kicked him and said, "You get up you SOB. I want to talk to you brave boys."

The man groaned and rolled over but didn't get up.

The marshal grabbed him and yanked him up and pushed him down the hall to the interrogation room.

As marshals trapped a rebel, they dragged him into the building. The marshals were rough.

This was not a lark. For the moment, it was war—and the marshals were losing. For two hours, the Lyceum Building on the Ole Miss campus was under siege. And the marshals inside were running out of the only ammunition they had— teargas.

The Oxford National Guard unit of 60 men arrived and the tenseness eased. But the sniper with the .22 was now on a rooftop across the park, plinking away at us.

"Can't you get that damn sniper?"

"I couldn't reach him with the pistol even if I was sure where he is. That little .22 doesn't even have a muzzle blast I can see."

"Bam-bam-bam," and the marshals ducked for cover and the mob charged.

Now National Guardsmen—some students at Ole Miss and lifelong Oxford residents—were being carried through the front doors with broken legs and arms and bloody faces.

"Those aren't students out there," a Guardsman said. "They wouldn't shoot."

I went back outside. The mob had turned over two cars and had set them afire.

A flash of light cut an arc through the trees, and landed with a crash. Then a burst of gasoline flame. The rebs were using Molotov cocktails now.

They jeered and shouted and overturned another car and set it afire.

"Bam-bam." The sniper was still up there someplace.

Then the regular army troops arrived.

And then the regular army men were being carried through the front doors with broken and sprained arms and legs. The mob was not frightened—but it was smaller.

As the night grew old, more and more prisoners were adults from Memphis, not from Oxford, not even Mississippi.

Finally, the army troops moved against the rebels and they retreated. Soldiers caught some and turned them over to the marshals for arrest.

Inside the Lyceum marshals slept now in grotesque positions on the floor. All of the wounded had been taken away. It looked as if the riot was over.

But it was just starting.

Dawn broke in grayness and a light rain began. It was peaceful on the campus with the troops broken into squads and waiting in the rain. The blood on the porch was dry now.

I went to town thinking it was all over.

But new cries rang from Oxford's town square. "Go home nigger lover. Get out."

The sleepless mob was at it again—and reinforced. As the Army troop trucks rolled by, the crowd smashed the windows with pop bottles and pieces of pipe. They ripped old railings from buildings and hurled the wood chunks.

"We just got here," a carload of men from out-of-town yelled to a rebel-flag-waver on the street.

"About time. We need some help."

As the troops moved in on foot with bayonets and teargas, the mob threw bottles and ran, retreating just out of range.

A grayhaired Oxford restaurant owner stared with tears in his eyes and said: "These aren't our people. They are outsiders. My people wouldn't do that."

I nodded and ducked for cover. I was blinded again by teargas. At least that sniper was gone.

The Miami Herald, October 2, 1962

Courthouse Square Is Authentic Picture of Occupied Town

by Kenneth L. Dixon

In Occupied Oxford, Miss.—This dateline is no joke.

Oxford is occupied—as thoroughly as any occupied town I saw on foreign soil in World War II.

By dawn today, the campus at Ole Miss appeared to contain more soldiers than students. A huge bivouac stretched from the grove in the Lyceum building on down toward the main entrance.

Out at the Oxford-University airport a much larger encampment was stretched out along the ground lining both sides of the single strip runway.

Already an Army field kitchen was set up, starting to serve breakfast to the troops. It had come in during the night, along with the hundreds of other military units that poured steady streams into this town that has become the center of the nation's and the world's attention.

When the sun came up, the campus had been almost cleared of the skeletons of burned cars and trucks, but the broken glass and stones still remained to remind all of the terror of night before last.

A vagrant breeze still brought traces of tear gas—some of which was exploded last night when the troops saw any sign of a crowd gathering in the area of Baxter Hall where Negro James Meredith became the first member of his race to officially spend the night on the Ole Miss campus as a student.

He spent the night there—but whether he slept or not is anybody's guess.

More tear gas was exploded in downtown Oxford about 6 o'clock this morning—just two blocks from Courthouse Square. An hour later, soldiers were not sure whether it had been done by one of their own troops or by someone who had stolen some of the tear gas bombs reported missing last night.

Courthouse Square last night was an authentic picture of an occupied town. Lights blazed on all sides of the courthouse itself throughout the long night, and the deserted parking and street areas surrounding it saw soldiers being put through bayonet drills—lunging and charging to the cries of "Yaaah—Huh! Yaaah—Huh!" of squad leaders.

Most of the practicing troops had just arrived, riding into town half asleep in the canvas covered backs of huge Army trucks.

Once on the scene they soon became adjusted to the situation. A couple of hundred of them spent the night on the grounds surrounding the courthouse, sleeping on the grass with raincoats spread over them and helmets or packs for pillows.

This morning they rose and stretched and rubbed their eyes and took up their posts—helping occupy this American town with American troops.

It was clearly apparent most of them didn't like their present job—but just as clear that they were going to follow orders and do it.

They snapped into a combat crouch and pointed their bayonetted carbines straight at the driver of each car stopped at the roadblocks. They methodically went through glove compartments and trunks, searched under the seats to be sure that no contraband weapons were being smuggled in. But once the search was over, many of them thanked the drivers courteously and seemed almost apologetic about the incident.

This morning their almost eager friendliness was apparent. Where yesterday they were defensively terse in dealing with townspeople and newsmen, today they were more relaxed and willing to engage in conversation.

Suddenly they seemed to realize what occupying troops have discovered throughout the world and throughout the centuries.

As the streets gradually became lined with mostly silent civilians, they clearly sensed that although they held a town in captivity, they were the real captives.

The Meridian Star, October 2, 1962

How a Secret Deal Prevented
a Massacre at Ole Miss

by George B. Leonard,
T. George Harris, and
Christopher S. Wren

BETWEEN noon and midnight of September 30, 1962, this nation came within one man's nod of a state-sized civil war. The riot that exploded at the University of Mississippi in Oxford brought death to two men and injuries to hundreds. But it was a pep rally compared with what almost happened.

A group of Mississippi leaders had been secretly planning to form a wall of unarmed bodies that would not yield until knocked down and trod upon by Federals. Many segregationists were prepared to go to jail. Many were ready to fight with fists, rocks and clubs. Some resolved to stand until shot down. Others planned to defy the orders of their leaders and conceal pistols on their persons.

"In retrospect, I'm thankful that 5,000 to 10,000—maybe 15,000 to 20,000—fellow Mississippians didn't go there and get killed," said Dr. M. Ney Williams, 40, a director of the Citizens' Council and adviser to Gov. Ross Barnett in the crisis. This earnest segregationist may have overstated, but he is one of a small group who knew the situation's real potential. No one who understood Mississippi's "wall-of-flesh" strategy estimates that less than "hundreds" would have been killed had the plan been carried out.

What the segregationists did not know is this: While Barnett was encouraging their efforts, he was—throughout the four days before the riot—secretly suggesting schemes to Attorney General Robert Kennedy that would allow Negro James Meredith to enter Ole Miss.

This strange story has never been told. To uncover the facts behind the Battle of Ole Miss, three LOOK editors spent weeks interviewing more than 105 individuals in Jackson and

Oxford, Miss., Atlanta, Ga., and Washington, D.C. From this search, LOOK has pieced together a chronicle of courage and cross-purposes, of passion and patience, of a massacre barely avoided.

The untold story begins after Mississippi's legal fight to keep Meredith out of Ole Miss had failed. By Thursday, September 27, Governor Barnett was legally on the defensive. He was under orders from the 5th U.S. Circuit Court, meeting the next day in New Orleans, to show cause why he should not be held in contempt of court. Three times already, he had blocked Meredith's attempts to enroll. Barnett knew that if he did not let the Negro into Ole Miss he probably would be held in contempt—and face a huge fine and possibly jail.

Other pressures were bearing down on Ross Barnett, an ambitious man who wanted to be loved by all. He was, of course, getting pressure from Robert Kennedy through a series of personal phone calls. But an unexpected pressure was building up in Mississippi. The state's permanent leadership— the bankers, educators, lawyers and businessmen whose power is not limited to a governor's term—had begun meeting in homes and offices, phoning one another for sobering talks. Now, on the 27th, Thursday morning, the grapevine and the telephone brought Barnett a word of caution, in contrast to the usual counsel of defiance. We back your principles, Governor, the permanent leaders said in essence, but we hope your actions will not harm Ole Miss.

Was it too late for reason to prevail? The signs were bad. By noon, a great force had gathered at Ole Miss. Barnett and Lt. Gov. Paul Johnson were there. Near the university's East Gate, some 250 state troopers and county sheriffs were lined up, surrounded and infiltrated by a restless crowd of more than 2,000 students and others. All were waiting for James Meredith and whatever U.S. marshals he might have with him. Here was Mississippi's "wall of flesh."

In this dangerous impasse, Robert Kennedy awaited a call from Ross Barnett, who, through a representative earlier that day, had suggested a way out. The call did not come. Now, at 2:50 p.m., Washington time, Kennedy took the initiative and put a call through to Barnett.

"Hello," said Kennedy.

"Hello, General. How are you?" Barnett said hospitably.

The two got right down to the business of the Governor's plan. Both understood its purpose: to allow Barnett to be overwhelmed by the Federals while crying "Never" for the segregationists' benefit.

The plan called for Barnett and Johnson to stand at the university's gate, backed up by unarmed state patrolmen. Kennedy would have Chief U.S. Marshal James McShane and 25 to 30 marshals bring Meredith to the gate. Barnett would refuse to let Meredith in. At this point, McShane would draw his gun, and the other marshals would slap their hands on their holsters. Barnett would then step aside and allow Meredith to register. The Mississippi highway patrol would maintain law and order.

In his talk with Kennedy, the Governor worried about how the scene would look to "a big crowd." If only one man drew his gun, Barnett felt that he could not back down. So Kennedy reluctantly agreed to have all the marshals draw their guns. Under Federal guns, Ross Barnett could surrender to prevent bloodshed.

Kennedy knew his own duty—to uphold the courts and to do everything in his power to avoid bloodshed. He did not wish to use Federal troops against, as he put it, "my fellow Americans." And, for the sake of a long-term solution, he wanted to leave law enforcement in state and local hands.

The plan, however bizarre, would accomplish these purposes. The Attorney General set about making plans to send Meredith and an escort of marshals down to Oxford from their base at the Naval Air Station near Memphis, Tenn.

But an hour later, Barnett called back and asked for a postponement until Saturday the 29th. He seemed shaky and unsure of his control over his people. He put Lieutenant Governor Johnson on. Johnson spoke worriedly of "intense citizens," sheriffs and deputies not directly under state control. It might take time to "move them." Everything was held in suspense until Barnett phoned again. Be there at 5 p.m., Mississippi time, he told Kennedy. It was then 2:20 at Oxford. Barnett repeatedly promised there would be no violence.

*

Thirteen green U.S. border-patrol sedans glided down Highway 55, the new expressway running south from Memphis. Twelve contained a total of more than two dozen marshals. They had unloaded pistols and had been briefed on their role in the coming charade. The other car was driven by border patrolman Charles Chamblee of New Orleans. With him in the front seat was Chief Marshal McShane, his rugged face tight and determined.

In back, James Meredith, cool as always, sat next to John Doar, 40, of the U.S. Department of Justice. Meredith wore the armor of the new Negro's determination to ignore personal risk. The NAACP had selected him for legal backing from among eleven students ready to apply to Ole Miss. Looking at Meredith, Doar thought here is a man who can stand almost any amount of pressure.

As the convoy rolled on, Robert Kennedy phoned Ross Barnett. Kennedy wanted specific assurances that Barnett would maintain order after Meredith got on campus. Barnett's answers were disturbing. He spoke generally of keeping order "all over the state. . . . We always do that." It was then 3:35 p.m. in Oxford.

At that point, Kennedy could not possibly realize the Governor's dilemma. Barnett had set forces in motion he could not control. The brigade at the gate didn't know that he was negotiating surrender with "the enemy." Their job, as many saw it, was to stop the Federal marshals even at the cost of their lives. But they were confused as to how they would fight. Barnett feared the "hotheads" would call the turn.

Judge Russell D. Moore, III, a blocky ex-marine in command at Oxford for the Governor, had originally disarmed all highway patrolmen and sheriffs. "We didn't want any of our officers to be incited into drawing a pistol and shooting someone," he said later. In its purest form, Mississippi strategy called for passive resistance. But Moore got word that the Federals were bringing in "the goon squad," equipped with billies and gas. So he broke out helmets, night sticks and gas masks for the highway patrol, and let his sheriffs carry blackjacks, keep their gas guns handy and bring in police dogs. Moore later said he was confident that the disciplined patrolmen would have accepted an order to give way if the Federals had drawn guns.

Oxford Sheriff Joe Ford knew, however, that the visiting sheriffs would be harder to control. "If the marshals had come with their guns drawn, they might have got by the patrol," he said later, "but when they got to the sheriffs, they would have had to use them." Then, too, at least one deputy carried a hidden pistol. "We're not going to just stand up here," another said, "and let that nigger in." Both troopers and sheriffs had their regular weapons locked in car trunks—near at hand. No matter what Barnett said, the crowd's emotion would have set off violence. "It would," Moore said later, "have been a donnybrook."

At 4:35 p.m., Oxford time, Barnett phoned Kennedy again. The Governor was, he said, worried. He was nervous. He felt unable to control the crowd. The way things were going, he thought a hundred people were liable to be killed, and that would "ruin all of us." It would, he said, be embarrassing to him.

"I don't know if it would be *embarrassing*," Kennedy said. "That would not be the feeling." He hurriedly ended the conversation and ordered the convoy to turn back. It was then just 30 miles from Oxford.

The next day, Friday, September 28, in New Orleans, the Circuit Court gave Barnett until 11 a.m. Tuesday to purge himself of contempt of court. This meant, among other things, allowing Meredith to register. Otherwise, Barnett would be fined $10,000 a day and jailed.

The Governor had his deadline. But Robert Kennedy had a worse one. Getting Meredith into Ole Miss would be difficult, perhaps dangerous. But arresting the Governor of Mississippi in his state capitol! This would not only be regrettable, but immeasurably more dangerous. Kennedy imagined the mob around the capitol building—troopers, sheriffs, "hotheads" and racists from all over. Two days before, ex-General Edwin Walker had spoken over a Shreveport (La.) radio station, calling for 10,000 volunteers from every state to come to the aid of Ross Barnett. Robert Kennedy knew he would have to do everything in his power to get Meredith into Ole Miss by 11 a.m. Tuesday.

That Friday afternoon, he met with five military leaders headed by Gen. Maxwell Taylor, Chairman of the Joint Chiefs, who, like most of the others, had worked on the Little Rock paratroop operation under President Eisenhower. They considered using—if necessary—two battalions of MP's, a battle group from the 2nd Infantry Division at Fort Benning, Ga., and logistic support.

Saturday, September 29. A lovely early-autumn day in Washington. Robert Kennedy was in his office by 10 a.m., surrounded by the small group of Justice Department officials who, informally, had become the "Mississippi task force." They included wiry, brilliant Burke Marshall, 40, head of the Civil Rights Division; Deputy Attorney General Nicholas de B. Katzenbach, 40, a big-boned law scholar; and Edwin Guthman, 43, Kennedy's assistant for public information.

At 11:50, the Attorney General got a call from the Governor's mansion. He was not expecting any change in the situation, and none was forthcoming. Kennedy put down the phone and looked grimly at the men around him.

"We'd better get moving," he said, "with the military."

He picked up the phone and, at 12:15, reached President Kennedy at the White House. The President told him to come over. Before leaving, Robert Kennedy shook his head. "Maybe we waited too long."

"No," Guthman replied. "The result would have been the same, and the record is clear that we've done everything to avoid this step."

Kennedy nodded. His face was somber and sad.

At the White House, the President, with his brother and Marshall, got to work on his television address (tentatively set for Sunday night), on military planning, and drafted a proclamation federalizing the Mississippi National Guard. Meanwhile, Governor Barnett was on the phone again. He had a new twist. He proposed that, on Monday morning, he, Johnson, the troopers and sheriffs stand defiantly at the entrance to Ole Miss. While they waited, Meredith would be sneaked into Jackson, where facilities would be set up to register him.

A "surprised" Barnett would complain bitterly of Federal trickery. But on Tuesday, he would allow Meredith to come to Ole Miss. He promised the President that the highway patrol would maintain law and order.

All Saturday afternoon, the men in Washington considered the proposal. In a 7 p.m. telephone call, the President himself and Governor Barnett agreed to this plan. The Governor assured him that Meredith would be safely on the campus by Tuesday morning. So the President held back his proclamation and canceled the TV time set aside for his speech.

Robert Kennedy and Burke Marshall returned to the Justice Department. Kennedy went home around 10. Just after he left, the phone rang. It was Barnett. "Well, here we go again," Ed Guthman thought wearily as he heard Nick Katzenbach tell the operator he could reach the Attorney General at home.

Guthman was right. The Governor called off the plan. Robert Kennedy's anger rose; this seemed a clear breach of an agreement between the Governor and the President of the United States. But the two men ended the conversation amiably, with the understanding that the Federals would arrive with Meredith at Oxford Monday morning—in force. The Governor said he would call again Sunday morning, at 11, Washington time.

There is a special loneliness in the White House late on a night of crisis. John F. Kennedy sat at the long table in the Indian Treaty Room, hunched over a piece of paper. Assistant Attorney General Norbert A. Schlei sat next to him. They were alone. The President took a pen and signed the proclamation federalizing the Mississippi National Guard. Before writing the date, he hesitated. "Is it past midnight?" he asked. Schlei checked his watch. "It's just 20 seconds past 12."

At Jackson's municipal stadium, about an hour earlier, Ross Barnett stood at the peak of his glory. It was half time in the night football game between Old Miss and Kentucky. The Rebels led 7 to 0. Some 41,000 spectators sensed the electricity in the air. Hundreds of Confederate flags waved defiantly.

Ross Barnett stood on the field, buoyed by the high-pitched clamor, smiling because he felt the warmth and love of 41,000 people. He paused before a microphone. The crowd fell silent. Barnett's face was sculptured by the stadium lights. The silence heightened. Barnett raised one arm, his fist clenched in command and defiance.

It was one of those rare moments of historical suspense that were to occur several times in the next 27 hours. A variation of only two or three words in what he said would have radically altered the flow of events. A few measured words of reason would have deflected tragedy. One phrase such as "repel the invaders" would have caused much worse tragedy on the following day.

The crowd waited. "I love Mississippi," Barnett said. The crowd did not roar; it screamed. "I love her people." Another scream. His voice was resonant, throbbing with emotion. "I love our customs." The scream was almost hysterical. Every Mississippian knew what "our customs" meant. Barnett never went beyond this point. He heightened the people's hysteria, but did not tell them what to do.

In the second half, a reporter came to Governor Barnett's box. He had word that the President had federalized the Mississippi National Guard, and asked if the Governor would care to comment. The Governor said no. Events, he knew, were closing in from both directions.

Second Lt. Donnie G. Bowman, a big, easy-going Texan, stretched and looked at his men dozing in the canvas seats of the darkened C-130 troop transport. He had been in flight over an hour. The 23-year-old platoon leader was one of 452 men of the 503rd MP Battalion pulled out of Fort Bragg, N.C., as part of a "Task Force Alpha."

That Saturday afternoon, while watching the Notre Dame–Oklahoma game, Bowman had been phoned to report to company headquarters. His wife Karlyn drove him there, with their eight-week-old daughter on the seat between them. Bowman, a member of the Army's STRAC alert force, was accustomed to sudden orders.

As Bowman watched his 56-man platoon loading into a squat C-130, he was given an unopened crate of riot shotguns. He began to suspect where he might be going.

*

Other planes and cars were on the move Saturday night. One car was a white compact on Highway 51 between Jackson and Oxford. In it sat a tall, erect man in a white Texas hat. He had been given a ticket to the Ole Miss–Kentucky game, but, hearing that action was developing fast at Oxford, had returned it and driven north with friends. The white car arrived in Oxford near midnight, and ex-General Edwin Walker, using an assumed name, checked into the Mansel Motel.

Sunday morning, September 30. Another beautiful day in Mississippi and Washington. Robert Kennedy and most of his Mississippi task force were at work by 9 a.m. Their deadline pressed them hard. Racial agitators from many states were converging on Oxford. Kennedy considered putting Meredith on campus that day. He knew that most of those coming to fight the Government did not expect the action until Monday or Tuesday.

The marshals at Memphis had been roused at dawn and told to be ready to load on planes by noon, just in case. Meredith, who had spent Saturday at Dillard University in New Orleans, was flying to Memphis in a border-patrol Cessna 310. They glided down to the Naval Air Station airport while C-130 transports brought in more troops.

Shortly before Meredith landed, Kennedy had another call from Barnett. The Governor suggested a new plan, basically his Thursday scheme, but more grandiose. On Monday morning, October 1, he would wait at the university gate, backed by a phalanx of state troopers, who would be backed by sheriffs, who would be backed by citizens and students. Meredith should arrive with a large Army force. The Governor would read a proclamation barring him from Ole Miss. Then, Kennedy's men should draw their guns. Barnett would, he said, step aside.

Kennedy could hardly believe his ears. He felt his indignation rising, but he spoke to Barnett in a cold, controlled tone. Barnett was responsible, Kennedy said, for more than his own political future. He had a responsibility to his state and the nation.

Kennedy then shifted to a new tack. Unless the Governor

cooperated, he said, and helped maintain law and order while Meredith went on campus, the President would go on television and tell the country that Barnett had broken his word. To prove it, the President could tell all about the behind-scenes dickering.

This had a devastating effect. The Governor's resistance seemed to melt away. Again and again, Barnett asked that the President say nothing on TV that would unveil the nature of the secret phone calls.

Kennedy suggested that Meredith be flown onto the campus by helicopter on Monday, while U.S. marshals and state troopers, working together, controlled the crowd. Barnett, whose supporters still had plans for that day, voiced a fear that on Monday hundreds of people would be killed. He spoke of Mississippi's mood and of the hundreds of agitators on their way from other states. Because of Monday's danger, the two agreed that Meredith would be brought in that very day before dark. Kennedy also stipulated that Meredith should be safely on the campus *before* the President's speech (now scheduled for 5:30, Mississippi time). Barnett was to send Col. T. B. Birdsong, head of the highway patrol, up to Oxford, to help get Meredith on the campus. Two more phone calls over the next couple of hours confirmed the arrangements. Kennedy was repeatedly assured that order would be upheld.

At noon, no one on the flight from Atlanta for Jackson could help noticing the huge man with the bushy red beard and untrimmed red mustache. There was something jolly about him. He exuded the confidence and humor that come from fame—or from a deep love and appreciation of life. And he was hungry. The stewardess brought him a cola and a couple of tiny sandwiches. Amused, she tried to guess his job and destination. "Oh, I know," she drawled, "you're going down to the nigger thing."

The bearded man smiled painfully. He turned to his companion, chubby little photographer Sammy Schulman, and said in French, "These people. It'll take them a hundred years to start forgetting."

The stewardess walked away. Paul Guihard, half English,

half French reporter for *Agence France-Presse*, later made a note for what was to be his last assignment.

He scribbled: "Hostess: 'about the nigger.'"

Meredith ate lunch calmly at the Naval Air Station cafeteria. His companion, John Doar, was on the phone to receive orders from the Justice Department: Be ready to take off with Meredith by 3:30. Later came the order to be over Oxford at 5:50. Circle until ordered to land.

Doar could hear the engines of four transports that would take the first 170 marshals to Oxford. A convoy of 30 U.S. border-patrol cars with two-way radios was ready to take 60 more men to Ole Miss.

In the executive mansion in Jackson, four somber men were commissioned by the Governor to go to Oxford as his representatives. They were: George M. Yarbrough, president pro tem of the senate and the state's third-ranking officer; County Judge Russell Moore, who had already been in command of the brigade at the campus; State Representative C. B. (Buddie) Newman and State Senator John C. McLaurin. The Governor gave Senator Yarbrough, head of the committee, an official order "to do all things necessary that the peace and security of the people of the State of Mississippi are fully protected."

The group, as Moore understood it, was to set up for Monday the same forces that had been on hand on Thursday. "We thought we might all be killed," McLaurin said later. Newman quickly made out a will, got the others to witness it.

When they left the mansion that day, they thought they had plenty of time. "We were going up there to get the defenses prepared," McLaurin explained afterwards. The group understood that the marshals and Meredith would arrive on Monday.

Yarbrough called the highway patrol to have it ready at Oxford. Judge Moore used the patrol radio to call 70 of the state's 82 sheriffs to bring deputies and meet him at Oxford courthouse at 10:30 that night. Three fire trucks, all high-pressure pumpers, were ready to rush to Oxford. "With those hoses," McLaurin knew, "you can knock a man down at 200 feet."

Yarbrough took a light plane to his huge cattle farm at Red Banks in northern Mississippi. The other three planned to fly to Oxford about sundown. McLaurin first drove to his home in Brandon, a Jackson suburb, and went out into the yard to say good-bye to his four-year-old son. All four planned to meet on the Oxford campus at 6:30.

Upon landing at Jackson, Paul Guihard and Sammy Schulman rented a white car and drove to the Citizens' Council meeting then in progress in front of the Governor's mansion. A crowd of some 2,000 was in a festive mood. Women volunteers brought in sandwiches and coffee. Students cheered and joked with the crowd. WRBC, the Rebel Broadcasting Company, played Mississippi fight songs, which blared from car and transistor radios; the announcer periodically called upon everyone to blow car horns. John R. Wright, handsome young undertaker and chairman of the Citizens' Council membership committee, bellowed a grim rumor on an electronic bull horn: The marshals were on their way to Jackson to arrest the Governor. "Reliable sources" had brought the rumor at dawn, and spy reports from Memphis said the planes were on the way. (Actually, they were headed for Oxford.) Wright called for a wall of flesh around the mansion to protect their Governor.

Paul Guihard plunged into the crowd. Schulman had warned him that racists could be deadly to newsmen, but the big man felt entirely safe. He was the kind of man everyone likes at first sight.

In fact, when Guihard pressed his way into the Citizens' Council office, racist Louis W. Hollis took half an hour, in the midst of a bedlam of activity, to give Guihard a private interview. He's on our side, Hollis thought, unable to conceive that any man worth trusting and liking could disagree on segregation. Guihard dictated his last story to his agency in French over the Citizens' Council telephone. "The crowd laughed and sang under the warm autumn sun," he said, "and it was apparent it hadn't the vaguest idea of the enormity of its actions. . . ."

A few minutes after Paul Guihard disappeared into the

crowd at Jackson, a Jetstar from Washington touched down at the Oxford airport. The Justice Department task force, Nick Katzenbach in charge, stepped out. Katzenbach telephoned the Attorney General. The operation was still on.

Between the airport and the campus, the convoy of marshals led by Katzenbach met the state-patrol head, Col. T. B. Birdsong. Katzenbach and Chief Marshal McShane got out to exchange pleasantries. Much of the Government's hope for that night lay with the elderly colonel's steadfastness and ability.

The convoy—seven olive-drab trucks—rolled on. A marshal with a smile as broad as his shoulders rode the running board of the third truck. Clarence Albert (Al) Butler, 33, was one of four group leaders. With practiced eyes, he judged the mood and intent of the crowd that lined both sides of the road.

"You'll be sorry," a young man shouted. Butler smiled. "Nigger lover," another yelled. Butler smiled. Compared with other mobs he had seen, this one did not seem so bad. Some people even applauded. Maybe it was sarcastic, but they applauded.

Ahead, Butler spied a boy of about five wearing a cowboy hat. Butler, not liking the look of fear on the child's face, waved and called, "Hi, Cowboy." Cowboy laughed and waved back.

Highway patrolmen stood guard at the Sorority Row entrance to the university. Obeying Birdsong's orders, they let the marshals through. The trucks rolled past stately white sorority houses, then swung around a grove that sloped gently up to the classic white-columned Lyceum. This was the university's administration building, the marshals' first objective. The only sign of life was an occasional squirrel gathering acorns in streaks of sun and shadow on the grass of the grove. Butler was dazzled by the beauty and stillness of the place.

At 4:15 p.m., the marshals dismounted and formed a cordon around the Lyceum. Butler's group of 48 held the area directly in the front, facing the grove. Butler paced up and down in the street before his men. A crowd gathered. Within a half hour, Butler estimated the number at around 500, almost all students. The first shots fired were verbal, and Butler was a main target.

"Marshal, where is your wife tonight? Home with a nigger?"

Butler's broad grin quickly earned him the name "Smiley."
"You have a nigger mistress, Smiley. You have nigger children."

Nick Katzenbach quickly set up a phone line from the Lyceum to Robert Kennedy's office in Washington and another to the White House. He told the Attorney General that Meredith could now come onto the campus, preferably via plane to the airport, then by car from there.

The airport. It was like a bad dream. The waiting Katzenbach looked up at the twilight sky to see three almost identical light planes circling. Which was Meredith's? The first, a blue and white Cessna 310, landed. Katzenbach and Guthman ran toward it. Not their man. They turned and ran to the next plane. It was Meredith. With the help of Birdsong, they drove him onto the campus without incident and took him to his room in Baxter Hall.

Unknown to Katzenbach and Guthman, the blue and white plane they had approached contained three of the Governor's group: Moore, McLaurin and Newman. They were to meet Yarbrough on campus. These men, upon first flying into the Oxford airport traffic pattern, had stared in shock at the military planes and trucks on the ground. "It's completely occupied," State Senator John McLaurin said. He thought, "Bobby and Jack jumped the gun." He did not know that Governor Barnett had made a deal with Robert Kennedy.

The Governor's men debated taking off again. Fear rose when Katzenbach and Guthman ran out to their plane, peered in the window—and turned away in disappointment. Moore expected, he said, "search and seizure."

"We got through the Federal lines untouched," McLaurin reported when he recounted the day's events.

The three met Yarbrough at the Alumni House at 6:30 and phoned Governor Barnett. They reported the early invasion, but, McLaurin later said, "apparently he knew about it already."

When they got word that Meredith was safely on campus,

Robert Kennedy and Burke Marshall drove to the White House. The President's office was crowded with TV equipment and technicians. The speech had been delayed to 10 p.m., Washington time, to be sure Meredith was first safely on the campus. Robert Kennedy and Marshall met the President and several of his assistants in the Cabinet Room.

All agreed on the content and tone of the proposed address to the nation. Robert Kennedy suggested adding an appeal to the students of Ole Miss. The reports coming over the phone from the Lyceum were still fairly reassuring.

Standing in front of the Lyceum, however, Marshal Al Butler was beginning to worry. Just as darkness fell, he was hit on the left leg with a poorly made Molotov cocktail, a soda bottle filled with lighter fluid. The fuse went out when the bottle smashed on the pavement. A few minutes later, an empty bottle hit his left arm.

The crowd swelled to 1,000, then to over 2,000. Students flipped lighted cigarettes onto the canvas tops of the Army trucks parked in front of the Lyceum. One truck was set aflame by a burning piece of paper. The driver put out the fire.

The Mississippi state troopers stood, widely spaced, between the marshals and the mob. When Butler asked the troopers to move the crowd back, they did. But members of the mob began slipping through the line of Mississippi lawmen.

The verbiage thrown at the marshals now reached the limits of obscenity. Butler was particularly shocked to hear foul epithets from the lips of pretty young girls in the crowd. Butler kept smiling. He would be thankful, he thought, if words were all he had to contend with. Nor did he particularly mind the spittle aimed at him, or the coins thrown by jeering mob members.

"Here, Marshal, pick these up. . . . Smiley will pick 'em up."

The mob edged forward. Pieces of pipe, brick and cinder block, along with the usual bottles, crashed against the steps of the Lyceum and occasionally bruised or cut a marshal. Shortly after seven, Butler and another group leader, Don Forsht, asked permission to use tear gas.

"Hold it off for a while," Chief Marshal McShane said, "and maybe things will ease up."

Down in Jackson before 7 p.m., Ross Barnett finished a surrender statement and had it read over the phone for Robert Kennedy's approval: "My heart still says 'Never,' but my calm judgment abhors the bloodshed that will follow. . . . Mississippi will continue to fight the Meredith case and all similar cases through the courts. . . ."

Gloom spread through the Governor's mansion. Most of the men there, unaware of Barnett's negotiations with the Kennedys, had spent the day making plans for a Monday confrontation with the Federals. Among others, the inner circle included George Godwin, Jackson advertising man who handled the Governor's press releases during the crisis; Dr. M. Ney Williams of the Citizens' Council; William Simmons, racist intellectual and the Council's full-time staff brain; and Fred Beard, TV station manager who was arranging television facilities for Monday. Beard had worked out the words he hoped Barnett would deliver Monday at the Ole Miss gate: "We do not submit to the illegality of your take-over. We are a peaceable people. We will not take up arms against the Federal Government. If you move over us, you will move over us by pushing us aside."

Barnett's surrender statement on the radio chilled the Citizens' Council members, still patiently forming a wall of flesh around the mansion. In the Council office, Executive Director Louis Hollis, 62, could not believe the radio report. He ran across the street to the mansion and burst in upon Barnett. "Governor, everybody thinks you've surrendered," he cried, tears in his eyes. "Everybody in the office is crying. You've got to tell them you haven't surrendered."

Oxford. Inside the Lyceum, Nick Katzenbach was desperately trying to reestablish the highway-patrol roadblocks withdrawn from the entrances to the university at 6:30. Colonel Birdsong courteously refused Katzenbach's pleas. He said he had only about 25 patrol cars, with two men each. The men were unarmed and couldn't do much good. "How about the deputy sheriffs?" Katzenbach suggested. Birdsong said he had no control over them. The Colonel offered to send "some" men to the gates, if Katzenbach would dispatch a larger number of marshals to accompany them. Katzenbach said he couldn't spare them.

While this debate seesawed, "outsiders" already were streaming in through the unguarded gates. This small stream was to become a flood before midnight. Some of the newcomers were Mississippians who had heard of the marshals' arrival. Others were agitators from as far away as Los Angeles. Many of them had figured on a Monday or Tuesday battle, but now moved directly into action.

Senator Yarbrough, a man of awesome presence, led his group to the Lyceum. "Who's in charge?" they demanded. John Doar took them to Katzenbach, McShane and Guthman. South met North.

The man in between was Colonel Birdsong. He pleaded with Katzenbach to tell Yarbrough that he had not given the marshals police protection. "I've been telling these people that all I've done is escort you onto the campus," Birdsong said. "Will you please clarify this?"

Yarbrough stepped up to Katzenbach. "You've occupied it, and now you can just have it," he said bluntly, insisting that what happened from then on was the responsibility of the Federal Government. "I want to avoid bloodshed," Yarbrough said, "and to do so, we must withdraw the highway patrol."

"I have the same interest, that is, to provide law and order," responded Katzenbach, eager to avoid a clash. "But while Federal marshals are here, this in no way displaces the state authority. All law-enforcement officers must cooperate to maintain law and order. I want to be very clear about the fact that I think the withdrawal of the state troopers will not avoid violence, but is the one decisive thing that will lead to violence."

Yarbrough said that was not his judgment, and bluntly insisted he would withdraw the patrol. It was just a question of when. Soon, the argument turned on whether he would pull them out at eight or nine.

At 7:40, Robert Kennedy came on the open line. He ordered Katzenbach to inform Yarbrough that, if he didn't keep

the patrol on hand, the President, then about to go on television, would tell the whole world what had happened.
Yarbrough, unaware of the Governor's deals, was unimpressed.
Kennedy reached the Governor's mansion in Jackson on another phone. Minutes later, Yarbrough got a call from Jackson.
He answered in glum monosyllables, turned to Katzenbach
and said that he would not pull out the state patrol.

At Katzenbach's urging, the Senator went out to talk to the
crowd. They thought him a marshal and booed. "I don't like
this any more than you do," he said. "I'm Senator George
Yarbrough, and I represent the Governor. I'm on your side. I
live just 40 miles from here at Red Banks." The crowd
quieted down. "We don't want any violence. Get back off the
street and, if you will, go back to your dormitories."

"We want Ross!" yelled the crowd.

"All right," Yarbrough responded. "If y'all get off this
street, I'll go see if I can get the Governor to come up here."
As he turned back to the Lyceum, he noticed that the highway patrolmen "began to get more earnest than they had
been before." The troopers, he later said, were moving the
crowd back across the street toward the trees.

Inside, Yarbrough told Doar he would phone Barnett to
come and quiet the students. "But first," he said, "I want assurances that the Governor will not be arrested." Doar called
Kennedy, handed the receiver to Yarbrough. "I don't think
it's best," said Kennedy, "for the Governor to come up there
now." Even if Barnett's presence did quiet the students, it
would also draw hundreds more into the fight.

Chief Marshal McShane looked at the mob and sensed danger. He thought the state troopers were unable or unwilling to
move the crowd back. Some troopers seemed mixed with the
crowd as far back as the fourth or fifth rank. About the time
Yarbrough reentered the Lyceum, McShane saw a two-foot
length of pipe arch over the crowd and strike a marshal's helmet. He shouted "Gas!"—the order for gas masks. As the
marshals put on their masks, the crowd fell back for a moment.

Just then, a bottle hit Al Butler on the arm. A milky liquid
sprayed on his hand, then ran under his sleeve. Hours later,
Butler realized that acid was searing his flesh.

"Fire!"

McShane's command was almost lost in the roar of the mob. The marshals near the center of the line fired first. Ragged salvos followed from right, then left. The cartridges in the marshals' guns emitted a blast of raw tear gas over a range of 35 feet. Wax wadding in the cartridges struck several people, who thought they had been hit by projectiles. Several gas canisters thrown by hand also hit people, including state troopers who were directly in the line of fire.

It was 7:58 p.m. in Oxford. The Battle of Ole Miss was on.

Nick Katzenbach rushed to the phone and asked for the Attorney General. "Bob," Katzenbach said, "I'm very sorry to report that we've had to fire tear gas. I'm very unhappy about it, but we had no choice."

Robert Kennedy, in the Cabinet Room, took the news with deep regret. "I think I should really go tell the President about it," he said. "He's just going on the air."

Kennedy rushed toward the President's office to give him the news. But it was too late. The TV cameras already were in action.

Angry state troopers straggled back crying and retching from the gas. Two had been hit by canisters; one, Welby Brunt, almost died. Yarbrough squelched a rumor that Birdsong had been killed.

When some patrolmen went for their guns, Yarbrough knew it was "getting ready to get rough." He ordered the guns locked back in the trunks. Though he sympathized with the troopers, he knew better than to allow gunplay to start. He resented having to keep the patrolmen in the gassed area. At his Alumni House headquarters, he phoned the Governor's mansion and agreed that he, McLaurin, Newman and Moore should pull out. (They reported back to Jackson about 11 p.m.)

They kept coming back. Even after barrages of tear gas, the crowd surged back, throwing stones, bricks, chunks of concrete. Marshals with long riot experience had not seen a mob like this. McShane's men did not realize that, as the more reasonable students withdrew, they were replaced by outsiders, fresh and ready for a new charge.

Reporter Fred Powledge of the Atlanta *Journal* was trapped in an automobile between the marshals and the mob. Powledge had been slugged earlier. The crowd was on the prowl for reporters.

Now, crouched down in the car, he tried to figure what to do next. If he ran toward the marshals, they would think he was attacking them, and he would be plugged with tear gas. But if he went toward the mob, he would be a dead rat in a gang of cats.

He slumped lower in the seat and switched on the car radio. The President was speaking, addressing himself to the students of Ole Miss:

"The eyes of the nation and all the world are upon you and upon all of us. And the honor of your university—and state— are in the balance. . . ."

Pomp! Pomp! Pomp! Three tear-gas guns went off.

". . . I am certain the great majority of the students will uphold that honor. . . ."

A volley of stones whistled over the car.

". . . There is, in short, no reason why the books on this case cannot now be quickly and quietly closed in the manner directed by the Court. . . ."

A cloud of tear gas floated over the car. Powledge, in spite of his own predicament, felt sorry for the President.

The feeling was short-lived. He heard a voice behind him: "Let's get that son of a bitch in the car." There seemed to be no escape. Just then, three marshals rushed toward him. The first jumped up in the air and fired over the top of the car. Powledge saw "a beautiful burst of smoke" billowing over his attackers. Someone yelled, "Kennedy is a son of a bitch." The crowd fell back.

Paul Guihard and Sammy Schulman were approaching Oxford when the President ended his speech. "Oh, hell," Guihard said, "the story's all over, but we might as well go up and clean it up."

The ride from Jackson had been a strange one. The road was crowded with cars bearing Confederate flags and Barnett bumper stickers; most headed north. Neither Guihard nor Schulman realized their significance. Guihard, in a mellow mood, started talking about his past life—his desire to become an actor, his early newspapering days, his ambitions as a playwright. As a modern writer, Guihard might have scoffed at the idea of a man reviewing his life just before death.

At Oxford, the pair found that the story was far from over. They heard battle sounds as they parked their car near the far end of the grove. Friendly students told them to hide their cameras, since "some bums up there are smashing them."

"I'll see what's doing," Guihard told Schulman, "and see you back here at the car in an hour then."

At that moment, the mob suddenly rushed toward them, away from the marshals. Guihard walked straight into the crowd. Some ten minutes later, he stood near a girls' dormitory, diagonally across the grove. An assassin stood close behind him and fired a .38 pistol. The bullet pierced Paul Guihard's back and entered his heart.

Lt. Donnie Bowman of the 503rd MP's viewed the President's telecast in the officers' club at the Naval Air Station at Memphis. Told that the crisis was over, Bowman returned to his quarters and crawled tiredly into bed. In minutes, he was asleep.

"We want a leader! We want a leader!"

A crowd of students and outsiders milled about the Confederate statue at the foot of the grove, 170 yards from the Lyceum. Small bands rushed in several directions. Some ran to get bricks from the construction site of the new science building. One rolled a wheelbarrow load. But no one seemed able to take charge and lead the attacks.

At 9 p.m., a great cheer went up. The state troopers were pulling out. A long line of patrol cars curved around the grove and past the Confederate monument. Fred Powledge started his car and fell in line behind the last patrol car. He decided that, if anyone tried to stop him, he would run over him slowly. One rioter leaned toward the car to see who was trying to escape. Powledge shifted into low, nudged the rioter with his fender. The man fell back. Powledge was free.

"We have a leader," the crowd exulted. A tall, erect figure stood near the monument. His dark suit made him almost invisible up to the neck, but his white Western hat gave off a ghostly glow in the gloom.

"General Walker's here!" People raced to spread the news. The ex-General mounted the base of the monument. The crowd fell silent.

"I want to compliment you all on the protest you make tonight," he said. "You have a right to protest under the Constitution." This night, he said, was the long way around to Cuba. He told the crowd they had been sold out by the man who brought the marshals onto the campus, Colonel Birdsong.

Father Duncan Gray, Jr., rector of St. Peter's Episcopal Church in Oxford, tried to climb onto the monument to rebut Walker. He was pulled down and propelled to the edge of the mob. A huge sheriff shepherded him to safety. Walker climbed off the monument and, surrounded by the crowd, walked slowly toward the Lyceum.

Radio, TV and telephone carried the riot news back to the executive mansion in Jackson. By 9 o'clock, the Governor's militant advisers saw a new hope. Maybe the rioters could drive the marshals out. Outside reinforcements, the advisers guessed, might tip the balance.

Some prayed for guidance. Some demanded that Barnett act. He could issue a call to battle. He could announce that he was on his way to Oxford. Any such move, they knew, would summon thousands of angry, armed Mississippians to the campus. A great many might be killed? They would die in a just war, and their bloody shirts would warn the country of the onrushing Kennedy dictatorship. Some of Barnett's men were ready to rush to Oxford and sacrifice their own lives.

Against the fervor for bloodshed, one man fought with equal fervor for reason. He was brilliant, red-haired Thomas Watkins, 52, corporation lawyer and for years a friend of Barnett. He was the man among the Governor's advisers most trusted by the state's business leadership, and through him, many had sent their cautions against destructive tactics. Now, he served the whole state. Passionately, he argued reason's case before a wavering judge—Ross Barnett.

Watkins won. Again, a massacre was barely averted.

"Your men are pulling out," Nick Katzenbach told Colonel Birdsong in the Lyceum. "Get them back."

"Your information must be wrong," Birdsong said. "They are not leaving." His men had been badly gassed, he said, and it was hard to control them.

"If they want to get away from the gas," Katzenbach said, "let them go down to the entrances and set up roadblocks."

"They can't do that. And now that they've been gassed, I'm not sure that they are willing to." Birdsong seemed honestly surprised that the troopers had left. Most of the patrol cars regrouped just off campus; others waited at strategic spots.

For the next few hours, the patrolmen held a series of debates over their car radios. Several troopers said the mob should be controlled. Others replied sarcastically that the students should demonstrate. One patrol car 20 miles out reported intercepting a convoy of 20 to 30 cars, with about four men in each, headed for Oxford to help the students. Some troopers favored stopping the convoy; others were opposed. The convoy was not stopped. Some patrol cars reported "a large number of civilians" entering the campus on foot from cars abandoned on Route 6. One trooper radioed in that a chartered bus with some 50 armed men aboard was heading for the campus via Route 6.

When President Kennedy heard that the state patrol had pulled out, he phoned Governor Barnett to get the men back. The Governor agreed. Later, Burke Marshall told Tom Watkins that the patrol was not returning.

"I can't believe it," Watkins said.

"They're not there, Tom."

"We'll get them back."

Worse shocks were to hit the White House. *The marshals were running out of tear gas.* Katzenbach told Robert Kennedy that only five or ten minutes' supply was left. And

Marshal Graham E. Same of Indianapolis had been shot in the neck. His condition was critical.

At about this time, the battle came to a halt briefly. Father Wofford Smith, Episcopal chaplain of the university, rushed up to the marshals waving a white handkerchief. Father Smith had heard that the marshals had wounded a student with a shotgun. Inside the Lyceum, he found that the marshals had no shotguns.

The scene there horrified him. Wounded marshals lay on the floor all up and down the hall. As the chaplain stood there half dazed, he got an urgent call to go outside. Some of the students were asking for a peace conference. Father Smith tells the story:

"A marshal led me out the front door of the Lyceum and down the front steps. I walked in front waving a handkerchief and shouting as loudly as I could to the crowd, which, at this point, was a great mob. They threw rocks, glass and cursed violently and shouted, and the marshal took a flashlight and walked beside me out into the street, shining the light on my clerical collar. And the mob momentarily ceased its activities of throwing things and formed a line running north and south near the front of the circle. I called out, 'You said you wanted to talk. I'm here to talk.' And the marshal kept shouting, 'Here's your priest. He will talk to you.' And the marshals also shouted to them to stay back and let one man come forward. At this point, a young student, apparently a freshman, because his head had been shaved, stepped forward. I asked him, 'Son, what is your name?' He said, 'I'd rather not say.' I said, 'I don't blame you. You people said you wanted to talk. We must talk this situation out. This situation has reached proportions that I'm sure you don't wish as a student of this university.' And I pled with him not to bring any more shame upon the school. He said that he could not help but agree, although this was the only way that they had to display their disapproval with the fact that the Court and the marshals had forced the enrollment of a Negro in the school. He said he did not feel that he was in a position to negotiate because he was only a freshman, at which point the marshal shouted out through the crowd, 'Send us a senior.' A boy walked forward to our group and identified himself as a senior.

I asked him if he played football. He said yes. Then I knew that he was one of the boys on the team, having recognized him from the night before, down in Jackson. He said that he was there to demonstrate and to protest. Then I asked him if he would co-operate and break this up. He said that this was the only way they had to demonstrate, and I said, 'Well, why are you attacking these men at this point?' He said, 'Because we want to get Meredith,' and I said, 'To my knowledge, Meredith is not in this building.' I told him they had no right to attack these innocent marshals, that they were policemen just like the policemen in any hometown. The senior did say that he would talk to the mob, which he did."

The senior faced the mob, arms outspread.

"Here's the deal," he shouted. "Here's the deal. The marshals will quit using tear gas if we'll stop throwing rocks and bricks."

Silence, then a loud voice from deep within the mob: "Give us the nigger and we'll quit."

Someone let fly with a brick. This was followed by a broadside of stones, bricks and bottles. The marshals fired a barrage of tear gas. The battle was on again.

Tear gas fast was running out. But U.S. border patrolman Charles Chamblee was en route from the airport with fresh supplies. He drove a green border-patrol car and led a rented van full of tear gas. The two vehicles came onto the campus at breakneck speed, crashing through roadblocks set by the rioters.

"Truck! Truck! Truck!" the mob shouted along the road curving up to the Lyceum. From both sides, stones and bricks crashed against the van. It made it. Twice more that night, Chamblee ran the gantlet. Stopped once by state troopers, he used his club to beat them out of the way. Every time the marshals were almost out of gas, Chamblee miraculously appeared, his battered van filled with fresh supplies.

Ex-General Walker had been one of those scrambling back from the tear-gas barrage that ended the peace conference. Now, he stood near the rear of the mob, stock still, hands at his sides, tie askew. Rioters rushed up to him, asking his advice and moral support. Walker answered in an even voice, his eyes fixed straight ahead.

"Sir, that minister with the marshals—he wasn't for us, was he?"

"No, he was against us. They all are. They're all selling us out."

Some of the students had tears in their eyes—not just from the tear gas. They likened themselves to the Hungarian Freedom Fighters. They believed they were fighting tyranny. For weeks, they had known only one side of the controversy. They had courage.

Bullets began to splatter against the Lyceum. Anyone appearing at a window drew fire. The marshals crouched behind the trucks in front of the Lyceum. Some asked permission to return fire with their pistols. The request was phoned to the White House. Permission denied.

Strangely, only a few rioters attacked Baxter Hall, which was far more vulnerable than the Lyceum. Only 24 marshals guarded it, and its only sure communication with the Lyceum was the radio in a border-patrol car parked outside. But the marshals at Baxter had secret permission to use pistols as a last resort. Meredith was there.

Katzenbach held off asking for troops as long as he could. Before 10 p.m., as the gunfire became intense, he told Robert Kennedy they had better get the Army. Then, Katzenbach phoned the National Guard armory in Oxford and asked Capt. Murray Falkner, nephew of the late novelist William Faulkner, to bring his men to the Lyceum.

Al Butler gasped for breath. "Mr. Katzenbach," he said, "that's not a riot out there anymore. It's an armed insurrection."

At 10:45, Butler saw the lights of four jeeps and three trucks coming up toward the grove. It was Falkner, running a gantlet of brickbats, Molotov cocktails and roadblocks. His 55 Mississippi guardsmen tried unsuccessfully to fend off the volleys of bricks and bottles. A Molotov cocktail hit Falkner's jeep, but did not go off. Falkner raised his left arm to shield his face; a brick struck the arm, breaking two bones. By the time they reached the Lyceum, 13 guardsmen were wounded.

Six vehicles had broken windshields. One jeep collected six bullet holes.

Those guardsmen who could stand joined the marshals on the left front of the Lyceum. Untrained in riot control, with no ammunition, no tear gas and only 15 bayonets, they had to take everything the mob could deliver. Earlier, most of the guardsmen had sympathized with the rioters. In ten minutes, sympathy vanished.

Five minutes before Falkner's men arrived, the rioters had brought a stolen fire truck up into the grove and had tried to shoot water at the marshals. A tear-gas foray beat the mob back, and a marshal fired four bullets into the hose to reduce the water pressure.

At 10:53, Al Butler heard a motor start up somewhere beyond the lower end of the grove. He heard the clank of treads. A wild Rebel yell soared up. Butler waited to see what horror was on its way.

He saw it coming out of the smoke and haze—a bulldozer, accompanied by almost the entire mob, headed straight for the Lyceum. Butler waved a signal. The marshals charged, firing all the way. An overwhelming cloud of gas enveloped the machine, and rioters fell back, cursing and vomiting. Two marshals leaped up on the bulldozer and pulled the driver off.

Butler started to disable the bulldozer, but left it to meet an attack on the right flank. Another rioter mounted the machine, aimed it toward the marshals and jumped off. It struck a tree. Finally, Marshal Carl Ryan of Indianapolis moved the machine close to the Federal line and turned it about to face the rioters with its lights on.

Butler had hardly returned to the front of the Lyceum when he heard another wild Rebel yell. The fire truck came roaring up through the grove and swung left in a dizzy circle. On the truck's second pass, Butler grabbed the handrail and swung aboard. It veered left and sent him rolling head over heels for some 20 yards. On the third pass, two marshals shot the truck's tires. They grabbed the driver, a thin young man dressed in a white sailor suit, and dragged him away.

Down in Jackson, Governor Barnett strove to prove he had

not surrendered. "I will never yield a single inch in my determination to win the fight we are all engaged in," he declared
in his last press release that night. "I call on all Mississippians
to keep the faith and courage. We will never surrender." But
he had sent Lieutenant Governor Johnson to Oxford, as a less
inflammatory substitute for himself. Johnson quickly ordered
the highway patrol back in action. He stationed them on
roadblocks, where, by his estimate, they stopped 600 or 800
cars loaded with armed riders. "If we hadn't done that," he
believes, "there wouldn't have been a marshal left that night."

The rioters burned their first car, a professor's station
wagon, as a fiery roadblock. The entire north side of the
grove was bathed in an eerie light. The crowd fell silent. The
lull was a godsend to the marshals, who again were almost
out of tear gas.

As the rioters stood there holding bricks and stones, the
horn of the burning automobile started blowing. For ten
minutes, it wailed, as if the car were crying out in agony. Shiv-
ering, many dropped their bricks and began drifting away. By
midnight, most students had returned to dormitories or fraternity houses, shaken by what they had done.

The outsiders took over the fight. Hidden snipers increased
their fire. One lay in a flower bed on the northeast border of
the grove and emptied his .22 rifle at the Lyceum. Miraculously, no marshals were killed. At least five cars were burning
at one time. Some 200 more Mississippi guardsmen made a
heroic entry through roadblocks, brick barrages, gunfire, plus
—this time—a wall of flaming gasoline. But they, like Captain
Falkner's group, were not equipped or trained for riot control
and had little effect.

Several hundred yards to the southeast, Ray Gunter, 23, an
Oxford juke-box repairman, watched the fight. Quietly, he
slumped forward, a .38 bullet in his forehead. He died on the
way to the hospital.

Nick Katzenbach spent more and more time on the phone,
asking, "Where's the Army?" Repeatedly, he was told the
troops were "twenty minutes away." The big delay actually
was a multitude of small delays. The great Army wheels were
slow to start.

In the White House, the President, the Attorney General and Burke Marshall moved from telephone to telephone, from the President's office to the Cabinet Room. They felt frustration, along with concern and horror. Angrily, the President told the Army to get moving.

Lieutenant Bowman's helicopter seemed to creep through the night sky. It was 12:30 a.m., Monday, before Bowman reached Oxford; the last helicopter did not touch down until after one. There were more delays in the confusion and dark. Maj. Gen. Charles E. Billingslea was on hand to supervise the Army forces. President Kennedy reached him by radio at 1:35 and relayed word to move "forthwith."

At 2:04, four gray Navy buses stopped just inside the Sorority Row entrance of the campus. Donnie Bowman led his men, grim and tight-lipped, out of the first and second buses. The marshals there told the MP's the buses could never make it through the mob. The men would have to march in. A small knot of onlookers ominously heckled the soldiers: "You'll get hurt up there." A state patrolman turned his powerful flashlight into the eyes of one of Bowman's five Negro soldiers and said, "What you doing down here, nigger?"

The soldiers fixed bayonets on their loaded rifles. About every fifth man carried a loaded riot shotgun. The MP's slipped on gas masks and moved into wedge formation. In silence, they began the half-mile march to Lyceum, past the dimly lit sorority houses and ghostly trees. The only sound was the shuffle of boots and the grunt of breath through gas masks.

From nowhere, a volley of bricks and rocks hit them. *Ambush*. Molotov cocktails exploded just in front of them. The soldiers marched through the flames. A Molotov cocktail shattered against an MP's helmet, but failed to ignite. Gasoline trickled down his face and shirt. Several men were knocked down. Others picked them up and dragged them on. "Take it, men, just take it," said Lt. Col. John Flanagan, the commander of the 503rd MP Battalion.

Bowman couldn't believe it. He was being assaulted by fellow Americans, fellow Southerners. He swung his platoon around the overturned, flaming hulks of several cars. As the soldiers—still in formation, bayonets at ready—hove into sight, the marshals cheered.

General Billingslea had followed the MP's to the Lyceum in a border-patrol sedan. He reported to Nick Katzenbach, who told him the President wanted him on the open line. The General's voice, on the phone that had brought so much bad news, led the President and his brother to sense that the battle was ending, though, actually, it had many hours to go. They knew the nation had experienced one of the most tragic riots in its history. They did not know—and will not know until they read this story—how narrowly they had averted civil war.

Forty-five minutes later, the President went to bed, made a last check on his bedside phone, and slept. It was 5:30 a.m. in Washington.

EPILOGUE

In Jackson, gleaming new buildings and modern schools thrust up toward a blue Mississippi sky. After a hundred years in economic eclipse Mississippi can glimpse a future of progress and prosperity. But the climate of the heart changes slowly. Few Northerners know how much courage it takes in Mississippi to move against the wind.

Some men tried. We call these men the "permanent leadership," not politicians, but bankers, lawyers, businessmen, educators. They believe in segregation and fear incursions of Federal power. But they are unwilling to let their communities be wrecked in the race struggle. Though Barnett never let them in on the dangerous wall-of-flesh strategy, the permanent leaders saw the danger of inflamed public passion. In the days before the riot, they made several moves: They silenced an inflammatory TV commentator. They talked reason and restraint with the editors of Jackson's nervous newspapers. Their timely cautions to the Governor helped (unknown to them) nudge him into secret negotiations with Robert Kennedy. Two days after the riot 128 of them made a public stand for law and order: "Violence at any point in our beloved State must not be permitted to further arise."

It took courage to make the statement. The tragedy is that

the permanent leaders could not speak out before the riot. Now, in their quiet and substantial way, they are working to repair the state's torn fabric. Many wonder whether they can get the job done in time to avoid new tragedy.

Look, December 31, 1962

Kennedy: The Reluctant Emancipator

by Howard Zinn

THE dispatch of federal troops to Oxford, Mississippi, tends to obscure the true cautiousness of John F. Kennedy in the movement for Negro rights. Oxford diverted attention from Albany, Georgia. In the former, the national government moved boldly and with overwhelming force. In the latter, which twice this past year has been the scene of Negro demonstrations, mass arrests and official violence, the federal government showed cautiousness to the point of timidity. The two situations, occurring in comparable Black Belt areas, point up the ambiguous, uncomfortable role of the Administration in civil rights. Oxford is fresh in the memory today and has been the object of an international uproar. Albany, now in the backwash of national attention, deserves to be brought forward for a good look.

I had the benefit of two such looks: last December, when that Black Belt city erupted with racial demonstrations for the first time in a long history going back to slavery days; and again last summer, when trouble burst out once more. Both times, the Southern Regional Council, which studies race matters throughout the South from its headquarters in Atlanta, had asked me to investigate and report. What I saw convinced me that the national government has an undeserved reputation, both among Southern opponents and Northern supporters, as a vigorous combatant for Negro rights.

To be fair, this much should be said at the outset in behalf of the Administration: fundamentally, it is behaving no differently from any of its predecessors. We have always lived in a white society, where even liberalism is tinged with whiteness. I am measuring the actions of the Kennedys not against past performances, but against the needs of our time. My object is not to denounce, but to clarify. It is important for American citizens to know exactly how far they can depend on the national government, and how much remains for them to do. In the field of racial equality, this government simply cannot be depended upon for vigorous initiatives. It will, however, respond to popular indignation and pressure. When I say that it often responds slowly and reluctantly, my intention is not to vilify John F. Kennedy, but to light a flame under the rest of us.

The Kennedy Administration has set limits, never publicized but nevertheless implicit in its actions, to its own power in the field of desegregation. It will act to keep law and order in cases of extreme and admitted defiance of federal authority, as in Oxford. But it will not act against violation of federal law in other cases—in Albany, Georgia, for instance—where the circumstances are less stark.

There is a rough analogy between Lincoln's insistence (in that famous letter to Horace Greeley) that he was more concerned with *union* than with slavery, and Kennedy's unspoken but obvious preoccupation with *law and order* above either desegregation or the right of free assembly. This explains why the Justice Department, while over a period of nine months 1,000 Negroes were being jailed in Albany for peaceful demonstrations against racial discrimination, gave tacit support to the chief of police for maintaining "law and order." Only after eight months of pressure and complaint did it enter the picture as "friend of the court" in a defensive suit. But it never took the initiative in behalf of Albany Negroes.

The analogy with Lincoln is only a rough one because even the "law and order" principle is applied by Kennedy rather narrowly, with shadowy situations interpreted against the Negro rather than for him. In the case of Ole Miss, the law was unquestionably clear and the imminence of disorder equally clear. But in Albany, there was legal doubt. True, there was an Interstate Commerce Commission ruling and explicit court decisions calling for desegregation of the bus and train terminals. But did not the chief of police say on three successive occasions, when arresting young people who had used the "white" section of the terminal, that it was not a matter of race, but of keeping "order"? A forthright national government might have dismissed this argument as easily as it did Barnett's contention that race was not the basic reason for barring James Meredith from Ole Miss. But the Kennedy Administration chose not to challenge Albany's Chief Pritchett.

And when, last December, more than 700 Negro men, women and children were packed into jails in the Albany area for protesting segregation by marching through downtown streets and holding prayer meetings in front of City Hall, the government might have gone to court, on the basis of the First Amendment, to defend the right of free assembly. It might be contended, however, that with Negroes in jail, Albany had more "order." Also, constitutional lawyers disagree over the right of the government to take the initiative in enforcing the First Amendment. The Kennedy Administration has talked of the New Frontier, but perhaps this frontier does not extend into the South or into the field of constitutional law.

Albany is a quiet commercial town in southwest Georgia surrounded by farm land that, in pre-Civil War days, was slave plantation country. Negroes, once a majority in the community, now make up 40 per cent of its population of 56,000. Interestingly enough, like many Southern cities just beginning the process of desegregation, Albany has been free of white mob violence of the kind that made headlines at Oxford, Little Rock and a few other places. When, last December, Negroes marched downtown in large but peaceful groups to sing and pray in front of City Hall, whites stood by and watched with curiosity—resentful, perhaps, but quiet. It was the city and county officials who, by jailing the peaceful demonstrators, repeatedly violated the Fourteenth Amendment, which not only prohibits the application of local law on the basis of color, but also—according to constitutional doctrine accepted since the 1920s—bars deprivation by local officials of the rights of free speech, assembly and petition.

The fact that it was local police who violated constitutional doctrine is important because it is against local governments, rather than private persons, that the federal government has the clearest right to act in defense of the rights of citizens.

A shaky truce ended the December demonstrations, which

had been provoked by arrests at the train terminal, but were rooted, of course, in the total segregation and white domination that make Albany, Georgia, such a hard place for Negroes to live in. By January, the truce began to fall apart. That month, an eighteen-year-old Negro girl named Ola Mae Quarterman sat in the front seat of an Albany bus, refused to move on the command of the driver, was arrested by a policeman and convicted in city court for using "obscene" language. The driver testified that she had told him: "I paid my damn twenty cents, and I can sit where I want." Subsequently Miss Quarterman told a federal court, to which her case had gone on appeal, that she had used the word "damn" in relation to her twenty cents, not in relation to the driver. (Anywhere but in the Deep South a judge might have thought it incredible that she should be forced to defend her words by making such a distinction.) The city's counsel insisted her race had nothing to do with her arrest, and in cross-examination asked if it were not true that the cause of her arrest was her "vulgar language." She replied softly, "That's what they said."

There followed several hundred arrests as the city police moved promptly against every Negro who, in any way and under any circumstances, challenged segregation patterns: two young men who sat in the Trailways terminal restaurant; four men picketing a store downtown; thirty youngsters asking service at a lunch counter; twenty-nine people praying in front of City Hall; thirty-two Negroes on the way to City Hall; 150 more on the way to City Hall; seven praying in front of City Hall; ten more, eighteen more, sixteen more, all praying in front of City Hall; fourteen praying at the Carnegie Library—all thrown into jail.

After a thousand arrests, Police Chief Laurie Pritchett emerged into national prominence as some sort of hero. He had kept the peace. Somehow, the standard for American democracy accepted by the Administration became the standard for the nation: the sole criterion was the prevention of violence. The fact that violence had at no time been imminent in the demonstrations was overlooked.

There is a statute in the U.S. Criminal Code, Section 242, going back to 1866, which makes it a crime for a local law-enforcement officer deliberately to subject "any inhabitant of any State . . . to the deprivation of any rights, privileges, or immunities secured or protected by the Constitution and laws of the United States. . . ." Under any reasonable interpretation, this law was broken in Albany at least thirty times from November 1, 1961, when police for the first time ignored the ICC ruling desegregating the bus terminal, to the middle of August, 1962, when three youngsters trying to attend service at a white church were arrested. To select one instance with at least fifty witnesses: a county judge watched quietly from his bench as deputy sheriffs dragged and pushed out of his courtroom five young people—one Negro and four whites—who had taken seats in the "wrong" section (by race). One was a young woman whom a deputy dragged over a row of seats and pushed through a revolving door.

The U.S. Department of Justice maintains an FBI office in Albany. Affidavits have flowed into that FBI office in a steady stream, attesting to violations by local officials of the constitutional rights of Negroes. But nothing was done. As recently as last week, the Rev. Martin Luther King, Jr., publicly charged that the FBI agents in Albany have been favoring the segregationists. [As to the role of the FBI in the investigation of complaints by Negroes in the South charging violations of civil rights, and of the attitude of Negroes toward the bureau, see Volume V of the 1961 *Report of the Civil Rights Commission*, particularly the notes on pages 211 and 219.—Ed.]

The Department of Justice, citing a 1943 case in which the conviction of a Georgia sheriff in the brutal killing of a Negro named Bobby Hall was overturned by a narrow Supreme Court interpretation of Section 242, takes the position that it should prosecute only in *extreme* cases of police brutality. This policy allows transgressors of Negro rights who stop short of premeditated murder to act with reasonable assurance that the federal government will not move. Last summer, at least three acts of brutality occurred in the Albany area, were duly reported to the FBI, and thus far have resulted in no federal action. I will describe these three in some detail as told to me by the principals.

On July 23, 1962, about 5:30 P.M., Mrs. Slater King, wife of a Negro leader in the Albany Movement, drove from Albany to the Camilla jail in neighboring Mitchell County, carrying food to a girl who had been arrested with a hundred other Negroes while on a march to City Hall. Mrs. King was in her sixth month of pregnancy, and had her three children along. "All you niggers get away from the fence," one of the deputies standing nearby called out as a group of visiting women approached the jailhouse. Mrs. King walked slowly towards her car. A deputy pointed her out, cursed her, threatened to arrest her if she didn't hurry. She turned and said, "If you want to arrest me, go ahead." She was then kicked, hit twice on the side of the head and was knocked unconscious.

Several days later, William Hansen, a twenty-year-old white field worker for the Student Non-Violent Coordinating Committee, and a veteran of jails in Mississippi and Maryland for participating in desegregation actions, was put in the Dougherty County jail in Albany after a prayer session in front of City Hall. A prison trustee, to whom the jailer had earlier suggested that Hansen needed to be "straightened out," beat the Cincinnati youth into senselessness as he sat on the floor reading. His jaw and several ribs were broken. Bleeding profusely from the mouth, he asked the jailer for medical aid, and was told this was not within the jailer's jurisdiction. Finally, a message shouted through the cell window brought about his transfer to the city jail, where he was hospitalized.

That same Saturday afternoon, C. B. King, thirty-six, the first and only Negro attorney in the city of Albany and the legal backbone of the Albany Movement, heard of Hansen's beating. He visited Sheriff Cull Campbell of Dougherty County to check on Hansen's condition. A Negro minister who was waiting to meet King in the Sheriff's office at the time later described what happened. Sheriff Campbell, seeing King in his office, said, "Nigger, haven't I told you to wait outside?" As King turned to reply, the Sheriff picked up a walking stick and hit him viciously on the head, breaking the cane. King staggered from the office, blood streaming from his head and crossed the street to City Hall, where Chief Pritchett had him taken to a hospital. Pritchett, who had just arrested twenty-eight Negroes for praying and singing in front of City Hall, called the beating of King "very regrettable." *The New York Times* reporter, Claude Sitton, noted that "Chief Pritchett had more than 160 city, county and state law-enforcement officers standing by to prevent violence." Sheriff Campbell readily admitted the beating, when I questioned him a month after the incident: "Yeh, I knocked hell out of him, and I'll do it again. I let him know I'm a white man and he's a damn nigger."

All of the above three incidents were reported to the FBI, which dutifully recorded them. Thus far, the federal government has taken no action.

The few things that the national government *did* do in Albany give a clue to the boundaries it has drawn for itself in the field of civil rights. It went into a frantic day of telephone calls when Martin Luther King, Jr., was jailed in Albany; King, of course, is a politically important symbol. President Kennedy, in answer to questions on Albany at two different press conferences, made two statements. In one, he criticized Albany officials for refusing to negotiate with Negroes; in the other, he denounced the burning of Negro churches that had been used for voter-registration activities in the Albany area. The President's plea for negotiation, like his careful speech on the eve of Meredith's registration at Ole Miss, carefully skirted the moral issue of racial equality and stuck to procedural questions: the law, negotiation. The President has still not followed the advice of his own Civil Rights Commission to give "moral leadership" and to use "education and persuasion." His statement on church-burning covered two points on which the Administration is especially sensitive: its antipathy to nationally publicized violence and its careful defense of voting rights (but not other rights) guaranteed by the Constitution. The only federal suit initiated by the Justice Department in the Albany area was in defense of voter-registration activity.

There is a plausible legal argument to the effect that voting rights are protected by specific legislation (the Civil Rights Acts of 1957 and 1960), while the First Amendment rights of free speech, assembly, etc., and the Fourteenth Amendment right to color-blind treatment by local officials, are not. However, a national administration less timorous than the present one could find solid legal sanction for the widespread use of injunctions to protect free assembly and to attack legal segregation. In the Debs case of 1895, the Supreme Court supported the issuance of injunctions without specific statutory basis, saying: "Every government has a right to apply to its own courts in matters which the Constitution has entrusted to the care of the national government." This ruling has never been overturned.

A truly bold national administration might do the following: (1) prosecute vigorously, under Sec. 242, violations of Negro rights by local officers; (2) create a corps of special agents—not encumbered, as is the FBI, by intimate relations with local police officers—to prevent, as well as to investigate, violations of constitutional rights; (3) use the power of injunction freely, both to prevent policemen from curtailing the right of assembly and petition and to break down legal enforcement of segregation; (4) tell the South and the nation frankly that racial discrimination is morally wrong as well as illegal, and that the nation intends to wipe it out.

At this moment, because of the limitations that the Administration has imposed upon itself, there is a vast no-man's-land for American Negroes into which they are invited by the Constitution, but where federal authority will not protect them. It was into this no-man's-land that the Negro population of Albany ventured, and found itself deserted. The future may bring one or two more Oxfords, but there are a hundred potential Albanys. Throughout the Deep South, Negroes are on the move towards dangerous territory. And so far, though these men, women and children live in a nation whose power encircles the globe and reaches into space, they are very much on their own.

The Nation, December 1, 1962

Down at the Cross
Letter from a Region in My Mind

by James Baldwin

Take up the White Man's burden—
Ye dare not stoop to less—
Nor call too loud on Freedom
To cloak your weariness;
By all ye cry or whisper,
By all ye leave or do,
The silent, sullen peoples
Shall weigh your Gods and you.
                    —*Kipling*

Down at the cross where my Saviour died,
Down where for cleansing from sin I cried,
There to my heart was the blood applied,
Singing glory to His name!
                    —*Hymn*

I UNDERWENT, during the summer that I became fourteen, a prolonged religious crisis. I use the word "religious" in the common, and arbitrary, sense, meaning that I then discovered God, His saints and angels, and His blazing Hell. And since I had been born in a Christian nation, I accepted this Deity as the only one. I supposed Him to exist only within the walls of a church—in fact, of *our* church—and I also supposed that God and safety were synonymous. The word "safety" brings us to the real meaning of the word "religious" as we use it. Therefore, to state it in another, more accurate way, I became, during my fourteenth year, for the first time in my life, afraid—afraid of the evil within me and afraid of the evil without. What I saw around me that summer in Harlem was what I had always seen; nothing had changed. But now, without any warning, the whores and pimps and racketeers on the Avenue had become a personal menace. It had not before occurred to me that I could become one of them, but now I realized that we had been produced by the same circumstances. Many of my comrades were clearly headed for the Avenue, and my father said that I was headed that way, too. My friends began to drink and smoke, and embarked—at first avid, then groaning—on their sexual careers. Girls, only slightly older than I was, who sang in the choir or taught Sunday school, the children of holy parents, underwent, before my eyes, their incredible metamorphosis, of which the most bewildering aspect was not their budding breasts or their rounding behinds but something deeper and more subtle, in their eyes, their heat, their odor, and the inflection of their voices. Like the strangers on the Avenue, they became, in the twinkling of an eye, unutterably different and fantastically *present.* Owing to the way I had been raised, the abrupt discomfort that all this aroused in me and the fact that I had no idea what my voice or my mind or my body was likely to do next caused me to consider myself one of the most depraved people on earth. Matters were not helped by the fact that these holy girls seemed rather to enjoy my terrified lapses, our grim, guilty, tormented experiments, which were at once as chill and joyless as the Russian steppes and hotter, by far, than all the fires of Hell.

Yet there was something deeper than these changes, and less definable, that frightened me. It was real in both the boys and the girls, but it was, somehow, more vivid in the boys. In the case of the girls, one watched them turning into matrons before they had become women. They began to manifest a curious and really rather terrifying single-mindedness. It is hard to say exactly how this was conveyed: something implacable in the set of the lips, something farseeing (seeing what?) in the eyes, some new and crushing determination in the walk, something peremptory in the voice. They did not tease us, the boys, any more; they reprimanded us sharply, saying, "You better be thinking about your soul!" For the girls also saw the evidence on the Avenue, knew what the price would be, for them, of one misstep, knew that they had to be protected and that we were the only protection there was. They understood that they must act as God's decoys, saving the souls of the boys for Jesus and binding the bodies of the boys in marriage. For this was the beginning of our burning time, and "It is better," said St. Paul—who elsewhere, with a most unusual and stunning exactness, described himself as a "wretched man"—"to marry than to burn." And I began to feel in the boys a curious, wary, bewildered despair, as though they were now settling in for the long, hard winter of life. I did not know then what it was that I was reacting to; I put it to myself that they were letting themselves go. In the same way that the girls were destined to gain as much weight as their mothers, the boys, it was clear, would rise no higher than their fathers. School began to reveal itself, therefore, as a child's game that one could not win, and boys dropped out of school and went to work. My father wanted me to do the same. I refused, even though I no longer had any illusions about what an education could do for me; I had already encountered too many college-graduate handymen. My friends were now "downtown," busy, as they put it, "fighting the man." They began to care less about the way they looked, the way they dressed, the things they did; presently, one found them in twos and threes and fours, in a hallway, sharing a jug of wine or a bottle of whiskey, talking, cursing, fighting, sometimes weeping: lost, and unable to say what it was that oppressed them, except that they knew it was "the man"—the white man. And there seemed to be no way whatever to remove this cloud that stood between them and the sun, between them and love and life and power, between them and whatever it was that they wanted. One did not have to be very bright to realize how little one could do to change one's situation; one did not have to be abnormally sensitive to be worn down to a cutting edge by the incessant and gratuitous humiliation and danger one encountered every working day, all day long. The humiliation did not apply merely to working days, or workers; I was thirteen and was crossing Fifth Avenue on my way to the Forty-second Street library, and the cop in the middle of the street muttered as I passed him, "Why don't you niggers stay uptown where you belong?" When I was ten, and didn't look, certainly, any older, two policemen amused themselves with me by frisking me, making comic (and terrifying) speculations concerning my ancestry and probable sexual prowess, and for good measure, leaving me flat on my back in one of Harlem's empty lots. Just before and then during the Second World War, many of my friends fled into the service, all to be changed there, and rarely for the better, many to be ruined, and many to die. Others fled to other states and cities—that is, to other ghettos. Some went on wine or whiskey or the needle, and are still on it. And others, like me, fled into the church.

For the wages of sin were visible everywhere, in every wine-stained and urine-splashed hallway, in every clanging ambulance bell, in every scar on the faces of the pimps and their whores, in every helpless, newborn baby being brought into this danger, in every knife and pistol fight on the Avenue, and in every disastrous bulletin: a cousin, mother of six, suddenly gone mad, the children parcelled out here and there; an indestructible aunt rewarded for years of hard labor by a slow, agonizing death in a terrible small room; someone's bright son blown into eternity by his own hand; another turned robber and carried off to jail. It was a summer of dreadful speculations and discoveries, of which these were not the worst. Crime became real, for example—for the first time—not as *a* possibility but as *the* possibility. One would never defeat one's circumstances by working and saving one's pennies; one would never, by working, acquire that many pennies, and, besides, the social treatment accorded even the most successful Negroes proved that one needed, in order to be free, something more than a bank account. One needed a handle, a lever, a means of inspiring fear. It was absolutely clear that the police would whip you and take you in as long as they could get away with it, and that everyone else—housewives, taxi-drivers, elevator boys, dishwashers, bartenders, lawyers, judges, doctors, and grocers—would never, by the operation of any generous human feeling, cease to use you as an outlet for his frustrations and hostilities. Neither civilized reason nor Christian love would cause any of those people to treat you as they presumably wanted to be treated; only the fear of your power to retaliate would cause them to do that, or to seem to do it, which was (and is) good enough. There appears to be a vast amount of confusion on this point, but I do not know many Negroes who are eager to be "accepted" by white people, still less to be loved by them; they, the blacks, simply

don't wish to be beaten over the head by the whites every instant of our brief passage on this planet. White people in this
country will have quite enough to do in learning how to accept and love themselves and each other, and when they have
achieved this—which will not be tomorrow and may very well
be never—the Negro problem will no longer exist, for it will
no longer be needed.

People more advantageously placed than we in Harlem
were, and are, will no doubt find the psychology and the view
of human nature sketched above dismal and shocking in the
extreme. But the Negro's experience of the white world cannot possibly create in him any respect for the standards by
which the white world claims to live. His own condition is
overwhelming proof that white people do not live by these
standards. Negro servants have been smuggling odds and
ends out of white homes for generations, and white people
have been delighted to have them do it, because it has as-
suaged a dim guilt and testified to the intrinsic superiority of
white people. Even the most doltish and servile Negro could
scarcely fail to be impressed by the disparity between his situation and that of the people for whom he worked; Negroes
who were neither doltish nor servile did not feel that they
were doing anything wrong when they robbed white people.
In spite of the Puritan-Yankee equation of virtue with well-
being, Negroes had excellent reasons for doubting that
money was made or kept by any very striking adherence to the
Christian virtues; it certainly did not work that way for black
Christians. In any case, white people, who had robbed black
people of their liberty and who profited by this theft every
hour that they lived, had no moral ground on which to stand.
They had the judges, the juries, the shotguns, the law—in a
word, power. But it was a criminal power, to be feared but not
respected, and to be outwitted in any way whatever. And
those virtues preached but not practiced by the white world
were merely another means of holding Negroes in subjection.

It turned out, then, that summer, that the moral barriers
that I had supposed to exist between me and the dangers of a
criminal career were so tenuous as to be nearly nonexistent. I
certainly could not discover any principled reason for not becoming a criminal, and it is not my poor, God-fearing parents

who are to be indicted for the lack but this society. I was icily determined—more determined, really, than I then knew—never to make my peace with the ghetto but to die and go to Hell before I would let any white man spit on me, before I would accept my "place" in this republic. I did not intend to allow the white people of this country to tell me who I was, and limit me that way, and polish me off that way. And yet, of course, at the same time, I *was* being spat on and defined and described and limited, and could have been polished off with no effort whatever. Every Negro boy—in my situation during those years, at least—who reaches this point realizes, at once, profoundly, because he wants to live, that he stands in great peril and must find, with speed, a "thing," a gimmick, to lift him out, to start him on his way. *And it does not matter what the gimmick is.* It was this last realization that terrified me and —since it revealed that the door opened on so many dangers —helped to hurl me into the church. And, by an unforeseeable paradox, it was my career in the church that turned out, precisely, to be my gimmick.

For when I tried to assess my capabilities, I realized that I had almost none. In order to achieve the life I wanted, I had been dealt, it seemed to me, the worst possible hand. I could not become a prizefighter—many of us tried but very few succeeded. I could not sing. I could not dance. I had been well conditioned by the world in which I grew up, so I did not yet dare take the idea of becoming a writer seriously. The only other possibility seemed to involve my becoming one of the sordid people on the Avenue, who were not really as sordid as I then imagined but who frightened me terribly, both because I did not want to live that life and because of what they made me feel. Everything inflamed me, and that was bad enough, but I myself had also become a source of fire and temptation. I had been far too well raised, alas, to suppose that any of the extremely explicit overtures made to me that summer, sometimes by boys and girls but also, more alarmingly, by older men and women, had anything to do with my attractiveness. On the contrary, since the Harlem idea of seduction is, to put it mildly, blunt, whatever these people saw in me merely confirmed my sense of my depravity.

It is certainly sad that the awakening of one's senses should lead to such a merciless judgment of oneself—to say nothing of the time and anguish one spends in the effort to arrive at any other—but it is also inevitable that a literal attempt to mortify the flesh should be made among black people like those with whom I grew up. Negroes in this country—and Negroes do not, strictly or legally speaking, exist in any other—are taught really to despise themselves from the moment their eyes open on the world. This world is white and they are black. White people hold the power, which means that they are superior to blacks (intrinsically, that is: God decreed it so), and the world has innumerable ways of making this difference known and felt and feared. Long before the Negro child perceives this difference, and even longer before he understands it, he has begun to react to it, he has begun to be controlled by it. Every effort made by the child's elders to prepare him for a fate from which they cannot protect him causes him secretly, in terror, to begin to await, without knowing that he is doing so, his mysterious and inexorable punishment. He must be "good" not only in order to please his parents and not only to avoid being punished by them; behind their authority stands another, nameless and impersonal, infinitely harder to please, and bottomlessly cruel. And this filters into the child's consciousness through his parents' tone of voice as he is being exhorted, punished, or loved; in the sudden, uncontrollable note of fear heard in his mother's or his father's voice when he has strayed beyond some particular boundary. He does not know what the boundary is, and he can get no explanation of it, which is frightening enough, but the fear he hears in the voices of his elders is more frightening still. The fear that I heard in my father's voice, for example, when he realized that I really *believed* I could do anything a white boy could do, and had every intention of proving it, was not at all like the fear I heard when one of us was ill or had fallen down the stairs or strayed too far from the house. It was another fear, a fear that the child, in challenging the white world's assumptions, was putting himself in the path of destruction. A child cannot, thank Heaven, know how vast and how merciless is the nature of power, with what unbelievable cruelty people treat each other. He reacts to the fear in his parents' voices because his parents hold up the world for him and he has no protection without them. I defended myself, as I imagined, against the fear my father made me feel by remembering that he was very old-fashioned. Also, I prided myself on the fact that I already knew how to outwit him. To defend oneself against a fear is simply to insure that one will, one day, be conquered by it; fears must be faced. As for one's wits, it is just not true that one can live by them—not, that is, if one wishes really to live. That summer, in any case, all the fears with which I had grown up, and which were now a part of me and controlled my vision of the world, rose up like a wall between the world and me, and drove me into the church.

As I look back, everything I did seems curiously deliberate, though it certainly did not seem deliberate then. For example, I did not join the church of which my father was a member and in which he preached. My best friend in school, who attended a different church, had already "surrendered his life to the Lord," and he was very anxious about my soul's salvation. (I wasn't, but any human attention was better than none.) One Saturday afternoon, he took me to his church. There were no services that day, and the church was empty, except for some women cleaning and some other women praying. My friend took me into the back room to meet his pastor—a woman. There she sat, in her robes, smiling, an extremely proud and handsome woman, with Africa, Europe, and the America of the American Indian blended in her face. She was perhaps forty-five or fifty at this time, and in our world she was a very celebrated woman. My friend was about to introduce me when she looked at me and smiled and said, "Whose little boy are you?" Now this, unbelievably, was precisely the phrase used by pimps and racketeers on the Avenue when they suggested, both humorously and intensely, that I "hang out" with them. Perhaps part of the terror they had caused me to feel came from the fact that I unquestionably wanted to be *somebody's* little boy. I was so frightened, and at the mercy of so many conundrums, that inevitably, that summer, *someone* would have taken me over; one doesn't, in Harlem, long remain standing on any auction block. It was my good luck—perhaps—that I found myself in the church racket instead of some other, and surrendered to a spiritual seduction

long before I came to any carnal knowledge. For when the
pastor asked me, with that marvellous smile, "Whose little
boy are you?" my heart replied at once, "Why, yours."

The summer wore on, and things got worse. I became
more guilty and more frightened, and kept all this bottled up
inside me, and naturally, inescapably, one night, when this
woman had finished preaching, everything came roaring,
screaming, crying out, and I fell to the ground before the
altar. It was the strangest sensation I have ever had in my life—
up to that time, or since. I had not known that it was going
to happen, or that it could happen. One moment I was on my
feet, singing and clapping and, at the same time, working out
in my head the plot of a play I was working on then; the next
moment, with no transition, no sensation of falling, I was on
my back, with the lights beating down into my face and all
the vertical saints above me. I did not know what I was doing
down so low, or how I had got there. And the anguish that
filled me cannot be described. It moved in me like one of
those floods that devastate counties, tearing everything down,
tearing children from their parents and lovers from each
other, and making everything an unrecognizable waste. All I
really remember is the pain, the unspeakable pain; it was as
though I were yelling up to Heaven and Heaven would not
hear me. And if Heaven would not hear me, if love could not
descend from Heaven—to wash me, to make me clean—then
utter disaster was my portion. Yes, it does indeed mean something—something unspeakable—to be born, in a white country, an Anglo-Teutonic, antisexual country, black. You very
soon, without knowing it, give up all hope of communion.
Black people, mainly, look down or look up but do not look
at each other, not at you, and white people, mainly, look
away. And the universe is simply a sounding drum; there is no
way, no way whatever, so it seemed then and has sometimes
seemed since, to get through a life, to love your wife and children, or your friends, or your mother and father, or to be
loved. The universe, which is not merely the stars and the
moon and the planets, flowers, grass, and trees, but *other
people*, has evolved no terms for your existence, has made no
room for you, and if love will not swing wide the gates, no
other power will or can. And if one despairs—as who has not?

—of human love, God's love alone is left. But God—and I felt this even then, so long ago, on that tremendous floor, un-willingly—is white. And if His love was so great, and if He loved all His children, why were we, the blacks, cast down so far? Why? In spite of all I said thereafter, I found no answer on the floor—not *that* answer, anyway—and I was on the floor all night. Over me, to bring me "through," the saints sang and rejoiced and prayed. And in the morning, when they raised me, they told me that I was "saved."

Well, indeed I was, in a way, for I was utterly drained and exhausted, and released, for the first time, from all my guilty torment. I was aware then only of my relief. For many years, I could not ask myself why human relief had to be achieved in a fashion at once so pagan and so desperate—in a fashion at once so unspeakably old and so unutterably new. And by the time I was able to ask myself this question, I was also able to see that the principles governing the rites and cus-toms of the churches in which I grew up did not differ from the principles governing the rites and customs of other churches, white. The principles were Blindness, Loneliness, and Terror, the first principle necessarily and actively culti-vated in order to deny the two others. I would love to be-lieve that the principles were Faith, Hope, and Charity, but this is clearly not so for most Christians, or for what we call the Christian world.

I was saved. But at the same time, out of a deep, adolescent cunning I do not pretend to understand, I realized immedi-ately that I could not remain in the church merely as another worshipper. I would have to give myself something to do, in order not to be too bored and find myself among all the wretched unsaved of the Avenue. And I don't doubt that I also intended to best my father on his own ground. Anyway, very shortly after I joined the church, I became a preacher—a Young Minister—and I remained in the pulpit for more than three years. My youth quickly made me a much bigger drawing card than my father. I pushed this advantage ruth-lessly, for it was the most effective means I had found of breaking his hold over me. That was the most frightening time of my life, and quite the most dishonest, and the result-ing hysteria lent great passion to my sermons—for a while. I relished the attention and the relative immunity from punishment that my new status gave me, and I relished, above all, the sudden right to privacy. It had to be recognized, after all, that I was still a schoolboy, with my schoolwork to do, and I was also expected to prepare at least one sermon a week. During what we may call my heyday, I preached much more often than that. This meant that there were hours and even whole days when I could not be interrupted—not even by my father. I had immobilized him. It took rather more time for me to realize that I had also immobilized myself, and had escaped from nothing whatever.

The church was very exciting. It took a long time for me to disengage myself from this excitement, and on the blindest, most visceral level, I never really have, and never will. There is no music like that music, no drama like the drama of the saints rejoicing, the sinners moaning, the tambourines racing, and all those voices coming together and crying holy unto the Lord. There is still, for me, no pathos quite like the pathos of those multicolored, worn, somehow triumphant and transfigured faces, speaking from the depths of a visible, tangible, continuing despair of the goodness of the Lord. I have never seen anything to equal the fire and excitement that sometimes, without warning, fill a church, causing the church, as Leadbelly and so many others have testified, to "rock." Nothing that has happened to me since equals the power and the glory that I sometimes felt when, in the middle of a sermon, I knew that I was somehow, by some miracle, really carrying, as they said, "the Word"—when the church and I were one. Their pain and their joy were mine, and mine were theirs— they surrendered their pain and joy to me, I surrendered mine to them—and their cries of "Amen!" and "Hallelujah!" and "Yes, Lord!" and "Praise His name!" and "Preach it, brother!" sustained and whipped on my solos until we all became equal, wringing wet, singing and dancing, in anguish and rejoicing, at the foot of the altar. It was, for a long time, in spite of—or, not inconceivably, because of—the shabbiness of my motives, my only sustenance, my meat and drink. I rushed home from school, to the church, to the altar, to be alone there, to commune with Jesus, my dearest Friend, who would never fail me, who knew all the secrets of my heart.

Perhaps He did, but I didn't, and the bargain we struck, actually, down there at the foot of the cross, was that He would never let me find out.

He failed His bargain. He was a much better Man than I took Him for. It happened, as things do, imperceptibly, in many ways at once. I date it—the slow crumbling of my faith, the pulverization of my fortress—from the time, about a year after I had begun to preach, when I began to read again. I justified this desire by the fact that I was still in school, and I began, fatally, with Dostoevski. By this time, I was in a high school that was predominantly Jewish. This meant that I was surrounded by people who were, by definition, beyond any hope of salvation, who laughed at the tracts and leaflets I brought to school, and who pointed out that the Gospels had been written long after the death of Christ. This might not have been so distressing if it had not forced me to read the tracts and leaflets myself, for they were indeed, unless one believed their message already, impossible to believe. I remember feeling dimly that there was a kind of blackmail in it. People, I felt, ought to love the Lord *because* they loved Him, and not because they were afraid of going to Hell. I was forced, reluctantly, to realize that the Bible itself had been written by men, and translated by men out of languages I could not read, and I was already, without quite admitting it to myself, terribly involved with the effort of putting words on paper. Of course, I had the rebuttal ready: These men had all been operating under divine inspiration. *Had* they? *All* of them? And I also knew by now, alas, far more about divine inspiration than I dared admit, for I knew how I worked myself up into my own visions, and how frequently—indeed, incessantly—the visions God granted to me differed from the visions He granted to my father. I did not understand the dreams I had at night, but I knew that they were not holy. For that matter, I knew that my waking hours were far from holy. I spent most of my time in a state of repentance for things I had vividly desired to do but had not done. The fact that I was dealing with Jews brought the whole question of color, which I had been desperately avoiding, into the terrified center of my mind. I realized that the Bible had been written by white men. I knew that, according to many Christians, I was a descendant of Ham, who had been cursed, and that I was therefore predestined to be a slave. This had nothing to do with anything I was, or contained, or could become; my fate had been sealed forever, from the beginning of time. And it seemed, indeed, when one looked out over Christendom, that this was what Christendom effectively believed. It was certainly the way it behaved. I remembered the Italian priests and bishops blessing Italian boys who were on their way to Ethiopia.

Again, the Jewish boys in high school were troubling because I could find no point of connection between them and the Jewish pawnbrokers and landlords and grocery-store owners in Harlem. I knew that these people were Jews—God knows I was told it often enough—but I thought of them only as white. Jews, as such, until I got to high school, were all incarcerated in the Old Testament, and their names were Abraham, Moses, Daniel, Ezekiel, and Job, and Shadrach, Meshach, and Abednego. It was bewildering to find them so many miles and centuries out of Egypt, and so far from the fiery furnace. My best friend in high school was a Jew. He came to our house once, and afterward my father asked, as he asked about everyone, "Is he a Christian?"—by which he meant "Is he saved?" I really do not know whether my answer came out of innocence or venom, but I said coldly, "No. He's Jewish." My father slammed me across the face with his great palm, and in that moment everything flooded back—all the hatred and all the fear, and the depth of a merciless resolve to kill my father rather than allow my father to kill me—and I knew that all those sermons and tears and all that repentance and rejoicing had changed nothing. I wondered if I was expected to be glad that a friend of mine, or anyone, was to be tormented forever in Hell, and I also thought, suddenly, of the Jews in another Christian nation, Germany. They were not so far from the fiery furnace after all, and my best friend might have been one of them. I told my father, "He's a better Christian than you are," and walked out of the house. The battle between us was in the open, but that was all right; it was almost a relief. A more deadly struggle had begun.

Being in the pulpit was like being in the theatre; I was behind the scenes and knew how the illusion was worked. I knew the other ministers and knew the quality of their lives. And I don't mean to suggest by this the "Elmer Gantry" sort of hypocrisy concerning sensuality; it was a deeper, deadlier, and more subtle hypocrisy than that, and a little honest sensuality, or a lot, would have been like water in an extremely bitter desert. I knew how to work on a congregation until the last dime was surrendered—it was not very hard to do—and I knew where the money for "the Lord's work" went. I knew, though I did not wish to know it, that I had no respect for the people with whom I worked. I could not have said it then, but I also knew that if I continued I would soon have no respect for myself. And the fact that I was "the young Brother Baldwin" increased my value with those same pimps and racketeers who had helped to stampede me into the church in the first place. They still saw the little boy they intended to take over. They were waiting for me to come to my senses and realize that I was in a very lucrative business. They knew that I did not yet realize this, and also that I had not yet begun to suspect where my own needs, *coming up* (they were very patient), could drive me. They themselves did know the score, and they knew that the odds were in their favor. And, really, I knew it, too. I was even lonelier and more vulnerable than I had been before. And the blood of the Lamb had not cleansed me in any way whatever. I was just as black as I had been the day that I was born. Therefore, when I faced a congregation, it began to take all the strength I had not to stammer, not to curse, not to tell them to throw away their Bibles and get off their knees and go home and organize, for example, a rent strike. When I watched all the children, their copper, brown, and beige faces staring up at me as I taught Sunday school, I felt that I was committing a crime in talking about the gentle Jesus, in telling them to reconcile themselves to their misery on earth in order to gain the crown of eternal life. Were only Negroes to gain this crown? Was Heaven, then, to be merely another ghetto? Perhaps I might have been able to reconcile myself even to this if I had been able to believe that there was any loving-kindness to be found in the haven I represented. But I had been in the pulpit too long and I had seen too many monstrous things. I don't refer merely to the glaring fact that the minister eventually acquires

houses and Cadillacs while the faithful continue to scrub
floors and drop their dimes and quarters and dollars into the
plate. I really mean that there was no love in the church. It
was a mask for hatred and self-hatred and despair. The trans-
figuring power of the Holy Ghost ended when the service
ended, and salvation stopped at the church door. When we
were told to love everybody, I had thought that that meant
everybody. But no. It applied only to those who believed as we
did, and it did not apply to white people at all. I was told by
a minister, for example, that I should never, on any public
conveyance, under any circumstances, rise and give my seat to
a white woman. White men never rose for Negro women.
Well, that was true enough, in the main—I saw his point. But
what was the point, the purpose, of *my* salvation if it did not
permit me to behave with love toward others, no matter how
they behaved toward me? What others did was their responsibility, for which they would answer when the judgment
trumpet sounded. But what *I* did was *my* responsibility, and I
would have to answer, too—unless, of course, there was also
in Heaven a special dispensation for the benighted black, who
was not to be judged in the same way as other human beings,
or angels. It probably occurred to me around this time that
the vision people hold of the world to come is but a reflection, with predictable wishful distortions, of the world in
which they live. And this did not apply only to Negroes, who
were no more "simple" or "spontaneous" or "Christian" than
anybody else—who were merely more oppressed. In the same
way that we, for white people, were the descendants of Ham,
and were cursed forever, white people were, for us, the descendants of Cain. And the passion with which we loved the
Lord was a measure of how deeply we feared and distrusted
and, in the end, hated almost all strangers, always, and
avoided and despised ourselves.

But I cannot leave it at that; there is more to it than that.
In spite of everything, there was in the life I fled a zest and a
joy and a capacity for facing and surviving disaster that are
very moving and very rare. Perhaps we were, all of us—pimps,
whores, racketeers, church members, and children—bound
together by the nature of our oppression, the specific and peculiar complex of risks we had to run; if so, within these limits

we sometimes achieved with each other a freedom that was close to love. I remember, anyway, church suppers and outings, and, later, after I left the church, rent and waistline parties where rage and sorrow sat in the darkness and did not stir, and we ate and drank and talked and laughed and danced and forgot all about "the man." We had the liquor, the chicken, the music, and each other, and had no need to pretend to be what we were not. This is the freedom that one hears in some gospel songs, for example, and in jazz. In all jazz, and especially in the blues, there is something tart and ironic, authoritative and double-edged. White Americans seem to feel that happy songs are *happy* and sad songs are *sad*, and that, God help us, is exactly the way most white Americans sing them—sounding, in both cases, so helplessly, defenselessly fatuous that one dare not speculate on the temperature of the deep freeze from which issue their brave and sexless little voices. Only people who have been "down the line," as the song puts it, know what this music is about. I think it was Big Bill Broonzy who used to sing "I Feel So Good," a really joyful song about a man who is on his way to the railroad station to meet his girl. She's coming home. It is the singer's incredibly moving exuberance that makes one realize how leaden the time must have been while she was gone. There is no guarantee that she will stay this time, either, as the singer clearly knows, and, in fact, she has not yet actually arrived. Tonight, or tomorrow, or within the next five minutes, he may very well be singing "Lonesome in My Bedroom," or insisting, "Ain't we, ain't we, going to make it all right? Well, if we don't today, we will tomorrow night." White Americans do not understand the depths out of which such an ironic tenacity comes, but they suspect that the force is sensual, and they are terrified of sensuality and do not any longer understand it. The word "sensual" is not intended to bring to mind quivering dusky maidens or priapic black studs. I am referring to something much simpler and much less fanciful. To be sensual, I think, is to respect and rejoice in the force of life, of life itself, and to be *present* in all that one does, from the effort of loving to the breaking of bread. It will be a great day for America, incidentally, when we begin to eat bread again, instead of the blasphemous and tasteless foam rubber that we have substituted for it. And I am not being frivolous now, either. Something very sinister happens to the people of a country when they begin to distrust their own re-actions as deeply as they do here, and become as joyless as they have become. It is this individual uncertainty on the part of white American men and women, this inability to renew themselves at the fountain of their own lives, that makes the discussion, let alone elucidation, of any conundrum—that is, any reality—so supremely difficult. The person who distrusts himself has no touchstone for reality—for this touchstone can be only oneself. Such a person interposes between himself and reality nothing less than a labyrinth of attitudes. And these at-titudes, furthermore, though the person is usually unaware of it (is unaware of so much!), are historical and public attitudes. They do not relate to the present any more than they relate to the person. Therefore, whatever white people do not know about Negroes reveals, precisely and inexorably, what they do not know about themselves.

White Christians have also forgotten several elementary his-torical details. They have forgotten that the religion that is now identified with their virtue and their power—"God is on our side," says Dr. Verwoerd—came out of a rocky piece of ground in what is now known as the Middle East before color was invented, and that in order for the Christian church to be established, Christ had to be put to death, by Rome, and that the real architect of the Christian church was not the disrep-utable, sun-baked Hebrew who gave it his name but the mer-cilessly fanatical and self-righteous St. Paul. The energy that was buried with the rise of the Christian nations must come back into the world; nothing can prevent it. Many of us, I think, both long to see this happen and are terrified of it, for though this transformation contains the hope of liberation, it also imposes a necessity for great change. But in order to deal with the untapped and dormant force of the previously sub-jugated, in order to survive as a human, moving, moral weight in the world, America and all the Western nations will be forced to reëxamine themselves and release themselves from many things that are now taken to be sacred, and to dis-card nearly all the assumptions that have been used to justify their lives and their anguish and their crimes so long.

"The white man's Heaven," sings a Black Muslim minister, "is the black man's Hell." One may object—possibly—that this puts the matter somewhat too simply, but the song is true, and it has been true for as long as white men have ruled the world. The Africans put it another way: When the white man came to Africa, the white man had the Bible and the African had the land, but now it is the white man who is being, reluctantly and bloodily, separated from the land, and the African who is still attempting to digest or to vomit up the Bible. The struggle, therefore, that now begins in the world is extremely complex, involving the historical role of Christianity in the realm of power—that is, politics—and in the realm of morals. In the realm of power, Christianity has operated with an unmitigated arrogance and cruelty—necessarily, since a religion ordinarily imposes on those who have discovered the true faith the spiritual duty of liberating the infidels. This particular true faith, moreover, is more deeply concerned about the soul than it is about the body, to which fact the flesh (and the corpses) of countless infidels bears witness. It goes without saying, then, that whoever questions the authority of the true faith also contests the right of the nations that hold this faith to rule over him—contests, in short, their title to his land. The spreading of the Gospel, regardless of the motives or the integrity or the heroism of some of the missionaries, was an absolutely indispensable justification for the planting of the flag. Priests and nuns and school-teachers helped to protect and sanctify the power that was so ruthlessly being used by people who were indeed seeking a city, but not one in the heavens, and one to be made, very definitely, by captive hands. The Christian church itself—again, as distinguished from some of its ministers—sanctified and rejoiced in the conquests of the flag, and encouraged, if it did not formulate, the belief that conquest, with the resulting relative well-being of the Western populations, was proof of the favor of God. God had come a long way from the desert—but then so had Allah, though in a very different direction. God, going north, and rising on the wings of power, had become white, and Allah, out of power, and on the dark side of Heaven, had become—for all practical purposes, anyway—black. Thus, in the realm of morals the role of Christianity has been, at best, ambivalent. Even leaving out of account the remarkable arrogance that assumed that the ways and morals of others were inferior to those of Christians, and that they therefore had every right, and could use any means, to change them, the collision between cultures—and the schizophrenia in the mind of Christendom—had rendered the domain of morals as chartless as the sea once was, and as treacherous as the sea still is. It is not too much to say that whoever wishes to become a truly moral human being (and let us not ask whether or not this is possible; I think we must *believe* that it is possible) must first divorce himself from all the prohibitions, crimes, and hypocrisies of the Christian church. If the concept of God has any validity or any use, it can only be to make us larger, freer, and more loving. If God cannot do this, then it is time we got rid of Him.

I had heard a great deal, long before I finally met him, of the Honorable Elijah Muhammad, and of the Nation of Islam movement, of which he is the leader. I paid very little attention to what I heard, because the burden of his message did not strike me as being very original; I had been hearing variations of it all my life. I sometimes found myself in Harlem on Saturday nights, and I stood in the crowds, at 125th Street and Seventh Avenue, and listened to the Muslim speakers. But I had heard hundreds of such speeches—or so it seemed to me at first. Anyway, I have long had a very definite tendency to tune out the moment I come anywhere near either a pulpit or a soapbox. What these men were saying about white people I had often heard before. And I dismissed the Nation of Islam's demand for a separate black economy in America, which I had also heard before, as willful, and even mischievous, nonsense. Then two things caused me to begin to listen to the speeches, and one was the behavior of the police. After all, I had seen men dragged from their platforms on this very corner for saying less virulent things, and I had seen many crowds dispersed by policemen, with clubs or on horseback. But the policemen were doing nothing now. Obviously, this was not because they had become more human but because they were under orders and because they were afraid. And indeed they were, and I was delighted to see it. There they stood, in twos and threes and fours, in their Cub Scout uniforms and with their Cub Scout faces, totally unprepared, as is the way with American he-men, for anything that could not be settled with a club or a fist or a gun. I might have pitied them if I had not found myself in their hands so often and discovered, through ugly experience, what they were like when *they* held the power and what they were like when *you* held the power. The behavior of the crowd, its silent intensity, was the other thing that forced me to reassess the speakers and their message. I sometimes think, with despair, that Americans will swallow whole any political speech whatever—we've been doing very little else, these last, bad years—so it may not mean anything to say that this sense of integrity, after what Harlem, especially, has been through in the way of demagogues, was a very startling change. Still, the speakers had an air of utter dedication, and the people looked toward them with a kind of intelligence of hope on their faces—not as though they were being consoled or drugged but as though they were being jolted.

Power was the subject of the speeches I heard. We were offered, as Nation of Islam doctrine, historical and divine proof that all white people are cursed, and are devils, and are about to be brought down. This has been revealed by Allah Himself to His prophet, the Honorable Elijah Muhammad. The white man's rule will be ended forever in ten or fifteen years (and it must be conceded that all present signs would seem to bear witness to the accuracy of the prophet's statement). The crowd seemed to swallow this theology with no effort—all crowds do swallow theology this way, I gather, in both sides of Jerusalem, in Istanbul, and in Rome—and, as theology goes, it was no more indigestible than the more familiar brand asserting that there is a curse on the sons of Ham. No more, and no less, and it had been designed for the same purpose; namely, the sanctification of power. But very little time was spent on theology, for one did not need to prove to a Harlem audience that all white men were devils. They were merely glad to have, at last, divine corroboration of their experience, to hear—and it was a tremendous thing to hear—that they had been lied to for all these years and generations, and that their captivity was ending, for God was black. Why were they *hearing* it now, since this was not the first time it had been said? I had heard it many times, from various prophets, during all the years that I was growing up. Elijah Muhammad himself has now been carrying the same message for more than thirty years; he is not an overnight sensation, and we owe his ministry, I am told, to the fact that when he was a child of six or so, his father was lynched before his eyes. (So much for states' rights.) And now, suddenly, people who have never before been able to hear this message hear it, and believe it, and are changed. Elijah Muhammad has been able to do what generations of welfare workers and committees and resolutions and reports and housing projects and play-grounds have failed to do: to heal and redeem drunkards and junkies, to convert people who have come out of prison and to keep them out, to make men chaste and women virtuous, and to invest both the male and the female with a pride and a serenity that hang about them like an unfailing light. He has done all these things, which our Christian church has spectacularly failed to do. How has Elijah managed it?

Well, in a way—and I have no wish to minimize his peculiar role and his peculiar achievement—it is not he who has done it but time. Time catches up with kingdoms and crushes them, gets its teeth into doctrines and rends them; time reveals the foundations on which any kingdom rests, and eats at those foundations, and it destroys doctrines by proving them to be untrue. In those days, not so very long ago, when the priests of that church which stands in Rome gave God's blessing to Italian boys being sent out to ravage a defenseless black country—which until that event, incidentally, had not considered itself to be black—it was not possible to believe in a black God. To entertain such a belief would have been to entertain madness. But time has passed, and in that time the Christian world has revealed itself as morally bankrupt and politically unstable. The Tunisians were quite right in 1956— and it was a very significant moment in Western (and African) history—when they countered the French justification for remaining in North Africa with the question "Are the *French* ready for self-government?" Again, the terms "civilized" and "Christian" begin to have a very strange ring, particularly in the ears of those who have been judged to be neither civilized nor Christian, when a Christian nation surrenders to a foul and violent orgy, as Germany did during the Third Reich. For the crime of their ancestry, millions of people in the middle of the twentieth century, and in the heart of Europe—God's citadel—were sent to a death so calculated, so hideous, and so prolonged that no age before this enlightened one had been able to imagine it, much less achieve and record it. Furthermore, those beneath the Western heel, unlike those within the West, are aware that Germany's current role in Europe is to act as a bulwark against the "uncivilized" hordes, and since power is what the powerless want, they understand very well what we of the West want to keep, and are not deluded by our talk of a freedom that we have never been willing to share with them. From my own point of view, the fact of the Third Reich alone makes obsolete forever any question of Christian superiority, except in technological terms. White people were, and are, astounded by the holocaust in Germany. They did not know that they could act that way. But I very much doubt whether black people were astounded—at least, in the same way. For my part, the fate of the Jews, and the world's indifference to it, frightened me very much. I could not but feel, in those sorrowful years, that this human indifference, concerning which I knew so much already, would be my portion on the day that the United States decided to murder its Negroes systematically instead of little by little and catch-as-catch-can. I was, of course, authoritatively assured that what had happened to the Jews in Germany could not happen to the Negroes in America, but I thought, bleakly, that the German Jews had probably believed similar counsellors, and, again, I could not share the white man's vision of himself for the very good reason that white men in America do not behave toward black men the way they behave toward each other. When a white man faces a black man, especially if the black man is helpless, terrible things are revealed. I know. I have been carried into precinct basements often enough, and I have seen and heard and endured the secrets of desperate white men and women, which they knew were safe with me, because even if I should speak, no one would believe me. And they would not believe me precisely because they would know that what I said was true.

The treatment accorded the Negro during the Second
World War marks, for me, a turning point in the Negro's relation to America. To put it briefly, and somewhat too simply,
a certain hope died, a certain respect for white Americans
faded. One began to pity them, or to hate them. You must
put yourself in the skin of a man who is wearing the uniform
of his country, is a candidate for death in its defense, and who
is called a "nigger" by his comrades-in-arms and his officers;
who is almost always given the hardest, ugliest, most menial
work to do; who knows that the white G.I. has informed the
Europeans that he is subhuman (so much for the American
male's sexual security); who does not dance at the U.S.O. the
night white soldiers dance there, and does not drink in the
same bars white soldiers drink in; and who watches German
prisoners of war being treated by Americans with more human dignity than he has ever received at their hands. And
who, at the same time, as a human being, is far freer in a
strange land than he has ever been at home. *Home!* The very
word begins to have a despairing and diabolical ring. You
must consider what happens to this citizen, after all he has endured, when he returns—home: search, in his shoes, for a job,
for a place to live; ride, in his skin, on segregated buses; see,
with his eyes, the signs saying "White" and "Colored," and
especially the signs that say "White Ladies" and "Colored
Women"; look into the eyes of his wife; look into the eyes of
his son; listen, with his ears, to political speeches, North and
South; imagine yourself being told to "wait." And all this is
happening in the richest and freest country in the world, and
in the middle of the twentieth century. The subtle and deadly
change of heart that might occur in you would be involved
with the realization that a civilization is not destroyed by
wicked people; it is not necessary that people be wicked but
only that they be spineless. I and two Negro acquaintances,
all of us well past thirty, and looking it, were in the bar of
Chicago's O'Hare Airport several months ago, and the bartender refused to serve us, because, he said, we looked too
young. It took a vast amount of patience not to strangle him,
and great insistence and some luck to get the manager, who
defended his bartender on the ground that he was "new" and
had not yet, presumably, learned how to distinguish between

a Negro boy of twenty and a Negro "boy" of thirty-seven.
Well, we were served, finally, of course, but by this time no
amount of Scotch would have helped us. The bar was very
crowded, and our altercation had been extremely noisy; not
one customer in the bar had done anything to help us. When
it was over, and the three of us stood at the bar trembling
with rage and frustration, and drinking—and trapped, now, in
the airport, for we had deliberately come early in order to
have a few drinks and to eat—a young white man standing
near us asked if we were students. I suppose he thought that
this was the only possible explanation for our putting up a
fight. I told him that he hadn't wanted to talk to us earlier
and we didn't want to talk to him now. The reply visibly hurt
his feelings, and this, in turn, caused me to despise him. But
when one of us, a Korean War veteran, told this young man
that the fight we had been having in the bar had been his
fight, too, the young man said, "I lost my conscience a long
time ago," and turned and walked out. I know that one
would rather not think so, but this young man is typical. So,
on the basis of the evidence, had everyone else in the bar lost
his conscience. A few years ago, I would have hated these
people with all my heart. Now I pitied them, pitied them in
order not to despise them. And this is not the happiest way to
feel toward one's countrymen.

But, in the end, it is the threat of universal extinction hanging over all the world today that changes, totally and forever,
the nature of reality and brings into devastating question the
true meaning of man's history. We human beings now have
the power to exterminate ourselves; this seems to be the entire sum of our achievement. We have taken this journey and
arrived at this place in God's name. This, then, is the best that
God (the white God) can do. If that is so, then it is time to
replace Him—replace Him with what? And this void, this despair, this torment is felt everywhere in the West, from the
streets of Stockholm to the churches of New Orleans and the
sidewalks of Harlem.

God is black. All black men belong to Islam; they have
been chosen. And Islam shall rule the world. The dream, the
sentiment is old; only the color is new. And it is this dream,
this sweet possibility, that thousands of oppressed black men

and women in this country now carry away with them after the Muslim minister has spoken, through the dark, noisome ghetto streets, into the hovels where so many have perished. The white God has not delivered them; perhaps the Black God will.

While I was in Chicago last summer, the Honorable Elijah Muhammad invited me to have dinner at his home. This is a stately mansion on Chicago's South Side, and it is the headquarters of the Nation of Islam movement. I had not gone to Chicago to meet Elijah Muhammad—he was not in my thoughts at all—but the moment I received the invitation, it occurred to me that I ought to have expected it. In a way, I owe the invitation to the incredible, abysmal, and really cowardly obtuseness of white liberals. Whether in private debate or in public, any attempt I made to explain how the Black Muslim movement came about, and how it has achieved such force, was met with a blankness that revealed the little connection that the liberals' attitudes have with their perceptions or their lives, or even their knowledge—revealed, in fact, that they could deal with the Negro as a symbol or a victim but had no sense of him as a man. When Malcolm X, who is considered the movement's second-in-command, and heir apparent, points out that the cry of "violence" was not raised, for example, when the Israelis fought to regain Israel, and, indeed, is raised only when black men indicate that they will fight for *their* rights, he is speaking the truth. The conquests of England, every single one of them bloody, are part of what Americans have in mind when they speak of England's glory. In the United States, violence and heroism have been made synonymous except when it comes to blacks, and the only way to defeat Malcolm's point is to concede it and then ask oneself why this is so. Malcolm's statement is *not* answered by references to the triumphs of the N.A.A.C.P., the more particularly since very few liberals have any notion of how long, how costly, and how heartbreaking a task it is to gather the evidence that one can carry into court, or how long such court battles take. Neither is it answered by references to the student sit-in movement, if only because not all Negroes are students and not all of them live in the South. I, in any case, certainly refuse to be put in the position of denying the truth of Malcolm's statements simply because I disagree with his conclusions, or in order to pacify the liberal conscience. Things are as bad as the Muslims say they are—in fact, they are worse, and the Muslims do not help matters—but there *is* no reason that black men should be expected to be more patient, more forbearing, more farseeing than whites; indeed, quite the contrary. The real reason that non-violence is considered to be a virtue in Negroes—I am not speaking now of its racial value, another matter altogether—is that white men do not want their lives, their self-image, or their property threatened. One wishes they would say so more often. At the end of a television program on which Malcolm X and I both appeared, Malcolm was stopped by a white member of the audience who said, "I have a thousand dollars and an acre of land. What's going to happen to me?" I admired the directness of the man's question, but I didn't hear Malcolm's reply, because I was trying to explain to someone else that the situation of the Irish a hundred years ago and the situation of the Negro today cannot very usefully be compared. Negroes were brought here in chains long before the Irish ever thought of leaving Ireland; what manner of consolation is it to be told that emigrants arriving here—voluntarily—long after you did have risen far above you? In the hall, as I was waiting for the elevator, someone shook my hand and said, "Goodbye, Mr. James Baldwin. We'll soon be addressing you as Mr. James X." And I thought, for an awful moment, My God, if this goes on much longer, you probably will. Elijah Muhammad had seen this show, I think, or another one, and he had been told about me. Therefore, late on a hot Sunday afternoon, I presented myself at his door.

I was frightened, because I had, in effect, been summoned into a royal presence. I was frightened for another reason, too. I knew the tension in me between love and power, between pain and rage, and the curious, the grinding way I remained extended between these poles—perpetually attempting to choose the better rather than the worse. But this choice was a choice in terms of a personal, a private better (I was, after all, a writer); what was its relevance in terms of a social worse? Here was the South Side—a million in captivity—stretching from this doorstep as far as the eye could see. And they didn't even read; depressed populations don't have the time or energy to spare. The affluent populations, which should have been their help, didn't, as far as could be discovered, read, either—they merely bought books and devoured them, but not in order to learn: in order to learn new attitudes. Also, I knew that once I had entered the house, I couldn't smoke or drink, and I felt guilty about the cigarettes in my pocket, as I had felt years ago when my friend first took me into his church. I was half an hour late, having got lost on the way here, and I felt as deserving of a scolding as a schoolboy.

The young man who came to the door—he was about thirty, perhaps, with a handsome, smiling face—didn't seem to find my lateness offensive, and led me into a large room. On one side of the room sat half a dozen women, all in white; they were much occupied with a beautiful baby, who seemed to belong to the youngest of the women. On the other side of the room sat seven or eight men, young, dressed in dark suits, very much at ease, and very imposing. The sunlight came into the room with the peacefulness one remembers from rooms in one's early childhood—a sunlight encountered later only in one's dreams. I remember being astounded by the quietness, the ease, the peace, the taste. I was introduced, they greeted me with a genuine cordiality and respect—and the respect increased my fright, for it meant that they expected something of me that I knew in my heart, for their sakes, I could not give—and we sat down. Elijah Muhammad was not in the room. Conversation was slow, but not as stiff as I had feared it would be. They kept it going, for I simply did not know which subjects I could acceptably bring up. They knew more about me, and had read more of what I had written, than I had expected, and I wondered what they made of it all, what they took my usefulness to be. The women were carrying on their own conversation, in low tones; I gathered that they were not expected to take part in male conversations. A few women kept coming in and out of the room, apparently making preparations for dinner. We, the men, did not plunge deeply into any subject, for, clearly, we were all waiting for the appearance of Elijah. Presently, the men, one by one, left the room and returned. Then I was asked if I would like to wash, and I, too, walked down the hall to the bathroom. Shortly after I came back, we stood up, and Elijah entered.

I do not know what I had expected to see. I had read some of his speeches, and had heard fragments of others on the radio and on television, so I associated him with ferocity. But, no—the man who came into the room was small and slender, really very delicately put together, with a thin face, large, warm eyes, and a most winning smile. Something came into the room with him—his disciples' joy at seeing him, his joy at seeing them. It was the kind of encounter one watches with a smile simply because it is so rare that people enjoy one another. He teased the women, like a father, with no hint of that ugly and unctuous flirtatiousness I knew so well from other churches, and they responded like that, with great freedom and yet from a great and loving distance. He had seen me when he came into the room, I knew, though he had not looked my way. I had the feeling, as he talked and laughed with the others, whom I could only think of as his children, that he was sizing me up, deciding something. Now he turned toward me, to welcome me, with that marvellous smile, and carried me back nearly twenty-four years, to that moment when the pastor had smiled at me and said, "Whose little boy are you?" I did not respond now as I had responded then, because there are some things (not many, alas!) that one cannot do twice. But I knew what he made me feel, how I was drawn toward his peculiar authority, how his smile promised to take the burden of my life off my shoulders. *Take your burdens to the Lord and leave them there.* The central quality in Elijah's face is pain, and his smile is a witness to it —pain so old and deep and black that it becomes personal and particular only when he smiles. One wonders what he would sound like if he could sing. He turned to me, with that smile, and said something like "I've got a lot to say to *you*, but we'll wait until we sit *down*." And I laughed. He made me think of my father and me as we might have been if we had been friends.

In the dining room, there were two long tables; the men sat at one and the women at the other. Elijah was at the head of our table, and I was seated at his left. I can scarcely remember what we ate, except that it was plentiful, sane, and simple—so sane and simple that it made me feel extremely decadent, and I think that I drank, therefore, two glasses of milk. Elijah mentioned having seen me on television and said that it seemed to him that I was not yet brainwashed and was trying to become myself. He said this in a curiously unnerving way, his eyes looking into mine and one hand half hiding his lips, as though he were trying to conceal bad teeth. But his teeth were not bad. Then I remembered hearing that he had spent time in prison. I suppose that I *would* like to become myself, whatever that may mean, but I knew that Elijah's meaning and mine were not the same. I said yes, I was trying to be me, but I did not know how to say more than that, and so I waited.

Whenever Elijah spoke, a kind of chorus arose from the table, saying "Yes, that's right." This began to set my teeth on edge. And Elijah himself had a further, unnerving habit, which was to ricochet his questions and comments off someone else on their way to you. Now, turning to the man on his right, he began to speak of the white devils with whom I had last appeared on TV: What had they made *him* (me) feel? I could not answer this and was not absolutely certain that I was expected to. The people referred to had certainly made me feel exasperated and useless, but I did not think of them as devils. Elijah went on about the crimes of white people, to this endless chorus of "Yes, that's right." Someone at the table said, "The white man sure *is* a devil. He proves that by his own actions." I looked around. It was a very young man who had said this, scarcely more than a boy—very dark and sober, very bitter. Elijah began to speak of the Christian religion, of Christians, in the same soft, joking way. I began to see that Elijah's power came from his single-mindedness. There is nothing calculated about him; he means every word he says. The real reason, according to Elijah, that I failed to realize that the white man was a devil was that I had been too long exposed to white teaching and had never received true instruction. "The so-called American Negro" is the only reason Allah has permitted the United States to endure so long; the white man's time was up in 1913, but it is the will of Allah that this lost black nation, the black men of this country, be redeemed from their white masters and returned to the true

faith, which is Islam. Until this is done—and it will be accomplished very soon—the total destruction of the white man
is being delayed. Elijah's mission is to return "the so-called
Negro" to Islam, to separate the chosen of Allah from this
doomed nation. Furthermore, the white man knows his history, knows himself to be a devil, and knows that his time is
running out, and all his technology, psychology, science, and
"tricknology" are being expended in the effort to prevent
black men from hearing the truth. This truth is that at the
very beginning of time there was not one white face to be
found in all the universe. Black men ruled the earth and the
black man was perfect. This is the truth concerning the era
that white men now refer to as prehistoric. They want black
men to believe that they, like white men, once lived in caves
and swung from trees and ate their meat raw and did not have
the power of speech. But this is not true. Black men were
never in such a condition. Allah allowed the Devil, through
his scientists, to carry on infernal experiments, which resulted,
finally, in the creation of the devil known as the white man,
and later, even more disastrously, in the creation of the white
woman. And it was decreed that these monstrous creatures
should rule the earth for a certain number of years—I forget
how many thousand, but, in any case, their rule now is ending, and Allah, who had never approved of the creation of the
white man in the first place (who knows him, in fact, to be
not a man at all but a devil), is anxious to restore the rule of
peace that the rise of the white man totally destroyed. There
is thus, by definition, no virtue in white people, and since
they are another creation entirely and can no more, by breeding, become black than a cat, by breeding, can become a
horse, there is no hope for them.

There is nothing new in this merciless formulation except
the explicitness of its symbols and the candor of its hatred. Its
emotional tone is as familiar to me as my own skin; it is but
another way of saying that *sinners shall be bound in Hell a
thousand years.* That sinners have always, for American Negroes, been white is a truth we needn't labor, and every
American Negro, therefore, risks having the gates of paranoia
close on him. In a society that is entirely hostile, and, by its
nature, seems determined to cut you down—that has cut

down so many in the past and cuts down so many every day
—it begins to be almost impossible to distinguish a real from
a fancied injury. One can very quickly cease to attempt this
distinction, and, what is worse, one usually ceases to attempt
it without realizing that one has done so. All doormen, for
example, and all policemen have by now, for me, become exactly the same, and my style with them is designed simply to
intimidate them before they can intimidate me. No doubt I
am guilty of some injustice here, but it is irreducible, since I
cannot risk assuming that the humanity of these people is
more real to them than their uniforms. Most Negroes cannot
risk assuming that the humanity of white people is more real
to them than their color. And this leads, imperceptibly but inevitably, to a state of mind in which, having long ago learned
to expect the worst, one finds it very easy to believe the worst.
The brutality with which Negroes are treated in this country
simply cannot be overstated, however unwilling white men
may be to hear it. In the beginning—and neither can this be
overstated—a Negro just cannot *believe* that white people are
treating him as they do; he does not know what he has done
to merit it. And when he realizes that the treatment accorded
him has nothing to do with anything he has done, that the attempt of white people to destroy him—for that is what it is—
is utterly gratuitous, it is not hard for him to think of white
people as devils. For the horrors of the American Negro's life
there has been almost no language. The privacy of his experience, which is only beginning to be recognized in language,
and which is denied or ignored in official and popular speech
—hence the Negro idiom—lends credibility to any system
that pretends to clarify it. And, in fact, the truth about the
black man, as a historical entity and as a human being, *has*
been hidden from him, deliberately and cruelly; the power of
the white world is threatened whenever a black man refuses to
accept the white world's definitions. So every attempt is made
to cut that black man down—not only was made yesterday
but is made today. Who, then, is to say with authority where
the root of so much anguish and evil lies? Why, then, is it not
possible that all things began with the black man and that he
was perfect—especially since this is precisely the claim that
white people have put forward for themselves all these years?

Furthermore, it is now absolutely clear that white people are a minority in the world—so severe a minority that they now look rather more like an invention—and that they cannot possibly hope to rule it any longer. If this is so, why is it not also possible that they achieved their original dominance by stealth and cunning and bloodshed and in opposition to the will of Heaven, and not, as they claim, by Heaven's will? And if *this* is so, then the sword they have used so long against others can now, without mercy, be used against them. Heavenly witnesses are a tricky lot, to be used by whoever is closest to Heaven at the time. And legend and theology, which are designed to sanctify our fears, crimes, and aspirations, also reveal them for what they are.

I said, at last, in answer to some other ricocheted questions, "I left the church twenty years ago and I haven't joined anything since." It was my way of saying that I did not intend to join their movement, either.

"And what are you now?" Elijah asked.

I was in something of a bind, for I really could not say—could not allow myself to be stampeded into saying—that I was a Christian. "I? Now? Nothing." This was not enough. "I'm a writer. I like doing things alone." I heard myself saying this. Elijah smiled at me. "I don't, anyway," I said, finally, "think about it a great deal."

Elijah said, to his right, "I think he ought to think about it *all* the deal," and with this the table agreed. But there was nothing malicious or condemnatory in it. I had the stifling feeling that *they* knew I belonged to them but knew that I did not know it yet, that I remained unready, and that they were simply waiting, patiently, and with assurance, for me to discover the truth for myself. For where else, after all, could I go? I was black, and therefore a part of Islam, and would be saved from the holocaust awaiting the white world whether I would or no. My weak, deluded scruples could avail nothing against the iron word of the prophet.

I felt that I was back in my father's house—as, indeed, in a way, I was—and I told Elijah that *I* did not care if white and black people married, and that I had many white friends. I would have no choice, if it came to it, but to perish with them, for (I said to myself, but not to Elijah), "I love a few

people and they love me and some of them are white, and
isn't love more important than color?"

Elijah looked at me with great kindness and affection, great
pity, as though he were reading my heart, and indicated, skep-
tically, that I *might* have white friends, or think I did, and
they *might* be trying to be decent—now—but their time was
up. It was almost as though he were saying, "They had their
chance, man, and they goofed!"

And I looked around the table. I certainly had no evidence
to give them that would outweigh Elijah's authority or the evidence of their own lives or the reality of the streets outside.
Yes, I knew two or three people, white, whom I would trust
with my life, and I knew a few others, white, who were struggling as hard as they knew how, and with great effort and
sweat and risk, to make the world more human. But how
could I say this? One cannot argue with anyone's experience
or decision or belief. All my evidence would be thrown out of
court as irrelevant to the main body of the case, for I could
cite only exceptions. The South Side proved the justice of the
indictment; the state of the world proved the justice of the
indictment. Everything else, stretching back throughout recorded time, was merely a history of those exceptions who
had tried to change the world and had failed. Was this true?
Had they failed? How much depended on the point of view?
For it would seem that a certain category of exceptions never
failed to make the world worse—that category, precisely, for
whom power is more real than love. And yet power *is* real, and
many things, including, very often, love, cannot be achieved
without it. In the eeriest way possible, I suddenly had a
glimpse of what white people must go through at a dinner
table when they are trying to prove that Negroes are not subhuman. I had almost said, after all, "Well, take my friend
Mary," and very nearly descended to a catalogue of those
virtues that gave Mary the right to be alive. And in what hope?
That Elijah and the others would nod their heads solemnly
and say, at least, "Well, *she's* all right—but the *others!*"

And I looked again at the young faces around the table,
and looked back at Elijah, who was saying that no people in
history had ever been respected who had not owned their
land. And the table said, "Yes, that's right." I could not deny

the truth of this statement. For everyone else has, *is*, a nation, with a specific location and a flag—even, these days, the Jew. It is only "the so-called American Negro" who remains trapped, disinherited, and despised, in a nation that has kept him in bondage for nearly four hundred years and is still unable to recognize him as a human being. And the Black Muslims, along with many people who are not Muslims, no longer wish for a recognition so grudging and (should it ever be achieved) so tardy. Again, it cannot be denied that this point of view is abundantly justified by American Negro history. It is galling indeed to have stood so long, hat in hand, waiting for Americans to grow up enough to realize that you do not threaten them. On the other hand, how is the American Negro now to form himself into a separate nation? For this—and not only from the Muslim point of view—would seem to be his only hope of not perishing in the American backwater and being entirely and forever forgotten, as though he had never existed at all and his travail had been for nothing.

Elijah's intensity and the bitter isolation and disaffection of these young men and the despair of the streets outside had caused me to glimpse dimly what may now seem to be a fantasy, although, in an age so fantastical, I would hesitate to say precisely what a fantasy is. Let us say that the Muslims were to achieve the possession of the six or seven states that they claim are owed to Negroes by the United States as "back payment" for slave labor. Clearly, the United States would never surrender this territory, on any terms whatever, unless it found it impossible, for whatever reason, to hold it—unless, that is, the United States were to be reduced as a world power, exactly the way, and at the same degree of speed, that England has been forced to relinquish her Empire. (It is simply not true—and the state of her ex-colonies proves this— that England "always meant to go.") If the states were Southern states—and the Muslims seem to favor this—then the borders of a hostile Latin America would be raised, in effect, to, say, Maryland. Of the American borders on the sea, one would face toward a powerless Europe and the other toward an untrustworthy and non-white East, and on the North, after Canada, there would be only Alaska, which is a Russian border. The effect of this would be that the white people of

the United States and Canada would find themselves ma-
rooned on a hostile continent, with the rest of the white
world probably unwilling and certainly unable to come to
their aid. All this is not, to my mind, the most imminent of
possibilities, but if I were a Muslim, this is the possibility that
I would find myself holding in the center of my mind, and
driving toward. And if I were a Muslim, I would not hesitate
to utilize—or, indeed, to exacerbate—the social and spiritual
discontent that reigns here, for, at the very worst, I would
merely have contributed to the destruction of a house I
hated, and it would not matter if I perished, too. One has
been perishing here so long!

And what were they thinking around the table? "I've
come," said Elijah, "to give you something which can never
be taken away from you." How solemn the table became
then, and how great a light rose in the dark faces! This is the
message that has spread through streets and tenements and
prisons, through the narcotics wards, and past the filth and
sadism of mental hospitals to a people from whom everything
has been taken away, including, most crucially, their sense of
their own worth. People cannot live without this sense; they
will do anything whatever to regain it. This is why the most
dangerous creation of any society is that man who has nothing to lose. You do not need ten such men—one will do. And
Elijah, I should imagine, has had nothing to lose since the day
he saw his father's blood rush out—rush down, and splash, so
the legend has it, down through the leaves of a tree, on him.
But neither did the other men around the table have anything
to lose. "Return to your true religion," Elijah has written.
"Throw off the chains of the slavemaster, the devil, and return to the fold. Stop drinking his alcohol, using his dope—
protect your women—and forsake the filthy swine." I remembered my buddies of years ago, in the hallways, with their
wine and their whiskey and their tears; in hallways still, frozen
on the needle; and my brother saying to me once, "If Harlem
didn't have so many churches and junkies, there'd be blood
flowing in the streets." *Protect your women:* a difficult thing to
do in a civilization sexually so pathetic that the white man's
masculinity depends on a denial of the masculinity of the
blacks. *Protect your women:* in a civilization that emasculates

the male and abuses the female, and in which, moreover, the male is forced to depend on the female's bread-winning power. *Protect your women:* in the teeth of the white man's boast "We figure we're doing you folks a favor by pumping some white blood into your kids," and while facing the Southern shotgun and the Northern billy. Years ago, we used to say, "*Yes*, I'm black, goddammit, and I'm beautiful!"—in defiance, into the void. But now—now—African kings and heroes have come into the world, out of the past, the past that can now be put to the uses of power. And black has *become* a beautiful color—not because it is loved but because it is feared. And this urgency on the part of American Negroes is *not to be forgotten!* As they watch black men elsewhere rise, the promise held out, at last, that they may walk the earth with the authority with which white men walk, protected by the power that white men shall have no longer, is enough, and more than enough, to empty prisons and pull God down from Heaven. It has happened before, many times, before color was invented, and the hope of Heaven has always been a metaphor for the achievement of this particular state of grace. The song says, "I know my robe's going to fit me well. I tried it on at the gates of Hell."

It was time to leave, and we stood in the large living room, saying good night, with everything curiously and heavily unresolved. I could not help feeling that I had failed a test, in their eyes and in my own, or that I had failed to heed a warning. Elijah and I shook hands, and he asked me where I was going. Wherever it was, I would be driven there—"because, when we invite someone here," he said, "we take the responsibility of protecting him from the white devils until he gets wherever it is he's going." I was, in fact, going to have a drink with several white devils on the other side of town. I confess that for a fraction of a second I hesitated to give the address —the kind of address that in Chicago, as in all American cities, identified itself as a white address by virtue of its location. But I did give it, and Elijah and I walked out onto the steps, and one of the young men vanished to get the car. It was very strange to stand with Elijah for those few moments, facing those vivid, violent, so problematical streets. I felt very close to him, and really wished to be able to love and honor him as a witness, an ally, and a father. I felt that I knew something of his pain and his fury, and, yes, even his beauty. Yet precisely because of the reality and the nature of those streets —because of what he conceived as his responsibility and what I took to be mine—we would always be strangers, and possibly, one day, enemies. The car arrived—a gleaming, metallic, grossly American blue—and Elijah and I shook hands and said good night once more. He walked into his mansion and shut the door.

The driver and I started on our way through dark, murmuring—and, at this hour, strangely beautiful—Chicago, along the lake. We returned to the discussion of the land. How were we—Negroes—to get this land? I asked this of the dark boy who had said earlier, at the table, that the white man's actions proved him to be a devil. He spoke to me first of the Muslim temples that were being built, or were about to be built, in various parts of the United States, of the strength of the Muslim following, and of the amount of money that is annually at the disposal of Negroes—something like twenty billion dollars. "That alone shows you how strong we are," he said. But, I persisted, cautiously, and in somewhat different terms, this twenty billion dollars, or whatever it is, depends on the total economy of the United States. What happens when the Negro is no longer a part of this economy? Leaving aside the fact that in order for this to happen the economy of the United States will itself have had to undergo radical and certainly disastrous changes, the American Negro's spending power will obviously no longer be the same. On what, then, will the economy of this separate nation be based? The boy gave me a rather strange look. I said hurriedly, "I'm not saying it *can't* be done—I just want to know *how* it's to be done." I was thinking, In order for this to happen, your entire frame of reference will have to change, and you will be forced to surrender many things that you now scarcely know you have. I didn't feel that the things I had in mind, such as the pseudo-elegant heap of tin in which we were riding, had any very great value. But life would be very different without them, and I wondered if he had thought of this.

How can one, however, dream of power in any other terms than in the symbols of power? The boy could see that freedom depended on the possession of land; he was persuaded that, in one way or another, Negroes must achieve this possession. In the meantime, he could walk the streets and fear nothing, because there were millions like him, coming soon, now, to power. He was held together, in short, by a dream—though it is just as well to remember that some dreams come true—and was united with his "brothers" on the basis of their color. Perhaps one cannot ask for more. People always seem to band together in accordance to a principle that has nothing to do with love, a principle that releases them from personal responsibility.

Yet I could have hoped that the Muslim movement had been able to inculcate in the demoralized Negro population a truer and more individual sense of its own worth, so that Negroes in the Northern ghettos could begin, in concrete terms, and at whatever price, to change their situation. But in order to change a situation one has first to see it for what it is: in the present case, to accept the fact, whatever one does with it thereafter, that the Negro has been formed by this nation, for better or for worse, and does not belong to any other—not to Africa, and certainly not to Islam. The paradox—and a fearful paradox it is—is that the American Negro can have no future anywhere, on any continent, as long as he is unwilling to accept his past. To accept one's past—one's history—is not the same thing as drowning in it; it is learning how to use it. An invented past can never be used; it cracks and crumbles under the pressures of life like clay in a season of drought. How can the American Negro's past be used? The unprecedented price demanded—and at this embattled hour of the world's history —is the transcendence of the realities of color, of nations, and of altars.

"Anyway," the boy said suddenly, after a very long silence, "things won't ever again be the way they used to be. I know *that*."

And so we arrived in enemy territory, and they set me down at the enemy's door.

No one seems to know where the Nation of Islam gets its money. A vast amount, of course, is contributed by Negroes, but there are rumors to the effect that people like Birchites and certain Texas oil millionaires look with favor on the movement. I have no way of knowing whether there is any truth to the rumors, though since these people make such a point of keeping the races separate, I wouldn't be surprised if for this smoke there was some fire. In any case, during a recent Muslim rally, George Lincoln Rockwell, the chief of the American Nazi party, made a point of contributing about twenty dollars to the cause, and he and Malcolm X decided that, racially speaking, anyway, they were in complete agreement. The glorification of one race and the consequent debasement of another—or others—always has been and always will be a recipe for murder. There is no way around this. If one is permitted to treat any group of people with special disfavor because of their race or the color of their skin, there is no limit to what one will force them to endure, and, since the entire race has been mysteriously indicted, no reason not to attempt to destroy it root and branch. This is precisely what the Nazis attempted. Their only originality lay in the means they used. It is scarcely worthwhile to attempt remembering how many times the sun has looked down on the slaughter of the innocents. I am very much concerned that American Negroes achieve their freedom here in the United States. But I am also concerned for their dignity, for the health of their souls, and must oppose any attempt that Negroes may make to do to others what has been done to them. I think I know —we see it around us every day—the spiritual wasteland to which that road leads. It is so simple a fact and one that is so hard, apparently, to grasp: *Whoever debases others is debasing himself.* That is not a mystical statement but a most realistic one, which is proved by the eyes of any Alabama sheriff—and I would not like to see Negroes ever arrive at so wretched a condition.

Now, it is extremely unlikely that Negroes will ever rise to power in the United States, because they are only approximately a ninth of this nation. They are not in the position of the Africans, who are attempting to reclaim their land and break the colonial yoke and recover from the colonial experience. The Negro situation is dangerous in a different way, both for the Negro qua Negro and for the country of which he forms so troubled and troubling a part. The American Negro is a unique creation; he has no counterpart anywhere, and no predecessors. The Muslims react to this fact by referring to the Negro as "the so-called American Negro" and substituting for the names inherited from slavery the letter "X." It is a fact that every American Negro bears a name that originally belonged to the white man whose chattel he was. I am called Baldwin because I was either sold by my African tribe or kidnapped out of it into the hands of a white Christian named Baldwin, who forced me to kneel at the foot of the cross. I am, then, both visibly and legally the descendant of slaves in a white, Protestant country, and this is what it means to be an American Negro, this is who he is—a kidnapped pagan, who was sold like an animal and treated like one, who was once defined by the American Constitution as "three-fifths" of a man, and who, according to the Dred Scott decision, had no rights that a white man was bound to respect. And today, a hundred years after his technical emancipation, he remains—with the possible exception of the American Indian—the most despised creature in his country. Now, there is simply no possibility of a real change in the Negro's situation without the most radical and far-reaching changes in the American political and social structure. And it is clear that white Americans are not simply unwilling to effect these changes; they are, in the main, so slothful have they become, unable even to envision them. It must be added that the Negro himself no longer believes in the good faith of white Americans—if, indeed, he ever could have. What the Negro *has* discovered, and on an international level, is that power to intimidate which he has always had privately but hitherto could manipulate only privately—for private ends often, for limited ends always. And therefore when the country speaks of a "new" Negro, which it has been doing every hour on the hour for decades, it is not really referring to a change in the Negro, which, in any case, it is quite incapable of assessing, but only to a new difficulty in keeping him in his place, to the fact that it encounters him (again! again!) barring yet another door to its spiritual and social ease. This is probably, hard and odd as it may sound, the most important thing that one human being can do for another—it is certainly *one* of the most important things; hence the torment and necessity of love—and this is the enormous contribution that the Negro has made to this otherwise shapeless and undiscovered country. Consequently, white Americans are in nothing more deluded than in supposing that Negroes could ever have imagined that white people would "give" them anything. It is rare indeed that people give. Most people guard and keep; they suppose that it is they themselves and what they identify with themselves that they are guarding and keeping, whereas what they are actually guarding and keeping is their system of reality and what they assume themselves to be. One can give nothing whatever without giving oneself—that is to say, risking oneself. If one cannot risk oneself, then one is simply incapable of giving. And, after all, one can give freedom only by setting someone free. This, in the case of the Negro, the American republic has never become sufficiently mature to do. White Americans have contented themselves with gestures that are now described as "tokenism." For hard example, white Americans congratulate themselves on the 1954 Supreme Court decision outlawing segregation in the schools; they suppose, in spite of the mountain of evidence that has since accumulated to the contrary, that this was proof of a change of heart—or, as they like to say, progress. Perhaps. It all depends on how one reads the word "progress." Most of the Negroes I know do not believe that this immense concession would ever have been made if it had not been for the competition of the Cold War, and the fact that Africa was clearly liberating herself and therefore had, for political reasons, to be wooed by the descendants of her former masters. Had it been a matter of love or justice, the 1954 decision would surely have occurred sooner; were it not for the realities of power in this difficult era, it might very well not have occurred yet. This seems an extremely harsh way of stating the case—ungrateful, as it were —but the evidence that supports this way of stating it is not easily refuted. I myself do not think that it can be refuted at all. In any event, the sloppy and fatuous nature of American good will can never be relied upon to deal with hard problems. These have been dealt with, when they have been dealt with at all, out of necessity—and in political terms, anyway, necessity means concessions made in order to stay on top. I think this is a fact, which it serves no purpose to deny, *but, whether it is a fact or not, this is what the black population of the world, including black Americans, really believe.* The word "independence" in Africa and the word "integration" here are almost equally meaningless; that is, Europe has not yet left Africa, and black men here are not yet free. And both of these last statements are undeniable facts, related facts, containing the gravest implications for us all. The Negroes of this country may never be able to rise to power, but they are very well placed indeed to precipitate chaos and ring down the curtain on the American dream.

This has everything to do, of course, with the nature of that dream and with the fact that we Americans, of whatever color, do not dare examine it and are far from having made it a reality. There are too many things we do not wish to know about ourselves. People are not, for example, terribly anxious to be equal (equal, after all, to what and to whom?) but they love the idea of being superior. And this human truth has an especially grinding force here, where identity is almost impossible to achieve and people are perpetually attempting to find their feet on the shifting sands of status. (Consider the history of labor in a country in which, spiritually speaking, there are no workers, only candidates for the hand of the boss's daughter.) Furthermore, I have met only a very few people—and most of these were not Americans—who had any real desire to be free. Freedom is hard to bear. It can be objected that I am speaking of political freedom in spiritual terms, but the political institutions of any nation are always menaced and are ultimately controlled by the spiritual state of that nation. We are controlled here by our confusion, far more than we know, and the American dream has therefore become something much more closely resembling a nightmare, on the private, domestic, and international levels. Privately, we cannot stand our lives and dare not examine them; domestically, we take no responsibility for (and no pride in) what goes on in our country; and, internationally, for many millions of people, we are an unmitigated disaster. Whoever doubts this last statement has only to open his ears, his heart, his mind, to the testimony of—for example—any Cuban peasant or any Spanish poet, and ask himself what *he* would feel about us if *he* were the victim of our performance in pre-Castro Cuba or in Spain. We defend our curious role in Spain by referring to the Russian menace and the necessity of protecting the free world. It has not occurred to us that we have simply been mesmerized by Russia, and that the only real advantage Russia has in what we think of as a struggle between the East and the West is the moral history of the Western world. Russia's secret weapon is the bewilderment and despair and hunger of millions of people of whose existence we are scarcely aware. The Russian Communists are not in the least concerned about these people. But our ignorance and indecision have had the effect, if not of delivering them into Russian hands, of plunging them very deeply in the Russian shadow, for which effect— and it is hard to blame them—the most articulate among them, and the most oppressed as well, distrust us all the more. Our power and our fear of change help bind these people to their misery and bewilderment, and insofar as they find this state intolerable we are intolerably menaced. For if they find their state intolerable, but are too heavily oppressed to change it, they are simply pawns in the hands of larger powers, which, in such a context, are always unscrupulous, and when, eventually, they do change their situation—as in Cuba —we are menaced more than ever, by the vacuum that succeeds all violent upheavals. We should certainly know by now that it is one thing to overthrow a dictator or repel an invader and quite another thing really to achieve a revolution. Time and time and time again, the people discover that they have merely betrayed themselves into the hands of yet another Pharaoh, who, since he was necessary to put the broken country together, will not let them go. Perhaps, people being the conundrums that they are, and having so little desire to shoulder the burden of their lives, this is what will always happen. But at the bottom of my heart I do not believe this. I think that people can be better than that, and I know that people can be better than they are. We are capable of bearing a great burden, once we discover that the burden is reality and arrive where reality is. Anyway, the point here is that we are living in an age of revolution, whether we will or no, and that America is the only Western nation with both the power and, as I hope to suggest, the experience that may help to make these revolutions real and minimize the human damage.

Any attempt we make to oppose these outbursts of energy is tantamount to signing our death warrant.

Behind what we think of as the Russian menace lies what we do not wish to face, and what white Americans do not face when they regard a Negro: reality—the fact that life is tragic. Life is tragic simply because the earth turns and the sun inexorably rises and sets, and one day, for each of us, the sun will go down for the last, last time. Perhaps the whole root of our trouble, the human trouble, is that we will sacrifice all the beauty of our lives, will imprison ourselves in totems, taboos, crosses, blood sacrifices, steeples, mosques, races, armies, flags, nations, in order to deny the fact of death, which is the only fact we have. It seems to me that one ought to rejoice in the *fact* of death—ought to decide, indeed, to *earn* one's death by confronting with passion the conundrum of life. One is responsible to life: It is the small beacon in that terrifying darkness from which we come and to which we shall return. One must negotiate this passage as nobly as possible, for the sake of those who are coming after us. But white Americans do not believe in death, and this is why the darkness of my skin so intimidates them. And this is also why the presence of the Negro in this country can bring about its destruction. It is the responsibility of free men to trust and to celebrate what is constant—birth, struggle, and death are constant, and so is love, though we may not always think so—and to apprehend the nature of change, to be able and willing to change. I speak of change not on the surface but in the depths— change in the sense of renewal. But renewal becomes impossible if one supposes things to be constant that are not— safety, for example, or money, or power. One clings then to chimeras, by which one can only be betrayed, and the entire hope—the entire possibility—of freedom disappears. And by destruction I mean precisely the abdication by Americans of any effort really to be free. The Negro can precipitate this abdication because white Americans have never, in all their long history, been able to look on him as a man like themselves. This point need not be labored; it is proved over and over again by the Negro's continuing position here, and his indescribable struggle to defeat the stratagems that white Americans have used, and use, to deny him his humanity. America could have used in other ways the energy that both groups have expended in this conflict. America, of all the Western nations, has been best placed to prove the uselessness and the obsolescence of the concept of color. But it has not dared to accept this opportunity, or even to conceive of it as an opportunity. White Americans have thought of it as their shame, and have envied those more civilized and elegant European nations that were untroubled by the presence of black men on their shores. This is because white Americans have supposed "Europe" and "civilization" to be synonyms—which they are not—and have been distrustful of other standards and other sources of vitality, especially those produced in America itself, and have attempted to behave in all matters as though what was east for Europe was also east for them. What it comes to is that if we, who can scarcely be considered a white nation, persist in thinking of ourselves as one, we condemn ourselves, with the truly white nations, to sterility and decay, whereas if we could accept ourselves *as we are*, we might bring new life to the Western achievements, and transform them. The price of this transformation is the unconditional freedom of the Negro; it is not too much to say that he, who has been so long rejected, must now be embraced, and at no matter what psychic or social risk. He is *the* key figure in his country, and the American future is precisely as bright or as dark as his. And the Negro recognizes this, in a negative way. Hence the question: Do I really *want* to be integrated into a burning house?

White Americans find it as difficult as white people elsewhere do to divest themselves of the notion that they are in possession of some intrinsic value that black people need, or want. And this assumption—which, for example, makes the solution to the Negro problem depend on the speed with which Negroes accept and adopt white standards—is revealed in all kinds of striking ways, from Bobby Kennedy's assurance that a Negro can become President in forty years to the unfortunate tone of warm congratulation with which so many liberals address their Negro equals. It is the Negro, of course, who is presumed to have become equal—an achievement that not only proves the comforting fact that perseverance has no color but also overwhelmingly corroborates the white man's

sense of his own value. Alas, this value can scarcely be cor-
roborated in any other way; there is certainly little enough in
the white man's public or private life that one should desire
to imitate. White men, at the bottom of their hearts, know
this. Therefore, a vast amount of the energy that goes into
what we call the Negro problem is produced by the white
man's profound desire not to be judged by those who are not
white, not to be seen as he is, and at the same time a vast
amount of the white anguish is rooted in the white man's
equally profound need to be seen as he is, to be released from
the tyranny of his mirror. All of us know, whether or not we
are able to admit it, that mirrors can only lie, that death by
drowning is all that awaits one there. It is for this reason that
love is so desperately sought and so cunningly avoided. Love
takes off the masks that we fear we cannot live without and
know we cannot live within. I use the word "love" here not
merely in the personal sense but as a state of being, or a state
of grace—not in the infantile American sense of being made
happy but in the tough and universal sense of quest and daring and growth. And I submit, then, that the racial tensions
that menace Americans today have little to do with real
antipathy—on the contrary, indeed—and are involved only
symbolically with color. These tensions are rooted in the very
same depths as those from which love springs, or murder.
The white man's unadmitted—and apparently, to him, unspeakable—private fears and longings are projected onto the
Negro. The only way he can be released from the Negro's
tyrannical power over him is to consent, in effect, to become
black himself, to become a part of that suffering and dancing
country that he now watches wistfully from the heights of his
lonely power and, armed with spiritual traveller's checks, visits surreptitiously after dark. How can one respect, let alone
adopt, the values of a people who do not, on any level whatever, live the way they say they do, or the way they say they
should? I cannot accept the proposition that the four-hundred-
year travail of the American Negro should result merely in
his attainment of the present level of the American civilization. I am far from convinced that being released from the
African witch doctor was worthwhile if I am now—in order to
support the moral contradictions and the spiritual aridity of

my life—expected to become dependent on the American psychiatrist. It is a bargain I refuse. The only thing white people have that black people need, or should want, is power —and no one holds power forever. White people cannot, in the generality, be taken as models of how to live. Rather, the white man is himself in sore need of new standards, which will release him from his confusion and place him once again in fruitful communion with the depths of his own being. And I repeat: The price of the liberation of the white people is the liberation of the blacks—the total liberation, in the cities, in the towns, before the law, and in the mind. Why, for example —especially knowing the family as I do—I should *want* to marry your sister is a great mystery to me. But your sister and I have every right to marry if we wish to, and no one has the right to stop us. If she cannot raise me to her level, perhaps I can raise her to mine.

In short, we, the black and the white, deeply need each other here if we are really to become a nation—if we are really, that is, to achieve our identity, our maturity, as men and women. To create one nation has proved to be a hideously difficult task; there is certainly no need now to create two, one black and one white. But white men with far more political power than that possessed by the Nation of Islam movement have been advocating exactly this, in effect, for generations. If this sentiment is honored when it falls from the lips of Senator Byrd, then there is no reason it should not be honored when it falls from the lips of Malcolm X. And any Congressional committee wishing to investigate the latter must also be willing to investigate the former. They are expressing exactly the same sentiments and represent exactly the same danger. There is absolutely no reason to suppose that white people are better equipped to frame the laws by which I am to be governed than I am. It is entirely unacceptable that I should have no voice in the political affairs of my own country, for I am not a ward of America; I am one of the first Americans to arrive on these shores.

This past, the Negro's past, of rope, fire, torture, castration, infanticide, rape; death and humiliation; fear by day and night, fear as deep as the marrow of the bone; doubt that he was worthy of life, since everyone around him denied it;

sorrow for his women, for his kinfolk, for his children, who
needed his protection, and whom he could not protect; rage,
hatred, and murder, hatred for white men so deep that it often turned against him and his own, and made all love, all
trust, all joy impossible—this past, this endless struggle to
achieve and reveal and confirm a human identity, human authority, yet contains, for all its horror, something very beautiful. I do not mean to be sentimental about suffering—enough
is certainly as good as a feast—but people who cannot suffer
can never grow up, can never discover who they are. That
man who is forced each day to snatch his manhood, his identity, out of the fire of human cruelty that rages to destroy it
knows, if he survives his effort, and even if he does not survive it, something about himself and human life that no
school on earth—and, indeed, no church—can teach. He
achieves his own authority, and that is unshakable. This is because, in order to save his life, he is forced to look beneath
appearances, to take nothing for granted, to hear the meaning
behind the words. If one is continually surviving the worst
that life can bring, one eventually ceases to be controlled by a
fear of what life can bring; whatever it brings must be borne.
And at this level of experience one's bitterness begins to be
palatable, and hatred becomes too heavy a sack to carry. The
apprehension of life here so briefly and inadequately sketched
has been the experience of generations of Negroes, and it
helps to explain how they have endured and how they have
been able to produce children of kindergarten age who can
walk through mobs to get to school. It demands great force
and great cunning continually to assault the mighty and in-
different fortress of white supremacy, as Negroes in this country have done so long. It demands great spiritual resilience
not to hate the hater whose foot is on your neck, and an even
greater miracle of perception and charity not to teach your
child to hate. The Negro boys and girls who are facing mobs
today come out of a long line of improbable aristocrats—the
only genuine aristocrats this country has produced. I say "this
country" because their frame of reference was totally American. They were hewing out of the mountain of white supremacy the stone of their individuality. I have great respect
for that unsung army of black men and women who trudged

down back lanes and entered back doors, saying "Yes, sir" and
"No, Ma'am" in order to acquire a new roof for the schoolhouse, new books, a new chemistry lab, more beds for the
dormitories, more dormitories. They did not like saying "Yes,
sir" and "No Ma'am," but the country was in no hurry to educate Negroes, these black men and women knew that the
job had to be done, and they put their pride in their pockets
in order to do it. It is very hard to believe that they were in
any way inferior to the white men and women who opened
those back doors. It is very hard to believe that those men
and women, raising their children, eating their greens, crying
their curses, weeping their tears, singing their songs, making
their love, as the sun rose, as the sun set, were in any way inferior to the white men and women who crept over to share
these splendors after the sun went down. But we must avoid
the European error; we must not suppose that, because the
situation, the ways, the perceptions of black people so radically differed from those of whites, they were racially superior.
I am proud of these people not because of their color but because of their intelligence and their spiritual force and their
beauty. The country should be proud of them, too, but, alas,
not many people in this country even know of their existence.
And the reason for this ignorance is that a knowledge of the
role these people played—and play—in American life would
reveal more about America to Americans than Americans wish
to know.

The American Negro has the great advantage of having
never believed that collection of myths to which white Americans cling: that their ancestors were all freedom-loving
heroes, that they were born in the greatest country the world
has ever seen, or that Americans are invincible in battle and
wise in peace, that Americans have always dealt honorably
with Mexicans and Indians and all other neighbors or inferi-
ors, that American men are the world's most direct and virile,
that American women are pure. Negroes know far more
about white Americans than that; it can almost be said, in
fact, that they know about white Americans what parents—or,
anyway, mothers—know about their children, and that they
very often regard white Americans that way. And perhaps this
attitude, held in spite of what they know and have endured,

helps to explain why Negroes, on the whole, and until lately, have allowed themselves to feel so little hatred. The tendency has really been, insofar as this was possible, to dismiss white people as the slightly mad victims of their own brainwashing. One watched the lives they led. One could not be fooled about that; one watched the things they did and the excuses that they gave themselves, and if a white man was really in trouble, deep trouble, it was to the Negro's door that he came. And one felt that if one had had that white man's worldly advantages, one would never have become as bewildered and as joyless and as thoughtlessly cruel as he. The Negro came to the white man for a roof or for five dollars or for a letter to the judge; the white man came to the Negro for love. But he was not often able to give what he came seeking. The price was too high; he had too much to lose. And the Negro knew this, too. When one knows this about a man, it is impossible for one to hate him, but unless he becomes a man—becomes equal—it is also impossible for one to love him. Ultimately, one tends to avoid him, for the universal characteristic of children is to assume that they have a monopoly on trouble, and therefore a monopoly on *you*. (Ask any Negro what he knows about the white people with whom he works. And then ask the white people with whom he works what they know about *him*.)

How can the American Negro past be used? It is entirely possible that this dishonored past will rise up soon to smite all of us. There are some wars, for example (if anyone on the globe is still mad enough to go to war), that the American Negro will not support, however many of his people may be coerced—and there is a limit to the number of people any government can put in prison, and a rigid limit indeed to the practicality of such a course. A bill is coming in that I fear America is not prepared to pay. "The problem of the twentieth century," wrote W.E.B. Du Bois around sixty years ago, "is the problem of the color line." A fearful and delicate problem, which compromises, when it does not corrupt, all the American efforts to build a better world—here, there, or anywhere. It is for this reason that everything white Americans think they believe in must now be reëxamined. What one would not like to see again is the consolidation of peoples on the basis of their color. But as long as we in the West place on color the value that we do, we make it impossible for the great unwashed to consolidate themselves according to any other principle. Color is not a human or a personal reality; it is a political reality. But this is a distinction so extremely hard to make that the West has not been able to make it yet. And at the center of this dreadful storm, this vast confusion, stand the black people of this nation, who must now share the fate of a nation that has never accepted them, to which they were brought in chains. Well, if this is so, one has no choice but to do all in one's power to change that fate, and at no matter what risk—eviction, imprisonment, torture, death. For the sake of one's children, in order to minimize the bill that *they* must pay, one must be careful not to take refuge in any delusion—and the value placed on the color of the skin is always and everywhere and forever a delusion. I know that what I am asking is impossible. But in our time, as in every time, the impossible is the least that one can demand—and one is, after all, emboldened by the spectacle of human history in general, and American Negro history in particular, for it testifies to nothing less than the perpetual achievement of the impossible.

When I was very young, and was dealing with my buddies in those wine- and urine-stained hallways, something in me wondered, *What will happen to all that beauty?* For black people, though I am aware that some of us, black and white, do not know it yet, are very beautiful. And when I sat at Elijah's table and watched the baby, the women, and the men, and we talked about God's—or Allah's—vengeance, I wondered, when that vengeance was achieved, *What will happen to all that beauty then?* I could also see that the intransigence and ignorance of the white world might make that vengeance inevitable—a vengeance that does not really depend on, and cannot really be executed by, any person or organization, and that cannot be prevented by any police force or army: historical vengeance, a cosmic vengeance, based on the law that we recognize when we say, "Whatever goes up must come down." And here we are, at the center of the arc, trapped in the gaudiest, most valuable, and most improbable water wheel the world has ever seen. Everything now, we must assume, is in our hands; we have no right to assume otherwise.

If we—and now I mean the relatively conscious whites and the relatively conscious blacks, who must, like lovers, insist on, or create, the consciousness of the others—do not falter in our duty now, we may be able, handful that we are, to end the racial nightmare, and achieve our country, and change the history of the world. If we do not now dare everything, the fulfillment of that prophecy, re-created from the Bible in song by a slave, is upon us: *God gave Noah the rainbow sign, No more water, the fire next time!*

from *The Fire Next Time* (1963)

My Negro Problem—and Ours

by Norman Podhoretz

If we—and . . . I mean the relatively conscious whites and the relatively conscious blacks, who must, like lovers, insist on, or create, the consciousness of the others—do not falter in our duty now, we may be able, handful that we are, to end the racial nightmare, and achieve our country, and change the history of the world.

—James Baldwin

Two IDEAS puzzled me deeply as a child growing up in Brooklyn during the 1930's in what today would be called an integrated neighborhood. One of them was that all Jews were rich; the other was that all Negroes were persecuted. These ideas had appeared in print; therefore they must be true. My own experience and the evidence of my senses told me they were not true, but that only confirmed what a day-dreaming boy in the provinces—for the lower-class neighborhoods of New York belong as surely to the provinces as any rural town in North Dakota—discovers very early: *his* experience is unreal and the evidence of his senses is not to be trusted. Yet even a boy with a head full of fantasies incongruously synthesized out of Hollywood movies and English novels cannot altogether deny the reality of his own experience—especially when there is so much deprivation in that experience. Nor can he altogether gainsay the evidence of his own senses—especially such evidence of the senses as comes from being repeatedly beaten up, robbed, and in general hated, terrorized, and humiliated.

And so for a long time I was puzzled to think that Jews were supposed to be rich when the only Jews I knew were poor, and that Negroes were supposed to be persecuted when it was the Negroes who were doing the only persecuting I knew about—and doing it, moreover, to *me*. During the early years of the war, when my older sister joined a left-wing youth organization, I remember my astonishment at hearing her passionately denounce my father for thinking that Jews were worse off than Negroes. To me, at the age of twelve, it seemed very clear that Negroes were better off than Jews—indeed, than *all* whites. A city boy's world is contained within three or four square blocks, and in my world it was the whites, the Italians and Jews, who feared the Negroes, not the other way around. The Negroes were tougher than we were, more ruthless, and on the whole they were better athletes. What could it mean, then, to say that they were badly off and that we were more fortunate? Yet my sister's opinions, like print, were sacred, and when she told me about exploitation and economic forces I believed her. I believed her, but I was still afraid of Negroes. And I still hated them with all my heart.

It had not always been so—that much I can recall from early childhood. When did it start, this fear and this hatred? There was a kindergarten in the local public school, and given the character of the neighborhood, at least half of the children in my class must have been Negroes. Yet I have no memory of being aware of color differences at that age, and I know from observing my own children that they attribute no significance to such differences even when they begin noticing them. I think there was a day—first grade? second grade?—when my best friend Carl hit me on the way home from school and announced that he wouldn't play with me any more because I had killed Jesus. When I ran home to my mother crying for an explanation, she told me not to pay any attention to such foolishness, and then in Yiddish she cursed the *goyim* and the *schwartzes*, the *schwartzes* and the *goyim*. Carl, it turned out, was a *schwartze*, and so was added a third to the categories into which people were mysteriously divided.

Sometimes I wonder whether this is a true memory at all. It is blazingly vivid, but perhaps it never happened: can anyone really remember back to the age of six? There is no uncertainty in my mind, however, about the years that followed. Carl and I hardly ever spoke, though we met in school every day up through the eighth or ninth grade. There would be embarrassed moments of catching his eye or of his catching mine—for whatever it was that had attracted us to one another as very small children remained alive in spite of the fantastic barrier of hostility that had grown up between us, suddenly and out of nowhere. Nevertheless, friendship would have been impossible, and even if it had been possible, it would have been unthinkable. About that, there was nothing anyone could do by the time we were eight years old.

Item: The orphanage across the street is torn down, a city housing project begins to rise in its place, and on the marvelous vacant lot next to the old orphanage they are building a playground. Much excitement and anticipation as Opening Day draws near. Mayor LaGuardia himself comes to dedicate this great gesture of public benevolence. He speaks of neighborliness and borrowing cups of sugar, and of the playground he says that children of all races, colors, and creeds will learn to live together in harmony. A week later, some of us are swatting flies on the playground's inadequate little ball field. A gang of Negro kids, pretty much our own age, enter from the other side and order us out of the park. We refuse, proudly and indignantly, with superb masculine fervor. There is a fight, they win, and we retreat, half whimpering, half with bravado. My first nauseating experience of cowardice. And my first appalled realization that there are people in the world who do not seem to be afraid of anything, who act as though they have nothing to lose. Thereafter the playground becomes a battleground, sometimes quiet, sometimes the scene of athletic competition between Them and Us. But rocks are thrown as often as baseballs. Gradually we abandon the place and use the streets instead. The streets are safer, though we do not admit this to ourselves. We are not, after all, sissies—that most dreaded epithet of an American boyhood.

Item: I am standing alone in front of the building in which I live. It is late afternoon and getting dark. That day in school the teacher had asked a surly Negro boy named Quentin a question he was unable to answer. As usual I had waved my arm eagerly ("Be a good boy, get good marks, be smart, go to college, become a doctor") and, the right answer bursting from my lips, I was held up lovingly by the teacher as an example to the class. I had seen Quentin's face—a very dark, very cruel, very Oriental-looking face—harden, and there had been enough threat in his eyes to make me run all the way home for fear that he might catch me outside.

Now, standing idly in front of my own house, I see him approaching from the project accompanied by his little brother who is carrying a baseball bat and wearing a grin of malicious anticipation. As in a nightmare, I am trapped. The surroundings are secure and familiar, but terror is suddenly present and there is no one around to help. I am locked to the spot. I will not cry out or run away like a sissy, and I stand there, my heart wild, my throat clogged. He walks up, hurls the familiar epithet ("Hey, mo'f——r"), and to my surprise only pushes me. It is a violent push, but not a punch. A push is not as serious as a punch. Maybe I can still back out without entirely losing my dignity. Maybe I can still say, "Hey, c'mon Quentin, whaddya wanna do *that* for. I dint do nothin' to *you*," and walk away, not too rapidly. Instead, before I can stop myself, I push him back—a token gesture—and I say, "Cut that out, I don't wanna fight, I ain't got nothin' to fight about." As I turn to walk back into the building, the corner of my eye catches the motion of the bat his little brother has handed him. I try to duck, but the bat crashes colored lights into my head.

The next thing I know, my mother and sister are standing over me, both of them hysterical. My sister—she who was later to join the "progressive" youth organization—is shouting for the police and screaming imprecations at those dirty little black bastards. They take me upstairs, the doctor comes, the police come. I tell them that the boy who did it was a stranger, that he had been trying to get money from me. They do not believe me, but I am too scared to give them Quentin's name. When I return to school a few days later, Quentin avoids my eyes. He knows that I have not squealed, and he is ashamed. I try to feel proud, but in my heart I know that it was fear of what his friends might do to me that had kept me silent, and not the code of the street.

Item: There is an athletic meet in which the whole of our junior high school is participating. I am in one of the seventh-grade rapid-advance classes, and "segregation" has now set in with a vengeance. In the last three or four years of the elementary school from which we have just graduated, each grade had been divided into three classes, according to "in-telligence." (In the earlier grades the divisions had either been arbitrary or else unrecognized by us as having anything to do with brains.) These divisions by IQ, or however it was arranged, had resulted in a preponderance of Jews in the "1" classes and a corresponding preponderance of Negroes in the "3's," with the Italians split unevenly along the spectrum. At least a few Negroes had always made the "1's," just as there had always been a few Jewish kids among the "3's" and more among the "2's" (where Italians dominated). But the junior high's rapid-advance class of which I am now a member is overwhelmingly Jewish and entirely white—except for a shy lonely Negro girl with light skin and reddish hair.

The athletic meet takes place in a city-owned stadium far from the school. It is an important event to which a whole day is given over. The winners are to get those precious little medallions stamped with the New York City emblem that can be screwed into a belt and that prove the wearer to be a dis-tinguished personage. I am a fast runner, and so I am as-signed the position of anchor man on my class's team in the relay race. There are three other seventh-grade teams in the race, two of them all Negro, as ours is all white. One of the all-Negro teams is very tall—their anchor man waiting silently next to me on the line looks years older than I am, and I do not recognize him. He is the first to get the baton and crosses the finishing line in a walk. Our team comes in second, but a few minutes later we are declared the winners, for it has been discovered that the anchor man on the first-place team is not a member of the class. We are awarded the medallions, and the following day our home-room teacher makes a speech about how proud she is of us for being supe-rior athletes as well as superior students. We want to believe that we deserve the praise, but we know that we could not have won even if the other class had not cheated.

That afternoon, walking home, I am waylaid and sur-rounded by five Negroes, among whom is the anchor man of the disqualified team. "Gimme my medal, mo'f——r," he grunts. I do not have it with me and I tell him so. "Anyway, it ain't yours," I say foolishly. He calls me a liar on both counts and pushes me up against the wall on which we sometimes play handball. "Gimme my mo'f——n' medal," he says again. I repeat that I have left it home. "Le's search the li'l mo'f——r," one of them suggests, "he prolly got it *hid* in his mo'f——n' *pants*." My panic is now unmanageable. (How many times had I been surrounded like this and asked in soft tones, "Len' me a nickle, boy." How many times had I been called a liar for pleading poverty and pushed around, or searched, or beaten up, unless there happened to be someone in the marauding gang like Carl who liked me across that enormous divide of hatred and who would therefore say, "Aaah, c'mon, le's git someone else, *this* boy ain't got no money on 'im.") I scream at them through tears of rage and self-contempt, "Keep your f——n' filthy lousy black hands offa me! I swear I'll get the cops." This is all they need to hear, and the five of them set upon me. They bang me around, mostly in the stomach and on the arms and shoulders, and when several adults loitering near the candy store down the block notice what is going on and begin to shout, they run off and away.

I do not tell my parents about the incident. My teammates, who have also been waylaid, each by a gang led by his opposite number from the disqualified team, have had their medallions taken from them, and they never squeal either. For days, I walk home in terror, expecting to be caught again, but nothing happens. The medallion is put away into a drawer, never to be worn by anyone.

Obviously experiences like these have always been a common feature of childhood life in working-class and immigrant neighborhoods, and Negroes do not necessarily figure in them. Wherever, and in whatever combination, they have lived together in the cities, kids of different groups have been at war, beating up and being beaten up: micks against kikes against wops against spicks against polacks. And even relatively homogeneous areas have not been spared the warring of the young: one block against another, one gang (called in my day, in a pathetic effort at gentility, an "S.A.C.," or social-athletic club) against another. But the Negro-white conflict had—and no doubt still has—a special intensity and was conducted with a ferocity unmatched by intramural white battling.

In my own neighborhood, a good deal of animosity existed between the Italian kids (most of whose parents were immigrants from Sicily) and the Jewish kids (who came largely from East European immigrant families). Yet everyone had friends, sometimes close friends, in the other "camp," and we often visited one another's strange-smelling houses, if not for meals, then for glasses of milk, and occasionally for some special event like a wedding or a wake. If it happened that we divided into warring factions and did battle, it would invariably be half-hearted and soon patched up. Our parents, to be sure, had nothing to do with one another and were mutually suspicious and hostile. But we, the kids, who all spoke Yiddish or Italian at home, were Americans, or New Yorkers, or Brooklyn boys: we shared a culture, the culture of the street, and at least for a while this culture proved to be more powerful than the opposing cultures of the home.

Why, *why* should it have been so different as between the Negroes and us? How was it borne in upon us so early, white and black alike, that we were enemies beyond any possibility of reconciliation? Why did we hate one another so?

I suppose if I tried, I could answer those questions more or less adequately from the perspective of what I have since learned. I could draw upon James Baldwin—what better witness is there?—to describe the sense of entrapment that poisons the soul of the Negro with hatred for the white man whom he knows to be his jailer. On the other side, if I wanted to understand how the white man comes to hate the Negro, I could call upon the psychologists who have spoken of the guilt that white Americans feel toward Negroes and that turns into hatred for lack of acknowledging itself as guilt. These are plausible answers and certainly there is truth in them. Yet when I think back upon my own experience of the Negro and his of me, I find myself troubled and puzzled, much as I was as a child when I heard that all Jews were rich and all Negroes persecuted. How could the Negroes in my neighborhood have regarded the whites across the street and around the corner as jailers? On the whole, the whites were not so poor as the Negroes, but they were quite poor enough, and the years were years of Depression. As for white hatred of the Negro, how could guilt have had anything to do with it? What share had these Italian and Jewish immigrants in the enslavement of the Negro? What share had they—downtrodden people themselves breaking their own necks to eke out a living—in the exploitation of the Negro?

No, I cannot believe that we hated each other back there in Brooklyn because they thought of us as jailers and we felt guilty toward them. But does it matter, given the fact that we all went through an unrepresentative confrontation? I think it matters profoundly, for if we managed the job of hating each other so well without benefit of the aids to hatred that are supposedly at the root of this madness everywhere else, it must mean that the madness is not yet properly understood. I am far from pretending that I understand it, but I would insist that no view of the problem will begin to approach the truth unless it can account for a case like the one I have been trying to describe. Are the elements of any such view available to us?

At least two, I would say, are. One of them is a point we frequently come upon in the work of James Baldwin, and the other is a related point always stressed by psychologists who have studied the mechanisms of prejudice. Baldwin tells us that one of the reasons Negroes hate the white man is that the white man refuses to *look* at him: the Negro knows that in white eyes all Negroes are alike; they are faceless and therefore not altogether human. The psychologists, in their turn, tell us that the white man hates the Negro because he tends to project those wild impulses that he fears in himself onto an alien group which he then punishes with his contempt. What Baldwin does *not* tell us, however, is that the principle of facelessness is a two-way street and can operate in both directions with no difficulty at all. Thus, in my neighborhood in Brooklyn, *I* was as faceless to the Negroes as they were to me, and if they hated me because I never looked at them, I must also have hated them for never looking at *me*. To the Negroes, my white skin was enough to define me as the enemy, and in a war it is only the uniform that counts and not the person.

So with the mechanism of projection that the psychologists talk about: it too works in both directions at once. There is no question that the psychologists are right about what the Negro represents symbolically to the white man. For me as a child the life lived on the other side of the playground and down the block on Ralph Avenue seemed the very embodiment of the values of the street—free, independent, reckless, brave, masculine, erotic. I put the word "erotic" last, though it is usually stressed above all others, because in fact it came last, in consciousness as in importance. What mainly counted for me about Negro kids of my own age was that they were "bad boys." There were plenty of bad boys among the whites —this was, after all, a neighborhood with a long tradition of crime as a career open to aspiring talents—but the Negroes were *really* bad, bad in a way that beckoned to one, and made one feel inadequate. *We* all went home every day for a lunch of spinach-and-potatoes; *they* roamed around during lunch hour, munching on candy bars. In winter *we* had to wear itchy woolen hats and mittens and cumbersome galoshes; *they* were bare-headed and loose as they pleased. *We* rarely played hookey, or got into serious trouble in school, for all our street-corner bravado; *they* were defiant, forever staying out (to do what delicious things?), forever making disturbances in class and in the halls, forever being sent to the principal and returning uncowed. But most important of all, they were *tough*; beautifully, enviably tough, not giving a damn for anyone or anything. To hell with the teacher, the truant officer, the cop; to hell with the whole of the adult world that held *us* in its grip and that we never had the courage to rebel against except sporadically and in petty ways.

This is what I saw and envied and feared in the Negro: this is what finally made him faceless to me, though some of it, of course, was actually there. (The psychologists also tell us that the alien group which becomes the object of a projection will tend to respond by trying to live up to what is expected of them.) But what, on his side, did the Negro see in me that made me faceless to *him*? Did he envy me my lunches of spinach-and-potatoes and my itchy woolen caps and my prudent behavior in the face of authority, as I envied him his noon-time candy bars and his bare head in winter and his magnificent rebelliousness? Did those lunches and caps spell for him the prospect of power and riches in the future? Did they mean that there were possibilities open to me that were denied to him? Very likely they did. But if so, one also sup-

poses that he feared the impulses within himself toward sub-
mission to authority no less powerfully than I feared the impulses in myself toward defiance. If I represented the jailer to
him, it was not because I was oppressing him or keeping him
down: it was because I symbolized for him the dangerous and
probably pointless temptation toward greater repression, just
as he symbolized for me the equally perilous tug toward
greater freedom. I personally was to be rewarded for this repression with a new and better life in the future, but how
many of my friends paid an even higher price and were given
only gall in return.

We have it on the authority of James Baldwin that all Negroes hate whites. I am trying to suggest that on their side all
whites—all American whites, that is—are sick in their feelings
about Negroes. There are Negroes, no doubt, who would say
that Baldwin is wrong, but I suspect them of being less honest than he is, just as I suspect whites of self-deception who
tell me they have no special feeling toward Negroes. Special
feelings about color are a contagion to which white Americans seem susceptible even when there is nothing in their
background to account for the susceptibility. Thus everywhere we look today in the North, we find the curious phenomenon of white middle-class liberals with no previous
personal experience of Negroes—people to whom Negroes
have always been faceless in virtue rather than faceless in vice
—discovering that their abstract commitment to the cause of
Negro rights will not stand the test of a direct confrontation.
We find such people fleeing in droves to the suburbs as the
Negro population in the inner city grows; and when they stay
in the city we find them sending their children to private
school rather than to the "integrated" public school in the
neighborhood. We find them resisting the demand that gerry-
mandered school districts be re-zoned for the purpose of
overcoming de facto segregation; we find them judiciously
considering whether the Negroes (for their own good, of
course) are not perhaps pushing too hard; we find them
clucking their tongues over Negro militancy; we find them
speculating on the question of whether there may not, after
all, be something in the theory that the races are biologically
different; we find them saying that it will take a very long

time for Negroes to achieve full equality, no matter what any-one does; we find them deploring the rise of black national-ism and expressing the solemn hope that the leaders of the Negro community will discover ways of containing the impa-tience and incipient violence within the Negro ghettos.

But that is by no means the whole story; there is also the phenomenon of what Kenneth Rexroth once called "crow-jimism." There are the broken-down white boys like Vivaldo Moore in Baldwin's *Another Country* who go to Harlem in search of sex or simply to brush up against something that looks like primitive vitality, and who are so often punished by the Negroes they meet for crimes that they would have been the last ever to commit and of which they themselves have been as sorry victims as any of the Negroes who take it out on them. There are the writers and intellectuals and artists who romanticize Negroes and pander to them, assuming a guilt that is not properly theirs. And there are all the white liberals who permit Negroes to blackmail them into adopting a dou-ble standard of moral judgment, and who lend themselves—again assuming the responsibility for crimes they never com-mitted—to cunning and contemptuous exploitation by Ne-groes they employ or try to befriend.

And what about me? What kind of feelings do I have about Negroes today? What happened to me, from Brooklyn, who grew up fearing and envying and hating Negroes? Now that Brooklyn is behind me, do I fear them and envy them and hate them still? The answer is yes, but not in the same pro-portions and certainly not in the same way. I now live on the upper west side of Manhattan, where there are many Negroes and many Puerto Ricans, and there are nights when I experi-ence the old apprehensiveness again, and there are streets that I avoid when I am walking in the dark, as there were streets that I avoided when I was a child. I find that I am not afraid of Puerto Ricans, but I cannot restrain my nervousness when-ever I pass a group of Negroes standing in front of a bar or sauntering down the street. I know now, as I did not know when I was a child, that power is on my side, that the police are working for me and not for them. And knowing this I feel ashamed and guilty, like the good liberal I have grown up to be. Yet the twinges of fear and the resentment they bring and the self-contempt they arouse are not to be gainsaid.

But envy? Why envy? And hatred? Why hatred? Here again the intensities have lessened and everything has been complicated and qualified by the guilts and the resulting over-compensations that are the heritage of the enlightened middle-class world of which I am now a member. Yet just as in childhood I envied Negroes for what seemed to me their superior masculinity, so I envy them today for what seems to me their superior physical grace and beauty. I have come to value physical grace very highly, and I am now capable of aching with all my being when I watch a Negro couple on the dance floor, or a Negro playing baseball or basketball. They are on the kind of terms with their own bodies that I should like to be on with mine, and for that precious quality they seem blessed to me.

The hatred I still feel for Negroes is the hardest of all the old feelings to face or admit, and it is the most hidden and the most overlarded by the conscious attitudes into which I have succeeded in willing myself. It no longer has, as for me it once did, any cause or justification (except, perhaps, that I am constantly being denied my right to an honest expression of the things I earned the right as a child to feel). How, then, do I know that this hatred has never entirely disappeared? I know it from the insane rage that can stir in me at the thought of Negro anti-Semitism; I know it from the disgusting prurience that can stir in me at the sight of a mixed couple; and I know it from the violence that can stir in me whenever I encounter that special brand of paranoid touchiness to which many Negroes are prone.

This, then, is where I am; it is not exactly where I think all other white liberals are, but it cannot be so very far away either. And it is because I am convinced that we white Americans are—for whatever reason, it no longer matters—so twisted and sick in our feelings about Negroes that I despair of the present push toward integration. If the pace of progress were not a factor here, there would perhaps be no cause for despair: time and the law and even the international political situation are on the side of the Negroes, and ultimately, therefore, victory—of a sort, anyway—must come. But from everything we have learned from observers who ought to know, pace has become as important to the Negroes as substance. They want equality and they want it *now*, and the white world is yielding to their demand only as much and as fast as it is absolutely being compelled to do. The Negroes know this in the most concrete terms imaginable, and it is thus becoming increasingly difficult to buy them off with rhetoric and promises and pious assurances of support. And so within the Negro community we find more and more people declaring—as Harold R. Isaacs recently put it in these pages—that they want *out*: people who say that integration will never come, or that it will take a hundred or a thousand years to come, or that it will come at too high a price in suffering and struggle for the pallid and sodden life of the American middle class that at the very best it may bring.

The most numerous, influential, and dangerous movement that has grown out of Negro despair with the goal of integration is, of course, the Black Muslims. This movement, whatever else we may say about it, must be credited with one enduring achievement: it inspired James Baldwin to write an essay which deserves to be placed among the classics of our language. Everything Baldwin has ever been trying to tell us is distilled here into a statement of overwhelming persuasiveness and prophetic magnificence. Baldwin's message is and always has been simple. It is this: "Color is not a human or personal reality; it is a political reality." And Baldwin's demand is correspondingly simple: color must be forgotten, lest we all be smited with a vengeance "that does not really depend on, and cannot really be executed by, any person or organization, and that cannot be prevented by any police force or army: historical vengeance, a cosmic vengeance based on the law that we recognize when we say, 'Whatever goes up must come down.'" The Black Muslims Baldwin portrays as a sign and a warning to the intransigent white world. They come to proclaim how deep is the Negro's disaffection with the white world and all its works, and Baldwin implies that no American Negro can fail to respond somewhere in his being to their message: that the white man is the devil, that Allah has doomed him to destruction, and that the black man is about to inherit the earth. Baldwin of course knows that this nightmare inversion of the racism from which the black man has suffered can neither win nor even point to the neighborhood in which victory might be located. For in his view the neighborhood of victory lies in exactly the opposite direction: the transcendence of color through love.

Yet the tragic fact is that love is not the answer to hate— not in the world of politics, at any rate. Color is indeed a political rather than a human or a personal reality and if politics (which is to say power) has made it into a human and a personal reality, then only politics (which is to say power) can unmake it once again. But the way of politics is slow and bitter, and as impatience on the one side is matched by a setting of the jaw on the other, we move closer and closer to an explosion and blood may yet run in the streets.

Will this madness in which we are all caught never find a resting-place? Is there never to be an end to it? In thinking about the Jews I have often wondered whether their survival as a distinct group was worth one hair on the head of a single infant. Did the Jews have to survive so that six million innocent people should one day be burned in the ovens of Auschwitz? It is a terrible question and no one, not God himself, could ever answer it to my satisfaction. And when I think about the Negroes in America and about the image of integration as a state in which the Negroes would take their rightful place as another of the protected minorities in a pluralistic society, I wonder whether they really believe in their hearts that such a state can actually be attained, and if so *why* they should wish to survive as a distinct group. I think I know why the Jews once wished to survive (though I am less certain as to why we still do): they not only believed that God had given them no choice, but they were tied to a memory of past glory and a dream of imminent redemption. What does the American Negro have that might correspond to this? His past is a stigma, his color is a stigma, and his vision of the future is the hope of erasing the stigma by making color irrelevant, by making it disappear as a fact of consciousness.

I share this hope, but I cannot see how it will ever be realized unless color does *in fact* disappear: and that means not integration, it means assimilation, it means—let the brutal word come out—miscegenation. The Black Muslims, like their racist counterparts in the white world, accuse the "so-called Negro leaders" of secretly pursuing miscegenation as a goal. The racists are wrong, but I wish they were right, for I believe that the wholesale merging of the two races is the most desirable alternative for everyone concerned. I am not claiming that this alternative can be pursued programmatically or that it is immediately feasible as a solution; obviously there are even greater barriers to its achievement than to the achievement of integration. What I am saying, however, is that in my opinion the Negro problem can be solved in this country in no other way.

I have told the story of my own twisted feelings about Negroes here, and of how they conflict with the moral convictions I have since developed, in order to assert that such feelings must be acknowledged as honestly as possible so that they can be controlled and ultimately disregarded in favor of the convictions. It is *wrong* for a man to suffer because of the color of his skin. Beside that clichéd proposition of liberal thought, what argument can stand and be respected? If the arguments are the arguments of feeling, they must be made to yield; and one's own soul is not the worst place to begin working a huge social transformation. Not so long ago, it used to be asked of white liberals, "Would you like your sister to marry one?" When I was a boy and my sister was still unmarried, I would certainly have said no to that question. But now I am a man, my sister is already married, and I have daughters. If I were to be asked today whether I would like a daughter of mine "to marry one," I would have to answer: "No, I wouldn't *like* it at all. I would rail and rave and rant and tear my hair. And then I hope I would have the courage to curse myself for raving and ranting, and to give her my blessing. How dare I withhold it at the behest of the child I once was and against the man I now have a duty to be?"

Commentary, February 1963

Letter from Birmingham Jail

by Martin Luther King Jr.

MY DEAR FELLOW CLERGYMEN:

While confined here in the Birmingham city jail I came across your recent statement calling my present activities "unwise and untimely." Seldom do I pause to answer criticism of my work and ideas. If I sought to answer all the criticisms that cross my desk, my secretaries would have little time for anything other than such correspondence in the course of the day, and I would have no time for constructive work. But since I feel that you are men of genuine good will and that your criticisms are sincerely set forth, I want to try to answer your statement in what I hope will be patient and reasonable terms.

I think I should indicate why I am here in Birmingham, since you have been influenced by the view which argues against "outsiders coming in." I have the honor of serving as president of the Southern Christian Leadership Conference, an organization operating in every southern state, with headquarters in Atlanta, Georgia. We have some 85 affiliate organizations across the south, and one of them is the Alabama Christian Movement for Human Rights. Frequently we share staff, educational and financial resources with our affiliates. Several months ago the affiliate here in Birmingham asked us to be on call to engage in a nonviolent direct action program if such were deemed necessary. We readily consented, and when the hour came we lived up to our promise. So I, along with several members of my staff, am here because I was invited here. I am here because I have organizational ties here.

I

But more basically, I am in Birmingham because injustice exists here. Just as the prophets of the eighth century B.C. left their villages and carried their "thus saith the Lord" far afield and just as the Apostle Paul left his village of Tarsus and carried the gospel of Jesus Christ to the far corners of the Greco-Roman world, so am I compelled to carry the gospel of freedom beyond my own home town. Like Paul, I must constantly respond to the Macedonian call for aid.

Moreover, I am cognizant of the interrelatedness of all communities and states. I cannot sit idly by in Atlanta and not be concerned about what happens in Birmingham. Injustice anywhere is a threat to justice everywhere. We are caught in an inescapable network of mutuality, tied in a single garment of destiny. Whatever affects one directly affects all indirectly. Never again can we afford to live with the narrow, provincial "outside agitator" idea. Anyone who lives inside the United States can never be considered an outsider anywhere within its bounds.

You deplore the demonstrations taking place in Birmingham. But your statement, I am sorry to say, fails to express a similar concern for the conditions that brought about the demonstrations. I am sure that none of you would want to rest content with the superficial kind of social analysis that deals merely with effects and does not grapple with underlying causes. It is unfortunate that demonstrations are taking place in Birmingham, but it is even more unfortunate that the city's white power structure left the Negro community with no alternative.

II

In any nonviolent campaign there are four basic steps: collection of the facts to determine whether injustices exist, negotiation, self-purification and direct action. We have gone through all these steps in Birmingham. There can be no gainsaying the fact that racial injustice engulfs this community. Birmingham is probably the most thoroughly segregated city in the United States. Its ugly record of police brutality is widely known. Its unjust treatment of Negroes in the courts is a notorious reality. There have been more unsolved bombings of Negro homes and churches in Birmingham than in any other city in the nation. These are the hard, brutal facts of the case. On the basis of these conditions Negro leaders sought to negotiate with the city fathers. But the latter consistently refused to engage in good-faith negotiation.

Then last September came the opportunity to talk with leaders of Birmingham's economic community. In the course of the negotiations certain promises were made by the merchants—for example, the promise to remove the stores' humiliating racial signs. On the basis of these promises the Rev. Fred Shuttlesworth and the leaders of the Alabama Christian Movement for Human Rights agreed to a moratorium on all demonstrations. As the weeks and months went by we realized that we were the victims of a broken promise. The signs remained.

As in so many past experiences, our hopes had been blasted, and our disappointment was keenly felt. We had no alternative except to prepare for direct action, whereby we would present our very bodies as a means of laying our case before the conscience of the local and the national community. Mindful of the difficulties involved, we decided to undertake a process of self-purification. We began a series of workshops on nonviolence, and we repeatedly asked ourselves: "Are you able to accept blows without retaliating?" "Are you able to endure the ordeal of jail?" We decided to schedule our direct action program for the Easter season, realizing that except for Christmas this is the main shopping period of the year. Knowing that a strong economic withdrawal program would be the by-product of direct action, we felt that this would be the best time to bring pressure to bear on the merchants.

But Birmingham's mayoral election was coming up in March, and when we discovered that Commissioner of Public Safety Eugene "Bull" Connor was to be in the run-off, we decided to postpone our demonstrations until the day after the run-off so that they could not be used to cloud the issues. It is evident, then, that we did not move irresponsibly into direct action. Like many others, we wanted to see Mr. Connor defeated, and to this end we endured postponement after postponement. Having aided in this community need, we felt that our direct action program could be delayed no longer.

III

You may well ask, "Why direct action? Why sit-ins, marches, etc.? Isn't negotiation a better path?" You are quite right in calling for negotiation. Indeed, this is the very purpose of direct action. Nonviolent direct action seeks to foster such a tension that a community which has constantly refused to negotiate is forced to confront the issue. It seeks so to dramatize the issue that it can no longer be ignored. My citing the creation of tension as part of the work of the nonviolent resister may sound rather shocking. But I readily acknowledge that I am not afraid of the word "tension." I have earnestly opposed violent tension, but there is a type of constructive, nonviolent tension which is necessary for growth. Just as Socrates felt that it was necessary to create a tension in the mind so that individuals could shake off the bondage of myths and half-truths and rise to the realm of creative analysis and objective appraisal, so must we see the need for nonviolent gadflies to create the kind of tension in society that will help men rise from the dark depths of prejudice and racism to the majestic heights of understanding and brotherhood.

The purpose of our direct action program is to create a situation so crisis-packed that it will inevitably open the door to negotiation. I therefore concur with you in your call for negotiation. Too long has our beloved southland been bogged down in a tragic effort to live in monologue rather than dialogue.

One of the basic points in your statement is that the action that I and my associates have taken in Birmingham is untimely. Some have asked, "Why didn't you give the new city administration time to act?" The only answer that I can give to this query is that the new Birmingham administration must be prodded about as much as the outgoing one before it will act. We are sadly mistaken if we feel that the election of Albert Boutwell as mayor will bring the millenium to Birmingham. While Mr. Boutwell is a much more gentle person than Mr. Connor, they are both segregationists, dedicated to maintenance of the status quo. I have hope that Mr. Boutwell will be reasonable enough to see the futility of massive resistance to desegregation. But he will not see this without pressure from devotees of civil rights. My friends, I must say to you that we have not made a single gain in civil rights without determined legal and nonviolent pressure. Lamentably, it is a historical fact that privileged groups seldom give up their privileges voluntarily. Individuals may see the moral light and voluntarily give up their unjust posture; but, as Reinhold Niebuhr has reminded us, groups tend to be more immoral than individuals.

We know through painful experience that freedom is never voluntarily given by the oppressor; it must be demanded by the oppressed. Frankly, I have yet to engage in a direct action campaign that was "well timed" in the view of those who have not suffered unduly from the disease of segregation. For years now I have heard the word "Wait!" It rings in the ear of every Negro with piercing familiarity. This "Wait" has almost always meant "Never." As one of our distinguished jurists once said, "Justice too long delayed is justice denied."

IV

We have waited for more than 340 years for our constitutional and God-given rights. The nations of Asia and Africa are moving with jet-like speed toward gaining political independence, but we still creep at horse-and-buggy pace toward gaining a cup of coffee at a lunch counter. Perhaps it is easy for those who have never felt the stinging darts of segregation to say "Wait." But when you have seen vicious mobs lynch your mothers and fathers at will and drown your sisters and brothers at whim; when you have seen hate-filled policemen curse, kick and even kill your black brothers and sisters with impunity; when you see the vast majority of your 20 million Negro brothers smothering in an air-tight cage of poverty in the midst of an affluent society; when you suddenly find your tongue twisted as you seek to explain to your six-year-old daughter why she can't go to the public amusement park that has just been advertised on television, and see tears welling up when she is told that Funtown is closed to colored children, and see ominous clouds of inferiority beginning to form in her little mental sky, and see her beginning to distort her personality by unconsciously developing a bitterness toward white people; when you have to concoct an answer for a five-year-old son asking, "Daddy, why do white people treat colored people so mean?"; when you take a cross-country drive and find it necessary to sleep night after night in the uncomfortable corners of your automobile because no motel will accept you; when you are humiliated day in and day out by nagging signs reading "white" and "colored"; when your first name becomes "nigger," your middle name becomes "boy" (however old you are) and your last name becomes "John," and your wife and mother are never given the respected title "Mrs."; when you are harried by day and haunted by night by the fact that you are a Negro, never quite knowing what to expect next, and are plagued with inner fears and outer resentments; when you are forever fighting a degenerating sense of "nobodiness"—then you will understand why we find it difficult to wait. There comes a time when the cup of endurance runs over, and men are no longer willing to be plunged into an abyss of injustice where they experience the bleakness of corroding despair. I hope, sirs, you can understand our legitimate and unavoidable impatience.

V

You express a great deal of anxiety over our willingness to break laws. This is certainly a legitimate concern. Since we so diligently urge people to obey the Supreme Court's decision of 1954 outlawing segregation in the public schools, at first glance it may seem rather paradoxical for us consciously to break laws. One may well ask, "How can you advocate breaking some laws and obeying others?" The answer lies in the fact that there are two types of laws: just and unjust. I agree with St. Augustine that "an unjust law is no law at all."

Now what is the difference between the two? How does one determine whether a law is just or unjust? A just law is a man-made code that squares with the moral law or the law of God. An unjust law is a code that is out of harmony with the moral law. To put it in the terms of St. Thomas Aquinas, an unjust law is a human law that is not rooted in eternal law and natural law. Any law that uplifts human personality is just. Any law that degrades human personality is unjust. All segregation statutes are unjust because segregation distorts the soul and damages the personality. It gives the segregator a false sense of superiority and the segregated a false sense of inferiority. Segregation, to use the terminology of the Jewish philosopher Martin Buber, substitutes an "I-it" relationship for an "I-thou" relationship and ends up relegating persons to the status of things. Hence segregation is not only politically, economically and sociologically unsound, it is sinful. Paul Tillich has said that sin is separation. Is not segregation an existential expression of man's tragic separation, his awful estrangement, his terrible sinfulness? Thus it is that I can urge men to disobey segregation ordinances, for such ordinances are morally wrong.

Let us consider some of the ways in which a law can be unjust. A law is unjust, for example, if the majority group compels a minority group to obey the statute but does not make it binding on itself. By the same token a law in all probability is just if the majority is itself willing to obey it. Also, a law is unjust if it is inflicted on a minority that, as a result of being denied the right to vote, had no part in enacting or devising the law. Who can say that the legislature of Alabama which set up that state's segregation laws was democratically elected? Throughout Alabama all sorts of devious methods are used to prevent Negroes from becoming registered voters, and there are some counties in which, even though Negroes constitute a majority of the population, not a single Negro is registered. Can any law enacted under such circumstances be considered democratically structured?

Sometimes a law is just on its face and unjust in its application. For instance, I have been arrested on a charge of parading without a permit. Now there is nothing wrong in having an ordinance which requires a permit for a parade. But such an ordinance becomes unjust when it is used to maintain segregation and to deny citizens the First-amendment privilege of peaceful assembly and protest.

I hope you are able to see the distinction I am trying to point out. In no sense do I advocate evading the law, as would the rabid segregationist. That would lead to anarchy. One who breaks an unjust law must do so *openly, lovingly,* and with a willingness to accept the penalty. I submit that an individual who breaks a law that conscience tells him is unjust and who willingly accepts the penalty of imprisonment in order to arouse the conscience of the community over its injustice is in reality expressing the highest respect for law.

Of course, there is nothing new about this kind of civil disobedience. It was evidenced sublimely in the refusal of Shadrach, Meshach and Abednego to obey the laws of Nebuchadnezzar, on the ground that a higher moral law was at stake. It was practiced superbly by the early Christians who were willing to face hungry lions rather than submit to certain unjust laws of the Roman empire. To a degree, academic freedom is a reality today because Socrates practiced civil disobedience. We should never forget that everything Adolf Hitler did in Germany was "legal" and everything the Hungarian freedom fighters did in Hungary was "illegal." It was "illegal" to aid and comfort a Jew in Hitler's Germany. Even so, I am sure that had I lived in Germany at the time I would have aided and comforted my Jewish brothers. If today I lived in a communist country where certain principles dear to the Christian faith are suppressed, I would openly advocate disobeying that country's antireligious laws.

VI

I must make two honest confessions to you, my Christian and Jewish brothers. First, I must confess that over the past few years I have been gravely disappointed with the white moderate. I have almost reached the regrettable conclusion that the Negro's great stumbling block in his stride toward freedom is not the White Citizen's Counciler or the Ku Klux Klanner but the white moderate who is more devoted to "order" than to justice; who prefers a negative peace which is the absence of tension to a positive peace which is the presence of justice; who constantly says "I agree with you in the goal you seek, but I cannot agree with your methods"; who paternalistically believes he can set the timetable for another man's freedom; who lives by a mythical concept of time and who constantly advises the Negro to wait for a "more convenient season." Shallow understanding from people of good will is more frustrating than absolute misunderstanding from people of ill will. Lukewarm acceptance is much more bewildering than outright rejection.

I had hoped that the white moderate would understand that law and order exist for the purpose of establishing justice and that when they fail in this purpose they block social progress. I had hoped that the white moderate would understand that the present tension in the south is a necessary phase of the transition from an obnoxious negative peace, in which the Negro passively accepted his unjust plight, to a substantive and positive peace, in which all men will respect the dignity and worth of human personality. Actually, we who engage in nonviolent direct action are not the creators of tension. We merely bring to the surface the hidden tension that is already alive. We bring it out in the open where it can be seen and dealt with. Like a boil that can never be cured so long as it is covered up but must be opened with all its pus-flowing ugliness to the natural medicines of air and light, injustice must be exposed, with all the tension its exposure creates, to the light of human conscience and the air of national opinion before it can be cured.

In your statement you assert that our actions, even though peaceful, must be condemned because they precipitate violence. But is this a logical assertion? Isn't this like condemning a robbed man because his possession of money precipitated an act of robbery? Isn't this like condemning Socrates because his unswerving commitment to truth and his philosophical inquiries precipitated the act by the misguided populace in which they made him drink hemlock? Isn't this like condemning Jesus because his unique God-consciousness and never-ceasing devotion to God's will precipitated the evil act of crucifixion? We must come to see that, as the federal courts have consistently affirmed, it is wrong to urge an individual to cease his efforts to gain his basic constitutional rights because the quest may precipitate violence. Society must protect the robbed and punish the robber.

I had also hoped that the white moderate would reject the myth concerning time in relation to the struggle for freedom. I have just received a letter from a white brother in Texas. He writes: "All Christians know that the colored people will receive equal rights eventually, but it is possible that you are in too great a religious hurry. It has taken Christianity almost 2,000 years to accomplish what it has. The teachings of Christ take time to come to earth." Such an attitude stems from a tragic misconception of time, from the strangely irrational notion that there is something in the very flow of time that will inevitably cure all ills. Actually, time itself is neutral; it can be used either destructively or constructively. More and more I feel that the people of ill will have used time much more effectively than have the people of good will. We will have to repent in this generation not merely for the hateful words and actions of the bad people but for the appalling silence of the good people. Human progress never rolls in on wheels of inevitability; it comes through the tireless efforts of men willing to be co-workers with God, and without this hard work time itself becomes an ally of the forces of social stagnation. We must use time creatively, in the knowledge that the time is always ripe to do right. Now is the time to make real the promise of democracy and transform our pending national elegy into a creative psalm of brotherhood. Now is the time to lift our national policy from the quicksand of racial injustice to the solid rock of human dignity.

VII

You speak of our activity in Birmingham as extreme. At first I was rather disappointed that fellow clergymen would see my nonviolent efforts as those of an extremist. I began thinking about the fact that I stand in the middle of two opposing forces in the Negro community. One is a force of complacency made up of Negroes who, as a result of long years of oppression, are so completely drained of self-respect and a sense of "somebodiness" that they have adjusted to segregation, and of a few middle class Negroes who, because of a degree of academic and economic security and because in some ways they profit by segregation, have unconsciously become insensitive to the problems of the masses. The other force is one of bitterness and hatred, and it comes perilously close to advocating violence. It is expressed in the various black nationalist groups that are springing up across the nation, the largest and best-known being Elijah Muhammad's Muslim movement. Nourished by the Negro's frustration over the continued existence of racial discrimination, this movement is made up of people who have lost faith in America, who have absolutely repudiated Christianity, and who have concluded that the white man is an incorrigible "devil."

I have tried to stand between these two forces, saying that we need emulate neither the "do-nothingism" of the complacent nor the hatred of the black nationalist. For there is the more excellent way of love and nonviolent protest. I am grateful to God that, through the influence of the Negro church, the way of nonviolence became an integral part of our struggle.

If this philosophy had not emerged, by now many streets of the south would, I am convinced, be flowing with blood. And I am further convinced that if our white brothers dismiss as "rabble-rousers" and "outside agitators" those of us who employ nonviolent direct action and if they refuse to support our nonviolent efforts, millions of Negroes will, out of frustration and despair, seek solace and security in black nationalist ideologies—a development that would inevitably lead to a frightening racial nightmare.

VIII

Oppressed people cannot remain oppressed forever. The yearning for freedom eventually manifests itself, and that is what has happened to the American Negro. Something within has reminded him of his birthright of freedom, and something without has reminded him that it can be gained. Consciously or unconsciously, he has been caught up by the *Zeitgeist*, and with his black brothers of Africa and his brown and yellow brothers of Asia, South America and the Caribbean, the U.S. Negro is moving with a sense of great urgency toward the promised land of racial justice. If one recognizes this vital urge that has engulfed the Negro community, he should readily understand why public demonstrations are taking place. The Negro has many pent-up resentments and latent frustrations, and he must release them. So let him march; let him make prayer pilgrimages to the city hall; let him go on freedom rides—and try to understand why he must do so. If his repressed emotions are not released in nonviolent ways, they will seek expression through violence; this is not a threat but a fact of history. I have not said to my people, "Get rid of your discontent." Rather, I have tried to say that this normal and healthy discontent can be channeled into the creative outlet of nonviolent direct action. And now this approach is being termed extremist.

But though I was initially disappointed at being categorized as an extremist, as I continued to think about the matter I gradually gained a measure of satisfaction from the label. Was not Jesus an extremist for love: "Love your enemies, bless them that curse you, do good to them that hate you, and pray for them which despitefully use you, and persecute you." Was not Amos an extremist for justice: "Let justice roll down like waters and righteousness like an everflowing stream." Was not Paul an extremist for the Christian gospel: "I bear in my body the marks of the Lord Jesus." Was not Martin Luther an extremist: "Here I stand; I can do no other so help me God." And John Bunyan: "I will stay in jail to the end of my days before I make a butchery of my conscience." And Abraham Lincoln: "This nation cannot survive half slave and half free." And Thomas Jefferson: "We hold these truths to be self-evident, that all men are created equal . . ." So the question is not whether we will be extremists but what kind of extremists we will be. Will we be extremists for hate or for love? Will we be extremists for the preservation of injustice or for the extension of justice? Perhaps the south, the nation and the world are in dire need of creative extremists.

I had hoped that the white moderate would see this need. Perhaps I was too optimistic; perhaps I expected too much. I suppose I should have realized that few members of the oppressor race can understand the deep groans and passionate yearnings of the oppressed race, and still fewer have the vision to see that injustice must be rooted out by strong, persistent and determined action. I am thankful, however, that some of our white brothers have grasped the meaning of this social revolution and committed themselves to it. They are still all too few in quantity, but they are big in quality. Some—such as Ralph McGill, Lillian Smith, Harry Golden and James

McBride Dabbs—have written about our struggle in eloquent and prophetic terms. Others have marched with us down nameless streets of the south. They have languished in filthy, roach-infested jails, suffering the abuse and brutality of police-men who view them as "dirty nigger lovers." Unlike so many of their moderate brothers and sisters, they have recognized the urgency of the moment and sensed the need for powerful "action" antidotes to combat the disease of segregation.

IX

Let me take note of my other major disappointment. Though there are some notable exceptions, I have also been disappointed with the white church and its leadership. I do not say this as one of those negative critics who can always find something wrong with the church. I say this as a minister of the gospel, who loves the church; who was nurtured in its bosom; who has been sustained by its spiritual blessings and who will remain true to it as long as the cord of life shall lengthen.

When I was suddenly catapulted into the leadership of the bus protest in Montgomery, Alabama, a few years ago I felt we would be supported by the white church. I felt that the white ministers, priests and rabbis of the south would be among our strongest allies. Instead, some have been outright opponents, refusing to understand the freedom movement and misrepresenting its leaders; all too many others have been more cautious than courageous and have remained silent and secure behind stained-glass windows.

In spite of my shattered dreams I came to Birmingham with the hope that the white religious leadership of this com-munity would see the justice of our cause and with deep moral concern would serve as the channel through which our just grievances could reach the power structure. But again I have been disappointed.

I have heard numerous southern religious leaders admonish their worshipers to comply with a desegregation decision be-cause it is the *law*, but I have longed to hear white ministers declare, "Follow this decree because integration is morally *right* and because the Negro is your brother." In the midst of blatant injustices inflicted upon the Negro I have watched

white churchmen stand on the sideline and mouth pious ir-
relevancies and sanctimonious trivialities. In the midst of a
mighty struggle to rid our nation of racial and economic injustice I have heard many ministers say, "Those are social issues with which the gospel has no real concern," and I have
watched many churches commit themselves to a completely
otherworldly religion which makes a strange, unbiblical distinction between body and soul, between the sacred and the
secular.

We are moving toward the close of the 20th century with a
religious community largely adjusted to the status quo—a
taillight behind other community agencies rather than a headlight leading men to higher levels of justice.

X

I have traveled the length and breadth of Alabama, Mississippi and all the other southern states. On sweltering summer days and crisp autumn mornings I have looked at the
south's beautiful churches with their lofty spires pointing
heavenward, and at her impressive religious education buildings. Over and over I have found myself asking: "What kind
of people worship here? Who is their God? Where were their
voices when the lips of Governor Barnett dripped with words
of interposition and nullification? Where were they when
Governor Wallace gave a clarion call for defiance and hatred?
Where were their voices of support when bruised and weary
Negro men and women decided to rise from the dark dungeons of complacency to the bright hills of creative protest?"

Yes, these questions are still in my mind. In deep disappointment I have wept over the laxity of the church. But be
assured that my tears have been tears of love. There can be
no deep disappointment where there is not deep love. Yes, I
love the church. How could I do otherwise? I am in the
rather unique position of being the son, the grandson and
the great-grandson of preachers. Yes, I see the church as the
body of Christ. But, oh! How we have blemished and scarred
that body through social neglect and through fear of being
nonconformists.

There was a time when the church was very powerful—in

the time when the early Christians rejoiced at being deemed
worthy to suffer for what they believed. In those days the
church was not merely a thermometer that recorded the ideas
and principles of popular opinion; it was a thermostat that
transformed the mores of society. Whenever the early Christians entered a town the power structure immediately sought
to convict them for being "disturbers of the peace" and "outside agitators." But the Christians pressed on, in the conviction that they were "a colony of heaven," called to obey God
rather than man. Small in number, they were big in commitment. By their effort and example they brought an end to
such ancient evils as infanticide and gladiatorial contest.

XI

Things are different now. So often the contemporary
church is a weak, ineffectual voice with an uncertain sound.
So often it is an archdefender of the status quo. Far from being disturbed by the presence of the church, the power structure of the average community is consoled by the church's
silent—and often even vocal—sanction of things as they are.

But the judgment of God is upon the church as never before. If today's church does not recapture the sacrificial spirit
of the early church, it will lose its authenticity, forfeit the loyalty of millions, and be dismissed as an irrelevant social club
with no meaning for the 20th century. Every day I meet
young people whose disappointment with the church has
turned into outright disgust.

Perhaps I have once again been too optimistic. Is organized
religion too inextricably bound to the status quo to save our
nation and the world? Perhaps I must turn my faith to the inner spiritual church, the church within the church, as the true
ecclesia and the hope of the world. But again I am thankful to
God that some noble souls from the ranks of organized religion have broken loose from the paralyzing chains of confor-
mity and joined us as active partners in the struggle for
freedom. They have left their secure congregations and walked
the streets of Albany, Georgia, with us. They have gone down
the highways of the south on torturous rides for freedom. Yes,
they have gone to jail with us. Some have been kicked out of

their churches, have lost the support of their bishops and fellow ministers. But they have acted in the faith that right defeated is stronger than evil triumphant. Their witness has been the spiritual salt that has preserved the true meaning of the gospel in these troubled times. They have carved a tunnel of hope through the dark mountain of disappointment.

I hope the church as a whole will meet the challenge of this decisive hour. But even if the church does not come to the aid of justice, I have no despair about the future. I have no fear about the outcome of our struggle in Birmingham, even if our motives are at present misunderstood. We will reach the goal of freedom in Birmingham and all over the nation, because the goal of America is freedom. Abused and scorned though we may be, our destiny is tied up with America's destiny. Before the pilgrims landed at Plymouth we were here. Before the pen of Jefferson etched across the pages of history the mighty words of the Declaration of Independence, we were here. For more than two centuries our forebears labored in this country without wages; they made cotton king; they built the homes of their masters while suffering gross injustice and shameful humiliation—and yet out of a bottomless vitality they continued to thrive and develop. If the inexpressible cruelties of slavery could not stop us, the opposition we now face will surely fail. We will win our freedom because the sacred heritage of our nation and the eternal will of God are embodied in our echoing demands.

XII

Before closing I feel impelled to mention one other point in your statement that has troubled me profoundly. You warmly commended the Birmingham police force for keeping "order" and "preventing violence." I doubt that you would have so warmly commended the police force if you had seen its angry dogs sinking their teeth into six unarmed, nonviolent Negroes. I doubt that you would so quickly commend the policemen if you were to observe their ugly and inhuman treatment of Negroes here in the city jail; if you were to watch them push and curse old Negro women and young Negro girls; if you were to see them slap and kick old Negro men and young boys; if you were to observe them, as they did on two occasions, refuse to give us food because we wanted to sing our grace together. I cannot join you in your praise of the Birmingham police department.

It is true that the police have exercised discipline in handling the demonstrators. In this sense they have conducted themselves rather "nonviolently" in public. But for what purpose? To preserve the evil system of segregation. Over the past few years I have consistently preached that nonviolence demands that the means we use must be as pure as the ends we seek. I have tried to make clear that it is wrong to use immoral means to attain moral ends. But now I must affirm that it is just as wrong, or perhaps even more so, to use moral means to preserve immoral ends. Perhaps Mr. Connor and his policemen have been rather nonviolent in public, as was Chief Pritchett in Albany, Georgia, but they have used the moral means of nonviolence to maintain the immoral end of racial injustice. As T. S. Eliot has said, there is no greater treason than to do the right deed for the wrong reason.

XIII

I wish you had commended the Negro sit-inners and demonstrators of Birmingham for their sublime courage, their willingness to suffer and their amazing discipline in the midst of great provocation. One day the south will recognize its real heroes. They will be the James Merediths, with a noble sense of purpose facing jeering and hostile mobs and the agonizing loneliness that characterizes the life of the pioneer. They will be old, oppressed, battered Negro women, symbolized in a 72-year-old woman in Montgomery, Alabama, who rose up with a sense of dignity and with her people decided not to ride segregated buses, and who responded with ungrammatical profundity to one who inquired about her: "My feet is tired, but my soul is rested." They will be the young high school and college students, the young ministers of the gospel and a host of their elders courageously and nonviolently sitting in at lunch counters and willingly going to jail for conscience' sake. One day the south will know that when these disinherited children of God sat down at lunch counters they were in reality standing up for what is best in the American dream and for the most sacred values in our Judeo-Christian heritage, thereby bringing our nation back to those great wells of democracy which were dug deep by the founding fathers in their formulation of the Constitution and the Declaration of Independence.

Never before have I written so long a letter. I can assure you that it would have been much shorter if I had been writing from a comfortable desk, but what else can one do when he is alone for days in a narrow jail cell, other than write long letters, think long thoughts and pray long prayers?

If I have said anything in this letter that overstates the truth and indicates an unreasonable impatience, I beg you to forgive me. If I have said anything that *under*states the truth and indicates my having a patience that allows me to settle for anything less than brotherhood, I beg God to forgive me.

I hope this letter finds you strong in the faith. I also hope that circumstances will soon make it possible for me to meet each of you, not as an integrationist or a civil rights leader but as a fellow clergyman and a Christian brother. Let us all hope that the dark clouds of racial prejudice will soon pass away and the deep fog of misunderstanding will be lifted from our fear-drenched communities and in some not too distant tomorrow the radiant stars of love and brotherhood will shine over our great nation with all their scintillating beauty.

The Christian Century, June 12, 1963

Eyewitness: The Police Terror at Birmingham

by Len Holt

COMING from the airport May 6, we drove past the post office and onto Ruth Ave. toward the A. G. Gaston Motel, integration headquarters. Then we saw why the downtown area was "cop-less." On the roofs of the three and four story buildings surrounding Kelly-Ingram Park were clusters of policemen with short-wave radios over their shoulders. At the four intersections surrounding the park were dozens of white-helmeted officers.

With the Birmingham police were reinforcements from such nearby cities as Bessemer, Fairfield, and Leeds. Also on hand were deputy sheriffs of Jefferson County and a sprinkling of State Troopers. The officers seemed fearful. This fear was expressed in marathon chatter and forced joviality as they waited for the ordeal that was to come: another massive demonstration.

Pressing on each cop were the eyes of 4,000 Negro spectators—women, men, boys, girls and mothers with babies. They were on the porches, lawns, cars and streets surrounding the park. They didn't talk much, just looked . . . and waited.

Frequently both policemen and Negro spectators turned toward the 16th St. Baptist Church. From the more than 2,000 persons inside the church, and 300 pressing toward its doors on the outside—mostly grammar and high school students—came the loud songs of Freedom: "We Shall Overcome," "Ain't Gonna Let Nobody Turn Me Round."

The temperature hit 90 degrees. Everybody was sweating. "Freedom! Freedom!" A roar arose from the church. The cops almost as one, faced the church. Some unleashed clubs from their belts. The faces of those I could see had turned crimson. Jeremiah X, Muslim minister from Atlanta standing near me, commented: "At any moment those cops expect 300 years of hate to spew forth from that church."

"Y'all niggers go on back. We ain't letting no more get on those steps," a police captain ordered as I approached the church. I turned away. The time was 1:10 p.m. Four fire engines arrived at the intersections and set themselves up for "business." Each disgorged its high-pressure hoses, and nozzle mounts were set up in the street. I was to learn the reason for the mounts later, when I watched the powerful water stripping bark off trees and tearing bricks from the walls as the firemen knocked Negroes down.

Before I could get back to the motel the demonstrations began; 60 demonstrators were on their way, marching two abreast, each with a sign bearing an integration slogan. Dick Gregory, the nightclub comedian, was leading the group.

At a signal, 40 policemen converged, sticks in hand. Up drove yellow school buses.

"Do you have a permit to parade?" asked the police captain.

"No," replied Gregory.

"No what?" asked the captain in what seemed to be a reminder to Gregory that he had not used a "sir."

"No. No. A thousand times No," Gregory replied.

The captain said, "I hereby place you all under arrest for parading without a permit, disturbing the peace and violating the injunction of the Circuit Court of Jefferson County."

Bedlam broke loose. The young demonstrators began shouting a freedom song. They broke into a fast step that seemed to be a hybrid of the turkey-trot and the twist as they sang to the tune of "The Old Grey Mare":

> "I ain't scared of your jail
> cause I want my freedom!
> . . . want my freedom!"

And for the next two hours this scene was repeated over and over as group after group of students strutted out of the church to the cheers of the spectators, the freedom chants of those being carried away in buses and a continuous banging on the floors and sides of the buses—a cacophony of freedom.

That day, the dogs were kept out of sight. The Birmingham riot tank was on the side street. The fire hoses were kept shut. The police clubs did not flail. The thousands of spectators also kept calm. The police savagery of the preceding week was contained.

Back at the Gaston Motel, there was a joyous air. Leaders in the organizational work, such as Dorothy Cotten, James Bevel and Bernard Lee of the Southern Christian Leadership Conference; Isaac Wright, CORE field secretary; and James Forman, William Porter, William Ricks, Eric Rainey and students of the Student Non-Violent Coordinating Committee, joined others in the motel parking lot in a parade and song fest.

Victory was suggested by the absence of the dogs, the lack of violence. Added to this was the news that a judge had continued the cases of 40 persons because "there was no room at the inn" for those sentenced. The threat of the Movement to fill the jails had been realized in Birmingham.

Rejoicing was short-lived. At 6 p.m. word got back to the motel that the 1,000 students arrested earlier had neither been housed nor fed. With Jim Forman of SNCC I drove to the jail. There we saw youths throwing candy bars over the fence to the students; spectators had passed the hat to purchase the candy. While we were there it began to rain. The students got soaked. The spectators, too, got wet. There was no shelter for the kids. The cops and their dog got into the squad car. They stayed dry.

Forman begged the cops to put the kids inside, in the halls, in the basement of the jail, anywhere. Nothing was done. A new day had not yet come to Birmingham.

That night the weather turned cool. We learned that the students were still in the jail yard, unsheltered and unfed. The same message got to others in the Negro community. An estimated 500 cars and 1,200 people drove to the jail with blankets and food. The police responded by bringing up dogs and fire hoses. The food and blankets were given to the kids. The crowd waited until all of the children were finally taken inside.

Later that night Forman and Dorothy Cotton of the Southern Christian Leadership Conference met with the student leaders. In the planning emphasis was placed on the need for speed and mobility. Heretofore the demonstrators seldom got downtown, or if they did, never in a large group. It was decided that instead of starting the demonstrations every day at 1 p.m., when the fire hoses were in place and the police were all on duty, an element of surprise would be introduced. The next demonstration would begin earlier. Picket signs would be taken downtown to prearranged spots in cars where the students could pick them up.

That night five of us slept in a motel room designed for two. We were crowded, but so were the 2,000 students crammed 75 or more in cells for eight in the city jail. Our room was hot that night, but not so hot as the unventilated sweat boxes in which Cynthia Cook, 15, and other girls were placed as punishment by the jail personnel when they refused to say "sir." Those on the outside were tired, but not so tired as the hundreds who had been forced to make marathon walks because they sang "We Shall Overcome" in jail. And there were beatings for many.

At 6 a.m. Tuesday SNCC and CORE fellows hurried to the schools to get out the students. Before 10—and before the police lines and firehoses were in place—600 students had been to the church and given assignments downtown. Cars were dispatched with picket signs. The clock struck noon. The students struck. Almost simultaneously, eight department stores were picketed.

I was standing near a police motorcycle, and could hear the pandemonium at police headquarters. Police not due to report until after 12:30 were being called frantically. Policemen speeded, sirens screaming, from Kelly-Ingram Park to downtown. Inside the 16th St. Baptist Church the folk laughed and sang "We Shall Overcome."

Over the police radio I heard Bull Connor's voice. He was mad. He had been betrayed. Never before had the students demonstrated before 1 p.m. I suspect the merchants were mad. And the kids downtown, all 600 of them, sang "We Shall Overcome." And they did overcome. No arrests were made. When the police finally got to the area, they merely ripped up the signs and told the youngsters to go home. The jails were full.

For the students, "home" was back to the 16th St. Baptist Church. There they were reassigned to go to Woolworth's and six other department stores, sit on the floor, and not move unless arrested. Since the jails were full, the cops still weren't arresting. A policeman went to the church to tell somebody from the Movement to ask the students to leave. When the announcement was made in the church, 2,000 persons went downtown. These thousands were joined by 2,000 spectators and made a wild, hilarious parade through downtown Birmingham, singing "We Shall Overcome."

Then the nearly 4,000 persons returned to the church from the "victory march." And while the throngs joyously sang inside, preparations were being made outside. The cars with dogs drove up. About 300 police officers surrounded the church and park area. Fire hoses were set up.

For a few minutes I left the area of the church and went to a nearby office. When I emerged I saw 3,000 Negroes encircled in the Kelly-Ingram Park by policemen swinging clubs. The hoses were in action with the pressure wide open. On one side the students were confronted by clubs, on other, powerful streams of water. The firemen used the hoses to knock down the students. As the streams hit trees, the bark was ripped off. Bricks were torn loose from the walls.

The hoses were directed at everyone with a black skin, demonstrators and non-demonstrators. A stream of water slammed the Rev. Fred Shuttlesworth against the church wall, causing internal injuries. Mrs. Colia LaFayette, 25-year-old, SNCC field secretary from Selma, Ala., was knocked down and two hoses were brought to bear on her to wash her along the sidewalk. A youth ran toward the firemen screaming oaths to direct their attention from the sprawling woman.

Meanwhile, over the public address system inside the church, I could hear a speaker admonishing the people to be non-violent . . . "We want to redeem the souls of people like Bull Connor."

I wondered how long it would be before some Negro lost his restraint. It had almost happened Monday, the day before, when cops flung a Negro woman to the ground and two of them had put their knees in her breast and twisted her arm. This was done in the presence of the woman's 19-year-old son and thousands of Negro spectators. Four 200-pound Negro men barely managed to restrain the son.

The terrible Tuesday, May 7, ended finally. There was much talk about an impending "settlement." This news discouraged all but the most cursory plans for the next day. Everyone realized the influx of state troopers would make downtown demonstrations difficult.

A strange thing about the demonstrations up until Wednesday was that all of the brutality had been police brutality. Where were the thugs who with razor blades, a few years previously, had cut off the penis of a Negro? Where were the men who stabbed Mrs. Ruby Shuttlesworth when she attempted to enroll her child in the white high school? Where were the whites who repeatedly bombed Birmingham churches and synagogues?

On Wednesday, after almost five weeks of protesting, the non-uniformed racists had not spoken. On May 12th, Mother's Day, they spoke . . . and the cup of non-violence of Birmingham Negroes overflowed. America learned that the patience of 100 years is not inexhaustible. It is exhausted.

The National Guardian, May 16, 1963

Waiting in the Rain at the Birmingham Jail

by Raymond R. Coffey

BIRMINGHAM, Ala.—Inside the compound, negro boys and girls standing under a chill rain asked a reporter to pass them cigarets through the 12-foot-high barb-topped fence.

Outside, a potbellied bondsman in a snug little concrete-block office sat sipping a can of beer and doing no business at all.

A few feet away a tall, slim, mustached father, waiting for word of sight of his 12-year-old son, told other Negroes huddling out of the rain under umbrellas and trees that "my 5-year-old boy wants to get arrested, too, but he's too young."

Up near the fence a police captain, his blue shirt soaked through to the skin, remarked wearily that "if we get any more I don't know where we'll put them."

This was the scene Monday night at the Birmingham city jail.

More than 800 Negroes—the greatest single-day total yet in a mass arrest in Southern antisegregation conflicts—had been piled into white paddy wagons and yellow school buses and rolled off to the jail for booking.

Among them was Chicago Negro comedian Dick Gregory.

Faced with a staggering problem in getting the Negroes—mostly school children, some of them 7 and 8 years old—booked on charges of parading without a permit, police more than six hours after the arrests had not managed to get them all fed and bedded down.

The juveniles, starting with the youngest, were being checked in at the jail and then taken off again in the school buses to a barracks-type setup in a building at the state fairgrounds.

The adults were being lodged in city and county jails here. But the booking process was not fast enough to beat the rain and darkness.

About 200 or 300 Negroes, arrested around 2 p.m., were still standing in the compound in the rain after 7 p.m. Some of the Negro youths complained to a reporter that they had not been fed or given a drink of water.

"But we still want freedom," said one husky youth. "When I get out I'll start demonstrating all over again."

A small crowd of Negro adults gathered outside the compound and occasionally one would dart to the fence and throw over a bag of sandwiches despite police orders to stand back.

One policeman, apparently touched with sympathy, turned his back when a Negro man walked to the fence and pushed through a pack of cigarets.

The negro father watching for his 12-year-old son was asked how he felt about his boy's arrest and defiance of white authority.

"It's fine with me," he said. "His father's been a slave all his life."

The beer drinking bondsman, a white man, said bond for those arrested was being set at $300 to $500 for the misdemeanor charge.

"But they don't want to get out and we wouldn't mess with them if they did," he said. "The appeal bonds are $2,500 and these civil rights cases go on forever."

On either side of the compound gate were separate but equal signs announcing jail visiting hours for whites and Negroes.

A policeman standing under the white visiting sign said the jail's capacity is "more than 600" and conceded it was "very overcrowded."

More than 2,500 Negroes have been arrested in the demonstrations here and authorities have had to lodge some of them at the county jail and in jails in nearby Bessemer, as well as at the fairgrounds.

If these and other local facilities are inadequate, Gov. George Wallace has offered to put up any overflow in state prisons.

A reporter also went to the fairgrounds and asked if he might see some of the youngsters being held there.

"No," said a policeman at gate. "If you want to see something, there's a lot of good movies downtown."

The massive arrests of Negroes came Monday at the climax of an "empty-the-schools" demonstration directed by the Rev. Martin Luther King and other leaders of the month-long antisegregation campaign here.

Chicago Daily News, May 7, 1963

Rioting Negroes Routed by Police at Birmingham

by Claude Sitton

BIRMINGHAM, Ala., May 7—The police and firemen drove hundreds of rioting Negroes off the streets today with high-pressure hoses and an armored car.

The riot broke out after 2,500 to 3,000 persons rampaged through the business district in two demonstrations and were driven back.

The Negroes rained rocks, bottles and brickbats on the law-enforcement officials as they were slowly forced backward by the streams of water. The pressure was so high that the water skinned bark off trees in parks and along sidewalks.

Policemen from surrounding cities and members of the Alabama Highway Patrol rushed to a nine-block area near the main business district to help quell the riot.

An undetermined number of persons were injured in the demonstrations against segregation. They included the Rev. Fred L. Shuttlesworth, a Negro leader, and two city policemen and a Jefferson County deputy sheriff.

[The National Association for the Advancement of Colored People called for peaceful picketing in 100 cities around the country to protest the actions of the Birmingham officials. In Greenfield Park, N.Y., a group of Conservative rabbis left for Birmingham in a "testimony on behalf of the human rights and dignity" of Negroes.]

Clarence B. Hanson Jr., publisher of The Birmingham News, the city's afternoon daily, appealed today in a telegram to President Kennedy to persuade Negro leaders to halt the demonstrations. The text of the telegram was carried on the front page of the newspaper.

Burke Marshall, chief of the Justice Department's Civil Rights Division, met privately with white business, professional and civic leaders from Birmingham and Jefferson County. The group was reported to be in telephone contact with Negro leaders. Later, a spokesman said the group had "high hopes" for developments in the next day or two that would ease the tension here.

In the demonstrations today, only 28 persons, including four juveniles, were arrested, as compared with some 1,000 yesterday. The police apparently wanted to avoid further arrests. Sheriff Melvin Bailey conceded that, from the standpoint of prison space, "we've got a problem."

Gov. George C. Wallace ordered 250 highway patrolmen to this Southern steel center, which has been torn by racial strife for five weeks. Some of the patrolmen have been trained in controlling riots.

Brig. Gen. Henry V. Graham of the Alabama National Guard arrived here after the situation was under control. He served as State Adjutant General under former Gov. John Patterson and enforced martial law in Montgomery, the state capital, in the Freedom Rider riots of 1961.

It could not be learned immediately whether his presence indicated that Governor Wallace was considering the use of the National Guard here.

In Montgomery, Governor Wallace addressed the opening session of the state legislature. He promised to "take whatever action I am called upon to take" to preserve law and order.

"I am beginning to tire of agitators, integrationists, and others who seek to destroy law and order in Alabama," he said.

The Rev. Dr. Martin Luther King Jr. called the reluctance of the police to arrest Negroes a victory. The Atlanta minister, president of the Southern Christian Leadership Conference, is leading the integration campaign.

Dr. King and his lieutenants appeared to have little control of the demonstrations, which were joined by hundreds of bystanders. One conference official accused leaders of the Student Nonviolent Coordinating Committee, an Atlanta-based integration group, of "whipping up" the emotions of the many teen-age participants.

The rioting broke out at about 2:45 P.M., Central Standard time, when Negroes jammed along sidewalks on the south side of the Kelly Ingram Park began hurling stones at the policemen and firemen.

Safety Commissioner Eugene Connor, who is in charge of the Fire and Police Departments, gave the order to turn the hoses on them. For almost an hour a seesaw struggle was waged around the park and in side streets and alleys.

The rioters were driven back at one point, only to appear again at another point to rain stones on the authorities. A deputy sheriff was struck by a stone opposite the 16th Street Baptist Church, the departure point for the demonstrations. He was carried to a hospital in a police cruiser.

A monitor, an extremely high-pressure fire nozzle fed by two, two-and-a-half-inch hoses, skidded out of control on its tripod mount opposite the church and struck two policemen. One suffered rib fractures and the other a leg injury.

Mr. Shuttlesworth, head of the Alabama Christian Movement for Human Rights, who also serves as pastor of a church in Cincinnati, Ohio, was struck by a stream of water and was hurled against the side of the church. He was carried inside and was later removed in a stretcher to an ambulance, which drove him to the Holy Family Hospital. Doctors said he had suffered chest injuries but was not hurt seriously.

Commissioner Connor, who arrived after the minister was driven away, said, "I waited a week to see Shuttlesworth get hit with a hose. I'm sorry I missed it."

A newsman noted that Mr. Shuttlesworth had been carried away in an ambulance.

"I wish they'd carried him away in a hearse," commented the commissioner.

Mr. Connor pointed out that several policemen had been injured and said, "We've just started to fight, if that's what they want. We were trying to be nice to them but they won't let us be nice."

The armored car, looking much like a tank with six wheels instead of tracks, roared backward and forward on 16th Street, forcing Negroes to the curb. Warnings to disperse were sounded repeatedly from loudspeakers atop the vehicle. There were a number of gun ports in the armor, but no guns were in evidence.

The stream from one fire hose picked a man up and flipped

him over, then sent him skittering along the grass in the park. Gutters along the southern edge of the elm-shaded square were overflowing.

Hundreds of whites massed along 18th Street to the east but made no effort to break through the police lines, thrown up at intersections to seal off the area.

Shortly after 3 P.M., Mr. Shuttlesworth marched into sight on the southern edge of the park at the head of 300 Negroes, many of them children. As they turned north, a monitor nozzle opened up and drove them all to cover.

Two Negro leaders, accompanied by Capt. George Wall of the police, walked along 16th Street for two blocks urging the crowd to go home. Their efforts had little apparent effect.

A few minutes later, 15 patrolmen armed with nightsticks charged behind a row of tenements opposite the church, confiscated a pile of stones and drove off the rioters who had been throwing them.

Five German shepherds, trained as police dogs, were brought up but were not used. They had been in past disturbances.

Before the demonstrations and the subsequent rioting, Dr. King voiced confidence over recent developments here. He and Mr. Shuttlesworth held a news conference at the Gaston Motel, headquarters for what Negroes call The Movement.

"Activities which have taken place in Birmingham over the last few days, to my mind, mark the nonviolent movement coming of age," Dr. King said. "This is the first time in the history of our struggle that we have been able, literally, to fill the jails.

"In a very real sense, this is the fulfillment of a dream."

Dr. King contended, as he has in the past, that imprisonment of Negroes "will lay the whole issue before the conscience of the community and the nation."

He said further that there would be no let-up in the demonstrations until the demands of the Negroes are met. He said white leaders seemed to recognize that the demands were just.

"But, at this point, I would not say that negotiations have been satisfactory," he said. "The demonstrations will go on until some progress has been made."

Less than two hours later, the first group of demonstrators, 14 schoolchildren, marched out of the 16th Street Church. Some clutched paper lunch bags, others had books. One child in a later group carried a suitcase.

The first 14 walked by twos east on Sixth Avenue past the Jockey Boy restaurant to 17th Street, where a policeman turned them north. Two other policemen at the next corner took their placards but allowed them to continue.

Juvenile authorities, their detention home and make-shift centers bulging with more than 1,000 demonstrators, began releasing children to their parents today on signed appearance bonds. Previously, cash bonds of $100 were required.

More than 100 juveniles were released, officials said, most of them under 13 years old. One was a 7-year-old girl arrested yesterday.

Dale Oltman, the chief probation officer of Juvenile Court, said authorities had called parents to encourage them to pick up their children. "We were concerned about having these younger children in detention," he said. "We felt they should be home with their parents."

The New York Times, May 8, 1963

9-Block Area Lies Devastated; Buildings Still Burn After Riot

by Hedrick Smith

B̲ᴵᴿᴹᴵᴺᴳᴴᴬᴹ, Ala., May 12—Dawn broke in Birmingham today to the sound of crackling flames eating through buildings, the gush of high-powered fire hoses and the shouts of state troopers.

Much of a nine-block area looked as if a vicious storm had struck.

Smashed and disabled police cruisers were abandoned in the streets. Seven stores and homes lay charred by fire. There was a hole in the brick wall of the A. G. Gaston Motel, caused by an explosion. Plate-glass windows were shattered in store after store in the Negro area.

Heaps of rocks and bricks littered the streets. Glass smithereens crackled under the feet of officers moving along sidewalks.

In front of the 16th Street Baptist Church, site of many Negro mass meetings during the civil rights drive here, smoke drifted upward from an overturned taxi. Less than a block away the tires of a motorcycle smoldered in the early light.

Troopers moved through the area in squads of a dozen to 20, ordering residents into their homes and outsiders away.

By 7 A.M., about 300 troopers and civilians were enforcing an uneasy peace in a 28-block area. They sealed off the section around the motel to everyone but officials and residents.

The blue-helmeted troopers, with night sticks, carbines, small arms and shotguns, later blocked every street and alleyway leading to the area.

"We're only passing folks who live in there," a highway patrolman said. Officials repeatedly rejected requests by newsmen to visit the battle-scarred section.

"It's for your own protection," a spokesman for the Police Department said.

At some check-points, officers were stopping and searching passing cars for weapons.

Seven miles away, in the suburb of Ensley, blasts punched a floor-to-ceiling hole in the home of the Rev. A. D. King, a leader in the desegregation drive. He is a younger brother of the Rev. Dr. Martin Luther King Jr., the Atlanta integrationist.

Four agents of the Federal Bureau of Investigation sifted the dirt outside his shattered home for clues to the bombings. In an undamaged back room, 10-year-old Albert King watched baseball on television.

Most of Birmingham superficially carried on activities as usual. Women wore bright dresses and men were well attired for Mother's Day. Homeowners were in their front yards, mowing the lawn or reading the newspaper.

Mayor-elect Albert Boutwell, whose authority has been challenged in the courts by the present three-member City Commission, issued a statement condemning the bombings and rioting.

"I want to make it plain to the hoodlums that this city will not tolerate violence, especially the dastardly hit-and-run bombers who wreak vengeance without regard for life and property," he declared.

It was a sweltering day. Troopers, clad in navy-blue shirts and light-blue trousers, looked hot and bored. Some sat on the hoods of their gray patrol cruisers, parked in intersections to block off approaches to the scene of the rioting. Others sat on curbs or chairs and benches beside their cars.

A big green police truck made its way around the check-points, delivering sandwiches, soft drinks and coffee to the officers.

On guard with the troopers were men in civilian clothes wearing khaki helmets and arm bands reading, "Alabama Department of Public Safety."

The sealed-off area was about four blocks northwest of the main business district. Along its borders troopers stared at passers-by and were studied in return. Negro residents kept a wary eye on the officers.

Shortly before 2 P.M., four officers at the 14th Street and Fifth Avenue check-point stopped two Negroes in a car. They lifted the hood, opened all the doors, checked the trunk, then searched the occupants before letting them continue.

Across the street, at least a dozen Negroes watched the procedure. They peered through doors and windows in their wooden-frame homes.

Hardest hit by the three-hour riot was the area near the two-story Gaston Motel. In addition to the motel, headquarters for the integration effort, three big house trailers were damaged by blasts.

The windows in the motel lobby and restaurant were shattered as were store windows across the street. Rocks thrown by rioting Negroes smashed windows in other stores.

A block and a half away, two small neighborhood stores were razed by a fire touched off two hours after the bombing.

All that remained of the stores, at the corner of 15th Street and Sixth Avenue, were metal display shelves and the brick bases.

Behind them was the blackened, wooden frame skeleton of a two-story home. A charred icebox sat on the remains.

Flames from the buildings had risen 100 feet as firemen battled them with a high-pressure hose just before dawn. Soon their stone chimneys tumbled. A telephone pole nearby caught fire, giving the appearance of a flaming cross.

Four other small, one-story stores in the neighborhood were razed by fire. Near the 16th Street Baptist Church, a taxi was pitched on its side, as the driver fled, and set afire by Negroes.

The driver, W. A. Bowman, a 50-year-old white, was admitted to University Hospital with stab wounds.

Nearly a score of police cars were smashed or damaged in this section and near Mr. King's home in Ensley.

The rioters shattered the windshield of a police paddywagon, jerked the seats from its cab, cut the tires and routed the occupants. Other police cars had broken windshields and dents from rocks.

When daylight came, wrecking crews gradually cleared the disabled cars and some debris from the streets in this section. Some owners boarded store windows for safety and to prevent looting.

The two blasts that demolished the front half of Mr. King's $26,000 home were felt four blocks away.

They tore a hole eight feet high and four feet across the brick-veneer fronting and blew out a large picture window.

The front door was knocked 10 feet into the living room. The metal porch railing was ripped from the concrete base and lay dangling over a three-foot hole in the ground.

The explosions knocked food from the ice box and showered debris 40 feet.

The bedrooms, in the rear of the house, were not damaged. Mr. King, his wife and their five children took refuge there after the first explosion, which apparently came on the front lawn.

Scores of Negroes from the surrounding community streamed to the King home to view the ruins in the morning.

Women and children walked through the wreckage.

Mr. King said his family was staying with friends temporarily. He appeared exhausted by his ordeal—the bombings and his efforts to persuade Negro rioters to stop attacking policemen earlier.

He said there should be "some tangible protests" against the bombings, but he added that the outbreak would not upset the desegregation agreement worked out earlier this week.

The New York Times, May 13, 1963

from
We Shall Overcome

by Michael Dorman

In the aftermath of the bombings and rioting, tension gripped Birmingham anew. And with it came nagging questions—the most important being whether the biracial agreement would be honored.

Dr. Martin Luther King flew back to Birmingham from Atlanta on Sunday and expressed confidence that the agreement would stand up. He said that no new demonstrations were planned because of the bombings. "I do not feel the events of last night nullified the agreement at all," King said. "I do not think the bombings were perpetrated or even sanctioned by the majority of the white people in Birmingham."

Nonetheless, there were strong doubts in some quarters about the possible effects of the night of violence on the implementation of the agreement. In addition, there was widespread fear that more violence might be in the offing. This fear led to a flurry of activity among federal officials. Assistant Attorney General Marshall, resting up from his Birmingham assignment at his farm in Berkeley Springs, West Virginia, was awakened by a phone call at 2 A.M. Sunday and told of the Birmingham violence. Attorney General Kennedy got the word a little later at his home in McLean, Virginia. President Kennedy, spending the weekend at Camp David, Maryland, was briefed on the Birmingham situation when he woke up.

The Attorney General, Marshall and other government officials phoned Birmingham white and Negro leaders from their homes to get the facts on the violence and try to calm things down. At 1 P.M., a government helicopter was sent to Marshall's farm to take him to Washington. He met first with the Attorney General at McLean. They then went to the Justice Department for a meeting with other officials. The Attorney General had taken his large black Newfoundland dog,

Brumus, to the office with him. While Kennedy conferred solemnly with his aides, Brumus romped around the office.

Meanwhile, President Kennedy flew back to Washington from Camp David by helicopter. He immediately went into conference at the White House with Defense Secretary Mc-Namara, Army Secretary Vance, Army Chief of Staff General Wheeler, and Theodore C. Sorenson, the President's special counsel. The presence of the military officials at the meeting gave rise to speculation that the President was considering using troops in the Birmingham crisis. But there was no immediate word from the White House on the President's plans.

Just before 6 P.M., Attorney General Kennedy, Marshall and Deputy Attorney General Katzenbach arrived at the White House to join the meeting. The President and the Attorney General had conferred by phone throughout the afternoon.

At 8:48, the President strode into the "Fish Room" of the White House to appear before the press and television cameras. Gravely, he read a statement:

I am deeply concerned about the events which occurred in Birmingham, Alabama, last night. The home of Reverend A. D. King was bombed and badly damaged. Shortly thereafter, the A. G. Gaston Motel was also bombed.

These occurrences led to rioting, personal injuries, property damage and various reports of violence and brutality. This government will do whatever must be done to preserve order, to protect the lives of its citizens and to uphold the law of the land. I am certain that the vast majority of the citizens of Birmingham, both white and Negro—particularly those who labored so hard to achieve the peaceful constructive settlement of last week—can feel nothing but dismay at the efforts of those who would replace conciliation and good will with violence and hate.

The Birmingham agreement was and is a fair and just accord. It recognized the fundamental right of all citizens to be accorded equal treatment and opportunity. It was a tribute to the process of peaceful negotiation and to the good faith of both parties. The federal government will not permit it to be sabotaged by a few extremists on either side who think they can defy both the law and the wishes of responsible citizens by inciting or inviting violence.

I call upon all the citizens of Birmingham, both Negro and white, to live up to the standards their responsible leaders set in reaching the agreement of last week, to realize that violence only breeds more violence and that good will and good faith are most important now to restore the atmosphere in which last week's agreement can be carried out. There must be no repetition of last night's incidents by any group. To make certain that this government is prepared to carry out its statutory and constitutional obligations, I have ordered the following three initial steps:

1. I am sending Assistant Attorney General Burke Marshall to Birmingham this evening to consult with local citizens. He will join Assistant Deputy Attorney General Joseph F. Dolan and other Justice Department officials who were sent back to Birmingham this morning.

2. I have instructed Secretary of Defense McNamara to alert units of the armed forces trained in riot control and to dispatch selected units to military bases in the vicinity of Birmingham.

3. Finally, I have directed that the necessary preliminary steps to calling the Alabama National Guard into federal service be taken now so that units of the Guard will be promptly available should their services be required.

It is my hope, however, that the citizens of Birmingham themselves maintain standards of responsible conduct that will make outside intervention unnecessary and permit the city, the state and the country to move ahead in protecting the lives and the interests of those citizens and the welfare of our country.

The President's action did not order federal troops into actual operations in Birmingham. It provided only that they be sent to bases near Birmingham, to be available in case of further violence. Three thousand GIs with riot-control training were dispatched to Maxwell Air Force Base at Montgomery and Fort McClellan at Anniston from other bases outside Alabama.

Similarly, the Alabama National Guard was not actually called into federal service, but the preliminary legal steps toward federalization of the Guard were taken, so that the actual federalization could be accomplished in a matter of minutes if it became necessary.

Alabama's segregationist Governor Wallace was incensed by Kennedy's action. He fired off a telegram to the President, questioning Kennedy's authority to send the troops into Alabama. Wallace insisted in the telegram that "we have sufficient state and local forces" to handle the Birmingham

situation, and asked Kennedy to leave the entire matter to the
state and local governments.

The U.S. Constitution, Wallace said, "states that the federal
government may send troops to quell domestic violence upon
application of the state legislature or the governor of a state.
The legislature of this state has made no request, nor have I.
May I ask by what authority you would send federal troops
into this state?"

In Washington, federal officials replied that Kennedy had
acted under a law giving the President power to quell civil
disturbances. The law, dating to 1871 and last revised in 1956,
is Section 133 of Title 10 of the United States Code. The section is headed "Interference with State and Federal Law." It
provides:

The President, by using the militia or the armed forces, or both,
or by any other means, shall take such measures as he considers necessary to suppress, in a state, any insurrection, domestic violence, unlawful combination or conspiracy if it—

1. So hinders the execution of the laws of that state, and of the
United States within that state, that any part or class of its people is
deprived of a right, privilege, immunity or protection named in the
Constitution and secured by law and the constituted authorities of
that state are unable, fail or refuse to protect that right, privilege or
immunity or to give that protection; or

2. Opposes or obstructs the execution of the laws of the United
States or impedes the course of justice.

In any situation covered by Clause 1, the state shall be considered
to have denied the equal protection of the laws secured by the
Constitution.

Sunday night passed without resumption of violence. But a
state of virtual martial law existed in Negro sections of Birmingham, where 1,200 helmeted peace officers kept close
watch for the possibility of further trouble.

On Monday, May 13, Dr. Martin Luther King set about trying to prevent such trouble. Few of the Negroes who had
participated in the Saturday night rioting had been members
of the integration movement. Rather, most of them had been
the habitués of pool halls, nightclubs and taverns. King felt
these Negroes had been missing his nonviolence message by
spending their time in such places, instead of at church. So,

like a wandering minstrel in search of an audience, he set out with a group of his aides on a tour of pool halls aimed at putting the message across. I went along.

At the smoke-filled New Home Billiard Parlor, the staccato clickety-clack of the cue sticks and pool balls was mingling with the mournful moan of a rock 'n roll record when King arrived. On one green wall hung a sign reading: "No Gambling. No Drinking. No Minors Allowed." About 100 Negroes, ranging from teen-agers to elderly men, clustered about the tables. The talk was boisterous, the language far from the kind you hear in church. It seemed hardly the place for an impromptu revival meeting. But a revival meeting was exactly what came about once King strode into the unlikely setting.

The pool-shooters obviously were surprised to see the renowned minister in their midst. But they obeyed respectfully when the pool hall manager told them: "All right, fellas, put your sticks down and come over here for a few minutes." They clustered around King and the Reverend Abernathy, some leaning on their cues, others sitting on the edges of the pool tables.

Abernathy, a spell-binding preacher, began the session in classic revival-meeting style, whipping the crowd to a fever pitch. "Every group needs a leader," he boomed. "Governor Wallace is not our leader. Bull Connor is not our leader."

"Right!" the pool-shooters shouted.

"Do you know who our leader is?" Abernathy asked.

"King!" came the reply.

"That's right. God sent Martin Luther King to be our leader. Are you willing to do whatever Martin Luther King tells you to do?"

"Yes!"

"Let's hear the King," Abernathy said.

"King, King, King, King, King, King, King, King, King, King, King!" the pool-shooters chanted.

Then King began to preach, his soft, melodious voice a sharp contrast to the deep rumble of Abernathy's. "We are engaged in a mighty struggle for dignity and human freedom," he said. "On Saturday night, after my brother's home and the Gaston Motel were bombed, we had a temporary reign of terror. Rocks were thrown; policemen were beat up; knives were used; stores were burned. I can well understand how deep-seated resentments can rise to the surface. But this is not the way we ought to act. We must make it clear that we can stand up to all injustices without fighting back with violence."

"Amen," shouted an elderly pool-shooter.

King continued: "As difficult as it is, we must not meet force with force. We must say, 'We don't care how many bombs you throw. We're not going to return violence.' For I believe that violence is immoral. But, more than that, it is impractical. We can't win with violence. Bull Connor is happy when we use force. He can cope with force. But he doesn't know how to handle nonviolence."

From the pool-shooters came: "Amen, brother, amen."

King urged them to spread his message to all their friends. "We must get rid of our knives," he said. "We don't need any guns. Try to get the idea of nonviolence over to the entire Negro community. That way, we can win. That way, we will win. I'm convinced that we shall overcome."

The pool-shooters then linked arms, some of them a bit self-consciously, and sang "We Shall Overcome."

The procedure was repeated at a second pool hall. When King set out for a third, a large crowd of Negroes fell in behind to walk with him. Two state troopers, evidently thinking a protest march was in progress, halted the procession. "Reverse and go back the way you came," one of the troopers ordered brusquely, brandishing a carbine. King, fearing the possibility of violence, decided to cancel the stop at the third pool hall.

As he turned and walked away, most of the Negroes behind him dispersed. But a few bystanders stood still. The two troopers, and four others who joined them, roughly pushed several of the Negroes, including an elderly woman, and told them to clear the area. With that, a sullen-faced young Negro who had followed King out of one of the pool halls turned to me and said: "I don't care what King says. I don't give a damn about that nonviolence stuff."

How many other Birmingham Negroes shared this view was an open question. But it did not take long to learn that racial violence had not ended completely in the city. On Monday night scattered incidents were reported. A white youth was attacked by a group of Negroes and slashed on the arm with a knife. A Negro man was hospitalized after being struck in the face with a steel ball fired from a white youth's slingshot. Windshields of autos belonging to both whites and Negroes were smashed, as were windows in about a dozen buildings owned by members of both races. But this violence did not swell into any major conflagration, and no move was made by federal officials to send troops into the city.

from *We Shall Overcome* (1965)

Police Dogs in Ala. Spur N.C. Unrest

by Cliff MacKay

GREENSBORO, N.C. —"When a police dog bites us in Birmingham, people of color bleed all over America."

That was the terse explanation given Saturday by Jesse Jackson, 21-year-old A. and T. College student president, for the social upheaval which is sweeping this state and the South.

There have been no biting police dogs used in North Carolina, but that memorable picture from Birmingham has served to launch a tidal wave of racial unrest that thus far has overwhelmed ten cities and still shows no signs of abating.

On one thing all of North Carolina's freedom fighters are in agreement: there will be no turning back; the status quo is gone forever.

The state's largest city, Charlotte, under Mayor Stan Brookshire has already fallen in line with an announcement that "all public facilities will be integrated immediately." The Chamber of Commerce backed his statement.

Businessmen of Thomasville have assured NAACP President, the Rev. W. E. Banks, that all downtown establishments will no longer discriminate.

A Durham bi-racial committee has launched a series of meetings designed to end discriminatory practices in all places licensed to serve the public.

Greensboro's Mayor David Schenk has appointed a special committee headed by Dr. G. W. Evans and empowered it to seek a solution "to our pressing racial problems."

Fifteen hundred arrests afterward, it has finally dawned on Greensboro officials that fear of jail would not halt the protests.

A word from liberal Gov. Terry Sanford, and the Bennett and A. and T. College students were released from makeshift lockups here, sorely disappointing some 3,000 others who had been eagerly waiting to experience "the thrills" of going to jail.

The demonstrations only gained momentum. From Greensboro, they have spread to nearby High Point and Winston-Salem; to Raleigh and Durham, to Fayetteville, Thomasville, Edenton, Wilmington and Charlotte.

Their point proved by overflowing the jails, the youthful freedom fighters, sponsored by CORE, immediately developed new strategy—the silent march.

A dignified, highly-disciplined line of as high as 4,000 marchers nightly walks silently, almost prayerfully through the downtown area. Grim faces show no smiles. There is no conversation, not a cigarette glows. Just the slap-slap-slap of hundreds of marching feet.

Suddenly a rag-tag group of confederate flag wavers bursts on the scene, chanting the old segregationist cadence, "two, four, six, eight, we don't want to integrate."

There is a smattering of applause from white spectators crowding the sidewalks, but the vast majority turn their backs, shamed by the unfavorable comparison of the silent marchers with the loud-mouthed demonstrators.

The quiet line passes beneath the marquee of the center theatre where "The Ugly American" is being shown to white patrons only.

There are no jeers, no mutterings as it moves around the corner, down two blocks to City Hall where suddenly the marchers fall to their knees in a continuous three-deep circle and begin praying.

The prayers are for Mayor David Schenk, whom the demonstrators accuse of frustrating their drive to make Greensboro a discrimination-free city.

The Mayor did appoint a bi-racial advisory committee headed by Dr. G. H. Evans, to seek a solution to the city's problems. The committee suggested that a special City Council session be called to pass laws requiring full integration and fair employment.

But the mayor has refused to heed the plea of his own committee.

Instead, on Friday, he said: "The City Council members have discussed this matter and have authorized me to state that it is our considered opinion that equal treatment of all persons without regard to race, color, or religion or any other mark of class distinction should be encouraged."

But that satisfied nobody. Nine students, four girls from Bennett and five men from A. and T., began a sit-in at the Mayor's office, vowing to remain until he called a council session.

Two hours later husky police arrived, picked up the sitters, chairs and all, carrying them next door to the police station where they were booked for disorderly conduct and then released.

William Thomas, president of Greensboro CORE, says the mayor is playing a "waiting game" that he cannot win. He reasons the mayor hopes the protests will cease with the closing of schools on Saturday.

"But while most of the college students will go home, we have two high schools with students to take the place of every one that leaves. Also the adult community has now become involved and the protests will not stop."

A selective buying campaign organized by the Greensboro Ministerial Alliance under Rev. C. W. Anderson has been termed 92 per cent effective.

It is this boycott, observers say, that forced the Greensboro Chamber of Commerce and the Merchants Association to go on record in support of CORE demands for a fully desegregated city.

This includes not only free access to all establishments which serve the public, but fair employment practices at City Hall, the desegregation of public schools, the opening of hospital facilities, segregation-free housing and representation on important city boards.

Mr. Thomas is also asking for dismissal of all charges now outstanding against some 1,500 freedom fighters.

An order to all A. and T. students by acting President Lewis C. Dowdy to "remain on the campus" until further notice or face dismissal has been largely ignored.

Student President Jesse Jackson charges that Dr. Dowdy was "pressured" into issuing the directive. The students, with but eight days remaining until Commencement, joined the nightly marches over the weekend. Thus far none has been dismissed.

Dr. Willa Player, president of Bennett College, a Methodist school, has not sought to restrict the protest activities of her girls.

Jackson, 21, is the son of Mr. and Mrs. Charles Jackson of Greenville, S.C., majoring in socio-economics. He has not decided whether to take law or earn a masters in marketing. He's a junior.

Also a sociology major is William Thomas, the CORE president. A native of Greensboro, he attended the University of Illinois for a year, before enrolling at A. and T. where he's in his senior year.

The Afro-American (Baltimore), June 1, 1963

Alabama Admits Negro Students; Wallace Bows to Federal Force

by Claude Sitton

TUSCALOOSA, Ala., June 11—Gov. George C. Wallace stepped aside today when confronted by federalized National Guard troops and permitted two Negroes to enroll in the University of Alabama. There was no violence.

The Governor, flanked by state troopers, had staged a carefully planned show of defying a Federal Court desegregation order.

Mr. Wallace refused four requests this morning from a Justice Department official that he allow Miss Vivian Malone and James A. Hood, both 20 years old, to enter Foster Auditorium and register.

This was in keeping with a campaign pledge that he would "stand in the schoolhouse door" to prevent a resumption of desegregation in Alabama's educational system.

The official, Nicholas deB. Katzenbach, Deputy Attorney General, did not press the issue by bringing the students from a waiting car to face the Governor. Instead, they were taken to their dormitories.

However, the outcome was foreshadowed even then. Mr. Katzenbach told Mr. Wallace during the confrontation:

"From the outset, Governor, all of us have known that the final chapter of this history will be the admission of these students."

Units of the 31st (Dixie) Division, federalized on orders from President Kennedy, arrived on the campus four and a half hours later under the command of Brig. Gen. Henry V. Graham.

A Birmingham real estate executive in civilian life, General Graham is the former State Adjutant General who enforced modified martial law in Montgomery, the state capital, following the Freedom Rider riots in 1961.

In a voice that was scarcely audible, General Graham said that it was his "sad duty" to order the Governor to step aside.

Mr. Wallace then read the second of two statements challenging the constitutionality of court-ordered desegregation and left the auditorium with his aides for Montgomery.

This sequence of events, which took place in a circus atmosphere, appeared to have given the Governor the face-saving exit he apparently wanted.

Whether the courts find that he actually defied the order issued last Wednesday by District Judge Seybourn H. Lynne in Birmingham remained to be seen. Significantly, Edwin O. Guthman, special assistant for information to Attorney General Robert F. Kennedy, noted that the students had not presented themselves for admission until Mr. Wallace had left the campus.

It thus appeared that the Kennedy Administration had saved itself the political embarrassment of bringing a contempt-of-court action against a second Southern Governor.

Gov. Ross R. Barnett of Mississippi now faces a trial for contempt as a result of his repeated defiance of orders directing the admission of James H. Meredith, a Negro, to the University of Mississippi last fall.

Tonight Mr. Guthman, in a news conference, said that it would be up to the courts to determine if Mr. Wallace should be prosecuted. He declined repeatedly to say whether the Justice Department would bring charges.

Governor Wallace gave no indication whether he still planned a show of defiance Thursday, when another Negro is scheduled to register at the university's Huntsville branch.

He is Dave M. McGlathery, 27, a mathematician for the National Aeronautics and Space Administration at the George C. Marshall Space Flight Center in that northern Alabama city.

However, there was speculation among Wallace aides that the Governor would not seek to interfere with Mr. McGlathery's registration.

Mr. Guthman told newsmen that Federal officials did not now plan to send troops to Huntsville. "The situation will be handled by state and university officials," he said.

There were indications that the 500 to 600 Guardsmen

dispatched to Tuscaloosa might not be needed for a lengthy period.

Judge Lynne's preliminary injunction against Governor Wallace followed a finding by District Judge H. H. Grooms that the university must admit the three students under a permanent injunction issued by Judge Grooms in 1955.

That order brought the registration of Miss Autherine Lucy, the first Negro to attend a formerly white public education institution in this state.

Miss Lucy, now Mrs. H. L. Foster, went to classes for three days in 1956. She withdrew and was later expelled after her lawyers had accused university officials of conspiring with the rioters who opposed her presence.

The injunction against Governor Wallace prohibited him from taking any of the following steps:

¶ Preventing, blocking or interfering with—by physically interposing his person or that of any other person—the Negroes' admission.

¶ Preventing or seeking to prevent by any means the enrollment or attendance at the university of any person entitled to enroll under the Lucy injunction.

The long-awaited confrontation between Governor Wallace and the Federal officials came shortly after 11 o'clock [1 P.M., New York time] on the sunbaked north steps of Foster Auditorium, a three-story building of red brick with six limestone columns.

Approximately 150 of the 825 state troopers, game wardens and revenue agents under the command of Col. Albert J. Lingo, State Director of Public Safety, lined the concrete walkways at the auditorium.

Others in this group, brought here to prevent any outbreak of violence, stood guard at entrances to the campus and patrolled the treeshaded stretch, which reaches westward to the banks of the Black Warrior River.

Shortly after 9:30 A.M., the Governor's aides and legal advisers arrived at the auditorium accompanied by two of his brothers, Circuit Judge Jack Wallace of Barbour County, and Gerald Wallace, a Montgomery lawyer.

Maj. Gen. Albert N. Harrison, State Adjutant General, walked hurriedly in and out of the auditorium, conferring with the Governor's assistants and Colonel Lingo. He was dressed in civilian clothes, apparently realizing that he would not be asked to command the troops that might be used.

Governor Wallace and Seymore Trammell, State Finance Director, an ardent segregationist who is a top political adviser, rode up behind a highway patrol motorcycle escort shortly before 10 o'clock.

Mr. Wallace was dressed neatly in a light gray suit, a blue shirt, a blue and brown tie with a gold tie clip and black shoes. He joked with the some 150 newsmen waiting in the broiling sun that sent the temperatures near 100 degrees. Then he went inside to an air-conditioned office to await the arrival of the Negro students.

Four Federal officials entered the auditorium a few minutes later. However, the scheduled arrival time of 10:30 A.M. passed with no sign of the students.

At 10:48 A.M., a white sedan followed by two brown sedans pulled up before the auditorium. Mr. Katzenbach emerged and walked to the entrance accompanied by Macon L. Weaver, United States Attorney for the Northern District of Alabama, and Peyton Norville Jr., the Federal marshal for this area.

Governor Wallace stood waiting behind a lectern placed in the doorway by a state trooper. He wore a microphone around his neck that was connected to a public address system.

Mr. Katzenbach said he had a proclamation from President Kennedy directing Governor Wallace to end his defiant stand. He asked the Governor to give way, but Mr. Wallace interrupted him and began reading a lengthy statement.

"The unwelcomed, unwanted, unwarranted and force-induced intrusion upon the campus of the University of Alabama today of the might of the Central Government offers a frightful example of the oppression of the rights, privileges and sovereignty of this state by officers of the Federal Government," he asserted.

Mr. Wallace cited the provision of the 10th Amendment that provides that powers not delegated to the Federal Government are retained by the states.

"I stand here today, as Governor of this sovereign state, and refuse to willingly submit to illegal usurpation of power by the Central Government," he said.

The Governor implied that there might have been violence were it not for his presence when he said:

"I stand before you today in place of thousands of other Alabamians whose presence would have confronted you had I been derelict and neglected to fulfill the responsibilities of my office."

He concluded by asserting that he did "denounce and forbid this illegal and unwarranted action by the Central Government."

"I take it from that statement that you are going to stand in the door and that you are not going to carry out the orders of the court," said Mr. Katzenbach, "and that you are going to resist us from doing so. Is that correct?"

"I stand according to my statement," replied Mr. Wallace.

"Governor, I am not interested in a show," Mr. Katzenbach went on. "I don't know what the purpose of this show is. I am interested in the orders of these courts being enforced."

The Federal official then told the Governor that the latter had no choice but to comply.

"I would ask you once again to responsibly step aside," said Mr. Katzenbach. "If you do not, I'm going to assure you that the orders of these courts will be enforced."

The Deputy Attorney General then asserted:

"Those students will remain on this campus. They will register today. They will go to school tomorrow."

After several pleas in a similar vein, including the one in which he forecast the students' admission, Mr. Katzenbach waited for the Governor to reply. Mr. Wallace stood defiantly in the door, his head thrown back, his lips compressed tightly.

The Federal officials returned to the car in which Miss Malone and Mr. Hood had been waiting. Mr. Katzenbach and Miss Malone then walked unmolested to nearby Mary Burke Hall, the dormitory in which she will live.

John Doar, first assistant in the Justice Department's Civil Rights Division, drove with Mr. Hood to Palmer Hall. Several student council members shook hands with Mr. Hood.

Both students ate lunch later in university cafeterias without incident.

Word of General Graham's arrival at 1:50 P.M. by military plane from Birmingham brought another series of consultations and preparations inside and outside the building. Troopers dispersed several hundred students who had filtered into the area.

At 3:16 P.M., three National Guard troop carriers escorted by Tuscaloosa motorcycle patrolmen and followed by a jeep roared up to Mary Burke Hall. Infantrymen, dressed in green fatigues and armed with M-1 rifles, jumped down and formed beside the auditorium.

Another convoy arrived on a street northwest of the auditorium. General Graham pulled up beside it in a green, unmarked command car.

The troops took up positions in the vicinity of the auditorium. Colonel Lingo walked over and saluted the general, who returned the salute. They then shook hands.

Mr. Katzenbach and other officials conferred briefly with General Graham. A short time later, the officer strode purposefully toward the entrance, followed by four unarmed special forces soldiers, all sergeants.

As the military party approached, Mr. Trammell turned toward the entrance and clapped on his straw hat. At this signal, Mr. Wallace walked out the door after an aide had straightened his tie.

General Graham walked to within four feet of the Governor. Standing at attention and leaning forward, he began to speak in a grim voice.

"It is my sad duty—" and his voice sank so low that bystanders could barely hear it.

Governor Wallace pulled a crumpled piece of paper from his pocket and read a brief statement. He said that had the Guardsmen not been federalized, "I would at this point be your commander. I know that this [duty] is a bitter pill for you to swallow."

He then reiterated earlier requests that white Alabamians refrain from violence.

The Governor denounced what he termed a trend toward "military dictatorship" in the nation. "We shall now return to Montgomery to continue this constitutional fight," he said.

General Graham saluted the Governor smartly. After returning the salute, Mr. Wallace and his aides walked swiftly to waiting cars and were driven away, to the cheers of students.

Three minutes after their departure, Mr. Hood walked into the auditorium with Federal officials to register. Miss Malone followed a minute later.

N.A.A.C.P. Leader Slain in Jackson; Protests Mount

by Claude Sitton

JACKSON, Miss., June 12—A sniper lying in ambush shot and fatally wounded a Negro civil rights leader early today.

The slaying touched off mass protests by Negroes in which 158 were arrested. It also aroused widespread fear of further racial violence in this state capital.

The victim of the shooting was Medgar W. Evers, 37-year-old Mississippi field secretary of the National Association for the Advancement of Colored People. Struck in the back by a bullet from a high-powered rifle as he walked from his automobile to his home, he died less than an hour later—at 1:14 A.M. (3:14 A.M., New York time)—in University Hospital.

Agents of the Federal Bureau of Investigation joined Jackson, Hinds County and state authorities in the search for the killer.

A 51-year-old white man was picked up, questioned for several hours and released. Investigators discovered a .30-06-caliber rifle with a newly attached telescopic sight in a vacant lot near the honeysuckle thicket from which they believed the fatal shot had been fired.

[In New York, the N.A.A.C.P. offered a $10,000 reward for information leading to the arrest and conviction of Mr. Evers's killer. The Rev. Dr. Martin Luther King Jr. mourned Mr. Evers as a "pure patriot."]

The first demonstration today occurred at 11:25 A.M., when 13 ministers left the Pearl Street African Methodist Episcopal Church and walked silently toward the City Hall.

The police, who refused to let them proceed by twos at widely spaced intervals, arrested all 13. The group included many of the Negro leaders who had been working with white officials in efforts to resolve this city's month-old racial crisis.

An hour and a half later, approximately 200 Negro teenagers marched out of the Masonic Building on Lynch Street, site of Mr. Evers's office. Some 100 city policemen, Hinds County deputy sheriffs and state highway patrolmen, armed with riot guns and automatic rifles, halted them a block away.

A total of 145 demonstrators, including 74 aged 17 and under, were then arrested. One girl was struck in the face by a club, deputies wrestled a middle-aged woman spectator to the sidewalk and other Negroes were shoved back roughly.

Mrs. Evers spoke tonight to some 500 persons at a mass meeting in the Pearl Street church. Dressed in a pale green dress, she appeared tired but composed. Many women in the audience wept openly.

Referring to her husband's death, she said, "It was his wish that this [Jackson] movement would be one of the most successful that this nation has ever known."

Mrs. Evers, who had requested that she be given the opportunity to speak, said that her husband had spoken of death last Sunday and said that he was ready to go.

"I am left with the strong determination to try to take up where he left off," she said. "I hope that by his death that all here and those who are not here will be able to draw some of his strength, some of his courage and some of his determination to finish this fight.

"Nothing can bring Medgar back, but the cause can live on."

Leaflets distributed at the meeting urged Negroes to return to the church tomorrow "prepared for action."

Other speakers also called on the audience to mourn Mr. Evers's death by wearing a black patch on their clothing for at least 30 days and by boycotting downtown white merchants.

A fund designed to provide money for the education of the Evers children was started here at the meeting. Speakers called on persons all over the nation to contribute to it.

The slaying, coupled with the arrests, led to sorrow mixed with anger among Negroes. Whites in this strongly segregationist community publicly expressed shock. But privately they showed more concern over the possibility of Negro retaliation.

The sentiment of Negroes seemed to be summed up by a slogan lettered on a white N.A.A.C.P. T-shirt worn by one of the demonstrators. "White Man, You May Kill the Body, but Not the Soul," it declared.

There were well-founded reports that a number of Negroes had armed themselves.

Gov. Ross R. Barnett and other officials issued statements deploring Mr. Evers's slaying and offering rewards for the arrest and conviction of the guilty.

Many of them, including Governor Barnett and Mayor Allen C. Thompson, are members of the Citizens Councils, a racist organization with national headquarters here.

The Mississippi Publishers Corporation, publisher of The Clairon-Ledger and Jackson Daily News, offered a $1,000 reward. These newspapers have spearheaded the campaign to maintain 100 per cent segregation throughout the state.

In a statement, Governor Barnett said of the killing:

"Apparently it was a dastardly act and as Governor of the State of Mississippi, I shall cooperate in every way to apprehend the guilty party.

"Too many such incidents are happening throughout the country, including the race riot last night in Cambridge, Md."

Governor Barnett and other officials here have frequently attacked the N.A.A.C.P. as an organization inspired by Communist aims and dedicated to the subversion of "the Southern way of life."

Mayor Thompson broke off a brief visit to a Florida resort to fly back to Jackson. He and City Commissioners D. L. Luckey and Tom Marshall announced the city was offering a $5,000 reward.

"Along with all of the citizens of Jackson, the commissioners and I are dreadfully shocked, humiliated and sick at heart that such a terrible tragedy should happen in our city," Mr. Thompson said in a statement.

"We will not stop working night or day until we find the person or persons who are responsible for such a cowardly act, and we urge the cooperation of everyone in this search," the Mayor said.

Mayor Thompson declined to comment on the mood of white residents of the state capital. He said he had been too busy with the investigation to talk to many of them.

However, one policeman said of the slayer:

"He destroyed in one minute everything we've been trying to do here."

He then asserted, "We're just scared to death. That's the truth."

Jimmy Ward, editor of The Jackson Daily News, expressed concern over the damage that the incident might cause to Jackson's reputation.

He did so in his daily front-page column, which frequently contains jokes aimed at the N.A.A.C.P., other civil rights organizations and their leaders and members.

"Despite numerous, most earnest appeals for law and order at all times and most especially during the current racial friction in Jackson," Mr. Ward wrote, "some conscienceless individual has stooped to violence and has greatly harmed the good relations that have existed in Jackson. All Mississippians and especially this shocked community are saddened by the dastardly act of inhuman behavior last night."

Mr. Evers, a native of Decatur, Miss., and an Army veteran of World War II, had been one of the key leaders in the Negroes' drive here to win a promise from the city to hire some Negro policemen and to appoint a biracial committee.

He left a mass meeting at a church last night, stopped at the residence of a Negro lawyer and then drove to his home on the city's northern edge. Before leaving the church, he remarked to a newsman that "tomorrow will be a big day."

He arrived at his neat, green-paneled and buff-brick ranch-style home on Guynes Street shortly after midnight. The accounts of the authorities, his wife and neighbors showed that the following series of events had taken place:

He parked his 1962 light blue sedan in the driveway, behind his wife's station wagon.

As he turned to walk into a side entrance opening into a carport, the sniper's bullet struck him just below the right shoulder blade.

The slug crashed through a front window of the home, penetrated an interior wall, ricocheted off a refrigerator and struck a coffee pot. The battered bullet was found beneath a watermelon on a kitchen cabinet.

Mr. Evers staggered to the doorway, his keys in his hand,

and collapsed near the steps. His wife, Myrlie, and three children rushed to the door.

The screaming of the children, "Daddy! Daddy! Daddy!" awoke a neighbor, Thomas A. Young. Another neighbor, Houston Wells, said he had heard the shot and the screams of Mrs. Evers.

Mr. Wells, according to the police, said he had looked out a bedroom window, saw Mr. Evers's crumpled body in the carport and had rushed out into his yard. He said he had crouched behind a clump of shrubbery, fired a shot into the air and shouted for help.

The police, who arrived a short time later, helped neighbors place Mr. Evers in Mr. Wells's station wagon.

As the station wagon sped to University Hospital, those who accompanied the dying man said he had murmured weakly, "Sit me up," and later, "Turn me loose."

Dr. A. B. Britton, Mr. Evers's physician, a member of the Mississippi Advisory Committee to the Federal Civil Rights Commission, rushed to the hospital. He indicated that the victim had died from loss of blood and internal injuries.

Mr. Evers expressed a premonition several weeks ago that he might be shot, according to Dr. Britton. The physician said he and other friends believed that they should have taken steps then to protect him.

City detectives making the investigation found a newly cleared space in the honeysuckle thicket some 200 feet southwest of Mr. Evers's home. They speculated the killer had hidden there while awaiting the arrival of his victim.

Lights in the carport, according to investigators, silhouetted Mr. Evers's body and enabled the sniper to see through the telescopic sight.

The New York Times, June 13, 1963

from

Mississippi Black Paper

MONTGOMERY COUNTY

I am a Negro, 46 years of age, and reside in Ruleville, Sunflower County.

On the 9th of June, 1963, I, Miss Annell Ponder, and eight other women were returning from a voter registration workshop in South Carolina. We were on a Continental Trailways bus that stopped at Winona, Montgomery County, at the bus station. Annell Ponder and others of our party, including James West from Itta Bena, Rosemary Freeman from near Greenwood, and June Johnson, a 15-year-old girl, got off the bus to go to the restaurant. Two, Euvester Simpson and Ruth Day, also of our party, got off the bus to use the rest room. I remained on the bus.

The four that got off the bus to go to the restaurant—and had gone to the "white" side of the restaurant—were coming back to the bus. I got off the bus and asked them what happened. They said that there were some policemen and highway patrolmen in there. Annell said policemen with billy clubs told them to get out of there. I said that this can be reported and Annell said, "Yes, I am going to get the tag number." The four of them were standing outside to get the tag number, and Euvester Simpson was standing with them talking, when all five of them were put in the patrol car, which I think was the highway patrolman's car; he was also the one giving orders.

I got off the bus when all at once an officer from the patrol car said, "Get that one too." A county deputy, Officer A——, and one more got out of the car and opened the door to his car and said, "You are under arrest." I was going into the car when Officer A—— kicked me into the car. While driving me to the jail, they were questioning me and calling me "bitch."

We got to the jail, and I saw all five of the above [Annell Ponder, Rosemary Freeman, June Johnson, James West, and

Euvester Simpson] in the booking room. As soon as I got to the booking room, a tall policeman walked over to James West and jumped hard on James West's feet.

I was led into a room—a cell—with Euvester Simpson. While I was in the cell, I could hear screaming and the passing of kicks. Pretty soon I saw several white men bringing Annell Ponder past my cell. She was holding on to the jail walls, her clothes all torn, her mouth all swelled up, and her eyes were all bloody—only one eye looking like itself.

After a while they came for me: Officer B——, a highway patrolman (his name on a metal plate on his pocket); the policeman who had jumped on James West's feet; and another policeman with a crew-cut haircut.

They came into my cell and asked me why I was demonstrating, and said that they were not going to have such carryings-on in Mississippi. They asked me if I had seen Martin Luther King, Jr. I said I could not be demonstrating—I had just got off the bus—and denied that I had seen Martin Luther King. They said "Shut up" and always cut me off. They then asked me where I was from. I said Ruleville. They then left, saying that they were going to check it out.

They then returned. Officer B—— said: "You damn right you are from Ruleville. We are going to make you wish that you were dead, bitch." They led me to another cell. Before I had been led out of the cell, I saw a Negro—who I reckoned was a trusty, who stayed around the jail—bring a mop and bucket to take somewhere.

When I was brought to another cell I saw two Negroes who were in their 20s or a little younger. Officer B—— said, "Take this," talking to the youngest Negro. Officer B—— had in his hand a long, 2-foot blackjack made out of leather, wider at one end, and one end being filled with something heavy. The young Negro said: "You mean for me to beat her with this?" Officer B—— said, "You damn right. If you don't, you know what I will do for you."

The young Negro told me to get on the bunk and he began to beat me. I tried to put my hands to my side where I had polio when I was a child, so that I would not be beat so much on that side. The first Negro beat me until he got tired. Then the second Negro was made to beat me. I took the first part of it, but couldn't stand the second beating. I began to move and the first Negro was made to sit on my feet to keep me from kicking. I remember that I tried to smooth my dress which was working up from all of the beating. One of the white officers pushed my dress up. I was screaming and going on, and the young officer with the crew-cut began to beat me about the head and told me to stop my screaming. I then began to bury my head in the mattress and hugged it to kill out the sound of my screams. It was impossible to stop the screaming. I must have passed out—I remember trying to raise my head and heard one of the officers, Officer B——, who said, "That's enough."

He said, "Get up and walk." I could barely walk. My body was real hard, feeling like metal. My hands were navy blue, and I couldn't bend the fingers. I was taken back to the cell.

While I was back in the cell, I could talk to June Johnson, Annell Ponder, and Rosemary Freeman, who were in their cells. I learned that June Johnson had a hole in her head from her beating. I learned that the trusty had used the bucket and mop to mop the blood.

Then they got us up one night to take our pictures and Officer B——, who had taken the pictures, forced me to sign a statement which they already had made me write, that I had been treated all right. That night was the following Monday night. I tried to write the statement in such a way that anybody would know that I had been forced to write the statement.

The following Tuesday, we had our trial. There was no jury. We had no lawyer. We were charged and were found guilty of disorderly conduct and resisting arrest.

When we were put in the jail, and when I was put in the jail, I told them that nothing is right around here. The arresting officer had lied and said that I was resisting arrest. I told them that I was not leaving my cell, and that if they wanted me they had to kill me in the cell and drag me out. I would rather be killed inside my cell instead of outside the cell.

On that Tuesday, I heard some white men talk to Officers C—— and D—— and that they were FBI and had to report what they said. I was able to see Lawrence Guyot, a field secretary of SNCC who I had known before in voter registration work, and saw him in the booking room and saw that he had been beaten.

On the following Wednesday, James Bevel, Andrew Young, and Dorothy Cotton of SCLC (Southern Christian Leadership Conference) came to see us and to get us (the people who had been on the bus and were arrested) out. But before I left the jail I was able to see that Lawrence Guyot's head had been beaten out of shape.

On the 31st of August, 1962, I had been fired from my plantation job, Dee Marlow's Plantation, Ruleville, because I attempted to register to vote. I had been working for SNCC and SCLC before I had been beaten. At the present time, I am a candidate for Congress in the coming primary, for the Second Congressional District.

Doctor Searcy, Cleveland, Mississippi, said that I had been beaten so deeply that my nerve endings are permanently damaged, and I am sore.

SIGNED: *Fannie Lou Hamer*

MONTGOMERY COUNTY

I am 31, Negro, and a resident of Atlanta, Georgia.

I was returning on June 9, 1963, from a workshop in voter education and community development held in John's Island, South Carolina. I was returning on a Trailways bus together with Mrs. Fannie Lou Hamer, June Johnson, Euvester Simpson, James West, Rosemary Freeman, and four other people.

When we got to the Winona bus station at about 12 noon, the five people named above, excepting Mrs. Hamer, got off the bus, and June Johnson, James West, and Rosemary Freeman and I went into the lunchroom. This lunchroom was the one normally reserved for white people (all of the party were Negroes). We sat down at the counter and the waitress behind the counter wadded up some paper and threw it against the wall and said: "I can't take no more."

By this time a member of the Winona city police (apparently ——) and a member of the highway patrol entered the back of the room. They came up behind where we were sitting and tapped each of us on the shoulders and said: "Get up and get out of here." I was the last one on the line, and I asked him if he didn't know it was against the law to put us out. (This was after the ICC ruling against discrimination in ICC facilities.) He said: "Ain't no damn law, get up and get out of here."

So we went outside. We stood outside discussing what happened. Mrs. Hamer saw us and got off the bus and asked us why we had come out so quick. So we told her what happened, and she said: "Yeah, this is what we have to put up with. This is what we have to go against here in Mississippi."

Then we agreed that we would include what had happened here in a report we were going to make about incidents during the trip. Mrs. Hamer got back on the bus and the rest of us stayed in front of the station talking, saying that it didn't look good to get up and walk out of the lunchroom when we knew we had a right to be in there. We said if anything like that happened again, we would just go to jail.

Then I went back to the door and looked inside to get a better look at the police officers, so I could identify them. But they crouched back against the wall so I couldn't see them. So I decided I would get the number off the patrolman's car. It didn't have a number on the side so we walked around to the back, to get the license plate number.

As I was taking that down, the officers came out of the restaurant and said that we were under arrest, and said: "You all get in that car," indicating the highway patrol car. Mrs. Hamer saw us getting in the car and she got off the bus, and she called out to me and asked me what I wanted them to do. I told her to go ahead on the bus.

The officer driving the car we were in called out to another policeman and said: "Get that other one too." Mrs. Hamer was then placed in another car which followed us to the Montgomery County Jail.

When we got there they started questioning us and one of them asked me something and I said "Yes" or "No." Then he wanted to know if I had enough "respect" for him to say "sir" when I answered his questions. So I asked him what he said, and he repeated his question, using the term "nigger" to refer to me. I told him I didn't know him that well. He looked very angry and confused. Then the highway patrolman walked over and stepped hard on James West's foot and ground on it, though James had not done anything.

Then they questioned us more about the civil rights work, about the Greenwood voter registration project, and said we had come to demonstrate. After a while they put us in cells, two of us together in a cell. James West and June Johnson were kept out.

After we were in awhile, I heard them questioning June Johnson, asking her what did she think they were supposed to do about it, apparently referring to our presence in Winona and our activities in civil rights. June said that she felt they were supposed to protect us and take care of us. Then I began to hear sounds of violence. There was a whiskey still (metal) in the booking room and I could hear people scraping against this and the floor and walls, and could hear June screaming.

After a while they came to get me, bringing June to put in my cell. She was bleeding from the face and neck and crying. They took me into the booking room, and made me stand several different places consecutively. Finally I was standing in a corner. There was blood on the floor in this place. I started to tell the four white men and police officers in the room that we wanted them to understand that we didn't hate them. When I told them that they turned toward me and one of them (in blue uniform) said he wanted to hear me say "sir." I ignored him. Another young man in a crew-cut said: "You just came up here to stir up trouble." The man slapped me in the head with his fist. Then the officer in blue uniform hit me. Then the highway patrolman wanted to know why I took down his license plate number. I told him I wanted to make an accurate report if there was trouble. They wanted to know who we would make a report to. I told him the federal government.

They said: "Who do you mean, Bobby Kennedy?" and there was contempt in their voices. I said: "No, the federal government." Then they started again insisting I say "sir." Through all this conversation they kept hitting me. The policeman in blue uniform at one point took a sort of blackjack from the man who I believe was —— and from then on he used that in beating me. This went on for about 10 minutes, with questioning and my being beaten to the floor and getting up and being beaten down again. At one point the highway patrolman hit me in the stomach. They finally stopped beating me and put me in a maximum security cell. One of my teeth had been chipped and my lip was bleeding, and later when I tried to walk I staggered and fell.

I was kept in the cell for three days and no doctor was brought to see me.

After three days I was charged in a trial with disorderly conduct and resisting arrest. We were found guilty, and appealed. And the next day we were released. We would have been fined $100 on each charge, but we got out on $200 appeal bond.

Since then the Justice Department brought suit against the officers. They denied the charge and an all-white male jury found them innocent.

SIGNED: *Annell Ponder*

MONTGOMERY COUNTY

I am 16 years old and live in Greenwood, Mississippi. A group of civil rights workers was traveling from Charleston, South Carolina, to Greenwood, Miss., by bus on June 9, 1963. The group consisted of Mrs. Fannie Lou Hamer, Miss Annell Ponder, Mr. James West, Miss Euvester Simpson, Miss Rosemary Freeman, and myself. On the trip from Columbus, Miss., to Winona, Miss., our group sat in the front of the bus and occasionally sang freedom songs.

When we got to Winona, the bus stopped at the terminal there. Everybody went into the terminal except Mrs. Hamer. When we got inside the terminal, our group sat down on the "white" side. [A] Winona [police officer] came in and told us to "get over where you belong." We got up and went outside the terminal. Soon the [police officer] and a state trooper came outside and arrested us. When she saw us getting into the trooper's car, Mrs. Hamer got out of the bus and asked us, "Should I go on to Greenwood?" We told her to go ahead, but the trooper called out, "Get that woman," and an unidentified white man grabbed her and put her in his car. The trooper took us to the Montgomery County Jail. Mrs. Hamer arrived in the other car about the same time.

We were taken inside. The trooper said, "What you niggers come down here for—a damn demonstration?" We all shook our heads and answered "No." Then he said, "You damn niggers don't say 'No' to me—you say 'Yes, sir.'" While he was saying this, Officer A—— and the Winona [police officer] came in, accompanied by the same white man that brought Mrs. Hamer in.

Officer A—— walked over and stamped James West's toe and hit Euvester in the side with a ring of heavy keys. Then the trooper questioned us. While questioning Annell Ponder, he found out that she lived in Atlanta, Ga. He told her, "I knew you wasn't from Mississippi 'cause you don't know how to say 'Yes, sir' to a white man." Then he turned to the rest of us and said, "I been hearing about you black sons-of-bitches over in Greenwood, raising all that hell. You come over here to Winona, you'll get the hell whipped out of you."

He opened the door to the cell block and told everybody to get inside. I started to go in with the rest of them and he said, "Not you, you black-assed nigger." He asked me, "Are you a member of the NAACP?" I said yes. Then he hit me on the cheek and chin. I raised my arm to protect my face and he hit me in the stomach. He asked, "Who runs that thing?" I answered, "The people." He asked, "Who pays you?" I said, "Nobody." He said "Nigger, you're lying. You done enough already to get your neck broken." Then the four of them—Officer A——, the [Winona police officer], the state trooper, and the white man that had brought Mrs. Hamer in—threw me on the floor and beat me. After they finished stomping me, they said, "Get up, nigger." I raised my head and the white man hit me on the back of the head with a club wrapped in black leather. Then they made me get up. My dress was torn off and my slip was coming off. Blood was streaming down the back of my head and my dress was all bloody. They put me in a cell with Rosemary Freeman, and called Annell Ponder. I couldn't see what they did to Annell, but I could hear them trying to make her say "Yes, sir." When they brought her back, she was bloody and her clothes were torn.

About 5 minutes later the trooper came in and yanked Rosemary Freeman off the bed and bumped her up against the brick wall of the cell two or three times. Then he turned to me and said, "Pull your dress down and wash off. When I come back in 5 minutes, you'd better be clean." I started to wash up but a man in a blue uniform told me to wait until we left.

Then we heard the policemen shouting at Mrs. Hamer in her cell. Then they took her somewhere into a different part of the building.

A little while later we heard Mrs. Hamer hollering, "Don't beat me no more, don't beat me no more." Later they brought her back to her cell crying. She cried at intervals during the night, saying that the leg afflicted with polio was hurting her terribly.

We stayed in that jail day and night from Sunday till Tuesday, when they booked us and informed us that we were charged with disorderly conduct and resisting arrest. We then went back to jail until Wednesday afternoon, when a group of SNCC people came from Greenwood to get us out of jail. We got back to Greenwood about 7 P.M. on June 12, 1963.

SIGNED: *June E. Johnson*

Mississippi Black Paper (1965)

Portrait of Three Heroes

by Tom Dent

In January 1963, as press assistant for the NAACP Legal Defense Fund in New York, I went to Jackson, Mississippi, to arrange a press conference for James Meredith to announce he would return to the University of Mississippi for a second semester. I had met Meredith the previous summer, and had been close to him and Mississippi civil rights people during the time our "Ole Miss" suit developed toward its tragic, but necessary, climax. This January trip, then, was really a chance for me to see again those friends whom I had come to know and admire during those fateful days.

Meredith had been in his apartment only two weeks, the first tenant to occupy this new red-brick structure. It is located on an unpaved road parallel to the legendary railroad tracks. His place is small; four rooms sparsely furnished. Barely enough room for himself and his wife, June, their three-year-old son, John, and Meredith's sister (who helps take care of John while June attends classes).

Less than an hour before, flying over Mississippi, I had felt, even within the air-pressured confines of our jet cabin, a certain tension. A white man sat next to me while I read a New York Public Library copy of Richard Wright's *The Outsider*. Even though Richard Wright was born in Mississippi I could not talk about *The Outsider* with the man from Mississippi next to me. The distance between our lives was so great that the illusion of proximity created by sitting side-by-side on that airplane was only a cruel joke.

Now Meredith, Medgar Evers and I were in front of the apartment house, talking.

We were concerned with whether Meredith should get his car repaired, or junk it. It had stalled on him at the Oxford campus a few weeks ago, and while he stood with the hood up trying to locate the trouble he was the target of insults and derisive laughter from those models of young America—his fellow students at the University of Mississippi.

Oxford, Mississippi, is the town where novelist William Faulkner lived, wrote and died. In 1956 he 'praised' Negroes in *Harpers*: "They have become skilled artisans and craftsmen capable of holding their own in a culture of technocracy."

As we stood behind those railroad tracks a train passed slowly by, and I wondered how Faulkner would describe the life and significance of Meredith, or Evers, if he were alive. I wondered how he could possibly comprehend the life vitiating behind those railroad tracks in terms such as *skilled artisans and craftsmen*, which means people who perform competently a task which they are taught.

Skilled artisans or craftsmen do not challenge a *system*, nor do they ask questions. But whites never go beyond the railroad tracks (except for the police to quell 'disturbances'), thus the tracks symbolize the limits of a white southern reality—a very limited reality indeed.

The tragedy of Mississippi—that lazy, blind, comfortable swampland—is the tragedy of the South. Whites cannot understand what is happening to 'their Negroes' in their 'magnolia state,' nor what will happen. And Faulkner had been their most persuasive mind.

Robert Smith, an intimate of Meredith and Evers, drove up. He is a short, stout man in his early thirties who looks as if he eats well. He does. Smith and his father own a supermarket in Jackson and considerable real estate. But the Smiths have used their money more ethically than any Negroes I know; they have contributed money to the Civil Rights Movement. Almost every person who has come here to help Medgar Evers has stayed at Smith's home, travelled in his car. His home is a civil rights hotel. Evers, Meredith, Smith: a dedicated (and lonely) triumvirate.

"Well, you know if you want to make a telephone call, you can use the one in the back of the store," Robert told Jay (Meredith). "It's not tapped." We laughed.

The telephones of Evers, Meredith and Smith in Jackson were always bugged. "When I want to make an important call," Evers remarked, "I always stop and say 'and I hope the white folks are listening!'"

So Meredith and I drove off to Smith's store. Evers went back to work.

Even by big city standards Smith's supermarket is an impressive business. He sells groceries and meats, cosmetics, newspapers, drugs, clothing, a whole variety of stuff.

I needed some things for my three-day stay. I purchased them there.

"Just pick out what you need and take it," Smith told me.

Meredith loves people, but he doesn't have to go to *them* anymore. They come to him. When we returned to his apartment late that afternoon, we discovered (to my shock, anyway) a white man helping little John to the toilet. I thought Meredith had expected him. But I learned he had not been expected. He had merely found out where Meredith lived, come there and waited for him.

I recognized his name: Walter Lord, author of *A Night To Remember* and other historical documentaries.

When Lord told Meredith about his plans for a book on the Ole Miss case, Jay said "the only objection I can think of is that someone might think you're using me to make money for yourself." Lord blinked, perhaps not believing what he had heard. Embarrassed, he mumbled something like "the book will be in the bookstores if people want to buy it."

But Walter Lord was persistent. He stayed, even through dinner, trying to get Meredith to answer questions about Mississippi politics, or the "battle of Ole Miss," while the telephone rang, friends dropped in and the baby cried. A year before no one cared what Meredith thought. A year before a white man would never have come to the home of a Mississippi Negro to ask him what he thought. Did Walter Lord expect to understand the realities of Mississippi race oppression, or what Meredith knew, in one chaotic hour?

Meredith was used to this chaos, he even seemed to thrive on it. But I tried to keep press people away from the apartment so he could at least have some privacy. Press people are told "get a story," and rarely respect anyone's privacy unless made to. That night, two television cameramen came. They wanted to set up their cameras and shoot Meredith "in the intimacy of his home," even though Jay was then bathing.

I read some of the mail Jay had received; there were boxes of letters in his bedroom. White southerners, Negroes from the north and south, soldiers, school children, college students and student-associations, foreign students, social workers (the most predictable, self-conscious letters), religious crackpots, race baiters and race haters—all wrote. Meredith had touched something deep in these people.

The ones that most moved me were from white southern youths. They couldn't ignore the realities of racial oppression any longer and they felt guilty about it. The letters appeared to be attempts to somehow expiate their guilt: "Go boy go, we can't tell our friends how we feel, but we're for you."

Of slight build, medium height, and dark brown skin, James Meredith speaks in a slow, high-pitched voice. He has a way of staring at people when he speaks, as if he wants to see how he is registering. He can be diplomatic; sometimes very, very blunt.

Though his attorneys, Mrs. Constance Baker Motley and Jack Greenberg, worried about his safety that previous summer, Meredith had absolutely no fear of possible injury to himself. He was almost foolishly unconcerned. Thus, even after he came under federal protection he often tried to get away from the marshals, and drove places by himself without escort. No warning from anyone did much good. He simply wasn't afraid, and strongly resented having his movements circumscribed. He would simply shrug off our admonitions with, "Oh, they're not going to shoot me."

During the time he was considering applying to the University, (apparently, he had thought about it a long time because his wife said they often discussed returning to Mississippi, even while they were courting) Meredith grew a beard. Mrs. Motley finally asked him to cut it off. Meredith consented, but one day he explained why he grew the beard. "I knew," he told her, "that if this case was filed and I actually did enter Ole Miss, I would have to withstand the pressure of being different, of being *strange* in the eyes of many people. Growing the beard was my test, a way of finding out whether I could go through with it."

Jay was very proud of the two farms he owned in his home-town, Kosciusko. He had purchased this property with money saved while he was in the Air Force. Though it wasn't valu-able property, Meredith wanted to *own* something.

"Hell," he often said, "all I want is the right to what I can earn for myself. Someday, I'd like to own my whole block."

The next morning Medgar Evers heard that Governor Bar-nett had pardoned Clyde Kennard. He would be released that morning from University Hospital in Jackson, where he had been hospitalized during his jail sentence.

Briefly, this was Kennard's story: he had tried in September, 1959 to enter Mississippi Southern University in Hattiesburg where he lived. Such an attempt by a Negro was unheard of at that time. Kennard had made his intentions known; the po-lice were waiting for him. On the day he attempted to enroll he was denied admission, then arrested on a bogus "speeding and possession of liquor" charge (Mississippi is a 'dry' state).

The Supreme Court of Mississippi later threw out those charges, but the Hattiesburg police weren't through with Kennard. On Nov. 14, 1960, he was arrested on a charge of inducing a 19-year-old Negro to steal five bags of chicken feed (worth $25), and sentenced to *seven years* in jail. The NAACP Legal Defense Fund had unsuccessfully tried several legal moves to free him.

Dick Gregory became interested in Kennard's story through Medgar Evers. Gregory sent private investigators at his own expense to Hattiesburg to seek out the truth. His in-vestigators discovered that Kennard was innocent, located the boy who committed the theft, and Gregory even offered to bring the boy to Chicago and find him a job if he would tes-tify in Kennard's behalf. He refused because he feared retalia-tion against his family in Mississippi.

A few people knew that Kennard was now dying of incur-able cancer. It was only because of his rapidly deteriorating condition that Barnett had that morning pardoned him.

When we entered University Hospital I was immediately struck by the absurd layout of the place. The segregatory de-vices had apparently been designed by a psychotic with a fas-cination for labyrinthine geometrics. The entrance to the Negro side was half the size of the entrance to the white side, the two entrances divided by a partition. Negroes were waited-on on one side of the central waiting desk, whites on the other. The waiting rooms were, of course, segregated, with water fountains designated: 'white only,' 'colored only,' 'white personnel only.' The rest rooms: 'white men,' 'white male personnel,' 'colored men,' 'colored male personnel,' 'white ladies,' 'colored females.' The hospital was a huge maze with signs pointing to where Negroes could or could not go (whites, however, were free to violate these signs if they wished).

Medgar stood at the 'colored' desk waiting to get some papers signed for Kennard's release. Kennard stood almost unnoticeable beside him, wearing denim trousers and a hooded blue sweat shirt. He is short, extremely thin (about 90 pounds) with no shoulders. Soon he would be out of jail for the first time in two years, but no joy or exultation showed on his face.

Kennard was thirty-four, his hair cut closely, his skin a very dark brown. He was extremely polite and soft-spoken. I wanted very much to talk with him, so after a wait of about fifteen minutes and still no service, I asked Kennard to come outside with me so we might talk, away from the suffocating atmosphere of the hospital.

It had been an overcast day, and when we reached the hospital door it began to rain.

We sat in Medgar's blue Oldsmobile. Kennard spoke about Parchman Prison:

"There's segregation even in prison. Let's sue the jails, too. They had fifteen farms at Parchman and no Negro non-inmate employees. We were like slaves. They even fed us leftovers from what the white prisoners ate. The white prisoners had the best jobs, lived in the best buildings. Parchman is just a modernized slave-labor camp."

Two Negro ministers from Hattiesburg came over to the car. They had heard about Kennard's release on the radio, and had come to the hospital to offer him a ride home. Kennard knew them and greeted them warmly.

We asked Kennard if the other Negro prisoners at Parchman knew his story, why he had been there? He said they did; and added:

"The night I left to come to the hospital they held a prayer meeting in our barracks. I told them not to do it because it's against the rules and I didn't want them to get whipped because of me. But they sang and sang, and the guards took names and names. In Mississippi in prisons, it's legal to whip prisoners—the laws says ten strokes. We called the whip 'black Annie.' I know they were all whipped the next day."

We began to talk about the significance of Meredith, of recent changes in Mississippi. He made, curiously, an observation which I heard from Meredith and Evers: "The white people who run this state are stupid. If the whites with power were more intelligent they might save themselves great tragedy. But the way Mississippi is going now, it's going to fall very hard."

He was excited over Meredith, what was happening in Mississippi. Kennard seemed like a soldier who had been captured at the front; now freed, he was as excited over Meredith's success as if it were his own. I asked him if he had ever met Meredith. He said "no," but he would like to.

I told him that he, in a way, had laid the groundwork for Meredith. "Maybe," he replied sadly, "but we look in life for success most of the time."

Kennard and I and the ministers had spent almost two hours talking, but Medgar still hadn't come. We wondered what on earth had happened to him. When I went back into the hospital, I found Medgar waiting now at the 'colored only' *prescription desk* for Clyde's pills. He had to wait until every white patient's prescription had been filled before they would serve him. They also recognized Medgar as 'the NAACP man,' so they made him wait longer. Medgar was furious. I was depressed and furious. We had been at that hospital three hours.

Medgar Evers was a very cool professional. Of all the civil rights people in Mississippi, I always felt safest with him because he had such marvelous self-control, seemed to know what was happening at all times, and had defied the white people for so long with no loss of dignity.

In September, he had driven Mrs. Motley, her secretary, Roberta Thomas, and me to Meridian during the height of the Ole Miss crisis. We were driving in the morning, when the

Mississippi highways are constricted with periodic school zone speed limits, so that one moment you may go sixty, then suddenly you're in a fifteen-mile-per-hour zone. We were followed three-quarters of the way by patrol cars just waiting for Evers to overshoot a limit, but he never did.

We were on our way to the federal district court on the Thursday Meredith was first turned back from Oxford by Governor Barnett. We had to drive through the small town where Evers was born.

"When I was discharged from the service," he said while driving, "I came back by bus to this town. When we were almost there the driver asked me to move back, back to the back. Well, I wouldn't do it. Hell, I'd just been on a battlefield for my country. When we reached my home town, the driver signalled to some men in town. They came on the bus and beat me within an inch of my life." He laughed softly. "It was the worst beating I ever had. But after that I was a different man."

In Meridian ugly crowds, which looked like the pictures one had seen of lynch mobs, loitered around the federal courthouse. Mississippi was, that day in September, in a state of shock because of *us*, and I personally felt there was danger. The small mobs outside the courthouse were waiting, just waiting—to *see* more than act. But they *knew* Evers, and as we walked through them to get to his car their recognition of him was obvious. So was their hatred.

Evers was a *field* man, his office was wherever he was needed in the state.

He told us that he was followed by police radio or patrol cars wherever he went. Medgar was not one to take unnecessary chances. He had no martyr complex. In fact, he had some white friends in Jackson who tipped him off when they received inside information. They were in the confidence of the police.

When we left the hospital that afternoon, Medgar was angry. Yet, he was still Medgar, that is, he was not so bitter that he couldn't offer a ride to the Negro section, to two women who had been waiting at the prescription desk with him.

We spoke of suing the hospital. Medgar said to these two women: "We're going to sue that hospital. I want you women to testify that the clerk told you to get your pills from a 'for colored only' window." They giggled. "Come on, now," Medgar urged, his voice edgy, "we've got to *stop* this stuff. All you have to do is testify as to what actually happened, nothing else. Give me your names and addresses, write them down on this piece of paper. Here, here's a pencil."

Finally, one of the women in the car said, "so wha's gon' happen when we go back there for some more pills if they know we don' signed some lawsuit?"

So that's it. The white man has the *system* going for him, he owns everything and controls everything. And Negroes have to depend on that system too. I made in my notes this comment: "Poor Medgar, another unknown, defenseless, almost hopeless hero."

After Kennard departed for Hattiesburg we went to a restaurant down the street where we found Meredith. He was with author James Baldwin, who had flown in at noon, and Steve Schapiro, a young *Life* photographer who was doing a picture story on Baldwin.

Meredith left them and went to the rear of the restaurant where he danced with any girl who would dance with him. The girls were students at Jackson State College, only a block away. The tension never showed in Meredith's face, but it was there. During that period he was frantic, desperate for relaxation. And he loved to dance.

"Toooommm," he said with twinkle and slow drawl, "I must be crazy to leave music like this to go to a place like Ole Miss!"

Jack Greenberg had suggested Meredith preface his press conference with a written statement saying he had called the conference because this was the easiest way to announce he was returning. It was Tuesday, the night before the conference. Meredith said, "You know, Tom, I don't think I'll do that." I figured he had his reasons. That night we gathered at Meredith's apartment to rehearse what "Jay" would say in reply to questions the next morning. Medgar Evers, James Baldwin, Robert Smith and several Jackson ministers were there.

Meredith actually had kept the fact he was returning pretty much of a secret. Only his intimates knew. The complication had been getting someone to help take care of his son, because June was going to school too and she couldn't do both. The problem was solved when Meredith's sister came from Kosciusko to help out.

But the Jackson papers were letting their hopes get the better of them and were printing stories that day saying Meredith was going to withdraw. Meredith enjoyed tantalizing local reporters, and loving the dramatic, tried to keep everyone in the dark as long as he could.

Our rehearsal soon became a "bull-session," then the "bull-session" a fascinating monologue by Meredith about what actually happened the night he entered Ole Miss. It was all so very complicated; the full story of the dealings between Mississippi and the Federal government has not been told.

Meredith was proudest of his condemnation of the Army's use of segregated troops in the first occupation of Oxford. He told us the Justice Department people *begged* him not to release a statement. They felt that once he was in safely, he should be happy and keep his mouth shut. Meredith told us:

"The next day, the Army even found a *Chinese* soldier and put him in front of our dormitory. They had had Negroes on permanent *garbage* detail, with white sergeants.

"I saw one of those army trucks and I couldn't believe my eyes. I yelled: 'Maann, what you guys *doing*?' A Negro lieutenant there was on the truck. They had told him 'take a rest on the football field, we don't need you,'" Meredith said.

"If someone hadn't made some changes soon, *very soon*, I would have left. What the hell's the point of the whole thing if the Army does that?"

After a few hours sleep, Jay's son woke me up. It seemed as if I hadn't slept at all. "Daddy said to read this," he said, throwing two hand-written pages on the couch.

Meredith had decided to write a statement after all; in bed, after that long night. He knew what he wanted to get over: it was absurd that a student returning to school was a news item. Near the end he said "the Negro" would not return to Ole Miss, but that *he would*. I liked this because it coupled his announcement with a comment on how he wanted his actions to be interpreted.

Meredith was always in touch with his own sense of reality.

As in the case of the statement, he would never do or say anything that wasn't real to him, that he couldn't see a reason for, according to his own thinking.

What actually happened at the press conference was unforgettable. The time: 10:00 that morning. The place: Masonic Temple Hall, in the building where the NAACP office was located, in Jackson. I was surprised to discover we had a *full* audience of Negroes who wanted to hear the decision 'live.' It was really supposed to be a 'press only' conference. But we had all been so busy no one was policing the door. It was too late now. Evers sat with Meredith at a table facing the newsmen. Meredith was to read his statement, Evers would recognize questioners.

Meredith began slowly reading to a tense silence. When he reached the sentence, "the 'Negro' will not return . . ." two or three Jackson newsmen broke out of the room to be the first to telephone the good news. Meredith was marvelous. He paused, waited until they were out, then continued, "but I, James Meredith . . ."

I imagine everyone heard the cheering from our uninvited audience. It was like an explosion—unrestrained and instantaneous. I looked at Baldwin and we *understood*. That cheer, what a lie it made of the Mississippi 'contented Negro' myth! It was beautiful.

Well, Jay and Medgar went through with the rest, but that was the press conference. That was it. We were all limp.

The hall cleared. A few photographers took additional pictures. Meredith's wife, June, slipped quietly out of the hall to return to class.

Evers must return to the work he loves. Meredith must go back to Oxford where he cannot dance.

Within an hour Baldwin and I have left a still rainy Jackson for New York City.

Five months later, the body of Medgar Evers lay in the same Masonic Temple Hall where we had conducted that small triumph of a press conference.

We came to the hall that June day to mourn his murder, and to reflect on the meaning of his life and death. Medgar had been shot in the back in the driveway of his home and fell bleeding to death, beside his blue Oldsmobile.

He had been taken to the emergency room of the same hospital where he had been made to wait hours for Clyde Kennard's pills. But it was too late, they could not make him wait any longer.

Two weeks later a small newspaper item—no more than a paragraph—announced the death, in Chicago, of Clyde Kennard.

Freedomways, Spring 1965

from

Coming of Age in Mississippi

by Anne Moody

In mid-September I was back on campus. But didn't very much happen until February when the NAACP held its annual convention in Jackson. They were having a whole lot of interesting speakers: Jackie Robinson, Floyd Patterson, Curt Flood, Margaretta Belafonte, and many others. I wouldn't have missed it for anything. I was so excited that I sent one of the leaflets home to Mama and asked her to come.

Three days later I got a letter from Mama with dried-up tears on it, forbidding me to go to the convention. It went on for more than six pages. She said if I didn't stop that shit she would come to Tougaloo and kill me herself. She told me about the time I last visited her, on Thanksgiving, and she had picked me up at the bus station. She said she picked me up because she was scared some white in my hometown would try to do something to me. She said the sheriff had been by, telling her I was messing around with that NAACP group. She said he told her if I didn't stop it, I could not come back there any more. He said that they didn't need any of those NAACP people messing around in Centreville. She ended the letter by saying that she had burned the leaflet I sent her. "Please don't send any more of that stuff here. I don't want nothing to happen to us here," she said. "If you keep that up, you will never be able to come home again."

I was so damn mad after her letter, I felt like taking the NAACP convention to Centreville. I think I would have, if it had been in my power to do so. The remainder of the week I thought of nothing except going to the convention. I didn't know exactly what to do about it. I didn't want Mama or anyone at home to get hurt because of me.

I had felt something was wrong when I was home. During

the four days I was there, Mama had tried to do everything she could to keep me in the house. When I said I was going to see some of my old classmates, she pretended she was sick and said I would have to cook. I knew she was acting strangely, but I hadn't known why. I thought Mama just wanted me to spend most of my time with her, since this was only the second time I had been home since I entered college as a freshman.

Things kept running through my mind after that letter from Mama. My mind was so active, I couldn't sleep at night. I remembered the one time I did leave the house to go to the post office. I had walked past a bunch of white men on the street on my way through town and one said, "Is that the gal goin' to Tougaloo?" He acted kind of mad or something, and I didn't know what was going on. I got a creepy feeling, so I hurried home. When I told Mama about it, she just said, "A lotta people don't like that school." I knew what she meant. Just before I went to Tougaloo, they had housed the Freedom Riders there. The school was being criticized by whites throughout the state.

The night before the convention started, I made up my mind to go, no matter what Mama said. I just wouldn't tell Mama or anyone from home. Then it occurred to me—how did the sheriff or anyone at home know I was working with the NAACP chapter on campus? Somehow they had found out. Now I knew I could never go to Centreville safely again. I kept telling myself that I didn't really care too much about going home, that it was more important to me to go to the convention.

I was there from the very beginning. Jackie Robinson was asked to serve as moderator. This was the first time I had seen him in person. I remembered how when Jackie became the first Negro to play Major League baseball, my uncles and most of the Negro boys in my hometown started organizing baseball leagues. It did something for them to see a Negro out there playing with all those white players. Jackie was a good moderator, I thought. He kept smiling and joking. People felt relaxed and proud. They appreciated knowing and meeting people of their own race who had done something worth talking about.

When Jackie introduced Floyd Patterson, heavyweight champion of the world, the people applauded for a long, long time. Floyd was kind of shy. He didn't say very much. He didn't have to, just his being there was enough to satisfy most of the Negroes who had only seen him on TV. Archie Moore was there too. He wasn't as smooth as Jackie, but he had his way with a crowd. He started telling how he was run out of Mississippi, and the people just cracked up.

I was enjoying the convention so much that I went back for the night session. Before the night was over, I had gotten autographs from every one of the Negro celebrities.

I had counted on graduating in the spring of 1963, but as it turned out, I couldn't because some of my credits still had to be cleared with Natchez College. A year before, this would have seemed like a terrible disaster, but now I hardly even felt disappointed. I had a good excuse to stay on campus for the summer and work with the Movement, and this was what I really wanted to do. I couldn't go home again anyway, and I couldn't go to New Orleans—I didn't have money enough for bus fare.

During my senior year at Tougaloo, my family hadn't sent me one penny. I had only the small amount of money I had earned at Maple Hill. I couldn't afford to eat at school or live in the dorms, so I had gotten permission to move off campus. I had to prove that I could finish school, even if I had to go hungry every day. I knew Raymond and Miss Pearl were just waiting to see me drop out. But something happened to me as I got more and more involved in the Movement. It no longer seemed important to prove anything. I had found something outside myself that gave meaning to my life.

I had become very friendly with my social science professor, John Salter, who was in charge of NAACP activities on campus. All during the year, while the NAACP conducted a boycott of the downtown stores in Jackson, I had been one of Salter's most faithful canvassers and church speakers. During the last week of school, he told me that sit-in demonstrations were about to start in Jackson and that he wanted me to be the spokesman for a team that would sit-in at Woolworth's lunch counter. The two other demonstrators would be class-mates of mine, Memphis and Pearlena. Pearlena was a dedicated NAACP worker, but Memphis had not been very involved in the Movement on campus. It seemed that the organization had had a rough time finding students who were in a position to go to jail. I had nothing to lose one way or the other. Around ten o'clock the morning of the demonstrations, NAACP headquarters alerted the news services. As a result, the police department was also informed, but neither the policemen nor the newsmen knew exactly where or when the demonstrations would start. They stationed themselves along Capitol Street and waited.

To divert attention from the sit-in at Woolworth's, the picketing started at J. C. Penney's a good fifteen minutes before. The pickets were allowed to walk up and down in front of the store three or four times before they were arrested. At exactly 11 A.M., Pearlena, Memphis, and I entered Woolworth's from the rear entrance. We separated as soon as we stepped into the store, and made small purchases from various counters. Pearlena had given Memphis her watch. He was to let us know when it was 11:14. At 11:14 we were to join him near the lunch counter and at exactly 11:15 we were to take seats at it.

Seconds before 11:15 we were occupying three seats at the previously segregated Woolworth's lunch counter. In the beginning the waitresses seemed to ignore us, as if they really didn't know what was going on. Our waitress walked past us a couple of times before she noticed we had started to write our own orders down and realized we wanted service. She asked us what we wanted. We began to read to her from our order slips. She told us that we would be served at the back counter, which was for Negroes.

"We would like to be served here," I said.

The waitress started to repeat what she had said, then stopped in the middle of the sentence. She turned the lights out behind the counter, and she and the other waitresses almost ran to the back of the store, deserting all their white customers. I guess they thought that violence would start immediately after the whites at the counter realized what was going on. There were five or six other people at the counter.

A couple of them just got up and walked away. A girl sitting next to me finished her banana split before leaving. A middle-aged white woman who had not yet been served rose from her seat and came over to us. "I'd like to stay here with you," she said, "but my husband is waiting."

The newsmen came in just as she was leaving. They must have discovered what was going on shortly after some of the people began to leave the store. One of the newsmen ran behind the woman who spoke to us and asked her to identify herself. She refused to give her name, but said she was a native of Vicksburg and a former resident of California. When asked why she had said what she had said to us, she replied, "I am in sympathy with the Negro movement." By this time a crowd of cameramen and reporters had gathered around us taking pictures and asking questions, such as Where were we from? Why did we sit-in? What organization sponsored it? Were we students? From what school? How were we classified?

I told them that we were all students at Tougaloo College, that we were represented by no particular organization, and that we planned to stay there even after the store closed. "All we want is service," was my reply to one of them. After they had finished probing for about twenty minutes, they were almost ready to leave.

At noon, students from a nearby white high school started pouring in to Woolworth's. When they first saw us they were sort of surprised. They didn't know how to react. A few started to heckle and the newsmen became interested again. Then the white students started chanting all kinds of anti-Negro slogans. We were called a little bit of everything. The rest of the seats except the three we were occupying had been roped off to prevent others from sitting down. A couple of the boys took one end of the rope and made it into a hangman's noose. Several attempts were made to put it around our necks. The crowds grew as more students and adults came in for lunch.

We kept our eyes straight forward and did not look at the crowd except for occasional glances to see what was going on. All of a sudden I saw a face I remembered—the drunkard from the bus station sit-in. My eyes lingered on him just long enough for us to recognize each other. Today he was drunk too, so I don't think he remembered where he had seen me before. He took out a knife, opened it, put it in his pocket, and then began to pace the floor. At this point, I told Memphis and Pearlena what was going on. Memphis suggested that we pray. We bowed our heads, and all hell broke loose. A man rushed forward, threw Memphis from his seat, and slapped my face. Then another man who worked in the store threw me against an adjoining counter.

Down on my knees on the floor, I saw Memphis lying near the lunch counter with blood running out of the corners of his mouth. As he tried to protect his face, the man who'd thrown him down kept kicking him against the head. If he had worn hard-soled shoes instead of sneakers, the first kick probably would have killed Memphis. Finally a man dressed in plain clothes identified himself as a police officer and arrested Memphis and his attacker.

Pearlena had been thrown to the floor. She and I got back on our stools after Memphis was arrested. There were some white Tougaloo teachers in the crowd. They asked Pearlena and me if we wanted to leave. They said that things were getting too rough. We didn't know what to do. While we were trying to make up our minds, we were joined by Joan Trumpauer. Now there were three of us and we were integrated. The crowd began to chant, "Communists, Communists, Communists." Some old man in the crowd ordered the students to take us off the stools.

"Which one should I get first?" a big husky boy said.

"That white nigger," the old man said.

The boy lifted Joan from the counter by her waist and carried her out of the store. Simultaneously, I was snatched from my stool by two high school students. I was dragged about thirty feet toward the door by my hair when someone made them turn me loose. As I was getting up off the floor, I saw Joan coming back inside. We started back to the center of the counter to join Pearlena. Lois Chaffee, a white Tougaloo faculty member, was now sitting next to her. So Joan and I just climbed across the rope at the front end of the counter and sat down. There were now four of us, two whites and two Negroes, all women. The mob started smearing us with ketchup, mustard, sugar, pies, and everything on the counter.

Soon Joan and I were joined by John Salter, but the moment he sat down he was hit on the jaw with what appeared to be brass knuckles. Blood gushed from his face and someone threw salt into the open wound. Ed King, Tougaloo's chaplain, rushed to him.

At the other end of the counter, Lois and Pearlena were joined by George Raymond, a CORE field worker and a student from Jackson State College. Then a Negro high school boy sat down next to me. The mob took spray paint from the counter and sprayed it on the new demonstrators. The high school student had on a white shirt; the word "nigger" was written on his back with red spray paint.

We sat there for three hours taking a beating when the manager decided to close the store because the mob had begun to go wild with stuff from other counters. He begged and begged everyone to leave. But even after fifteen minutes of begging, no one budged. They would not leave until we did. Then Dr. Beittel, the president of Tougaloo College, came running in. He said he had just heard what was happening.

About ninety policemen were standing outside the store; they had been watching the whole thing through the windows, but had not come in to stop the mob or do anything. President Beittel went outside and asked Captain Ray to come and escort us out. The captain refused, stating the manager had to invite him in before he could enter the premises, so Dr. Beittel himself brought us out. He had told the police that they had better protect us after we were outside the store. When we got outside, the policemen formed a single line that blocked the mob from us. However, they were allowed to throw at us everything they had collected. Within ten minutes, we were picked up by Reverend King in his station wagon and taken to the NAACP headquarters on Lynch Street.

After the sit-in, all I could think of was how sick Mississippi whites were. They believed so much in the segregated Southern way of life, they would kill to preserve it. I sat there in the NAACP office and thought of how many times they had killed when this way of life was threatened. I knew that the killing had just begun. "Many more will die before it is over with," I thought. Before the sit-in, I had always hated the whites in Mississippi. Now I knew it was impossible for me to hate sickness. The whites had a disease, an incurable disease in its final stage. What were our chances against such a disease? I thought of the students, the young Negroes who had just begun to protest, as young interns. When these young interns got older, I thought, they would be the best doctors in the world for social problems.

Before we were taken back to campus, I wanted to get my hair washed. It was stiff with dried mustard, ketchup and sugar. I stopped in at a beauty shop across the street from the NAACP office. I didn't have on any shoes because I had lost them when I was dragged across the floor at Woolworth's. My stockings were sticking to my legs from the mustard that had dried on them. The hairdresser took one look at me and said, "My land, you were in the sit-in, huh?"

"Yes," I answered. "Do you have time to wash my hair and style it?"

"Right away," she said, and she meant right away. There were three other ladies already waiting, but they seemed glad to let me go ahead of them. The hairdresser was real nice. She even took my stockings off and washed my legs while my hair was drying.

There was a mass rally that night at the Pearl Street Church in Jackson, and the place was packed. People were standing two abreast in the aisles. Before the speakers began, all the sit-inners walked out on the stage and were introduced by Medgar Evers. People stood and applauded for what seemed like thirty minutes or more. Medgar told the audience that this was just the beginning of such demonstrations. He asked them to pledge themselves to unite in a massive offensive against segregation in Jackson, and throughout the state. The rally ended with "We Shall Overcome" and sent home hundreds of determined people. It seemed as though Mississippi Negroes were about to get together at last.

Before I demonstrated, I had written Mama. She wrote me back a letter, begging me not to take part in the sit-in. She even sent ten dollars for bus fare to New Orleans. I didn't have one penny, so I kept the money. Mama's letter made me mad. I had to live my life as I saw fit. I had made that decision when I left home. But it hurt to have my family prove to me how scared they were. It hurt me more than anything else —I knew the whites had already started the threats and intimidations. I was the first Negro from my hometown who had openly demonstrated, worked with the NAACP, or anything. When Negroes threatened to do anything in Centreville, they were either shot like Samuel O'Quinn or run out of town, like Reverend Dupree.

I didn't answer Mama's letter. Even if I had written one, she wouldn't have received it before she saw the news on TV or heard it on the radio. I waited to hear from her again. And I waited to hear in the news that someone in Centreville had been murdered. If so, I knew it would be a member of my family.

On Wednesday, the day after the sit-in, demonstrations got off to a good start. Ten people picketed shortly after noon on Capitol Street, and were arrested. Another mass rally followed the demonstrations that night, where a six-man delegation of Negro ministers was chosen to meet Mayor Thompson the following Tuesday. They were to present to him a number of demands on behalf of Jackson Negroes. They were as follows:

1. Hiring of Negro policemen and school crossing guards
2. Removal of segregation signs from public facilities
3. Improvement of job opportunities for Negroes on city payrolls—Negro drivers of city garbage trucks, etc.
4. Encouraging public eating establishments to serve both whites and Negroes
5. Integration of public parks and libraries
6. The naming of a Negro to the City Parks and Recreation Committee
7. Integration of public schools
8. Forcing service stations to integrate rest rooms

After this meeting, Reverend Haughton, the minister of Pearl Street Church, said that the Mayor was going to act on all the suggestions. But the following day, Thompson denied that he had made any promises. He said the Negro delegation "got carried away" following their discussion with him.

"It seems as though Mayor Thompson wants to play games with us," Reverend Haughton said at the next rally. "He is calling us liars and trying to make us sound like fools. I guess we have to show him that we mean business."

When Reverend Charles A. Jones, dean and chaplain at Campbell College, asked at the close of the meeting, "Where do we go from here?" the audience shouted, "To the streets." They were going to prove to Mayor Thompson and the white people of Jackson that they meant business.

Around ten the next morning, an entire day of demonstrations started. A little bit of everything was tried. Some Negroes sat-in, some picketed, and some squatted in the streets and refused to move.

All of the five-and-ten stores (H. L. Green, Kress, and Woolworth) had closed their lunch counters as a result of the Woolworth sit-in. However, this did not stop the new sit-ins. Chain restaurants such as Primos Restaurant in downtown Jackson were now targets. Since police brutality was the last thing wanted in good, respectable Jackson, Mississippi, whenever arrested demonstrators refused to walk to a paddy wagon, garbage truck, or whatever was being used to take people to jail, Negro trusties from Jackson's city jail carted them away. Captain Ray and his men would just stand back with their hands folded, looking innocent as lambs for the benefit of the Northern reporters and photographers.

The Mayor still didn't seem to be impressed with the continuous small demonstrations and kept the streets hot. After eighty-eight demonstrators had been arrested, the Mayor held a news conference where he told a group of reporters, "We can handle 100,000 agitators." He also stated that the "good colored citizens are not rallying to the support of the outside agitators" (although there were only a few out-of-state people involved in the movement at the time) and offered to give Northern newsmen anything they wanted, including transportation, if they would "adequately" report the facts.

During the demonstrations, I helped conduct several workshops, where potential demonstrators, high school and college students mostly, were taught to protect themselves. If, for instance, you wanted to protect the neck to offset a karate blow, you clasped your hands behind the neck. To protect the genital organs you doubled up in a knot, drawing the knees up to the chest to protect your breasts if you were a girl.

The workshops were handled mostly by SNCC and CORE field secretaries and workers, almost all of whom were very young. The NAACP handled all the bail and legal services and public relations, but SNCC and CORE could draw teenagers into the Movement as no other organization could. Whether they received credit for it or not, they helped make Jackson the center of attention throughout the nation.

During this period, civil rights workers who had become known to the Jackson police were often used to divert the cops' attention just before a demonstration. A few cops were always placed across the street from NAACP headquarters, since most of the demonstrations were organized there and would leave from that building. The "diverters" would get into cars and lead the cops off on a wild-goose chase. This would allow the real demonstrators to get downtown before they were noticed. One evening, a group of us took the cops for a tour of the park. After giving the demonstrators time enough to get to Capitol Street, we decided to go and watch the action. When we arrived there ourselves, we met Reverend King and a group of ministers. They told us they were going to stage a pray-in on the post office steps. "Come on, join us," Reverend King said. "I don't think we'll be arrested, because it's federal property."

By the time we got to the post office, the newsmen had already been informed, and a group of them were standing in front of the building blocking the front entrance. By now the group of whites that usually constituted the mob had gotten smart. They no longer looked for us, or for the demonstration. They just followed the newsmen and photographers. They were much smarter than the cops, who hadn't caught on yet.

We entered the post office through the side entrance and found that part of the mob was waiting inside the building. We didn't let this bother us. As soon as a few more ministers joined us, we were ready to go outside. There were fourteen of us, seven whites and seven Negroes. We walked out front and stood and bowed our heads as the ministers began to pray. We were immediately interrupted by the appearance of Captain Ray. "We are asking you people to disperse. If you don't, you are under arrest," he said.

Most of us were not prepared to go to jail. Doris Erskine, a student from Jackson State, and I had to take over a workshop the following day. Some of the ministers were in charge of the mass rally that night. But if we had dispersed, we would have been torn to bits by the mob. The whites standing out there had murder in their eyes. They were ready to do us in and all fourteen of us knew that. We had no other choice but to be arrested.

We had no plan of action. Reverend King and some of the ministers who were kneeling refused to move; they just kept on praying. Some of the others also attempted to kneel. The rest of us just walked to the paddy wagon. Captain Ray was using the Negro trusties. I felt so sorry for them. They were too small to be carrying all these heavy-ass demonstrators. I could tell just by looking at them that they didn't want to, either. I knew they were forced to do this.

After we got to jail we were mugged and fingerprinted, then taken to a cell. Most of the ministers were scared stiff. This was the first time some of them had seen the inside of a jail. Before we were mugged, we were all placed in a room together and allowed to make one call. Reverend King made the call to the NAACP headquarters to see if some of the ministers could be bailed out right away. I was so glad when they told him they didn't have money available at the moment. I just got my kicks out of sitting there looking at the ministers. Some of them looked so pitiful, I thought they would cry any minute, and here they were, supposed to be our leaders.

When Doris and I got to the cell where we would spend the next four days, we found a lot of our friends there. There were twelve girls altogether. The jail was segregated. I felt sorry for Jeanette King, Lois Chaffee, and Joan Trumpauer. Just because they were white they were missing out on all the fun we planned to have. Here we were going to school together, sleeping in the same dorm, worshipping together, playing together, even demonstrating together. It all ended in jail. They were rushed off by themselves to some cell designated for whites.

Our cell didn't even have a curtain over the shower. Every time the cops heard the water running, they came running to peep. After the first time, we fixed them. We took chewing gum and toilet tissue and covered the opening in the door. They were afraid to take it down. I guess they thought it might have come out in the newspaper. Their wives wouldn't have liked that at all. Peep through a hole to see a bunch of nigger girls naked? No! No! They certainly wouldn't have liked that. All of the girls in my cell were college students. We had a lot to talk about, so we didn't get too bored. We made cards out of toilet tissue and played Gin Rummy almost all day. Some of us even learned new dance steps from each other.

There were a couple of girls in with us from Jackson State College. They were scared they would be expelled from school. Jackson State, like most of the state-supported Negro schools, was an Uncle Tom school. The students could be expelled for almost anything. When I found this out, I really appreciated Tougaloo.

The day we were arrested one of the Negro trusties sneaked us a newspaper. We discovered that over four hundred high school students had also been arrested. We were so glad we sang freedom songs for an hour or so. The jailer threatened to put us in solitary if we didn't stop. At first we didn't think he meant it, so we kept singing. He came back with two other cops and asked us to follow them. They marched us down the hall and showed us one of the solitary chambers. "If you don't stop that damn singing, I'm gonna throw all of you in here together," said the jailer. After that we didn't sing any more. We went back and finished reading the paper.

We got out of jail on Sunday to discover that everyone was talking about the high school students. All four hundred who were arrested had been taken to the fairgrounds and placed in a large open compound without beds or anything. It was said that they were getting sick like flies. Mothers were begging to have their children released, but the NAACP didn't have enough money to bail them all out.

The same day we went to jail for the pray-in, the students at Lanier High School had started singing freedom songs on their lunch hour. They got so carried away they ignored the bell when the break was over and just kept on singing. The principal of the high school did not know what to do, so he called the police and told them that the students were about to start a riot.

When the cops came, they brought the dogs. The students refused to go back to their classrooms when asked, so the cops turned the dogs loose on them. The students fought them off for a while. In fact, I was told that mothers who lived near the school had joined the students in fighting off the dogs. They had begun to throw bricks, rocks, and bottles. The next day the papers stated that ten or more cops suffered cuts or minor wounds. The papers didn't say it, but a lot of students were hurt, too, from dog bites and lumps on the head from billy clubs. Finally, one hundred and fifty cops were rushed to the scene and several students and adults were arrested.

The next day four hundred of the high school students from Lanier, Jim Hill, and Brinkley High schools gathered in a church on Farish Street, ready to go to jail. Willie Ludden, the NAACP youth leader, and some of the SNCC and CORE workers met with them, gave a brief workshop on nonviolent protective measures and led them into the streets. After marching about two blocks they were met by helmeted police officers and ordered to disperse. When they refused, they were arrested, herded into paddy wagons, canvas-covered trucks, and garbage trucks. Those moving too slowly were jabbed with rifle butts. Police dogs were there, but were not used. From the way everyone was describing the scene it sounded like Nazi Germany instead of Jackson, USA.

On Monday, I joined a group of high school students and several other college students who were trying to get arrested. Our intention was to be put in the fairgrounds with the high school students already there. The cops picked us up, but they didn't want to put us so-called professional agitators in with the high school students. We were weeded out, and taken back to the city jail.

I got out of jail two days later and found I had gotten another letter from Mama. She had written it Wednesday the twenty-ninth, after the Woolworth sit-in. The reason it had taken so long for me to get it was that it came by way of New

Orleans. Mama sent it to Adline and had Adline mail it to me. In the letter she told me that the sheriff had stopped by and asked all kinds of questions about me the morning after the sit-in. She said she and Raymond told them that I had only been home once since I was in college, that I had practically cut off all my family connections when I ran away from home as a senior in high school. She said he said that he knew I had left home. "He should know," I thought, "because I had to get him to move my clothes for me when I left." She went on and on. She told me he said I must never come back there. If so he would not be responsible for what happened to me. "The whites are pretty upset about her doing these things," he told her. Mama told me not to write her again until she sent me word that it was O.K. She said that I would hear from her through Adline.

I also got a letter from Adline in the same envelope. She told me what Mama hadn't mentioned—that Junior had been cornered by a group of white boys and was about to be lynched, when one of his friends came along in a car and rescued him. Besides that, a group of white men had gone out and beaten up my old Uncle Buck. Adline said Mama told her they couldn't sleep, for fear of night riders. They were all scared to death. My sister ended the letter by cursing me out. She said I was trying to get every Negro in Centreville murdered.

I guess Mama didn't tell me these things because she was scared to. She probably thought I would have tried to do something crazy. Something like trying to get the organizations to move into Wilkinson County, or maybe coming home myself to see if they would kill me. She never did give me credit for having the least bit of sense. I knew there was nothing I could do. No organization was about to go to Wilkinson County. It was a little too tough for any of them. And I wasn't about to go there either. If they said they would kill me, I figured I'd better take their word for it.

Meantime, within four or five days Jackson became the hotbed of racial demonstrations in the South. It seemed as though most of the Negro college and high school students there were making preparations to participate. Those who did not go to jail were considered cowards by those who did. At this point, Mayor Allen Thompson finally made a decisive move. He announced that Jackson had made plans to house over 12,500 demonstrators at the local jails and at the state fairgrounds. And if this was not enough, he said, Parchman, the state penitentiary, 160 miles away, would be used. Governor Ross Barnett had held a news conference offering Parchman facilities to Jackson.

An injunction prohibiting demonstrations was issued by a local judge, naming NAACP, CORE, Tougaloo College, and various leaders. According to this injunction, the intent of the named organizations and individuals was to paralyze the economic nerve center of the city of Jackson. It used as proof the leaflets that had been distributed by the NAACP urging Negroes not to shop on Capitol Street. The next day the injunction was answered with another mass march.

The cops started arresting every Negro on the scene of a demonstration, whether or not he was participating. People were being carted off to jail every day of the week. On Saturday, Roy Wilkins, the National Director of NAACP, and Medgar Evers were arrested as they picketed in front of Woolworth's. Theldon Henderson, a Negro lawyer who worked for the Justice Department, and had been sent down from Washington to investigate a complaint by the NAACP about the fairgrounds facilities, was also arrested. It was said that when he showed his Justice Department credentials, the arresting officer started trembling. They let him go immediately.

Mass rallies had come to be an every night event, and at each one the NAACP had begun to build up Medgar Evers. Somehow I had the feeling that they wanted him to become for Mississippi what Martin Luther King had been in Alabama. They were well on the way to achieving that, too.

After the rally on Tuesday, June 11, I had to stay in Jackson. I had missed the ride back to campus. Dave Dennis, the CORE field secretary for Mississippi, and his wife put me up for the night. We were watching TV around twelve-thirty, when a special news bulletin interrupted the program. It said, "Jackson NAACP leader Medgar Evers has just been shot."

We didn't believe what we were hearing. We just sat there staring at the TV screen. It was unbelievable. Just an hour or so earlier we were all with him. The next bulletin announced that he had died in the hospital soon after the shooting. We didn't know what to say or do. All night we tried to figure out what had happened, who did it, who was next, and it still didn't seem real.

First thing the next morning we turned on the TV. It showed films taken shortly after Medgar was shot in his driveway. We saw the pool of blood where he had fallen. We saw his wife sobbing almost hysterically as she tried to tell what had happened. Without even having breakfast, we headed for the NAACP headquarters. When we got there, they were trying to organize a march to protest Medgar's death. Newsmen, investigators, and reporters flooded the office. College and high school students and a few adults sat in the auditorium waiting to march.

Dorie Ladner, a SNCC worker, and I decided to run up to Jackson State College and get some of the students there to participate in the march. I was sure we could convince some of them to protest Medgar's death. Since the march was to start shortly after lunch, we had a couple of hours to do some recruiting. When we got to Jackson State, class was in session. "That's a damn shame," I thought. "They should have dismissed school today, in honor of Medgar."

Dorie and I started going down each hall, taking opposite classrooms. We begged students to participate. They didn't respond in any way.

"It's a shame, it really is a shame. This morning Medgar Evers was murdered and here you sit in a damn classroom with books in front of your faces, pretending you don't even know he's been killed. Every Negro in Jackson should be in the streets raising hell and protesting his death," I said in one class. I felt sick, I got so mad with them. How could Negroes be so pitiful? How could they just sit by and take all this shit without any emotions at all? I just didn't understand.

"It's hopeless, Moody, let's go," Dorie said.

As we were leaving the building, we began soliciting aloud in the hall. We walked right past the president's office, shouting even louder. President Reddix came rushing out. "You girls leave this campus immediately," he said. "You can't come on this campus and announce anything without my consent."

Dorie had been a student at Jackson State. Mr. Reddix looked at her. "You know better than this, Dorie," he said.

"But President Reddix, Medgar was just murdered. Don't you have any feelings about his death at all?" Dorie said.

"I am doing a job. I can't do this job and have feelings about everything happening in Jackson," he said. He was waving his arms and pointing his finger in our faces. "Now you two get off this campus before I have you arrested."

By this time a group of students had gathered in the hall. Dorie had fallen to her knees in disgust as Reddix was pointing at her, and some of the students thought he had hit her. I didn't say anything to him. If I had I would have been calling him every kind of fucking Tom I could think of. I helped Dorie off the floor. I told her we'd better hurry, or we would miss the demonstration.

On our way back to the auditorium we picked up the Jackson DAILY NEWS. Headlines read JACKSON INTEGRATION LEADER EVERS SLAIN.

Negro NAACP leader Medgar Evers was shot to death when he stepped from his automobile here early today as he returned home from an integration strategy meeting.

Police said Evers, 37, was cut down by a high-powered bullet in the back of the driveway of his home.

I stopped reading. Medgar was usually followed home every night by two or three cops. Why didn't they follow him last night? Something was wrong. "They must have known," I thought. "Why didn't they follow him last night?" I kept asking myself. I had to get out of all this confusion. The only way I could do it was to go to jail. Jail was the only place I could think in.

When we got back to the auditorium, we were told that those who would take part in the first march had met at Pearl Street Church. Dorie and I walked over there. We noticed a couple of girls from Jackson State. They asked Dorie if President Reddix had hit her, and said it had gotten out on campus that he had. They told us a lot of students had planned to demonstrate because of what Reddix had done. "Good enough," Dorie said, "Reddix better watch himself, or we'll turn that school out."

I was called to the front of the church to help lead the marchers in a few freedom songs. We sang "Woke Up This

Morning With My Mind on Freedom" and "Ain't Gonna Let Nobody Turn Me 'Round." After singing the last song we headed for the streets in a double line, carrying small American flags in our hands. The cops had heard that there were going to be Negroes in the streets all day protesting Medgar's death. They were ready for us.

On Rose Street we ran into a blockade of about two hundred policemen. We were called to a halt by Captain Ray, and asked to disperse. "Everybody ain't got a permit get out of this here parade," Captain Ray said into his bull horn. No one moved. He beckoned to the cops to advance on us.

The cops had rifles and wore steel helmets. They walked right up to us very fast and then sort of engulfed us. They started snatching the small American flags, throwing them to the ground, stepping on them, or stamping them. Students who refused to let go of the flags were jabbed with rifle butts. There was only one paddy wagon on the scene. The first twenty of us were thrown into it, although a paddy wagon is only large enough to seat about ten people. We were sitting and lying all over each other inside the wagon when garbage trucks arrived. We saw the cops stuff about fifty demonstrators in one truck as we looked out through the back glass. Then the driver of the paddy wagon sped away as fast as he could, often making sudden stops in the middle of the street so we would be thrown around.

We thought that they were going to take us to the city jail again because we were college students. We discovered we were headed for the fairgrounds. When we got there, the driver rolled up the windows, turned the heater on, got out, closed the door and left us. It was over a hundred degrees outside that day. There was no air coming in. Sweat began dripping off us. An hour went by. Our clothes were now soaked and sticking to us. Some of the girls looked as though they were about to faint. A policeman looked in to see how we were taking it. Some of the boys begged him to let us out. He only smiled and walked away.

Looking out the back window again, we noticed they were now booking all the other demonstrators. We realized they had planned to do this to our group. A number of us in the paddy wagon were known to the cops. After the Woolworth sit-in, I had been known to every white in Jackson. I can remember walking down the street and being pointed out by whites as they drove or walked past me.

Suddenly one of the girls screamed. Scrambling to the window, we saw John Salter with blood gushing out of a large hole in the back of his head. He was just standing there dazed and no one was helping him. And we were in no position to help either.

After they let everyone else out of the garbage trucks, they decided to let us out of the paddy wagon. We had now been in there well over two hours. As we were getting out, one of the girls almost fell. A guy started to help her.

"Get ya hands off that gal. Whatta ya think, ya goin' to a prom or somethin'?" one of the cops said.

Water was running down my legs. My skin was soft and spongy. I had hidden a small transistor radio in my bra and some of the other girls had cards and other things in theirs. We had learned to sneak them in after we discovered they didn't search the women but now everything was showing through our wet clothes.

When we got into the compound, there were still some high school students there, since the NAACP bail money had been exhausted. There were altogether well over a hundred and fifty in the girls' section. The boys had been put into a compound directly opposite and parallel to us. Some of the girls who had been arrested after us shared their clothes with us until ours dried. They told us what had happened after we were taken off in the paddy wagon. They said the cops had stuffed so many into the garbage trucks that some were just hanging on. As one of the trucks pulled off, thirteen-year-old John Young fell out. When the driver stopped, the truck rolled back over the boy. He was rushed off to a hospital and they didn't know how badly he had been hurt. They said the cops had gone wild with their billy sticks. They had even arrested Negroes looking on from their porches. John Salter had been forced off some Negro's porch and hit on the head.

The fairgrounds were everything I had heard they were. The compounds they put us in were two large buildings used to auction off cattle during the annual state fair. They were about a block long, with large openings about twenty feet wide on both ends where the cattle were driven in. The openings had been closed up with wire. It reminded me of a concentration camp. It was hot and sticky and girls were walking around half dressed all the time. We were guarded by four policemen. They had rifles and kept an eye on us through the wired sides of the building. As I looked through the wire at them, I imagined myself in Nazi Germany, the policemen Nazi soldiers. They couldn't have been any rougher than these cops. Yet this was America, "the land of the free and the home of the brave."

About five-thirty we were told that dinner was ready. We were lined up single file and marched out of the compound. They had the cook from the city jail there. He was standing over a large garbage can stirring something in it with a stick. The sight of it nauseated me. No one was eating, girls or boys. In the next few days, many were taken from the fairgrounds sick from hunger.

When I got out of jail on Saturday, the day before Medgar's funeral, I had lost about fifteen pounds. They had prepared a special meal on campus for the Tougaloo students, but attempts to eat made me sicker. The food kept coming up. The next morning I pulled myself together enough to make the funeral services at the Masonic Temple. I was glad I had gone in spite of my illness. This was the first time I had ever seen so many Negroes together. There were thousands and thousands of them there. Maybe Medgar's death had really brought them to the Movement, I thought. Maybe his death would strengthen the ties between Negroes and Negro organizations. If this resulted, then truly his death was not in vain.

Just before the funeral services were over, I went outside. There was a hill opposite the Masonic Temple. I went up there to watch the procession. I wanted to see every moment of it.

As the pallbearers brought the body out and placed it in a hearse, the tension in the city was as tight as a violin string. There were two or three thousand outside that could not get inside the temple, and as they watched, their expression was that of anger, bitterness, and dismay. They looked as though any moment they were going to start rioting. When Mrs. Evers and her two older children got into their black limousine, Negro women in the crowd began to cry and say things like "That's a shame," . . . "That's a young woman," . . . "Such well-looking children," . . . "It's a shame, it really is a shame."

Negroes formed a seemingly endless line as they began the march to the funeral home. They got angrier and angrier; however, they went on quietly until they reached the downtown section where the boycott was. They tried to break through the barricades on Capitol Street, but the cops forced them back into line. When they reached the funeral home, the body was taken inside, and most of the procession dispersed. But one hard core of angry Negroes decided they didn't want to go home. With some encouragement from SNCC workers who were singing freedom songs outside the funeral home, these people began walking back toward Capitol Street.

Policemen had been placed along the route of the march, and they were still there. They allowed the crowd of Negroes to march seven blocks, but they formed a solid blockade just short of Capitol Street. This was where they made everyone stop. They had everything—shotguns, fire trucks, gas masks, dogs, fire hoses, and billy clubs. Along the sidewalks and on the fringes of the crowd, the cops knocked heads, set dogs on some marchers, and made about thirty arrests, but the main body of people in the middle of the street was just stopped.

They sang and shouted things like "Shoot, shoot" to the police, and then the police started to push them back slowly. After being pushed back about a block, they stopped. They wouldn't go any farther. So the cops brought the fire trucks up closer and got ready to use the fire hoses on the crowd. That really broke up the demonstration. People moved back faster and started to go home. But it also made them angrier. Bystanders began throwing stones and bottles at the cops and then the crowd started too; other Negroes were pitching stuff from second- and third-story windows. The crowd drew back another block, leaving the space between them and the fire trucks littered with rocks and broken glass. John Doar came out from behind the police barricade and walked toward the crowd of Negroes, with bottles flying all around him. He talked to some of the people at the front, telling them he was from the Justice Department and that this wasn't "the way." After he talked for a few minutes, things calmed down considerably, and Dave Dennis and a few others began taking bottles away from people and telling them they should go home. After that it was just a clean-up operation. One of the ministers borrowed Captain Ray's bull horn and ran up and down the street telling people to disperse, but by that time there were just a few stragglers.

After Medgar's death there was a period of confusion. Each Negro leader and organization in Jackson received threats. They were all told they were "next on the list." Things began to fall apart. The ministers, in particular, didn't want to be "next"; a number of them took that long-promised vacation to Africa or elsewhere. Meanwhile SNCC and CORE became more militant and began to press for more demonstrations. A lot of the young Negroes wanted to let the whites of Jackson know that even by killing off Medgar they hadn't touched the real core of the Movement. For the NAACP and the older, more conservative groups, however, voter registration had now become number one on the agenda. After the NAACP exerted its influence at a number of strategy meetings, the militants lost.

The Jackson *Daily News* seized the opportunity to cause more fragmentation. One day they ran a headline THERE IS A SPLIT IN THE ORGANIZATIONS, and sure enough, shortly afterward, certain organizations had completely severed their relations with each other. The whites had succeeded again. They had reached us through the papers by letting us know we were not together. "Too bad," I thought. "One day we'll learn. It's pretty tough, though, when you have everything against you, including the money, the newspapers, and the cops."

Within a week everything had changed. Even the rallies were not the same. The few ministers and leaders who did come were so scared—they thought assassins were going to follow them home. Soon there were rallies only twice a week instead of every night.

The Sunday following Medgar's funeral, Reverend Ed King organized an integrated church-visiting team of six of us from the college. Another team was organized by a group in Jackson. Five or six churches were hit that day, including Governor Ross Barnett's. At each one they had prepared for our visit with armed policemen, paddy wagons, and dogs—which would be used in case we refused to leave after "ushers" had read us the prepared resolutions. There were about eight of these ushers at each church, and they were never exactly the usherly type. They were more on the order of Al Capone. I think this must have been the first time any of these men had worn a flower in his lapel. When we were asked to leave, we did. We were never even allowed to get past the first step.

A group of us decided that we would go to church again the next Sunday. This time we were quite successful. These visits had not been publicized as the first ones were, and they were not really expecting us. We went first to a Church of Christ, where we were greeted by the regular ushers. After reading us the same resolution we had heard last week, they offered to give us cab fare to the Negro extension of the church. Just as we had refused and were walking away, an old lady stopped us. "We'll sit with you," she said.

We walked back to the ushers with her and her family. "Please let them in, Mr. Calloway. We'll sit with them," the old lady said.

"Mrs. Dixon, the church has decided what is to be done. A resolution has been passed, and we are to abide by it."

"Who are we to decide such a thing? This is a house of God, and God is to make all of the decisions. He is the judge of us all," the lady said.

The ushers got angrier then and threatened to call the police if we didn't leave. We decided to go.

"We appreciate very much what you've done," I said to the old lady.

As we walked away from the church, we noticed the family leaving by a side entrance. The old lady was waving to us.

Two blocks from the church, we were picked up by Ed King's wife, Jeanette. She drove us to an Episcopal church. She had previously left the other two girls from our team there. She circled the block a couple of times, but we didn't see them anywhere. I suggested that we try the church. "Maybe they got in," I said. Mrs. King waited in the car for us. We walked up to the front of the church. There were no ushers to be seen. Apparently, services had already started. When we walked inside, we were greeted by two ushers who stood at the rear.

"May we help you?" one said.

"Yes," I said. "We would like to worship with you today."

"Will you sign the guest list, please, and we will show you to your seats," said the other.

I stood there for a good five minutes before I was able to compose myself. I had never prayed with white people in a white church before. We signed the guest list and were then escorted to two seats behind the other two girls in our team. We had all gotten in. The church service was completed without one incident. It was as normal as any church service. However, it was by no means normal to me. I was sitting there thinking any moment God would strike the life out of me. I recognized some of the whites, sitting around me in that church. If they were praying to the same God I was, then even God, I thought, was against me.

When the services were over the minister invited us to visit again. He said it as if he meant it, and I began to have a little hope.

from *Coming of Age in Mississippi* (1968)

Epilogue in Albany:
Were the Mass Marches Worthwhile?

by Reese Cleghorn

Albany, Georgia

THE ebullient expectations that sent more than 1,500 Negroes to jail in Albany under the banners of Dr. Martin Luther King Jr. have been reduced to sullen despair one year after the last big marches. Almost every week more civil rights protestants are arrested in this hot city of palms, pines, 37,000 whites and 23,000 Negroes in southwestern Georgia, but the home addresses entered on the police dockets are less often Albany than New Rochelle, Brookline, Weston and Melrose. Today the banner taken to jail is usually that of the Student Non-Violent Coordinating Committee, a threadbare stepchild of the civil rights movement, born of the 1960 college student sit-ins, cut free by its young leaders' decision not to accept direction from older organizations or Dr. King, and nurtured at present by the willingness of students from Princeton, Temple and Barnard to spend a hot summer on the firing lines of social action.

Once the goal was to fill the jails. But the Albany City Jail, which had working agreements with fortresses in neighboring counties, proved a bottomless pit. Not since Albany has anyone taken Dr. King literally when he has talked of filling the jails of the South. Today in Albany the goal more often is to pass out handbills or picket, and it is the police rather than the students who usually decide whether to fill some of the jail.

Albany remains a monument to white supremacy. At this moment it represents at once the triumph of sophisticated segregation and the low point for the mass demonstration in this, the decade of the mass demonstration. It was here that the ambitious "jail-ins" began, and here that they were found wanting. Does the outcome suggest what may happen in other urban centers of the old Southern plantation country, where segregation is only beginning to be tested? Police Chief Laurie Pritchett, whose national acclaim has taken him to the podium of a Ford Foundation-sponsored seminar to tell other police chiefs how to handle racial protests, says about 30 police departments in the South have sent officers to learn from Albany.

Albany's Negroes are no less impressed than Southern police chiefs with the capacities of this constabulary. On July 6, Slater King, a Negro businessman who is acting president of the Albany Movement, remarked: "It is a police state we live in here, and the police seem to be getting jumpy." During the previous three weeks more than 100 Negroes and their white co-workers had been arrested for picketing, passing out handbills, disorderly conduct, and, in one instance, starting on a disorganized march.

Negroes once were allowed small-scale picketing in Albany, and Chief Pritchett insists they still may picket in small groups if they are not creating a disturbance. Slater King and other Negroes say, however, that picketing even in small numbers always seem to the police to be a disturbance of Albany's peace. A lack of acceptable picketing crippled the Negroes' efforts to boycott department stores.

Passing out handbills also is likely to bring arrest. Chapter 10, Section 12, of the city code prohibits public distribution of handbills, though it excepts the US mail, newspapers and commercial advertising; this mockery of the Bill of Rights thus is very precise, being limited principally to ideas. When six white and Negro rights workers passed out leaflets in May urging defeat of a bond issue as a protest against segregated facilities, they were hustled off to jail as summarily as if they had been putting dynamite under City Hall.

If the police are jumpy, they are not alone. There has been violence in the wake of the Negroes' nonviolent action, and both Negroes and whites are afraid of more and worse. A white businessman taking his maid home in a Negro section last month suffered a fractured skull when he was bombarded by bricks and bottles. Windows of stores owned by whites and Negroes have been smashed. Negroes have thrown rocks and bottles at police officers, on one occasion smashing a police car and injuring a sergeant inside.

Although Martin King preached nonviolence and even visited taprooms to stress that message, and Laurie Pritchett likes to talk about meeting nonviolence with nonviolence, both men know they are not the only protagonists on this scene. On the first day that Dr. King led his hymn-singing marchers toward City Hall, two well-established Negro teenage gangs lined the streets with concealed knives and other weapons, ready to move in if the nonviolent Negroes were attacked. That is a fact that television cameras, Dr. King and perhaps Chief Pritchett missed, but it is a fact. A talk with some of Albany's younger Negroes, the school dropouts who are jobless and sometimes hopeless, readily establishes that nonviolence is not a settled issue.

Whether it is a cause of, or response to, the recent out-breaks is a matter of dispute, but the police unquestionably have become increasingly ready to make arrests. Once they drew praise for controlling white hoodlums, but Negro bit-terness against them is growing. "You just can't drive people the way these people are being driven," a white human rela-tions worker has remarked.

Frustration for the Negroes is more intense because not one of the expectations aroused by the demonstrations of late 1961 and mid-1962 has been realized. "We can turn Albany upside down and then right side up," Dr. King had said. But Chief Pritchett attests correctly: "Albany is just as segregated as ever." In a caustic evaluation, Mrs. Ruby Hurley, South-eastern regional director of the National Association for the Advancement of Colored People, has observed: "Albany was successful only if the goal was to go to jail."

Except at the federally regulated airport, segregation was complete when the protests began in December of 1961. Later, transportation terminals yielded to Interstate Com-merce Commission insistence upon integration, but except for that, no barriers have fallen. After being closed for a time, the Albany city library is open now to Negroes as well as to whites, but only on a "take-out" basis.

The city bus line went out of business, and a number of parks, swimming pools and tennis courts were closed. In May the city offered three pools and a tennis court for sale. James H. Gray, a vocal segregationist of Massachusetts origin who publishes the city's only daily newspaper and owns its only television station, bought one pool and a tennis court and re-opened these on July 7 for whites only. Police were standing by to seize seven Negroes and two white men making an integration attempt the first day.

Since Albany has repealed its segregation laws in a tactical move, there is no ordinance to prevent anyone from buying recreation facilities and opening them on an integrated basis. But, again, it is not only economics but the police power which would prevent this. No one could operate integrated facilities in Albany without assurance of police cooperation. This was a fact faced by the owners of Albany's bus line: They asked the City Commission for assurance of police cooperation if the line were integrated, and, receiving no such assurance, shut down their operations. In Albany, no one is more important than a policeman.

Aside from desegregation demands, the Negroes most important request was for a biracial commission. Although Mayor Asa Kelley Jr. has urged discussion with the Negroes, the City Commission has repeatedly rejected the idea of a biracial group. The most recent refusal came on July 2, when Jerome Heilbron, a Justice Department lawyer, spent an hour and a half discussing race relations with the seven-member commission. His most optimistic appraisal of the confrontation afterward was that he had found the commissioners "polite and courteous."

From the start of the Albany conflict, the city administration's strategy seems to have been to stand immovable; to refuse even to negotiate; to "eliminate all demonstrations," in the words of Chief Pritchett; to prevent any intrusion by "white troublemakers"; and to maintain order with such effectiveness that the federal government would have no justification for intervention with marshals and troops. It is significant that the city simply does not deal with the Negroes except through Chief Pritchett. When some white citizens tried last fall to begin unofficial biracial talks, the City Commission reacted quickly, calling the move "a foolhardy enterprise" and a "usurpation of this commission's authority." The plan collapsed.

For the Negroes' part, they have never seemed able to make a sustained, carefully directed effort. The original protest marches were suddenly conceived and without specific, limited goals. They began with the arrest of a group of Freedom Riders at a bus terminal, gained momentum at protest rallies that even got beyond the control of leaders running them, and spilled into the streets in wave after wave of hymn-singing marchers. As the demonstrations continued, however, the number of those willing to be arrested grew small and the marches ended anti-climactically. In July of 1962 they were resumed when Dr. King was summoned from his home base in Atlanta to face trial on a charge of parading without a permit. By then, however, the pattern of Negro ultimatum and white rejection had been set, and the new arrests did nothing to change it.

If anything, the Negroes' ambitions have grown in ratio to the decline of their hopes. Now the demand is for an "open city," with no segregation and without job discrimination. Because of the frustration, however, Negro leadership in Albany is in disarray. The lot of a leader who cannot show his followers any gains in a year and a half is difficult, indeed. After a long trial of this kind, Dr. W. G. Anderson, the articulate osteopath who is president of the Albany Movement, moved to Detroit. Now Slater King, as his acting successor, has to face the rebellion of those who see the Albany Movement as moribund and defeated.

The young men and women of the Student Non-violent Coordinating Committee ("Snick," in the jargon of the movement) work in Albany but also are busy with the old plantation country that surrounds it. (George Washington Carver helped make this peanut land rich.) The "Snicks" are an irritant to the whites, and they show unlettered field hands that whites and Negroes can work together as equals; but they have not moved the power structure of Albany.

Neither has a decline in retail business, apparently caused by a reluctance of some people in neighboring small communities to enter a city of strife. Neither has a virtual standstill in industrial growth in what had been a booming little city, one which doubled its population between 1950 and

1960. "They're just not going to do anything, regardless," former Mayor Taxi Smith says of the city commissioners.

Part of the demoralization of the Negro community may be attributed to a diffusion of goals. "Some just want to demonstrate, without real purpose," a local Negro leader said. "Just to get 15 people and say let's go to jail doesn't accomplish anything. Nobody even knows about it until it's over. There are three things that we could do successfully if we organized properly: register, boycott and push on employment. Voter registration is almost dead. You can't demonstrate and register, too. The boycott of stores hasn't been effective. As for employment, we are working on it, slowly."

Negro employment on the lower levels actually is probably worse than before the marches. Slater King estimates that 20 percent of the maids and cooks lost jobs permanently because of animosity aroused by the protests. ("We've been good to her for 20 years," said one hurt white employer of a cook who had demonstrated. "Now she's done THIS to us.")

Week by week the city has summoned more of the Negroes who were released on bond, fining them. Another bond then must be posted for the appeal. So far, according to one official's estimate, between $250,000 and $275,000 in cash and security bonds has been posted.

Though the Albany campaign thus may be seen as negative in tangible results, another measure may be applied. Dr. King says this: "There is still a great deal of work that must be done in Albany. However, I think it must be said that we have achieved something. We have made it possible for the leaders of Albany to confront segregation and the Negroes of Albany have been made more aware. This movement gave a new sense of dignity and destiny to the Negro citizens of Albany. For this reason, Albany can never be the same again. Negroes have straightened their backs, and you can never dump your load until you have straightened your back."

King agrees with some of his critics on one point: that it was a mistake not to limit the goals. "Albany . . . was the first time we had made a full-scale assault on all forms of segregation, dealing with the whole structure of segregation," he said. "I think it would have been better to concentrate on one area." Were the mass marches worthwhile? "I think so. It has proved to be the only thing that can arouse the entire community and imbue the people with courage to endure a long, hard struggle."

An earnest white SNCC worker, Joyce Barrett, of Philadelphia, also spoke not long ago of accomplishments in the realm of the spirit. "If we never registered a voter, never got a change in the structure, it would still be worthwhile to bring a change in people, to help them find a new direction," she said. But Miss Barrett's words, voiced not long after she had come to Albany from human relations work in Philadelphia, perhaps had a less hopeful aspect after she had become intimate with the Albany jail. A few days ago she described Albany as a place of "bitterness, anger and frustration."

The chief hope for change, in structure if not in spirit, lies now in court action, which was neglected at first in the frenzy of the demonstrations. First fruit apparently will come in the schools, and other court action is pending. Charles Wittenstein, director of the American Jewish Committee in the Southeast and an experienced observer of racial events there, made some pointed remarks about this in a private gathering. Though his words were not intended to be made generally public, they have attracted much attention among civil rights workers in the South.

"If lunch counter desegregation represents the high water mark of direct action by use of picketing and boycotting," he said, "then Albany, Ga., represents its low water mark—indeed, its most dismal failure. We have seen an enormous amount of time, effort, money and sacrifice expended in an effort which has, to this day, failed to desegregate anything whatsoever. All it has succeeded in doing is to create bitterness locally and embarrassment of the United States internationally.

"The explanation for the failure is the lack of clear thinking about tactics. . . . The situation was ideally suited for neither direct action nor negotiation, but for litigation. Finally, a suit was filed by the NAACP, and it will be this suit, or one like it, that will eventually bring desegregation to Albany, not Martin Luther King, not the Student Non-violent Coordinating Committee, and not the courageous but futile demonstrations by Negroes of the Albany Movement, or their visiting Northern supporters."

Behind his desk in City Hall, Laurie Pritchett, a ruddy-faced, red-haired man in short shirt sleeves, who seems to like being told he is the man who beat Martin Luther King, says Albany always has been ready to abide by court orders. The police, says Pritchett, will do their duty.

The New Republic, July 20, 1963

Blazing Guns Mark Freedom Fight: Embattled Defenders Fire from Rooftops

by George W. Collins

CAMBRIDGE, Md. —The long smouldering powder-keg here finally exploded Thursday night and unchained violence swept the streets of Cambridge.

An unofficial count of the injured is put at 12, including three National Guardsmen and a 12-year-old boy. Of the known injured at this time, all are white except three.

Miraculously, no deaths had been reported at this time. How all survived, I'll never know.

Only an act of God could have stayed the hand of death during the long night when bullets literally rained on the county seat of Dorchester County.

Despite the presence of National Guardsmen and state policemen who bolstered the local police force, all the guns that had been accumulated in the Second Ward over the last year and a half appeared to have gone off in one mighty blast that echoed endlessly through the chilly night.

I was an eyewitness to an hour-long gun battle on Pine St. that shook the ground on which I stood—to be more exact, the ground on which I lay.

The gunplay was triggered by an invasion of the Second Ward by two carloads of white men who raced down Pine St. at intervals with guns blazing from the windows.

Racing through the streets at speeds upwards of 70 miles an hour the invaders used two late model cars that were packed with gunmen.

Nearly 100 colored men and boys armed to the teeth, crouched behind cars, buildings and in windows and on rooftops, retaliated.

For what seemed an eternity the Second Ward was a replica of the Old West as men and boys of all ages roamed the streets, stood in the shadows, and leaned out of windows with their weapons in full view.

At the height of the Pine St. gun battle not a guardsman, state trooper or city policeman was in sight.

Periodically, accidentally or intentionally, about five minutes after the invaders exchanged fire with the defenders, the three colored city policemen would cruise down the street, only to disappear in the darkness.

The battle, however, was not confined to Pine St. In the various sections of the Second Ward of this divided city—geographically and racially—colored defenders clashed with white invaders.

The nervous peace that has been kept by National Guardsmen since Friday is destined to be shortlived, it was announced Sunday. Demonstration leaders said they will defy the ban on demonstrations early this week.

"We will demonstrate, even if it means going to jail," announced Mrs. Gloria Richardson, chairman of the Cambridge Nonviolent Action Committee.

She said they will resume demonstrations because city and county officials have "thrown our demands out the window."

The demonstration leader said that officials will take no action on their demands because they think the presence of the guardsmen prevents them from protesting.

Unofficial account of the shooting of the three guardsmen indicates that while they were checking the perimeter of the Second Ward their black military vehicle was mistaken for a car of the invaders and the defenders opened up on them with an awesome array of firepower.

Two white men, and the 12-year-old boy, were injured when they were struck by buckshot blasts fired by colored men, General George M. Gelston, guard commander, reported.

Three persons, including two television network cameramen, were bitten by K-9 Corps dogs held by state police who said that the newsmen and spectators refused to disperse at the scene of the initial shooting when they were ordered to do so.

Other injuries were sustained earlier in the day when demonstrators staged a sit-in at Dizzyland Restaurant. About

15 demonstrators descended on the segregated eating place while an estimated 100 demonstrators watched from across the street.

Six were able to enter before the owner, Robert Fehsenfeld, locked the door.

As if by signal, when the door slammed shut, nearly 20 white men, already inside, pounced on the demonstrators and beat them unmercifully while late-arriving city police vainly tried to break down the door to rescue them.

Finally, Fehsenfeld, one of the leaders of the petition movement to have the recently adopted city charter amendment to integrate public accommodations, decided to open the door.

Two demonstrators, Dwight Campbell and Lester Green, were beaten into unconsciousness.

A third demonstrator, Andrew Moursund, 18, white student at Duke University, sustained a cut in the face which still oozed a stream of blood when police reached him.

Even then, the violence that was to come later was temporarily halted when police succeeded in dispersing the mob of blood-thirsty colored persons who rushed to the rescue of their comrade.

An ominous and brief peace then descended on Cambridge.

When guardsmen rolled into town at 5:30 p.m. it appeared that the worst was over.

This assumption, as it turned out, was the biggest miscalculation of the 18-month-old war of Cambridge.

Following a mass meeting at Bethel AME Church about 300 demonstrators, for the fourth straight night since the guardsmen lifted the ban, staged their standard mass march on the county courthouse.

They were greeted by the usual band of heckling segregationists, but nothing more serious than egg throwing and a chorus of verbal abuse marred the demonstration—while the demonstrators were at the courthouse, that is.

At about 8:30 p.m. freedom fighters began the return trek to the Second Ward. Then it happened.

One of their number, William Jackson, 17, was picked up by state police for having a paring knife in his possession. Word of his arrest—or detention, as it later proved—was slow to reach the element of Second Ward residents which has rejected the philosophy of non-violence.

When it did, the second phase of the violent night was born.

Hundreds of persons, giving Pine St. the appearance of a giant conveyor belt, moved rapidly toward the white side of town of black and white. They headed for the Armory where Jackson was being held.

Fortunately, Reginald Robinson and Fred Jackson, leaders of the Cambridge crusade, rushed to the Armory and began working for the release of the youth.

They succeeded with only seconds to spare. The maddened mob, chanting "Freedom, Freedom," with the volume of a thousand drums, were but a few yards from nearly 100 battle-ready state policemen when the youth and Robinson and Jackson walked between them.

I knew then that Cambridge was in for a long and violent night. It wasn't long in coming.

Whether there is violence, National Guard occupation or any other efforts to curtail them, Mrs. Richardson and Mr. Robinson say they will not stop the protests.

"We will demonstrate until the city fathers and the white power structure recognize our just demands," Mr. Robinson declared.

The Afro-American (Baltimore), July 20, 1963

CHRONOLOGY 1941–1973

BIOGRAPHICAL NOTES

NOTE ON THE TEXTS

NOTES

INDEX

Chronology 1941–1973

1941   A. Philip Randolph, president of the Brotherhood of
         Sleeping Car Porters, calls on January 15 for 10,000
         African-Americans to march on Washington, D.C., to de-
         mand an end to segregation in the armed forces and to
         racial discrimination in hiring for defense industries.
         March on Washington Committee is formed with Ran-
         dolph as its director and calls for the march to be held
         July 1. Randolph and Walter White, executive secretary of
         the National Association for the Advancement of Colored
         People (NAACP), meet at the White House on June 18
         with President Franklin D. Roosevelt, who attempts to
         forestall march, but Randolph insists on necessity of pres-
         idential action against hiring discrimination. Roosevelt is-
         sues Executive Order 8802 on June 25, prohibiting racial
         discrimination in hiring by federal departments and de-
         fense contractors and establishing a Fair Employment
         Practice Committee (FEPC) to monitor compliance with
         the order. Randolph announces postponement of the
         march on June 28. (Armed forces remain segregated, and
         most black servicemen will serve in supply and service
         units, although the army will form two black infantry di-
         visions, as well as black artillery, tank, and tank destroyer
         battalions. In July 1941 the army begins training its first
         black pilots; the first African-American marines are re-
         cruited in 1942; and the navy commissions its first black
         officers in 1944.) FEPC holds first in a series of public
         hearings, October 20–21. Japanese attack Pearl Harbor,
         December 7, bringing the United States into World
         War II.

1942   Members of the Fellowship of Reconciliation, a pacifist
         organization, form Chicago Committee of Racial Equal-
         ity to undertake "nonviolent direct action" against dis-
         crimination. March on Washington Committee holds
         large public rallies in New York, June 16, and Chicago,
         June 26, as part of continuing campaign against job dis-
         crimination. House of Representatives passes bill on Oc-
         tober 13 abolishing poll taxes in national elections, but bill
         is blocked in the Senate by a Southern filibuster. (Bills to

abolish poll taxes in national elections are also passed by the House in 1943, 1945, 1947, and 1949, but are blocked in the Senate.) William Dawson is elected to the House of Representatives from Chicago on November 3, succeeding the retiring Arthur Mitchell as the sole black member of Congress.

1943   Members of the Committee of Racial Equality conduct sit-in protests in Chicago restaurants. (Organization is renamed Congress of Racial Equality in 1944.) FEPC continues to be hampered by its lack of legal enforcement powers. Fighting between African-Americans and whites in a city park in Detroit leads to rioting, June 20–23, in which 34 people are killed. Confrontation between a white police officer and a black soldier in Harlem section of New York City results in riot, August 1–2, in which six people are killed.

1944   On April 3 U.S. Supreme Court decides, 8–1, in *Smith* v. *Allwright* that the exclusion of African-Americans from voting in the Texas Democratic primary is a violation of the Fifteenth Amendment. (Case for the plaintiff was argued by Thurgood Marshall, executive director of the NAACP Legal Defense and Educational Fund from its founding in 1939 until 1961.) *An American Dilemma: The Negro Problem and Modern Democracy*, extensive study of race relations by Swedish economist Gunnar Myrdal, is published. Roosevelt is reelected on November 7, defeating Thomas Dewey 432–99 in the electoral voting and carrying all 11 Southern states (Virginia, North Carolina, South Carolina, Georgia, Florida, Tennessee, Alabama, Mississippi, Louisiana, Arkansas, and Texas). Adam Clayton Powell Jr. is elected to Congress from a district in Harlem and becomes the second African-American serving in the House of Representatives.

1945   Poll tax is abolished in Georgia on February 5. Roosevelt dies on April 12 and Vice-President Harry S. Truman becomes president. Congress votes to end funding for the FEPC after June 30, 1946. Japan surrenders on August 14, ending World War II.

1946   Attempts to create a permanent FEPC fail in both houses of Congress. In *Morgan* v. *Virginia* the Supreme Court rules 7–1 on June 3 that a Virginia law requiring segregated seating on interstate buses is an unconstitutional burden on interstate commerce. (Decision does not address intrastate travel or segregation on interstate lines that is the result of bus company policy.) Four African-Americans, Roger and Dorothy Malcolm and George and Mae Dorsey, are shot to death by a white mob at Moore's Ford, near Monroe, Georgia, on July 25 after Roger Malcolm wounded a white man in a scuffle. Murders attract widespread public attention along with other incidents of racial violence against African-Americans, including the beating of army veteran Isaac Woodard by two police officers in Batesburg, South Carolina, on February 13, which left Woodard blind, and the torture, mutilation, and murder of army veteran John Jones by a mob in Minden, Louisiana, on August 8. (Despite an extensive federal investigation, no one is ever charged in the Moore's Ford murders; one man is acquitted of federal charges in the assault on Woodard, and five men, including two deputy sheriffs, are acquitted of federal charges in the murder of Jones.) During a meeting held with Walter White on September 19 to discuss racial violence, Truman proposes creating a presidential committee on civil rights, and on December 5 appoints its 15 members, with Charles Wilson, president of General Electric, serving as its chairman.

1947   Fellowship of Reconciliation organizes "Journey of Reconciliation," April 9–23, in which integrated group of 16 activists rides interstate buses in Virginia, North Carolina, Tennessee, and Kentucky to test compliance with the *Morgan* decision. Four of the riders are arrested in Chapel Hill, North Carolina, and later sentenced to serve 30-day terms on a chain gang. Jackie Robinson plays his first game for the Brooklyn Dodgers on April 15, becoming the first African-American player in major league baseball since the 1880s. Presidential committee on civil rights submits its report on October 29; its recommendations include the creation of a civil rights division in the Department of Justice, a permanent national civil rights commission, and a permanent FEPC with enforcement powers; ending segregation in the armed forces; and federal legislation to punish lynching, secure voting rights, and abolish segregation in interstate transport.

1948   Truman sends message to Congress on February 2 en-
            dorsing many of the recommendations of the civil rights
            committee but, in the face of strong Southern opposition,
            does not submit civil rights legislation to Congress. Ran-
            dolph warns Truman at White House meeting on March
            22 that he will lead a civil disobedience campaign against
            the draft unless the armed forces are integrated, and op-
            position to continued military segregation is also ex-
            pressed by delegation of African-American leaders in
            meeting with Secretary of Defense James Forrestal on
            April 26. In case of *Shelley* v. *Kraemer*, Supreme Court
            rules 6–0 on May 3 that judicial enforcement of racially
            restrictive property convenants is a violation of the equal
            protection clause of the Fourteenth Amendment. After
            liberals force a floor fight, Democratic national conven-
            tion adopts platform plank on civil rights, July 14, that
            calls for a federal anti-lynching law, a new FEPC, the abo-
            lition of poll taxes, and desegregation of the armed
            forces. Adoption of plank causes split in Democratic
            party, and on July 17 Southern "Dixiecrats" hold a States'
            Rights convention and nominate Governor Strom Thur-
            mond of South Carolina for president. Truman issues two
            executive orders on July 26: 9980, establishing a Fair Em-
            ployment Board to promote nondiscriminatory employ-
            ment practices in the federal civil service, and 9981,
            declaring "equality of treatment and opportunity" in the
            armed services to be presidential policy. Randolph praises
            9981 and ends call for civil disobedience on August 18.
            Truman names seven-member committee to oversee inte-
            gration of the armed forces, September 18, and appoints
            Charles Fahy, a former solicitor general, as its chairman. In
            the presidential election, November 2, Truman wins 303
            electoral votes, Thomas Dewey 189, and Thurmond 39.
            Thurmond carries Louisiana, Mississippi, Alabama, and
            South Carolina, while Truman wins the other seven
            Southern states and also carries key states of Ohio, Illinois,
            and California with strong support from black voters.

1949   Senate votes 63–23 on March 17 to increase the majority
            needed for cloture from two-thirds of the Senators pres-
            ent and voting to two-thirds of the Senate; change in the
            rules strengthens ability of Southerners to block civil
            rights legislation with filibusters. Administration proposes
            legislation to make lynching a federal crime, create a new

FEPC, abolish poll taxes in national elections, and end segregation in interstate transportation, but none of the bills are brought to a vote in the Senate. Fahy Committee approves integration plans of the air force and navy, but encounters resistance to desegregation from the army. William Hastie, a former dean of the Howard Law School and a leading civil rights lawyer, is appointed by Truman to the Third Circuit Court of Appeals on October 15, becoming the first African-American federal appellate judge.

1950   Fahy Committee accepts army integration plan in January and submits its final report on May 22. Supreme Court decides three civil rights cases on June 5, all by 9–0 votes. In *Sweatt* v. *Painter*, the Court rules that separate law school established by the University of Texas does not provide equal educational opportunity and orders the university to admit African-Americans to its previously all-white law school; in *McLaurin* v. *Oklahoma State Regents*, it rules that the University of Oklahoma could not impose segregated seating arrangements on a black graduate student; and in *Henderson* v. *United States*, it rules that segregated seating on railroad dining cars denies the equal access to public accommodations guaranteed by the Interstate Commerce Act. (Although the NAACP attorneys arguing *Sweatt* and *McLaurin* had asked the Court to overturn the 1896 *Plessy* v. *Ferguson* decision establishing the "separate but equal" doctrine of constitutionally permissible segregation, the decisions do not rule on its continuing validity.) Korean War begins June 25. After meeting with NAACP attorneys and branch presidents, Thurgood Marshall decides to litigate against segregation in the public schools in a direct challenge to *Plessy*. (Public schools are segregated by law in all 11 Southern states as well as Delaware, Maryland, West Virginia, Kentucky, Missouri, Oklahoma, and the District of Columbia; laws in Kansas, New Mexico, and Arizona allow individual school districts to segregate.)

1951   Poll tax is abolished in South Carolina on February 13. NAACP attorneys argue school segregation cases in federal and state courts in South Carolina, Kansas, and Delaware, May–October. Harry Moore, a NAACP leader who campaigned against police brutality and led voter registration drives, is killed and his wife, Harriette Moore, a schoolteacher, is fatally wounded when their home in Mims, Florida, is bombed on December 25.

1952   Fourth school case is argued in federal court in Virginia in February. Republican Dwight D. Eisenhower wins presidential election, November 4, defeating Adlai Stevenson 442–89 in the electoral voting and carrying four Southern states (Texas, Tennessee, Florida, and Virginia). Supreme Court hears arguments on appeal in the four school cases, now consolidated as *Brown* v. *Board of Education of Topeka*, as well as *Bolling* v. *Sharpe*, case challenging school segregation in the District of Columbia, December 9–11.

1953   Divided Supreme Court orders reargument in *Brown* on June 8. Armistice is signed in Korea on July 27. Frederick Vinson, chief justice of Supreme Court since 1946, dies on September 8. Eisenhower appoints California governor Earl Warren as chief justice, October 2. Poll tax is abolished in Tennessee on November 3 (poll taxes remain in Texas, Arkansas, Mississippi, Alabama, and Virginia). *Brown* and *Bolling* are reargued, December 7–9. Warren begins working with other justices to bring about unanimous decision.

1954   On May 17 the Supreme Court rules 9–0 in *Brown* that public school segregation violates the equal protection clause of the Fourteenth Amendment. Writing for the court, Warren declares that the "separate but equal" doctrine has no place in public education and requests further argument concerning implementation. In companion case of *Bolling*, the Court rules 9–0 that school segregation in the District of Columbia violates the due process clause of the Fifth Amendment. *Brown* decision is denounced by many Southern elected officials. "Citizens' Council" is organized in Indianola, Mississippi, July 11, to oppose desegregation by political, legal, and economic means; by the end of the year chapters of the organization are founded in Texas, Louisiana, Alabama, Georgia, and Virginia, as well as throughout Mississippi. Desegregation begins in District of Columbia and Baltimore schools. Department of Defense announces on October 30 that the armed forces have been fully desegregated.

1955   Desegregation begins in St. Louis schools in February. Supreme Court hears arguments on implementation of *Brown*, April 11–14, and rules 9–0 on May 31 that school cases should be remanded to lower federal courts and instructs them to issue desegregation orders "with all deliberate speed" without setting a deadline for compliance. (Implementation of school desegregation decision will be obstructed by resistance, evasion, and delay by school authorities and state governments, as well as by reluctance of some federal judges to issue effective desegregation orders.) Emmett Till, a 14-year-old African-American boy visiting from Chicago, is beaten and shot to death in Tallahatchie County, Mississippi, on August 28 after he allegedly whistled at a white woman; his murder and the acquittal on September 23 of the two white men charged with the crime attract widespread public attention. Interstate Commerce Commission rules on November 7 that segregated seating on interstate buses and trains is a violation of the Interstate Commerce Act. Supreme Court rules in *Holmes* v. *Atlanta*, November 7, that municipal recreation facilities cannot be racially segregated. Rosa Parks, an active member of the NAACP, is arrested in Montgomery, Alabama, on December 1 for violating the municipal bus segregation ordinance. Montgomery Improvement Association is organized at mass meeting held on December 5 to conduct boycott of city buses, and Martin Luther King Jr., the pastor since 1954 of the Dexter Avenue Baptist Church, is elected as its president.

1956   King family escapes injury when their home is bombed on January 30. University of Alabama admits Autherine Lucy as its first African-American student, February 3, after prolonged litigation in federal court. White students and Tuscaloosa residents riot on February 6, and Lucy is suspended, allegedly for her own safety; she is later expelled for criticizing the university. "Southern Manifesto" is introduced in Congress on March 12; signed by 19 senators and 77 representatives, it denounces *Brown* as an "abuse of judicial power" and endorses resistance to integration by "any lawful means." Bus boycott begins in Tallahassee, Florida, on May 26. Alabama attorney general John Patterson obtains injunction against the NAACP in state court, June 1, on the grounds that it has failed to comply with state corporate registration laws, and July 9 obtains order directing the NAACP to turn over its membership lists. (Several other Southern states undertake legal campaigns to restrict the operations of the NAACP and the Legal Defense Fund.) Special session of the Virginia legislature in August adopts program of "massive resistance" to school desegregation that calls for the closing of schools under desegregation orders. Governor Frank Clement orders the National Guard to restore order in Clinton, Tennessee, on September 2 after white mobs attempt to block the desegregation of the high school. Eisenhower wins reelection on November 6, defeating Stevenson in the electoral voting 457–73 and carrying five Southern states (Texas, Louisiana, Tennessee, Virginia, and Florida). Supreme Court affirms ruling of lower federal court in *Browder* v. *Gayle* declaring segregation on Alabama intrastate buses to be unconstitutional, November 13. Montgomery boycott ends on December 21 as municipal buses begin operating on a desegregated basis. The Rev. Fred Shuttlesworth, a leading civil rights activist in Birmingham, Alabama, escapes injury when his parsonage is bombed on December 25.

1957   Southern Negro Leadership Conference on Transportation and Nonviolent Integration (later known as the Southern Christian Leadership Conference) is organized in Atlanta on January 11 with King as its chairman. Ghana becomes independent, March 6, beginning period of decolonization in sub-Saharan Africa. Malcolm X (born Malcolm Little), minister of Temple No. 7 of the Nation of Islam since 1954, leads demonstration outside a police station in Harlem, April 14, to protest the beating of a Black Muslim and demand his transfer to a hospital. First federal civil rights bill since 1875 is passed on August 29 after it is significantly weakened in the Senate to avoid a filibuster. The act creates a federal civil rights commission with investigatory powers; replaces the existing civil rights section of the Department of Justice with a division headed by an assistant attorney general; makes conspiring to deny citizens their right to vote in federal elections a federal crime; and gives federal prosecutors the power to obtain injunctions against discrimnatory practices used to deny citizens their voting rights. Federal district court orders nine African-American students admitted to Central High School in Little Rock, Arkansas, on September 3, but Governor Orval Faubus uses the National Guard to prevent them from entering the school. After the district court orders Faubus to end his interference on September 20, the governor withdraws the Guard, and on September 23 the students are attacked by a large mob. Eisenhower sends more than 1,000 paratroopers of the 101st Airborne Division to Little Rock on September 24 and places the Arkansas National Guard under federal control. Students are escorted to class by armed soldiers on September 25. Airborne troops are withdrawn from Little Rock, November 27, as federalized Guard continues to protect the students.

1958   Buses in Tallahassee begin desegregated service in May. Supreme Court rules 9–0 in *NAACP* v. *Alabama*, June 30, upholding on First Amendment grounds the refusal of the organization to turn its membership lists over to the Alabama authorities (injunction against the Alabama NAACP remains in effect). On September 12 the Court decides *Cooper* v. *Aaron*, unanimously overturning a district court decision allowing the Little Rock school board to postpone desegregation until 1960 because of the threat of continued violence. In opinion signed by all nine justices, Warren writes that governors and state legislators are bound by the Constitution to uphold Supreme Court decisions. (In response to decision, Little Rock high schools are closed for most of the 1958–59 school year, then reopen with token desegregation.) Schools under desegregation orders are closed in Norfolk, Charlottesville, and Warren County, Virginia. Bus boycott is organized in Birmingham in November but fails to end segregation on city buses.

1959   Virginia supreme court rules on January 19 that school closing law passed in 1956 violates the state constitution. Youth March for Integrated Schools held in Washington, D.C., on April 18 is attended by 25,000 people. Mack Charles Parker, an African-American man accused of raping a white woman, is taken from jail in Poplarville, Mississippi, and lynched by a mob on April 25. After Virginia legislature repeals its compulsory school attendance laws, Prince Edward County closes it schools on June 26 to avoid desegregation. *The Hate That Hate Produced,* television documentary on the Nation of

Islam, airs July 13-17 and brings Malcolm X to wider public attention.

1960   King moves to Atlanta, where the SCLC has its head-quarters, and becomes co-pastor with his father at the Ebenezer Baptist Church. Four African-American students stage sit-in at segregated lunch counter in Greensboro, North Carolina, on February 1. Sit-in movement spreads rapidly, and by the end of the month 31 lunch counter sit-ins are held in North Carolina, Maryland, Virginia, South Carolina, Georgia, Florida, Tennessee, Louisiana, and Texas, resulting in hundreds of arrests. Lunch counters are desegregated in San Antonio, Texas, on March 19, and in Nashville, Tennessee, and Winston-Salem, Charlotte, and Greensboro, North Carolina by July. Student Nonviolent Coordinating Committee (SNCC) is founded at conference organized by Ella Baker, executive director of the SCLC, and held in Raleigh, North Carolina, April 15-17. Civil rights act is passed by Congress, April 21; it provides criminal penalties for forcibly obstructing federal court orders; makes interstate flight after committing a bombing or arson a federal crime; and allows federal courts to appoint referees to register voters in cases where a pattern or practice of voting discrimination has been proven at trial. Survey of school desegregation records substantial desegregation efforts in the District of Columbia, West Virginia, Delaware, Kentucky, Maryland, Missouri, Oklahoma, and Texas; token desegregation in Arkansas, Florida, North Carolina, Tennessee, and Virginia; and no desegregation in Alabama, Georgia, Louisiana, Mississippi, and South Carolina. King is arrested during an Atlanta sit-in on October 19 and sentenced to four months in state prison for violating his probation on a traffic charge. Democratic presidential nominee Senator John F. Kennedy calls Coretta Scott King to express concern, and his brother, Robert F. Kennedy, calls the judge handling the case. King is released on bond, October 27, and his father publicly endorses Kennedy. On November 8 Kennedy narrowly defeats Richard M. Nixon with crucial support from African-American voters in key states of Illinois and Texas. Kennedy wins 303 electoral votes and Nixon 219, while 15 electors vote for Senator Harry Byrd, a leading segregationist. Nixon carries Virginia, Tennessee, and

Florida, while Kennedy wins the remainder of the Southern states with the exception of Mississippi and Alabama,
whose unpledged electors vote mostly for Byrd. Limited
school desegregation begins in New Orleans under federal court order, November 14, as federal marshals escort
black elementary school pupils past hostile crowds. Supreme Court rules 9–0 in *Gomillion* v. *Lightfoot*, November 14, that the redrawing of the Tuskegee, Alabama, city
boundaries in order to exclude black voters violates the
Fifteenth Amendment. On December 5 the Court rules
7–2 in *Boynton* v. *Virginia* that segregation of facilities in
interstate bus terminals violates the Interstate Commerce
Act.

1961   Federal district court orders University of Georgia to admit Hamilton Holmes and Charlayne Hunter, January 6.
They are suspended after a riot on campus by white stu-
dents, January 11, but are reinstated by court order on
January 13. James Farmer becomes national director of
CORE on February 1 and begins planning "Freedom
Rides" to test compliance with the *Boynton* decision.
President Kennedy issues Executive Order 10925, March
6, establishing President's Committee on Equal Employ-
ment Opportunity to investigate racial discrimination by
government contractors and recommend action by the
Justice Department. First group of Freedom Riders leaves
Washington May 4 and travels through Virginia, North
Carolina, South Carolina, and Georgia to Atlanta. On
May 14 they leave Atlanta for Birmingham on two buses,
one of which is attacked by a mob and firebombed outside Anniston, Alabama; when the other bus arrives in
Birmingham, the Freedom Riders are beaten by Klansmen. Group from CORE leaves Birmingham by air, and a
new group of Freedom Riders is organized by SNCC activists in Nashville. Second group leaves Birmingham on
May 20 and is attacked by a mob in the Montgomery bus
station. Attorney General Robert F. Kennedy sends federal
marshals to Montgomery to protect Freedom Riders while
urging an end to the protest. Marshals use tear gas on May
21 against mob surrounding church of SCLC leader the
Rev. Ralph Abernathy during civil rights meeting. In effort to avoid further involvement by federal marshals,
Robert Kennedy arranges for Alabama and Mississippi
National Guard to escort 27 Freedom Riders from

Montgomery to Jackson, Mississippi, where they are arrested at the bus station, May 24. Despite opposition
from the Kennedy administration, Freedom Rides continue during the summer, with at least 1,000 people participating throughout the South and more than 300
people arrested in Jackson alone. (Many of the protestors
arrested in Mississippi receive 60-day sentences on state
prison farms.) Coalition of civil rights groups, including
CORE, SNCC, NAACP, and SCLC, plans new effort to
register African-Americans in the South; Voter Education
Project receives funding from foundations and assistance
from the Justice Department. In response to request from
Robert Kennedy, the Interstate Commerce Commission
issues new rules on September 22, effective November 1,
forbidding interstate carriers to use segregated terminals.
Herbert Lee, a farmer working with Robert Moses of
SNCC to register black voters, is killed in Liberty, Mississippi, on September 25 by E. H. Hurst, a state representative. (Coroner's jury rules the killing to be self-defense,
though Louis Allen, who witnessed the shooting, later
tells the FBI Lee did not attack Hurst. Allen is murdered
in 1964.) Coalition of civil rights groups and local
African-American organizations in Albany, Georgia, forms
Albany Movement, November 17, to conduct protest
campaign against segregation. In series of demonstrations, December 10–16, more than 700 people are arrested, including King and Abernathy. Demonstrations
are suspended December 18 to allow for negotiations with
the city government.

1962   Boycott of city buses begins in Albany, January 12, as negotiations fail to reach an agreement on desegregation.
Council of Federated Organizations (COFO) is organized in Mississippi in February by coalition of civil rights
groups, including NAACP, CORE, and SNCC, to register black voters. In March Robert Kennedy approves FBI
wiretapping of Stanley Levison, a close adviser to King
who had been identified by FBI informers as a major
clandestine fundraiser for the Communist party between
1952 and 1957. Justice Department officials begin warning
King against associating with Levison, but he continues
the relationship. Voter Education Project is launched in
April. (In 1962 approximately 29 percent of eligible
African-Americans in the South are registered to vote.)

Fifth Circuit Court of Appeals orders James Meredith admitted to the University of Mississippi, June 25. Mass demonstrations resume in Albany in late July but are suspended in August when local leadership decides to concentrate on voter registration. (Failure of the Albany Movement to achieve desegregation of public accommodations brings public attention to tensions among SCLC, SNCC, and NAACP activists over tactics and personalities.) Congress submits Twenty-fourth Amendment to the Constitution, abolishing poll taxes in federal elections, to the states for ratification on August 27. Mississippi Governor Ross Barnett gives televised address on September 13 in which he vows to resist any federal attempt to integrate the university. Barnett personally blocks attempts by Meredith to register on September 20 and 25 while secretly negotiating with Robert Kennedy to end the confrontation. Meredith, Deputy Attorney General Nicholas Katzenbach, and 400 federal marshals arrive on Oxford campus of the university on September 30 after President Kennedy federalizes the Mississippi National Guard. During the night a mob of more than 2,000 people repeatedly attack the marshals, who are reinforced by the Guard. Violence ends on morning of October 1 as U.S. army troops arrive from Memphis; two people are killed and more than 300 injured during the riot. Meredith registers on October 1 as army troops continue to arrive. (U.S. army deploys 12,000 men to Oxford area by October 2; the last troops are withdrawn on July 24, 1963.) Kennedy issues Executive Order 11063 on November 20, prohibiting racial discrimination in federally owned housing, in public housing built with federal funds, and in new housing built with loans from federal agencies.

1963   SCLC leaders meet in January to plan major campaign against segregation in Birmingham. Campaign begins with sit-in on April 3, and on April 12 King, Abernathy, and Birmingham civil rights leader Fred Shuttlesworth are arrested. King writes his "Letter from Birmingham Jail," justifying disobedience to unjust laws, before being released on bail on April 20. Mass marches by African-American high school students begin on May 2. Birmingham public safety commissioner Eugene (Bull) Connor orders police dogs and fire hoses used on the marchers, May 3, and the police make more than 2,400 arrests between May 2 and May 7. Demonstrations are suspended on May 8 for negotiations mediated by Justice Department officials. Agreement reached on May 10 establishes timetable for desegregation of downtown department stores, the establishment of a biracial civic committee, and the release on bond of jailed protestors. After Klansmen set off two bombs in Birmingham on night of May 11, rioting breaks out despite pleas of movement leaders for continued nonviolence. Supreme Court reverses convictions of sit-in protestors in series of cases decided on May 20, ruling that state enforcement of restaurant segregation is a violation of the Fourteenth Amendment. Campaign of sit-ins and demonstrations begins in Jackson, May 28, led by Medgar Evers, Mississippi field secretary of the NAACP since 1954. Two African-American students register at the University of Alabama at Tuscaloosa on June 11 after confrontation outside of administration building in which Katzenbach orders Governor George Wallace to cease his obstruction of the court order admitting the students. On the evening of June 11 President Kennedy gives televised address in which he calls racial discrimination "a moral crisis" and proposes passage of a new civil rights bill. Medgar Evers is assassinated outside his home early on June 12. National Guard is sent to Cambridge, Maryland, on June 14 after rioting breaks out during protest campaign against segregation. Administration submits civil rights bill prohibiting racial discrimination in public accommodations to Congress on June 19. Demonstrations are suspended in Jackson, June 20, after the city agrees to hire black police officers, promote black sanitation workers, and desegregate municipal facilities. Agreement is mediated by Justice Department in Cambridge, July 23, calling for limited school desegregation, the creation of a biracial committee, and holding a referendum on desegregating public accommodations. (During spring and summer of 1963, campaigns against segregation are also organized in Gadsen, Alabama; Savannah, Georgia; Plaquemine, Louisiana; Danville, Virginia; Raleigh, Greensboro, and Durham, North Carolina; and Charleston, South Carolina.) More than 200,000 people attend March for Jobs and Freedom in Washington, August 28, during which King delivers "I Have a Dream" speech. Klansmen bomb church in Birmingham on September 15, killing Denise McNair, age 11, Cynthia Wesley, 14, Carole Robertson, 14, and Addie Mae Collins, 14. After learning that King is continuing to communicate with Stanley Levison, Robert Kennedy authorizes FBI wiretapping of King on October 10. (Wiretapping continues until June 1966; the FBI will also repeatedly place microphones in King's hotel rooms.) President Kennedy is assassinated in Dallas on November 22 and Vice-President Lyndon B. Johnson becomes president. Johnson begins intensive effort to move civil rights bill through Congress.

1964   In January COFO leadership approves SNCC plan to bring hundreds of volunteers, mostly white Northern college students, to Mississippi during the summer. Ratification of the Twenty-fourth Amendment is completed on January 23. House of Representatives passes civil rights bill, 290–130, on February 10, and the Senate begins debate on the bill, March 9. Malcolm X resigns from the Nation of Islam on March 11. More than 280 people are arrested during sit-ins held in restaurants and hotels in St. Augustine, Florida, March 28–April 1. George Wallace enters three Democratic presidential primaries and receives 34 percent of the vote in Wisconsin (April 7), 30 percent in Indiana (May 5), and 43 percent in Maryland (May 19). Supreme Court rules 9–0 on May 25 that Prince Edward County, Virginia, must reopen its public school system, which has been closed since 1959. (In 1964, ten years after *Brown* decision, 55 percent of African-American students in the District of Columbia, Delaware, Kentucky, Maryland, Missouri, Oklahoma, and West Virginia attend integrated schools, while only 1.2 percent of black students in the 11 Southern states attend school with whites.) Series of mass demonstrations are held in St. Augustine, May 26–June 30. Supreme Court unanimously overturns Alabama ban on the NAACP, June 1, allowing the organization to operate in the state for the first time since 1956. Senate votes 71–29 on June 10 to limit further debate on the civil rights bill, ending the longest filibuster in Senate history, and passes revised civil rights bill, 73–27, on June 19. First of approximately 550 "Freedom Summer" volunteers begin arriving in Mississippi to register voters, work in community centers, and teach in "Freedom Schools" (another 400 volunteers go to Mississippi before the project ends in August). Civil rights workers Andrew Goodman, Michael Schwerner, and James Chaney are murdered near Philadelphia, Mississippi, June 21, by Klansmen who bury their bodies under an earthen dam. Malcolm X announces formation of the Organization of Afro-American Unity on June 28. House passes final version of civil rights bill on July 2 and Johnson signs it the same day. The act strengthens federal power to protect voting rights; prohibits discrimination in public accommodations; authorizes the attorney general to file suits for the desegregation of schools and public facilities; bars discrimination in federally assisted programs; prohibits discrimination by employers and unions; and establishes an Equal Employment Opportunity Commission with investigative and mediative powers. Senator Barry Goldwater, who voted against the civil rights bill, wins the Republican presidential nomination on July 15. Fatal shooting of an African-American youth by a police officer in New York City, July 16, leads to rioting in Harlem, July 18–21, in which one person is killed. The bodies of the three missing civil rights workers are discovered by the FBI on August 4. Newly founded Mississippi Freedom Democratic Party selects delegates on August 6 to attend the Democratic national convention and challenge the seating of the all-white regular Democrats, August 6. Convention credentials committee votes on August 25 to seat regular Democrats who pledge their loyalty to the national party while offering Freedom Democrats two at-large seats. Freedom Democrats reject offer, and all but three of the regular Mississippi Democrats walk out of the convention. King is awarded the Nobel Peace Prize on October 14. Johnson wins election on November 3, defeating Goldwater 486–52 in the electoral voting; Goldwater carries five Southern states (Louisiana, Mississippi, Alabama, Georgia, and South Carolina). FBI mails tape compiled from potentially compromising hotel room recordings to King on November 21, along with an anonymous letter in which he is urged to commit suicide in order to avoid public disgrace. On December 4 FBI agents arrest 19 people on federal civil rights charges in the murders of Goodman, Schwerner, and Chaney (seven defendants, including a deputy sheriff, are convicted by an all-white jury in 1967). In *Katzenbach* v. *McClung* and *Heart of Atlanta Motel* v. *United States*, both decided 9–0 on

December 14, the Supreme Court upholds the constitutionality of the public accommodations sections of the 1964 civil rights act.

1965   SCLC begins voter registration campaign in Selma, Alabama, intended to demonstrate need for a new federal voting rights law. Mass arrests begin at the Selma courthouse, January 19, and more than 700 people are arrested during a march on February 1. Jimmie Lee Jackson, a church deacon and woodcutter, is fatally wounded by a state trooper during a demonstration in nearby Marion, Alabama, on February 18. Malcolm X is assassinated in New York by members of the Nation of Islam on February 21. United States begins sustained bombing of North Vietnam on March 2. SCLC leaders organize 54-mile march from Selma to Montgomery, the state capital. Several hundred marchers are beaten and tear-gassed by state police and sheriff's deputies as they cross the Edmund Pettus bridge in Selma on March 7 (incident becomes known as "Bloody Sunday"). After a federal district judge issues a temporary restraining order against a second march, King leads 2,000 people across the bridge and then turns back into Selma on March 9. James Reeb, a Unitarian minister from Boston, is fatally beaten in Selma on the evening of March 9. Johnson addresses joint session of Congress on March 15 and calls for the passage of a new voting rights bill, which the administration submits on March 17. Federal judge lifts restraining order and enjoins state and local authorities from interfering with Selma to Montgomery march. Led by King, marchers leave Selma on March 21 under federal military protection. March ends with rally outside of state capitol in Montgomery on March 25 attended by 25,000 people. Viola Liuzzo, a civil rights volunteer from Detroit, is shot and killed by Klansmen in Lowndes County, Alabama, on the night of March 25. Senate votes 70–30 to end debate on voting rights bill, May 25, and passes the bill 77–19 on May 26. House of Representatives passes its version of the bill, 333–85, on July 9. Final version of bill is approved by the Senate on August 4 and signed by Johnson on August 6. The voting rights act prohibits the use of literacy tests in jurisdictions where less than 50 percent of the eligible population either was registered to vote on November 1, 1964, or voted in the 1964 presidential election (Alabama,

Georgia, Louisiana, Mississippi, South Carolina, Virginia, and parts of North Carolina); gives the federal government the power to register voters in these jurisdictions; and prohibits changes in voting procedures in the covered jurisdictions without approval from either the attorney general or a federal court panel. Justice Department begins registering voters in nine Southern counties on August 10. (Proportion of eligible African-Americans registered to vote in the South increases from 43 percent in 1964 to 62 percent in 1968.) Traffic stop by police leads to rioting in the Watts section of Los Angeles, August 11–16, in which 34 people are killed. Johnson issues Executive Order 11246 on September 24, requiring all federal contractors and subcontractors to take "affirmative action" to hire and promote persons without regard to race.

1966   Floyd McKissick is elected on January 3 to succeed James Farmer as national director of CORE. Civil rights activist Vernon Dahmer dies after his home is fire-bombed by Klansmen in Hattiesburg, Mississippi, on January 10. (At least 35 people are killed by white supremacist terrorism in the South between 1954 and 1967.) Robert C. Weaver becomes the first African-American cabinet member when he is sworn in on January 18 as Secretary of Housing and Urban Development. In *South Carolina* v. *Katzenbach*, March 17, the Supreme Court upholds 8–1 the constitutionality of the Voting Rights Act, and on March 24 it rules 6–3 in *Harper* v. *Virginia State Board of Elections* that the imposition of poll taxes in state and local elections violates the Fourteenth Amendment. Johnson submits new civil rights bill to Congress on April 28 that provides enforcement powers to the EEOC, expands federal protection for civil rights workers, prohibits discrimination in the sale, rental, or financing of housing, and seeks to prevent discrimination in jury selection. Lowndes County Freedom Organization, independent political party organized in Alabama by Stokely Carmichael and other SNCC activists, holds convention on May 3 and nominates all-black slate of candidates for county offices (LCFO slate is defeated in November election). John Lewis, national chairman of SNCC since 1966, is defeated for reelection by Carmichael on May 14. Carmichael announces that SNCC will no longer send white organizers into black communities. James Meredith begins one-man "walk against fear" through Mississippi on June 5 and is wounded in an ambush on June 6. King, McKissick, and Carmichael agree on June 7 to lead march along Meredith's intended route. Carmichael gives speech calling for "black power" at rally in Greenwood on June 16. "Meredith March" ends with rally in Jackson on June 26. SCLC and Chicago civil rights groups begin campaign against housing discrimination in Chicago with mass rally on July 10. (Leaders of the Chicago campaign include Jesse Jackson, who in 1967 becomes national director of Operation Breadbasket, SCLC program that uses boycotts to promote the hiring of African-Americans and create opportunities for black-owned businesses.) SCLC begins series of marches through white neighborhoods on July 30 that are often met with violence from mobs; during march on August 5 King is struck in the head by a rock. House of Representatives passes civil rights bill with weakened open housing provision 259–157 on August 9. King, Mayor Richard Daley, and Chicago realtors announce agreement on housing discrimination on August 26 that is denounced by SNCC and CORE as ineffectual. Attempt to close debate on civil rights bill fails in the Senate on September 19. (Open housing provision is opposed by Everett Dirksen, Republican leader whose support was crucial in the passage of 1964 and 1965 bills.) Black Panther Party is founded by Huey Newton and Bobby Seale in Oakland, California, on October 15. Edward Brooke, attorney general of Massachusetts, is elected to the Senate on November 8, becoming the first black senator since 1881 (all six African-American representatives are reelected in 1966).

1967   King gives speech strongly condemning American involvement in Vietnam, April 4, and addresses major antiwar rally in New York City on April 15. H. Rap Brown succeeds Stokely Carmichael as chairman of SNCC on May 12 and continues its commitment to "Black Power." Supreme Court rules 5–4 in *Reitman* v. *Mulkey*, May 29, that a California state constitutional amendment allowing racial discrimination by property owners violates the Fourteenth Amendment. In *Loving* v. *Virginia*, June 12, the Supreme Court rules 9–0 that laws prohibiting interracial marriage violate the Fourteenth Amendment. Johnson appoints Thurgood Marshall to be the first

African-American justice on the Supreme Court, June 13. Traffic arrest by police in Newark, New Jersey, leads to riot, July 12–17, in which 23 people are killed. Police raid on after-hours club in Detroit, July 23, leads to widespread rioting, and on July 25 Johnson sends 4,700 army paratroopers to reinforce the National Guard. Riot ends July 27 after 43 people are killed. Johnson appoints commission headed by Illinois Governor Otto Kerner to investigate recent civil disorders, July 27 (there are a total of 59 urban riots in 1967). House of Representatives passes bill extending protection for civil rights workers 326–93 on August 16. FBI director J. Edgar Hoover approves counterintelligence program (COINTELPRO) intended to disrupt black nationalist groups, August 25. Black Panther leader Huey Newton is arrested October 28 and charged in the shooting death of an Oakland police officer (incident is first in series of violent encounters between Black Panthers and the police). Carl Stokes wins election in Cleveland, Ohio, and Richard Hatcher is elected in Gary, Indiana, November 7, becoming the first black mayors of major cities. SCLC announces plans on December 4 for Poor People's Campaign.

1968   Three African-American students are shot to death by state highway patrolmen on campus of South Carolina State College in Orangeburg, February 8, after series of demonstrations prompted by continued segregation of a local bowling alley. Senate adds provision prohibiting racial discrimination in the sale, rental, or financing of housing to the civil rights bill passed by the House in 1967. Kerner Commission delivers report on March 1 warning that "the nation is moving toward two societies, one black, one white—separate and unequal." Senate votes to end debate on civil rights bill, March 4, after Dirksen reverses his earlier opposition to fair housing legislation, and passes the bill 71–20 on March 11. Johnson announces on March 31 that he will not seek reelection. King is assassinated in Memphis on April 4. Rioting in Washington, Chicago, Baltimore, Kansas City, and other cities, April 5–9, results in 46 deaths. House of Representatives passes Senate version of civil rights bill 250–172, April 10, and Johnson signs it on April 11. Abernathy succeeds King as president of the SCLC and leads Poor People's March to Washington, where protestors build "Resurrection City," plywood shantytown near the Washington Monument, on May 12. In *Green* v. *County School Board of New Kent County*, decided May 27, the Supreme Court rejects 9–0 "freedom of choice" desegregation plan adopted by a Virginia school district and orders it to take further action to end its dual school system. Senator Robert Kennedy is assassinated in Los Angeles on June 5 while campaigning for the Democratic presidential nomination. Supreme Court rules 7–2 in *Jones* v. *Alfred H. Mayer Co.*, June 17, that racial discrimination in housing sales violates the 1866 Civil Rights Act. Police evict remaining protestors from Resurrection City on June 24. Huey Newton is convicted of voluntary manslaughter on September 10. Richard M. Nixon wins presidential election on November 5, defeating Vice-President Hubert H. Humphrey and George Wallace, who ran as an independent. Nixon wins 301 electoral votes and carries Virginia, North Carolina, South Carolina, Florida, and Tennessee; Humphrey wins 191 electoral votes and carries Texas; and Wallace wins 46 electoral votes and carries Louisiana, Arkansas, Mississippi, Alabama, and Georgia. Black Panther leader Eldridge Cleaver flees the country on November 24 to avoid imprisonment for a parole violation and goes into exile in Algeria.

1969   Federal appellate judge Warren Burger succeeds Earl Warren as chief justice on June 23. Department of Labor announces "Philadelphia Plan," June 27, requiring federal building contractors in Philadelphia to meet specific "goals" for hiring minority workers. (Plan is criticized for establishing racial quotas, which are prohibited by the 1964 Civil Rights Act, but withstands challenge in the federal courts and is later extended to several other cities.) Nixon issues Executive Order 11478, August 8, requiring all federal agencies to adopt "affirmative programs for equal employment opportunity." Nomination of federal appellate judge Clement Haynsworth Jr. to the Supreme Court on August 18 is opposed by civil rights groups and labor unions. In *Alexander* v. *Holmes County Board of Education*, decided 8–0 on October 29, the Supreme Court declares the "all deliberate speed" standard is no longer constitutionally permissible and orders the immediate desegregation of 33 Mississippi school districts. (By close of the 1970–71 school year 33 percent of African-American students in the South will attend white-majority schools.) Haynsworth nomination is rejected by the Senate 55–45 on November 21, becoming the first Supreme Court appointment defeated in a confirmation vote since 1930.

1970   Nomination of federal appellate judge G. Harrold Carswell to the Supreme Court on January 19 meets with strong opposition from civil rights groups and is rejected by the Senate, 51–45, on April 8. Huey Newton is released from prison, August 5, after his manslaughter conviction is overturned on appeal.

1971   Congressional Black Caucus is founded, February 2, with 13 members (12 Representatives and one nonvoting delegate from the District of Columbia). Black Panther party splits into bitterly opposed factions headed by Newton and Cleaver. In *Griggs* v. *Duke Power Company*, March 8, the Supreme Court rules 8–0 in favor of black employees who challenged the use of standardized tests by an employer with a past history of discrimination. (Decision makes it easier to bring suit under the employment provisions of the 1964 Civil Rights Act in cases where there is no evidence of discriminatory intent.) On April 20 the Court rules 9–0 in *Swann* v. *Charlotte-Mecklenburg Board of Education*, upholding a court-ordered busing plan designed to achieve racial balance in a de jure segregated school system. Nomination of assistant attorney general William Rehnquist to the Supreme Court is approved 68–26 on December 10 despite opposition from civil rights groups. Jesse Jackson resigns from SCLC and announces on December 18 the formation of his own organization, Operation PUSH (People United to Save Humanity).

1972   Congress passes Equal Employment Opportunity Act, March 24, giving the Equal Employment Opportunity Commission the power to file class-action lawsuits and extending its jurisdiction to cover state and local governments and educational institutions. Nixon wins reelection on November 7, defeating George McGovern 520–17 in the electoral voting and carrying all 11 Southern states. Andrew Young, a former aide to King, is elected to the House of Representatives from Georgia, and Barbara Jordan is elected to the House from Texas; they are the first African-Americans elected to Congress from the South since 1898.

1973   Last American troops are withdrawn from South Vietnam on March 29. Tom Bradley wins election on May 29 and becomes the first African-American mayor of Los Angeles. In *Keyes* v. *Denver School District No. 1*, decided June 21, the Supreme Court upholds 7–1 desegregation order involving busing in Denver, Colorado, ruling that decisions by school officials had reinforced de facto segregation. Maynard Jackson wins election in Atlanta on October 16 and becomes the first African-American mayor of a major Southern city.

Biographical Notes

TREZZVANT ANDERSON (November 2, 1906–March 25, 1963) Born Trezzvant William Anderson in Charlotte, North Carolina. Attended Johnson C. Smith College in Charlotte, leaving a year before graduation; was feature editor of college newspaper, *The University Student*. Earned his living as a railway mail clerk in Charlotte (1927–30) and later in Washington, D.C. (1930–41). Also worked as contributing editor of Charlotte *Post* (1928–29), and as speechwriter and publicist for Caesar R. Blake Jr., Imperial Potentate of the Shriners (Ramses Temple), and J. Finley Wilson, Grand Exalted Ruler of the Elks (1929–30; 1931–52). Organized the first Negro Press Club in Washington, D.C., in 1930, acting as president until 1934. Drafted into U.S. Army in 1941; served as a war correspondent, 1943–46, publishing *Come Out Fighting: The Epic Tale of the 761st Tank Battalion, 1942–1945* (1945) while overseas. After the war, edited and published his own newspaper in Charlotte and worked briefly on an assembly line at Ford Motors in Detroit. Joined *Pittsburgh Courier* staff in 1947, working on rewrite desk in Pittsburgh. Beginning in 1957 became "The Courier Roving Reporter," based in Georgia and traveling throughout Southeast. Covered the desegregation crisis in Little Rock, evictions of tenant farmers in Tennessee, and the sit-in movement in Greensboro, North Carolina, among other stories. Died in Macon, Georgia.

JOE AZBELL (August 24, 1927–September 30, 1995) Born in Vernon, Texas. Ran away from home at 13, reading in public libraries by day and working at night in print shops and on newspapers in a number of states. At 18 joined U.S. Army Air Forces; worked on base newspapers and founded *Air University Dispatch*. After World War II, founded weekly *West Alabama News* in Selma; hired as state editor of *Montgomery Advertiser* in 1948 and later named city editor. Fired and soon rehired in 1953 after decision to stop presses for front-page coverage of Hank Williams' Montgomery funeral (special issue achieved record circulation). In 1955, tipped off by E. D. Nixon, published first newspaper account of Montgomery bus boycott. Left *Advertiser* in early 1960s. Published book *The Riotmakers* (1968). Founded successful real estate firm. Worked on 1968 and 1972 presidential campaigns of George Wallace as director of communications, and subsequently as independent political consultant. From 1968 until his death, wrote a weekly political column for *Montgomery Independent*.

BEN H. BAGDIKIAN (January 30, 1920–) Born Ben Haig Bagdikian in Marash, Turkey; came to United States as an infant and was naturalized in 1926. After graduation from Clark University, took job as reporter for Springfield, Massachusetts, *Morning Union* (1941–42); served in U.S. Army Air Forces. Joined reporting staff of *Providence Journal* in 1947, eventually becoming chief Washington correspondent; shared Pulitzer Prize for deadline reporting with group from *Providence Journal*. From 1963 to 1967 served as contributing editor for *Saturday Evening Post*, from 1970 to 1972 as assistant managing editor at *Washington Post*, and from 1972 to 1974 as national correspondent for *Columbia Journalism Review*. Beginning in 1976, taught journalism at University of California at Berkeley, retiring in 1990; served as dean of journalism school for three years (1985–88). Currently lives in Berkeley, California. His books include *In the Midst of Plenty: The Poor in America* (1964), *The Information Machines: Their Impact on Men and the Media* (1971), *The Shame of the Prisons* (1972), *The Effete Conspiracy, and Other Crimes by the Press* (1972), *Caged: Eight Prisoners and Their Keepers* (1976), *The Media Monopoly* (1983; 6th edition revised, 2000), and a memoir, *Double Vision: Reflections on My Heritage, Life, and Profession* (1995).

JAMES BALDWIN (August 2, 1924–November 30, 1987) Born James Arthur Jones in New York City; given name Baldwin after mother remarried in 1927. Graduated from De Witt Clinton High School; employed as waiter in Greenwich Village while working on novel. Wrote reviews for *The Nation*, *The New Leader*, *Commentary*, and *Partisan Review*; in 1948 moved to Paris, living alternately in France and the U.S. for remainder of life. First novel, *Go Tell It on the Mountain*, published in 1953, and first essay collection, *Notes of a Native Son*, in 1955. A play, *Amen Corner*, performed at Howard (later revived in New York, 1965, and London, 1986). Second novel, *Giovanni's Room*, appeared in 1956. Toured southern states in 1957 for *Partisan Review* and *Harper's*, visiting newly integrated public schools; in 1960 reported on Tallahassee sit-in movement and Congress of Racial Equality. *Nobody Knows My Name: More Notes of a Native Son* published 1961, novel *Another Country* in 1962. Traveled through South in 1963, lecturing for CORE; appeared on cover of *Time* magazine. Long essay *The Fire Next Time* won 1963 George Polk award. Met with Attorney General Robert Kennedy and Assistant Attorney General Burke Marshall, head of Justice Department civil rights division; assisted James Forman of SNCC in Selma voter registration drive. Play *Blues for Mr. Charlie* performed in New York; collection of stories, *Going To Meet the Man*, appeared in 1965. Worked on film adaptation of *Autobiography of Malcolm X*; published novel *Tell Me How Long the Train's Been Gone* (1968). Directed production of *Fortune and Men's Eyes* in Istanbul (1969); subject of documentary *James Baldwin from Another Place* (1970). Conversations with Margaret Mead published as *A Rap on Race* (1971). Published novels *No Name in the Street* (1972), *If Beale Street Could Talk* (1974), and *Just Above My Head* (1979), and long essay *The Devil Finds Work* (1976). Taught three semesters at Bowling Green College (1978–81), at University of California, Berkeley (1979), and University of Massachusetts at Amherst (1983–84). Died at St. Paul-de-Vence, France; buried in New York.

DAVID B. BITTAN (June 27, 1921–June 29, 2001) Born David Benjamin Bittan in Philadelphia; raised in Hammonton and Westmont, New Jersey.

Graduated from Overbrook High School. Served in the army for three years during World War II, contributing reports to *Stars and Stripes*. Graduated from Temple University (B.S., 1948), where he majored in journalism and edited college newspaper; also did graduate work at Trinity University. Began journalism career as reporter for papers in San Antonio and Port Arthur, Texas. Returned to New Jersey to work for *Trenton Times*. Worked as reporter for *Philadelphia Daily News* from the mid-1950s until the late 1990s; contributed Philadelphia-area stories to *New York Times* and wire services. Also wrote jazz criticism for *Downbeat*, *Variety*, and *Metronome*. Died in Merion Station, Pennsylvania.

TOLLY R. BROADY (September 20, 1917–September 20, 1986)   Born Tolly Rupert Broady in Low Moor, Virginia. Educated in Alleghany County, Virginia, public schools; graduated from Tuskegee Institute in 1940. Taught sociology at Tuskegee until 1942. Served in the U.S. Army from 1943 to 1945, after which he studied law (LL.B., Fordham, 1949; M.S. in labor law, New York University, 1954; Doctor of Law, Fordham, 1968), and sociology (M.A., NYU, 1953). Practiced law in Queens and Nassau counties in New York beginning in 1953; appointed administrative law judge in New York City in 1970. Served as counsel to New York State Conference of the NAACP.

STERLING A. BROWN (May 1, 1901–January 13, 1989)   Born Sterling Allen Brown in Washington, D.C. Educated at Williams College and at Harvard (M.A., 1923). During the 1920s taught at Virginia Seminary and College, Fisk University, and Lincoln University; joined faculty of Howard University in 1929, remaining until 1969. Also served as visiting professor at Vassar, University of Minnesota, and University of Illinois; worked as Negro Affairs editor for Federal Writers' Project, 1936–39, and on staff of Carnegie Corporation study of Negro in America, headed by Gunnar Myrdal and published as *An American Dilemma* (1944). Author of *The Negro in American Fiction* (1937), *Negro Poetry and Drama* (1937), *A Son's Return: Selected Essays of Sterling A. Brown* (1996), and three books of poetry: *Southern Road* (1932), *The Last Ride of Wild Bill and Eleven Narrative Poems* (1975), and *The Collected Poems of Sterling A. Brown* (1980). Edited influential anthology *The Negro Caravan* (1941). Died in Takoma Park, Maryland.

HODDING CARTER (February 3, 1907–April 4, 1972)   Born William Hodding Carter Jr. in Hammond, Louisiana; educated at Bowdoin (B.A., 1927) and the Graduate School of Journalism, Columbia University (1928). After a year as a teaching fellow at Tulane (1928–29), worked as reporter for *New Orleans Item-Tribune* (1929), United Press in New Orleans (1930), and Associated Press in Jackson, Mississippi (1931–32). Founded, edited, and published Hammond, Louisiana, *Daily Courier* (1932–36), and Greenville, Mississippi, *Delta Star* (1936–38). Founded *Delta Democrat-Times* by merger in 1938, serving as editor and publisher until the mid-1960s, when son Hodding Carter III gradually took on editorship. Awarded a Nieman fellowship at

Harvard in 1940, and helped to found daily *PM* in the same year. Served in Mississippi National Guard during the war; edited Middle East editions of *Yank* and *Stars and Stripes*. Won Pulitzer Prize in 1946 for editorials on racial intolerance. In 1955, censured by Mississippi legislature for criticism of White Citizens Councils. Died in Greenville. His books include *Lower Mississippi* (1942), *Civilian Defense for the United States* (1942, with Ernest R. Dupuy), *The Winds of Fear* (novel, 1944), *Flood Crest* (novel, 1947), *Southern Legacy* (1950), *Gulf Coast Country* (1951, with Anthony Ragusin), *Where Main Street Meets the River* (1953), *So Great a Good: A History of the Episcopal Church in Louisiana and Christ Church Cathedral* (1955, with Betty Carter), *The Angry Scar: The Story of Reconstruction* (1959), *First Person Rural* (1963), *The Ballad of Catfoot Grimes and Other Verses* (1964), *So the Heffners Left McComb* (1965), *Their Words Were Bullets: The Southern Press in War, Reconstruction, and Peace* (1969), and *Man and the River: The Mississippi* (1970). A biography by Ann Waldron, *Hodding Carter: The Reconstruction of a Racist*, was published in 1993.

REESE CLEGHORN (April 9, 1930–) Born George Reese Cleghorn in Lyerly, Georgia. Graduated from Emory in 1950 with journalism degree, after which served with the U.S. Air Force in Germany (1951–52). From 1954–58 was editor and reporter for Associated Press in New York and Atlanta; also received master's degree in public law and government from Columbia University, 1956. Reported on civil rights movement from Atlanta for *Atlanta Journal* and national magazines. Served as associate editor of *Atlanta Journal* (1963–69); project director for the Southern Regional Council (1969–71), editing monthly *South Today*; editorial page editor, *Charlotte Observer* (1971–76); and associate editor of *Detroit Free Press* (1976–80). Currently professor at Philip Merrill College of Journalism, University of Maryland, of which he was dean from 1981 to 2000, and president emeritus of *American Journalism Review*. Author of *Climbing Jacob's Ladder: The Arrival of Negroes in Southern Politics* (1967, with Pat Watters).

RAYMOND R. COFFEY (March 31, 1929–) Born in Racine, Wisconsin. Graduated from Marquette University in 1951. Served in U.S. Army (1951–53), then worked as reporter and later Springfield bureau chief for United Press International (1953–61). In 1961, joined staff of *Chicago Daily News* as reporter; also served as national correspondent, assistant managing editor, Washington bureau chief, and foreign correspondent, covering Vietnam War and Nigerian civil war. Won 1963 National Headliners Club award for civil rights reporting. Moved to *Chicago Tribune* when *Daily News* ceased publication in 1978, eventually becoming Washington bureau chief. Returned to Chicago in 1986; wrote a daily column for *Chicago Sun-Times* and was a member of *Sun-Times* editorial board until his retirement in 1999.

GEORGE COLLINS (October 14, 1925–) Born George W. Collins in Stamford, Connecticut. Attended Central Connecticut State University in

New Britain in 1942; served with U.S. Army Air Forces, 1943–48, as agent for Criminal Investigation Division. Returned to college, graduating in 1950 with a degree in journalism; contributed to *Brooklyn Eagle*. Took first job as reporter with Baltimore *Afro-American* in 1950, where he remained until 1968, eventually becoming editor-in-chief. Reported on rise of narcotics trade in Baltimore and civil rights movement in Maryland; arrested in 1963 while reporting Morgan State sit-in movement in Baltimore. Beginning in 1968 worked for WMAR-TV in Baltimore as investigative reporter, news anchor, producer, host, and commentator. Since 1986 has owned GWC Associates, a media consulting firm; since 2001 has been producing *@Issue*, a radio program on WEAA, a Morgan State University-based National Public Radio affiliate.

TOM DENT (March 20, 1932–June 6, 1998) Born Thomas Covington Dent in New Orleans; educated at Gilbert Academy, Morehouse College (B.A., political science, 1952), and Syracuse University (1952–56). Editor at Morehouse of literary journal *Maroon Tiger*. After two years in the U.S. Army (1957–59), moved to New York, where he worked as reporter for *New York Age* (1959–60), social worker for New York Welfare Department (1960–61), and as press attaché and public information director for the NAACP Legal Defense Fund (1961–63), assisting Thurgood Marshall. In 1962 co-founded Umbra Writer's Workshop in New York. Returned to New Orleans in 1965. As associate director of the Free Southern Theater (1966–70), an activist community theater project, organized performances throughout the South. Taught at Mary Homes College in West Point, Mississippi (1968–70), and later at University of New Orleans (1979–81); in 1969 co-founded *Callaloo: A Quarterly Journal of African and African-American Arts and Letters*. Wrote plays *Negro Study No. 34A* (1970), *Snapshot* (1970), and *Ritual Murder* (1976). Served as public relations director for New Orleans antipoverty agency (1971–74); earned an M.F.A. in creative writing from Goddard University in 1974. Beginning in the late 1970s was active in compiling oral histories of Mississippi civil rights workers, and in 1984 interviewed Acadian and New Orleans musicians. From 1984 to 1986 worked with Andrew Young on autobiography *An Easy Burden* (1996). Served as executive director of New Orleans Jazz and Heritage Foundation, sponsor of New Orleans Jazz and Heritage Festival, 1987–90. Author of two books of poetry, *Magnolia Street* (1976) and *Blue Lights and River Songs* (1982); co-edited *The Free Southern Theater* (1969, with Richard Schechner). In 1996 published *Southern Journey*, in which he revisited the scenes and characters of the southern civil rights movement. Died in New Orleans.

KENNETH L. DIXON (April 3, 1915–June 29, 1986) Born near Colchester, Illinois; educated at Western Illinois State Teachers College. Taught at rural schools. Wrote first newspaper story while a subscription salesman at *Macomb* (Illinois) *Daily Journal*. Edited newspapers in Carlsbad and Hobbs, New Mexico. During World War II worked as war correspondent for Associated

Press, filing stories on Anzio, the invasion of southern France, and the Battle of the Bulge. After the war wrote column "Assignment: America" for King Features and reported for International News Service from Europe and the Middle East. In 1948 joined staff of *Lake Charles American Press*, exposed a Louisiana gambling syndicate. Last worked as reporter and editorial writer for *Baton Rouge Morning Advocate*. Died in Baton Rouge, Louisiana.

ROBERT J. DONOVAN (August 21, 1912–   ) Born Robert John Donovan in Buffalo, New York. Graduated from high school in Buffalo; failure of father's business frustrated college plans. In 1933 took job as copyboy at *Courier-Express* in Buffalo; promoted to reporter. Joined staff of New York *Herald-Tribune* in 1937. Covered City Hall beginning in 1942. After wartime service in Europe, including stint at *Stars and Stripes* in Paris, reported from Washington for *Herald-Tribune* (1947–63). Covered 1948 Harry Truman campaign. Became Washington bureau chief for *Los Angeles Times* in 1963, and associate editor in 1970, serving until 1977. Currently lives in Washington, D.C. His books include *The Assassins* (1955), *Eisenhower: The Inside Story* (1956), *PT 109: John F. Kennedy in World War II* (1961), *The Future of the Republican Party* (1964), *Conflict and Crisis: The Presidency of Harry S. Truman, 1945–48* (1977), *Tumultuous Years: The Presidency of Harry S. Truman, 1949–53* (1982), *Nemesis: Truman and Johnson in the Coils of War in Asia* (1984), *The Second Victory: The Marshall Plan and the Postwar Revival of Europe* (1987), *Confidential Secretary: Ann Whitman's Twenty Years with Eisenhower and Rockefeller* (1988), *Unsilent Revolution: Television News and American Public Life, 1948–1991* (1992, with Ray Scherer), and *Boxing the Kangaroo: A Reporter's Memoir* (2000).

MICHAEL DORMAN (October 9, 1932–   ) Born in New York City. Began career in journalism at 17 as *Wall Street Journal* editorial assistant; worked for *New York Times* on night shift while attending New York University (graduated 1953). After college, reported for Associated Press (1953), *Houston Press* (1953–58), *Newsweek* (1959), and *Newsday* (1959–64); covered assassination of John Kennedy, civil rights protests, and state and national political campaigns. From 1964 to 1999 worked as freelance writer; his books include *We Shall Overcome* (1964), *The Secret Service Story* (1967), *The Second Man: The Changing Role of the Vice-Presidency* (1968), *King of the Courtroom: Percy Foreman for the Defense* (1969), *Under Twenty-One: A Young People's Guide to Legal Rights* (1970), *Payoff: The Role of Organized Crime in American Politics* (1972), *The Making of a Slum* (1972), *Confrontation: Politics and Protest* (1974), *Vesco: The Infernal Money Making Machine* (1975), *The George Wallace Myth* (1976), *Witch Hunt: The Underside of American Democracy* (1976), *Detectives of the Sky: Investigating Aviation Tragedies* (1976), *Dirty Politics from 1776 to Watergate* (1980) and *Blood and Revenge* (1991). In 1999 returned to *Newsday* as an editor.

BOB DUKE (July 27, 1932–January 25, 2001) Born Robert M. Duke in Bolling, Alabama. Served in U.S. Air Force during Korean War. Attended

Pensacola Junior College and later Florida State University in Tallahassee, receiving degree in journalism (1958). Was reporter at *Montgomery Advertiser, Tallahassee Democrat, Pensacola News-Journal, Albuquerque Tribune,* and papers in El Paso, Texas, and Birmingham, Alabama; worked for *Mobile Press-Register,* 1964–69. Beginning in 1969 was press secretary for Alabama Senator James Allen; later worked in the Scripps-Howard Washington bureau, as a financial writer and editor for newsletter division of American Banker-Bond Buyer, and as housing editor for CD Publications, a Maryland newsletter publisher. Died in Takoma Park, Maryland.

WILMA DYKEMAN (May 20, 1920–) Born in Asheville, North Carolina; educated at Biltmore Junior College in Asheville and Northwestern University. Returned to Appalachia after college, working as a writer, teacher, and lecturer. Currently lives in Newport, Tennessee. Her first book, *The French Broad* (a volume in the *Rivers of America* series), appeared in 1955. With husband James Stokely, reported on Montgomery bus boycott, school desegregation in Clinton, Tennessee, and other events in civil rights movement; co-authored *Neither Black Nor White* (1957) with Stokely. Also published novels (*The Tall Woman,* 1962; *The Far Family,* 1966; *Return the Innocent Earth,* 1973), biographies (*Seeds of Southern Change: The Life of Will Alexander,* 1962, with James Stokely; *Prophet of Plenty: The First Ninety Years of W. D. Weatherford,* 1966; *Too Many People, Too Little Love,* 1974, on Edna Rankin McKinnon, Appalachian family planning advocate), and regional histories (*The Southern Appalachian Region: A Survey,* 1962; *Tennessee: A Bicentennial History,* 1975; *Highland Homeland: The People of the Great Smokies,* 1978, with son James R. Stokely III; *With Fire and Sword: The Battle of Kings Mountain,* 1978; and *At Home in the Smokies: A History Handbook for Great Smoky Mountains National Park,* 1984). *Explorations,* a collection of essays about the Appalachians, appeared in 1984; *Tennessee Woman: An Infinite Variety* in 1993.

RALPH ELLISON (March 1, 1913–April 16, 1994) Born Ralph Waldo Ellison in Oklahoma City, Oklahoma. Educated at Frederick Douglass High School in Oklahoma City and at Tuskegee Institute (1933–36), where he studied music. Moved to New York in 1936; worked for Federal Writers' Project, researching history of African-Americans in Manhattan (1938–42), and edited *Negro Quarterly* (1942). To avoid the draft, worked as a cook in merchant marine (1943–45); published reviews and short stories. *Invisible Man* (1952), first novel, became bestseller and won National Book Award. Taught American literature at Bard College and New York University, and creative writing at Rutgers; published *Shadow and Act* (1964), a collection of essays, and *Going to the Territory* (1985), an anthology of essays and interviews. Died in New York. *Flying Home* (1996), a book of stories, and *Juneteenth* (1999), unfinished novel, published posthumously.

ELIZABETH HEAD FETTER (September 4, 1904–January 1973) Born Elizabeth Head in Philadelphia. Educated at Vassar (1922–25) and University of

Colorado, graduating in 1927. After college, was advertising copywriter for Philadelphia department stores (1928–30, 1933–34), and novelist and freelance magazine writer, publishing under pseudonym Hannah Lees. Her books include *Women Will Be Doctors* (1939), *Rx: Prescription for Murder* (1941), *Death in the Dolls' House* (1942), *Till the Boys Come Home* (1944), *The Dark Device* (1947), *Help Your Husband Stay Alive* (1957), and *The Sweet Death of Candor* (1969). Taught experimental writing at Bryn Mawr College, 1953–56; served as member of Philadelphia Council on Human Relations, 1952–59. Died in Philadelphia.

SAMUEL L. GANDY (November 28, 1914–June 23, 1988) Born Samuel Lucius Gandy in Anderson, South Carolina. Educated at Howard and University of Chicago. Served as director of religious activities at Virginia State College for 11 years, and later as Dean of Lawless Memorial Chapel at Dillard University. Edited *Human Possibilities: A Vernon Johns Reader* (1977). Died in Washington, D.C.

HARRY L. GOLDEN (May 6, 1903–October 2, 1981) Born Herschele Lewis Goldhirsch in New York City. Attended City College of New York for three years. Worked for sister's brokerage firm; founded own brokerage in mid-1920s. Declared bankruptcy in 1926, unable to return clients' investments after unsuccessful market speculation. Pled guilty to charges of mail fraud in 1929, spending more than three years in prison; edited prison newspaper. Worked for five years as hotel manager. In 1938 wrote and sold advertising for *New York Mirror*. Moved to Norfolk, Virginia, where he sold advertising for *Norfolk Times-Advocate*. Changed name to Golden. Worked for *Charlotte Labor Journal* and *Charlotte Observer* as advertising salesman. Founded small newspaper *Carolina Israelite* in 1941, noted for its humorous treatment of civil rights issues; worked on *Israelite* until 1968. Disclosure of prison term in 1958 increased popularity; later received presidential pardon from Richard Nixon. Author of *Only in America* (1958), *For 2¢ Plain* (1959), *Enjoy! Enjoy!* (1960), *You're Entitle'* (a biography of Carl Sandburg, 1962), *Mr. Kennedy and the Negroes* (1964), *So What Else Is New?* (1964), *A Little Girl Is Dead* (1965), and *The Best of Harry Golden* (1967). Died in Charlotte.

JOHN HOWARD GRIFFIN (June 16, 1920–September 9, 1980) Born in Dallas. Went to France at 15 to complete education; studied medicine at University of Poitiers, and worked as assistant to director of Asylum of Tours. After outbreak of war, aided in evacuation of Jewish children. Returned to U.S. in 1941. Enlisted in U.S. Army Air Forces; wounded during Japanese air raid, partially losing his sight. Wrote novels *The Devil Rides Outside* (1952) and *Nuni* (1956) about wartime experiences. Recovered sight in 1957. Proposed series of articles to editor of *Sepia*, eventually expanded and published as *Black Like Me* (1961). Finished book in Mexico after he was hanged in effigy in his Texas hometown. Later wrote *The Church and the Black Man* (1969), *A Time To Be Human* (1977), and books about Thomas Merton: *A Hidden*

Wholeness (1970), and posthumously published *Hermitage Journals* (1981) and *Follow the Ecstasy: Thomas Merton, the Hermitage Years, 1965–1968* (1983). Died in Fort Worth.

DAVID HALBERSTAM   (April 10, 1934–   )   Born in New York City; educated at Harvard (B.A., 1955). After college took reporting job in Mississippi with *West Point Daily Times Leader* (1955–56); later worked for *Nashville Tennesseean* (1956–60), and as *New York Times* staff writer (1960–67). Shared Pulitzer Prize and George Polk award for foreign reporting, 1964. Left *Times* in 1967 to become contributing editor for *Harper's*. His books include *The Noblest Roman* (novel, 1961), *The Making of a Quagmire* (1965), *One Very Hot Day* (novel, 1968), *The Unfinished Odyssey of Robert Kennedy* (1969), *Ho* (1971), *The Best and the Brightest* (1972), *The Powers That Be* (1979), *The Breaks of the Game* (1981), *The Amateurs* (1985), *The Reckoning* (1987), *Summer of '49* (1989), *The Next Century* (1991), *The Fifties* (1993), *October 1964* (1994), *The Children* (1998), *War in a Time of Peace* (2001), and *Firehouse* (2002).

FANNIE LOU HAMER   (October 6, 1917–March 14, 1977)   Born Fannie Lou Townsend in Montgomery County, Mississippi (married Perry Hamer in 1944). Picked cotton from the age of six; left school at thirteen to help support family. Worked as sharecropper on W. D. Marlow plantation near Ruleville, Mississippi; evicted in 1962 after attempting to register to vote. Became SNCC field worker later in 1962. Registered successfully early in 1963; in June, with June E. Johnson, Annell Ponder, and others, arrested and beaten in Winona, Mississippi. In 1964 ran unsuccessfully for Congress as candidate of Mississippi Freedom Democratic Party. Participated in Oxford, Ohio, training of Freedom Summer volunteers. Appeared before credentials committee of 1964 Democratic National Convention in Atlantic City on behalf of MFDP challenge to Mississippi delegation; traveled to Guinea with SNCC workers and joined Malcolm X in New York rallies. In 1965 filed lawsuit contesting several election results in Sunflower County, Mississippi; won case in federal appeals court, leading to new elections. Lost 1967 election for board of Sunflower County antipoverty agency. In 1968 served as delegate to Democratic National Convention in Chicago. Established Freedom Farm in 1969; later forced to sell to creditors. Established "pig bank" with National Council of Negro Women, loaning pigs to poor Mississippi families; worked to establish Head Start programs in Mississippi Delta. Filed 1970 lawsuit against Sunflower County alleging failure to desegregate schools; bombing of home attempted early in 1971. Ran unsuccessfully for Mississippi state senate. Died in Mound Bayou, Mississippi.

T. GEORGE HARRIS   (October 4, 1924–   )   Born in Simpson County, Kentucky. In 1942 took first job in journalism, working as reporter for *Clarkesville* (Tennessee) *Leaf Chronicle*. Served in U.S. Army during World War II, winning Bronze Star and Air Medal with cluster. Attended University of Kentucky in 1946; graduated from Yale in 1949. After college joined *Time* magazine staff as correspondent, becoming Chicago bureau chief for Time-Life-Fortune in 1955, contributing editor in 1958, and San Francisco bureau chief in 1960. Served as senior editor at *Look* (1962–68), founding editor of *Psychology Today* (1969–76, 1988–90), founding editor of *American Health* (1980–90), editor of *Harvard Business Review* (1992–93), and founding editor of *Spirituality and Health* (1996–   ). Author of *Romney's Way: A Plan and an Idea* (1967).

TOM HAYDEN (December 11, 1939–   ) Born Thomas Emmett Hayden in Detroit. At University of Michigan, worked on college paper, Michigan *Daily*, becoming editor; reported for *Daily* on disenfranchised sharecroppers in Fayette County, Tennessee. Turned down newspaper job after college to work as first field secretary for Students for a Democratic Society, assisting and reporting on work of SNCC; beaten in McComb, Mississippi, while investigating protests. Late in 1961 arrested after train ride from Atlanta to Albany, Georgia, testing ICC desegregation ruling. In 1962 organized conference at Port Huron, Michigan, and drafted SDS *Port Huron Statement*; served as SDS president (1962–63) while in graduate school at University of Michigan. Lived in Newark, New Jersey, from 1964 to 1968; led antipoverty Newark Community Union Project. Published *Rebellion in Newark: Official Violence and Ghetto Response* (1967) in wake of Newark riots. Active in antiwar movement, traveling to North Vietnam in 1965 and to Czechoslovakia and Cambodia in 1967. Defendant in "Chicago Eight" conspiracy trial. Moved to Los Angeles in 1971; elected to California state assembly in 1982, and state senate in 1992, serving until 1999. Currently lives in Los Angeles. Also author of *The Other Side* (1966, with Staughton Lynd), *Trial* (1970), *The Love of Possession Is a Disease with Them* (1972), *Vietnam: The Struggle for Peace, 1972–73* (1973), *The American Future: New Visions Beyond Old Frontiers* (1980), *Reunion: A Memoir* (1988), *The Lost Gospel of the Earth: A Call for Renewing Nature, Spirit and Politics* (1996), *Irish Hunger* (1997), and *Irish on the Inside: In Search of the Soul of Irish America* (2001).

JOHN HERBERS (November 4, 1923–   ) Born in Memphis, Tennessee. Educated at Emory University, graduating in 1949. Began career at Greenwood, Mississippi, *Morning Star* and Jackson, Mississippi, *Daily News*. From 1953 to 1963 reported from Mississippi for United Press International. Joined staff of *New York Times* in 1963; covered civil rights, Congress, presidential campaigns, and urban affairs. Appointed *Times* assistant national editor in 1975, deputy Washington bureau chief in 1977, and national Washington correspondent in 1979; retired in 1987. His books include *The Lost Priority: What Happened to the Civil Rights Movement in America?* (1970), *The Black Dilemma* (1973), *No Thank You, Mr. President* (1976), and *The New Heartland: America's Flight Beyond the Suburbs and How It Is Changing Our Future* (1986).

JAMES L. HICKS   (May 9, 1915–January 19, 1986)   Born in Akron, Ohio; educated at University of Akron and at Howard. Began journalism career in 1935 as reporter for *Call and Post* in Cleveland. Enlisted in U.S. Army as private; awarded three battle stars for service in New Guinea campaign, and was promoted to captain. After the war, joined Baltimore *Afro-American*; became Washington bureau chief for National Negro Press Association. Served as editor of *Amsterdam News* from 1955 to 1966 and from 1972 to 1977; worked in the interim as a public relations officer for National Urban League and as assistant commissioner of New York State Division of Human Rights. Reported for *Amsterdam News* on the Emmett Till case, on school desegregation in Clinton, Tennessee, Little Rock, Arkansas, and Oxford, Mississippi; was first African-American member of State Department Correspondents Association and first African-American reporter accredited to cover United Nations. In 1977 became editor of *New York Voice*, a Queens weekly. Died in Manhattan.

FRANK HOLLOWAY   (c. 1940–   )   Worked with SNCC in Selma, Alabama, voter registration campaigns. Currently lives in Riverdale, Georgia.

LEN HOLT   (1928–   )   Born in Tuscumbia, Alabama; raised in Chicago, where family had moved when he was three months old. Attended Phillips High School in Chicago, then enlisted in U.S. Navy, serving for two years as pharmacist's mate 3rd class (1945–47). After military service was educated at University of Redlands for three years (1948–51), and later at Howard University Law School, graduating in 1956. Worked as civil rights lawyer for Norfolk, Virginia, firm Jordan, Dawler, and Holt; became CORE field secretary. Traveled throughout South coordinating local groups and national office; with National Lawyers Guild, represented and arranged for representation of thousands of arrested protestors. Currently lives in Berkeley, California. Author of *The Summer That Didn't End: the Story of the Mississippi Civil Rights Project of 1964* (1965) and *An Act of Conscience* (1965).

BETTYE RICE HUGHES   Lived in Los Angeles area in 1961.

LANGSTON HUGHES   (February 1, 1902–May 22, 1967)   Born James Langston Hughes in Joplin, Missouri. Graduated from Central High School in Cleveland in 1920 and attended Columbia University (1921–22), afterward working as sailor on voyages to West Africa and France. *Weary Blues*, first book, published in 1926; completed college at Lincoln University in Pennsylvania (1926–29), and published second book of poetry, *Fine Clothes to the Jew* (1927). With Zora Neale Hurston, Wallace Thurman, and Gwendolyn Bennett, started literary magazine *Fire!!* (1926). Novel *Not Without Laughter* published 1930. Traveled throughout South and West in 1931 on reading tour, visiting Scottsboro Boys in prison; also went to Soviet Union and China (1933–34). Book of short stories, *The Ways of White Folks*, appeared in 1934. Plays *Mulatto* (1935), *Little Ham* (1936), *Joy to My Soul* (1937), *Don't You Want To Be Free?* (1938), and *Front Porch* (1938) staged; reported on Spanish

Civil War for Baltimore *Afro-American*. Wrote screenplay for film *Way Down South* (1939). *The Big Sea*, an autobiography, appeared in 1941 (second volume, *I Wonder As I Wander*, in 1956). Began writing weekly column, "Here to Yonder," for *Chicago Defender* in 1942, often featuring Harlem everyman "Simple" (later collected in *Simple Speaks His Mind*, 1950, *Simple Takes a Wife*, 1953, *The Best of Simple*, 1961, and *Simple's Uncle Sam*, 1965; last column, 1966). In 1943 published pamphlet of civil rights poems, *Jim Crow's Last Stand*. Beginning in 1945 collaborated with Kurt Weill and Elmer Rice as lyricist for musical *Street Scene*, performed on Broadway in 1947; published *Fields of Wonder* (1947), *One-Way Ticket* (1949), and *Montage of a Dream Deferred* (1951). Testified before House Un-American Activities Committee in 1953. Inducted into National Institute of Arts and Letters in 1961; beginning in 1962 wrote column for *New York Post*. Gospel musical *Tambourines to Glory* opened in New York in 1963. Died in New York. Last poems collected in *Ask Your Mama* (1961) and *The Panther and the Lash* (1967).

WILLIAM BRADFORD HUIE (November 13, 1910–November 22, 1986) Born in Hartselle, Alabama. Graduated from University of Alabama in 1930. Worked as reporter for *Birmingham Post* (1932–36) and as associate editor of *American Mercury* (1941–43). Served in the U.S. Navy (1943–45), after which he returned to *Mercury* as editor and publisher, remaining until 1952. Later in the 1950s interviewed major political figures for CBS series *Chronoscope*. With Zora Neale Hurston, covered Florida murder case of Ruby McCollum; published *Ruby McCollum: Woman in the Suwannee Jail* (1956). In wake of 1967 novel *The Klansman*, a cross was burned on his lawn. Died in Guntersville, Alabama. His books of fiction include *Mud on the Stars* (1942), *The Revolt of Mamie Stover* (1951), *Wolf Whistle and Other Stories* (1959), *The Americanization of Emily* (1959), *The Hero of Iwo Jima and Other Stories* (1962), *Hotel Mamie Stover* (1963), *In the Hours of the Night* (1975); nonfiction, *The Fight for Air Power* (1942), *Seabee Roads to Victory* (1944), *Can Do!: The Story of the Seabees* (1944), *The Case Against the Admirals: Why We Must Have a Unified Command* (1946), *The Execution of Private Slovik* (1954), *The Hiroshima Pilot: The Case of Major Claude Eatherly* (1964), *Three Lives for Mississippi* (1965), *He Slew the Dreamer: My Search with James Earl Ray for the Truth about the Murder of Martin Luther King* (1970), *A New Life To Live: Jimmy Putnam's Story* (editor, 1977), *It's Me, O Lord!* (1979), *The Ray of Hope* (1984), and *To Live and Die in Dixie* (1985).

CHARLAYNE HUNTER (February 27, 1942–) Born in Due West, South Carolina; attended high schools in Alaska and Georgia. Applied for admission to University of Georgia in 1960; attended Wayne State in Detroit while university and state of Georgia obstructed application. After successful litigation, entered university in 1961; she and Hamilton Holmes were the first African-American students to do so. Served as intern at Louisville *Times* during summer of 1961. Received B.A. in journalism, 1963. Worked at *The New Yorker*

magazine, becoming staff writer in 1964. In 1967 studied social science at
Washington University in St. Louis as Russell Sage fellow; edited articles and
reported on Poor People's Campaign for *Trans-Action*; also worked as news
anchor for WRC-TV in Washington, D.C. Joined staff of *New York Times* in
1968, becoming Harlem bureau chief. Took name Hunter-Gault after second
marriage in 1971; directed minority journalism program at Columbia University during 1970s. Left *Times* in 1978 to work for PBS's *MacNeil / Lehrer Report*, as national correspondent beginning in 1983. Won 1985 and 1988 George
Foster Peabody awards for reporting on Africa. Left *The News Hour with Jim
Lehrer* in 1997, moving to South Africa. Served as National Public Radio's
chief Africa correspondent (1997–99); since 1999 has been CNN's Johannesburg bureau chief. Author of *In My Place* (1992), a memoir.

HOMER A. JACK   (May 19, 1916–August 5, 1993)   Born Homer Alexander
Jack in Rochester, New York. Educated at Cornell, receiving a Ph.D. in biol-
ogy in 1940, but decided on career in the ministry; graduated from Meadville
Theological School in Chicago in 1944. Active in efforts to prevent U.S.
entry into World War II, helping to organize Rochester antiwar rally. Edited
Rochester No-War News. In 1942 attended meetings of Fellowship of Reconciliation; helped organize 1942 Chicago sit-in protest and 1947 Journey of
Reconciliation. Served as Unitarian minister in Lawrence, Kansas (1942–43),
executive secretary of Chicago Council Against Racial and Religious Discrimination (1943–48), minister of Unitarian Church of Evanston, Illinois (1948–
59), co-founder and associate director of American Committee on Africa
(1959–60), co-founder and executive director of National Committee for Sane
Nuclear Policy (1960–64), director of Social Responsibility Department of
Unitarian Universalist Association in Boston (1964–70), Secretary General of
the World Conference on Religion and Peace in New York (1970–83), and as
minister in Winnetka, Illinois (1984–late 1980s). Retired to Swarthmore,
Pennsylvania, to work on autobiography, published posthumously as *Homer's
Odyssey: My Quest for Peace and Justice* (1996); also author of *Disarmament
Workbook* (1978) and *Disarm—or Die* (1983). Died in Swarthmore.

JUNE E. JOHNSON   (December 31, 1947–   )   Born in Greenwood, Mississippi. Began attending SNCC meetings in her early teens; walked to school
with Bob Moses. In June 1963, after attending voter registration workshop,
was arrested and beaten in Winona, Mississippi, jail. Parents Lula Belle and
Theodore Johnson joined SNCC; family hosted visiting SNCC workers.
Graduated from Stillman College with a degree in sociology in 1972 and
earned master's degree in education from Jackson State University in 1974.
Worked as paralegal for North Mississippi Rural Legal Services (1972–73).
Throughout 1970s, was actively involved in lawsuits aimed at stopping discriminatory practices of Greenwood city and Leflore county governments, as
named plaintiff and as paralegal investigator. With Marion Wright Edelman
of the Children's Defense Fund, drew attention to failures of Mississippi
antipoverty agencies; investigated Mississippi prison conditions. In 1978 was

first African-American woman candidate for Leflore County Board of Supervisors. Moved to Washington, D.C., in 1982; worked in city government for the Office of Paternity and Child Support Enforcement (1983–86), and as a home hospital teacher. Was a research consultant for the film *Freedom Song* (2000), about Mississippi SNCC workers. Since 1995 has been program monitor in the Office of Early Childhood Development; serves as first vice-president of the Washington, D.C., Ward 6 Democrats.

MURRAY KEMPTON (December 16, 1917–May 5, 1997) Born James Murray Kempton in Baltimore. Worked as copyboy for H. L. Mencken at *Baltimore Evening Sun*. Educated at Johns Hopkins, where he was editor-in-chief of *Johns Hopkins News-Letter*. After graduation in 1939 worked for a short time as labor organizer, then joined staff of *New York Post*. Served in air force during World War II, returning to *Post* in 1949 as labor editor and later columnist. Also wrote for *Sun* and *World-Telegram* in New York. Edited *The New Republic*, 1963–64. In 1981 began writing regular column for *Newsday*, continuing until his death; also wrote for *New York Review of Books*. Won Pulitzer Prize for *Newsday* columns in 1985. His books include: *Part of Our Time: Some Ruins and Monuments of the Thirties* (1955), *America Comes of Middle Age: Columns 1950–1962* (1963), *The Briar Patch: The People of the State of New York v. Lumumba Shakur* (1973, winner of National Book Award), and *Rebellions, Perversities, and Main Events* (1994).

STETSON KENNEDY (October 5, 1916–) Born in Jacksonville, Florida. Studied at University of Florida (where he published column "News in the Nude" in *Florida Alligator*), the New School for Social Research, and the Sorbonne. From 1935 to 1942 worked as state director of folklore, oral history, and ethnic studies for Florida Federal Writers' Project; served on staff of *The Florida Guide* (1941). During World War II was based in Atlanta as editorial director of CIO political action committee; wrote column "Inside Out," syndicated in AFL/CIO newspapers (1945–48). Was research director, also in Atlanta, for Anti-Defamation League of B'nai Brith (1946–49); conducted 1946 undercover investigation of Ku Klux Klan for Georgia Bureau of Investigation, later publishing exposés *Southern Exposure* (1946) and *I Rode with the Ku Klux Klan* (1954, reissued in 1990 as *The Klan Unmasked*). Traveled widely overseas from 1952 to 1960, spending three years in communist countries; published reports in *Pittsburgh Courier*. Edited Florida edition of *Pittsburgh Courier*, 1960–62; later wrote *Courier* column "Up Front Down South" under pseudonym "Daddy Mention." Was federal projects and development officer, Florida Memorial College, St. Augustine (1963–65); deputy director of Jacksonville Neighborhood Youth Corps (1965–67); and director of planning, training, and evaluation for Greater Jacksonville Economic Opportunity, Inc. Currently working on autobiography *Dissident-at-Large*. His other books include *Palmetto County* (1942), *Jim Crow Guide to the U.S.A.* (1959) and *After Appomattox: How the South Won the War* (1994).

WILLIAM KENNEDY (pseud.)   See **STETSON KENNEDY**

MARTIN LUTHER KING JR.   (January 15, 1929–April 4, 1968)   Born in Atlanta. Graduated from Morehouse College in 1948, and from Crozer Theological Seminary in 1951 with a B.A. in divinity; later earned doctorate in systematic theology from Boston University (1955). Beginning in 1954 worked as pastor at Dexter Avenue Baptist Church in Montgomery, Alabama. In December 1955 became president of Montgomery Improvement Association, leading bus boycott; home bombed the following January. Became chairman of Southern Negro Leadership Conference (later Southern Christian Leadership Conference) in January 1957; appeared on cover of *Time* in February. Attended Ghanaian independence celebration; delivered speech, "Give Us the Ballot," at 1957 Prayer Pilgrimage for Freedom in Washington, D.C. Published *Stride Toward Freedom: The Montgomery Story* (1958). In September 1958 stabbed by mentally ill woman in New York City. Traveled to India in February 1959, meeting with Jawaharlal Nehru and followers of Gandhi. Moved to Atlanta in 1960, serving with father as co-pastor of Ebenezer Baptist Church; arrested during Atlanta sit-in protests. In May 1961 addressed mass rally at Montgomery church in wake of Freedom Ride; in December, arrested in Albany, Georgia, protest. Published *Strength To Love* (1963), a book of sermons, and "Letter from Birmingham Jail" after April 1963 arrest in Birmingham. Addressed March on Washington for Jobs and Freedom on August 28, 1963; eulogized children killed in September 1963 bombing of Sixteenth Street Baptist Church in Birmingham. Book *Why We Can't Wait* published (1964); arrested during sit-in in St. Augustine, Florida. Received Nobel Peace Prize in Oslo in December. With James Forman and John Lewis, led march from Selma to Montgomery (March 1965); in August announced opposition to war in Vietnam at Birmingham rally. Lived in Chicago slum for a week, part of SCLC campaign to bring southern civil rights movement north (January 1966); in June, walked in Mississippi "March Against Fear" after shooting of James Meredith. Published *Where Do We Go from Here: Chaos or Community* (1967); delivered antiwar speeches. Led 1968 march in support of striking Memphis sanitation workers; made final speech on April 3. Assassinated while standing on balcony of Lorraine Hotel, Memphis. Buried in Atlanta.

HANNAH LEES (pseud.)   See **ELIZABETH HEAD FETTER**

GEORGE B. LEONARD   (August 9, 1923–   )   Born George Burr Leonard Jr. in Macon, Georgia. Educated at University of North Carolina. Served as combat pilot in U.S. Army Air Forces in South Pacific during World War II, and as intelligence officer during Korean War. Joined staff of *Look* magazine in 1953, reporting on education, foreign affairs, and civil rights movement until 1970; afterward worked as freelance writer and contributing editor for *Esquire*. Currently co-owner of Aikido of Tamalpais dojo in Mill Valley, California; serves as president of the Esalen Institute. His books include *The*

Decline of the American Male (1958, with William Atwood and J. Robert Moskin), *Shoulder the Sky* (novel, 1959), *Education and Ecstasy* (1968), *The Man and Woman Thing, and Other Provocations* (1970), *The Transformation: A Guide to the Inevitable Changes in Humankind* (1972), *The Ultimate Athlete* (1975), *The Silent Pulse* (1978), *The End of Sex: Erotic Love after the Sexual Revolution* (1983), *Walking on the Edge of the World* (1988, memoir), *Mastery: The Keys to Long-Term Success and Fulfillment* (1992), *The Life We Are Given: A Long Term Program for Realizing the Potential of Body, Mind, Heart, and Soul* (1995, with Michael Murphy; program currently subject of studies at Stanford University Medical School), and *The Way of Aikido: Life Lessons from an American Sensei* (1999).

ANTHONY LEWIS (March 27, 1927–   )   Born in New York City. Graduated from Harvard in 1948. Began career in journalism as deskman for Sunday *New York Times* (1948–52). In 1952 worked for the Democratic National Committee, and joined staff of *Washington Daily News*; won 1955 Pulitzer Prize for articles on federal government's loyalty security program. Returned to *New York Times* in 1955, reporting from Washington (1955–64), from Europe as London bureau chief (1965–72), and as editorial columnist (1969–2001). Won second Pulitzer in 1963 for Supreme Court reporting. Lectured on the Constitution and the press at Harvard, 1974–89; has been a visiting lecturer at Columbia and universities of Arizona, California, Illinois, and Oregon. His books include *Gideon's Trumpet* (1964), *Portrait of a Decade: The Second American Revolution* (1964), and *Make No Law: The Sullivan Case and the First Amendment* (1992).

CHARLES H. LOEB (April 2, 1905–August 21, 1978)   Born Charles Harold Loeb in Baton Rouge, Louisiana; educated in New Orleans public schools and at Howard. In New Orleans, co-founded *Louisiana Weekly* and *Southern News Weekly*; later sold advertising for *Amsterdam News* and *Atlanta Daily World*. Joined staff of Cleveland *Call and Post* in 1933, working as advertising salesman, reporter, city editor, and managing editor; retired in the late 1960s. In 1944 served as war correspondent in southwest Pacific for National Newspaper Publishers Association; reported on surrender of Japan from U.S.S. *Missouri*. Reported for *Call and Post* on Montgomery bus boycott. Ran unsuccessfully for Congress in 1956. Author of *The Future Is Yours: The History of the Future Outlook League, 1935–1946* (1947).

LOUIS E. LOMAX (August 16, 1922–July 30, 1970)   Born in Valdosta, Georgia. Educated at Paine College in Augusta, graduating in 1942, and later at American University (M.A., 1944) and Yale (Ph.D., 1947). Taught philosophy briefly at Georgia State College in Savannah. Worked as a newspaper reporter, for Baltimore *Afro-American* and *Chicago American*, until 1958; later a freelance magazine journalist and author of books including *The Reluctant African* (1960), *The Negro Revolt* (1962), *When the Word Is Given: A Report on Elijah Muhammad, Malcolm X, and Black Muslim World* (1963),

Thailand: The War That Is, The War That Will Be (1967), and *To Kill a Black Man* (1968). In 1959, with Mike Wallace, interviewed Malcolm X for documentary on Nation of Islam, *The Hate That Hate Produced*. From 1964 to 1968 hosted twice-weekly Los Angeles television show on KTTV; lectured widely on college campuses. Died in automobile accident near Santa Rosa, New Mexico.

STUART H. LOORY   (May 22, 1932–   )   Born Stuart Hugh Loory in Wilson, Pennsylvania. Graduated from Cornell in 1954. After college, worked for three years as reporter for *Newark News*; received master's degree in journalism from Columbia in 1958, and did postgraduate work in Vienna. In 1959 hired by New York *Herald-Tribune*, serving as reporter, science writer (1961–63), Washington correspondent (1963–64), and Moscow-based foreign correspondent (1964–66). Worked briefly as science writer for *New York Times* in 1966, then as White House correspondent for *Los Angeles Times* (1967–71), earning place on President Nixon's enemies list. Was a fellow at Woodrow Wilson Center, 1971–72, and in 1973 executive editor for WNBC-TV news. Was first Kiplinger Professor of Public Affairs Reporting at Ohio State, 1973–75. Became associate and later managing editor of *Chicago Sun-Times* in 1975, remaining until 1980, when he joined staff of Turner Broadcasting Systems/Cable News Network (managing editor of CNN Washington bureau, 1980–82; Moscow bureau chief, 1983–86; senior correspondent, 1986; executive producer, 1987–90; editor-in-chief of *CNN World Report*, 1990–91; vice-president of CNN, 1990–95; executive vice-president, Turner International Broadcasting, Russia, 1993–97). Since 1997, has been first Lee Hills Chair in Free-Press Studies at University of Missouri at Columbia; currently editor of *IPI Global Journalist* for International Press Institute and moderator of *Global Journalist* on KBIA radio in Columbia, Missouri. Author of *The Secret Search for Peace in Vietnam* (1968, with David Kraslow), *Defeated: Inside America's Military Machine* (1973) and *Seven Days That Shook the World: The Collapse of Soviet Communism* (1991, with Ann Isme).

RALPH McGILL   (February 5, 1898–February 3, 1969)   Born Ralph Emerson McGill in Soddy, Tennessee; moved to Chattanooga as six-year-old. Attended Vanderbilt (1917–18, 1920–21), where he worked on student newspaper *Vanderbilt Hustler*; expelled after fraternity prank during senior year. Hired at *Nashville Banner*, reporting on sports, politics, and crime; became acting sports editor in 1923. Joined *Atlanta Constitution* in 1929 as assistant sports editor; later became associate editor, editor (1942–61) and publisher (1961–69). Traveled to Scandinavia in 1937 on Rosenwald fellowship to study farm marketing and rural schools; published *Two Georgians Explore Scandinavia* (with Thomas C. David, for Georgia State Department of Education) in 1938. In daily *Atlanta Constitution* columns, frequently addressed questions of segregation and racial justice. Column "A Church, a School," on Atlanta Temple bombing and school burning, won 1958 Pulitzer Prize for editorial leadership. Awarded Presidential Medal of Freedom, 1964. Died in Atlanta.

Author of *Israel Revisited* (1950) and *The South and the Southerner* (1963); his *Atlanta Constitution* columns have been collected in *The Fleas Come with the Dog* (1954), *A Church, a School* (1959), and posthumously in *Southern Encounters: Southerners of Note in Ralph McGill's South* (1983), and *No Place to Hide: The South and Human Rights* (1984).

CLIFF MACKAY (March 2, 1908–late 1960s or early 1970s) Born Clifford Wesley MacKay in Des Moines, Iowa. Educated at East High School in Des Moines and Drake University, from which he received a bachelor's degree in journalism. Began career as copy editor for *Des Moines Register*; worked as managing editor for *Iowa Bystander* (1928–29); reporter and theater editor, *Chicago Defender*; news editor, *Journal and Guide* (Norfolk, Virginia); and managing editor, *Atlanta Daily World* (early 1940s). Studied at American Press Institute, Columbia University, in 1946. Joined staff of Baltimore *Afro-American* in the early 1940s as managing editor; retired as editor-in-chief in 1968. Died in Baltimore.

GEORGE MCMILLAN (March 11, 1913–September 1, 1987) Born in Knoxville, Tennessee, where he attended high school. Moved to Washington, D.C., area in the 1930s. Employed by Office of War Information during the war, then enlisted in Marine Corps, working as combat correspondent. After the war, moved to Aiken, South Carolina; wrote *The Old Breed: A History of the First Marine Division in World War II* (1949), about division in which he served. Reported on civil rights movement as freelance journalist; his articles appeared in *New York Times, Saturday Evening Post, Washington Post, Look*, and other periodicals. Worked as writer-in-residence at Atlanta University in the late 1960s; lived in Cambridge, Massachusetts, during the 1970s. Published *The Making of an Assassin: The Life of James Earl Ray* (1976). Died in St. Helena, South Carolina.

JULIAN MAYFIELD (June 6, 1928–October 20, 1984) Born Julian Hudson Mayfield in Greer, South Carolina. Moved to Washington, D.C., with family in 1933. Enlisted in U.S. Army, serving until 1947; later educated at Lincoln University in Pennsylvania. In 1949–50 played lead in Kurt Weill and Maxwell Anderson musical *Lost in the Stars* (based on Alan Paton novel *Cry, the Beloved Country*); his own play *Fire* was produced off-Broadway, and he directed 1952 *Alice in Wonder*, by Ossie Davis. Published three novels: *The Hit* (1951), *The Long Night* (1958), and *The Grand Parade* (1961). In 1961 accepted position as writer in office of Ghanaian President Kwame Nkrumah; edited *African Review*, political and economic journal, and helped to establish first international branch of Organization of Afro-American Unity. Published "Ghanaian Sketches" in 1963 collection *Young Americans Abroad*. Moved from Ghana to Spain in 1965, and returned to U.S. in 1967; taught at Cornell and New York University. Co-wrote screenplay for, and starred in, Jules Dassin film *Up Tight* (1968). From 1971 to 1974 served as aide to Guyanese Prime Minister Forbes Burnham. Later taught at University of Maryland,

College Park (1975–78) and Howard University (1978–84). Died in Washington, D.C.

LUCILLE B. MILNER (June 9, 1888–August 14, 1975) Born Lucille Bernheimer in St. Louis. Graduated from School of Social Work at Columbia; worked as lobbyist for child welfare bills in Missouri. Studied labor movement as New York City factory worker. One of the founders of American Civil Liberties Union; served for 25 years as its executive secretary. Died in New York. Published *Education of an American Liberal*, a memoir, in 1954.

W. F. MINOR (May 17, 1922–) Born Wilson Floyd Minor in Hammond, Louisiana; after high school in Bogalusa, studied journalism at Tulane, graduating in 1943. Worked for *Bogalusa Enterprise* in 1939 and while in college as part-time reporter for New Orleans *Times-Picayune*. Served aboard U.S. Navy destroyer in the Pacific during World War II, and was awarded 12 battle stars; after the war, joined staff of *Times-Picayune*. Beginning in 1947 served as *Times-Picayune*'s Mississippi correspondent, a position he held until 1976, when the paper closed Jackson bureau; afterward worked as owner/editor of *Capitol Reporter* (1976–81) and as statewide syndicated columnist. Taught journalism at University of Mississippi (1983–84). Currently lives in Jackson, Mississippi. A selection of his columns was published in 2001 as *Eyes on Mississippi: A Fifty-Year Chronicle of Change.*

ANNE MOODY (September 15, 1940–) Born Essie Mae Moody in Wilkinson County, Mississippi. Educated at Natchez Junior College and Tougaloo (B.S., 1964). Worked for CORE as organizer (1961–63); participated in SNCC and CORE voter registration drives in Mississippi (1962–63), and 1963 Jackson, Mississippi, sit-in at Woolworth's lunch counter. After graduation from college, worked as civil rights project coordinator at Cornell (1964–65) and in New York City antipoverty programs (1967). Author of *Coming of Age in Mississippi* (1968), and *Mr. Death: Four Stories* (1975).

RELMAN MORIN (September 11, 1907–July 16, 1973) Born Relman George Morin in Freeport, Illinois. Began journalism career as office boy for *Los Angeles Times* (1924–26). After graduation from Pomona College (1929), worked as a reporter for *Shanghai Evening Post* and studied in China; later wrote movie columns for *Los Angeles Record* (1932–34). Joined Associated Press in 1934, remaining for almost 40 years: as Los Angeles editor (1934–37), Tokyo bureau chief (1937–40), Far East correspondent (1940–41), war correspondent (1942–45); and bureau chief in Paris (1945–47), Washington, D.C. (1947–48), and New York (1948–72). From December 1941 to August 1942 was imprisoned by the Japanese secret police on espionage charges; wrote *Circuit of Conquest* (1943) about his time in Asia. Won Pulitzer Prize in 1951 for coverage of the Korean War and in 1958 for his reporting of the Little Rock school crisis. Died in New York City. Author of *East Wind Rising: A Long View of the Pacific Crisis* (1960), *A Reporter Reports* (1960), *Churchill:*

Portrait of Greatness (1965), *Assassination: The Death of President John F. Kennedy* (1968), *Dwight D. Eisenhower: A Gauge of Greatness* (1969), and *The Associated Press Story of Election* 1968 (1969).

PAULI MURRAY (November 20, 1910–July 1, 1985) Born Anna Pauline Murray in Baltimore; orphaned at an early age, was raised in Durham, North Carolina, by maternal grandparents and an aunt. Educated at Hunter College, receiving bachelor's degree in 1933. Worked briefly for *Opportunity* magazine; hired in 1936 in WPA worker education and remedial reading projects. In 1938 attempted with NAACP support to enter graduate school at University of North Carolina, but was denied admission because of race. As member of Fellowship of Reconciliation was arrested in 1940 for failure to sit in back of Virginia bus. Studied law at Howard from 1941 to 1944; participated in founding of Congress of Racial Equality in 1942, and wrote articles and essays on civil rights movement, including 1943 report for *New York Call* on Harlem race riots. Refused permission in 1944 to apply for further study of law at Harvard because she was a woman (later received master's in law from University of California; passed California bar in 1945). Practiced law in New York; ran unsuccessfully for Brooklyn city council seat, 1948. Published *States' Laws on Race and Color* (1951) and family memoir *Proud Shoes: The Story of an American Family* (1956). From 1956 to 1960 worked for New York law firm Paul, Weiss; taught at Ghana School of Law (1960–61) and studied for doctorate in law at Yale (1962–65). Co-founded National Organization for Women, 1966; taught in Afro-American studies department at Brandeis beginning in 1967. Published *Dark Testament*, a book of poems, in 1970. Following 1973 decision of Episcopal Church to allow women deacons, studied for holy orders at General Theological Seminary, New York; became deacon in 1976 and ordained to priesthood in 1977. Died in Pittsburgh. An autobiography, *Song in a Weary Throat: An American Pilgrimage* (1987), was published after her death.

TOM O'CONNOR (July 28, 1914–July 24, 1952) Born Thomas O'Connor in Nampa, Idaho; graduated from Harvard College in 1936. Began career with *Los Angeles Post-Record* in 1935; also worked for *Los Angeles Evening News*, and served as president of Los Angeles Newspaper Guild. Went to New York in 1940 to work as reporter for *PM*; in 1941 won Heywood Broun Memorial Award for series on conditions in the coal mining industry. After service in the merchant marine during the war, returned to *PM*, where he was reporter and labor editor until paper went out of business in 1947. Later worked for *New York Star* (1947–48) and as city and managing editor for New York *Daily Compass* (1949–52). Appeared before the House Un-American Activities Committee in May 1952, having been named as a Communist by Alice K. Bennett, the ex-wife of a Los Angeles newspaperman; refused to testify or name others. Died of a heart attack at the offices of *Daily Compass* while watching a television broadcast of the Democratic National Convention.

ROI OTTLEY (August 2, 1906–October 1, 1960) Born in New York City. Educated at St. Bonaventure College, University of Michigan, and St. John's Law School (Brooklyn, New York). Worked for *Amsterdam News* as reporter, columnist, and editor, 1931–37. Joined New York City Writers' Project as editor in 1937. Published *New World A-Coming: Inside Black America* in 1943, incorporating Writers' Project reports; it became a bestseller and was adapted into a series of radio programs. Worked as a war correspondent for *PM, Pittsburgh Courier*, and *Liberty*; publicity director of national CIO War Relief Committee in 1943. Other books include *Black Odyssey: The Story of the Negro in America* (1948), *No Green Pastures* (1951), *The Lonely Warrior: The Life and Times of Robert S. Abbott* (1955). *White Marble Lady* (1965), a novel, and *The Negro in New York: An Informal Social History, 1626–1940* (1967, with William J. Weatherby) were published after his death.

JAMES PECK (December 19, 1914–July 12, 1993) Attended Harvard University for a year, dropping out to work as sailor. Helped organize National Maritime Union; beaten during 1936 strike. Reported for Federated Press on activities of union. A conscientious objector during World War II, was jailed for more than two years for antiwar activism; assisted War Resisters League, and wrote labor column for *The Conscientious Objector*. Organized strike against racial segregation while in prison. Joined Congress of Racial Equality in 1946; arrested with Bayard Rustin in Durham, North Carolina, during Journey of Reconciliation. Also participated in CORE Freedom Rides in 1961; beaten by mob in Birmingham, Alabama. Published *Freedom Ride* (1962) about his experiences. Served as editor of *CORElator* for 17 years; organized many civil rights protests. Demonstrated against nuclear tests and Vietnam War; arrested in 1971 May Day demonstration in Washington. Died in Minneapolis.

NORMAN PODHORETZ (January 16, 1930–) Born in Brooklyn, New York. Studied English literature at Columbia and Cambridge. Served in the U.S. Army (1953–55); during the later 1950s worked as a freelance writer and in short-term editing and publishing jobs. From 1960 until 1995 served as editor-in-chief of *Commentary*; currently editor-at-large. In 1995 became a senior fellow of the Hudson Institute. In addition to contributing articles to most major periodicals, has lectured widely and appeared often on radio and television. His books include *Doings and Undoings: The Fifties and After in American Writing* (1964), *Making It* (1968), *Breaking Ranks: A Political Memoir* (1979), *The Present Danger* (1980), *Why We Were in Vietnam* (1982), *The Bloody Crossroads: Where Literature and Politics Meet* (1986), *Ex-Friends* (1999), *My Love Affair with America: The Cautionary Tale of a Cheerful Conservative* (2000), and *The Prophets: Who They Were, What They Are* (2002).

JAMES POLING (January 7, 1907–February 1976) Born James W. Poling in Lima, Ohio. Graduated from University of Michigan with a degree in English literature, 1928. Worked as editor at Doubleday, Doran in New York.

During World War II served as air combat intelligence officer in the Pacific. After war wrote articles for *Argosy, Collier's,* and other magazines, and books including *The Final Face of Eve* (with Evelyn Lancaster, 1958), *Esquire's World of Jazz* (1962), *Animals in Disguise* (1966), *The Man Who Saved Robinson Crusoe* (1967), *The Story of Tools* (1969), *The Rockefeller Record* (editor, 1970), *All Battle Stations Manned: The U.S. Navy in World War II* (1971), and *Leaves: Their Amazing Lives and Strange Behavior* (1971).

JACK H. POLLACK (December 4, 1914–September 30, 1984) Born Jack Hersh Pollack in Philadelphia. Reported on sports for high school newspaper; majored in English at University of Pennsylvania, from which he graduated in 1936. After college, worked as freelance journalist; a one-act play, *The Renegade,* was performed by the New Theatre League. During World War II, employed as press liaison officer on alien registration with Department of Justice (1942), information specialist in Office of Civilian Defense (1943), and special assistant to executive director of War Manpower Commission (1945); wrote speeches for senators and other officials and served briefly as editor of magazine *This Month* (1946). Returned to freelance journalism after war, publishing widely in newspapers and popular magazines; co-founded Society of Magazine Writers. Also wrote *Croiset, the Clairvoyant* (1964), *Dr. Sam: An American Tragedy* (1972, about trial of Dr. Sam Sheppard), and *Earl Warren: The Judge Who Changed America* (1979). Lived in Westport, Connecticut, and Westhampton Beach, Long Island. Died in New York City.

ANNELL PONDER (August 22, 1932–) Born in McDonough, Georgia. Graduated from Clark College (B.A., 1955). Worked as teacher and librarian in Jonesboro, Georgia (1955–57); obtained master's in social work from Atlanta University (1959). From 1962 to 1967 worked as field supervisor for United Church of Christ and Southern Christian Leadership Conference, based in Atlanta and New York; assisted Septima Clark in citizenship education program. Taught at Atlanta University (1967–68) and during the 1970s and 1980s at elementary and middle schools in Atlanta and Decatur, Georgia; later moved to Milwaukee where she continued to teach through the 1990s.

TED POSTON (July 4, 1906–January 11, 1974) Born Theodore Roosevelt Poston in Hopkinsville, Kentucky; graduated from Tennessee Agricultural and Industrial College in 1928 with journalism degree. Moved to New York; worked for brother Ulysses on occasional paper, *New York Contender.* In 1931 wrote column "Harlem Shadows" for *Pittsburgh Courier;* hired by *Amsterdam News,* becoming city editor by 1935. Active in formation of Newspaper Guild, was fired for leading strike against paper; joined staff of Federal Writers' Project. In 1936 began writing freelance articles for *New York Post;* soon hired full-time, an unprecedented event for an African-American reporter. In 1940 became member of "Black Cabinet," informal network of African-Americans serving or advising the Roosevelt administration; as head of Negro News Desk in the Office of War Information was responsible for relations with Negro press. Returned to *Post* in late 1945, remaining until his retirement in 1972. Series of articles on "Little Scottsboro" case (1949) won George Polk award for national reporting; also covered Montgomery bus boycott, racial discrimination in New York City, the integration of Central High in Little Rock, and the trial of Medgar Evers' assassin. Died in New York City. *The Dark Side of Hopkinsville*, a book of short stories, published posthumously in 1991.

L. D. REDDICK (March 3, 1910–August 2, 1995)   Born Lawrence Dunbar Reddick in Jacksonville, Florida. Educated at Fisk and University of Chicago, earning doctorate in 1939. In the same year succeeded Arthur A. Schomburg as curator of Schomburg Collection of Negro Literature (now Schomburg Center for Research in Black Culture) at New York Public Library. Moved to Atlanta in 1948 to become professor of history and head of the library at University of Atlanta. In 1956 took a position as chair of history department at Alabama State College in Montgomery. Worked closely with Martin Luther King Jr. during the late 1950s and early 1960s, traveling with him to India and to Oslo for Nobel Prize ceremony. Dismissed from position at Alabama State in 1960 at the order of Governor John Patterson, who alleged Communist sympathies (a charge Reddick denied). Subsequently taught at Coppin State Teachers' College in Baltimore (1960–67), Temple (1967–76), Harvard (1977–78), and Dillard (1978–87). Died in New Orleans. Author of *Our Cause Speeds On* (1957), *Crusader Against Violence: A Biography of Martin Luther King, Jr.* (1959), *The Southerner as American* (1960), and *Worth Fighting For: A History of the Negro in the United States during the Civil War and Reconstruction* (1965, with Agnes McCarthy).

JAMES N. RHEA (July 22, 1918–March 13, 1989)   Born James Norbon Rhea in Johnson City, Tennessee. Graduated from Langston High School in Johnson City. Attended University of Michigan; studies deferred during service in U.S. Army, including two years in the Pacific. Graduated from University of Michigan in 1946. Worked for Norfolk, Virginia, *Journal and Guide* for three years after college. Joined staff of *Providence Journal-Bulletin* in 1950. In 1955 published series "Jim Crow Goes to Church," for which he won Brotherhood Award of National Conference of Christians and Jews. During 1960s and 1970s covered Rhode Island state courts; helped found newspaper guild local. In 1973 crossed picket lines during strike; grew increasingly estranged from colleagues and management of paper. Retired in 1983. Died in Providence.

MARTY RICHARDSON (June 6, 1906–June 27, 1957)   Born Martin Daniel Richardson in Jacksonville, Florida. Began journalism career with Cleveland *Call* in 1925. Published *Jacksonville World* and *Jacksonville Bulletin* during 1930s; campaigned against police brutality and for equal voting rights. In 1934 reported on Marianna, Florida, lynching of Claude Neale; was chased for three days by mob. Worked as supervisor of records and on writers' projects for WPA in Florida and Massachusetts; lived briefly in Atlanta and New York. During part of the 1930s, all of the 1940s, and the early 1950s, lived in Boston, where he was managing editor of *Boston Chronicle*. Later returned to Cleveland, where he worked as *Call and Post* managing editor until his death.

CARL T. ROWAN (August 11, 1925–September 23, 2000) Born Carl Thomas Rowan in Ravenscroft, Tennessee. Studied at Tennessee State (1942–43) and Washburn University (1943–44). Was one of the first African-Americans to serve as commissioned officer in U.S. Navy. Graduated from Oberlin (1947) and earned master's degree in journalism from University of Minnesota (1948). Began career in journalism as copywriter for *Minneapolis Tribune* (1948–50); later became staff writer (1950–61), reporting extensively on civil rights movement. Joined Kennedy administration in 1961, working as deputy assistant secretary of state for public affairs. Served as U.S. ambassador to Finland (1963–64), then as director of the United States Information Agency (1964–65). Returned to journalism in 1965, working as syndicated columnist for King Features and Field Syndicate (later News America); also appeared as panelist on public affairs television show *Inside Washington* (1967–96). Died in Washington, D.C. His books include *South of Freedom* (1953), *The Pitiful and the Proud* (1956), *Go South to Sorrow* (1957), *Wait Till Next Year: The Life Story of Jackie Robinson* (1960), *Just Between Us Blacks* (1974), *Breaking Barriers: A Memoir* (1991), and *Dream Makers, Dream Breakers: The World of Justice Thurgood Marshall* (1993).

ALBERT L. ROZIER JR. (January 14, 1932–May 14, 1990) Born Albert Lee Rozier Jr. in Apopka, Florida. Graduated from high school in Florida, 1951; served in military. Entered North Carolina Agricultural and Technical State College in 1956; graduated in 1961 with degree in electrical engineering. Edited A.&T. student newspaper *The Register*; published extra edition on Greensboro sit-in movement. After college, worked as systems engineer and technical writer, mainly on defense aerospace projects, for Boeing (Seattle, 1960–63), Lawrence Livermore National Laboratory (1963–67), General Electric (San Jose, California, 1967–70), Atlas Heating (San Jose, 1970–71), Aydin Corporation (Palo Alto, 1973–74), and Lockheed Missile and Space (Sunnyvale, California, 1975–76). Returned to Apopka in 1976; worked for Martin Marietta (Orlando, Florida, 1976–78), TRW (Orlando, 1978–80), and other firms in central Florida. Died in Apopka.

BAYARD RUSTIN (March 17, 1912–August 24, 1987) Born Bayard Taylor Rustin, West Chester, Pennsylvania. Attended Wilberforce College (1932–33) and Cheyney State Teachers College (1934–36); expelled from both. Moved to New York City in 1937, taking classes at City College until 1941 and working as recruiter for Young Communist League. Recorded album *Chain Gang* (1940) as member of Josh White and His Carolinians; granted conscientious objector status. Left Young Communist League mid-1941; volunteered services to A. Philip Randolph's March on Washington Committee. Joined staff of Fellowship of Reconciliation as field secretary; traveled widely as lecturer on Gandhian nonviolence, pacifism, and race discrimination; also worked with James Farmer as first field secretary of Congress of Racial Equality (1942–44). Between 1944 and 1946 served 28 months in prison for resistance to terms of conscientious objector service; participated in hunger strike against prison dining hall segregation. With George Houser, organized 1947 Journey of Reconciliation; arrested in Durham, North Carolina, later serving three-week sentence on chain gang. (Published articles in *New York Post* in 1949 about chain gang experience.) In 1947 staged impromptu protest in St. Paul, Minnesota, hotel lobby when reservations were not honored. Traveled to India in 1948, meeting with Nehru. In 1953 arrested in Pasadena on publicly reported "morals charge," discovered having sex with men in car; sentenced to 60 days in county jail and forced to resign from Fellowship of Reconciliation. Appointed executive secretary of War Resisters League (1953). In 1956 served as adviser to Martin Luther King and Montgomery Improvement Association on Gandhian nonviolence. Organized New York fundraisers for Montgomery bus boycott. Founded Southern Christian Leadership Conference with Ella Baker and Stanley Levison; organized Prayer Pilgrimage to Washington (1957). Forced to resign from SCLC in 1960. Debated Malcolm X at Howard University. Headed organization of 1963 March on Washington; appeared on cover of *Life* with A. Philip Randolph. In 1965 published *Commentary* essay "From Protest to Politics"; left War Resisters League to head A. Philip Randolph Institute, funded by AFL-CIO. Edited 1969 essay collection *Black Studies: Myths and Realities*, opposed to campus Black Studies programs. Formed Black Americans to Support Israel Committee (1975) and chaired Committee on Conscience of U.S. Holocaust Memorial Council. In 1981 addressed Polish Solidarity movement on techniques of nonviolence. Died in New York City. *Down the Line: The Collected Writings of Bayard Rustin* published in 1971.

HARRISON E. SALISBURY (November 14, 1908–July 5, 1993) Born Harrison Evans Salisbury in Minneapolis, Minnesota; graduated from University of Minnesota in 1930. In 1928 took job as reporter for *Minneapolis Journal.* After college joined United Press International, working as reporter, London manager, Moscow manager, and foreign editor. From 1949 to 1954 served as *New York Times* Moscow correspondent; received Pulitzer Prize in 1955 for articles on Soviet Union. Later based in New York as reporter (1955–61), national editor (1962–64), assistant managing editor (1964–70), and op-ed page editor (1971–75). Covered southern civil rights movement in 1960. In addition to two novels, *The Northern Palmyra Affair* (1962) and *The Gates of Hell* (1975), and a book of photographs, *Children of Russia* (1967), he is the author of: *Russia on the Way* (1946), *American in Russia* (1955), *The Shook-up Generation* (1958), *To Moscow—and Beyond: A Reporter's Narrative* (1960), *Moscow Journal: The End of Stalin* (1961), *A New Russia?* (1962), *The Key to Moscow* (1963), *Russia* (1965), *Orbit of China* (1967), *Behind the Lines—Hanoi* (1967), *The Coming War Between Russia and China* (1969), *The 900 Days: The Siege of Leningrad* (1969), *The Many Americans Shall Be One* (1971), *To Peking—and Beyond: A Report on the New Asia* (1973), *Travels Around America* (1976), *Black Night, White Snow: Russia's Revolutions, 1905–1917* (1978), *The Unknown War* (1978), *Russia in Revolution: 1900–1930* (1978), *Without Fear or Favor: The New York Times and Its Times* (1980), *China: 100 Years of Revolution* (1983), *A Journey for Our Times: A Memoir* (1983), *The Long March: The Untold Story* (1985), *A Time of Change: A Reporter's Tale of Our Time* (1988), *The Great Black Dragon Fire: A Chinese Inferno* (1989), *Tienanmen Diary: Thirteen Days in June* (1989), *The New Emperors: China in the Era of Mao and Deng* (1992), and the posthumous *Heroes of My Time* (1993).

THOMAS SANCTON   (January 11, 1915–   )   Born in the Panama Canal Zone. Raised in New Orleans. After graduating from Tulane University in 1935, worked for New Orleans *Times-Picayune*; published short stories in *Harper's* and other magazines. Moved to New York, where he helped edit national Associated Press wire. Studied at Harvard as Nieman fellow, 1942–43. Named managing editor of *The New Republic* in 1943; wrote extensively on race and the South while with *The New Republic* and later as Washington editor of *The Nation*. Moved back to the South in 1949 to work for *New Orleans Item*. Published novels *Count Roller Skates* (1956; reprinted as *The Magnificent Rascal*, 1958) and *By Starlight* (1960). Following sale of *Item* in 1960 started public relations firm. Currently at work in New Orleans on a memoir of his New York years and early involvement in civil rights movement.

GEORGE S. SCHUYLER   (February 25, 1895–August 31, 1977)   Born George Samuel Schuyler in Providence, Rhode Island; grew up in Syracuse, New York. Enlisted in U.S. Army in 1912. In 1918, having been commissioned as first lieutenant, went AWOL after refusal of service by white bootblack; served nine months of five-year sentence. Worked in odd jobs in New York City and Syracuse. In 1923 hired as reporter for socialist paper *The Messenger*; joined staff of *Pittsburgh Courier* in 1924, retiring as editor in 1966. Investigated Liberian slave trade for *New York Evening Post* in 1930, basis of novel *Slaves Today: A Story of Liberia* (1931). Also published satirical science fiction novel *Black No More: Being an Account of the Strange and Wonderful Workings of Science in the Land of the Free, A.D. 1933–1940* (1931) and pseudonymous serial novels in *Courier* (some published posthumously: *Black Empire*, 1991; *Ethiopian Stories*, 1995). His articles appeared in magazines including *The Nation*, *Negro Digest*, *American Mercury*, and *Common Ground*; wrote syndicated column (1965–77) for North American Newspaper Alliance and an autobiography, *Black and Conservative* (1966). Died in New York City. *Rac(e)ing to the Right*, an essay collection, appeared in 2001.

CLAUDE SITTON   (December 4, 1925–   )   Born Claude Fox Sitton in Atlanta, Georgia. Served in U.S. Navy in the Pacific, 1943–46. Graduated from Emory University in 1949. After college worked as a wire service reporter, first for International News Service (1949–50), and then United

Press (1950–55). After two years as United States Information Officer in Accra, Ghana (1955–57), joined *New York Times* staff as chief southern correspondent; reported widely on civil rights movement (1958–64). From 1964 to 1968 was *New York Times* national news director. Became editorial director of Raleigh *News and Observer* and *Raleigh Times* in 1968; also served as editor of *News and Observer* and vice-president of News and Observer publishing company from 1970 until retirement in 1990. Taught at Emory University from 1991 to 1994, and was a member of Board of Counselors of Emory's Oxford College (1993–2001). Won Pulitzer Prize for commentary (1983), George Polk career award (1991), and John Chancellor award for excellence in journalism (2000). Lives in Oxford, Georgia.

HEDRICK SMITH (July 9, 1933–   ) Born Hedrick Laurence Smith in Kilmacolm, Scotland. Began newspaper career with *Greenville* (South Carolina) *News.* Educated at Williams College (B.A., 1955) and Balliol College, Oxford (1955–56), after which he served for three years in the U.S. Air Force. Worked for United Press International in Memphis, Nashville, and Atlanta from 1959 to 1962, then for *New York Times* (Washington, D.C., and the South, 1962–63; Vietnam, 1963–64; Cairo, 1964–66; Washington diplomatic correspondent, 1966–71; Moscow bureau chief, 1971–74; deputy national editor, 1975–76; Washington bureau chief, 1976–79; chief Washington correspondent, 1980–85; *Times Magazine* Washington correspondent, 1987–88). Won Pulitzer Prize for international reporting in 1974 for stories from Russia and Eastern Europe; shared 1972 Pulitzer for role in publication of Pentagon Papers. Since 1989 has been a producer of television documentaries, including *The Power Game: How Washington Works* (1989), *Inside Gorbachev's USSR* (1991), *Challenge to America* (1994), *Across the River* (1995), *Surviving the Bottom Line* (1998), and *Duke Ellington's Washington* (2000). Founded Hedrick Smith Productions in 1990. His books include *The Russians* (1976), *The Power Game: How Washington Works* (1988), *The New Russians* (1990), and *Rethinking America* (1995).

LILLIAN SMITH (December 12, 1897–September 28, 1966) Born Lillian Eugenia Smith in Jasper, Florida; graduated from high school there. Family moved to Clayton, Georgia, after business failure. Studied music at Peabody Conservatory in Baltimore (1917–20); worked as head of music department at missionary school in China (1922–25). Returned to Georgia to run Laurel Falls Camp, begun by father in 1920; continued as camp director until 1948. Spent winter semester of 1927–28 at Columbia University Teachers College; taught in Harlem school. With Paula Snelling, edited journals *Pseudopodia* (1936), *North Georgia Review* (1937–41), and *South Today* (1942–45). Published controversial bestselling novel *Strange Fruit* in 1944; wrote regular column for *Chicago Defender* (1948–49). Raised funds for CORE and SNCC; lectured and published articles about civil rights in magazines including *Ebony*, *Redbook*, and *Life*. Her other books include *Killers of the Dream* (1949), *The Journey* (1954), *Now Is the Time* (1955), *One Hour* (novel, 1959), and *Our Faces, Our Words* (1964); a collection of letters, *How Am I To Be Heard?*, was published in 1993.

WENDELL SMITH (June 27, 1914–November 26, 1972) Born in Detroit. Attended Southeastern High School, where he excelled in baseball and basketball; decided to become sportswriter in 1933. After graduating from West Virginia State College with a degree in physical education (1937), was hired by *Pittsburgh Courier*; became assistant sports editor in 1938. Led campaign in *Courier* for integration of major league baseball; wrote *Jackie Robinson: My Own Story* (1948), an as-told-to biography. From 1947 to 1963 worked for *Chicago Today* (later *Chicago American*) as sportswriter; nominated for Pulitzer Prize for stories about segregation in baseball. From 1963 until his death, reported on sports for Chicago television stations; contributed weekly column to *Chicago Sun-Times*. Died in Chicago. Inducted into Baseball Hall of Fame in 1994.

JOHN STEINBECK (February 27, 1902–December 20, 1968) Born in Salinas, California; attended Stanford intermittently (1920–25), afterward working in construction in New York and as reporter for *New York American*. First novel, *Cup of Gold*, published in 1929, followed by *The Pastures of Heaven* (1932), *To a God Unknown* (1933), and *Tortilla Flat* (1935), the last a commercial success; *Of Mice and Men* (1937) became bestseller. Commissioned by *San Francisco News* in 1936 to write articles on migrant farm workers; *The Grapes of Wrath* (1939) won Pulitzer Prize in 1940. During World War II worked as war correspondent for New York *Herald-Tribune*. Published *Sea of Cortez*, about marine biological expedition, in 1941; *The Moon Is Down* and *Bombs Away* in 1942; and *Cannery Row* in 1945. His subsequent novels include *The Wayward Bus* (1947), *The Pearl* (1947), *Burning Bright* (1950), *East of Eden* (1952), *Sweet Thursday* (1954), *The Short Reign of Pippin IV* (1957) and *The Winter of Our Discontent* (1961); also published *A Russian Journal* (1948), *Once There Was a War* (1958), *Travels with Charley: In Search of America* (1962), *Letters to Alicia* (1965), and *America and Americans* (1966). Died in New York.

JAMES STOKELY (October 8, 1913–June 20, 1977) Born James Rorex Stokely Jr. in Newport, Tennessee; educated at University of Tennessee (B.S., 1934) and Princeton. Married Wilma Dykeman in 1940; author, with Dykeman, of *Neither Black nor White* (1957), *Seeds of Southern Change* (1962), *Highland Homeland: The People of the Great Smokies* (1978), and many magazine articles. Owned and managed Stokely Apple Orchard in Newport and in Asheville, North Carolina (1940–53; 1944–53). Died in Newport.

RICHARD B. STOLLEY (October 3, 1928–   ) Born Richard Brockway Stolley in Peoria, Illinois. While in high school, worked as sports editor for Pekin, Illinois, *Daily Times* (1944–46). Served in U.S. Navy (1946–48); studied journalism at Northwestern (B.S., 1952; M.A., 1953). After short stint in

1953 as reporter for *Chicago Sun-Times*, joined staff of *Life* magazine, working as Atlanta bureau chief (1956–60), Los Angeles bureau chief (1961–64),
Washington bureau chief (1964–68), senior editor based in Europe (1968–70),
assistant managing editor (1971–73), and later managing editor of *Life*
monthly (1982–86). Founded and served as managing editor of *People* magazine (1974–82); was director of special projects for Time, Inc. (1987–89), editorial director of Time, Inc. (1989–93), and executive producer of TV show
Extra (1995–96). Currently senior editorial adviser for Time Warner; lives in
New York City.

L. O. SWINGLER   (c. 1905–September 25, 1962)   Born Lewis Ossie Swingler
in Crittenden, Arkansas; moved to Tulsa, Oklahoma, as a child, and educated at Booker T. Washington High School. Graduated from University of
Nebraska–Lincoln with a journalism degree, 1931. Moved to Memphis in
1931 to edit biweekly *Memphis World*, remaining, with an interruption during
the war, until 1951. Was a co-founder of the Negro Newspaper Publishers Association. Also edited *The Sphinx*, a publication of Alpha Phi Alpha fraternity
(1936–43, 1946–50). Served in the U.S. Army at Fort Benning, where he
edited *The Bayonet*, a service paper. Co-founded *Tri-State Defender* in Memphis in 1951; succeeded as editor-in-chief by L. Alex Wilson in 1955. After a
failed attempt to start his own paper, *The Mid-South Times*, took job as executive secretary of the Abe Scharff YMCA in Memphis; later worked as
high school teacher in Marked Tree, Arkansas, and Mound Bayou, Mississippi. Died in Mound Bayou. Buried in Memphis National Cemetery.

FRED TRAVIS   (October 7, 1917–March 9, 1998)   Born Fred Richardson
Travis in Murfreesboro, Tennessee. Began career in journalism at 18, working
for Murfreesboro *Daily News Journal*; later worked for *Rutherford Courier*,
becoming editor in 1938. Joined staff of Chattanooga *Times* in 1940; moved
to Nashville as *Times* bureau chief and state capital correspondent in 1946,
serving until 1980. From 1980 to 1996 wrote columns about Tennessee politics for state syndication. Died in Hermitage, Tennessee.

RICK TUTTLE   No biographical information has been forthcoming.

DAN WAKEFIELD   (May 21, 1932–   )   Born in Indianapolis, Indiana;
worked for high school newspaper and as sports correspondent for *Indianapolis Star*. Graduated from Columbia in 1955. Worked as staff writer for
The Nation (1956–60), contributing editor for *Atlantic Monthly* (1968–80),
contributing editor for *GQ* (1990–94), and senior writer for *Yoga Journal*
(1994–98). Awarded Neiman fellowship in journalism at Harvard University,
1963–64. Created television series *James at 15* (1977). Has taught in writing
programs at Boston University, University of Massachusetts at Boston, Emerson College, Iowa Writers' Workshop, and Florida International University,
and has led workshops in spiritual autobiography at religious institutions. His
books include *Island in the City: The World of Spanish Harlem* (1959), *Revolt*

in the South (1962), *The Addict: An Anthology* (1963), *Between the Lines* (1965), *Supernation at Peace and War* (1968), *All Her Children: The Making of a Soap Opera* (1975), *Returning: A Spiritual Journey* (1988), *New York in the Fifties* (1992), *Expect a Miracle* (1995), *Creating from the Spirit* (1996), *How Do We Know When It's God?* (1999), and the novels *Going All the Way* (1970), *Starting Over* (1973), *Home Free* (1977), *Under the Apple Tree* (1982), and *Selling Out* (1985).

ROBERT PENN WARREN   (April 24, 1905–September 15, 1989)   Born in Guthrie, Kentucky. At Vanderbilt, from which he graduated in 1925, helped to found magazine *The Fugitive*; later attended University of California (1925–27), Yale (1927), and New College, Oxford, as Rhodes scholar (1928–30). Taught at Southwestern College (1930), Vanderbilt (1931–34), Louisiana State University (1934–40), University of Iowa (1941–42), University of Minnesota (1942–49), Yale (1950–55; 1962–73), and Hunter College (1974). Appointed Poet Laureate consultant in poetry to Library of Congress, 1986. Died in West Wardsboro, Vermont. Author of almost 50 books, including novels and short fiction (*Night Rider*, 1939; *At Heaven's Gate*, 1943; *All the King's Men*, 1946; *Blackberry Winter*, 1946; *The Circus in the Attic and Other Stories*, 1947; *World Enough and Time*, 1950; *Band of Angels*, 1955; *The Cave*, 1959; *The Gods of Mount Olympus*, 1959; *Wilderness: A Tale of the Civil War*, 1961; *Flood: A Romance of Our Time*, 1964; *Meet Me in the Green Glen*, 1971; and *A Place to Come To*, 1977); poetry (including *Promises: Poems 1954–56*, 1957 and *Now and Then: Poems 1976–1978*, 1978, both winners of Pulitzer Prize and the former winning National Book Award, and the posthumous *Collected Poems of Robert Penn Warren*, 1998); nonfiction (*John Brown: The Making of a Martyr*, 1929; *Segregation: The Inner Conflict in the South*, 1956; *Remember the Alamo!*, 1958; *Selected Essays*, 1958; *The Legacy of the Civil War: Meditations on the Centennial*, 1961; *Who Speaks for the Negro?*, 1965; *Homage to Theodore Dreiser*, 1971; *Democracy and Poetry*, 1975; and *New and Selected Essays*, 1989); and plays (*Proud Flesh*, 1947; *All the King's Men*, 1960; *Ballad of a Sweet Dream of Peace: An Easter Charade*, 1981).

CHRISTOPHER S. WREN   (February 22, 1936–   )   Born Christopher Sale Wren in Los Angeles; graduated from Dartmouth in 1957. After service in U.S. Army, obtained master's degree in journalism (Columbia University, 1961). Began career as reporter for *Look*, covering civil rights movement and Vietnam War; became a senior editor and Washington editor for the magazine, which ceased publication in 1971. Reported on national affairs for *Newsweek*. Joined *New York Times* staff in 1973 as metropolitan reporter; later worked as Moscow correspondent and bureau chief (1973–77), as bureau chief in Cairo (1977–81), Beijing (1981–84), Ottawa (1984–87), and Johannesburg (1988–92), as assistant financial desk editor (1994–95), and as United Nations correspondent (1995–   ) and foreign correspondent covering drug policy. Humorous memoir of overseas assignments published in 2000 as *The Cat Who Covered the World: The Adventures of Henrietta and Her Foreign*

Correspondent. Other books include *Quotations from Chairman LBJ* (with Jack Shepherd, 1968), *The Almanack of Poor Richard Nixon* (with Jack Shepherd, 1968), *The Super Summer of Jamie McBride* (with Jack Shepherd, 1971), *Winners Got Scars Too: The Life and Legends of Johnny Cash* (1971), *The End of the Line: The Failure of Communism in the Soviet Union and China* (1990) and *Hacks* (1996). Lives in New York City.

HOWARD ZINN (August 24, 1922–   ) Born in Brooklyn. Served as bombardier during World War II. Received Ph.D. in history from Columbia in 1958, and was postdoctoral fellow in East Asian studies at Harvard. Appointed chairman of history department at Spelman College beginning in 1956; worked alongside SNCC activists in Alabama, Georgia, and Mississippi. Published articles about civil rights movement in *The Nation, Harper's, Freedomways,* and other magazines, and books *The Southern Mystique* (1964) and *SNCC: The New Abolitionists* (1964). From 1964 to 1988 was professor of history at Boston University. Flew to Hanoi with Father Daniel Berrigan during Vietnam War; wrote *Vietnam: The Logic of Withdrawal* (1967) and *Disobedience and Democracy: Nine Fallacies on Law and Order* (1968), and later edited *The Pentagon Papers: Critical Essays* with Noam Chomsky. Also author of *La Guardia in Congress* (1959), *The Politics of History* (1970), *Post-War America* (1973), *A People's History of the United States* (1980), *Declarations of Independence: Cross-Examining American Ideology* (1990), *Failure to Quit: Reflections of an Optimistic Historian* (1993), and *The Zinn Reader: Writings on Disobedience and Democracy* (1997). An autobiography, *You Can't Be Neutral on a Moving Train: A Personal History of Our Times,* appeared in 1994.

Note on the Texts

This volume collects newspaper reports, magazine articles, book excerpts, the book *Segregation* by Robert Penn Warren, and one wire service article, published between 1941 and 1965 and dealing with events connected with the African-American civil rights movement in the period between May 1941 and July 1963. Excerpts from books are taken from first editions; in some cases, these excerpts include material that had earlier appeared in periodicals in different form. For example, *Segregation*, a portion of which originally appeared in *Life* magazine, is reprinted here from the first edition, published by Random House in 1956. The pieces included have been arranged in the approximate chronological order of the latest events they refer to or describe.

Original wire copy for the Associated Press article included in this volume (Relman Morin, "Violence at Central High," September 23, 1957) is not known to be extant; this article has been reprinted from the most complete version available, in a 1995 Associated Press anthology. The excerpt from *Mississippi Black Paper* that appears in this volume corrects an error in the text from which it is reprinted, published by Random House in 1965. A ten-paragraph section of Fannie Lou Hamer's affidavit (from page 837, line 28, to page 839, line 14, in this volume) was originally printed within Annell Ponder's affidavit, after the phrase "when I tried to walk I staggered and fell" (at 842.5–6 in this volume).

The following is a list of sources of the texts included in this volume, listed alphabetically by author.

Trezzvant Anderson. Over 500 Negro Arrests in Albany: *The Pittsburgh Courier*, December 23, 1961. Reprinted by permission of GRM Associates, Inc., agents for *The Pittsburgh Courier*. Copyright © 1961 by *The Pittsburgh Courier*; copyright renewed 1989 by *The New Pittsburgh Courier*.

Joe Azbell. At Holt Street Baptist Church: *The Montgomery* (Alabama) *Advertiser*, December 7, 1955. Reprinted by permission of *The Advertiser* (Montgomery, Alabama).

James Baldwin. They Can't Turn Back: *Mademoiselle*, August 1960; Fifth Avenue, Uptown: A Letter from Harlem: James Baldwin, *Nobody Knows My Name: More Notes of a Native Son* (New York: The Dial Press, 1961), pp. 56–71; Down at the Cross: Letter from a Region in My Mind: James Baldwin, *The Fire Next Time* (New York: The Dial Press, 1963), pp. 25–120. Copyright © 1960, 1961, 1963 by James Baldwin; copyrights renewed. Reprinted by arrangement with the James Baldwin Estate.

David B. Bittan. Ordeal in Levittown: *Look*, August 19, 1958.

Tolly R. Broady. "Will Two Good White Men Vouch for You?" *The Crisis*, January 1947. Reprinted by permission of The Crisis Publishing Co., Inc., the publisher of the magazine of the National Association for the Advancement of Colored People.

Sterling A. Brown. Out of Their Mouths: *Survey Graphic*, November 1942. Reprinted by permission of John L. Dennis.

Hodding Carter. Mrs. Means Married Woman: Hodding Carter, *Where Main Street Meets the River* (New York: Rinehart & Co., 1953), pp. 253–61. Copyright © 1952, 1953 by Hodding Carter. Reprinted by permission of Hodding Carter III.

Reese Cleghorn. Epilogue in Albany: Were the Mass Marches Worthwhile?: *The New Republic*, July 20, 1963. Reprinted by permission of *The New Republic*, © 1963 The New Republic, Inc.

Raymond R. Coffey. Waiting in the Rain at the Birmingham Jail: *Chicago Daily News*, May 7, 1963. Reprinted with special permission from the Chicago Sun-Times, Inc., © 1963 and © 2002.

George W. Collins: Everybody Eats But Americans: *The Afro-American* (Baltimore), September 2, 1961; Blazing Guns Mark Freedom Fight: Embattled Defenders Fire from Rooftops: *The Afro-American* (Baltimore), July 20, 1963. Reprinted by permission of the Afro-American Newspapers Archives and Research Center.

Tom Dent. Portrait of Three Heroes: *Freedomways*, Spring 1965. Reprinted by permission of the Estate of Tom Dent.

Kenneth L. Dixon. Courthouse Square Is Authentic Picture of Occupied Town: *The Meridian* (Mississippi) *Star*, October 2, 1962.

Robert J. Donovan. Supreme Court, 9–0, Bans Segregation in Schools: New York *Herald-Tribune*, May 18, 1954. Copyright © 1954 by The New York Times Co. Reprinted by permission.

Michael Dorman. From *We Shall Overcome*: Michael Dorman, *We Shall Overcome* (New York: Dell Publishing, 1965), pp. 199–205. Copyright © 1964 by Michael Dorman. Reprinted by permission of McIntosh & Otis, Inc.

Bob Duke. 2 Mob Victims Ready To Die for Integration: *The Montgomery* (Alabama) *Advertiser*, May 21, 1961. Reprinted by permission of *The Montgomery Advertiser*.

Wilma Dykeman and James Stokely. Montgomery Morning: *The Nation*, January 5, 1957. Reprinted by permission of *The Nation*.

Ralph Ellison. Eyewitness Story of Riot: False Rumors Spurred Mob: *New York Post*, August 2, 1943. Copyright © 1943 by The New York Post. Reprinted by permission.

Samuel L. Gandy. Tallahassee Spirit: Tired of Being Pushed Around: *Journal and Guide* (Norfolk, Virginia), July 28, 1956. Reprinted courtesy of *New Journal and Guide*.

Harry L. Golden. A Rabbi in Montgomery: *Congress Weekly*, May 13, 1957; How To Solve the Segregation Problem: *The Carolina Israelite* (How To Solve the Segregation Problem, May–June, 1956; How To Solve the Segre-

gation Problem: The White Baby Plan, March–April, 1957; The Golden
Vertical Negro Plan in Operation, September–October 1957; The Golden
Carry-the-Books Plan, January–February, 1958; Golden Out-of-Order Plan
in Operation, May–June, 1958). Reprinted by permission of the Estate of
Harry L. Golden.

John Howard Griffin. From *Black Like Me*: John Howard Griffin, *Black Like
Me* (Boston: Houghton Mifflin, 1961), pp. 52–76. Copyright © 1960, 1961,
1977 by John Howard Griffin. Reprinted by permission of Houghton Mifflin Company. All rights reserved.

David Halberstam. "A Good City Gone Ugly": *The Reporter*, March 31, 1960;
"Good Jelly's" Last Stand: *The Reporter*, January 19, 1961. Copyright ©
1960, 1961 by David Halberstam. Reprinted by permission of David
Halberstam.

Tom Hayden. From *Revolution in Mississippi*: Tom Hayden, *Revolution in
Mississippi* (n.p.: Students for a Democratic Society, 1962), pp. 8–15.
Reprinted by permission of Tom Hayden.

John Herbers. The Reporter in the Deep South: *Nieman Reports,* April 1962.
Reprinted with permission of John Herbers.

James L. Hicks. "We Were Kicked, Beaten": *New York Amsterdam News*,
September 28, 1957; On the Mississippi Warfront: Oxford's a Town All
Shook Up: *New York Amsterdam News*, October 6, 1962. Reprinted by per-
mission of the *New York Amsterdam News.*

Frank Holloway. Travel Notes from a Deep South Tourist: *New South*, July–
August 1961. Reprinted by permission of the Southern Regional Council.

Len Holt. Eyewitness: The Police Terror at Birmingham: *The National
Guardian*, May 16, 1963. Reprinted by permission of Len Holt.

Bettye Rice Hughes. A Negro Tourist in Dixie: *The Reporter*, April 26, 1962.

Langston Hughes. Adventures in Dining: *Chicago Defender*, June 2, 1945; A
Brickbat for Education—A Kiss for the Bedroom in Dixie: *Chicago Defender*, March 24, 1956. Reprinted by permission of Harold Ober Associates Incorporated.

William Bradford Huie. The Shocking Story of Approved Killing in Mississippi: *Look*, January 24, 1956. Reprinted by permission of Martha Hunt
Huie.

Charlayne Hunter. A Walk through a Georgia Corridor: *The Urbanite*, June
1961. Reprinted with permission of Charlayne Hunter-Gault.

Homer A. Jack. Cicero Nightmare: *The Nation*, July 28, 1951. Reprinted by
permission of *The Nation.*

Murray Kempton. He Went All the Way; "When the Riots Came" (The Alabama Story; The Way It's Got To Be); "If You Got the Guts . . ."; The
Book; Tear Gas and Hymns; The Hostile Witness: from *America Comes of
Middle Age: Columns 1950–1962* (Boston: Little, Brown, 1963), pp. 135–37,
148–54, 161–64; 178–85, 196–98. (Title "When the Riots Came," from a
phrase within the excerpt, supplied for this volume.) Copyright © The
Literary Estate of Murray Kempton, Barbara Epstein, executor. Reprinted
by permission.

William Kennedy (Stetson Kennedy, pseud.). Dixie's Race Signs "Gone with the Wind": *The Pittsburgh Courier*, December 9, 1961. Reprinted by permission of GRM Associates, Inc., agents for *The Pittsburgh Courier*. Copyright © 1961 by *The Pittsburgh Courier*; copyright renewed 1989 by *The New Pittsburgh Courier*.

Martin Luther King Jr. Letter from Birmingham Jail: *The Christian Century*, June 12, 1963. Reprinted by arrangement with the Estate of Martin Luther King Jr., c/o Writers House as agent for the proprietor, New York, New York. Copyright © 1963, Dr. Martin Luther King Jr., copyright renewed 1991, Coretta Scott King.

Hannah Lees (Elizabeth Head Fetter, pseud.). The Not-Buying Power of Philadelphia's Negroes: *The Reporter*, May 11, 1961. Reprinted by permission of Alexander Fetter.

George B. Leonard, T. George Harris, and Christopher S. Wren. How a Secret Deal Prevented a Massacre at Ole Miss: *Look*, December 31, 1962. Reprinted by permission of T. George Harris, George B. Leonard, and Christopher S. Wren.

Anthony Lewis. President Sends Troops to Little Rock, Federalizes National Guard; Tells Nation He Acted To Avoid Anarchy: *The New York Times*, September 25, 1957. Copyright © 1957 by The New York Times Co. Reprinted by permission.

Charles H. Loeb. Our G.I.'s in S. Pacific Fiercely Resent "Uncle Tom" Roles: *New York Amsterdam News*, September 1, 1945. Reprinted by permission of the *New York Amsterdam News*.

Louis E. Lomax. The Negro Revolt Against "The Negro Leaders": *Harper's*, June 1960. Reprinted by permission of Mrs. Louis Lomax.

Stuart H. Loory. Reporter Tails "Freedom" Bus, Caught in Riot: New York *Herald-Tribune*, May 21, 1961. Copyright © 1961 by The New York Times Co. Reprinted by permission.

Ralph McGill. Men Who Shame Our State and Flag: *The Atlanta Constitution*, August 18, 1949. Copyright © 1949, The Atlanta Journal-Constitution. Reprinted with permission from *The Atlanta Journal-Constitution*.

Cliff MacKay. Police Dogs in Ala. Spur N.C. Unrest: *The Afro-American* (Baltimore), June 1, 1963. Reprinted by permission of the Afro-American Newspapers Archives and Research Center.

George McMillan. Race Justice in Aiken: *The Nation*, November 23, 1946. Reprinted by permission of *The Nation*. The Ordeal of Bobby Cain: *Collier's*, November 23, 1956.

March on Washington Committee. Call to Negro America: "To March on Washington for Jobs and Equal Participation in National Defense": *The Black Worker*, May, 1941. Reprinted by permission of the A. Philip Randolph Institute.

Julian Mayfield. Challenge to Negro Leadership: The Case of Robert Williams: *Commentary*, April 1961. Reprinted by permission of *Commentary*; all rights reserved.

Lucille B. Milner. Jim Crow in the Army: *The New Republic*, March 13, 1944.

Reprinted by permission of *The New Republic*, © 1944, The New Republic, Inc.

W. F. Minor. Meredith Blocked at Ole Miss: *Times-Picayune* (New Orleans), September 21, 1962. Permission to reprint granted by The Times-Picayune Publishing Corporation. All rights reserved.

From *Mississippi Black Paper*: *Mississippi Black Paper* (New York: Random House, 1965), pp. 17–24. Copyright © 1965 by Misseduc Foundation, Inc. Used by permission of Random House, Inc.

Anne Moody. From *Coming of Age in Mississippi*: Anne Moody, *Coming of Age in Mississippi* (New York: The Dial Press, 1968), pp. 233–55. Copyright © 1968 by Anne Moody. Used by permission of Doubleday, a division of Random House, Inc.

Relman Morin. Violence at Central High: Associated Press wire copy, September 23, 1957, as reprinted in *Twentieth-Century America: A Primary Source Collection from the Associated Press, vol. 5: The Eisenhower Years* (Danbury, CT: Grolier Educational, 1995), pp. 116–19. Reprinted with permission of The Associated Press.

Pauli Murray. A Blueprint for First Class Citizenship: *The Crisis*, November 1944. Reprinted by permission of The Crisis Publishing Co., Inc., the publisher of the magazine of the National Association for the Advancement of Colored People.

Tom O'Connor. Lynch Law Back in Georgia—4 Murdered: *PM*, July 28, 1946.

Roi Ottley. Negro Morale: *The New Republic*, November 10, 1941. Reprinted by permission of *The New Republic*, © 1941, The New Republic, Inc.

James Peck. Not So Deep Are the Roots: *The Crisis*, September 1947. Reprinted by permission of The Crisis Publishing Co., Inc., the publisher of the magazine of the National Association for the Advancement of Colored People.

Norman Podhoretz. My Negro Problem—and Ours: *Commentary*, February 1963. Copyright © 1963 by Norman Podhoretz. Reprinted by permission of Norman Podhoretz.

James Poling. Thurgood Marshall and the 14th Amendment: *Collier's*, February 23, 1952.

Jack H. Pollack. Literacy Tests: Southern Style: *The American Mercury*, May 1947.

Ted Poston. Florida's Legal Lynching: *The Nation*, September 24, 1949. Reprinted by permission of *The Nation*. From "The Negroes of Montgomery" ("No Sir, I Don't Guess So"; "They Are No Longer Afraid"): *New York Post*, June 15, 19, 1956 (articles 5 and 8 of a series, June 11–24, 1956; the first subtitle supplied for this volume from a phrase within the excerpt; the second Poston's original title); Martin Luther King: Where Does He Go from Here?: *New York Post*, April 14, 1957; The 19-Day Ordeal of Minnie Jean Brown: *New York Post*, February 9, 1958. Copyright © 1956, 1957, 1958 by The New York Post. Reprinted by permission.

L. D. Reddick. The Bus Boycott in Montgomery: *Dissent*, Winter 1956. Reprinted by permission of Ella R. Reddick.

James N. Rhea and Ben H. Bagdikian. From "We Went South": *The Providence Journal and Evening Bulletin*, October 20, 22, 1957. (From a 19-article series, October 20–30, 1957, published under separate bylines, in side-by-side columns, with a common title; individual article titles, drawn from phrases within each article, supplied for this volume.) Reprinted by permission of The Providence Journal Company.

Marty Richardson. Charge Two with Lynch Death of 14-Year-Old: *Cleveland Call and Post*, September 10, 1955. Reprinted by permission of M. Daniel Richardson.

Carl T. Rowan. From "Jim Crow's Last Stand": *Minneapolis Tribune*, November 29, 30; December 1, 2, 4, 8, 1953 (parts 1–4, 6, 10 of an 11-part series, November 29–December 9, 1953). Copyright © 1953, *Minneapolis Tribune*. Reprinted here with the permission of the Star Tribune. No further republication or redistribution is permitted without the approval of the Star Tribune.

Albert L. Rozier Jr. Students Hit Woolworth's for Lunch Service: *The Register* (North Carolina A&T), February 5, 1960. Reprinted by permission of Ellen Rozier.

Bayard Rustin. Non-Violence vs. Jim Crow: *Fellowship*, July 1942. Reprinted by permission of *Fellowship: The Journal of the Fellowship of Reconciliation*, Box 271, Nyack, New York, 10960.

Harrison E. Salisbury. Fear and Hatred Grip Birmingham: *The New York Times*, April 12, 1960. Copyright © 1960 by The New York Times Co. Reprinted by permission.

Thomas Sancton. The Race Riots: *The New Republic*, July 5, 1943. Reprinted by permission of *The New Republic*, © 1943, The New Republic, Inc.

George S. Schuyler. Jim Crow in the North: *The American Mercury*, June 1949. Copyright © 1949 by George Schuyler, © renewed 1977. Reprinted by permission of GRM Associates, Inc., agents for the Estate of George Schuyler.

Claude Sitton. Negro Sitdowns Stir Fear of Wider Unrest in South: *The New York Times*, February 15, 1960; Sheriff Harasses Negroes at Voting Rally in Georgia: *The New York Times*, July 27, 1962; Rioting Negroes Routed by Police at Birmingham: *The New York Times*, May 8, 1963; Alabama Admits Negro Students; Wallace Bows to Federal Force: *The New York Times*, June 12, 1963; N.A.A.C.P. Leader Slain in Jackson; Protests Mount: *The New York Times*, June 13 1963. Copyright © 1960, 1962, 1963 by The New York Times Co. Reprinted by permission.

Hedrick Smith. 9–Block Area Lies Devastated; Buildings Still Burn After Riot: *The New York Times*, May 13, 1963. Copyright © 1963 by The New York Times Co. Reprinted by permission of *The New York Times*.

Lillian Smith: When I Was a Child: Lillian Smith, *Killers of the Dream* (New York: W.W. Norton, 1949), pp. 15–31. Copyright 1949, © 1961 by Lillian Smith. Used by permission of W.W. Norton & Company, Inc.

Wendell Smith. It Was a Great Day in Jersey: *The Pittsburgh Courier*, April 27, 1946. Reprinted by permission of Wyonella Smith / National Baseball Library, Cooperstown: Wendell Smith Papers.

John Steinbeck. "Ain't Those Cheerleaders Something": John Steinbeck, *Travels with Charley: In Search of America* (New York: The Viking Press, 1962), pp. 220–29. (Title, from a phrase within the excerpt, supplied for this volume.) Copyright © 1961, 1962 by The Curtis Publishing Co., © 1962 by John Steinbeck, renewed © 1990 by Elaine Steinbeck, Thom Steinbeck, and John Steinbeck IV. Used by permission of Viking Penguin, a division of Penguin Putnam Inc.

Richard B. Stolley. A Sequel to Segregation: *Life*, December 10, 1956. Reprinted by permission of Richard B. Stolley.

L. O. Swingler. Thrown from Train, Attacked: *Atlanta Daily World*, August 27, 1942. Reprinted by permission of *Atlanta Daily World*.

Fred Travis. The Evicted: *The Progressive*, February 1961.

Rick Tuttle. It Was War—and Marshals Were Losing: *The Miami Herald*, October 2, 1962. Copyright © 1961 by The Miami Herald. Reprinted by permission.

Dan Wakefield. Justice in Sumner: *The Nation*, October 1, 1955; Respectable Racism: *The Nation*, October 22, 1955; Eye of the Storm: *The Nation*, May 7, 1960. Reprinted by permission of *The Nation*.

Robert Penn Warren. *Segregation: The Inner Conflict in the South* (New York: Random House, 1956). Copyright © 1956 by Robert Penn Warren. Reprinted by permission of William Morris Agency, Inc., on behalf of the author.

Howard Zinn. Finishing School for Pickets: *The Nation*, August 6, 1960; Kennedy: The Reluctant Emancipator: *The Nation*, December 1, 1962. Reprinted by permission of *The Nation*.

Great care has been taken to trace all owners of copyrighted material included in this book; if any have been inadvertently omitted or overlooked, acknowledgment will gladly be made in future printings.

This volume presents the texts listed here without change except for the correction of typographical errors, but it does not attempt to reproduce features of their typographic design. The following is a list of typographical errors, cited by page and line number: 4.13, Douglas; 11.13, land. After; 11.18, you? [no close quote]; 12.31, "Well, he; 19.23, Glosters'; 20.3, man, used; 20.20, 'These; 20.34, matress; 21.35, trail; 22.16, College; 25.38, Condentially; 26.33, it?"; 27.30, died; 29.13, jail.'"; 29.24, now.'"; 31.7, its; 49.31, lineoleum; 51.10, rabble; 51.23–24, sitlation; 62.10, degredation; 64.32, 1995, introduced; 64.39, lobbyed; 65.27, was the; 66.1, D.C.—; 66.3, continuped; 66.27, wi h; 67.18, Faculty-Administration; 67.26, that must; 67.27, th ecommunity; 67.32, toward a; 72.9, Fetchitt; 75.34, broze; 76.35, downed; 77.3, Rurrett; 78.35, statue; 92.24, get. And; 92.28, occured; 95.13, succeded; 95.34, occured; 96.25, featured the; 137.10, 1947; 148.25, plead; 156.10, divertisements; 158.24, fear; 165.14, than the; 169.17, "It that; 175.15, ours. [no close quote]; 180.35, folks."; 186.15, this? expression; 200.30, charasteristic; 200.32, Carringan's; 209.29, flaunt; 209.35, such as like; 211.9, it's; 211.31, lnown; 213.23, be; 225.39, propaganda.); 229.30, introduction; 229.38, right"; 242.31, these; 250.26, younder; 250.36, instead or; 259.2, seem; 259.26, commision; 267.30, you? And; 267.31, me. [no close quote]; 267.36, me. [no close quote]; 273.3, tell,; 273.27, doctor's; 276.1, other,; 276.3, MIT; 278.3, "'Jedge,'"; 278.30, Begley; 279.14, its; 281.12, busses; 281.15, moset; 328.17, You re; 359.15, folk's; 363.15, invited; 364.1, he hair; 364.33, Yolando; 366.3, Ghana"; 366.23, whisky. [no close quote]; 366.37, Montomery; 367.7, least while; 379.1, already about; 379.28, school we; 380.2, lot I; 380.8, whom; 380.10, " "Leave ... alone. By; 380.12, kick-; 380.19, We; 380.23, here; 380.39, out of their; 381.4, He ran back to the corner and yelled: "Here men. I; 384.29, necessary with; 385.11, At either side on the; 389.40, Dryodes; 390.1, Dryodes; 390.8, Everyone; 392.39, "n"; 393.4, races...."; 393.11, persons." 396.5, her since; 396.20, Winnie; 397.19, over.'; 397.23, and Minnie; 401.28, o fthe; 402.7, drug-tore conters; 402.12, segregation." 402.37, etc,; 403.31, 'whites"; 404.39, Aprons; 431.9, McLain; 431.24, Blair the; 432.15, custom. [no close quote]; 434.5, minister's; 435.26–27, Company Other; 437.30, Greensboro voluntarily; 437.37, church,; 449.1, Octavius; 515.41, self deluded; 535.9, politician,; 574.14, crow; 575.29, "Life,"; 577.10, ride the; 578.38, shortly; 579.4, yesterday during; 579.12, Zwerag; 584.13, reproach,; 585.33, behicle; 586.2, occuring; 586.7, cameraman . . . assaulted a [lines transposed]; 586.21, "freedom rides"; 586.25, Southerners'; 586.30, tak; 587.4, that; 589.15–16, "'Course . . . either.'"; 589.21, eight; 603.21, other The; 605.12, escape They; 606.13, Guard; 608.14, stripped; 609.13, stop; 609.15, official walked ... door."; 609.19, in by; 610.1, Okora; 610.31, gobbled; 611.13, Phillips,; 613.20, accent?; 613.35, amazement?; 613.40, business"; 615.15, huddle; 616.9, burgon; 616.11, "something" light; 617.14, quarter ride; 617.27, I'M; 621.6, priviledged; 621.27, roads"; 624.34, collar;; 627.29 not,'; 628.25, enlightment; 628.27, desreves; 628.29 an; 630.6, Committe; 630.12, asks the; 630.16, desegration; 630.32, rooom; 631.6, detonation; 631.11, an an; 631.18, King's Jr.; 639.4, *Absolom, Absolom*; 639.5, Quinten; 639.12, 80 years; 640.11, capitol; 649.26, equal."; 650.38, off."; 651.2, reckon."; 651.14, December.; 651.21, them."; 655.6, Hanson; 661.35, Natinal; 662.34, troopers suddenly; 663.2, Years; 663.3, othere; 664.10, happeded; 665.19, dying?; 666.22, said,"; 670.24, seats sure; 702.32, precedessors; 784.29, Klu; 796.28, I [no open quote]; 797.7, 18, 24, 34, Foreman; 797.34, Cotten; 801.6, sigarets; 801.6, barba-topped; 801.12, that my; 807.29, jails,"; 820.22, Banks'; 821.15, waver; 822.7, arrived; 822.12, 'waiting; 822.23, Mechants; 825.28 defence; 828.8, unwaranted; 829.18–19, purposely; 832.22, those are; 845.20, year old; 852.3, fifteen mile; 854.14, Feweral; 873.37, said, 887.38, structures; 892.32, ban; 893.23, recognizes.

Notes

In the notes below, the reference numbers denote page and line of this volume (the line count includes headings). No note is made for material included in standard desk-reference works. Biblical references are keyed to the King James Version. Footnotes and bracketed editorial notes within the texts were in the originals. For historical background see the Chronology in this volume; for further background and references to other studies, see *Encyclopedia of African-American Civil Rights*, edited by Charles D. Lowery and John F. Marszalek (Westport, Connecticut: Greenwood Press, 1992) and Ralph E. Luker, *Historical Dictionary of the Civil Rights Movement* (Lanham, Maryland: The Scarecrow Press, 1997).

8.17–18   National Negro Congress] Founded in 1936 with A. Philip Randolph as its president, the National Negro Congress was intended to bring together representatives of existing African-American labor, political, fraternal, and religious organizations. In 1940 Randolph resigned his position after accusing the Communist party of seeking to take over the Congress.

17.32   F.O.R.] Fellowship of Reconciliation, a pacifist organization founded in 1915.

23.3   *Out of Their Mouths*] This essay was originally published with a headnote:

> The author of "Southern Road" draws this "fair sampling of current talk among American Negroes from a store of conversations harvested up and down the Atlantic Seaboard, from Massachusetts to Mississippi, but mainly in the Deep South."
> He writes: "Whether in army camps or juke joints or dorms or offices or commissaries or cabins or Jim Crow coaches or bus stations, I naturally found more wartime grousing than beatitudes.
> "A few were recorded on the spot at interviews; far more were bootlegged into many small notebooks, which sometimes got me into embarrassing predicaments and occasionally got me out of them. In their rendering, I found no better advice than Chaucer's, written six centuries ago:
>
>> "Who-so shall tell a tale after a man,
>> He must rehearse, as nigh as ever he can
>> Every word, if it be in his charge,
>> Although he speak never so rudely and large,
>> Or else he must tell his tale untrue,
>> Or feign something, or find words new!"

24.21   Japs before Singapore] Japanese troops landed in northern Malaya on December 8, 1941, and captured Singapore on February 15, 1942.

25.26–33   "Little Orphan . . . found the car."] "Little Orphan Annie," a comic strip by Harold Gray (1894–1968), featured a home front organization for children, the Junior Commandos, in its storylines, beginning in June 1942. On August 2, 1942, a strip appeared in which a black child, George, volunteers information about an abandoned railroad car. The Junior Commandos salvage the car for scrap iron; Annie, a colonel, promotes George to sergeant. (The Asp, Punjab, and the Chinaman were recurring characters in the series.)

28.26–27   it happened . . . Roland Hayes.] Hayes (1887–1976), an acclaimed classical tenor, was beaten by police in Rome, Georgia, in July 1942 after his Northern-born wife refused to move to the rear section of a shoe store.

29.22   Frontenac head] An overhead-valve cylinder head, developed in 1921 for the Ford Model T engine, used to increase engine performance.

30.3   FEPC] Fair Employment Practice Committee; see Chronology, 1941.

30.16–18   *The day that Life . . . Desdemona*] Paul Robeson was pictured alongside actress Uta Hagen on August 31, 1942, in *Life*.

30.24   Rosenwald] Julius Rosenwald (1862–1932), an Illinois businessman and philanthropist, endowed the Rosenwald Fund, which supported both white and African-American schools and colleges in the South. In 1941 Governor Eugene Talmadge accused Marvin Pittman, the president of Georgia Teachers College, of using Rosenwald funds to buy subversive books for the college library.

31.22   *(big as John Henry) . . . Field*] In ballad, folklore, and possibly historical fact, "Big John" Henry, a steel-driver working on the Big Bend railroad tunnel near Talcott, West Virginia, in the early 1870s, won a test of strength against a newly introduced steam drill, but died in the process. African-American fighter pilots were trained at Tuskegee, Alabama, beginning in 1941.

32.34   Bob Considine] Robert Considine (1906–75), newspaper columnist and political reporter.

33.29–32   that Pegler . . . tyranny."] Westbrook Pegler (1894–1969), a newspaper columnist, was a persistent critic of the "Double V" campaign begun by *The Pittsburgh Courier* in February 1942 for military "victory abroad" and "victory at home" in the struggle for civil rights.

35.10   that pretty white suit . . . you] Louis donated more than $100,000 in prize money from two of his heavyweight title fights in 1942 to army and navy relief funds and was also an active participant in war bond campaigns.

37.18 Belle Isle] Island in the Detroit River used as a city park.

39.24–25 The Black Legion] A midwestern terrorist organization hostile to African-Americans, Jews, Catholics, and labor organizers that was responsible during the 1930s for a number of bombings, murders, and other acts of violence; its members wore black outfits decorated with skull and crossbones.

39.30–31 Gerald L. K. Smith] Gerald Lyman Kenneth Smith (1898–1976), Christian fundamentalist preacher and supporter of extreme right-wing organizations.

42.1 Beaumont] Beaumont, Texas.

43.8–11 One leading . . . explosion,"] Virginius Dabney, editor of the *Richmond Times-Dispatch*, "Nearer and Nearer the Precipice," *Atlantic Monthly*, January 1943.

45.35 the Wagner Act] The National Labor Relations Act (1935), legislation designed to protect the rights of workers to unionize.

45.40 the TNEC reports] The Temporary National Economic Committee, created by Congress in 1938 to investigate monopolies and the concentration of economic power in the production and distribution of goods and services, issued a number of reports between 1939 and 1941.

47.39–48.4 the fatalism . . . avoid it."] These remarks were attributed to Stephens by Richard Malcolm Johnston (1822–98) in *Life of Alexander H. Stephens* (1878) by Johnston and William Hand Browne.

50.18 riot of 1935] A riot broke out in Harlem on March 19, 1935, after a false rumor spread that the police had killed a young shoplifter. The police made 75 arrests and 64 people were injured in the riot.

56.18 voided laws . . . cities] In *Buchanan* v. *Warley* (1917).

56.19–21 separate railroad . . . the same.] In *Plessy* v. *Ferguson* (1896), which established the "separate but equal" doctrine.

68.9 Mitchell Case] In *Mitchell* v. *United States* (1941) the Supreme Court unanimously ruled that the denial of equal accommodations to interstate rail passengers on racial grounds violated the provision of the Interstate Commerce Act that prohibited treating passengers with "undue or unreasonable prejudice." The case was brought by Arthur Mitchell, the only African-American member of Congress, after he was forced to leave a first-class Pullman car and move into a segregated coach car while traveling from Chicago to Hot Springs, Arkansas, in 1937. In his opinion for the Court, Chief Justice Charles Hughes wrote that the case presented "not a question of segregation but one of equality of treatment," and the decision did not overturn the "separate but equal" doctrine established in *Plessy* v. *Ferguson*.

72.30   Rochester]   Rochester Van Jones, a Pullman porter on the Jack Benny radio show beginning in June 1937, played by Eddie Anderson (1905–77).

74.13   Johnny Wright]   Wright, a pitcher for the Homestead Grays before being signed by the Dodgers, never played in the major leagues.

74.20   Wendell Willkie's "One World"]   Title of 1943 bestseller by Willkie, based on his 1942 world tour as President Roosevelt's envoy, that advocated the creation of an international organization to promote world peace.

78.18   minority candidate Talmadge]   In the 1946 primary Talmadge lost the popular vote but won a majority of the county-unit votes. (Under the electoral system adopted in 1917 by the Georgia Democratic party for statewide primaries, counties were allocated two, four, or six unit votes depending on their population. The system was declared unconstitutional by the U.S. Supreme Court in *Gray* v. *Sanders* in 1963.)

78.22–23   the murderers . . . to trial.]   No one was ever charged in the murders.

85.9   James K. Vardaman]   Vardaman (1861–1930) was governor of Mississippi, 1904–8, and a U.S. senator, 1913–19.

86.7   the Bilbo hearings]   Following the 1946 Democratic primary in Mississippi a group of black voters petitioned the Senate, charging that Senator Theodore G. Bilbo (1877–1947) had incited racial violence during his campaign in an effort to intimidate potential African-American voters. In December 1946 a Senate select committee held four days of hearings in Jackson and heard testimony from more than 100 witnesses regarding Mississippi registration and voting procedures. The majority of the committee recommended in January 1947 that Bilbo be allowed to take his seat, but the minority issued a report accusing him of having violated the Constitution and federal law during his campaign.

87.5–6   a 1944 Supreme . . . unconstitutional]   See Chronology, 1944.

88.34–38   "Four score . . . earth."]   The beginning and ending of Lincoln's Gettysburg Address (1863).

92.10–11   a U.S. Supreme . . . travel.]   *Morgan* v. *Virginia* (1946); see Chronology.

94.2–3   Conrad Lynn]   Conrad J. Lynn (1908–95), an African-American attorney from New York and author of *Black Justice Exposed* (1947), *Monroe: Turning Point* (1962), and *How To Stay Out of the Army* (1968).

96.39   Igal Roodenko]   Roodenko (1917–91) had been a conscientious objector during World War II, and was later active (1947–77) in the War Resisters League.

97.23   Lottie Taylor case]   Lottie E. Taylor was arrested for disorderly conduct in Fairfax, Virginia, on September 12, 1946, after she refused to move to the back of a bus in accordance with the bus company's segregation policy. Her subsequent conviction was overturned by the Virginia Supreme Court on March 1, 1948, on the grounds that her refusal to give up her seat did not qualify as disorderly conduct as defined by state law.

106.23–26   "God is . . . the sea."]   Psalm 46:1–2.

106.27–28   "I have fought . . . the faith."]   Cf. 2 Timothy 4:7.

114.25   labor unions]   A footnote in the original magazine printing of this essay reads: "For a detailed discussion of this touchy problem, see 'Race Discrimination in Unions,' by Herbert R. Northrup, in the July 1945 MERCURY.—THE EDITORS."

115.40–116.1   The decision . . . covenants]   See Chronology, 1948.

117.37   "Wings over Jordan" choir]   A Cleveland gospel choir founded in the mid-1930s and broadcast widely on the CBS and Mutual radio networks (1939–47; 1948–49).

118.23   Four Freedoms]   President Roosevelt named "four essential human freedoms" in his State of the Union address of January 6, 1941: freedom of speech; freedom of worship; freedom from want; and freedom from fear.

126.7–8   fight the convictions . . . Supreme Court]   In April 1951 the Supreme Court unanimously overturned the convictions of Shepherd and Irvin on the grounds that they had been deprived of a fair trial by inflammatory pretrial publicity (Greenlee did not appeal his conviction). On November 6, 1951, Lake County sheriff Willis McCall killed Shepherd and seriously wounded Irvin while transporting them from Raiford state prison to Tavares. McCall testified that he had fired in self-defense and was exonerated by the coroner's jury; Irvin claimed that McCall had deliberately shot him and Shepherd. In February 1952 Irvin was retried with Thurgood Marshall serving as his attorney. He was again convicted and sentenced to death, but his sentence was commuted to life imprisonment by Governor LeRoy Collins. Greenlee was paroled in 1962 and Irvin was released in 1968.

128.23   Scottsboro case.]   On March 25, 1931, nine black youths, aged 13 to 20, were accused of raping two young white women on a freight train in northern Alabama. They were tried in Scottsboro, Alabama, beginning on April 6, 1931, and on April 9 eight of the defendants were sentenced to death (the case of the 13-year-old resulted in a mistrial when a jury deadlocked over whether to impose the death penalty). In 1932, the U.S. Supreme Court overturned the verdicts on the grounds that the inadequate counsel provided to the accused at their trial violated their right to due process under the Fourteenth Amendment. Two defendants were retried and again sentenced to death in 1933, despite the recantation by one of the alleged victims of her previous testimony. The U.S. Supreme Court overturned one of the new convictions in 1935, ruling that the systematic exclusion of blacks from grand and trial jury duty violated the right to equal protection under the law under the Fourteenth Amendment. All of the defendants were then re-indicted by Alabama authorities. Four of the defendants were retried and convicted between January 1936 and July 1937; one was sentenced to death (commuted in 1938 to life imprisonment), one to 99 years in prison, and two to 75-year terms. A fifth defendant received 20 years for assaulting a deputy while in custody, and charges against the remaining four were dropped in July 1937. Four of the imprisoned men were paroled between 1943 and 1950; a fifth escaped in 1948 to Michigan, where the governor refused to have him extradited to Alabama.

156.9–10   like Barkis . . . willing]   In Charles Dickens' *David Copperfield* (1850), Barkis, a coachman, indicates his eagerness to marry Peggoty, a maid, by sending the message "Barkis is willin'."

219.30–34   Charles E. Wilson . . . to him]   Wilson (1890–1961), the president of General Motors since 1941, was named secretary of defense by President Eisenhower in 1953. During his Senate confirmation hearing Wilson was asked if he could make a decision in the interests of the country that adversely affected General Motors; he answered that he could, but that "I cannot conceive of one because for years I thought what was good for our country was good for General Motors, and vice versa."

230.20   Dexter]   A Montgomery street.

232.6–7   true account . . . Till.]   William Bradford Huie paid Milam and the Bryants between $3,600 and $4,000 for their account of the crime. In *A Death in the Delta: The Story of Emmett Till* (1988), historian Stephen J. Whitfield wrote that it is likely that Milam and Bryant concealed the involvement of one or two accomplices in the abduction and murder of Till.

232.35   *Shane*]   Western (1953) directed by George Stevens and starring Alan Ladd.

236.4   "grease gun"]   Popular name for the American M3 submachine gun.

241.26   capitulated . . . what it wanted.]   See Chronology, 1956.

246.20–22   victory . . . University of Alabama.]   In 1988 the university rescinded its expulsion of Lucy. She subsequently reenrolled and was awarded an M.A. in elementary education in 1992.

280.12   widely publicized Live Oaks trial]   Ruby McCollum, a black woman, went on trial at the Suwanee County courthouse in Live Oak, Florida, in November 1952 for the murder on August 3, 1952, of Dr. C. LeRoy Adams, a white physician and state senator who was the father of her youngest child. During the trial the prosecution claimed that a dispute over a medical bill was the motive for the murder and successfully challenged attempts by the defense to present testimony regarding the personal relationship between McCollum and Adams. McCollum was found guilty and sentenced to death, but her conviction was overturned by the Florida supreme court because of a procedural error made by the trial judge. In September 1954 she was found unfit to be retried due to insanity and was confined in a mental hospital until her release in 1976. Among the reporters who covered her trial was Zora Neale Hurston, who wrote about the case for *The Pittsburgh Courier* (October 1952–April 1953) and whose reporting was extensively quoted by William Bradford Huie in his book *Ruby McCollum* (1956).

288.3   Castoria]   A patent medicine used as a children's cathartic.

289.1–2   the men who rode with Forrest]   General Nathan Bedford Forrest (1821–71), Confederate cavalry commander.

290.28–30   movie . . . Williams]   *Baby Doll* (1956), directed by Elia Kazan and written by Tennessee Williams using material from his play *27 Wagons Full of Cotton*.

291.8   movie over at Oxford?"]   *Intruder in the Dust* (1949), directed by Clarence Brown.

293.3–7   *Life* . . . rape-murder]   An editorial that appeared in *Life* on October 10, 1955, stated that Emmett Till's father had been killed while fighting in France during World War II. *Life* retracted the statement on October 31, 1955, after military records were released showing that Private Louis Till had been hanged by the U.S. Army in Italy in 1945 for the murder of an Italian woman and the rape of two other Italian women. (Emmett Till's parents were divorced in 1943, two years after his birth.)

297.34   tobacco night riders]   Vigilantes who engaged in violence between 1905 and 1909 against the monopolistic American Tobacco Company and tobacco farmers who refused to join planters' associations opposed to the company.

297.40   Blackstone]   *Blackstone's Commentaries on the Laws of England* (1769), by William Blackstone.

298.4–5   Gerald L. K. Smith]   See note 39.30–31.

299.19–20   Court-packing plan]   In 1937 President Roosevelt proposed expanding the membership of the Supreme Court after it had struck down several New Deal measures. His proposal encountered severe political opposition and was never enacted.

332.4–8   William Lloyd Garrison . . . forever?"]   From, respectively, Garrison's first editorial (1831) in *The Liberator*, an abolitionist newspaper; a dispatch written by Grant on May 11, 1864, during the battle of Spotsylvania; and newspaper accounts of the June 1918 battle of Belleau Wood, which attributed versions of "Come on, you bastards . . . " to Gunnery Sergeant Daniel Daly (1874–1937).

342.2 *A Sequel to Segregation*] When first published in *Life* magazine, this article was accompanied by a sidebar, titled "What Has Happened to Causeys Now": "When the Causeys' difficulties were reported to LIFE, one of LIFE's reporters immediately investigated. His report agreed with the family's feeling that it could not continue to live in Choctaw County. Later one of our senior editors visited the county and talked to the people mentioned in this article, confirming for himself the earlier findings. At that point the Causey family, with the help of LIFE, was resettled in a place of its own choosing in another part of the South. The series on segregation was conceived and published in order to examine and explain one of the most controversial social problems before the United States today. In asking the Causeys to illustrate one phase of Negro life in the South, LIFE did not anticipate subsequent developments, nor did the Causeys. In justice to them and to our readers, the editors felt it was necessary to report further on the Causey family."

346.11 LIFE's reporter . . . story] Robert Wallace and Gordon Parks.

358.19 the famous ninety] On February 21, 1956, a grand jury indicted 89 people involved in the boycott campaign for violating a state anti-boycott law.

358.27 the night . . . last decision] November 13, 1956; see Chronology.

369.20 Scottsboro boys] See note 128.23.

370.1 *shochet*] Kosher slaughterer.

387.7–8 like Old Satch . . . North] Louis "Satchmo" Armstrong (1900–77), who left his native New Orleans for Chicago in 1922.

407.22 *Old Man River*] Song by Jerome Kern and Oscar Hammerstein II, from the musical *Show Boat* (1927).

409.7–8 J. Robert Oppenheimer] Oppenheimer (1904–67), the physicist who directed the design of the first atomic bombs at Los Alamos, 1943–45, had his security clearance revoked by the Atomic Energy Commission in 1954 after being accused of disloyalty.

410.3 *Black Like Me*] Griffin, a white man, had used medication and ultraviolet radiation to darken his skin so that he could "pass" as an African-American.

414.27–30 *Tantum ergo* . . . famous text.] "Down in adoration falling, this great sacrament we hail," the opening words of a two-stanza section of the *Pange lingua* (Eucharistic or Vesper hymn) sung or recited, in Catholic ritual, in Benediction of the Blessed Sacrament.

414.35 *Confiteor*] Penitential prayer (beginning with *Confiteor*, "I confess") offered, in Roman Catholicism, at the beginning of Mass.

421.16 the Parker youth's lynching] See Chronology, 1959.

426.8–10   Trilling's remark . . . prison.]   In his preface to *The Opposing Self: Nine Essays in Criticism* (1955), Trilling attributes to Matthew Arnold a "sense of modern culture as a kind of prison."

428.25   P. D. East]   P. D. East (1921–71) was editor of *The Petal Paper* (Petal, Mississippi) and author of *The Magnolia Jungle: The Life, Times, and Education of a Southern Editor* (1960).

449.1   Octavus Roy Cohen . . . stories]   Florian Slappey, a dandified "sepia gentleman" who travels from his native Birmingham to New York's Harlem and to Europe in a series of detective misadventures, is the main character in more than a dozen *Saturday Evening Post* stories, two book collections (*Florian Slappey Goes Abroad*, 1928, and *Florian Slappey*, 1938), and a Broadway play (*Come Seven*, 1920) by Octavus Roy Cohen (1891–1959).

465.8   his book]   *Stride Toward Freedom: The Montgomery Story* (1958).

493.6–7   Bandung Conference]   The first conference of nonaligned nations, held in Bandung, Indonesia, in April 1955.

496.1   'A little child . . . them,']   Isaiah 11:6.

504.8   Little Rock Nine]   The nine African-American students who integrated Central High School were Minnie Jean Brown, Elizabeth Eckford, Ernest Green, Thelma Mothershed, Melba Patillo, Gloria Ray, Terrence Roberts, Jefferson Thomas, and Carlotta Walls.

505.15–20   the Senate's watered-down . . . eighty-three years.]   See Chronology, 1957.

509.9–10   his appearance . . . Kenya natives.]   Marshall served as an adviser to the Kenyan delegation in independence negotiations held at Lancaster House, London, in January 1960.

515.12   Stuyvesant Town]   A large publicly subsidized housing development in lower Manhattan. Restricted to white tenants when it opened in 1947, the project began to admit African-Americans in August 1950.

515.31   inhabitants . . . this description]   This essay was first published in *Esquire* in July 1960, then revised for inclusion in *Nobody Knows My Name* (1961).

526.31   Charley . . . doctor]   Steinbeck's French poodle Charley had been in the care of an Amarillo veterinarian, recovering from treatment for prostatitis.

528.27   Rocinante]   Steinbeck's name for his pickup truck, after Don Quixote's horse.

533.26   Lyle Saxon]   Saxon (1891–1946) was a feature writer for the New Orleans *Times-Picayune* from 1918 to 1926, and author of books about

Louisiana and the South including *Father Mississippi* (1927), *Fabulous New Orleans* (1928), and *Old Louisiana* (1929).

533.28–29   Roark Bradford . . . leadeth us] Bradford (1896–1948) was a journalist and author of black dialect and Southern plantation fiction. His collection *Ol' Man Adam an' His Chillun* (1928), in which a black preacher retells stories from the Bible, was adapted for the stage in 1930 as *The Green Pastures*.

537.5–6   famous Silas Green show] The "Silas Green from New Orleans Minstrel Show" was a black-owned traveling tent show that featured comic sketches and jazz and ragtime performers, including Ma Rainey and Bessie Smith. It drew large audiences touring Southern states through the late 1950s.

547.10–11   case . . . Supreme Court] The Haywood County lawsuit was settled out of court on May 1, 1962, and the Fayette County suit was resolved by a consent decree on July 26, 1962. In both cases the defendants agreed to permanently cease all attempts to interfere with the right to register and vote.

550.21   Tuskegee . . . boycotts] The Tuskegee Civic Association launched a boycott of white-owned businesses in Tuskegee, Alabama, on June 25, 1957, in response to an attempt by the state legislature to redraw the boundaries of the city to ensure white political control. The U.S. Supreme Court ruled the revised boundaries to be unconstitutional in *Gomillion* v. *Lightfoot* (1960).

559.27–29   the Southern day . . . night] In "Nobody Knows My Name: A Letter from the South" (*Partisan Review*, Winter 1959): "In the Southern night everything seems possible, the most private unspeakable longings; but then arrives the Southern day, as hard and brazen as the night was soft and dark. It brings what was done in the dark to light."

564.35   Robert Williams] After white mobs attacked civil rights demonstrators in Monroe, North Carolina, on August 27, 1961, armed supporters of Williams detained a white couple inside his home for about two hours. Indicted on kidnapping charges as a result of the incident, Williams fled to Cuba in the fall of 1961 and began broadcasting "Radio Free Dixie," a weekly program that mixed political news and speeches with African-American music. In 1965 Williams and his wife, Mabel, moved to Beijing, where he met with Mao Zedong and Zhou Enlai. The Williams returned to the United States in 1969 and settled in Michigan, visiting North Carolina after the kidnapping charges were dropped in 1976. Williams died in 1996.

580.6   last night] May 21, 1961.

582.24–25   a Princess phone] A compact telephone model first sold in 1959.

595.4   Hollowell] Donald L. Hollowell, a leading Atlanta civil rights attorney whose clients included Martin Luther King, was a member of the

NOTES   969

legal team that had represented Holmes and Hunter in their desegregation
suit.

619.8   Moses]   Bob Moses (b.1935), the first SNCC field representative to
work in Mississippi.

622.26–27   riots in San Francisco or Japan]   A demonstration protesting
hearings by the House Un-American Activities Committee in San Francisco
ended in violence on May 13, 1960, when the police made 68 arrests. Violent
protests by Japanese leftists against the signing of a security treaty with the
United States forced President Eisenhower to cancel his planned state visit to
Japan in June 1960.

628.16   Hupmobile]   Brand name for cars manufactured by the Hupp
Motor Car Company, 1909–40.

631.10   Fayette County . . . "Tent City"]   See pages 541–49 in this volume.

645.36   William Graham]   Possibly a setting error for William Graham
Sumner (1840–1910), professor of social and political science at Yale,
1872–1910, and an exponent of Social Darwinism who criticized Reconstruction as a futile attempt to change Southern mores by legislation.

649.17–18   "If God . . . slaughter."]   Romans 8:31 and 8:36.

654.4   Friday]   August 3, 1962. Hearings in federal district court regarding the injunction sought by the city of Albany against mass civil rights
protests began on July 30 and continued until August 8. The Albany Movement suspended mass demonstrations on August 14, 1962, before a decision
was handed down in the case.

654.16–17   Elliott . . . fear him]   Elliott had issued a temporary restraining order against demonstrations on July 20, 1962, which was overturned by
Judge Elbert Tuttle of the Fifth Circuit Court of Appeals on July 24.

655.6–7   Bill Hansen . . . being struck]   See pages 707–8 in this volume.

657.5   Thursday]   September 20, 1962.

661.9   Thursday]   September 27, 1962.

665.20–21   Same . . . critical condition.]   Marshal Same recovered from
his wound.

673.1   General]   Traditional form of addressing the attorney general of
the United States.

675.36   ex-General Edwin Walker]   Walker (1909–93), who led federal
troops during the Little Rock school integration crisis in 1957–58, was removed from his command in 1961 for distributing right-wing literature to his
troops and resigned his commission.

678.34   STRAC]   Strategic Army Corps.

703.17   letter to Horace Greeley] Written on August 22, 1862, and printed in the New York *Tribune* on August 25, 1862.

709.1   the Debs case] In 1895 the Supreme Court unanimously refused to grant a writ of habeas corpus to Eugene Debs, president of the American Railway Union, who had been sentenced to six months' imprisonment for contempt of court after he defied a federal circuit court injunction forbidding the union from striking railroads using Pullman cars. Writing for the Court, Justice David Brewer upheld the injunction as a constitutionally valid means of removing obstructions to interstate commerce.

710.5–12   Take up . . . you.] Penultimate stanza of "The White Man's Burden" (1899).

712.2–4   "It is better . . . to burn."] 1 Corinthians 7:9.

723.2   "Elmer Gantry"] Novel (1927) by Sinclair Lewis portraying a hypocritical preacher.

726.22   Dr. Verwoerd] Hendrik F. Verwoerd (1901–66), a former professor of psychology, served as minister of native affairs (1950–58) and prime minister (1958–66) of South Africa and was responsible for much of the legislation that constituted the apartheid system.

747.39   Birchites] Members of the John Birch Society, an extreme right-wing political organization founded in Indiana in 1958 by candy manufacturer Robert Welch (1899–1985) and named after John Birch (1918–45), an American intelligence officer killed by the Chinese Communists at the end of World War II.

759.33–35   "The problem . . . line."] *The Souls of Black Folk* (1903), "The Forethought."

762.4–10   *If we* . . . Baldwin] See page 761.1–6 in this volume.

772.7–8   Kenneth Rexroth . . . "crow-jimism."] In "Revolt: True and False" (*The Nation*, April 26, 1958), Rexroth refers to "that evil perversion we call, in jazz, 'Crow-jimism.'"

774.10–11   as Harold R. Isaacs . . . pages] In "Integration and the Negro Mood," *Commentary*, December 1962.

774.20–22   an essay . . . language] "Down at the Cross: Letter from a Region in My Mind" (see pages 710–61 in this volume), first published in *The New Yorker* on November 17, 1962, and later collected in *The Fire Next Time* (1963).

774.28–33   a vengeance . . . down.] See page 760.32–37 in this volume.

777.4–7   FELLOW CLERGYMEN . . . untimely."] In a note accompanying the 1964 first book printing of the "Letter from Birmingham Jail," King wrote: "This response to a published statement by eight fellow clergymen from Alabama (Bishop C.C.J. Carpenter, Bishop Joseph A. Durick, Rabbi Hilton L. Grafman, Bishop Paul Hardin, Bishop Holan B. Harmon, the Reverend George M. Murray, the Reverend Edward V. Ramage and the Reverend Earl Stallings) was composed under somewhat constricting circumstances. Begun on the margins of the newspaper in which the statement appeared while I was in jail, the letter was continued on scraps of writing paper supplied by a friendly Negro trusty, and concluded on a pad my attorneys were eventually permitted to leave me." King was arrested on April 12 (Good Friday) while marching on the Birmingham city hall and remained in jail until April 20, when he was released on bail. The statement by the eight clergymen, dated April 12, appeared in the *Birmingham News* and *Birmingham Post-Herald* on April 13, 1963.

778.6   Macedonian call for aid.]   Acts 16:9–10.

780.14–18   Socrates . . . gadflies.]   Cf. Socrates' first speech in Plato's *Apology*.

781.6–8   as Reinhold Niebuhr . . . individuals.]   In *Moral Man and Immoral Society: A Study in Ethics and Politics* (1932).

782.30–37   St. Augustine . . . natural law.]   Cf. Aquinas, *Summa Theologiae*, I-II, which cites Augustine, *De Libero Arbitrio* I.5.

783.8–9   Paul Tillich . . . separation.]   In the sermon "You Are Accepted," *The Shaking of the Foundations* (1948).

784.7–9   the refusal of Shadrach . . . Nebuchadnezzar]   Cf. Daniel 3.

788.12–24   "Love your enemies . . . created equal . . ."]   From, respectively, Matthew 5:44; Amos 5:24; Galatians 6:17; words attributed to Martin Luther before the Diet of Worms, April 1521; a paraphrase of *A Confession of My Faith, and a Reason of My Practice* (1671); the "House Divided" speech at Springfield, Illinois, June 16, 1858; and the Declaration of Independence.

788.40–789.1   James McBride Dabbs]   Dabbs (1896–1970), born in South Carolina, argued for racial integration in books including *The Southern Heritage* (1958) and *Who Speaks for the South?* (1964).

790.24   Wallace gave a clarion call]   In his January 14, 1963, inaugural address as governor of Alabama, George Wallace vowed to defy federal attempts at integration and pledged his support for "segregation now, segregation tomorrow, segregation forever."

793.18–19   As T. S. Eliot . . . reason.]   In the third and fourth lines of the final speech of Part I, *Murder in the Cathedral* (1935): "The last temptation is the greatest treason: / To do the right deed for the wrong reason."

795.24   16th St. Baptist Church]   The church was bombed on September 15, 1963; see Chronology.

800.6–9   the thugs . . . high school]   Six Klansmen abducted and castrated a black man in Birmingham on September 2, 1957. The victim was chosen at random and told the crime was being committed as a warning to the Rev. Fred Shuttlesworth and other African-Americans not to try to integrate the city's schools. On September 9, 1957, Ruby Shuttlesworth, the wife of Fred Shuttlesworth, was stabbed in the hip during a mob attack in which her husband was beaten with chains. She recovered from her wound.

800.13   May 12th]   See pages 809–12 in this volume.

813.7–8   the biracial agreement]   An agreement negotiated by civil rights leaders and Birmingham merchants with the help of the Justice Department was announced on May 10, 1963. In return for a halt in demonstrations, the merchants agreed to a timetable for desegregating rest rooms, fitting rooms, drinking fountains, and lunch counters; the hiring of African-American store clerks and cashiers; and the establishment of a biracial civic committee.

821.23   "The Ugly American"]   Film (1963) directed by George Englund and starring Marlon Brando, about the American ambassador to a fictional Southeast Asian country. It was based on the novel (1958) by William J. Lederer and Eugene Burdick.

825.19–20   Barnett . . . trial for contempt]   The civil and criminal contempt charges against Barnett were dropped in 1965.

831.25–26   arrest and conviction of Mr. Evers's killer.]   Byron de la Beckwith, an avowed white supremacist, was arrested in Greenwood, Mississippi, on June 22, 1963, and charged with the murder of Evers. Two trials in 1964 ended in mistrials when all-white juries voted 7–5 and 8–4 for his acquittal. The case was reopened in 1990, and a third trial before a racially mixed jury in 1994 resulted in his conviction. Beckwith died in prison in 2001.

836.3   *Mississippi Black Paper*]   A collection of 57 affidavits and statements documenting police brutality recorded by the Council of Federated Organizations and published in 1965. A note in the 1965 edition stated that they were collected "for the purpose of offering them in evidence in a suit brought against Sheriff Rainey—both as an individual and as a representative of similar public servants in all eighty-two counties of Mississippi—and other state officials. The purpose of the suit is to obtain the appointment of special federal commissioners to prevent violence against Negro citizens and civil rights workers in that state." (Lawrence Rainey was the sheriff of Neshoba County from 1963 to 1967. He was arrested in 1964 on federal civil rights charges connected with the murder of three civil rights workers near Philadelphia, Mississippi, but was acquitted in 1967.) In the aftermath of the incidents described in the affidavits of Fannie Lou Hamer, Annell Ponder, and June E. Johnson printed in this volume, the Justice Department filed criminal charges on September 9, 1963, against the sheriff of Montgomery County (Earl Partridge), the Winona police chief (Thomas J. Herrod, Jr.), a Winona policeman (William Surrell), a state highway patrolman (John L. Basinger), and a former state highway patrolman (Charles Thomas Perkins) for violating the civil rights of the prisoners. An all-white, all-male jury acquitted the defendants in December 1963.

836.29   Officer A——]   The publisher's note in the 1965 edition stated that the law enforcement officers named in the affidavits would be referred to by pseudonyms in *Mississippi Black Paper* "only because of the high cost of defending libel suits in Mississippi. The publishers of these documents are convinced that eventually, on appeal outside the state, they would win whatever actions could be brought against them if the full names of the officials involved were printed. But the legal cost of scores of such suits, even when victory was achieved, would be enormous, and therefore we have reluctantly, on the advice of our lawyers, resorted to pseudonyms."

847.20–21   a book . . . Ole Miss case]   Later published as *The Past That Would Not Die* (1965).

857.9–10   Curt Flood, Margaretta Belafonte]   Flood (1938–97), outfielder for the St. Louis Cardinals and civil rights activist; Marguerite Belafonte, first wife of Harry Belafonte and director of NAACP Freedom Fund.

859.5   Archie Moore]   Moore (1913–98) was the light heavyweight boxing champion from 1952 to 1962.

859.23   Maple Hill]   New Orleans restaurant where Moody had worked washing and busing dishes.

859.26   Raymond and Miss Pearl]   Father and paternal grandmother of Moody's half-brother James.

861.39   the bus station sit-in]   Toward the end of the 1962 Tougaloo summer session, Moody and a friend from her dormitory had been harrassed while they waited in the "white" area of the Jackson bus station.

862.22–23   Joan Trumpauer]   A white Tougaloo student who worked as a secretary for SNCC.

871.1   Adline]   Moody's younger sister.

890.6   Thursday]   July 11, 1963.

892.29–30   fourth straight night . . . the ban]   After an earlier outbreak of violence on June 11, the Maryland National Guard was sent to Cambridge and a ban on demonstrations was imposed. The ban was lifted and the Guard was withdrawn on July 8, 1963.

Index

Library of Congress Cataloging-in-Publication Data

Reporting civil rights
    p. cm.—(The Library of America; 137–138)
    Includes index.
    Contents: pt. 1. American journalism, 1941–1963—pt. 2 American
journalism, 1963–1973.
    ISBN 1–931082–28–6 (vol. 1: alk. paper)—ISBN 1–931082–29–4 (vol.
2: alk. paper)
    1. African Americans—Civil rights—History—20th century—
Sources. 2. African Americans—Civil rights—Press coverage. 3. Civil
rights movements—United States—History—20th century—Sources.
4. Civil rights movements—Press coverage—United States. 5.
Journalism—United States—History—20th century. 6. United
States—Race relations—Sources. 7. United States—Race relations—
Press coverage. I. Title: Reporting civil rights. II. Series.
E185.61.R47   2003
323.1′196073′0904 dc—21   2002027459

THE LIBRARY OF AMERICA SERIES

The Library of America fosters appreciation and pride in America's literary heritage by publishing, and keeping permanently in print, authoritative editions of America's best and most significant writing. An independent nonprofit organization, it was founded in 1979 with seed money from the National Endowment for the Humanities and the Ford Foundation.

1. Herman Melville, *Typee, Omoo, Mardi* (1982)
2. Nathaniel Hawthorne, *Tales and Sketches* (1982)
3. Walt Whitman, *Poetry and Prose* (1982)
4. Harriet Beecher Stowe, *Three Novels* (1982)
5. Mark Twain, *Mississippi Writings* (1982)
6. Jack London, *Novels and Stories* (1982)
7. Jack London, *Novels and Social Writings* (1982)
8. William Dean Howells, *Novels 1875–1886* (1982)
9. Herman Melville, *Redburn, White-Jacket, Moby-Dick* (1983)
10. Nathaniel Hawthorne, *Collected Novels* (1983)
11. Francis Parkman, *France and England in North America*, vol. I (1983)
12. Francis Parkman, *France and England in North America*, vol. II (1983)
13. Henry James, *Novels 1871–1880* (1983)
14. Henry Adams, *Novels, Mont Saint Michel, The Education* (1983)
15. Ralph Waldo Emerson, *Essays and Lectures* (1983)
16. Washington Irving, *History, Tales and Sketches* (1983)
17. Thomas Jefferson, *Writings* (1984)
18. Stephen Crane, *Prose and Poetry* (1984)
19. Edgar Allan Poe, *Poetry and Tales* (1984)
20. Edgar Allan Poe, *Essays and Reviews* (1984)
21. Mark Twain, *The Innocents Abroad, Roughing It* (1984)
22. Henry James, *Literary Criticism: Essays, American & English Writers* (1984)
23. Henry James, *Literary Criticism: European Writers & The Prefaces* (1984)
24. Herman Melville, *Pierre, Israel Potter, The Confidence-Man, Tales & Billy Budd* (1985)
25. William Faulkner, *Novels 1930–1935* (1985)
26. James Fenimore Cooper, *The Leatherstocking Tales*, vol. I (1985)
27. James Fenimore Cooper, *The Leatherstocking Tales*, vol. II (1985)
28. Henry David Thoreau, *A Week, Walden, The Maine Woods, Cape Cod* (1985)
29. Henry James, *Novels 1881–1886* (1985)
30. Edith Wharton, *Novels* (1986)
31. Henry Adams, *History of the U.S. during the Administrations of Jefferson* (1986)
32. Henry Adams, *History of the U.S. during the Administrations of Madison* (1986)
33. Frank Norris, *Novels and Essays* (1986)
34. W.E.B. Du Bois, *Writings* (1986)
35. Willa Cather, *Early Novels and Stories* (1987)
36. Theodore Dreiser, *Sister Carrie, Jennie Gerhardt, Twelve Men* (1987)
37. Benjamin Franklin, *Writings* (1987)
38. William James, *Writings 1902–1910* (1987)
39. Flannery O'Connor, *Collected Works* (1988)
40. Eugene O'Neill, *Complete Plays 1913–1920* (1988)
41. Eugene O'Neill, *Complete Plays 1920–1931* (1988)
42. Eugene O'Neill, *Complete Plays 1932–1943* (1988)
43. Henry James, *Novels 1886–1890* (1989)
44. William Dean Howells, *Novels 1886–1888* (1989)
45. Abraham Lincoln, *Speeches and Writings 1832–1858* (1989)
46. Abraham Lincoln, *Speeches and Writings 1859–1865* (1989)
47. Edith Wharton, *Novellas and Other Writings* (1990)
48. William Faulkner, *Novels 1936–1940* (1990)
49. Willa Cather, *Later Novels* (1990)
50. Ulysses S. Grant, *Memoirs and Selected Letters* (1990)

This book is set in 10 point Linotron Galliard,
a face designed for photocomposition by Matthew Carter
and based on the sixteenth-century face Granjon. The paper
is acid-free Domtar Literary Opaque and meets the requirements
for permanence of the American National Standards Institute. The
binding material is Brillianta, a woven rayon cloth made by
Van Heek-Scholco Textielfabrieken, Holland. The compo-
sition is by The Clarinda Company. Printing and
binding by R.R.Donnelley & Sons Company.
Designed by Bruce Campbell.